ALLART VAN EVERDINGEN

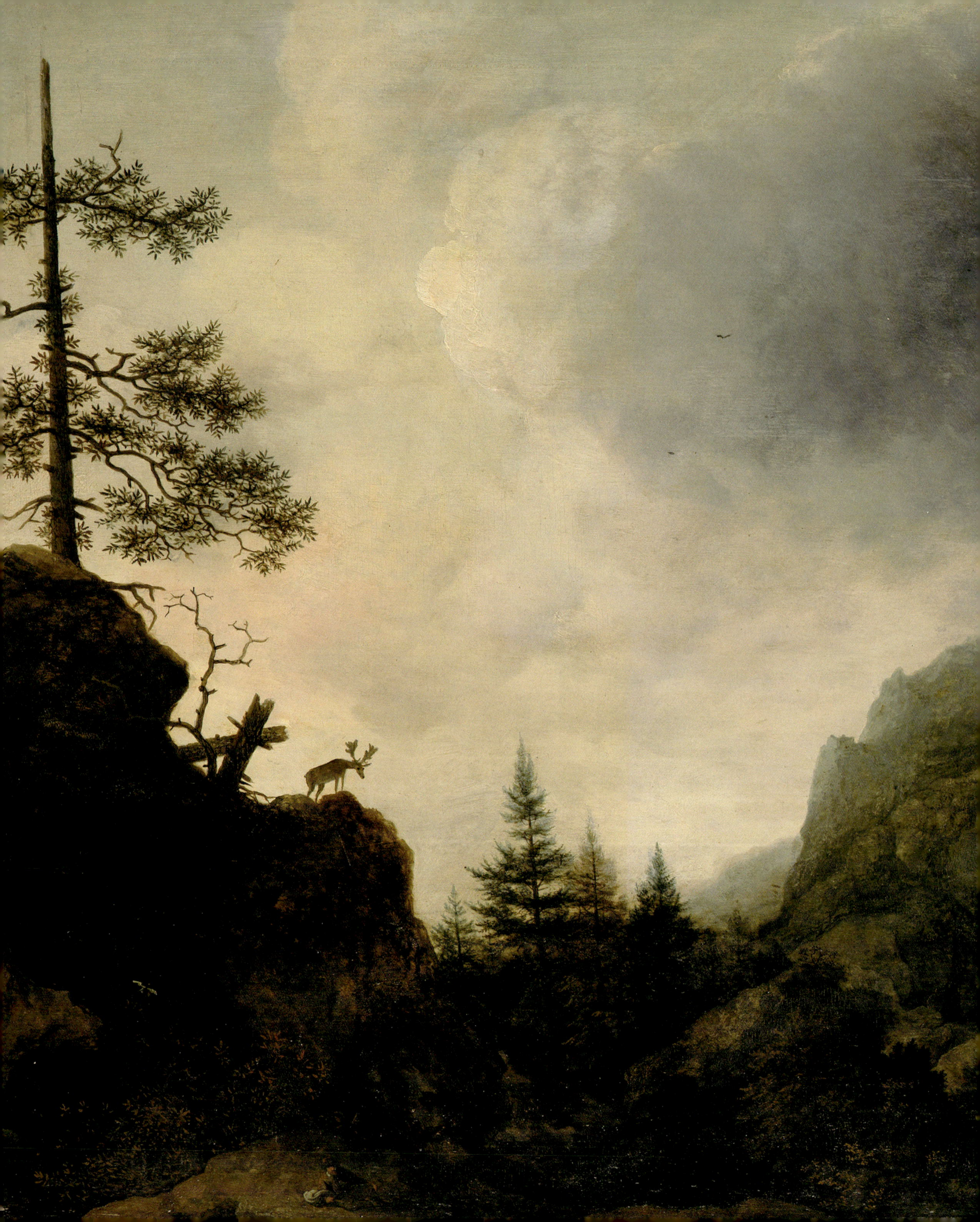

Allart van Everdingen

MASTER OF THE RUGGED LANDSCAPE

1621-1675

Compiled and edited by

Christi M. Klinkert and Yvonne Bleyerveld

Authors

Christi M. Klinkert

Yvonne Bleyerveld

Ellis Dullaart

Erik Hinterding

Paul Knolle

Cynthia Osiecki

Marjan Pantjes

Stedelijk Museum Alkmaar

nai010 publishers

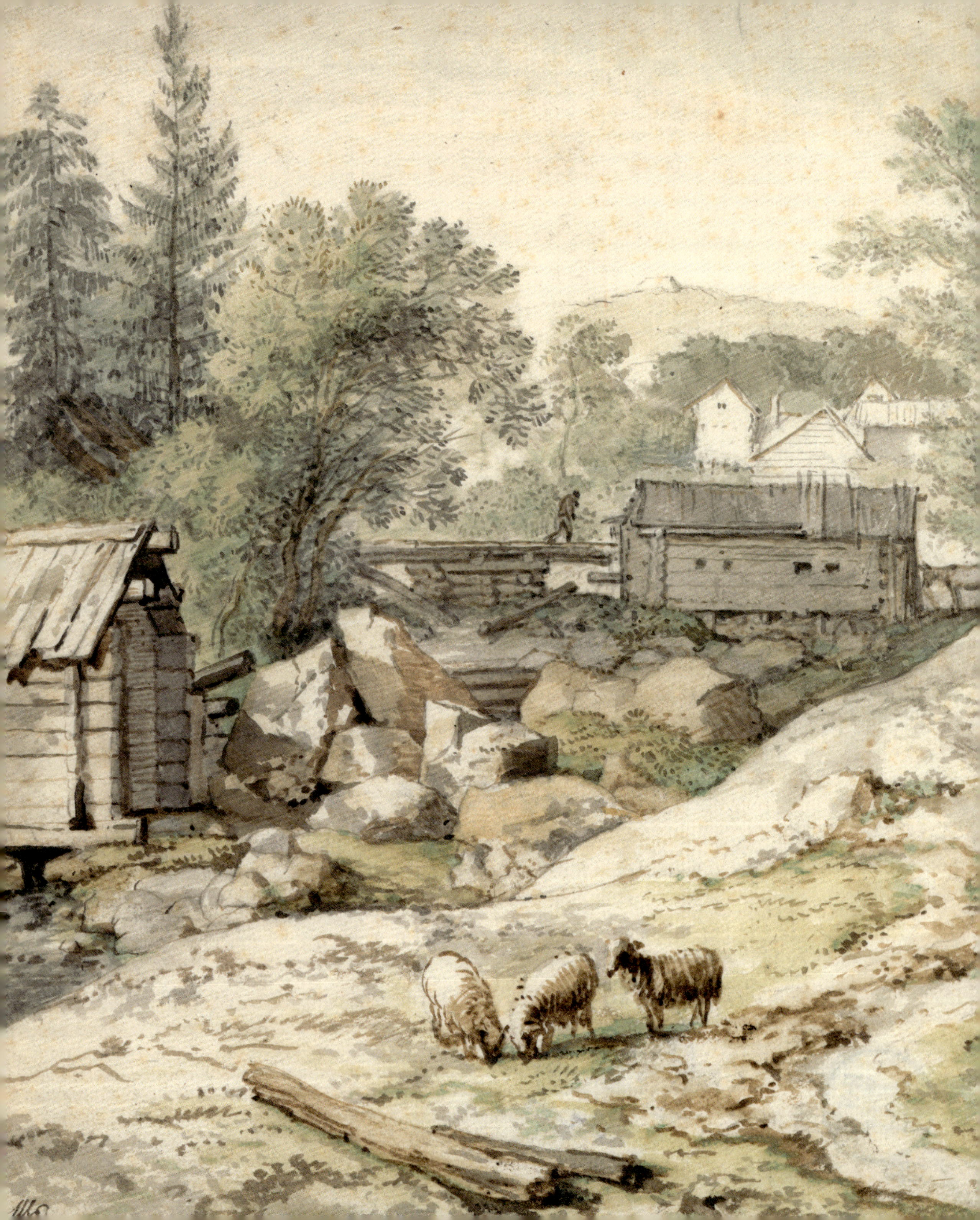

Contents

Foreword

How often do two siblings excel in one and the same discipline? It's a familiar phenomenon in sport. Think of the international footballers Erwin and Ronald Koeman, or the tennis stars Venus and Serena Williams. In music, too, we see brothers and sisters performing. Pop stars Beyoncé and Solange Knowles and classical pianists Arthur and Lucas Jussen are recent examples. Instances in fine art are perhaps less well-known, but the phenomenon does occur. In seventeenth-century Alkmaar, for example, where the brothers Caesar and Allart van Everdingen both trained as painters and became important artists in different genres. While Caesar van Everdingen (1616/1617-1678) focused on history works and portraits, his younger brother Allart van Everdingen (1621-1675) specialized in landscapes.

Of the two Van Everdingen brothers, Caesar acquired the greater reputation. His mythological scenes and tranquil figure works in bright, clear colours are regarded as the best examples of Dutch Classicism. Nowadays, Allart's work is less familiar. One undoubted factor in this is that one of his followers, Jacob van Ruisdael, became the most important landscape painter of the seventeenth century. Over time, Van Ruisdael's glory has rather cast Van Everdingen into the shade. This is a shame, because Allart's oeuvre is surprisingly rich and varied. It was high time that the work of this Dutch painter, draughtsman and etcher was examined and explored, and this is what we have done at the Stedelijk Museum Alkmaar. We present the results on the occasion of the quatercentenary of the artist's birth in a retrospective—the first ever devoted to him—and in this catalogue.

Allart van Everdingen fits seamlessly into the series of Alkmaar artists to whom the Stedelijk Museum Alkmaar has devoted monographic exhibitions in recent years—Claes Jacobsz van der Heck (2015-2016), Caesar van Everdingen (2016-2017) and Emanuel de Witte (2017-2018). These exhibitions and the accompanying catalogues have put neglected artists on the map and shone a light on the remarkable cultural wealth of seventeenth-century Alkmaar.

Allart van Everdingen, the originator of the rugged Scandinavian landscape, an entirely new genre in Dutch art, was an important innovator who was followed by artists until well into the nineteenth century. However, his significance extends further. During visits to potential lenders with curator Christi Klinkert, I have had the privilege of seeing Allart's work at close quarters in several European and American collections, and it became clear to me that Van Everdingen's talent was remarkably multifaceted. One moment you're face to face with imposing paintings of rocky landscapes, which you literally and figuratively look up to; the next you're in a print room bending over subtle drawings and etchings, built up with deft, assured lines. The Alkmaar artist was skilled in painting and drawing in a variety of formats, with brush, pen and etching needle.

What also struck me in Allart's paintings, drawings and etchings is that there is always more to find than you think at first sight. They invite you to look closely—if you do, you will be rewarded. I hope that reading this catalogue will give you a similar experience—if you have not already enjoyed seeing the exhibition in Alkmaar. It would be wonderful if our exhibition and book were to generate more recognition of and admiration for Van Everdingen's oeuvre and significance. He deserves it.

As we do for all our exhibitions, we undertook thorough preliminary research. Thanks to partnerships with the Rijksmuseum and the RKD – Netherlands Institute for Art History we were able to carry it out in a multidisciplinary team with a range of specialists. Not only did this lead us to new insights, which are presented in the exhibition and this book, we also encountered new questions that can form the basis for future research. I would like to extend my warmest thanks to our colleagues in Amsterdam and The Hague for the fruitful collaboration.

So that we could present a balanced and representative picture of Van Everdingen's oeuvre, we had to ask for the loan of many paintings, drawings and etchings. All the collectors and museums we approached welcomed us and promised their cooperation and so we were able to bring together a superb selection of works from the Netherlands and beyond. My thanks to all the lenders for their confidence in us.

For a medium-sized museum like the Stedelijk Museum Alkmaar, an exhibition of this calibre is an ambitious project and we would not have been able to achieve it without contributions from public and private funds. The Vereniging Rembrandt's Ekkart Fund (thanks to a gift from the Stichting Dames Spoorenberg), Fonds 21, Mondriaan Fund, Prins Bernhard Cultuurfonds, Samenwerkende Maritieme Fondsen (Vaderlandsch Fonds ter Aanmoediging van 's-Lands Zeedienst, Directie der Oostersche Handel en Reederijen, De Prins Hendrik Stichting and Admiraal van Kinsbergen-fonds) and TAQA Cultuurfonds gave us generous support. The Cultural Heritage Agency of the Netherlands provided an indemnity grant on behalf of the Minister of Education, Culture and Science. We are immensely grateful for this important financial support. In this regard I should also like to thank Alkmaar city council, who every year enable us to inspire new generations with the art and culture of our region.

Last but not least, I want to praise the Stedelijk Museum Alkmaar team, especially curator Christi Klinkert. As she was in the Caesar project, so she was the coordinating hub of the research, exhibition and book about Allart. Thanks to her knowledge, skill, perseverance and enthusiasm, after years of preparation we are able to present a unique exhibition and this lavishly illustrated catalogue. The Van Everdingen brothers could not have had a better champion.

Patrick van Mil
Director, Stedelijk Museum Alkmaar

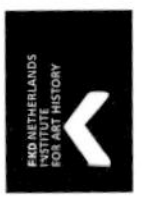 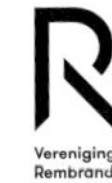 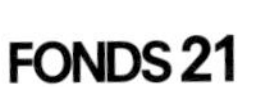 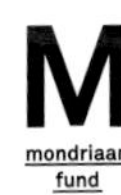 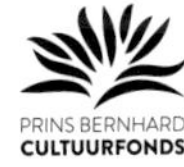 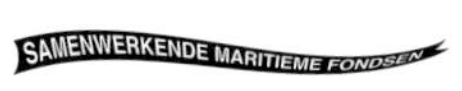 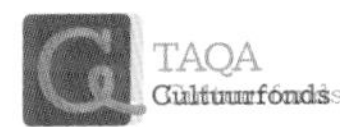 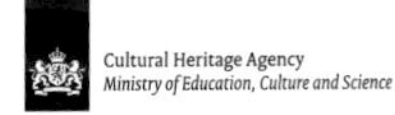

Acknowledgements

'Allart van Everdingen, isn't he the man who did those Scandinavian landscapes?' This was the reaction of many of our colleagues when they heard we were planning to devote an exhibition to this artist. And indeed, Van Everdingen painted, drew and etched an extraordinary number of rugged landscapes featuring waterfalls and log cabins. It was with these that he established his name, but he made much more—seascapes, Dutch river and village views, a series of tiny brunailles, and a set of illustrations for the tale of Reynard the Fox. We swiftly realized that we needed a team of researchers to do justice to all these aspects of his varied oeuvre.

Three experts enthusiastically agreed to help us get a grip on Allart's work: Erik Hinterding, curator of prints at the Rijksmuseum, Yvonne Bleyerveld and Ellis Dullaart, senior curator of prints and drawings and curator of Dutch and Flemish old master painting at the RKD – Netherlands Institute for Art History respectively. They were joined by the young art historian Marjan Pantjes, after we obtained a grant for her from the Vereniging Rembrandt's Ekkart Fund thanks to a gift from the Stichting Dames Spoorenberg. It was a privilege and a pleasure to work on the exhibition and accompanying book with them. I am also grateful to Cynthia Osiecki and Paul Knolle for their valuable contributions to the catalogue. My very particular thanks go to Yvonne for acting as researcher, author, co-compiler and co-editor of this book. Working together on Allart van Everdingen was just as much fun and just as fruitful as it was when we did the same for his older brother Caesar, 'the painter with the flattering brush', a few years ago.

Van Everdingen's oeuvre proved to raise more questions that we, a team of specialist art historians, could answer, so we approached outside experts. Their comprehensive responses turned our research into a feast of interdisciplinary collaboration. Ernst Berge Drange, curator at the Ryfylkemuseum in Bergen (Norway), was our walking encyclopaedia on seventeenth-century Norwegian history and architecture. Ron Brand, curator at the Maritime Museum Rotterdam, identified many ships, boats and other maritime details in Allart's pictures. Henryk van Hugten and Sterre Hoek, volunteers at the Rijksmuseum, took X-rays of the watermarks in the etchings for us. Anna Krekeler, conservator at the Rijksmuseum, helped us to interpret the infrared reflectograms of his paintings. Laurens Schoemaker, curator of historical topography at the RKD, analysed some town and village views. Biologist Frans Smeding found out exactly which trees and animals the artist had depicted. I thank them all for their important contributions to a better understanding of Van Everdingen's work.

Two years before the opening of the exhibition I followed in Allart's footsteps and went to Gothenburg, Mölndal, the waterfalls at Trollhättan and Bohus Fortress in Sweden, and to Langesund and Risør in Norway. Photographer Pascal Vossen accompanied me to record the buildings and landscape features that Van Everdingen could have seen at the time. Roar Isaksen, Thomas Juell, Roger Normann and Kristofer Torkildsen acted as our local guides. It was a rare and instructive experience to explore the Scandinavian landscape with them and compare what we saw around us with what Allart pictured. Some of Pascal's atmospheric photographs can be found in this catalogue and in the exhibition.

The other visual material for this book was meticulously collected and organized by Olga Kruisbrink. Lynne Richards produced an elegant translation of the texts with her usual speed and accuracy. Studio Berry Slok ensured a tasteful catalogue design. Eelco van Welie and Laurence Ostyn supervised the production of this book on behalf of nai010 publishers. Jelena Stefanovic of Studio OTW created a clean-lined exhibition design that shows off the artist's multifaceted work to best effect. Sappho

Panhuysen of Studio Vrijdag supplied the fresh typography. What a wonderful result we have achieved together!

As well as the people and institutions referred to above, my thanks also go to the many others who have helped us in one way or another to create the exhibition and the catalogue, especially Susan Anderson, Fahema Begum, Jaco Benckhuijsen, Mollie Berger Salah, Holm Bevers, Thomas Bionda, Niels de Boer, Wendy van Bohemen, Jeroen ter Brugge, Alexander de Bruin, Quentin Buvelot, Anne-Charlotte Cathelineau, Dionysia Christoforou, Peter van der Coelen, Dan Cox, Sabine Craft-Giepmans, Rik van Daele, Sjors Dekkers, Maaike Dirkx, Eric Domela Nieuwenhuis, Bernd Ebert, Michiel van Elsas, Merel van Erp, Lisette Frimannslund, Rob Fucci, Eva de la Fuente Pedersen, Silke Gatenbröcker, René Gerritsen, Hilliard Goldfarb, Inger Groeneveld, Jazzy de Groot, Stefaan Hautekeete, Signe Havsteen, Claudia Hofstee, Charlotte Hoitsma, Jonathan Hopson, Olenka Horbatsch, Karoline Hvalsøe, Angela Jager, Ruth Jongsma, Menno Jonker, Vera Jorissen, Pepijn Kamminga, Hildegard Kaul, Jan de Klerk, Hanneke Klinkert-Koopmans, Lisa Kloosterman, Antje-Fee Köllermann, Edouard Kopp, Gerbrand Korevaar, Everhard Korthals Altes, Hester Kuiper, Peter Kuipers Munneke, Fransje Kuyvenhoven, Celeste Langedijk, Leah Lehmbeck, Camilla Lengstrand, Clé Lesger, Lisa Lucassen, Ger Luijten, Austeja Mackelaite, Bas Maliepaard, Jan Nicolaisen, Bernice Notenboom, Nadine Orenstein, Sander Paarlberg, Sheldon Peck †, Domenico Pino, Sandra Pisot, Terje Planke, Michiel Plomp, Almut Pollmer-Schmidt, Mark Ponte, Harry de Raad, Marleen Ram, Sabine Rieger, Marrigje Rikken, Laura Ritter, Pieter Roelofs, Michiel Roscam Abbing, Manja Rottink, Juliane Rückert, Charlotte Rulkens, Tatjana van Run, Jochen Sander, Iris Schaefer, Anja Ševčik, Britton Smith, Walter Straten, Margareta Svensson, Alice Taatgen, Cécile Tainturier, Júlia Tátrai, Ilona van Tuinen, Simon Turner, Gabri van Tussenbroek, Paul Wackers, Kees Zandvliet, Diva Zumaya.

And lastly, a special thank you to the two expert advisers who have constantly stood by our side at the museum in recent years in everything related to this project: Alice I. Davies, author of the bulky catalogues of Allart van Everdingen's paintings and drawings, and Frits Duparc, former director of the Mauritshuis. Without their input, the exhibition could never have come about in this ambitious form.

Christi M. Klinkert
Curator, Stedelijk Museum Alkmaar

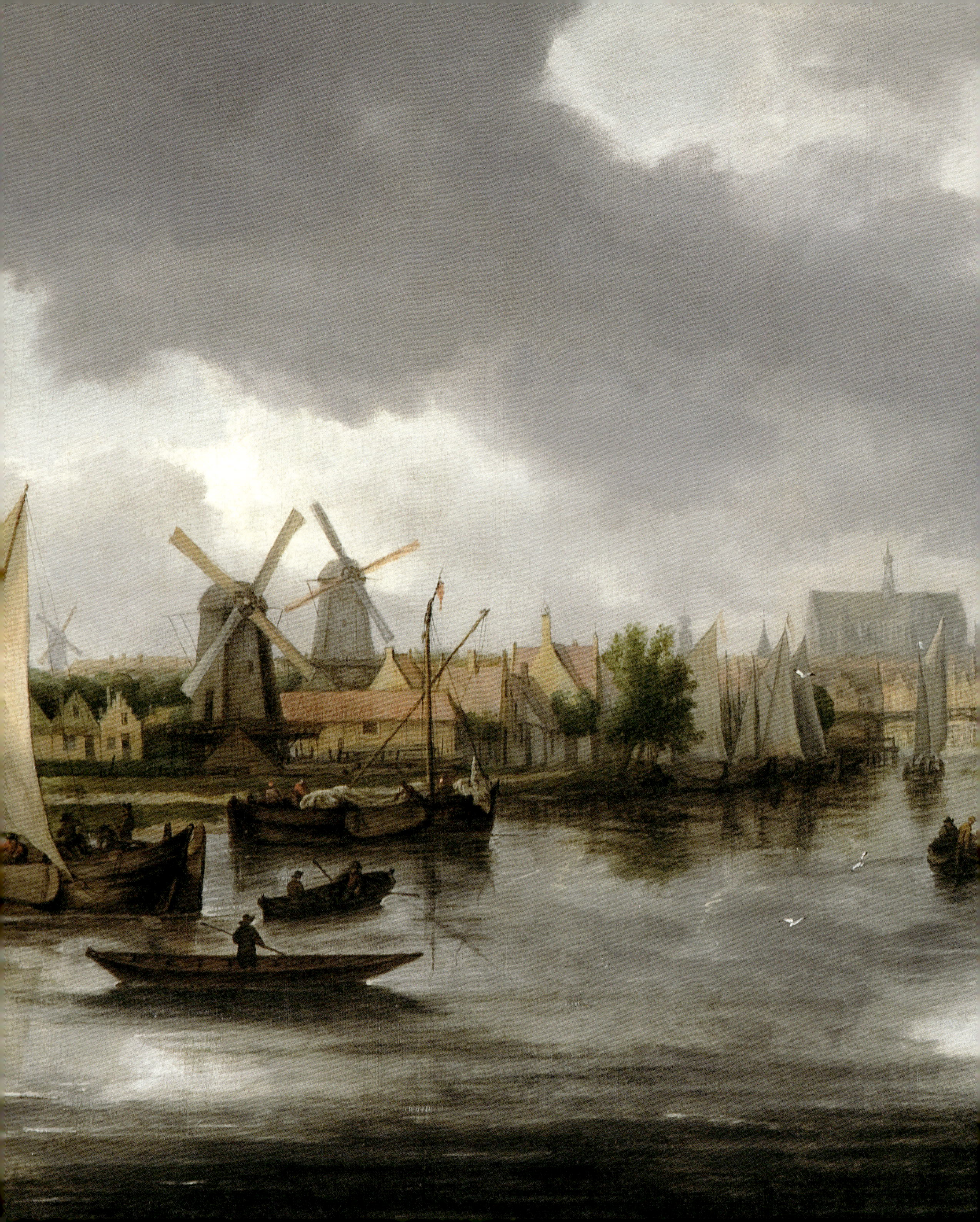

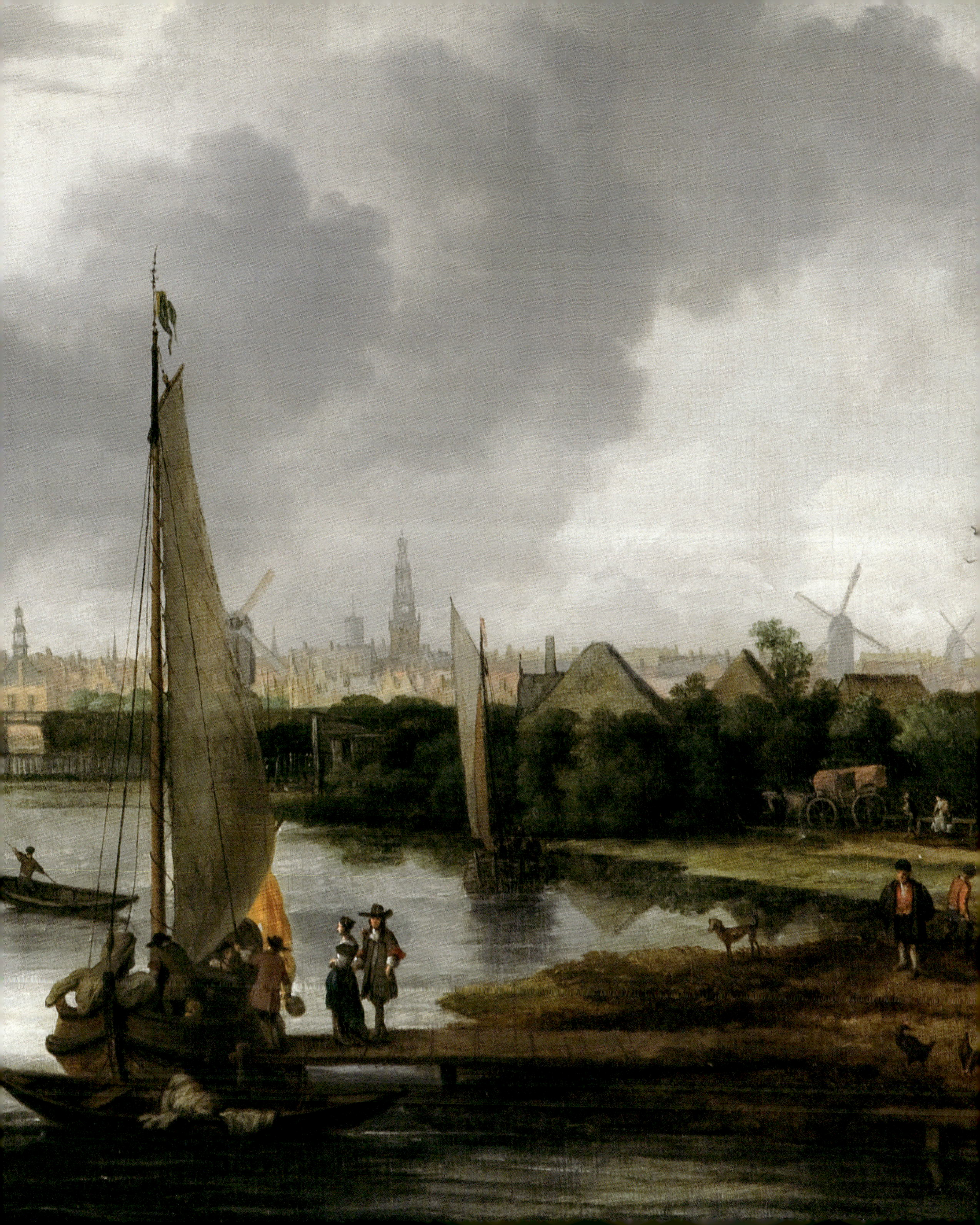

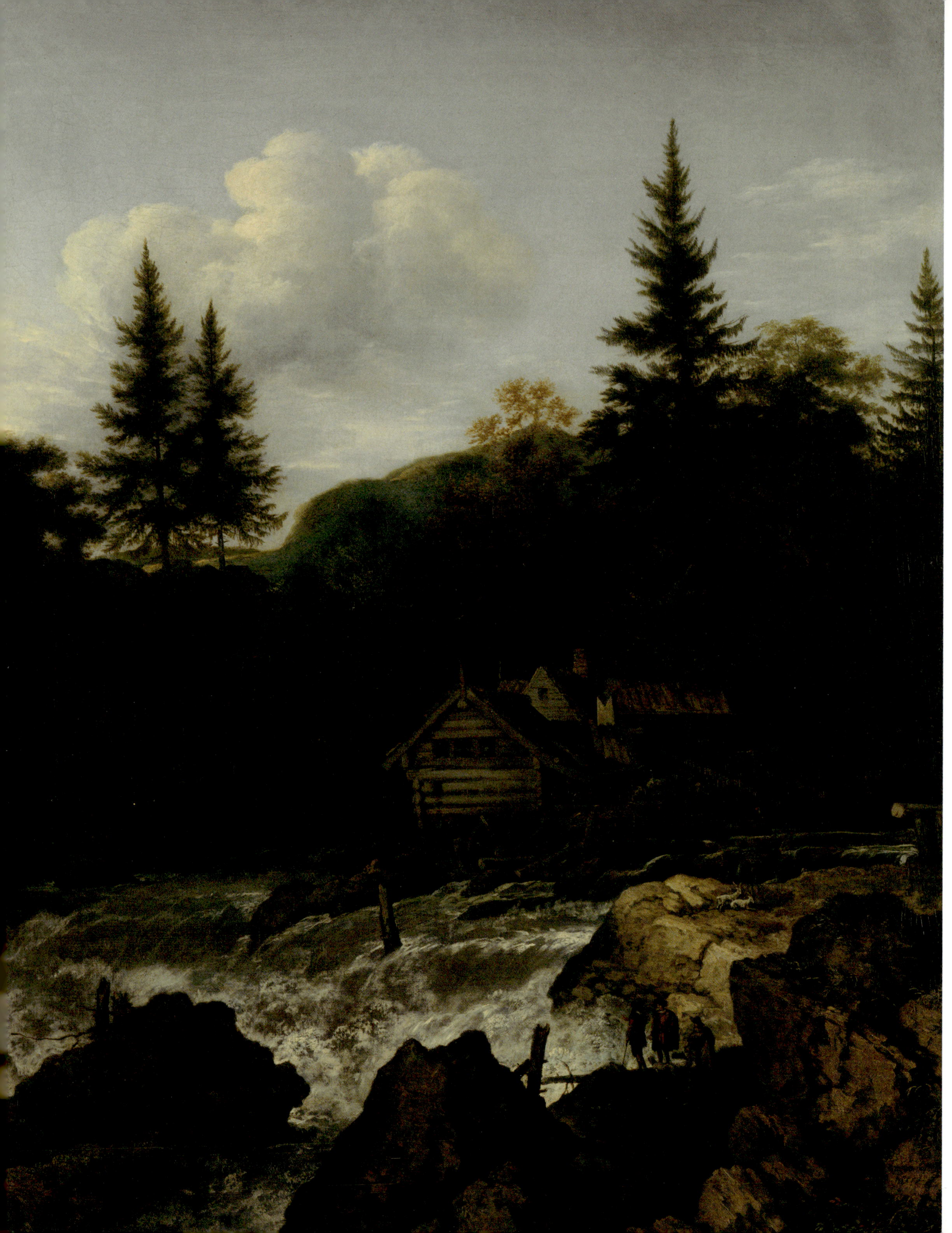

1
THE LIFE AND WORK
of Allart van Everdingen

Christi M. Klinkert

In 1644, a young Alkmaar artist boarded a ship bound for the Baltic. A terrible storm drove the vessel on to the Norwegian coast. The man remained in the region for a while, travelled about and made sketches of the rugged landscape he found there. Back in Holland, he transformed his impressions into paintings, drawings and prints.

This adventure is described in the biography of Allart van Everdingen (Alkmaar 1621-1675 Amsterdam) in Arnold Houbraken's *De groote schouburgh der Nederlantsche konstschilders en schilderessen* (*The Great Theatre of Dutch Painters*, volume 2, 1719).[1] Houbraken dished up this story to explain how the landscape painter came to specialize in Scandinavian scenes. That Van Everdingen was actually driven ashore in Norway by a storm at sea is unconfirmed, but there is no doubt that he went to that country, and that he owes his reputation chiefly to his pictures of waterfalls, log cabins, rock formations and conifers (fig. 1).

In Van Everdingen's day, Norway was a province of Denmark. When Allart visited the country, it covered a rather larger area than it does today: part of the present-day Swedish coastal region around the city of Gothenburg was then Norwegian. The Swedes and the Norwegians constantly fought over it; in the end the Swedes prevailed. The region to the southeast of Gothenburg was added to Sweden in 1645, followed by the region to the northwest in 1658.

Numerically, Scandinavian landscapes account for the greater part of Van Everdingen's substantial oeuvre.[2] It should be noted, however, that only a small number of landscapes are unmistakably and wholly Scandinavian; in most cases, they are mountain landscapes with some Scandinavian motifs. The artist also made a great many Dutch landscapes and a few seascapes and river scenes (marines). This latter category includes both Dutch and rocky coasts. Of the surviving etchings and paintings—a hundred and nine and around a hundred and eighty respectively—the great majority are devoted to the northern mountain landscape.[3] In the case of the drawings, this is true of about a third of the six hundred and fifty-plus surviving works.[4] Besides the many landscapes, Van Everdingen made a series of prints of the story of Reynard the Fox.[5]

In this catalogue, separate essays are devoted to Allart van Everdingen's paintings, drawings and etchings. The Reynard series also has an essay of its own. While this arrangement is certainly clear and comprehensible, it does not reflect the historical reality. The artist would have drawn, painted and etched more or less simultaneously throughout his career. Drawings, for instance, were used as preparatory studies for paintings and etchings. Van Everdingen worked out certain motifs on paper, canvas and panel. Relationships like these between particular drawings, etchings and paintings are obviously mentioned in the essays. In this biography, the oeuvre as a whole is discussed —albeit briefly and broadly. More detailed information can be found in the essays that follow.

It is difficult to establish a chronological order for Van Everdingen's extensive and varied output, because he seldom dated his works. Some thirty paintings are dated; two-thirds of those were made in the early period from 1640 to 1650.[6] The artist did not date any of his drawings and etchings.[7] He did sign as a rule, but in many different ways: 'Allart van Everdingen', 'A. van Everdingen', 'A. v. Everdingen', 'A. Everdingen', 'Van Everdingen', 'V. Everdingen', 'Everdingen', 'AVE', written in italics or capitals, with or without a point where a word is abbreviated. Most of the signatures with the last name

written out in full occur on the paintings (fig. 2). Van Everdingen usually signed his drawings and etchings just with his monogram (fig. 3).[8]

Birth and Training

Allart van Everdingen was born in Alkmaar in June 1621.[9] He and his twin sister Dieuwertje were baptized in the Grote Sint-Laurenskerk (Great St Lawrence's Church) there on 18 June 1621.[10] Dieuwertje did not live long: her burial —likewise in the Grote Kerk—was recorded on 6 September 1621. She was described there as 'a child of Everdingen, lawyer in Schoutenstraat'.[11] And it was in Schoutenstraat in Alkmaar that Allart grew up, the third son of the notary Pieter Cornelisz van Everdingen (1575-1662) and midwife Aechje Claesdr Moer (c. 1585-1640). Both parents had been married before and had children from those marriages; together they had another four children. Caesar van Everdingen (1616/1617-1678) was the oldest of that brood and, like Allart, became a celebrated painter.[12] He was followed by Jan (c. 1618/1619-1656), the twins Allart and Dieuwertje, and Scipio (1623-1653). Jan followed in his father's footsteps and Scipio became an apothecary.

< 2
Signature on Allart van Everdingen, *Mountain Landscape with a River and a Castle*, oil on canvas, 219 x 193 cm, Copenhagen, Statens Museum for Kunst, inv. no. KMSsp512 (cat. no. 67)

3
Signature on Allart van Everdingen, *Scandinavian Landscape with Two Log Cabins by the Water*, brush and brown ink, watercolour, 112 x 168 mm, Haarlem, Teylers Museum, inv. no. Q 030 (cat. no. 54)

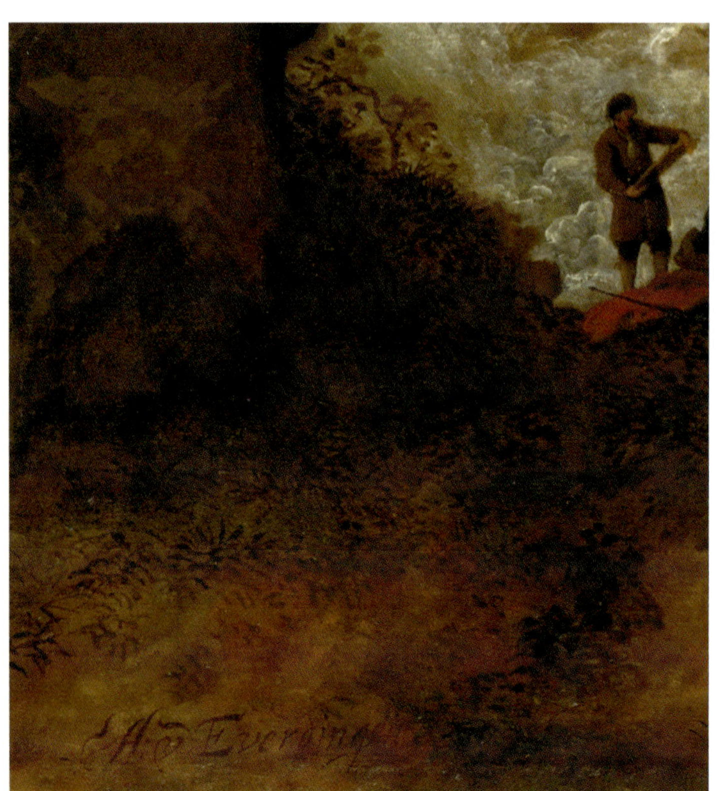

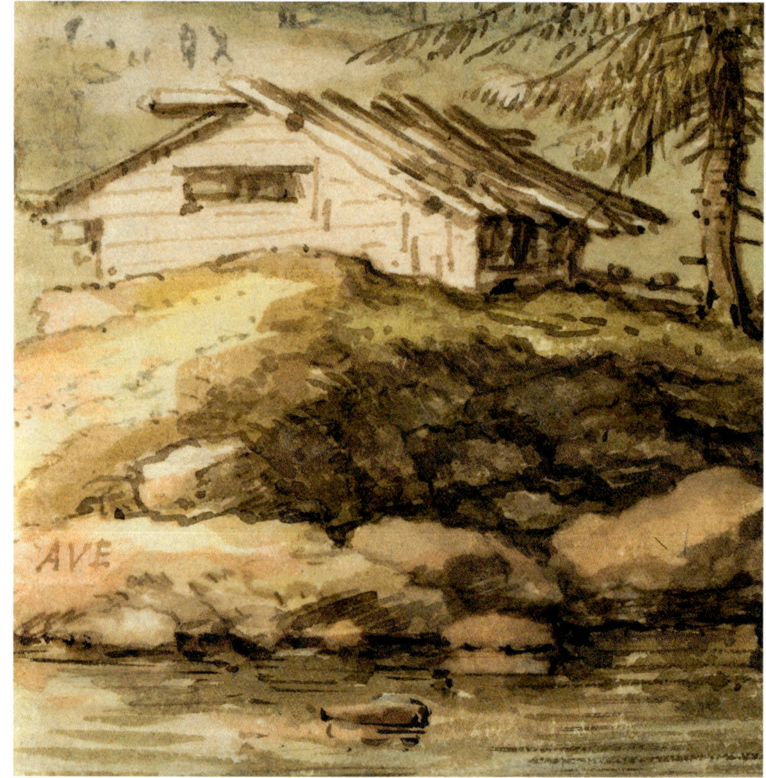

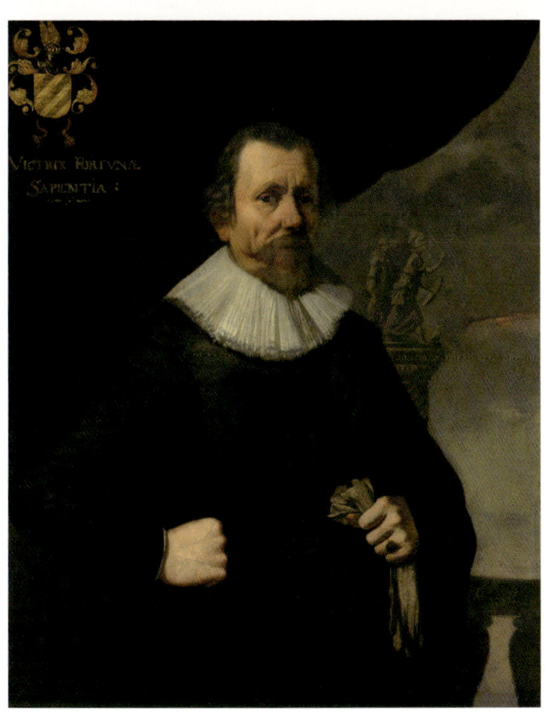
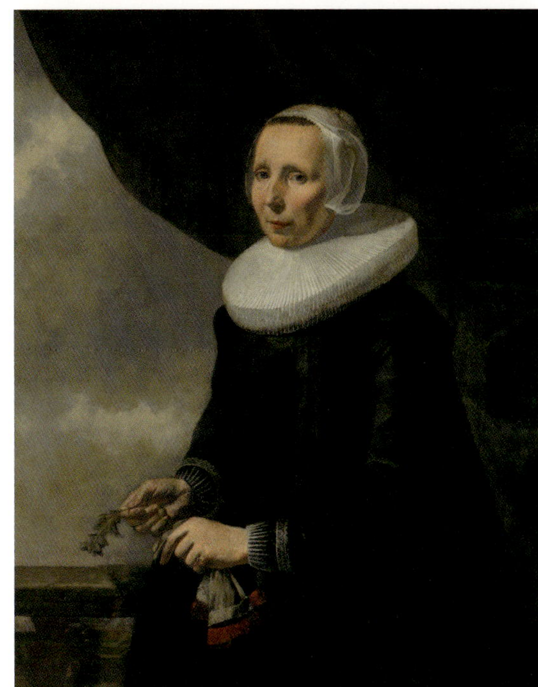

4 and 5
Caesar van Everdingen,
*Portrait of Pieter
Cornelisz van Everdingen*
and *Portrait of Aechje
Claesdr Moer*, 1636,
oil on panel, 94 x 74.6 cm
and 94.1 x 74.3 cm,
Stedelijk Museum
Alkmaar, inv. nos.
20929 and 20930

6
Caesar van Everdingen,
Self-Portrait c. 1670,
oil on canvas, 94.3 x
74.5 cm, Stedelijk
Museum Alkmaar,
inv. no. 20931

Caesar van Everdingen, a gifted figure painter, made portraits of his parents and himself (figs. 4-6).[13] He also painted Allart but, as far as we are aware, that work has not survived. We do, though, know that it existed and what it looked like from a drawing Jan Stolker (1724-1785) based on it (fig. 7). It is tempting to think that the woman who holds the portrait of Allart van Everdingen in this composition is his wife, but there is no way of proving this conjecture.[14]

The surname Van Everdingen had been adopted at the end of the fifteenth century by a distant ancestor who had leased a piece of land near the village of Everdingen in the Province of Utrecht. Allart's grandfather, Cornelis Loeffsz van Everdingen (c. 1545-1585), was among the Sea Beggars who took part in the capture of Den Briel in 1572. Soon after this, he was appointed captain of Holland's Northern Quarter and stationed in Alkmaar. His son Pieter set up his legal practice there in 1598 and married Aechje in 1615.[15] From 1618 onwards they lived with their children in Schoutenstraat, moving in June 1629 to Langestraat, in the building that is now number 96.[16]

In the absence of contemporary sources, it is impossible to say with certainty who trained Allart van Everdingen as an artist. His older brother Caesar was given his first painting lessons by a local artist and continued his training in Utrecht; Allart probably followed the same path.[17] It is quite conceivable that in the 1633 to 1636 period he was learning the basic skills—making paint, setting out palettes,

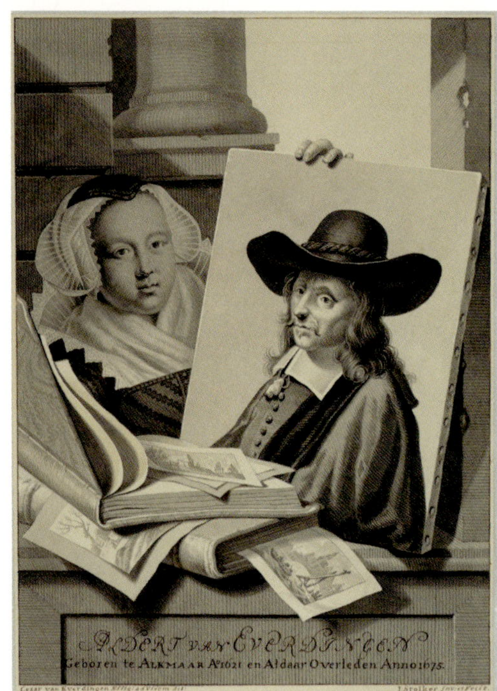

preparing canvases and panels, drawing from life and working out compositions—from Claes Jacobsz van der Heck (c. 1578-1652), then the most important painter in Alkmaar and known for his landscapes.[18] He would then most likely have gone to Utrecht, following Caesar. According to Houbraken, Allart van Everdingen was apprenticed to 'Roelant Savry' and concluded his training with 'Pieter Molyn' in Haarlem.

By 'Roelant Savry', Houbraken certainly meant Roelandt Savery (1576-1639), who after years in Haarlem, Amsterdam and Prague lived in Utrecht from 1618 until his death.[19] It is not entirely clear who 'Pieter Molyn' was. The most obvious candidate is Pieter de Molijn (1595-1661), an extremely productive Haarlem artist who drew and painted landscapes.[20] However, it could also be Pieter Mulier I (1595/1610-1659/1661), a Haarlem marine painter.[21] Houbraken had erroneously called Mulier I 'Pieter Molyn the Elder' elsewhere in his book and he may have made the same mistake in his biography of Van Everdingen.[22] We should also take into account the fact that Allart's earliest works are all seascapes, which suggests a period of training with a marine artist.

Houbraken probably got his information about Van Everdingen's training from Allart's son Pieter, given that they both lived in Amsterdam when the former was writing his lives of the

artists.[23] However, there is no hard evidence of his assertions. The Van Everdingen family's connections with the region make it likely that Allart did spend time in Utrecht. A notarial document dated 15 January 1639, in which Allart's father authorized his son 'living in Haerlem' to collect the sum of one hundred guilders from a Haarlem lawyer, confirms that Allart spent some time in Haarlem when he was a young man.[24]

Whether Allart van Everdingen was trained by Savery and De Molijn or Mulier I, in any event the influence of all three of these artists can be seen in his work. In 1606-1607 Roelandt Savery travelled through the Tyrol, commissioned by Emperor Rudolf II to draw the Alpine landscape.[25] The likeness between those drawn mountain landscapes (fig. 8) and the bare rocks in Allart's early seascapes and Scandinavian landscapes (fig. 47) is striking.[26] In drawing style and rural motifs, a river landscape signed and dated 'A. van Everdingen / 1644' (fig. 9) resembles De Molijn's Dutch landscapes (fig. 10).[27] And the way Allart rendered ships in distress on raging seas (fig. 11) bears a strong similarity to Pieter Mulier I's work (fig. 12).

His possible teachers were not the only artists to have an influence on Van Everdingen. The catalogue of Allart's collection of paintings,

< 7
Jan Stolker after Caesar van Everdingen, *Portrait of Allart van Everdingen*, pen and brush and grey and brown ink, 336 x 243 mm, Klassik Stiftung Weimar, Museen, inv. no. KK 5459

8
Roelandt Savery, *Mountain Landscape with a Waterfall*, c. 1606-1607, black chalk, brush and grey ink, watercolour, 383 x 413 mm, Amsterdam, Rijksmuseum, inv. no. RP-T-1931-182

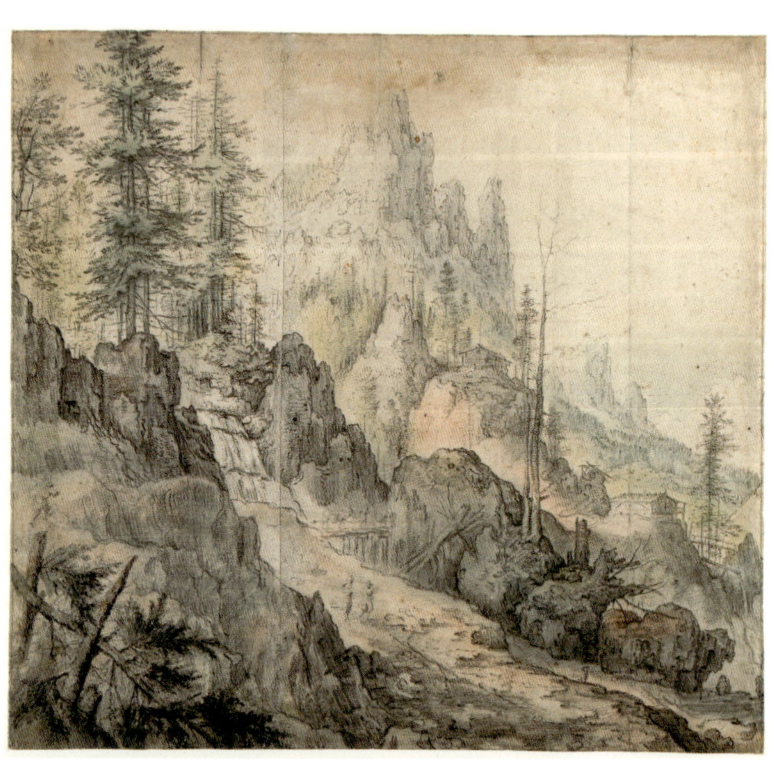

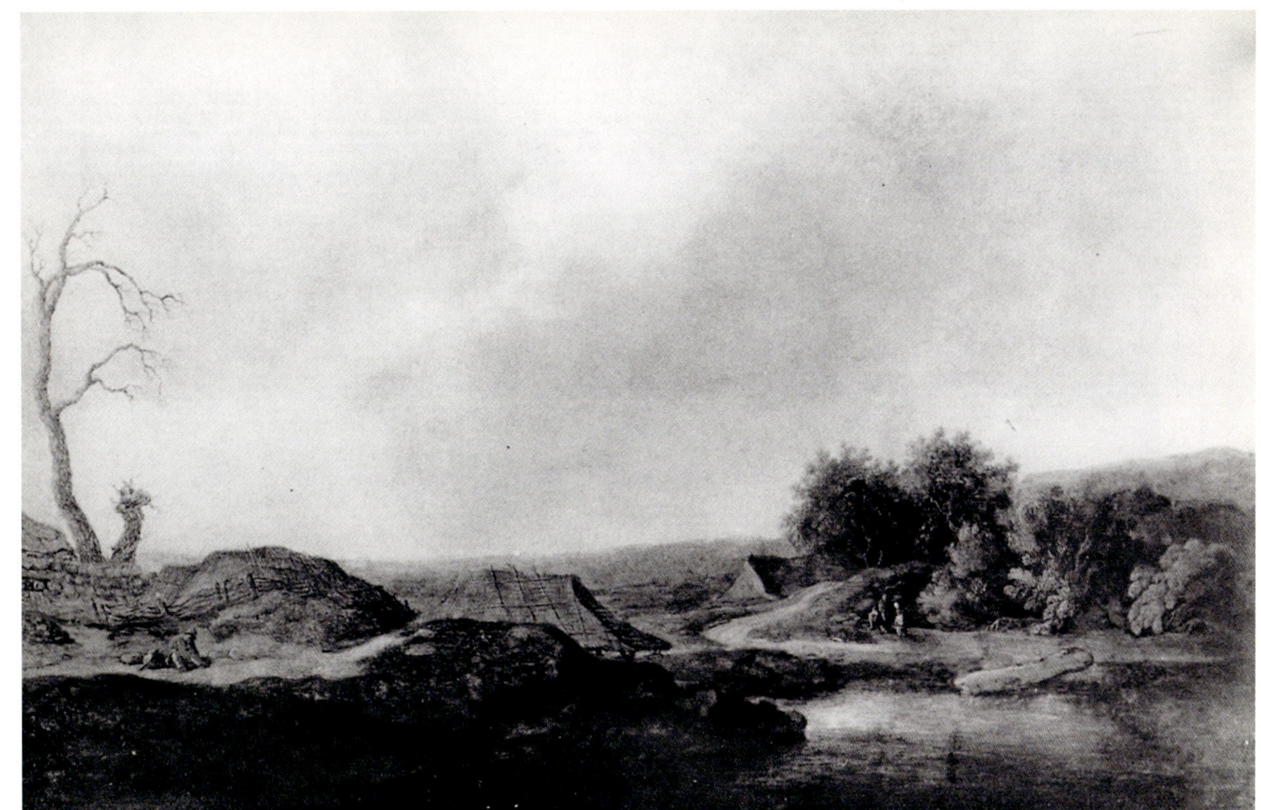

9
Allart van Everdingen,
*River Landscape with
Cottages*, 1644, oil
on panel, approx.
30 x 50 cm, where-
abouts unknown

10
Pieter de Molijn,
*Landscape with an
Open Gate*, c. 1630-
1635, oil on panel,
33.6 x 47.9 cm,
Washington, National
Gallery of Art, inv.
no. 1986.10.1

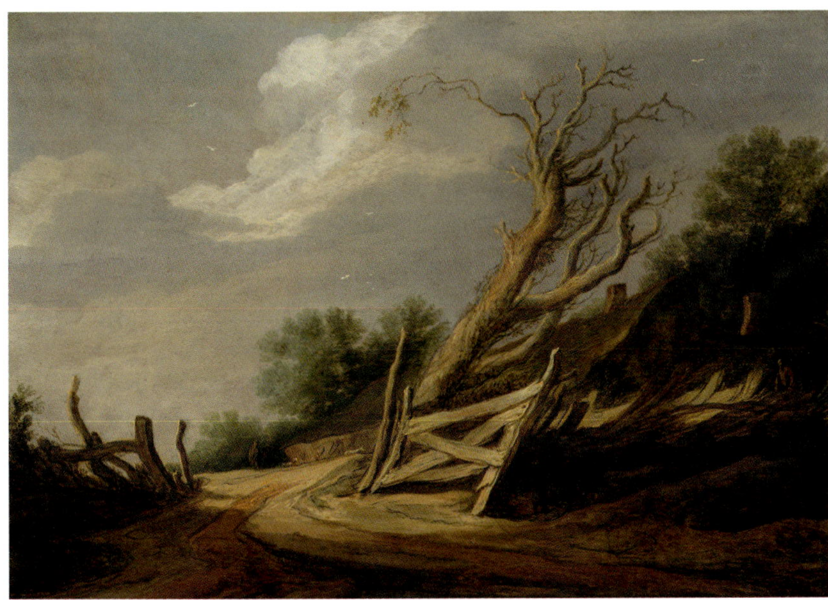

published in 1709 on the occasion of its sale, provides some interesting insights.[28] There are works by Savery, De Molijn and Mulier I, but also by other eminent landscape and marine painters like Hendrick Cornelisz Vroom (1562/1566-1640), his son Cornelis Hendricksz Vroom (1590/1591-1661) and Jan Porcellis (c. 1584-1632). Allart van Everdingen must have studied their paintings very closely and borrowed style idioms and motifs from them. These artists also contributed to his development. The individual essays on his painting, drawing and etching examine how these and other examples inspired Van Everdingen.

On 20 August 1639, Allart van Everdingen acted as a witness for his brother, the notary Jan, in Alkmaar.[29] Between September 1640 and the end of July 1642 he did this for him quite frequently, and occasionally for his father, Pieter, too.[30] This tells us that he must have been living in his birthplace again during that period and working as an independent artist.[31] His earliest known signed and dated painting —a seascape—bears the date 1640 (fig. 42).[32]

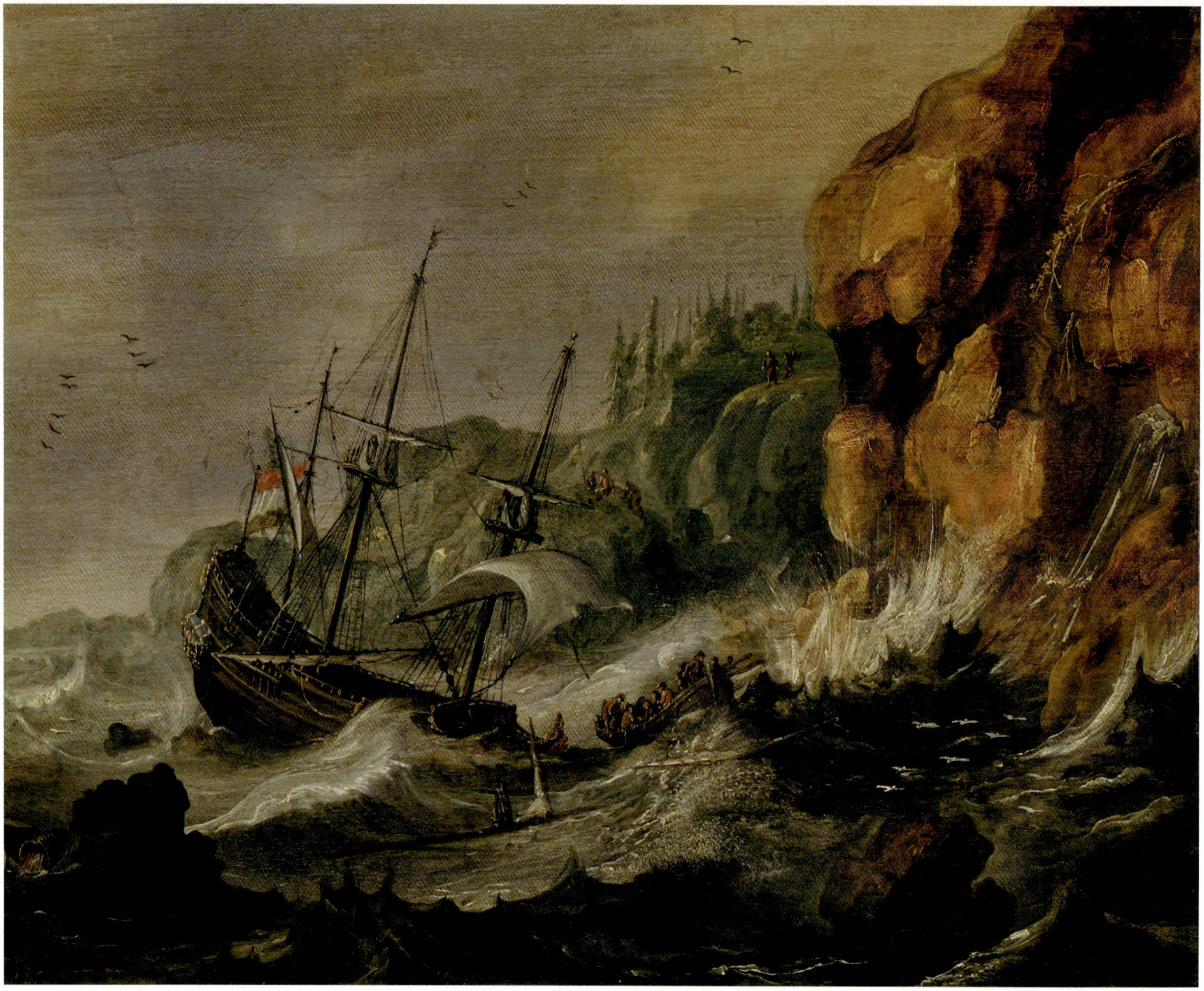

11
Allart van Everdingen, *Shipwreck off a Rocky Coast*, oil on panel, 34 x 42 cm, private collection (cat. no. 104)

12 >
Pieter Mulier I, *A Dutch Ship in a Storm off a Rocky Coast*, c. 1640, oil on panel, 39.4 x 52.1 cm, London, Greenwich, National Maritime Museum, Palmer Collection, inv. no. BHC0819

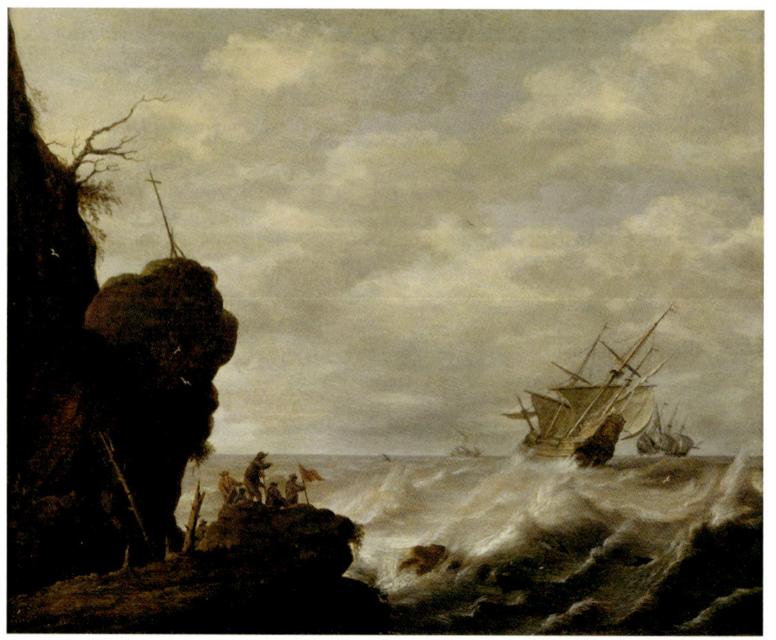

To the North

On 5 February 1645, Allart van Everdingen and Janneke Cornelisdr (1624-1708), daughter of Cornelis Brouwers and Lysbeth Pietersdr, gave notice of their intended marriage both in Alkmaar—where Allart was living 'in Langestraet'—and in Haarlem—where Janneke was residing 'in Grote Houtstraet'.[33] Van Everdingen must have taken his trip to Scandinavia, as reported by Arnold Houbraken, shortly before this. As far as can be determined, there is no trace of Allart in the Alkmaar and Haarlem archives from the summer of 1642 until early 1645.[34]

To be precise, Houbraken wrote the following about Van Everdingen's journey to the north in his *Groote schouburgh*: 'for having embarked on a ship for some place on the Baltic Sea, he encountered a dangerous storm, which caused him to land, willy-nilly, on the coast of Norway, not without harm.'[35] The phrase 'willy-nilly' ('whether he wanted to or not') implies that the author was unable to discover whether Allart was planning to visit Norway or had originally had another destination in mind—perhaps one of the Baltic states—but was forced by circumstances to disembark earlier. The note that he arrived 'not without harm' means that he had suffered some physical or material damage during the crossing: he had been ill, injured or lost some of his possessions on the way. It has been said in the art historical literature that Van Everdingen was shipwrecked.[36] Houbraken, however, says nothing about the loss of a vessel, he simply mentions heavy weather.

We cannot say for certain why Allart van Everdingen took ship, but the events on his journey can be reconstructed. For a young artist from Alkmaar in the seventeenth century, there were possibilities enough to find shelter in Norway through Dutch connections. Hundreds of ships from Western Europe—including the Republic—set sail for the Baltic region every year, among other things to load grain and timber.[37] Many of them put in at one of the ports along the Norwegian coast to avoid storms at sea and await more favourable winds, or to replenish their provisions and drinking water. As well as this, there had been a direct trading relationship between the Low Countries and Norway since the Middle Ages.[38] Dutch and Frisian merchants exported goods like beer, wine, salt, herrings, cheese, tiles, textiles, furniture, tobacco and clay pipes to Norway and imported wool, butter, fish and lobsters. The major import product, however, was timber, which was used primarily in building ships and houses. It was with justice said that Amsterdam 'stood on Norway', because it was built on Norwegian tree trunks. In normal circumstances, the sea voyage from the Netherlands to Norway took from something over a week to two weeks at most.[39] During the sailing season (April to December), Dutch captains sailed back and forth several times, generally to the same Norwegian port.[40] The Hollanders had traditionally concentrated chiefly on the south-eastern Norwegian coastal region, the Frisian skippers on the southwest.

Perhaps Van Everdingen's teacher Roelandt Savery, who himself spent time in Central Europe in the 1603/1604 to 1612/1613 period, aroused his pupil's curiosity about the wide world beyond the Republic.[41] Or maybe he advised him to specialize in an unusual type of landscape if he wanted commercial success. Allart may then have met one of the many Dutch businessmen who were active at that time in Scandinavia and the countries around the Baltic Sea.[42] There can be no doubt that he sailed on a merchantman from Amsterdam or Hoorn to Norway, where he would have been shown the ropes by the Dutchmen who worked there as agents for merchants.[43] He may have explored the region on foot or on horseback, but more probably mainly by boat. The Norwegian hinterland was relatively inaccessible; there were no good roads for heavy traffic, and people and materials were usually transported by water.[44] When his trip came to an end, it would have been a Dutch captain who took Van Everdingen back to his homeland.

Of course, Allart recorded the things that caught his eye in Norway—it is inconceivable that an artist would not do that—but regrettably no travel journal or sketchbook has survived. However, a number of related drawings in his oeuvre are assumed to have been made en route or based on sketches done on the spot (figs. 13 and 14).[45] Because the places recorded in them have been identified as existing locations in Scandinavia (figs. 15 and 16), Van Everdingen's route can be reconstructed. He visited the coastal towns of Langesund and Risør and the region around Gothenburg (Göteborg)—the

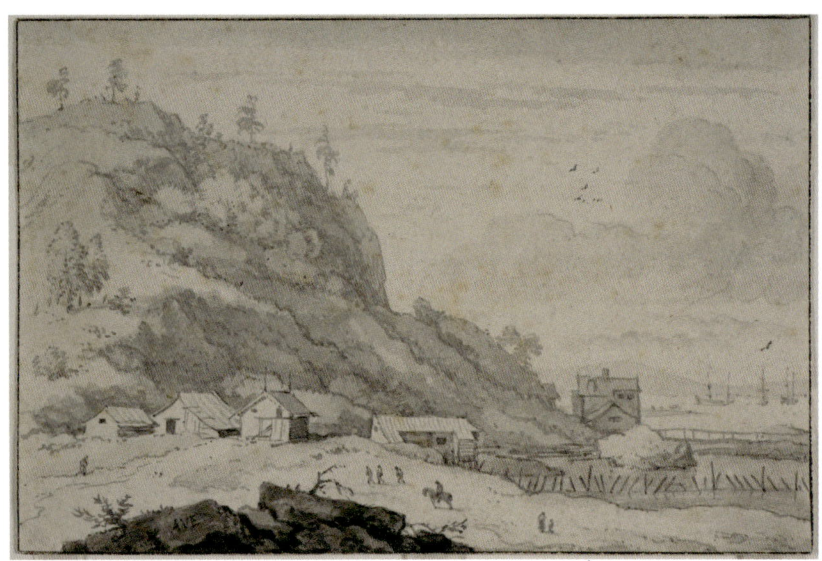

13
Allart van Everdingen, *View of Risør*, 1644 or shortly
thereafter, pen and brush and grey ink, grey wash,
115 x 176 mm, Stockholm, Nationalmuseum,
inv. no. NMH 851/1938

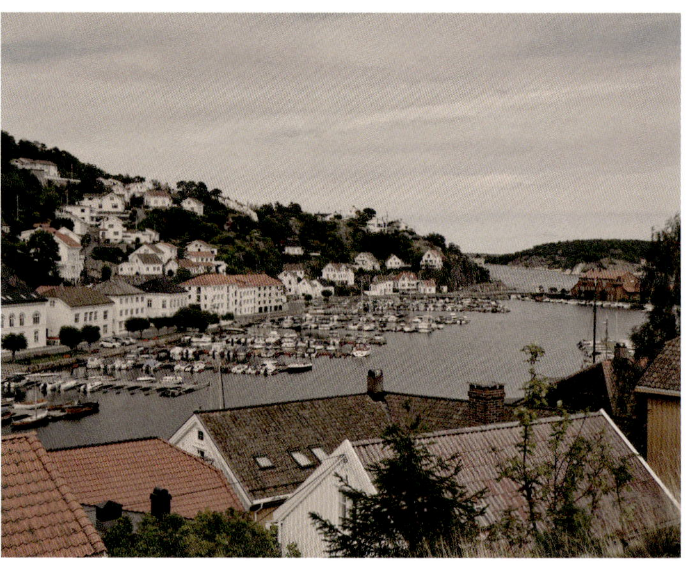

15
Risør Harbour (photograph Pascal Vossen,
August-September 2019)

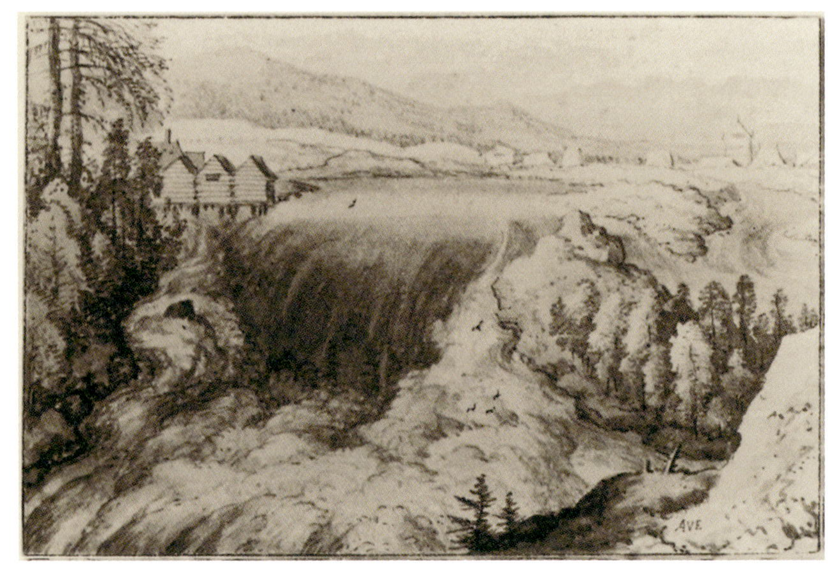

14
Allart van Everdingen, *Waterfall near Trollhättan*,
1644 or shortly thereafter, pen and brush and grey ink,
grey wash, 115 x 176 mm, Rotterdam, Museum
Boijmans Van Beuningen, inv. no. AvE 4 (PK)

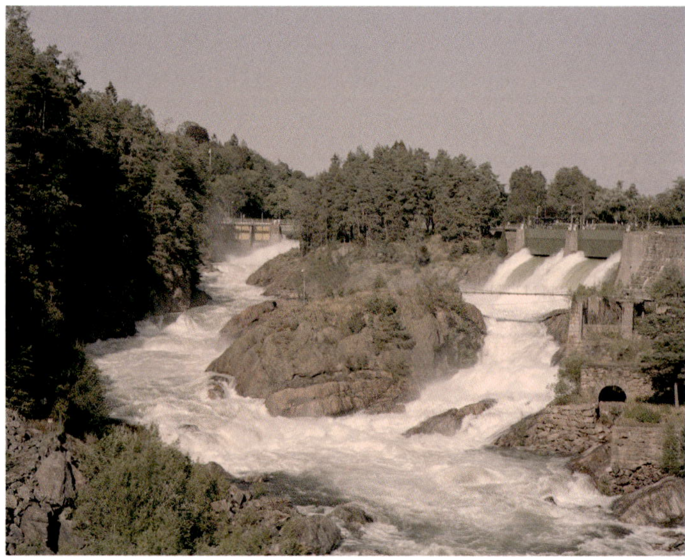

16
Waterfall near Trollhättan (photograph
Pascal Vossen, August-September 2019)

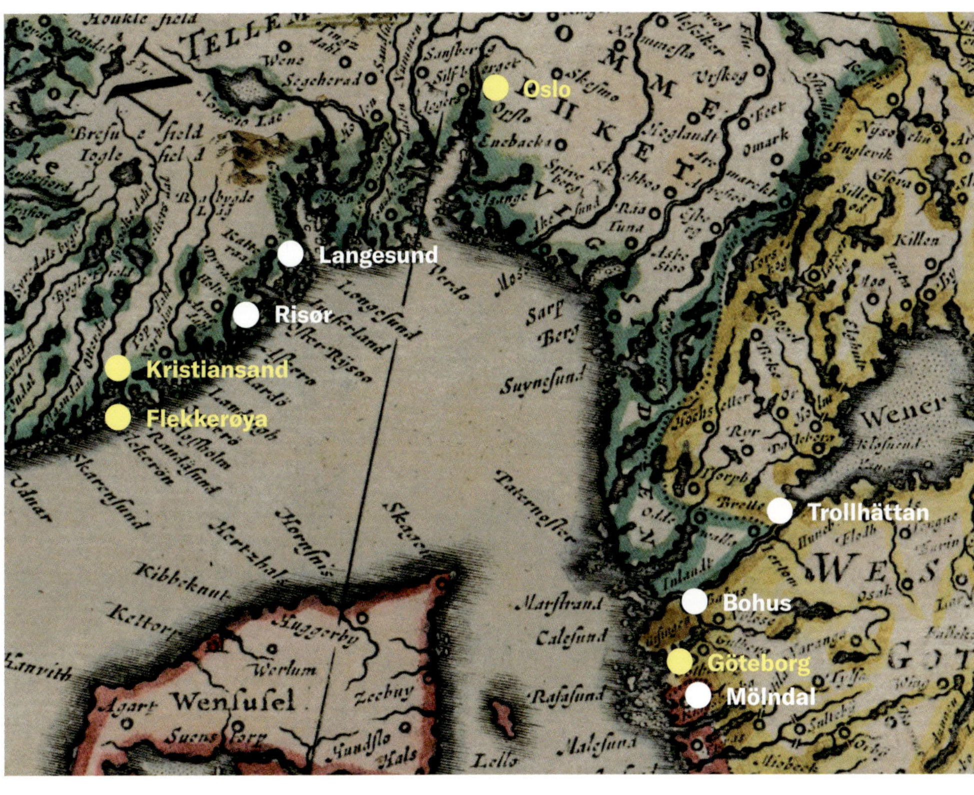

17

The Norwegian coastal region Allart van Everdingen visited, with the places he went to in white; detail of the map of Scandinavia and the Baltic States in *Toonneel des aerdriicx, Ofte nieuwe atlas, Dat is beschryving van alle Landen*, vol. 1, Amsterdam: Willem Jansz Blaeu and Joan Blaeu 1649, Erfgoed Leiden en Omstreken, library, sign. AB 447 large folio volume

18

Jan de Beijer, *View of Risør*, pen and reddish brown and grey ink, watercolour, 190 x 290 mm, Arendal, Aust-Agder Museum og Arkiv IKS - KUBEN, inv. no. AAM.B.0759

village of Mölndal, Bohus Fortress and the waterfalls near Trollhättan (fig. 17).[46] This is precisely the then Norwegian coastal strip and the Norwegian-Swedish border area in which Dutch merchants were active, particularly in the timber trade, and Dutch merchant vessels sailed back and forth.

None of the surviving 'travel sketches' is dated. There is, however, an early copy by Jan de Beijer (1703-1780) of one work (fig. 13), with the inscription 'oostrysen in noorwegen 1644' ('Oostrysen in Norway 1644') (fig. 18). De Beijer made other drawings after 'sketches from life' by Van Everdingen.[47] It may be assumed that he took the inscription quoted from one such original sketch and that it is a reliable date for Allart's journey. Indeed 1644 falls exactly in the period when there is no record of Van Everdingen in Holland. Nevertheless, it is also possible that he went on his northern adventure in 1643, perhaps even in the late summer of 1642. In this catalogue we stick to the most likely date, 1644. Given the distance Allart covered in Norway and the time taken by the crossing, we can say that he was away from home for no more than a few months. The fact that there is no snow in Van Everdingen's Norwegian scenes tells us that he must have seen the country between April and October, not in the winter.[48]

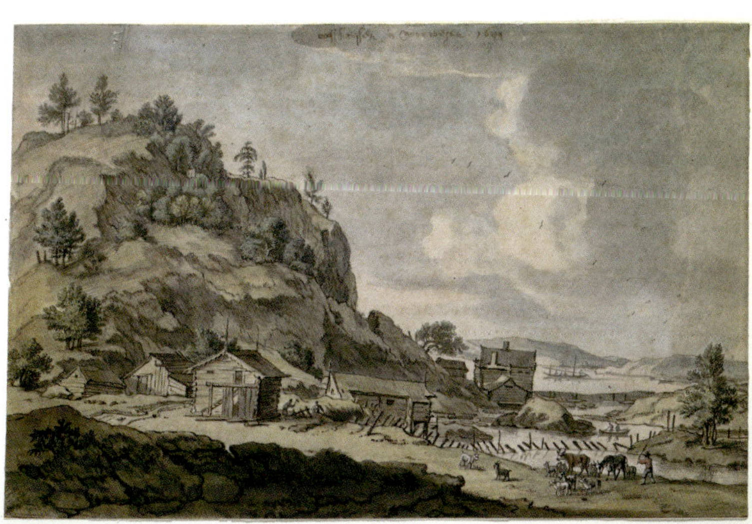

In Haarlem

On 21 February 1645, Allart van Everdingen married Janneke Cornelisdr in Haarlem. They settled in the town, in a house called 'Het Serpent' in Grote Houtstraat—on the site of the present-day number 21.[49] On 16 February 1646, a year after their wedding, their first child, Cornelis, was baptized. They had to bury their second, Aegje, shortly after her birth, in December 1647. A year later they had another daughter, whom they also called Aegje. A third daughter, Elisabeth, followed in 1651. Meanwhile, Allart had become a member of the Haarlem painters' guild in 1646. In 1648 he had also joined the Old or St George's Civic Guard in his home town, together with his brother Caesar, who had just come to live in Haarlem.

Around the middle of the seventeenth century, Haarlem was a prosperous town with a flourishing art scene. It was where Frans Hals made his lively, loosely painted portraits, Pieter Saenredam his tranquil church interiors, where Salomon de Bray painted impressive historical, biblical and mythological compositions, Jan Miense Molenaer cheerful domestic scenes and Salomon van Ruysdael peaceful riverscapes.[50] The depiction of the landscape, in particular, underwent significant developments in Haarlem. The pictorial tradition of the typically Dutch, naturalistic landscape, for instance, was given a major boost at the beginning of the seventeenth century, when Hendrick Goltzius and Esaias van de Velde left their studios and took their sketchbooks out to draw in the open air. At the time Van Everdingen set up his workshop, there was a fashion for more imposing, dramatic landscapes, which would reach its zenith in the work of Jacob van Ruisdael.[51]

It was in this inspiring environment that Allart van Everdingen painted his first Scandinavian

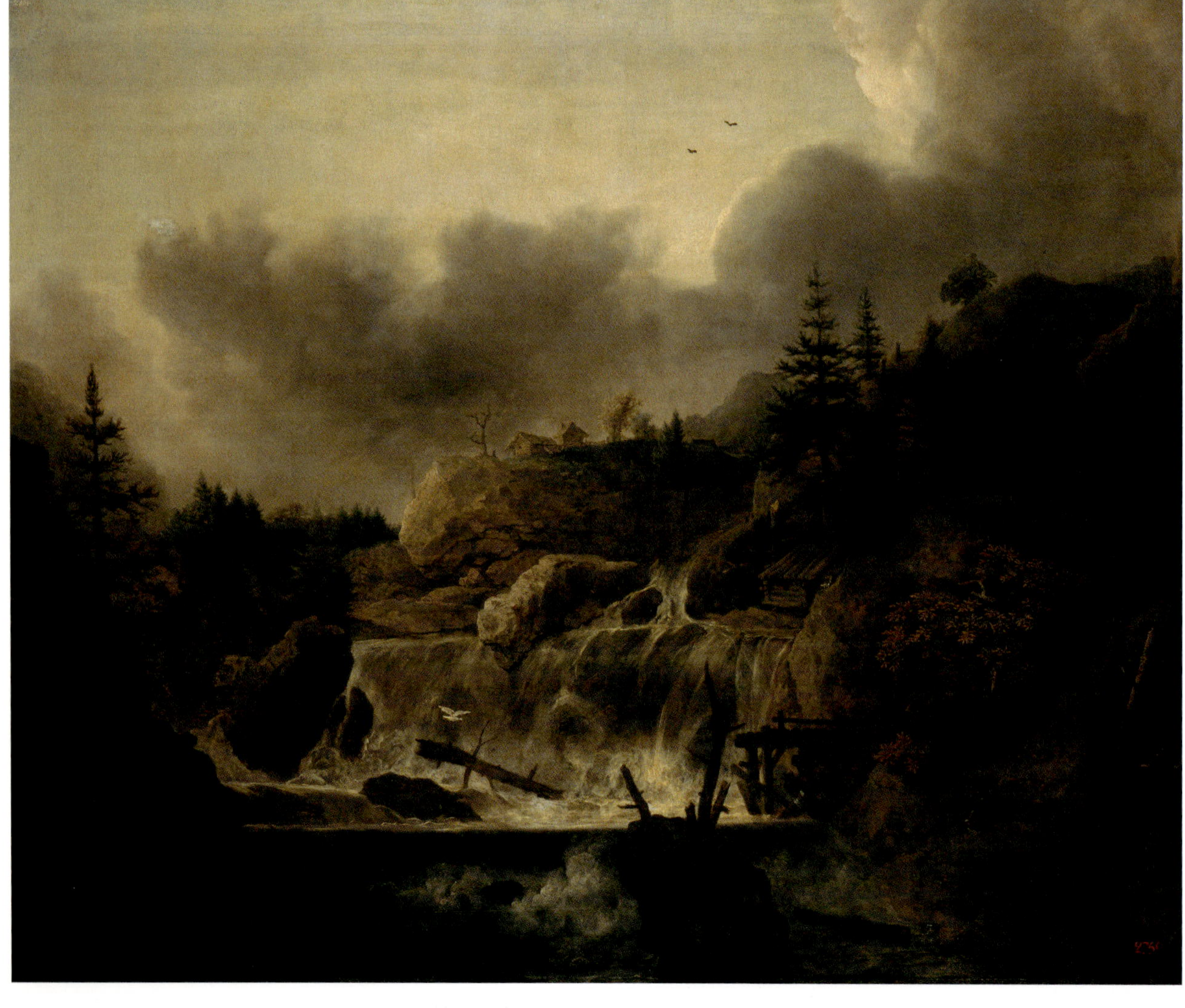

19
Allart van Everdingen, *Norwegian Landscape with a Waterfall*, 1647, oil on canvas, 111 x 135 cm, St Petersburg, The State Hermitage Museum, inv. no. ГЭ-1901

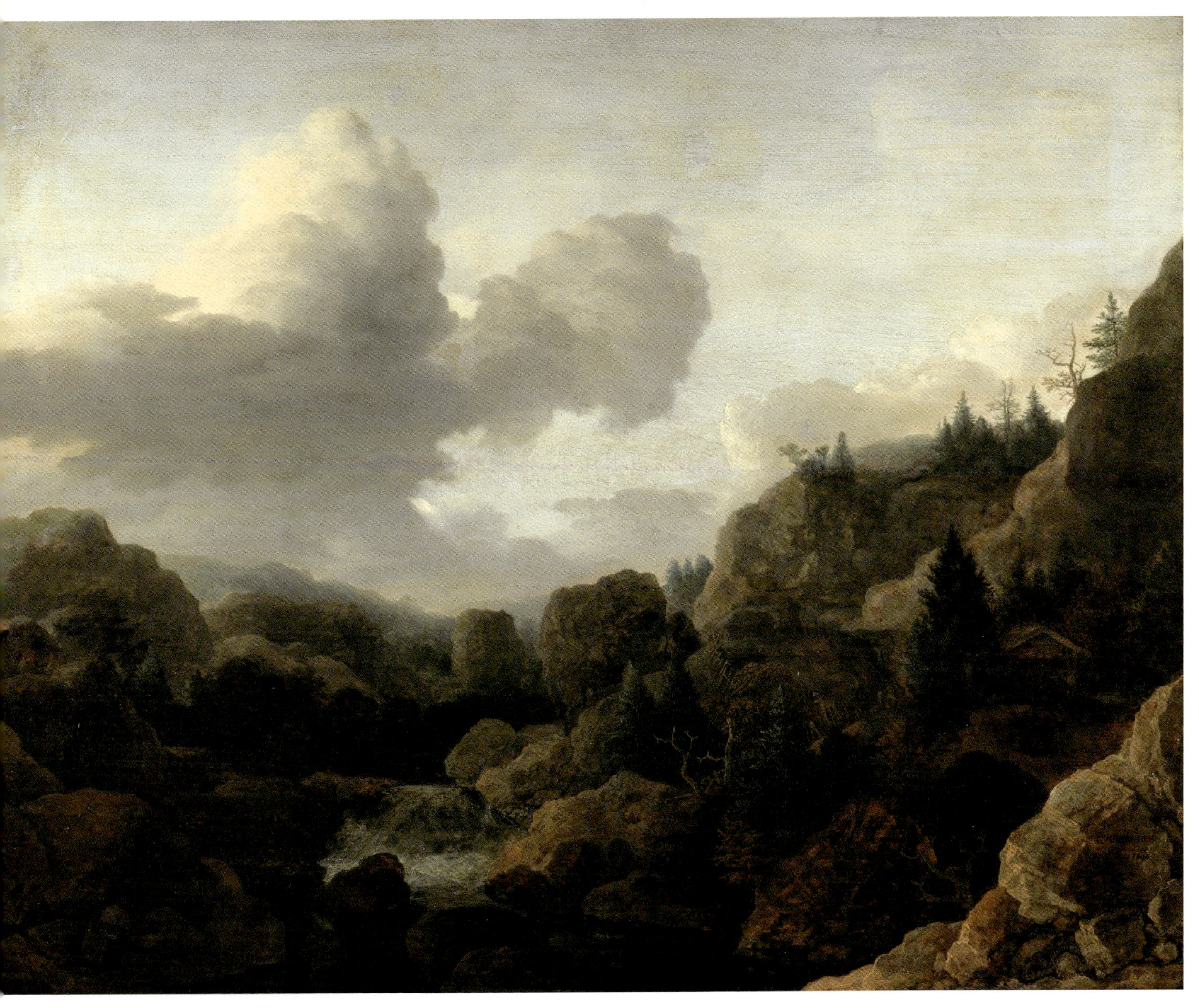

landscapes (figs. 19 and 20).[52] In so doing, he brought something new to the Dutch market. Surprisingly—given the strong trade links that had existed between the Low Countries and Norway since the Middle Ages—he was the first Dutch artist to produce convincing Norwegian scenes with rocks, waterfalls, log cabins and pine trees. It evidently did not take him long to decide to specialize in the genre, for his paintings in these early years were almost exclusively mountain landscapes of this kind. He also made a number of marines, such as this view of his home town of Haarlem (fig. 21).[53]

Where his early drawings are concerned, the proportion of Scandinavian to Dutch subjects is probably more balanced, although the lack of dates makes it difficult to establish which works on paper were made during the Haarlem period. The large number of Dutch landscapes in Van Everdingen's drawn oeuvre justify the assumption that he engaged with this subject from the start of his career (fig. 22).

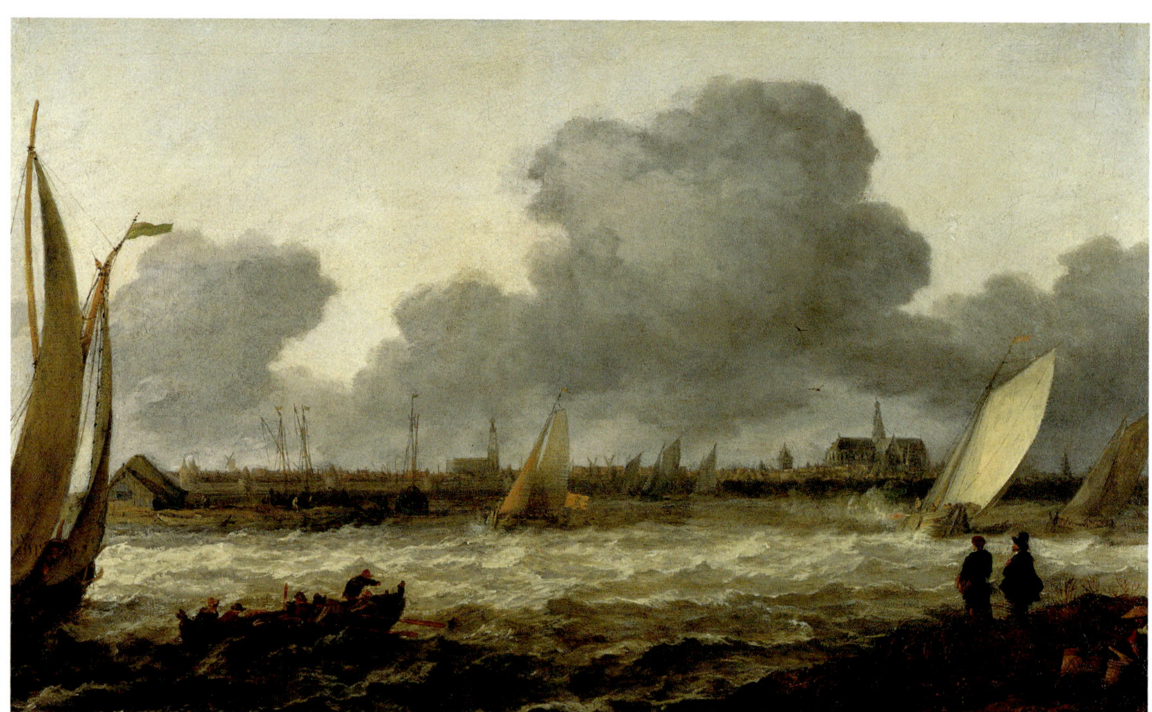

21
Allart van Everdingen,
*View of Haarlem from
the Noorder Buiten
Spaarne*, oil on canvas
on panel, 39 x 65.5 cm,
Haarlem, Frans Hals
Museum, inv. no. OS I-82
(cat. no. 52)

22
Allart van Everdingen,
*View of Haarlem from
the North*, pen and
brush and brown and
grey ink over black
chalk, brown and grey
wash, 156 x 271 mm,
Hamburger Kunsthalle,
inv. no. 21908
(cat. no. 57)

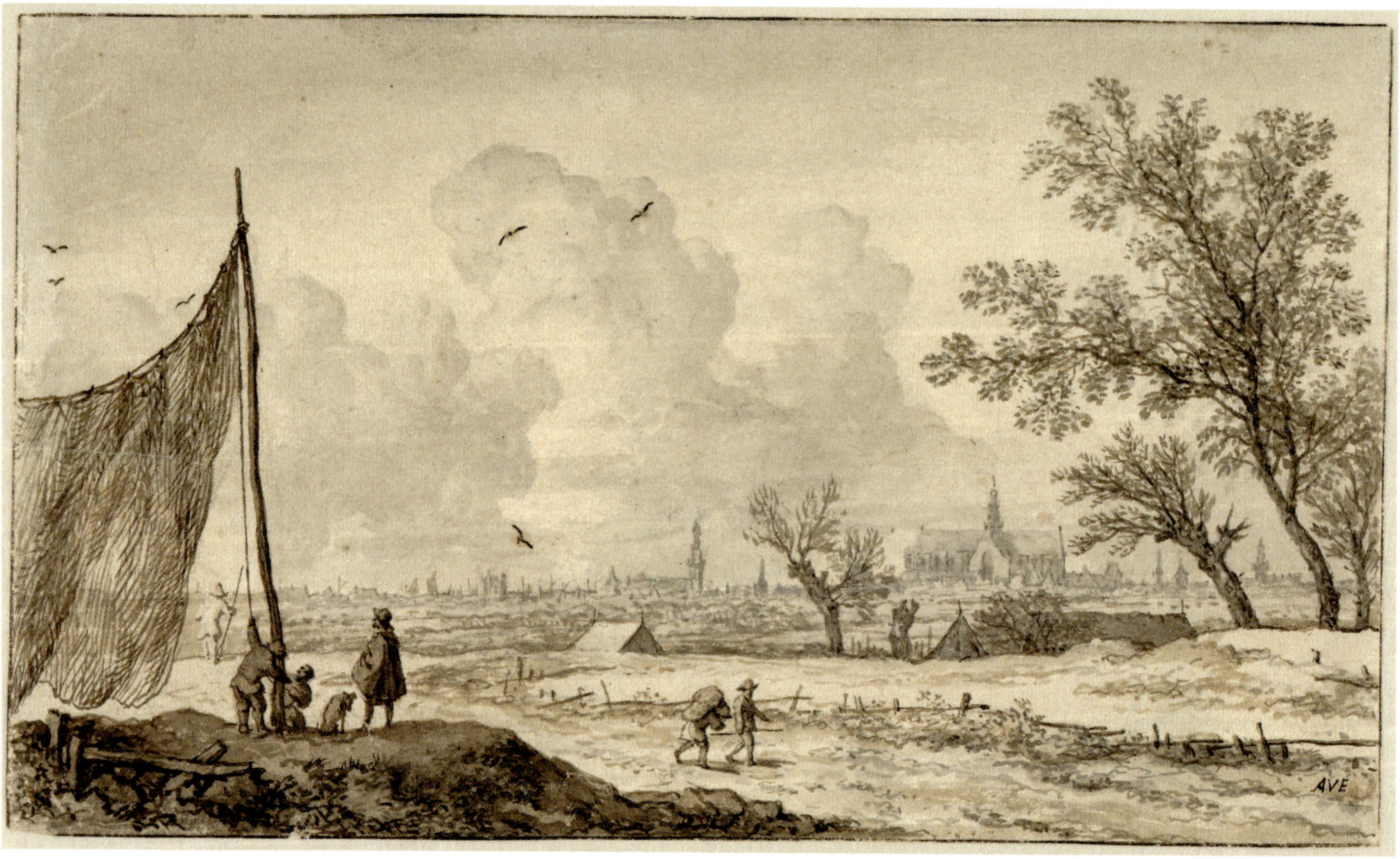

In Amsterdam

Allart van Everdingen moved to Amsterdam at some time between May and December 1652, although he was not registered as a burgher of the city until 10 April 1657.[54] He lived there until his death in 1675; in Koningsstraat near the Waag (Weigh House) in the first few years, later in Korte Keizersdwarsstraat and lastly in Bantammerstraat, close to the river IJ.[55] In their new home Allart and Janneke had four more daughters and two sons: Catrina in 1654, Petrus (Pieter) in 1657, Sara in 1659, Jacoba in 1661, Maria in 1663 and Johannes (Jan) in 1666. Again they lost a child, in August 1664; it was probably the infant Maria.

The ever-growing metropolis that was Amsterdam in the third quarter of the seventeenth century supported a larger market for works of art than Haarlem and acted like a magnet on artists of all kinds.[56] Rembrandt van Rijn and his pupils were active there, as were the painter of church interiors Emanuel de Witte, the still-life painter Willem Kalf and the marine specialist Willem van de Velde the Elder, to mention just a few. Van Everdingen probably thought there was scope for him to make a profit there with his highly unusual specialism.[57] And indeed in Amsterdam he became a successful and productive artist, known for his marines and landscapes (fig. 23), and particularly appreciated for his Scandinavian scenes (fig. 24).[58] Painting people was not Allart's strong point, so for the staffage of his landscapes—'populating' them with human and animal figures—he regularly called upon Nicolaes Berchem (1621/1622-1683), Johannes

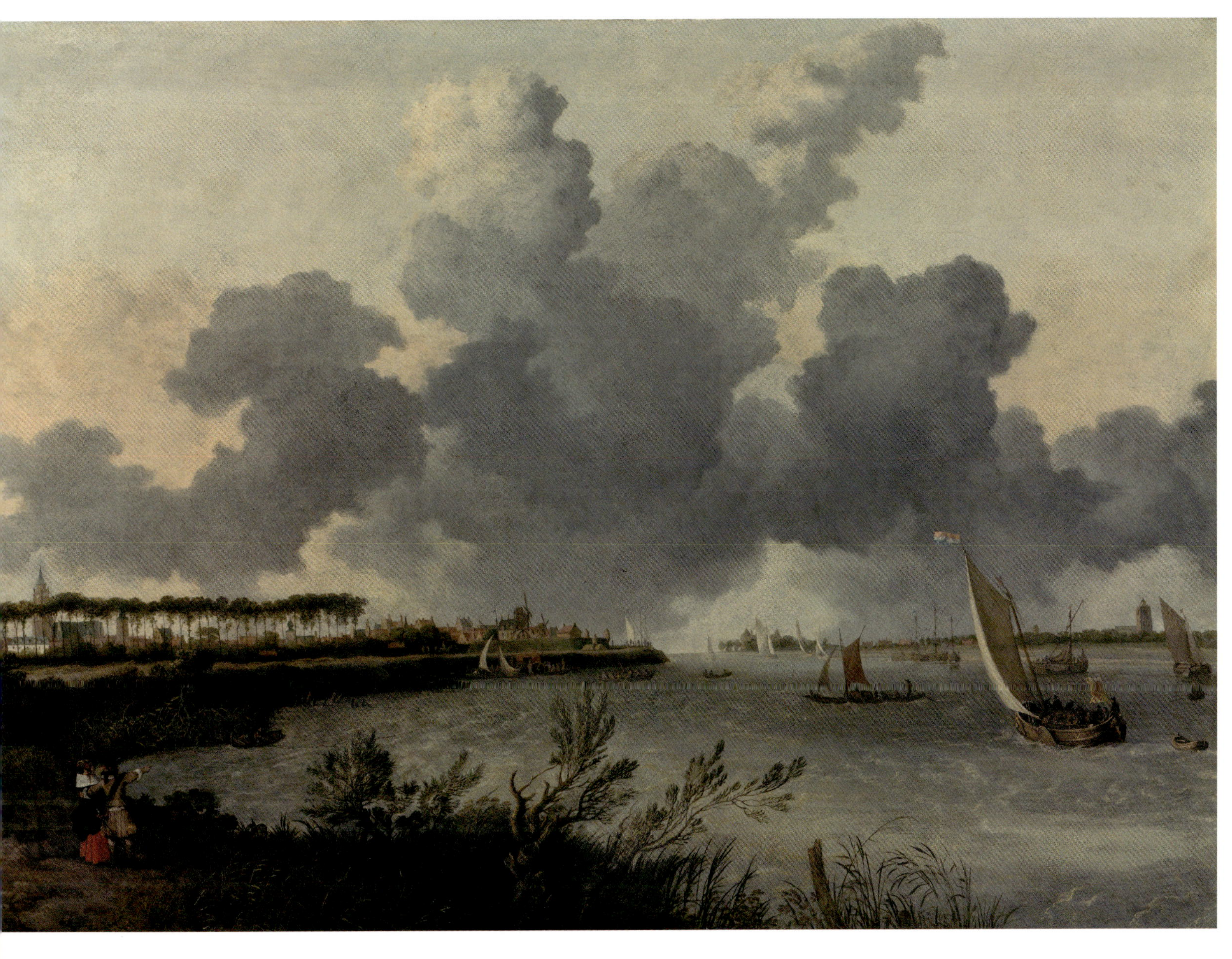

23
Allart van Everdingen, *View of Gorinchem from the Merwede*, oil on canvas, 97.7 x 135.5 cm, private collection

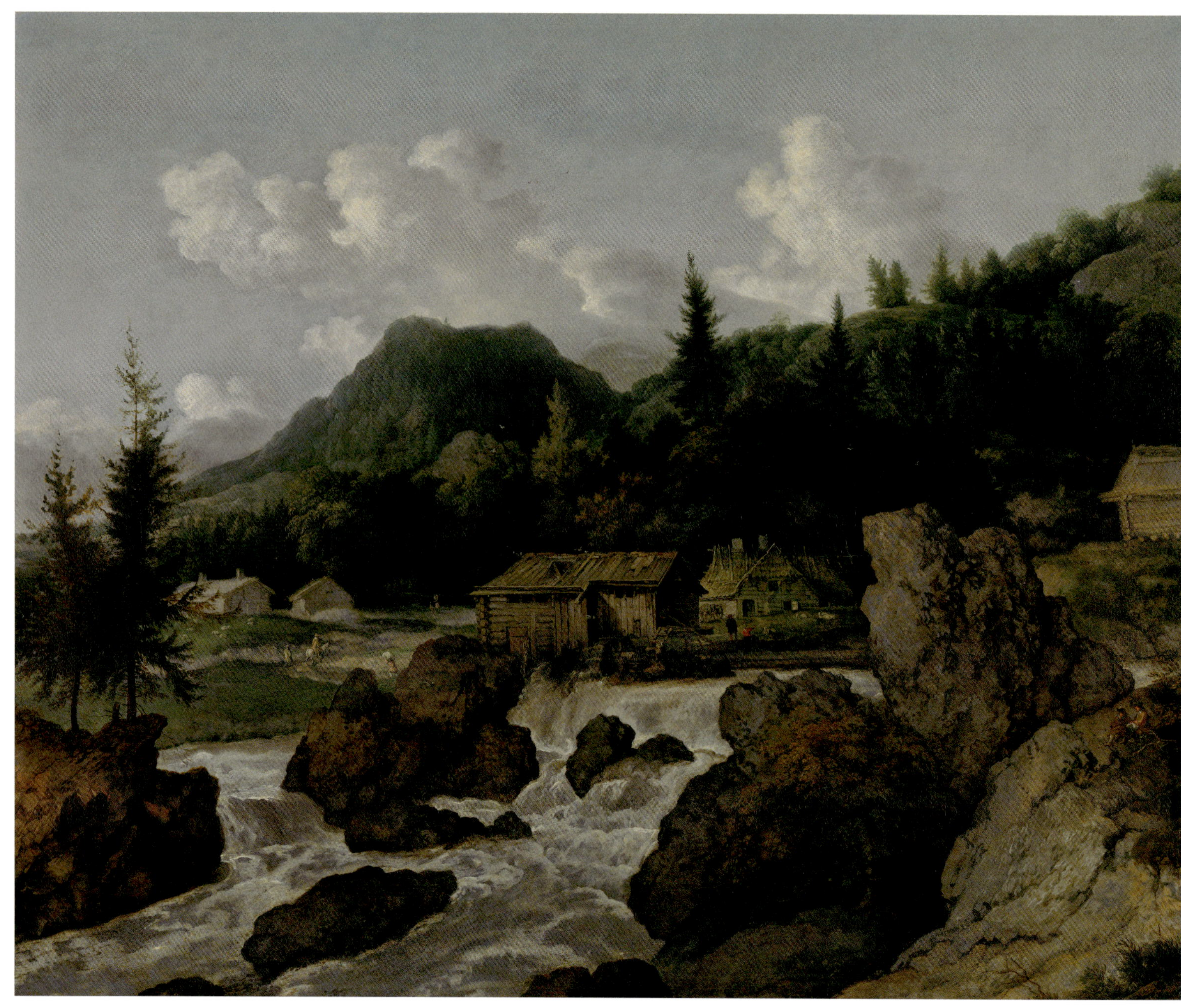

24
Allart van Everdingen,
Norwegian Landscape,
oil on canvas, 129.5
x 158 cm, Oslo,
Nasjonalmuseet,
inv. no. NG.M.03234

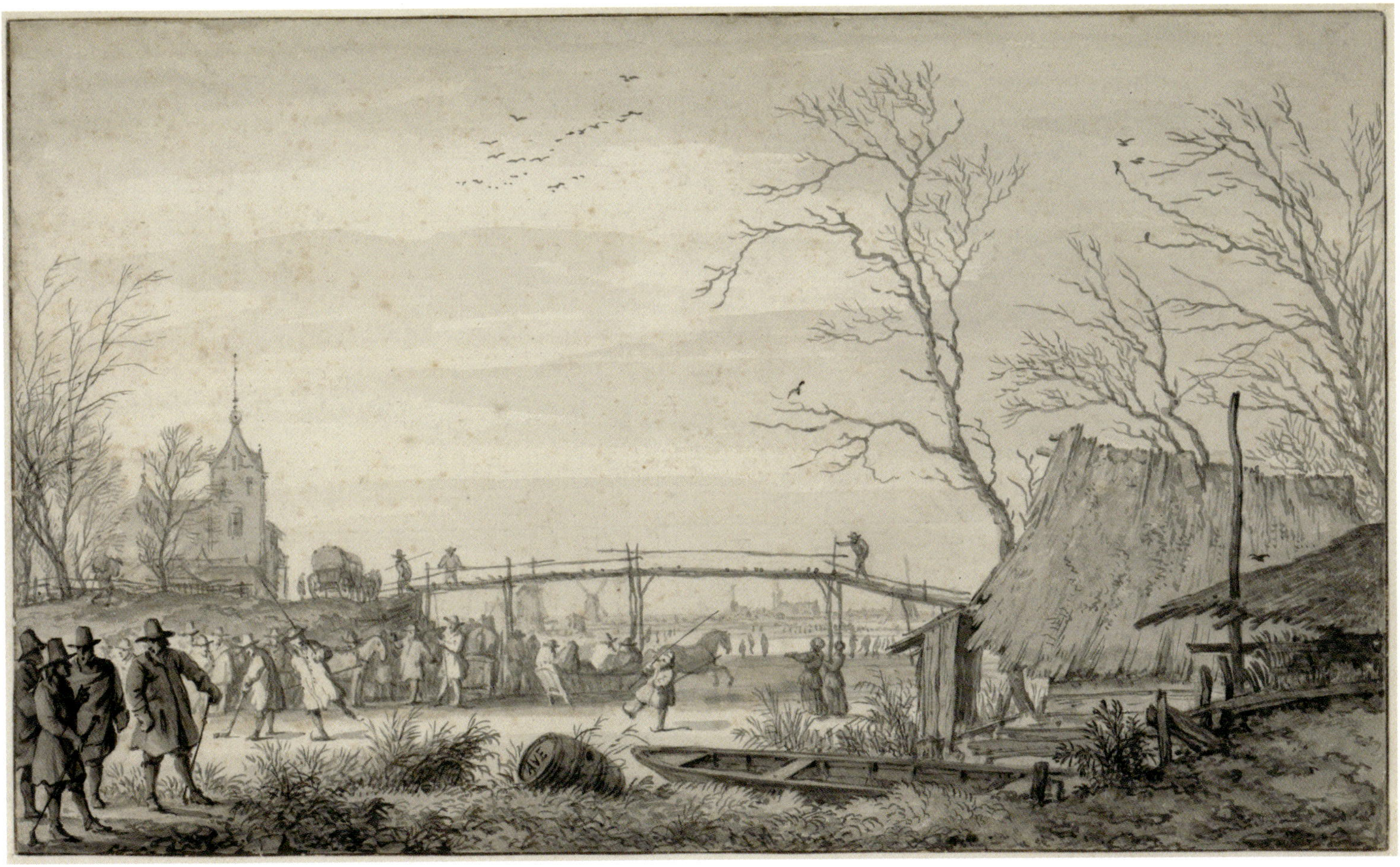

25
Allart van Everdingen, *Winter Landscape with Kolf Players*, pen and brush and black and brown ink over black chalk, grey wash, 179 x 303 mm, Paris, Fondation Custodia, Frits Lugt Collection, inv. no. 3659

v **26**
Allart van Everdingen, *River Landscape with a Church*, etching, 100 x 147 mm, Amsterdam, Rijksmuseum, inv. no. RP-P-OB-50.381 (Holl. 65 IIa) (cat. no. 20)

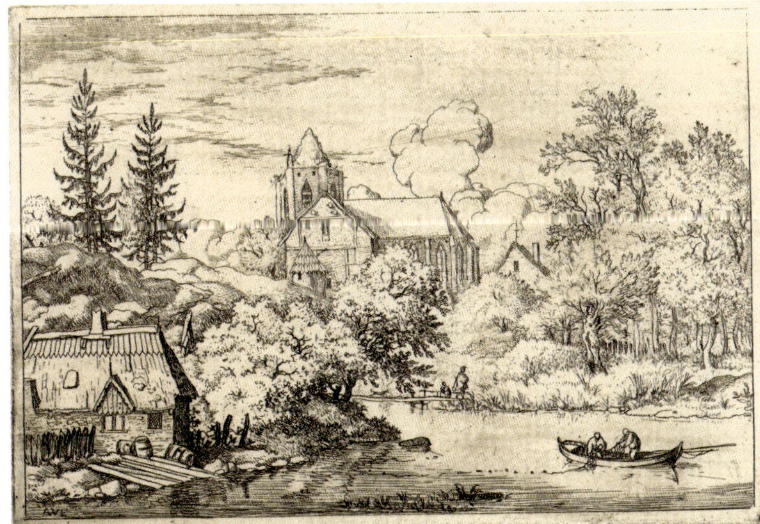

Lingelbach (1622-1674) and Adriaen van de Velde (1636-1672), all leading Amsterdam staffage painters at that time.[59] Alongside his paintings, Van Everdingen continued to make many drawings (fig. 25) and embarked on making etchings (fig. 26).[60] His series of prints illustrating the Reynard the Fox tale must have been made in Amsterdam (figs. 27 and 28).

In this period Van Everdingen took a trip to the Ardennes, most probably in the mid-sixteen-fifties, as we see from a group of drawings and etchings of springs in and around Spa (figs. 29 and 30) and a painting of Montjardin Castle (fig. 31).[61] Allart's picture of the impressive château looks very much like a faithful 'portrait'. It can reasonably be assumed that it was commissioned by the owner.

Around 1662, the brothers Louys (1605-1684) and Hendrick Trip (1607-1666) asked Van Everdingen to make several paintings to decorate the magnificent house they were having built on Kloveniersburgwal in Amsterdam (fig. 32).[62] The Trip family made its fortune from the trade in iron, copper and armaments from Sweden.

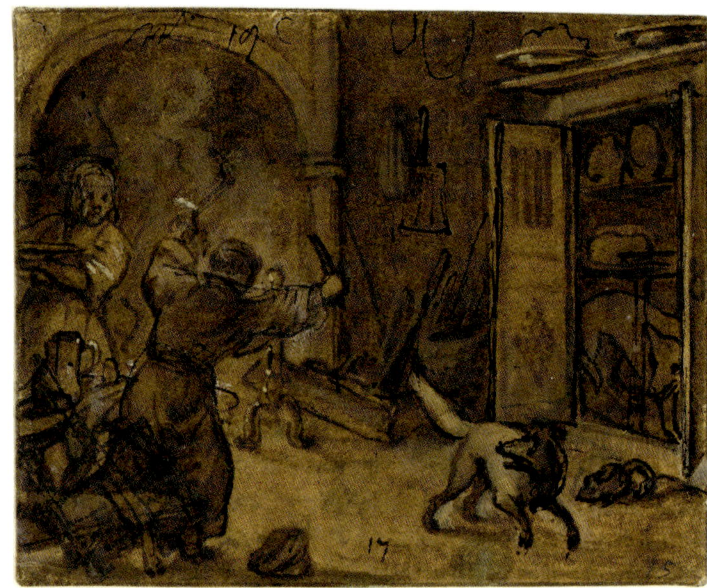

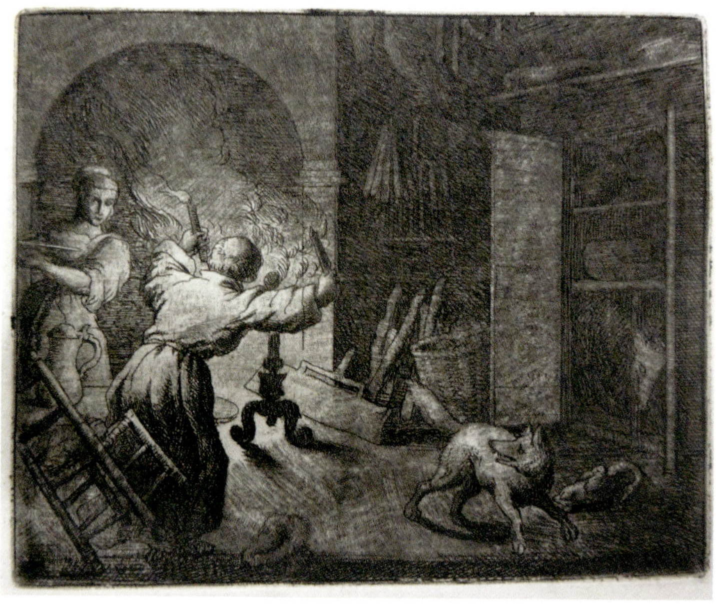

27
Allart van Everdingen, *Reynard the Fox Tries to Steal a Capon*, pen and brush and brown ink, brown wash, heightened with light grey, corrections in pen and dark brown ink, on brown prepared paper, 93 x 115 mm, London, The British Museum, inv. no. 1836,0811.201 (cat. no. 79)

28
Allart van Everdingen, *Reynard the Fox Tries to Steal a Capon*, etching and mezzotint, 95 x 117 mm, Petit Palais, Musée des Beaux-Arts de la Ville de Paris, inv. no. GDUT10392 (Dut. 20 IV) (cat. no. 100)

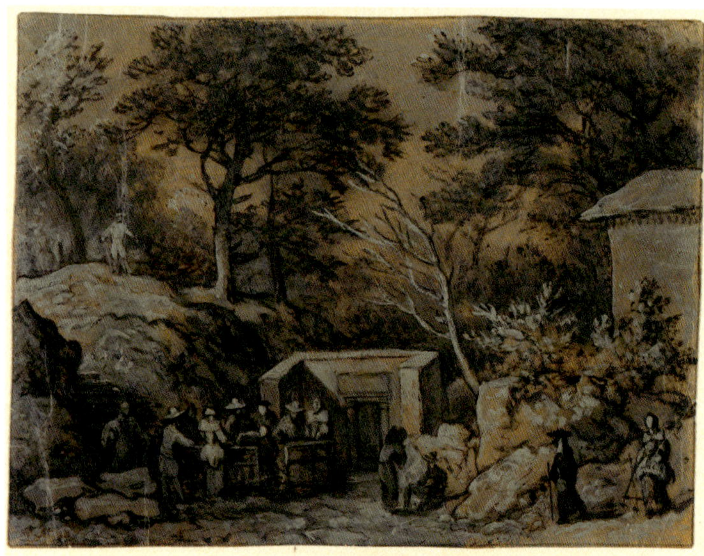

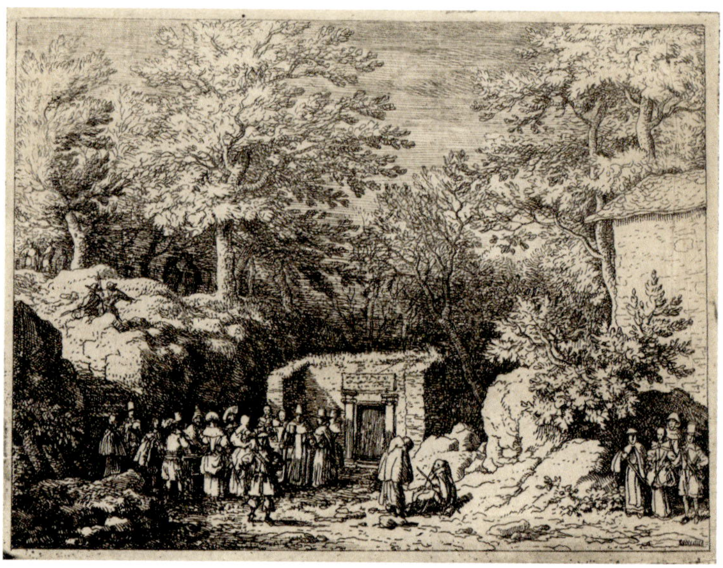

29
Allart van Everdingen, *The Spring at Sauvenière near Spa*, c. 1655, pen and brush and brown ink, light and dark grey oil paint, on reddish brown prepared paper, 128 x 170 mm, Hamburger Kunsthalle, inv. no. 21906 (cat. no. 64)

30
Allart van Everdingen, *The Spring at Sauvenière near Spa*, c. 1655, etching, 133 x 175 mm, Amsterdam, Rijksmuseum, inv. no. RP-P-OB-50.434 (Holl. 98 I) (cat. no. 24)

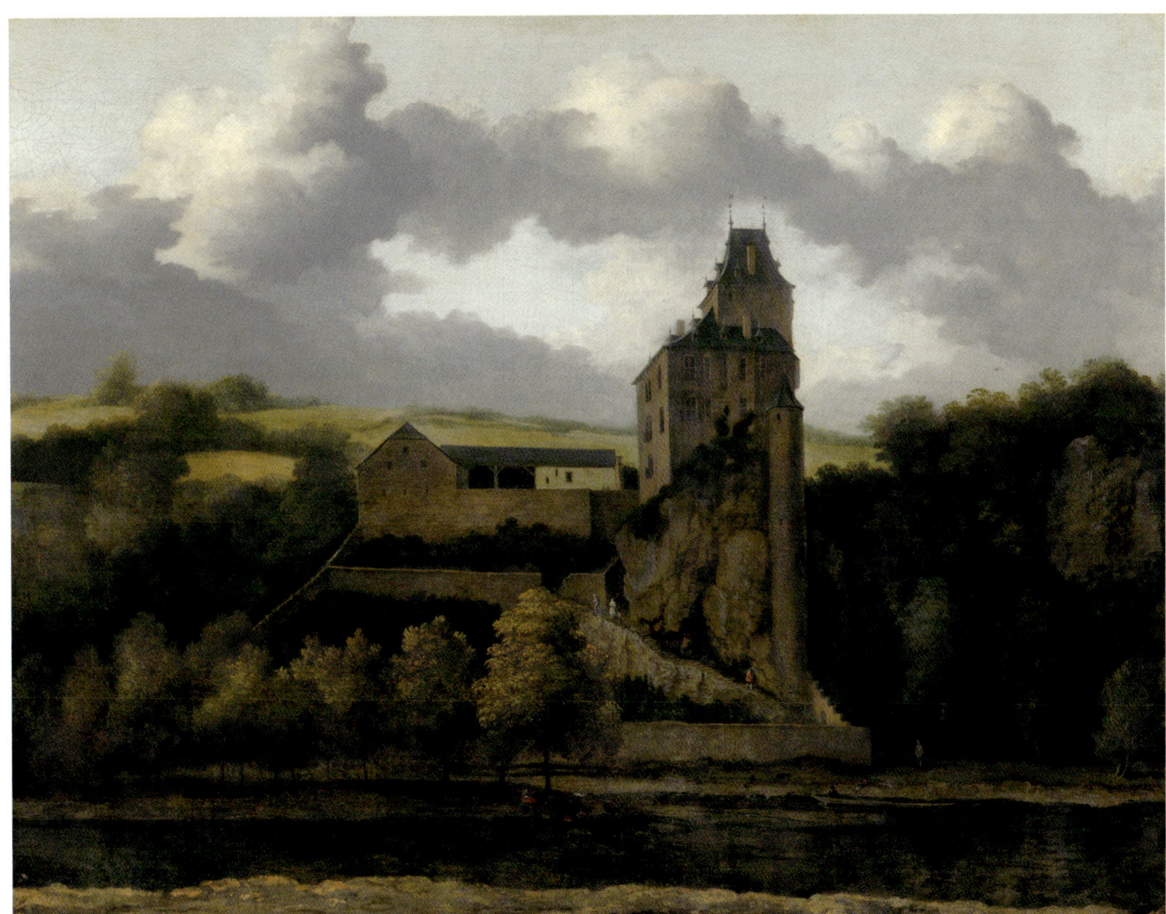

Hendrick leased a cannon foundry in Julita Bruk in the Swedish county of Södermanland. The Trip brothers naturally wanted pictures of the Scandinavian landscape they knew so well in their Trippenhuis, which went up between 1660 and 1662. Allart van Everdingen was the obvious choice to supply them, although it is highly unlikely that he ever visited the region where the Trips had their works.

Commissions like this were exceptional in Van Everdingen's practice; he doubtless sold the vast majority of his works on the open market.[63] He also dealt in paintings by other artists. His stock included works by his brother Caesar van Everdingen and Dutch masters like Frans Hals and Rembrandt, but he also had Italians like Raphael, Titian and Veronese—then at the highest and most expensive end of the art market.[64] It is clear that Allart was taken seriously as a dealer and connoisseur, for in 1655 he was involved in the valuation of paintings by Jan Miense Molenaer and in 1661 he was asked to give his opinion on a seascape attributed to Jan Porcellis.[65]

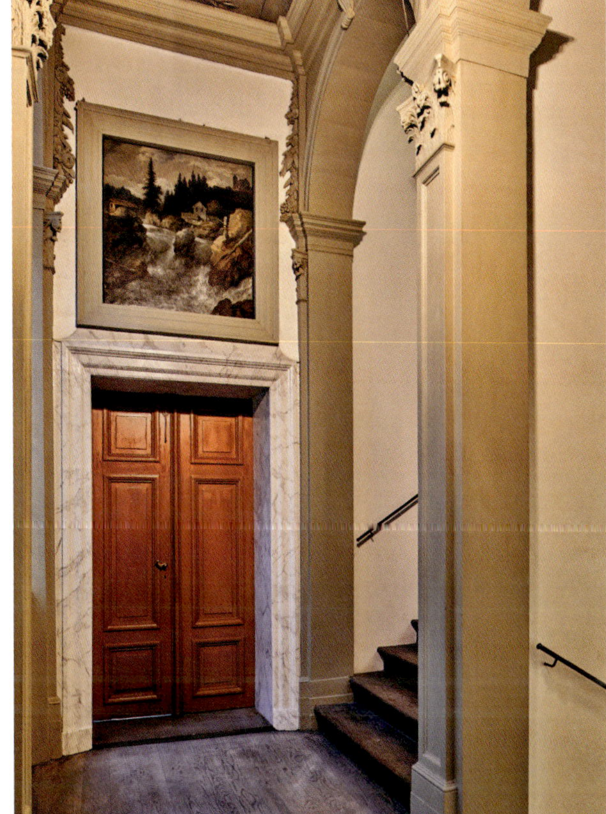

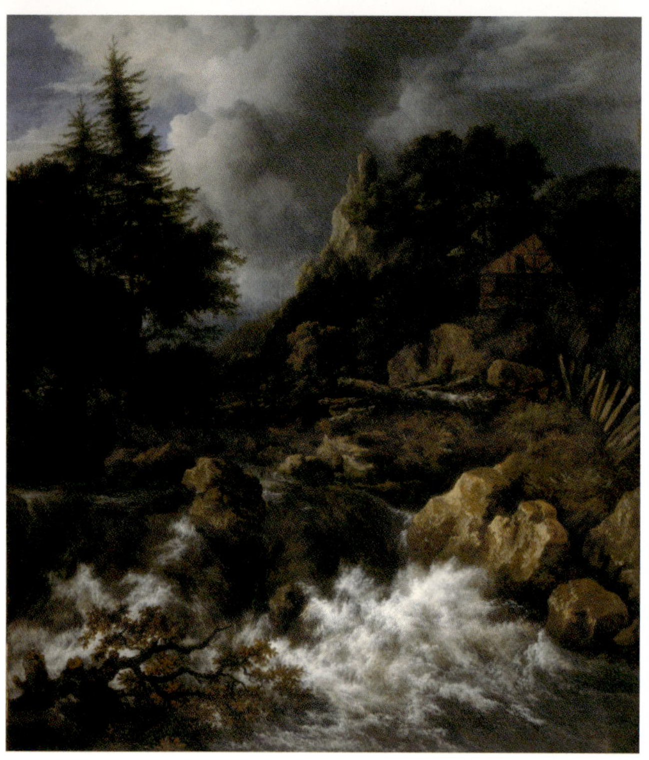

Jacob van Ruisdael (1628/1629-1682) was also consulted on this matter. He had likewise moved from Haarlem to Amsterdam a few years after Allart, in 1656 or 1657, when an interesting interaction developed between the two landscape painters.[66] Van Ruisdael must have noticed how successful Van Everdingen was with his Norwegian waterfalls, rocks and pine trees, for he started to use these motifs himself at the end of the sixteen-fifties (fig. 33).[67] In turn, Van Everdingen borrowed subjects from Van Ruisdael. The most obvious is the fortress perched on a high outcrop of rock or a mountain, which frequently appears in Allart's late work (fig. 34).[68] This is very reminiscent of Van Ruisdael's pictures of Bentheim Castle, which he had visited in 1650.[69]

< 33
Jacob van Ruisdael, *Waterfall with a House and a Castle*, c. 1665-1670, oil on canvas, 99.7 x 86.4 cm, Cambridge (Mass.), Harvard Art Museums/ Fogg Museum, inv. no. 1953.2

34
Allart van Everdingen, *Mountain Landscape with a River and a Castle*, 1669, oil on canvas, 150 x 200 cm, New York, Collection of Aliis Inserviendo Consumor Foundation

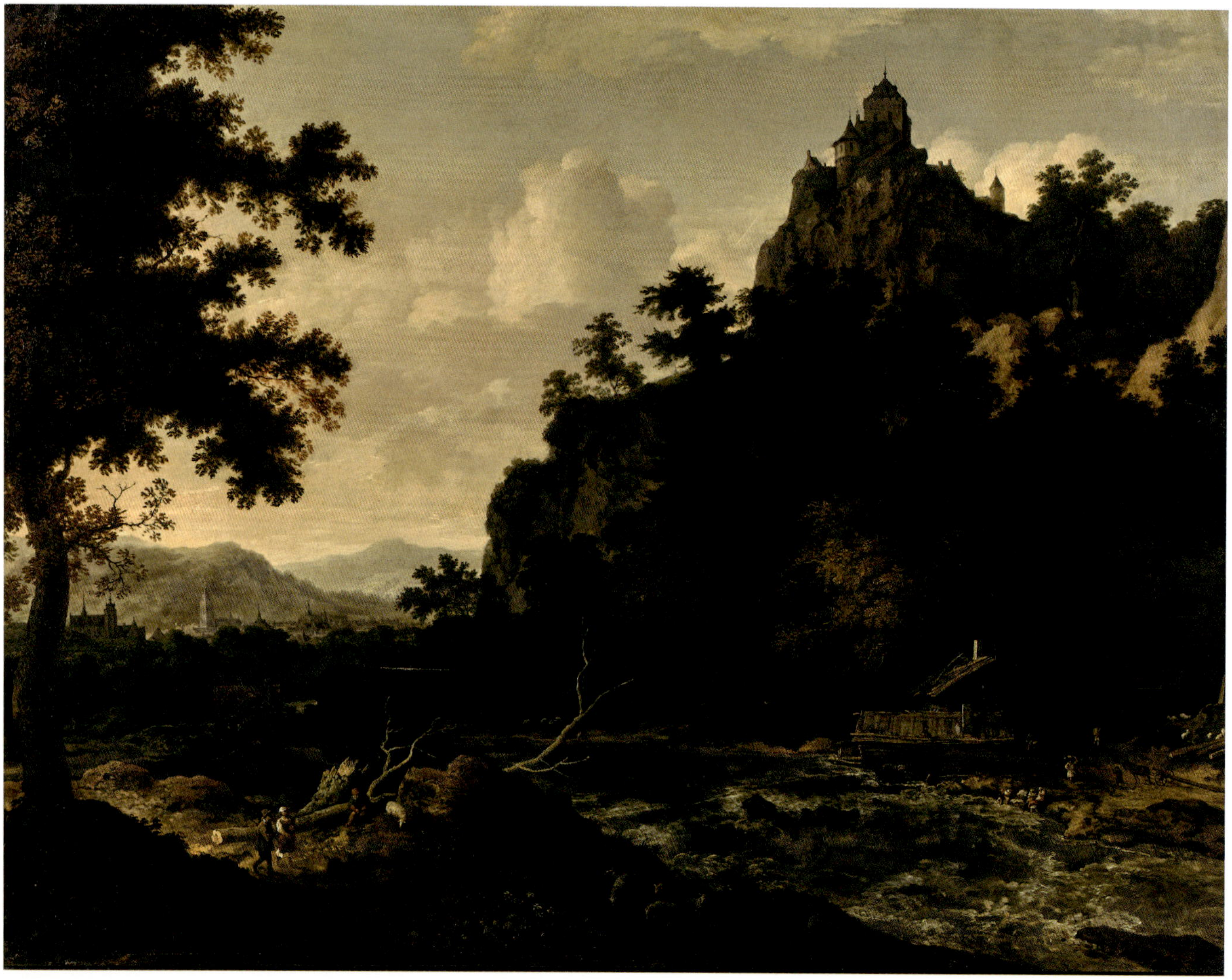

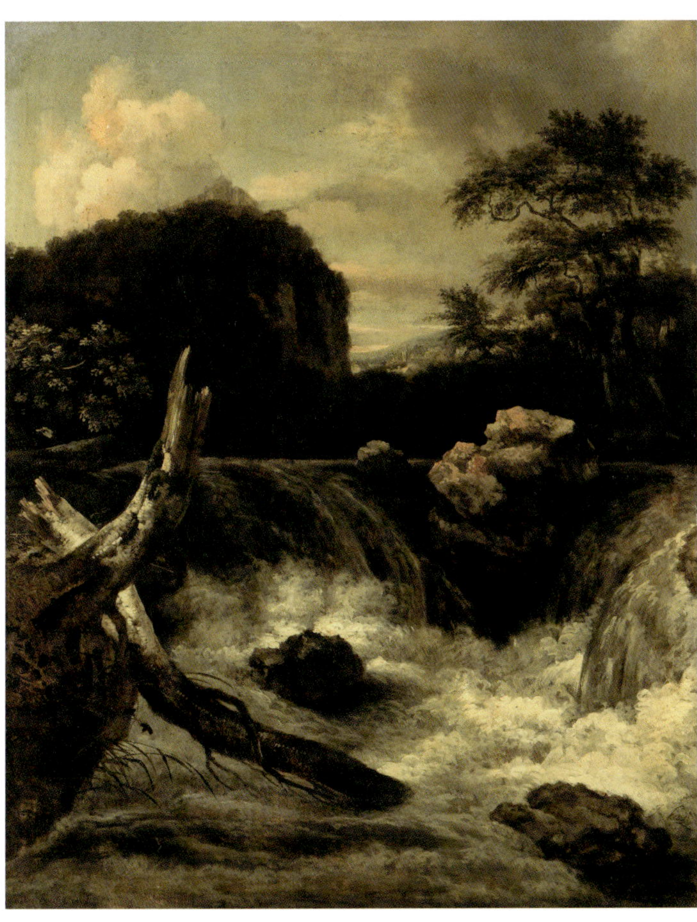

35
Jan van Kessel, *Waterfall*, oil on canvas, 94 x 74.5 cm, Amsterdam, Rijksmuseum, inv. no. SK-A-696

Van Ruisdael was not the only artist to be influenced by Allart van Everdingen. Various other landscape and marine painters adopted his subjects and compositions. Jan van Kessel (1641-1680) took this to the extreme: he imitated Van Everdingen's style and copied some of his paintings, doing it so convincingly that several works by Van Kessel have been attributed to Van Everdingen in the past (fig. 35).[70] Van Everdingen's work must have been brought to Van Kessel's notice by Van Ruisdael, whom he followed and whose pupil he may have been.[71]

The relationship between Van Everdingen and the marine painter Ludolf Backhuysen (1630-1708) is an intriguing one.[72] Houbraken wrote that 'Aldert van Everdingen was the first to push a palette with paint and brushes into his hand'.[73] Evidently Van Everdingen encouraged Backhuysen, who until then had been employed as an office clerk and draughtsman, to try painting.[74] As well as encouragement,

he certainly also provided inspiration, for Backhuysen's oeuvre is akin to Van Everdingen's in both composition and choice of subject. Both artists depicted shipwrecks and vessels in bad weather, sometimes near jagged rocks and cliffs (figs. 11 and 36).[75]

Allart must have had apprentices in Amsterdam whom he trained in his style, compositions and motifs. The landscape painter Gerard van Edema (c. 1652-c. 1700) is said to have been taught by him.[76] Like Van Everdingen he painted waterfalls and rocks, but Van Edema's landscapes look more Italian than northern.[77] Allart's sons Cornelis (1646-in or after 1692) and Pieter (1657-1739) van Everdingen followed in their father's artistic footsteps and undoubtedly had their initial training at home. None of Cornelis's work has survived, but there are a few drawn seascapes by Pieter (fig. 37).

Allart van Everdingen died in 1675 at the age of fifty-four and was buried in the Oude Kerk (Old Church) in Amsterdam on 8 November that year. On 3 March 1676 his widow placed an advertisement announcing the sale of his collection of paintings.[78] We do not know what was in the estate at that time, but some works remained unsold or were kept by the heirs. After Janneke's death in 1708 there was another sale, on 19 April 1709. The catalogue of this sale has survived —it has already been discussed above.[79] Among the ninety-one items being sold were more than twenty paintings by Allart himself, his gifted brother and his sons. For the rest, the list consists of very different works by Netherlandish, German and Italian painters. With fifteen paintings, Porcellis was by far the best represented. Van Everdingen must have been an expert on his work—a conclusion justified by his involvement in the attribution question in 1661 that was touched on above.

Recognition

Allart van Everdingen must have been a respected and prosperous man. This can be deduced from the commissions he received from the immensely rich Trip brothers, his sizable output and his large collection of paintings, and from the prices that were paid and estimated for his work in his lifetime.[80] In other words, what was paid for his paintings when they were sold and what values they were given in estate inventories. Regrettably, we do not know how much Van Everdingen's prints and drawings fetched in the seventeenth century.

At that time, landscape was not the most highly regarded genre in art—those were the prestigious history painting and the ingenious architectural work.[81] The average price for a landscape painting in the third quarter of the seventeenth century was something over twenty-four guilders. In comparison: skilled craftsmen (a category to which artists were reckoned to belong) earned about a guilder a day.[82] Van Everdingen was among the best-paid landscape painters. On average, his works were valued at more than thirty-six guilders; Van Ruisdael was a little ahead of him at over forty-two guilders. The highest price fixed for a work by Van Ruisdael in the seventeenth century (a hundred guilders), however, was much lower than the highest price for a Van Everdingen (a hundred and fifty guilders).

It has been assumed that the attraction of mountain landscapes like Allart van Everdingen's was that they came across as strange, awe-inspiring and even alarming to Dutch buyers. The owner of one of these works could sit in his safe, comfortable chair and contemplate exotic, inhospitable regions.[83] It is very possible that Van Everdingen's Norwegian scenes were particularly interesting to the merchants who did business in Norway and to the Norwegians who had emigrated to Amsterdam in the wake of the trade between Norway and the Republic.[84] In that case, it would not be the awe-inspiring

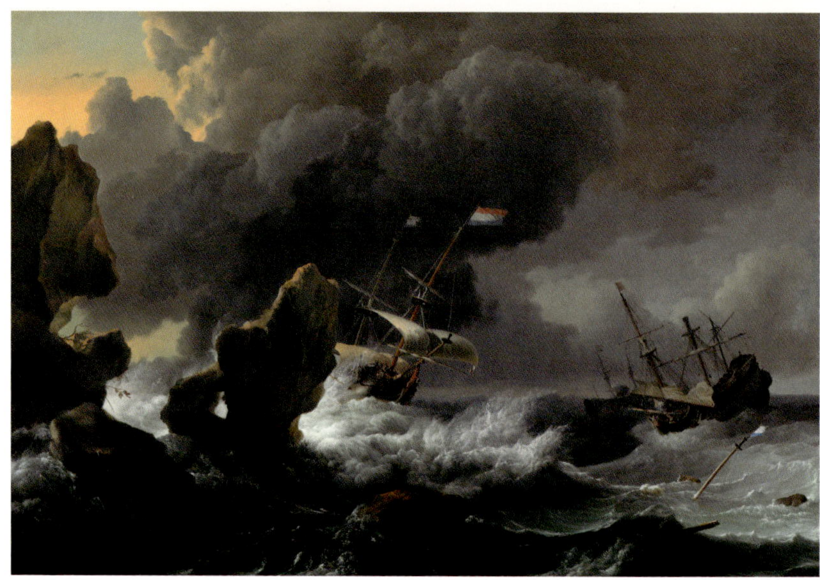

foreignness, but the pleasant familiarity of the scenes that would have appealed.[85] This was certainly true of the Trip brothers.

In the seventeenth century, Van Everdingen's paintings were probably bought chiefly by well-to-do Dutchmen, such as merchants, patricians and craftsmen.[86] Some works were acquired by eminent foreign collectors, among them the portrait painter Sir Peter Lely (1618-1680) and the English king James II (1633-1701).[87]

In the eighteenth century, Van Everdingen's works found their way to the German principalities. In 1784, for instance, Johann Wolfgang (von) Goethe (1749-1832) admired the early Scandinavian landscape with a fallow deer

36
Ludolf Backhuysen, *Ships in Distress off a Rocky Coast*, 1667, oil on canvas, 114.3 x 167.3 cm, Washington, National Gallery of Art, inv. no. 1985.29.1

37
Pieter van Everdingen, *View of Amsterdam from the IJ, with on the left the Gallows Field and the Toll Booth on the Volewijck Peninsula*, pen and brush and black ink over black chalk, grey wash, 105 x 224 mm, Amsterdam City Archives, accession no. 10097, fig. no. 010097002163

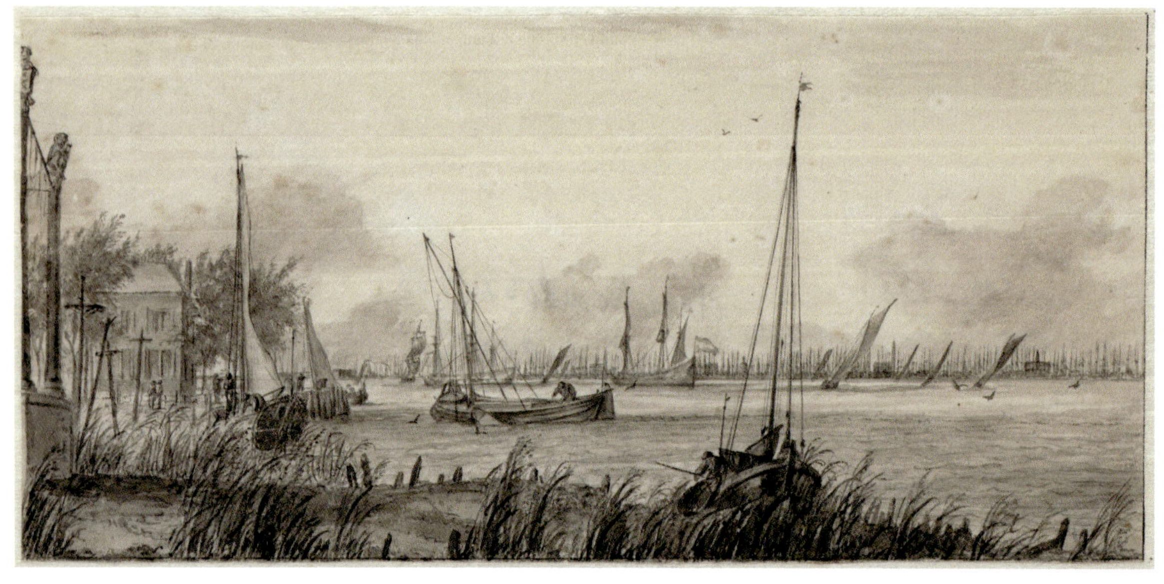

(fig. 48) in Salzdahlum Castle near Braunschweig.[88] The writer and philosopher himself owned almost all of Van Everdingen's print oeuvre, and as an amateur artist sometimes copied works by him. Goethe was not alone in his regard: in the eighteenth and nineteenth centuries, Van Everdingen's rugged landscapes struck a chord with other artists in the German-speaking regions. The desolate atmosphere prevailing in these scenes, the impressive waterfalls and the formidable rocks must have impressed upon them man's insignificance in the face of the power of nature. This mixed feeling of 'delightful horror' inspired Romantic artists like Caspar David Friedrich (1774-1840) and Johan Christian Dahl (1788-1857) to create their impressive landscapes (fig. 38).[89]

Allart van Everdingen's works have not played a prominent role in museums up to the present day. In so far as they are represented in public collections, by no means all of them hang in the gallery and they did not appear in high-profile exhibitions until well into the twentieth century.[90] In 1987 Peter Sutton included two early Scandinavian compositions by Van Everdingen in his influential exhibition *Masters of Dutch 17th-Century Landscape Painting* (*Onze meesters van het landschap. Schilderijen uit de Gouden Eeuw*), which ran in Amsterdam, Boston and Philadelphia. In the accompanying catalogue a good deal of attention was paid to the artist's unusual oeuvre.[91] After that, Van Everdingen's work often appeared—although always in dribs and drabs—in exhibitions about landscapes or seascapes.[92] The retrospective opening in Stedelijk Museum Alkmaar in 2021 is the first ever devoted to Allart van Everdingen.

38
Johan Christian Dahl,
*Mountain Landscape
with a Waterfall*, 1817,
oil on canvas, 187.5 x
250.3 cm, Copenhagen,
Statens Museum for
Kunst, inv. no. KMS43

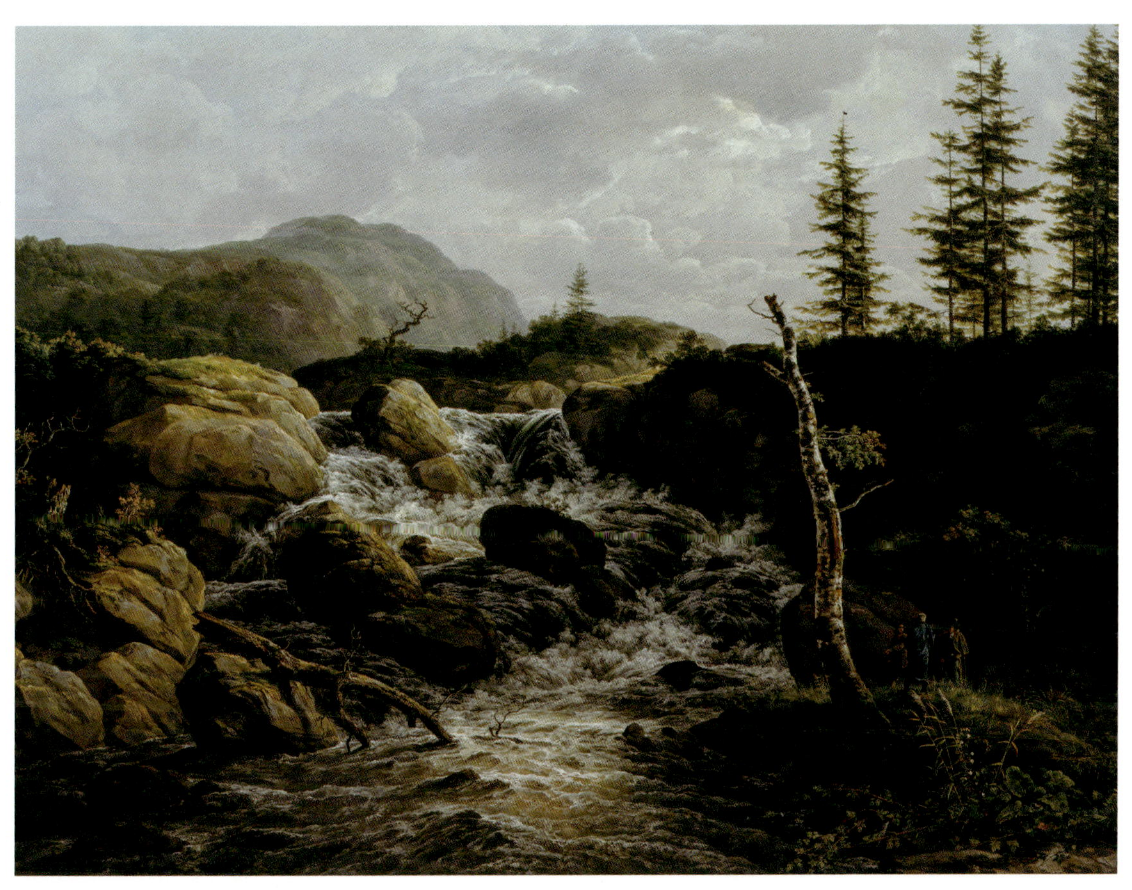

1 Houbraken 1718-1721, vol. 2, pp. 95-96. This passage is cited in English and discussed in Davies 2001, pp. 157-158.

2 For the size and subjects of Van Everdingen's oeuvre see Davies 2001, pp. 13-14.

3 The paintings are catalogued in Davies 2001, the etchings in Hollstein (Allart van Everdingen).

4 The drawings are catalogued in Davies 2007.

5 Davies 2007, pp. 118-127 and cat. nos. 594-654 (sketches); Dutuit 1881, cat. nos. 1-57 (prints).

6 For all the dated paintings see Davies 2001, pp. 203-204.

7 Alice Davies mentioned three dated drawings (see Davies 2001, p. 45 and Davies 2007, p. 10). Yvonne Bleyerveld rejects the attribution of these works (see her contribution in this catalogue, esp. note 9).

8 On Van Everdingen's way of signing see Davies 2001, pp. 44-45.

9 All the biographical details in this chapter are taken from Houbraken 1718-1721, vol. 2, pp. 95-96, Davies 2001, pp. 15-39 and Van Thiel-Stroman in Köhler et al. 2006, pp. 148-151, unless otherwise stated.

10 Regionaal Archief Alkmaar, accession no. 10.3.001: Doop, Trouw- en Begraafboeken Alkmaar, inv. no. 2, fol. 21v.

11 Idem, inv. no. 40, fol. 10v: 'een kindt van Everdingen, procureur uuijt de schoutenstraet'.

12 For Caesar van Everdingen see Huys Janssen 2002 and Alkmaar/Helsinki 2016.

13 Huys Janssen in De Vries 1997, cat. nos. 21, 22 and 28; Huys Janssen 2002, cat. nos. 7, 8 and 14; Klinkert in Alkmaar/Helsinki 2016, cat. nos. 1a, 1b and 32.

14 Davies 2001, p. 20. Two of the three sheets in the foreground have been identified as drawings by Allart (Davies 2007, p. 140; they are cat. nos. 542 and 543). On Stolker's portrait drawings, which were a speciality of the artist, see Niemeijer 1980, pp. 179-186.

15 On Allart van Everdingen's forefathers see Davies 2001, pp. 15-18, Huys Janssen 2002, pp. 25-27 and Van Thiel-Stroman in Köhler et al. 2006, p. 149.

16 This information is taken from Willem van den Berg's actual Historical Land Registry of Alkmaar 1493-1910, version 18.05, May 2016 (database under development), Utrecht 1989-2016, Kad. A729 (Schoutenstraat 17) and Kad.A398 (Langestraat 96). See also Regionaal Archief Alkmaar, accession no. 10.3.006: Oud-rechterlijke archieven van Alkmaar, inv. no. 143, fol. 53 (concerns Kad.A729); inv. no. 144, fol. 240v (concerns Kad.A729); inv. no. 146, fol. 325v (concerns Kad.A398).

17 For Caesar's first teacher see Klinkert 2016, pp. 15-16.

18 For Van der Heck see Alkmaar 2015. For the training of artists in the seventeenth century see De Jager 1990.

19 For Roelandt Savery see Prague/Kortrijk 2010.

20 For De Molijn see Allen 1987, Beck 1998 and Van Thiel-Stroman in Köhler et al. 2006, pp. 246-249.

21 For Mulier I see Keyes 1976, Giltaij in Rotterdam/Berlin 1996, pp. 235-237, Van Thiel-Stroman in Köhler et al. 2006, pp. 254-255 and Van der Veen in De Beer 2019, vol. 2, pp. 439-443.

22 Houbraken 1718-1721, vol. 3, p. 183. This was previously noted by Jeroen Giltaij in Rotterdam/Berlin 1996, p. 252 (cat. no. 52).

23 Davies 2001, p. 158. Davies regards it as unlikely that Houbraken spoke to Van Everdingen's son because of the errors he made in his description of Allart's family (for instance, he wrote that Allart's father was Jan, not Pieter van Everdingen). Houbraken's reliability is stressed, however, in Cornelis 1995 (esp. p. 164) and Erftemeijer 2011, pp. 475-476.

24 Regionaal Archief Alkmaar, accession no. 10.3.003: Notariële archieven Alkmaar (notary Jacob Cornelisz van der Gheest), inv. no. 59, fol. 608: 'wone[nde] tot Haerlem'. This was a legacy that Eefken Jansdr Dobben left to Pieter van Everdingen's children. See also Van Thiel-Stroman in Köhler et al. 2006, p. 149. Cf. Davies 2001, p. 25, with an erroneous interpretation of the source.

25 Bartilla 2010, pp. 63-64 (dating of the journey 'in de zomermaanden van 1606 of 1607': 'in the summer months of 1606 or 1607') and Kotková 2010, pp. 39-40 ('de twee jaar durende reis … in 1606-1607': 'the two-year journey … in 1606-1607').

26 The monogram 'AVE' was added lower left on the drawing by Savery (fig. 8). It has been suggested on these grounds that Allart van Everdingen owned this work by his teacher and worked up the dark passage lower left (Spicer 1979, vol. 2, cat. no. C19; Davies 2001, p. 25). Schapelhouman rightly observed that this dark area is an integral part of the drawing and not a later addition. The monogram 'AVE' was probably put on later, when Van Everdingen's drawings were highly sought after by collectors. See Schapelhouman 1987, cat. no. 77.

27 Van Everdingen's painting: Davies 2001, cat. no. 169.

28 See Davies 2001, pp. 199-202, for a reproduction of this catalogue.

29 Regionaal Archief Alkmaar, accession no. 10.3.003: Notariële archieven Alkmaar (notary Jan van Everdingen), inv. no. 144, fol. 25.

30 Van Thiel-Stroman in Köhler et al. 2006, p. 149 (with all the relevant deeds in note 20 on p. 150; they are held in the Regionaal Archief Alkmaar, accession no. 10.3.003: Notariële archieven Alkmaar, inv. nos. 142, 144 and 164).

31 The surviving register of the Alkmaar painters' guild has not a single entry for the 1638-1642 period; evidently this information has been lost (Davies 2001, p. 26). This is all the more regrettable, since that is precisely the period in which Allart must have enrolled, probably in 1640.

32 Davies 2001, cat. no. 1 (whereabouts unknown, so the dating cannot be verified).

33 Van Thiel-Stroman in Köhler et al. 2006, p. 150 (NB: in the sources cited in note 22 on p. 151 it is wrongly stated that the notification

in Alkmaar is dated 3 February 1645). The Alkmaar source is Regionaal Archief Alkmaar, accession no. 10.3.001: Doop, Trouw- en Begraafboeken Alkmaar, inv. no. 24, notice under the heading dated 5 February 1645.

34 There are supposedly two paintings by him dated 1643 and 1644: Davies 2001, cat. nos. 2 and 169. The first of these two works recently appeared on the market (sale London (Bonhams), 5 December 2018, no. 11); at that time neither date nor signature could be found on the canvas. Doubt as to the attribution is expressed in De Beer 2019a, p. 115. The whereabouts of the second work are unknown and the date cannot be seen clearly on the photograph in Davies 2001.

35 Houbraken 1718-1721, vol. 2, p. 96: 'want hy zig naar eenige plaats aan de Oost Zee te scheep begeven hebbende beliep hem eene gevarelyke storm, die hem willig of onwillig niet onbeschadigt op de kust van Norway deed belanden.'

36 Alice Davies, for instance, writes that Van Everdingen 'was shipwrecked on the coast of Norway in a perilous storm' (Davies 2001, p. 158). Jan Blanc repeats this wording almost verbatim in Blanc 2016, p. 13.

37 On the *moedernegotie* (mother of all trades) and its immense significance to the Republic's economy see Van Tielhof 2002. On p. 49 we read that 'the 1640s witnessed an enormous and unprecedented expansion, and the Baltic grain trade reached it greatest extent ever'—the precise period when Allart van Everdingen undertook his journey. Specifically on the role of the Dutch in the import of timber from the Baltic states and Scandinavia see Tossavainen 1994.

38 On these contacts see Schreiner 1934, Hart 1976, pp. 71-92, Bruijn 1985, Willemsen 1988, Lesger 1992, Sogner 1996, Sogner 2004 and Van Tussenbroek 2012, pp. 34-35. All the information about trading contacts between Norway and the Netherlands in the remainder of this section is taken from these publications, unless otherwise stated.

39 My thanks to Ron Brand for working out the duration of the sea voyage from the Netherlands to Norway.

40 In 1647 there were 387 registered Dutch vessels plying to and from Norway; by 1652 there were as many as one thousand (Sogner 2004, p. 45).

41 For Savery's stay at the court in Prague see Kotková 2010.

42 Van Everdingen could, for example, have got to know the art-loving Carl du Moulin (or connections of his), who was then living in Haarlem and Overveen and traded with Russia and Sweden, or Jochem Cromhuysen (or connections of his), who lived in Amsterdam and had trading posts in Riga. The most interesting possible contact, however, is the art collector Gabriel Marselis Jr (1609-1673). He was born in Hamburg, but settled in Amsterdam from 1634 to 1654 and was very active in Denmark and Norway. He traded with and loaned money to the king of

Denmark-Norway, a relationship that became much more intensive during the sixteen-forties. For the Marselis family see Amburger 1957 and Zandvliet 2006, pp. 67-68 (no. 29). My thanks to Inger Groeneveld for these suggestions.

43 For the Dutch agents who worked overseas and the Dutch communities that grew up because of overseas trade see Van Tielhof 2002, pp. 166-179.

44 Holan 1990, p. 28.

45 The works pictured are Davies 2007, cat. nos. 171 and 170 respectively. On p. 15 of Davies 2007, Alice Davies gave a summary of the drawings she believes Allart made during his trip through Scandinavia. In a personal email dated 22 April 2018 she stated that there is a minor error in this: cat. no. 153 should be 157. Furthermore, cat. no. 173 can be added to the series (according to Davies 2007, p. 62).

46 The literature on Van Everdingen's route through Scandinavia is discussed in Davies 2001, pp. 163-167.

47 Davies 2001, p. 26 and Davies 2007, pp. 11 and 136.

48 It is therefore implausible that Van Everdingen left in the spring of 1643 and returned at some point in 1644, as Van Thiel-Stroman asserts in Köhler et al. 2006, pp. 149-150.

49 Allart van Everdingen rented this house from Christoffel van Beringen. My thanks to Inger Groeneveld for finding out the exact location of 'Het Serpent'. There is currently a shoe shop on the site.

50 Haak 1984, pp. 179-188, 229-273 and 377-394; Van Thiel 2006.

51 Stechow 1968, pp. 15-81 and Buijsen 1992, pp. 56-57.

52 The works pictured are Davies 2001, cat. nos. 24 and 25. Van Everdingen's earliest mountain landscape with log cabins and a waterfall is dated 1636 (Davies 2001, cat. no. 23; whereabouts unknown).

53 Biesboer in Köhler et al. 2006, cat. no. 136.

54 The archive records on which this conclusion is based are discussed in Davies 2001, p. 101: payment of rent in Haarlem dated 25 April 1652 and a notarial document dated 30 December 1652 in which it is stated that Van Everdingen was living in Amsterdam. See also Van Thiel-Stroman in Köhler et al. 2006, p. 149.

55 Van Everdingen lived in Koningsstraat from around 1655 until at least 1663 and in Korte Keizersdwarsstraat in 1664; in the year of his death (1675) he was living in Bantammerstraat. See Davies 2001, p. 31 and Van Thiel-Stroman in Köhler et al. 2006, pp. 149-150. See also Amsterdam City Archives, DTB Begraven, archive no. 5001, inv. no. 1210, p. 114.

56 Haak 1984, pp. 273-311, 351-377 and 462-498.

57 On the commercial importance of a recognizable specialism in the seventeenth-century Dutch art market see Sluijter 1999 and Boers 2012, p. 26.

58 Davies 2001, pp. 101-107. The illustrated paintings are idem, cat. nos. 21 and 74. Cat. no. 21 was auctioned by Christie's London as part of the Eric Albada Jelgersma Collection (no. 16) on 6 December 2018.

59 Stechow 1968, p. 7 and Davies 2001, p. 14. On Berchem see Stefes 1997 and Haarlem/ Zurich/Schwerin 2006; on Lingelbach see Burger-Wegener 1976; on Van de Velde see Amsterdam/London 2016.

60 The drawing: Davies 2007, cat. no. 131.

61 Davies initially dated this trip to the sixteen-sixties (Davies 2001, p. 34), but later narrowed it down to 1656 (Davies 2007, pp. 10-11 and 113-114). She derived this specific date from a drawing in the British Museum in London (Davies 2007, cat. no. 73). The attribution of this work to Van Everdingen is doubtful, however, and the landscape it depicts cannot be securely located in the Ardennes. Hos 1961 argues that Allart's painting of Montjardin Castle must have been done before 1654, because the gardens in front of the building look less cultivated than in a drawing made of them by a visitor in 1654. This is not reliable evidence, however; it gives a demonstrably incorrect view of the castle itself. In the present publication Van Everdingen's trip to the Ardennes is dated to around 1655, on the grounds of, among other things, Allart's picture of the Pouhon spring and the market square in Spa. See Erik Hinterding's essay in this catalogue.

62 For the programme of decorations in the Trippenhuis see Van Run 2019. Specifically on Van Everdingen's paintings for this building see Davies 2001, pp. 125-131.

63 On the market for landscape paintings see Stechow 1968, pp. 6-7 and Chong 1987.

64 Davies 2001, pp. 199-202. On the art market in Van Everdingen's time see London/ Amsterdam 2006.

65 In 1655 Allart van Everdingen appraised some paintings that Jan Miense Molenaer wanted to use as payment for a house in Haarlem. He and Emanuel de Witte acted on behalf of the vendor of the house; Caesar van Everdingen and Pieter Soutman for the buyer, Molenaer. In 1661 the collector Laurens Mauritsz Douci asked Allart van Everdingen, Jacob van Ruisdael, Willem Kalf and Barent Cornelisz Kleeneknecht to establish the authenticity of a work by Jan Porcellis. See Davies 2001, pp. 32-33 and Van Thiel-Stroman in Köhler et al. 2006, pp. 149-150.

66 For Van Ruisdael see Los Angeles/Philadelphia/London 2005 (with further literature references) and Van Thiel-Stroman in Köhler et al. 2006, pp. 281-286. This paragraph is based on these sources.

67 For the relationship between Van Ruisdael and Van Everdingen see Stechow 1968, pp. 144-145, Davies 2001, pp. 174-179 and Slive 2005, pp. 8-11.

68 The pictured work by Van Everdingen is not in Davies 2001.

69 Los Angeles/Philadelphia/London 2005, cat. no. 14 and The Hague 2009.

70 For Van Kessel see Davies 1992. On the relationship between Van Kessel and Van Everdingen see Davies 2001, pp. 173-180. Van Everdingen was not the only artist whose work Van Kessel imitated; he also copied Van Ruisdael and other Amsterdam landscape painters.

71 On the relationship between Van Kessel and Van Ruisdael see Slive 2005, p. 13.

72 For Backhuysen see De Beer 2002.

73 Houbraken 1718-1721, vol. 2, p. 237: 'Aldert van Everdingen was d'eerste die hem [= Backhuysen] een palet met verf en pencelen in de vuist stak.'

74 Davies 2001, pp. 31-32 and De Beer 2002, pp. 34-37.

75 De Beer 2002, p. 69, cat. no. 26.

76 Davies 2001, pp. 32 and 181-183.

77 Idem, p. 182.

78 This sale was announced in the *Opregte Haerlemse Courant* of 3 March 1676 and took place in the Heerenlogement in Amsterdam (Davies 2001, p. 34 and Van Thiel-Stroman in Köhler et al. 2006, pp. 150-151).

79 See Davies 2001, pp. 199-202 for a reproduction of this catalogue.

80 All the figures in this section are taken from Chong 1987. Chong based his conclusions about the prices of landscape paintings in the seventeenth century on auction and sale catalogues, estate inventories and archive records of commissions from government bodies.

81 Brenninkmeyer-de Rooij 1984, pp. 64-65 and Chong 1987, p. 112.

82 Boers 2012, p. 29.

83 Sutton 1987, p. 48, De Jongh 1995, pp. 168-191, Davies 2001, p. 83 and Blanc 2016.

84 On the large community of Norwegian immigrants in seventeenth-century Amsterdam see Sogner 2004.

85 Quentin Buvelot makes a similar argument about Jacob van Ruisdael's paintings of Bentheim Castle in The Hague 2009, pp. 51-52.

86 Chong 1987, p. 112 and Sluijter 1999, p. 116.

87 Davies 2001, p. 37.

88 Idem, p. 11.

89 See among others Davies 2001, pp. 183-197, Haarlem 2009, Monrad 2001 and Oslo/ Dresden 2014.

90 Davies 2001, p. 12.

91 Amsterdam/Boston/Philadelphia 1987, specifically cat. nos. 27 and 28 (including a biography of the artist on pp. 307-308) and Sutton 1987, pp. 47-49.

92 For example, Tokyo/Kasama/Kumamoto/ Leiden 1992, cat. no. 54; Amsterdam 1993a, cat. no. 72; Giltaij in Rotterdam/Berlin 1996, cat. no. 52; Vogt in Brussels/Amsterdam/Aachen 2007, cat. nos. 38 and 39. The drawn work was also included in exhibitions and books on particular collections, see for example Schapelhouman and Schatborn 1987, cat. no. 47, and Blok in Paris 2014, cat. no. 78.

Spotlight 1

NORWAY AROUND 1644:
AT WAR   Cynthia Osiecki

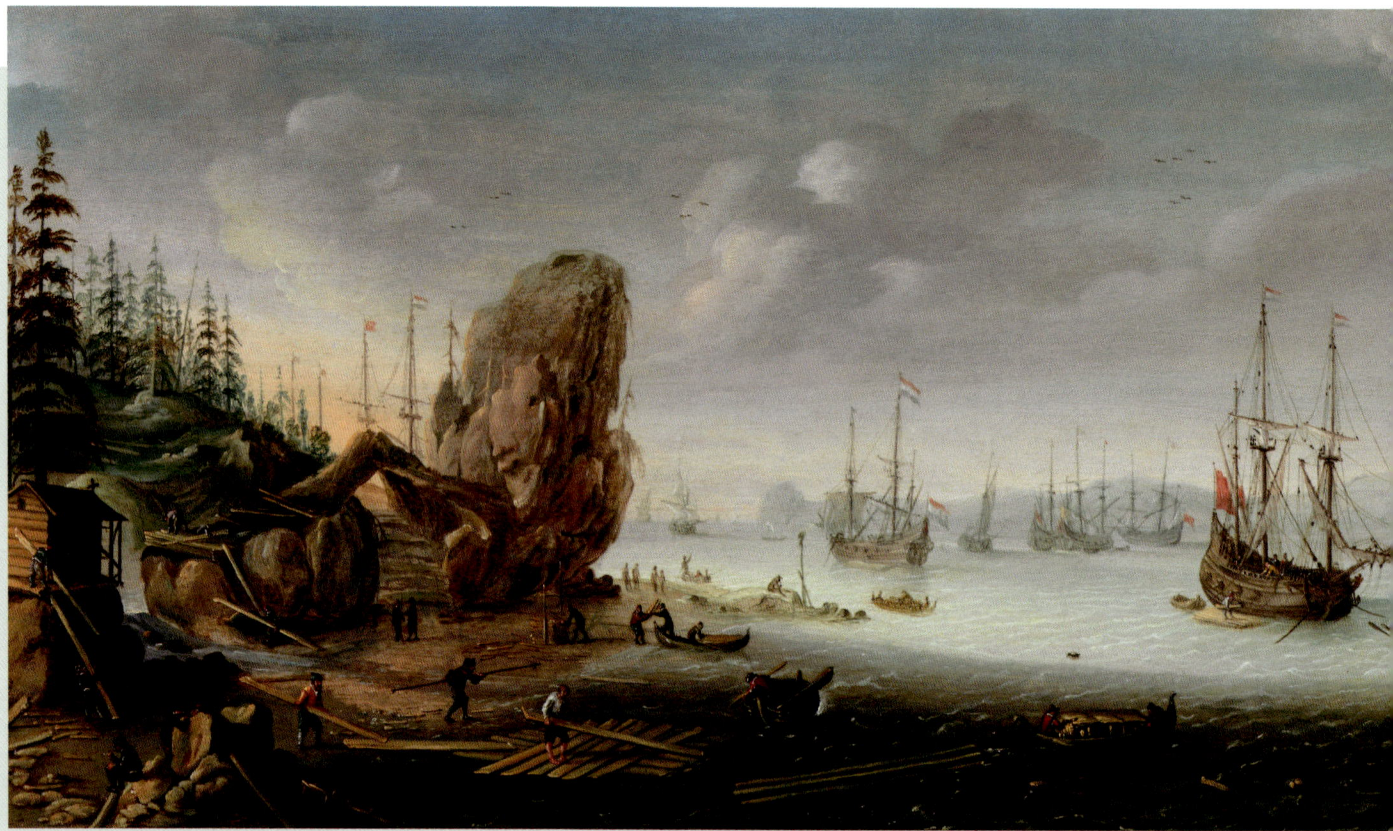

By the time Allart van Everdingen found himself on the Norwegian coast in 1644, Dutchmen had been active in the area for at least a century and a half. There had been extensive trade between the Low Countries and Norway since the Middle Ages.[1] In the seventeenth century, this Scandinavian country was a province of Denmark, ruled by the Danish king. In 1644 this was Christian IV (1577-1648), who was very active—economically, militarily and culturally—in the region Van Everdingen visited (fig. 17). How much of this would Allart have noticed? What did the political and cultural landscape look like when the Dutch artist travelled through southeastern Norway?

The Timber Trade between Norway and the Netherlands

In the seventeenth century Norway was inhospitable and sparsely populated, but its vast areas of forest gave it an important export product: timber. There was a huge demand for it in the Dutch Republic for building houses and ships, and there was regular traffic from the provinces of Friesland and Holland back and forth to Norway to load masts, balks and planks (fig. 39). The southern Norwegian coastal towns of Risør and Langesund, which Allart van Everdingen visited, were important timber ports. Dutch merchants liked to buy in products here because it was easy to evade the Danish king's

convoy.[6] With a view to strengthening his control of the timber trade, in 1641 Christian IV established the town of Kristiansand on the south coast of Norway, at the mouth of the River Otra.[7] These measures were effective and the income from tolls rose sharply. Special storage facilities for smuggled goods were set up both on Flekkerøya and in Kristiansand. These sheds filled up steadily—evidence that the customs checks were very strict.[8]

The Danish-Swedish War of 1643-1645

Between 1643 and 1645 the Kingdom of Denmark was embroiled in a war with Sweden, which is also known as the Torstenson War or Hannibal controversy.[9] In the course of the Thirty Years' War (1618-1648), Sweden had become the strongest military power on the European continent and was trying to gain the upper hand in Scandinavia, too. Denmark had pulled out of the Thirty Years' War in 1629, but in 1643 was attacked by the Swedes from the south and the north. The conflict revolved around control of the Baltic. Denmark lost the war in 1645 and was compelled to exempt the Swedes from Sound dues and cede large areas of land to the Swedish crown. It is noteworthy that Allart van Everdingen visited Scandinavia while this war was going on and even travelled through the Bohuslän region around Gothenburg—the Norwegian-Swedish border area where the Danes and the Swedes were fighting.[10]

In the Danish-Swedish War, the Republic was officially neutral—it maintained trading relationships with both Sweden and the Danish-Norwegian kingdom. However, the most important armaments manufacturer for the Republic, Louis de Geer (1587-1652), who had significant trade interests in Sweden, fought on the Swedish side with his private army, while the Rotterdam-born merchant Selius (or Selio) Marselis (1600-1663) went to the aid of the Danish king. When the king found himself in financial difficulties because of the hostilities, Marselis made him a substantial loan and gave him four fully equipped warships.[11] In return Marselis was given far-reaching privileges in the timber trade and licences for copper and iron mines in Norway. He settled in Christiania (now Oslo) in 1644 and became a pivotal figure in the timber trade between Norway and the Republic.

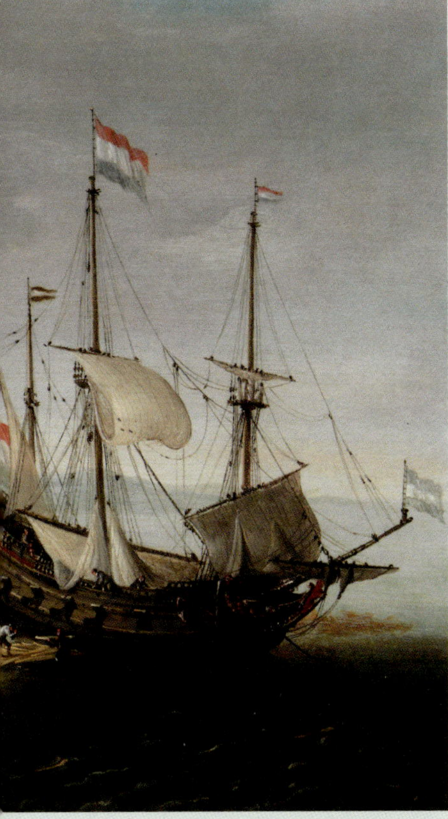

39
Cornelis Claesz van Wieringen, *Loading Timber on the Coast of Norway*, c. 1610-1630, oil on panel, 35.5 x 83.8 cm, private collection (on loan to the Maritime Museum Rotterdam, inv. no. P4600)

toll points in this region.[2] That was impossible in the Sound, the narrow sea strait between Denmark and Sweden; all the ship's captains on their way to and from the Baltic had to pay duty on their cargo.[3]

This state of affairs on the Norwegian coast was an irritant to Christian IV as he saw revenues slipping away.[4] In 1634, he had consequently had a toll post built on the island of Flekkerøya off the southernmost tip of Norway, and in 1635 he had an old fortress made habitable again to keep watch on the collection of tolls.[5] At that time Flekkerøya was one of the main Norwegian harbours, where many Dutch vessels stopped in order to travel back to their home ports in

Cultural Contacts between the Netherlands and Norway

Alongside the trading contacts, there was also cultural exchange between the Low Countries and the Danish-Norwegian kingdom. While Van Everdingen was travelling in the south of Norway, towns like Christiania and Kristiansand were being built. King Christian IV was an active sponsor of new buildings and art lover, whose projects and commissions lured several architects and artists from the Netherlands to Norway.[12]

After a great fire in Christiania in 1624, which left many wooden houses reduced to ash, Christian IV decided to have a modern town with brick houses built on the site. The Dutch master builder Cornelis Flint was summoned in 1625 to develop plans for it and at the same time to restore and modernize Akershus Fortress in Christiania.[13] The Amsterdam-born Adam van Breen (c. 1585-after 1642) was also involved in the latter project as builder and decorator.[14]

As well as Flint and Van Breen, the cartographer Isaac van Geelkercken (1615-1672), also came to Christiania in 1644. Trained in Leiden, he was a specialist in fortress construction, and the Danish court could certainly use his expertise in the war against Sweden.[15] Van Geelkercken was appointed as an engineer in the army and in the twelve years he was active in Norway he reinforced numerous fortifications, including those in Varberg, Halmstad and Laholm and on Flekkerøya.[16] In 1644 and 1645 he worked on the reinforcement and provisional repair of the badly neglected Bohus Fortress (fig. 40), the most important military border post between Norway and Sweden. Allart visited the area around Bohus while Van Geelkercken was working on it.[17] He most probably made a sketch of the fortress, which now only exists in an eighteenth-century copy (fig. 41).[18] Might the two Dutchmen have encountered one another there and shared their impressions of their time in the extraordinary Scandinavian landscape?

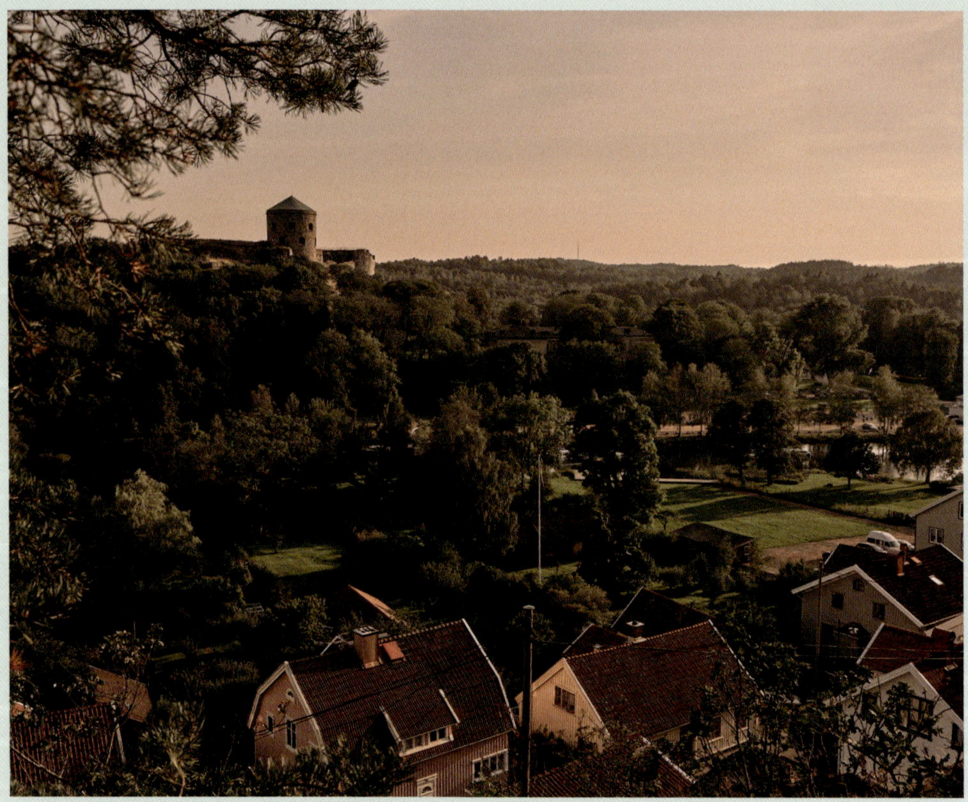

40
Bohus Fortress (photograph Pascal Vossen, August-September 2019)

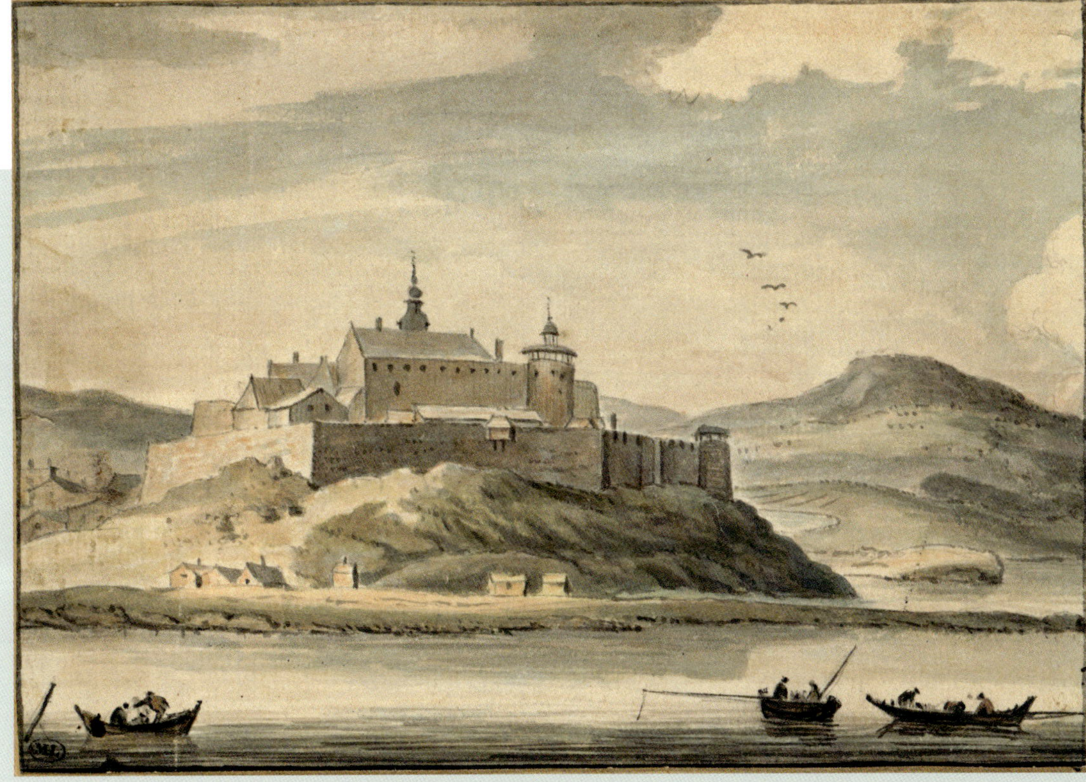

41
Anonymous (Dutch, eighteenth century), *Bohus Fortress*, copy after a lost drawing by Allart van Everdingen, brush and grey ink over graphite, watercolour, 111 x 159 mm, Paris, Musée du Louvre, inv. no. 23514

1 On the trade (in timber among other things) between the Low Countries and Norway see Schreiner 1934, Bødtker 1938, Hart 1976, pp. 71-92, Bruijn 1985, Willemsen 1988, Lesger 1992, Sogner 1996, Sogner 2004, Van Tussenbroek 2012, pp. 34-35, and Brand and Paul 2020.
2 Tønnessen 1989, p. 14
3 Mikkelsen 1988, p. 53.
4 Idem, pp. 52-53.
5 Munksgaard 1997, p. 5. Christian IV stayed on Flekkerøya at least six times—he evidently felt it was important to keep a personal watch on the collection of tolls there.
6 Stylegar 2016, pp. 13-14. They sailed in convoy as protection against privateers.
7 Munksgaard 1997, p. 5.

8 Tønnessen 1989, pp. 22-23.
9 On the war and the role Dutch seamen played in it see Van Nieuwenhuize 2021.
10 Nowadays this region belongs to Sweden but until the Treaty of Roskilde in 1658 it was part of Norway.
11 Marselis also tried to raise an army in the Republic to support the Danish king; he was less successful than Louis de Geer had been for Sweden (Murdoch 2010, p. 215). In 1640 Selius's brother Gabriel had acquired Bærumsverk, a Norwegian iron ore mine. This may explain why the brothers chose to convert the loan to the king into privileges in Norway (Bull, Sønstevold and Hammer 1927, pp. 106-108). On Gabriel and Selius Marselis see also Zandvliet 2006, pp. 67-68 (no. 29).

12 Denmark 1988, Gerson 1983, pp. 453-480, Bøggild Johannsen 1993, pp. 88-141 and Roding 1996, pp. 96-97.
13 This builder, who does not appear in dictionaries of art, worked on the rebuilding of Christiania between 1625 and 1632 (Daae 1871, p. 20, Mey 1878, p. 262 and Holden 2012, p. 21).
14 Gerson 1983, p. 476 and Buijsen et al. 1998, p. 108.
15 Hendriks 1998, p. 52.
16 Roding 1996, p. 101.
17 Widerberg 1924, pp. 11-12 and Hendriks 1998, p. 53.
18 Davies 2001, p. 27.

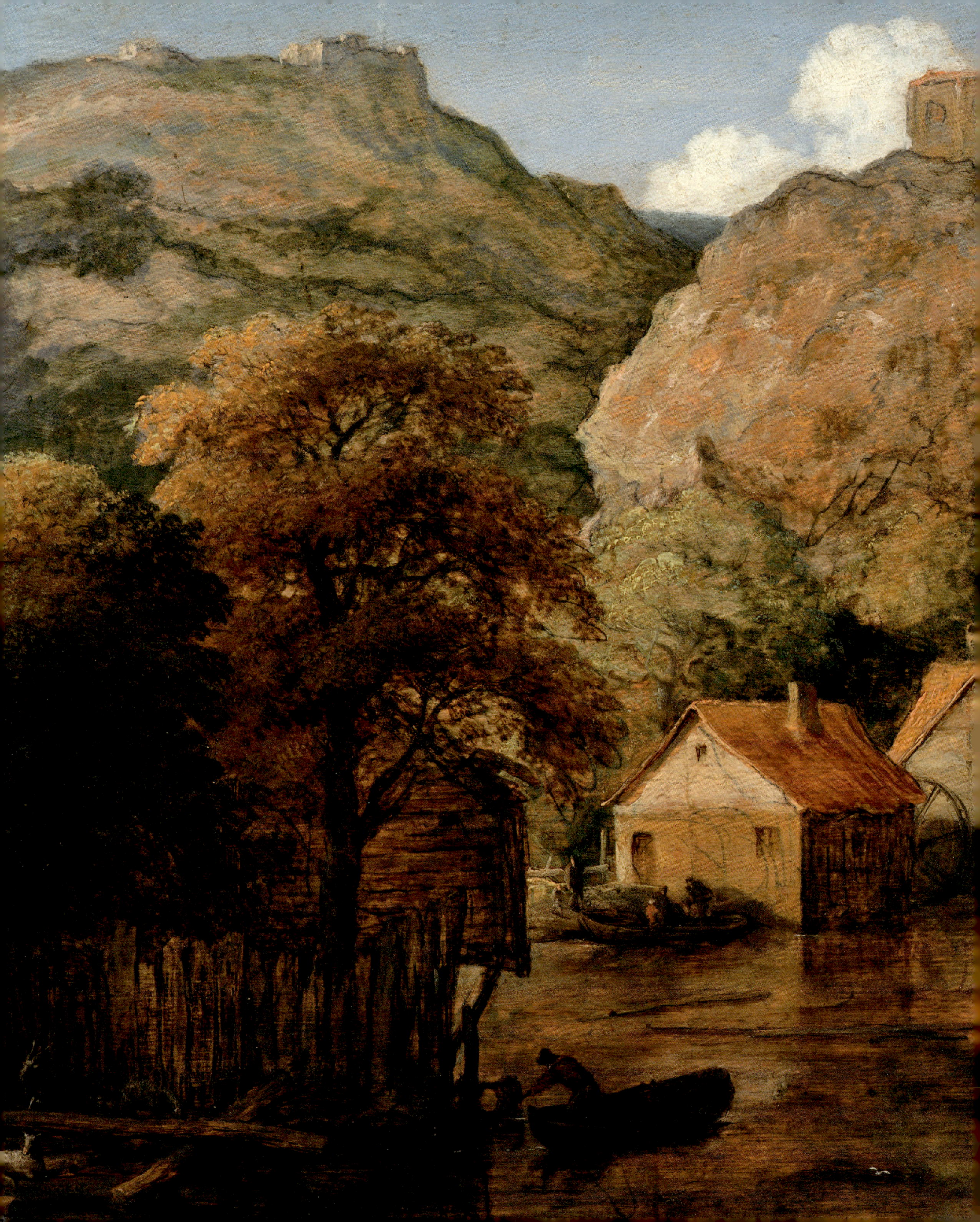

2 FROM EXPERIENCE TO IMAGINATION

Allart van Everdingen the Painter

Christi M. Klinkert

< Detail of cat. no. 89

Around a hundred and eighty of Allart van Everdingen's paintings survive.[1] Save for some twenty or so, they are landscapes—and aside from a handful of Dutch scenes they are chiefly pictures of mountainous regions, where rushing torrents or waterfalls find their way among massive rocks. The rest can be described as marines, with a river, lake or the sea as the subject.[2] In most of them, however, land is clearly visible in the shape of a rocky shore, the skyline of a Dutch town or the outlines of a Dutch village. One could conclude that Van Everdingen painted landscapes virtually exclusively, with rocks and water often key features.

Allart van Everdingen is regarded as the pre-eminent painter of the Scandinavian landscape: he was the first artist to sell realistic scenes of the region on the Dutch market. At least a hundred and forty of Van Everdingen's paintings depict convincing Scandinavian elements, such as log cabins or rocky outcrops with waterfalls. The artist developed this unusual specialism following a visit to Norway in 1644, soon after he completed his training and not long before his marriage, discussed at length in the previous contributions.

But just how Norwegian were Van Everdingen's paintings in truth? To what extent are they reliable visual records of his journey? And how realistic were his Dutch landscapes—pictures of places he saw every day? There can be no doubt that Allart had sketches he had made on the spot before him when he was composing his paintings. Some of the motifs in these drawings appear on a canvas or panel. But, as every other artist did, Van Everdingen altered elements of his drawings, combined them and rearranged them as he saw fit in order to arrive at a balanced and attractive composition in paint. He also drew inspiration from what other landscape painters had done before him.

In what follows, we examine thirty-two paintings by Allart van Everdingen, a representative selection of the surviving work. In discussing them, we look each time at how the artist decided upon his composition, seeking answers to such questions as which examples or sources he used, how he conceived his paintings and how he worked them out, which elements are convincingly true to life, which sprang from his imagination, which pictorial traditions Van Everdingen followed and in which respects he was an innovator.

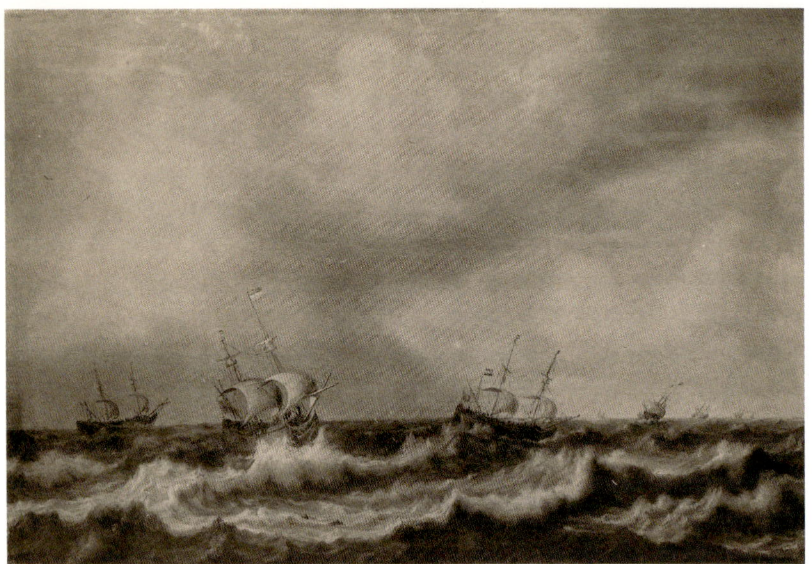

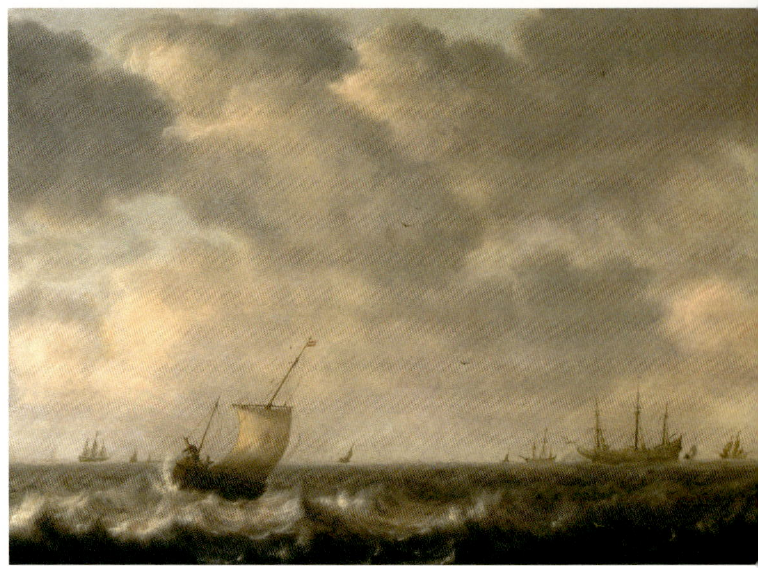

Allart seldom dated his work; altogether he gave some thirty paintings a date. Ten of them are discussed here, providing a set of chronological 'pegs' on which other, similar paintings can be hung. This makes it possible to sketch Van Everdingen's development as a painter.

Raging Seas

It is assumed that Allart van Everdingen completed his training in Haarlem in 1639 or 1640 and from then on produced paintings as an independent artist—for the first few years in his birthplace, Alkmaar. In the absence of dated works from this phase, it is difficult to establish exactly what the young artist was making at the time. A scene of three-masters in raging seas, on which 'A.v.Everdingen 1640.' is supposedly noted lower right, is regarded as his earliest work (fig. 42).[3] However this panel was last seen in 1942 and its present whereabouts are unknown, so the signature and date cannot be checked. All that can be said about it on the basis of the surviving black-and-white photograph is that it bears a strong resemblance to seascapes by the Haarlem artist Pieter Mulier I (1595/1610-1659/1661) (fig. 43), who may have been Van Everdingen's teacher.[4] The similarities lie in the strong chiaroscuro (the dark foregrounds are particularly striking), the relatively small vessels beneath towering skies and the breakers rolling in diagonally from left to right.

A work that is traceable, and recently studied, is another early sea scene with a three-master by Allart van Everdingen in a German private collection (fig. 44). It shows a ship—probably a merchant frigate—in danger off a rocky coast, flying a Dutch flag on the stern.[5] The crew is trying to row to safety in a small boat while onlookers watch from the tall cliffs. The white birds at the lower right create a decorative pattern that merges almost imperceptibly into the foaming crests of the waves.

It is tempting to think that Van Everdingen based this dramatic scene on his own experiences at sea. According to artists' biographer

< 42
Allart van Everdingen, *Ships at Sea in Stormy Weather*, 1640, oil on panel, 69 x 105 cm, whereabouts unknown

43
Pieter Mulier I, *Turbulent Sea*, oil on panel, 34 x 47 cm, The Hague, Museum Bredius, inv. no. 88-1946

< 44
Allart van Everdingen, *Shipwreck off a Rocky Coast*, oil on panel, 34 x 42 cm, private collection (cat. no. 104)

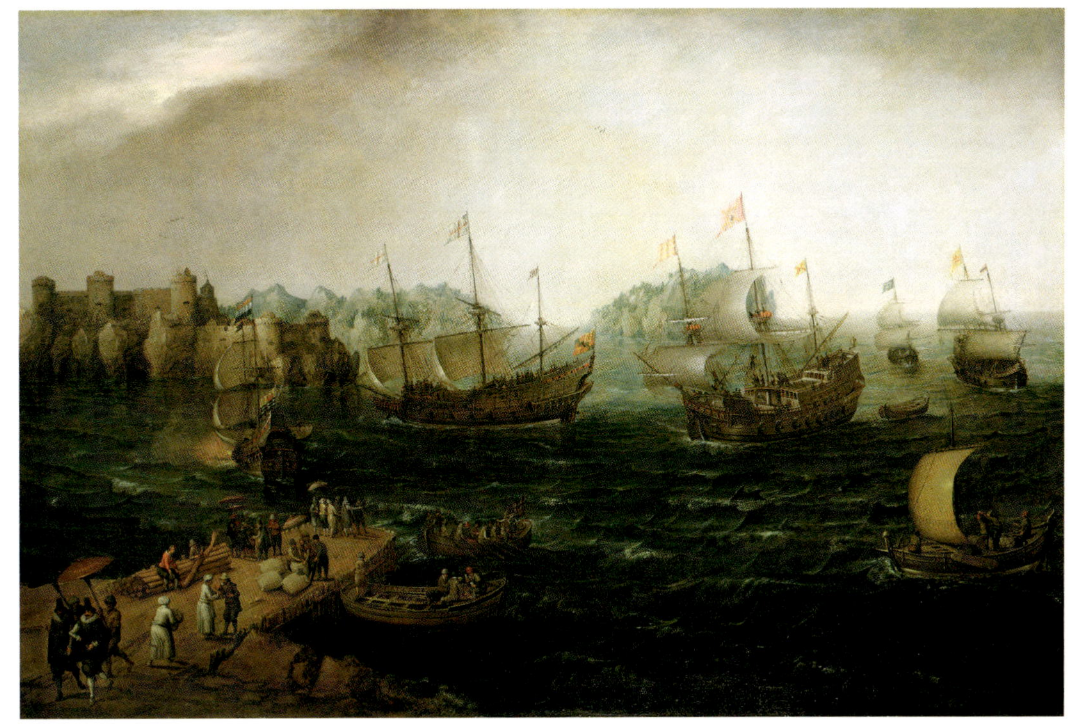

45
Hendrick Cornelisz Vroom, *Ships Trading in the East*, 1614, oil on canvas, 97.8 x 151.2 cm, London, Greenwich, National Maritime Museum, Palmer Collection, inv. no. BHC0727

46
Adam Willaerts, *Shipwreck on a Rocky Coast*, 1614, oil on panel, 64.5 x 85.2 cm, Amsterdam, Rijksmuseum, inv. no. SK-A-1955

Arnold Houbraken, at the beginning of his career Allart was caught in 'a perilous storm' while he was on board a ship heading for the Baltic; it carried the vessel to the coast of Norway.[6] However, Van Everdingen's painting of ships in danger fits seamlessly into the prevailing pictorial traditions and could have been created without the aid of sketches from life.

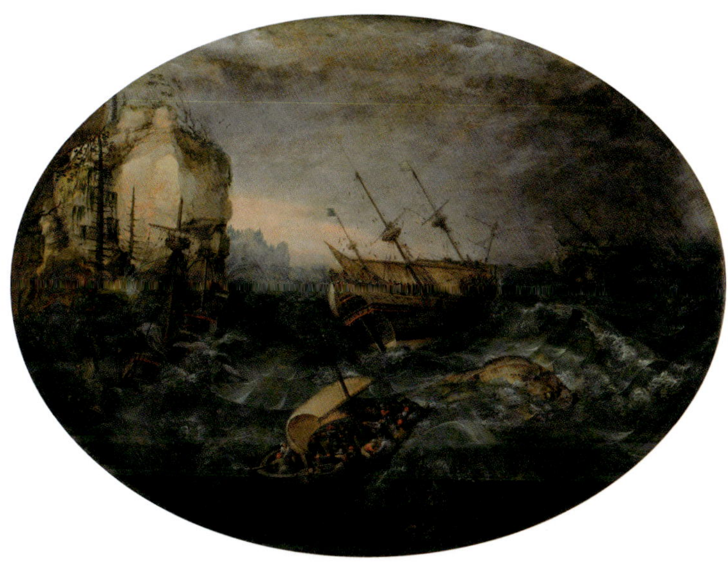

In the first decades of the seventeenth century, the marine (sea or river view) developed and flourished in the Low Countries—an area that owed much of its power and prosperity to shipping.[7] The Haarlem artist Hendrick Cornelisz Vroom (1562/1566-1640) is regarded as the pioneer of this genre. Around 1600 he was one of the first to make ships at sea a specific genre in its own right and an accepted subject for paintings (fig. 45).[8] Vroom used a colourful palette and presented his vessels in detail and distributed evenly across the picture plane. Van Everdingen must have seen examples of Vroom's work while he was training in Haarlem. Before that, when he was probably an apprentice in Utrecht, he may have come across the marine painter Adam Willaerts (1577-1664), a follower of Vroom. In the early seventeenth century Willaerts began painting similar colourful, detailed scenes of ships in harbours, off rocky shores and in storms (fig. 46). In terms of its viewpoint, palette and level of detail, Allart's early panel (fig. 44) is reminiscent of Vroom's and Willaerts's marines. The dark foreground and the way the waves are rendered, with sharp peaks and white crests, are more of a piece with Mulier I's work (figs. 43 and 12).

Rugged Scandinavia

In February 1645, Allart van Everdingen married Janneke Cornelisdr and moved from Alkmaar to Haarlem. From then on, he appears to have devoted his efforts as a painter first and foremost to processing his impressions of his time in Norway. Among his earliest Norwegian paintings are some works dated 1647 (figs. 47 and 48; see also figs. 19 and 20). The landscapes they depict are inhospitable and inaccessible. There are buildings, people walk about here and there, and there are animals, but they look insignificant amidst the immense rock formations. The desolation of the scenes is intensified by the low horizon and the artist's high vantage point: it is as if we are staring into the depths or far into the distance from a mountain top. Perhaps Van Everdingen actually stood in such places and admired the awe-inspiring views, but if he did, he left no drawings of mountain vistas as evidence.

Allart's probable teacher in Utrecht, Roelandt Savery (1576-1639), had, though, made drawings of this kind during his travels through the Tyrol in 1606-1607.[9] It seems that Van Everdingen must have had some of Savery's sketches in mind when he composed his first Scandinavian scenes. Both artists placed a massive rock face in the middle ground of their compositions against a low-lying river landscape in the background to create a strong sense of depth (figs. 47 and 49). In Van Everdingen's day, dividing the picture plane along clear diagonal lines was a tried and tested recipe in landscape painting, widely used by Flemish painters like Lucas van Valckenborch (1535/1536-1597) (fig. 50) and Joos de Momper II (1564-1635).[10]

The spruce trees growing here and there on the bare rocks stand out in both these early Norwegian landscapes by Van Everdingen.[11] In one of them, (fig. 47), a fallen trunk lies in the foreground to emphasize the rugged nature

47
Allart van Everdingen, *Mountain Landscape with a River Valley*, 1647, oil on canvas, 82.5 x 111 cm, Copenhagen, Statens Museum for Kunst, inv. no. KMSsp513 (cat. no. 66)

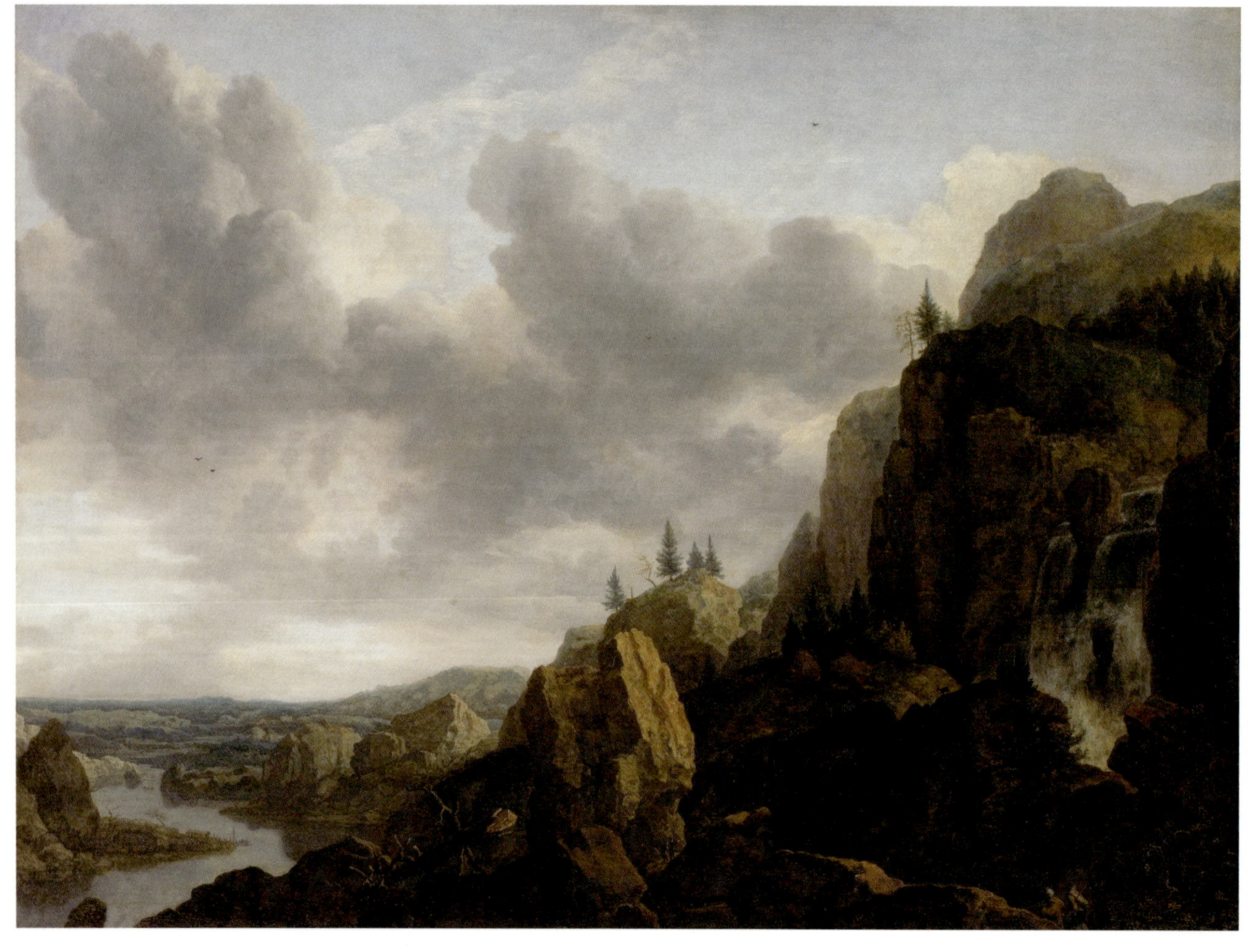

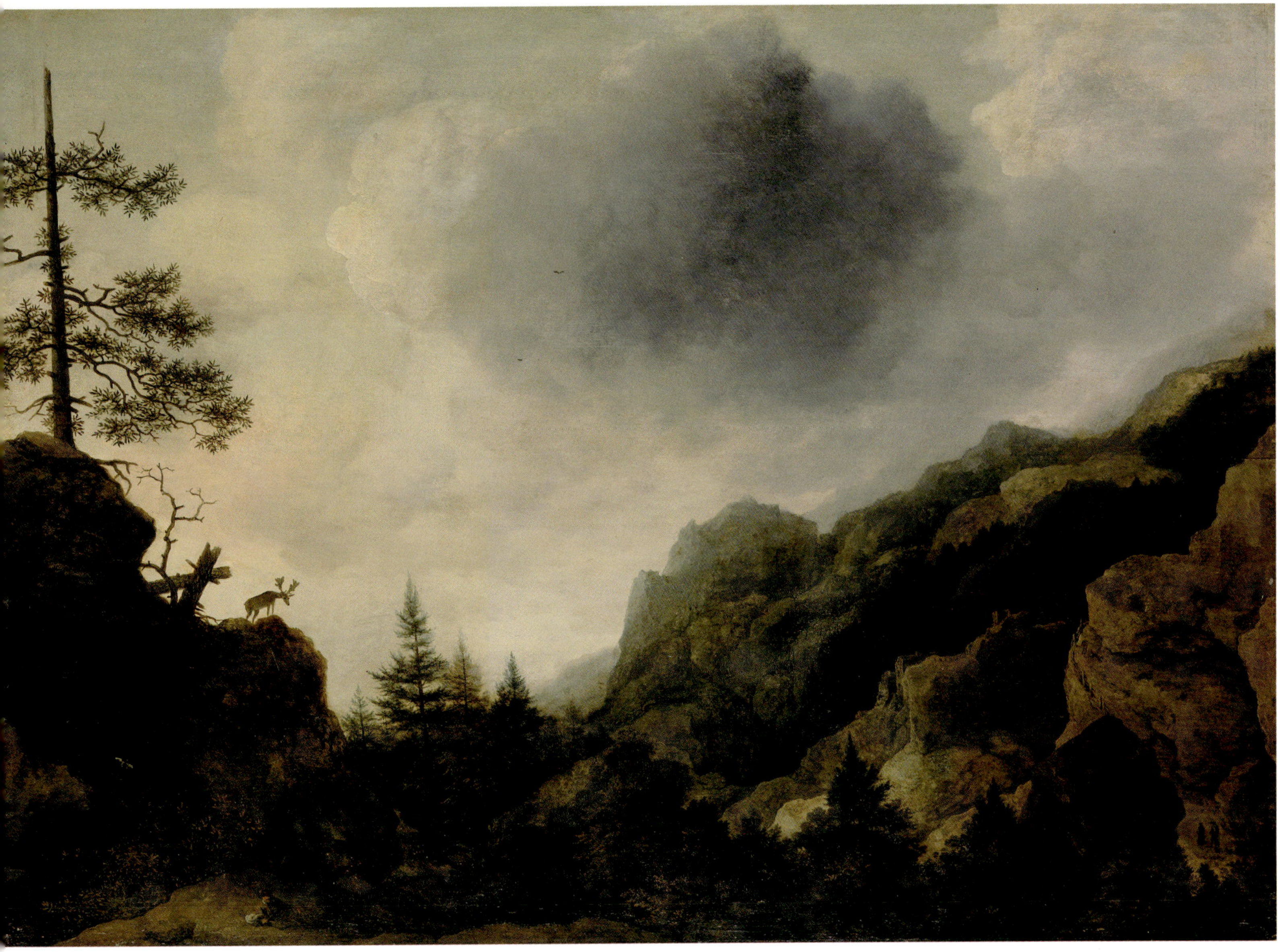

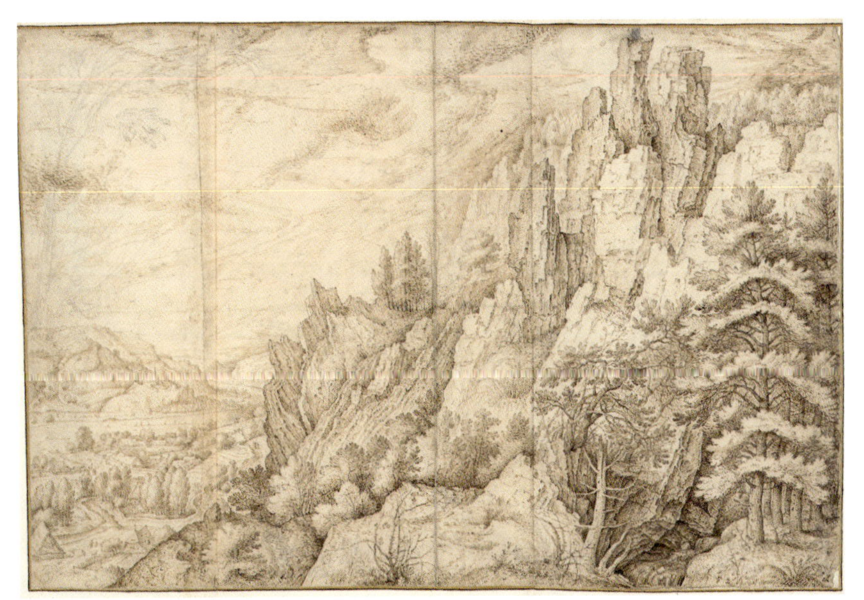

48
Allart van Everdingen,
*Mountain Landscape
with a Fallow Deer*,
1647, oil on panel, 64.3 x
89 cm, Braunschweig,
Herzog Anton Ulrich-
Museum, Kunstmuseum
des Landes Nieder-
sachsen, inv. no. GG 364
(cat. no. 46)

> 49
Roelandt Savery,
Valley in Bohemia,
1606, pen and brown
ink, 510 x 575 mm,
Vienna, Österreichische
Nationalbibliothek,
Atlas van der Hem,
vol. XLVI, fol. 13

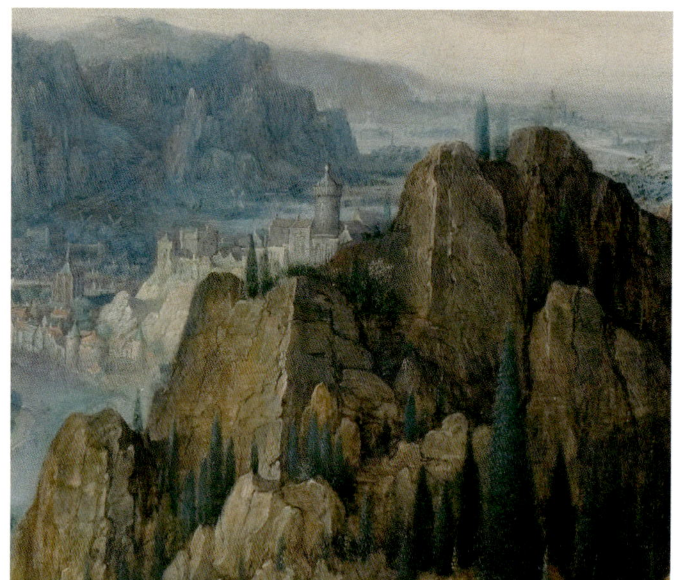

50

Lucas van Valckenborch, *Mountainous Landscape with the Temptation of Christ*, c. 1583, oil on panel, 27 x 38.2 cm, Enschede, Rijksmuseum Twenthe, inv. no. 0058

> 51

Roelandt Savery, *Alpine Landscape with Rocks and a Waterfall, an Artist and a Rainbow*, c. 1606-1607, red and black chalk, grey, green and blue wash, 550 x 430 mm, Vienna, Österreichische National-bibliothek, Atlas van der Hem, vol. XLVI, fol. 10

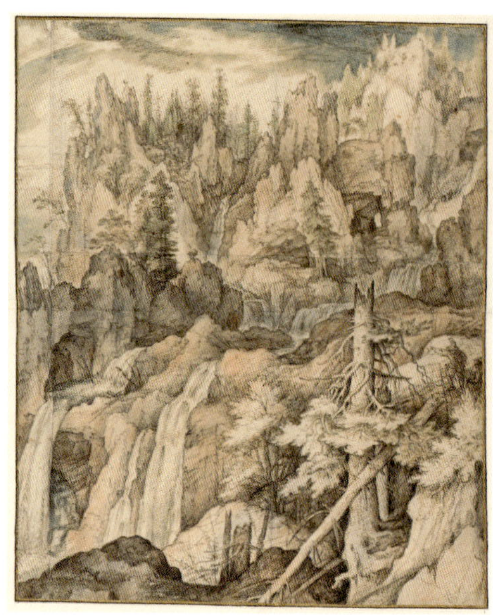

of the terrain. Allart undoubtedly saw fallen trunks himself in Scandinavia, but their positioning diagonally in the foreground of the picture plane as a signpost in the composition is something he must have learnt from Savery (fig. 51).

On the extreme left of the painting *Mountain Landscape with a Fallow Deer* (fig. 48) there is a very remarkable tree: a dead straight trunk with a few branches on which individual leaves stand out sharply against the grey clouds. With a little effort it is possible to recognize it as an ash —a species that grows throughout Europe.[12] Van Everdingen probably took this motif directly from the work of the Haarlem artist Cornelis Hendricksz Vroom (1590/1591-1661), the oldest son of the marine painter Hendrick Vroom.[13] Trees as dark, decorative silhouettes were his trademark (fig. 52). Allart also used them more than once (fig. 53).[14] In the panel with the strange ash tree, a fallow deer likewise stands out against the light sky.[15] Van Everdingen often introduced animals into his compositions, but there are very few paintings where he did it in precisely this way (fig. 54).

There is a waterfall in *Mountain Landscape with a River Valley* (fig. 47). Cascading down the dark rocks on the far right, it does not show up at first glance. It appears, moreover, to have

been taken from a drawing by Savery (fig. 51) rather than from life. The same type of high waterfall, with two or more long, vertical streams, also occurs in paintings, drawings and prints of the landscape near Tivoli in Italy.[16] Van Everdingen would certainly have seen such compositions, for this famous Italian beauty spot was repeatedly pictured from the second half of the sixteenth century, not least by Cornelis van Poelenburch (1594/1595-1667) (fig. 55).

52

Cornelis Hendricksz Vroom, *River Landscape Seen through Trees*, c. 1638, oil on panel, 50 x 67 cm, The Hague, Maurits-huis, inv. no. 1156

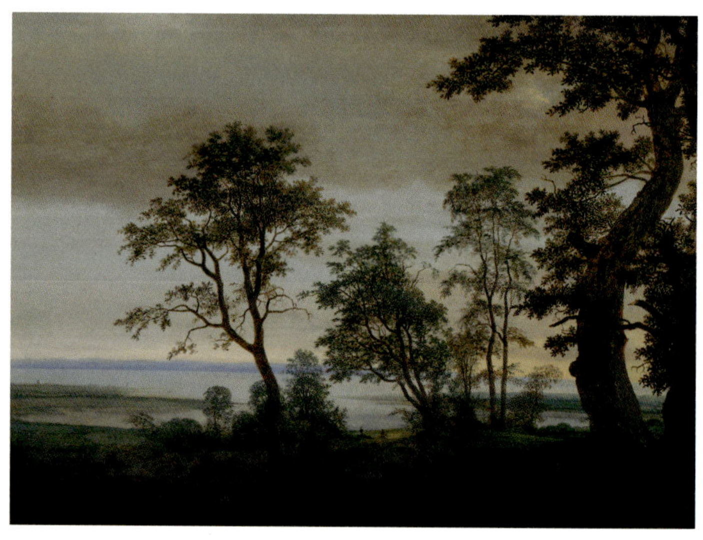

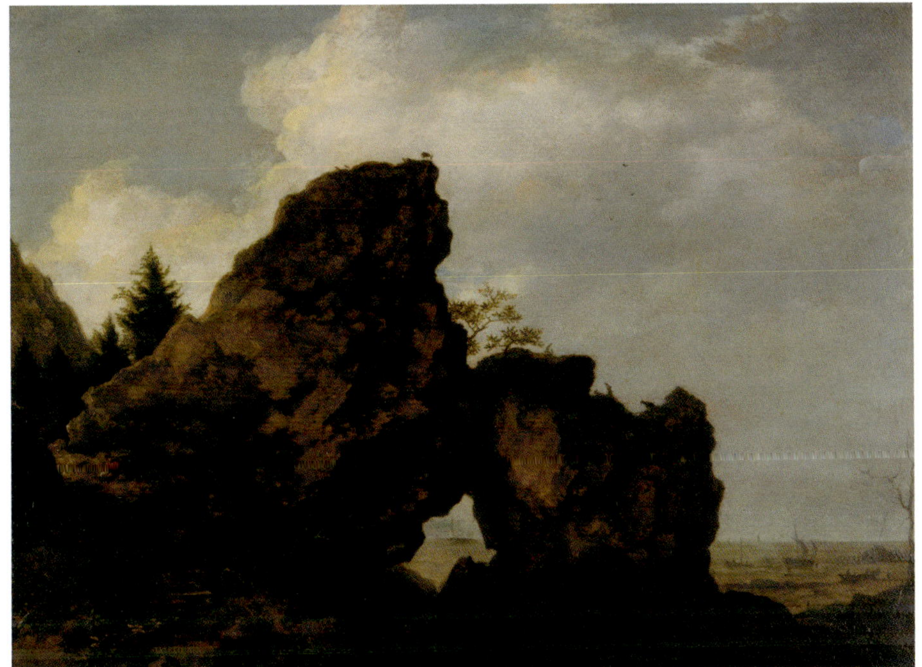

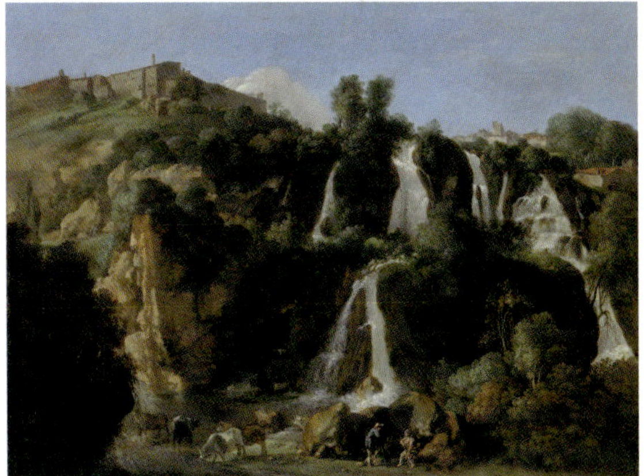

55
Cornelis van Poelenburch,
Waterfalls at Tivoli, c. 1622,
oil on copper, 24.1 x 33.3 cm,
Munich, Bayerische Staats-
gemäldesammlungen, Alte
Pinakothek, inv. no. 5273

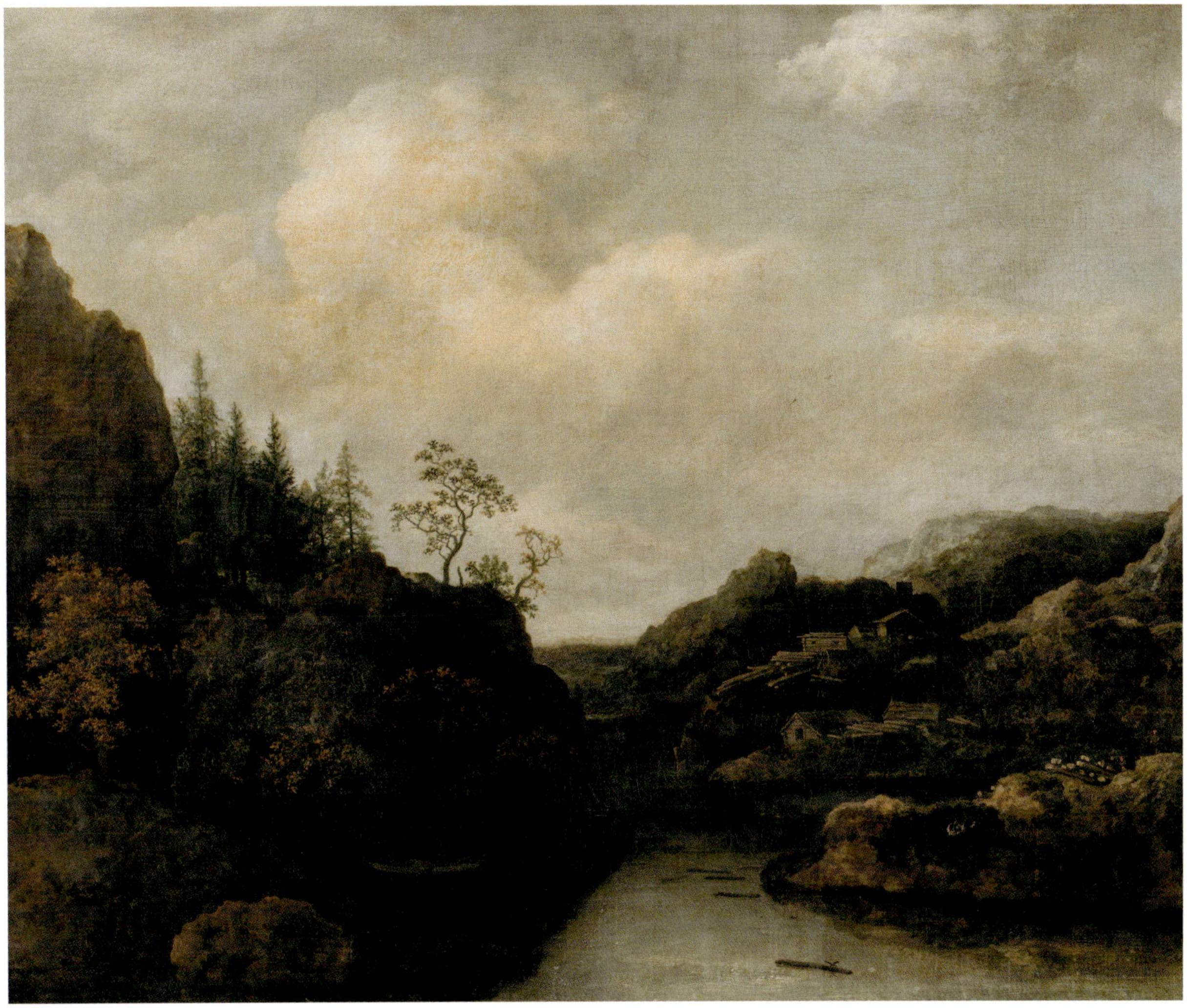

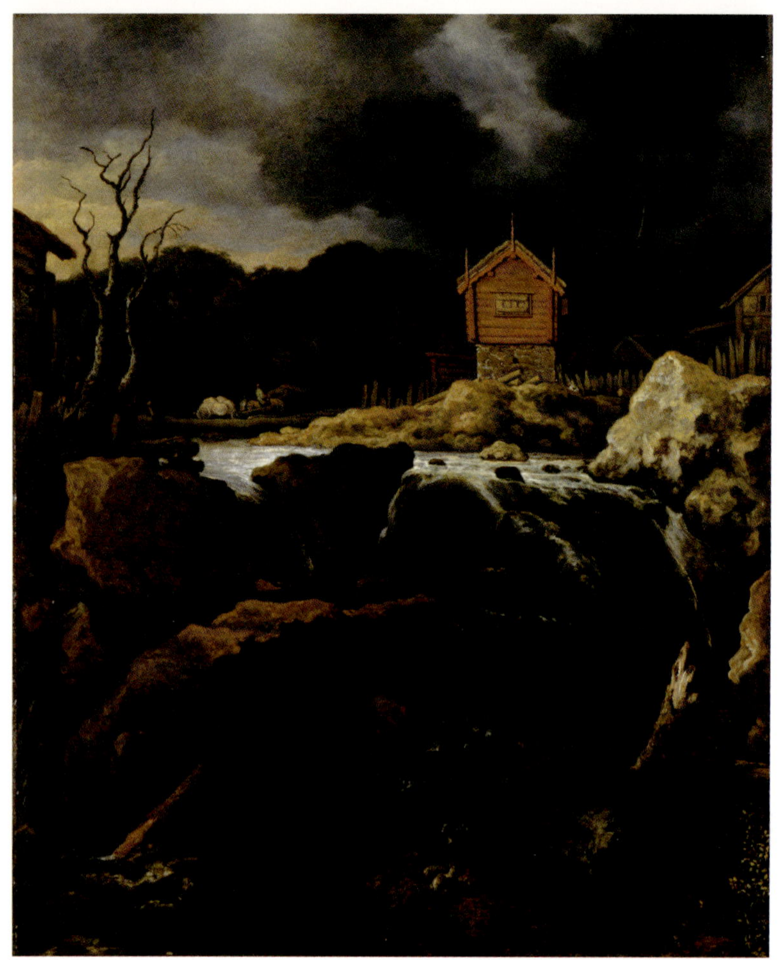

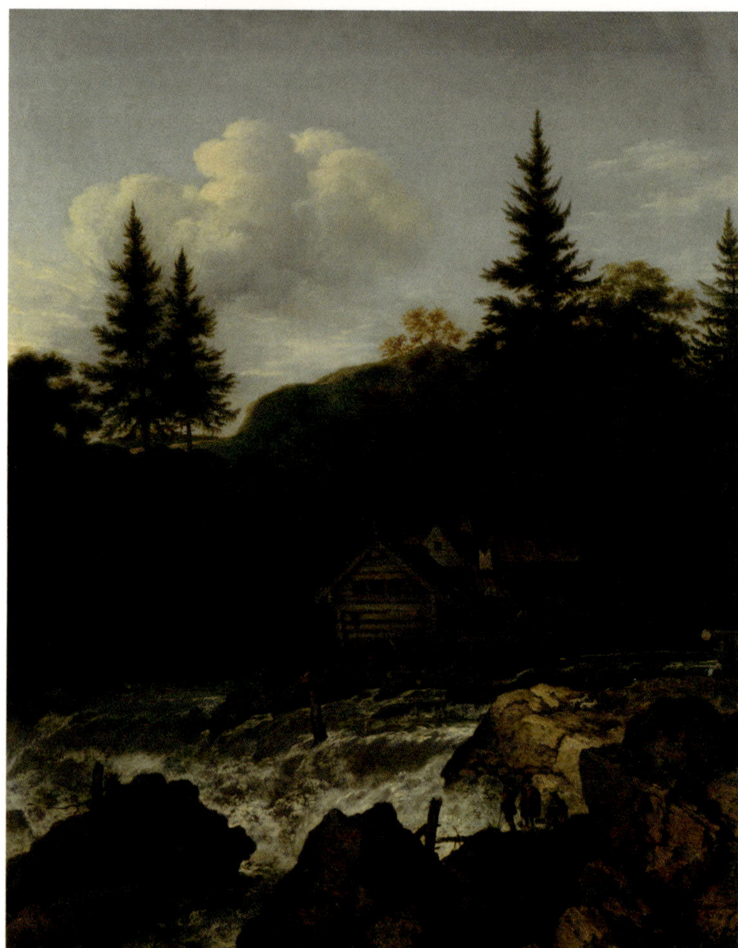

The waterfalls in Allart's *Rocky Landscape with a Waterfall* of 1648 (fig. 56) and *Norwegian Landscape with a Waterfall and a Watermill* of 1650 (fig. 57) are very different.[17] No decorative incidentals, these, but realistic torrents that dominate the foreground. The vertical format of these paintings immediately strikes one—landscapes, after all, are almost always horizontal. Van Everdingen must have realized that this unusual orientation was more effective for waterfalls; it puts them almost automatically in the centre. After 1648 he continued to paint waterfalls in vertical format.

Rivers in mountain landscapes full of conifers, foaming as they pass through rapids or go over a waterfall, can still be found in the region Van Everdingen visited in 1644 (fig. 58). The similarity between that natural beauty and Allart's depictions of it is remarkable, albeit that the Alkmaar artist usually made the Norwegian rocks, rounded as they are by glaciers, more angular and rugged in his paintings, and kept the figures in his landscapes very small in relation to the trees and rocks.

Houses in Scandinavia were traditionally built of wood—a raw material available in abundance (fig. 59). Watermills were often built on to these log cabins and used, for instance, to grind wheat. Allart certainly saw buildings like this with his own eyes; drawings he made on the spot or based on 'travel sketches' attest to this (figs. 96-100). The brightly lit log cabin in *Rocky Landscape with a Waterfall* (fig. 56) was derived from one such drawing (fig. 60). The little wooden building looks convincingly Scandinavian and must have impressed Allart's Dutch buyers as being foreign and northern.[18]

As well as waterfalls and log cabins, Van Everdingen's mountain landscapes also feature a remarkable number of tall trees, standing

< 56
Allart van Everdingen, *Rocky Landscape with a Waterfall*, 1648, oil on canvas, 85 x 70 cm, Hannover, Dr Amir Pakzad Family Collection (on loan to the Landesmuseum Hannover)

57
Allart van Everdingen, *Norwegian Landscape with a Waterfall and a Watermill*, 1650, oil on canvas, 112.8 x 88.2 cm, Munich, Bayerische Staatsgemäldesammlungen, Alte Pinakothek, inv. no. 387 (cat. no. 90)

58
Waterfall near Treungen (photograph
Pascal Vossen, August-September 2019)

59
Authentic Norwegian log cabins, the earliest dating
from c. 1675, in Grimdalstunet, Dalen (photograph
Pascal Vossen, August-September 2019)

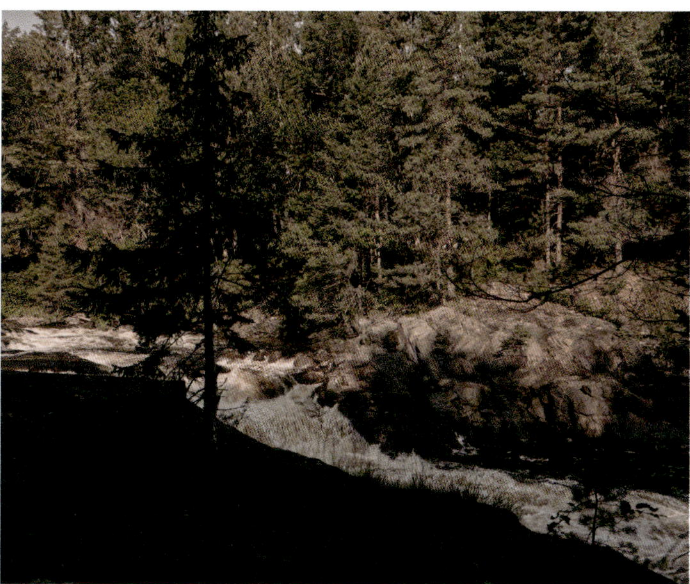

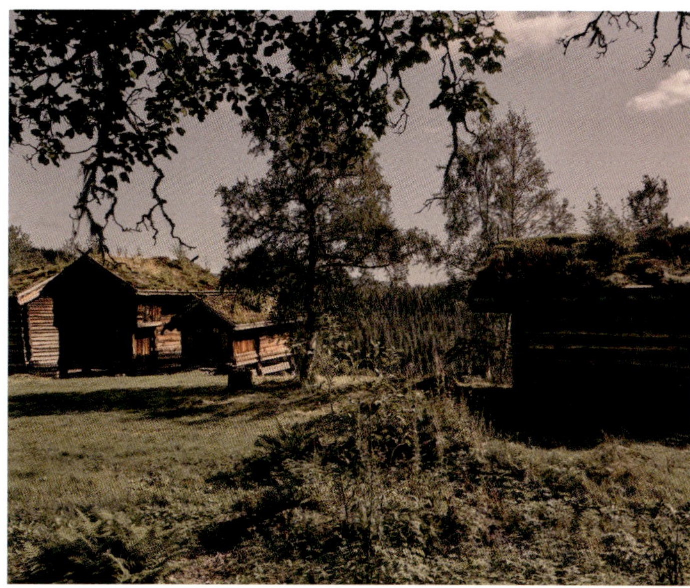

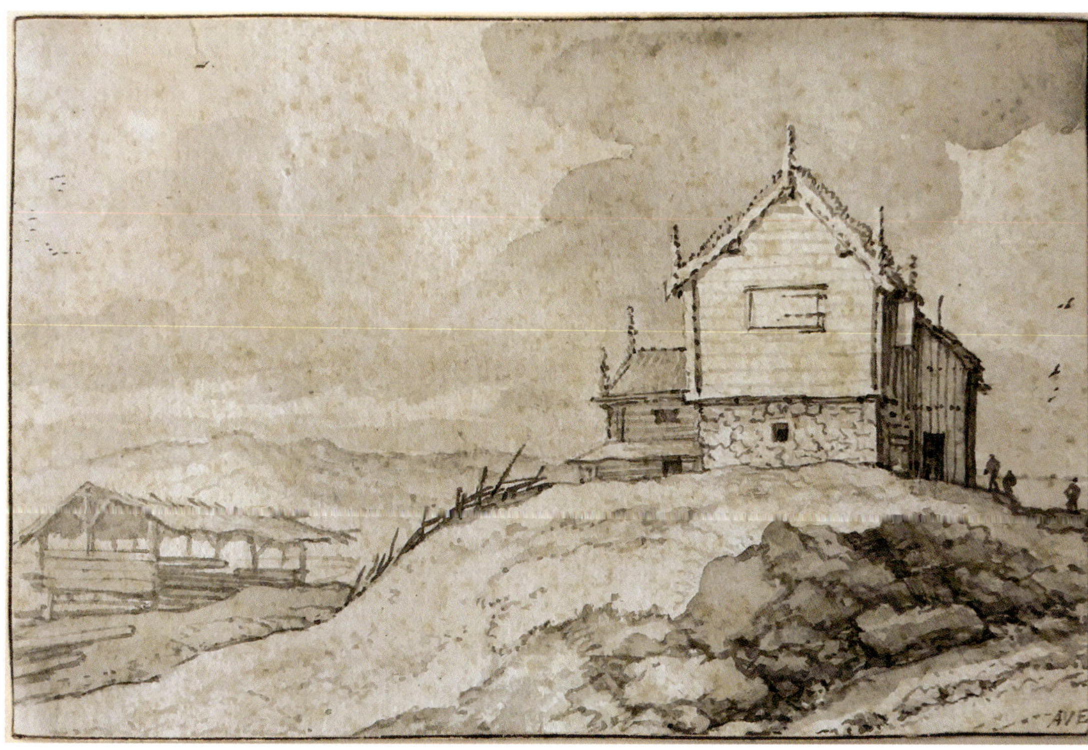

60
Allart van Everdingen,
*Norwegian Landscape
with a Log Cabin*, 1644
or shortly thereafter,
pen and brush in grey
ink over traces of black
chalk, grey wash, 116 x
176 mm, Boston, Alice
I. Davies Collection
(cat. no. 45)

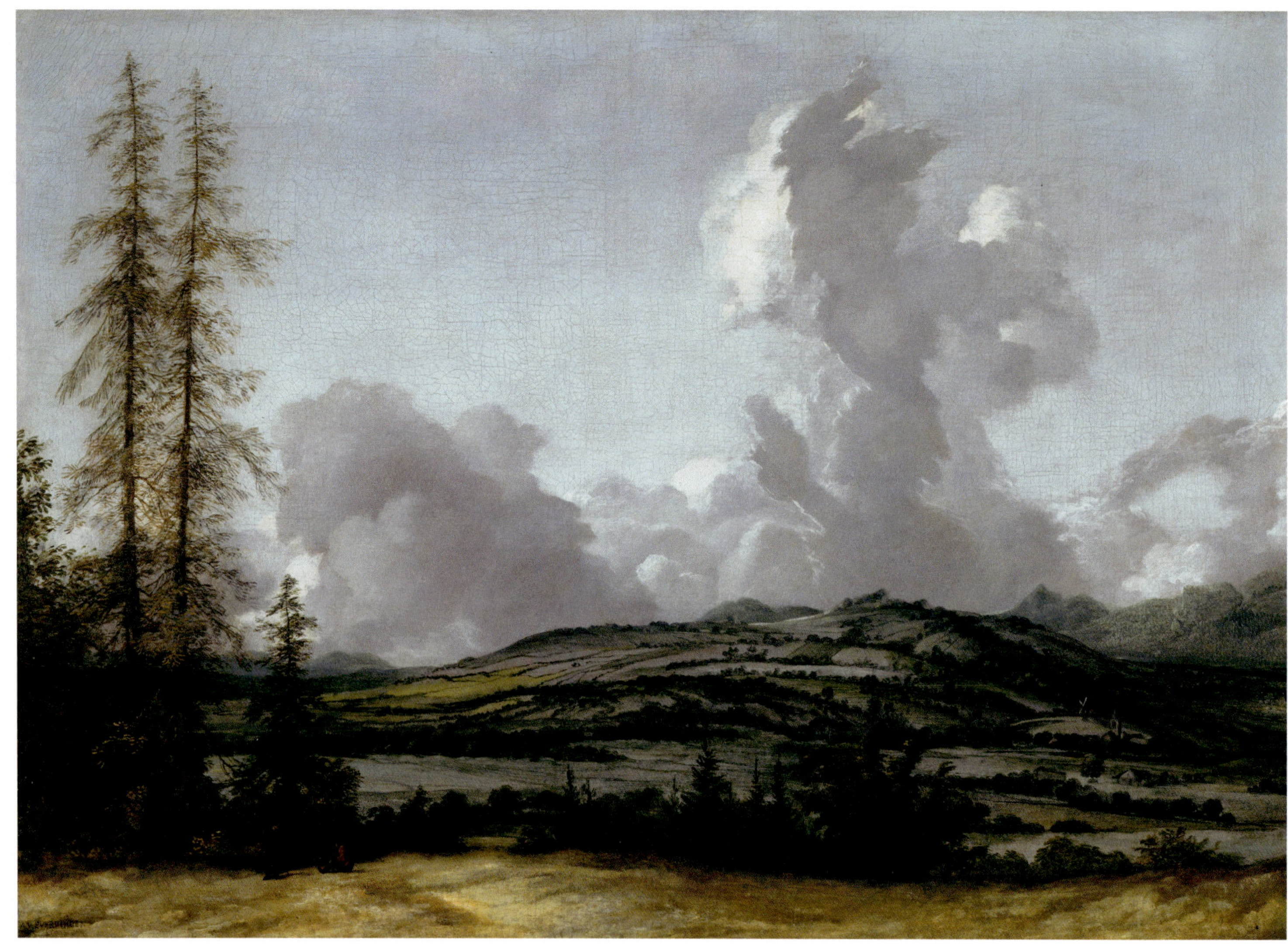

alone.[19] The striking spruces in the 1650 painting *Norwegian Landscape with a Waterfall and a Watermill* (fig. 57), for instance, create a fine contrast with the plunging waterfall and lend balance to the composition. In *Hilly Landscape* (fig. 61) the slender larches lead the eye upwards.[20] Opposite these trees is an extraordinary cloud formation. Its shape was probably dictated by the function it performs in the composition—as a visual counterweight to the larches—rather than observation of an actual situation. Clouds like these certainly do occur in reality, but always high up in the sky. When seventeenth-century artists pictured them, they placed them lower, as it were pressed down on to the horizon. What

usually stretches horizontally above our heads, illuminated from above with a dark underside, seems to have become a vertical tower lit from behind with grey at the front.[21]

With his Norwegian scenes of spruce and log cabins by waterfalls, Van Everdingen introduced a completely new genre on to the market. No other artist had pictured Scandinavia in this naturalistic way. Allart must have been aware of this, for he signed and dated these early landscapes, establishing his position as the first artist to paint works like these. After 1650, when his reputation as the 'inventor' of the Norwegian landscape was secure, Van Everdingen dated his works only occasionally.

61
Allart van Everdingen, *Hilly Landscape*, oil on canvas, 72.8 x 102.2 cm, Hamburger Kunsthalle, inv. no. HK-56 (cat. no. 56)

> 62
Allart van Everdingen, *Trees by the Water*, oil on canvas, 76.6 x 66.5 cm, Stedelijk Museum Alkmaar, inv. no. 20918 (cat. no. 1)

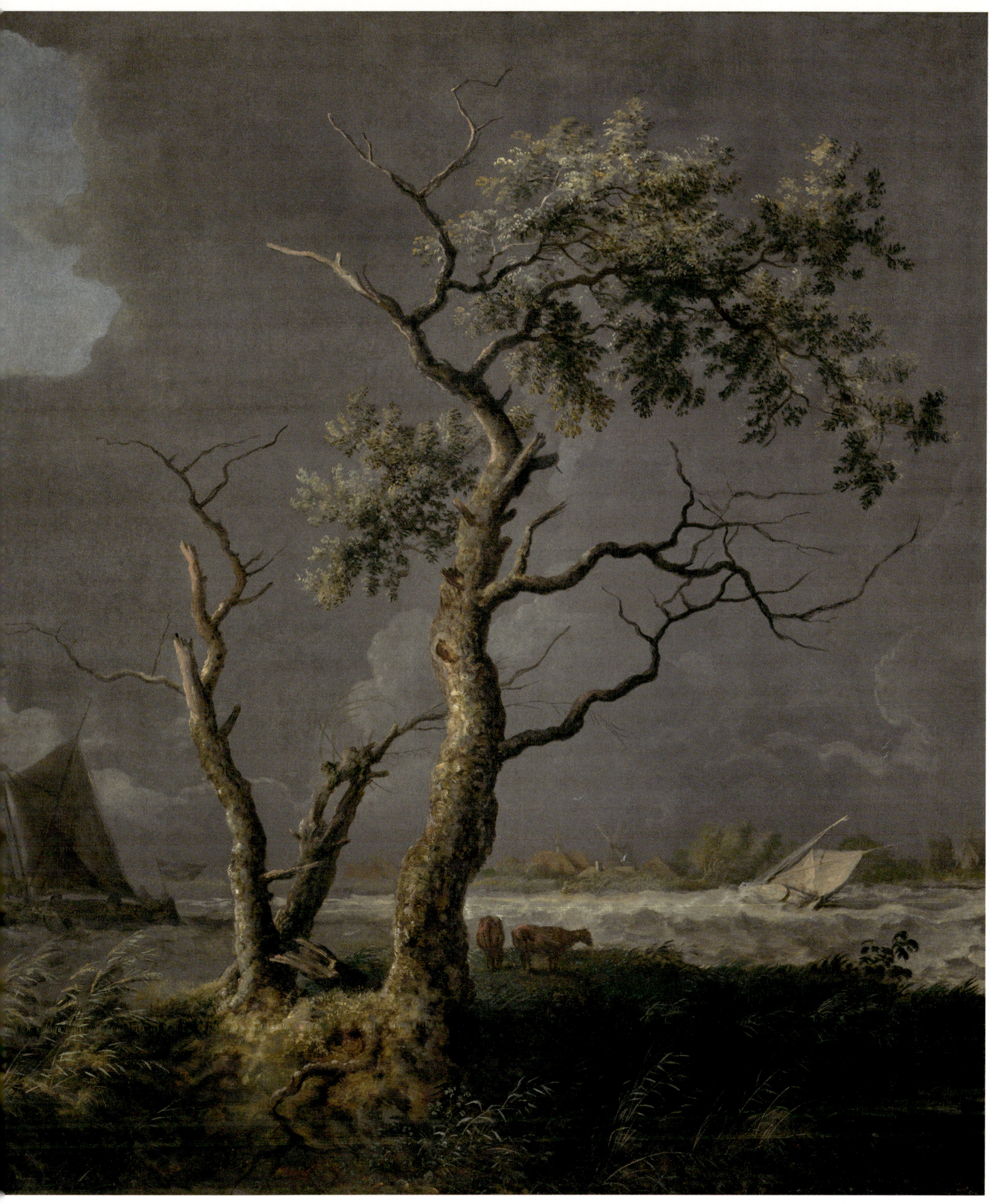

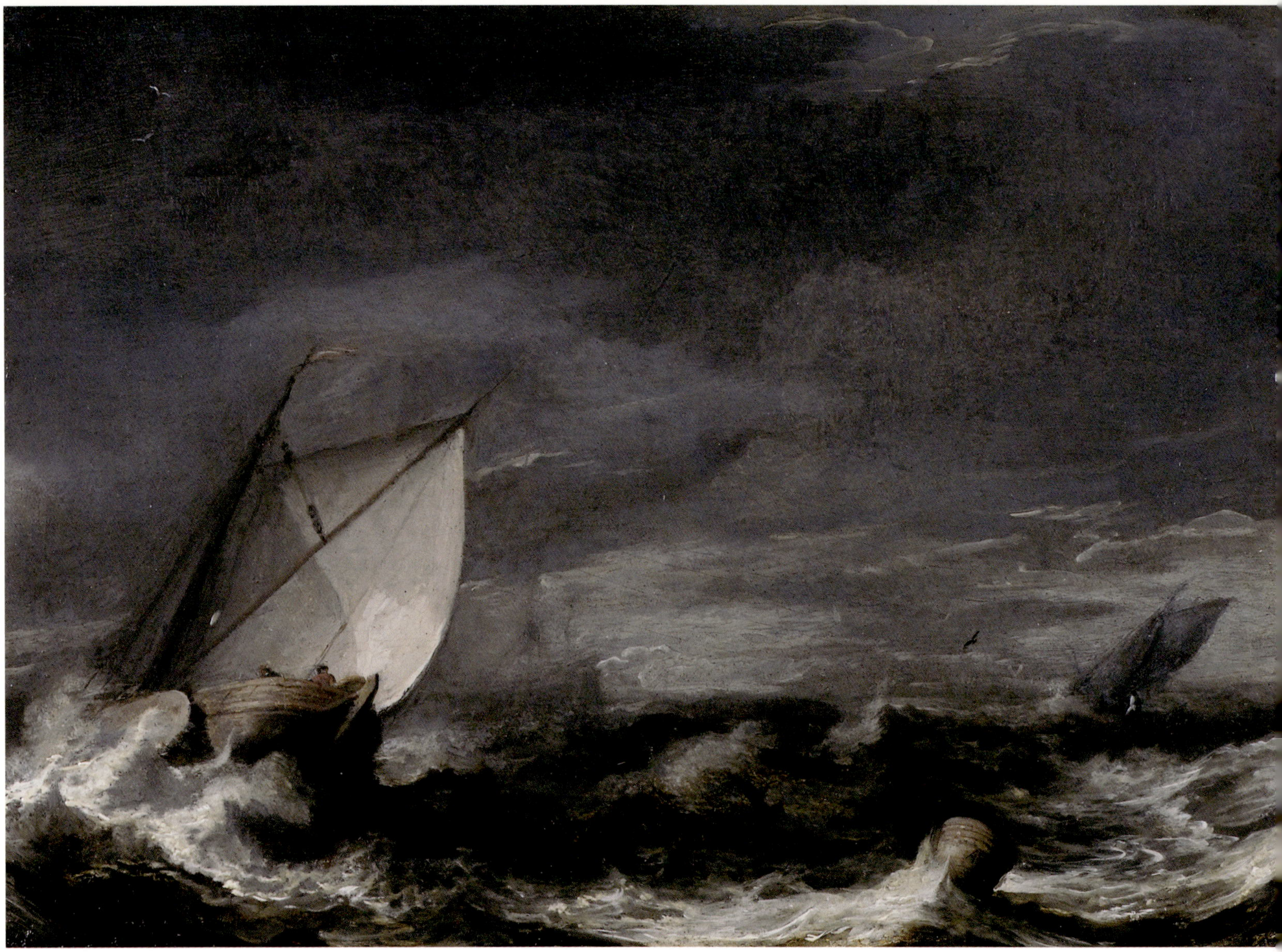

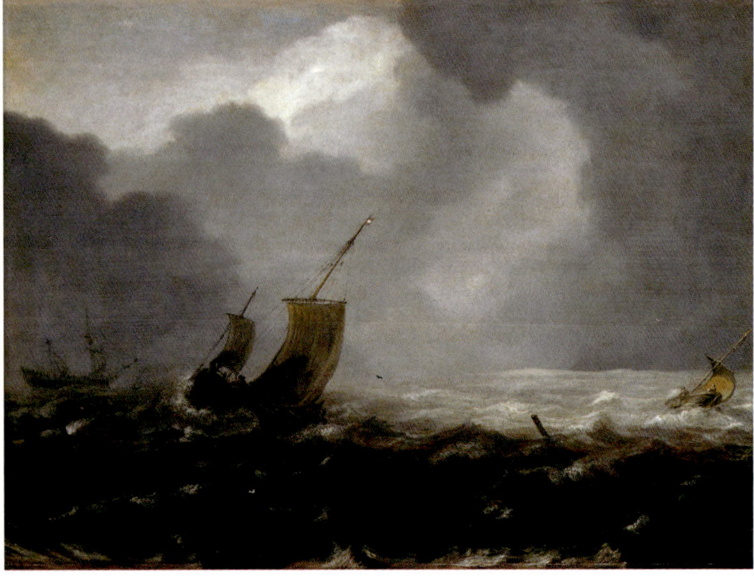

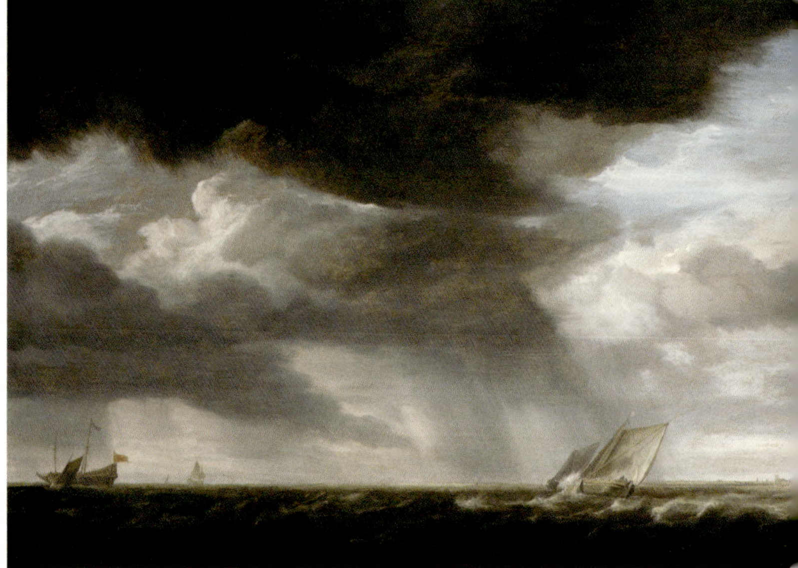

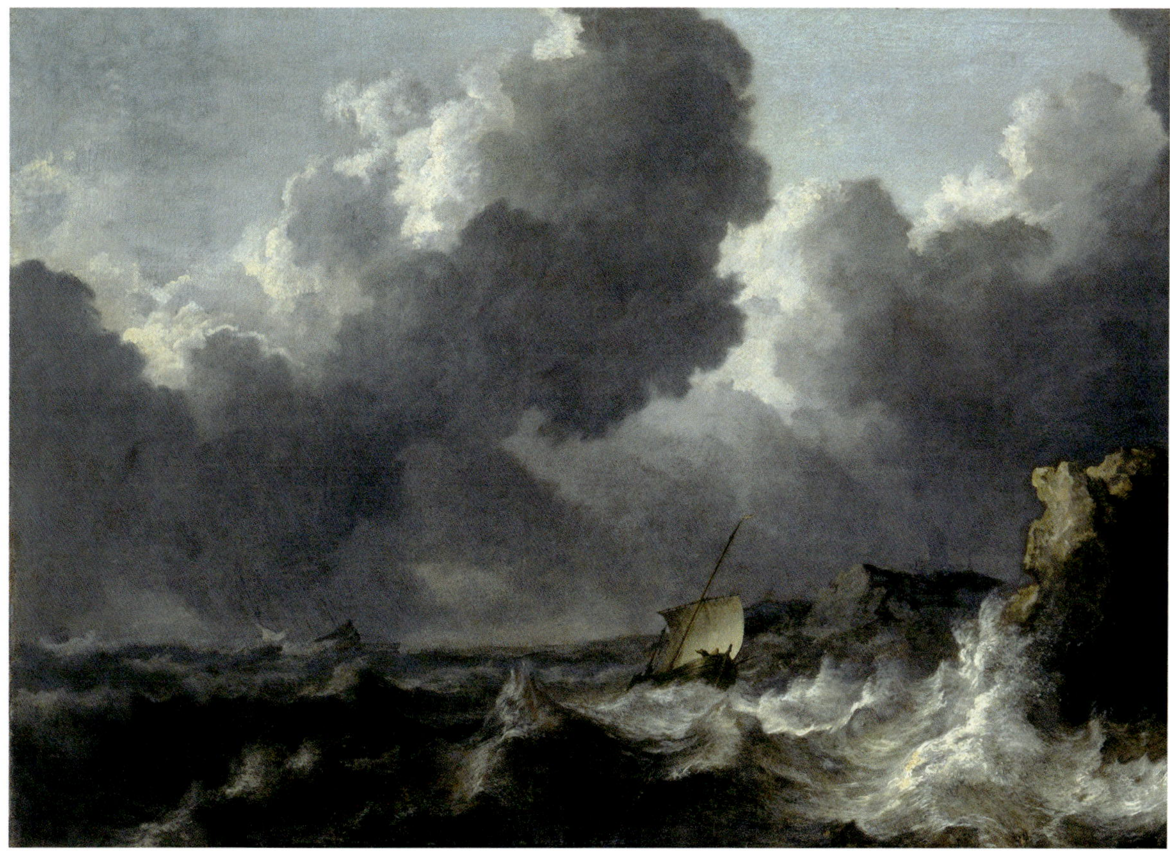

A Change of Course in the Marines

Trees—probably elms—and clouds also domi-nate the scene in *Trees by the Water* (fig. 62).[22] The brown and olive-green tints of the vegeta-tion, the gnarled trunks and snaking branches, and the leaden clouds create an ominous atmosphere. This painting is not really about the landscape, but rather the weather, the elements and—witness the small ships in the background—the way people cope with them. Dutch people, to be precise, because there is nothing exotic about this low country. The work perfectly illustrates the change of course Van Everdingen made in Haarlem. From then on, most of his marines were of Dutch waters with mid-size vessels in a stiff breeze—very different from the seascapes with three-masters wallow-ing in towering waves with which he began his career around 1640.

There can be no doubt that he took inspir-ation for his Dutch seascapes and river views from the work of Jan Porcellis (c. 1584-1632), an innovative and highly successful marine painter who lived in Haarlem from 1622 until his death.[23] Allart knew his oeuvre well: he himself owned no fewer than fifteen paintings by the artist, and in 1661 he was asked to pass judge-ment on a work attributed to Porcellis.[24] Some of Van Everdingen's later marines (figs. 63 and 64) are very akin to Porcellis's (fig. 65)—the same limited palette, the same type of simple vessel heeling over in the waves, the same emphasis on atmosphere, and the same subtle transition from water to sky.[25] Porcellis drew

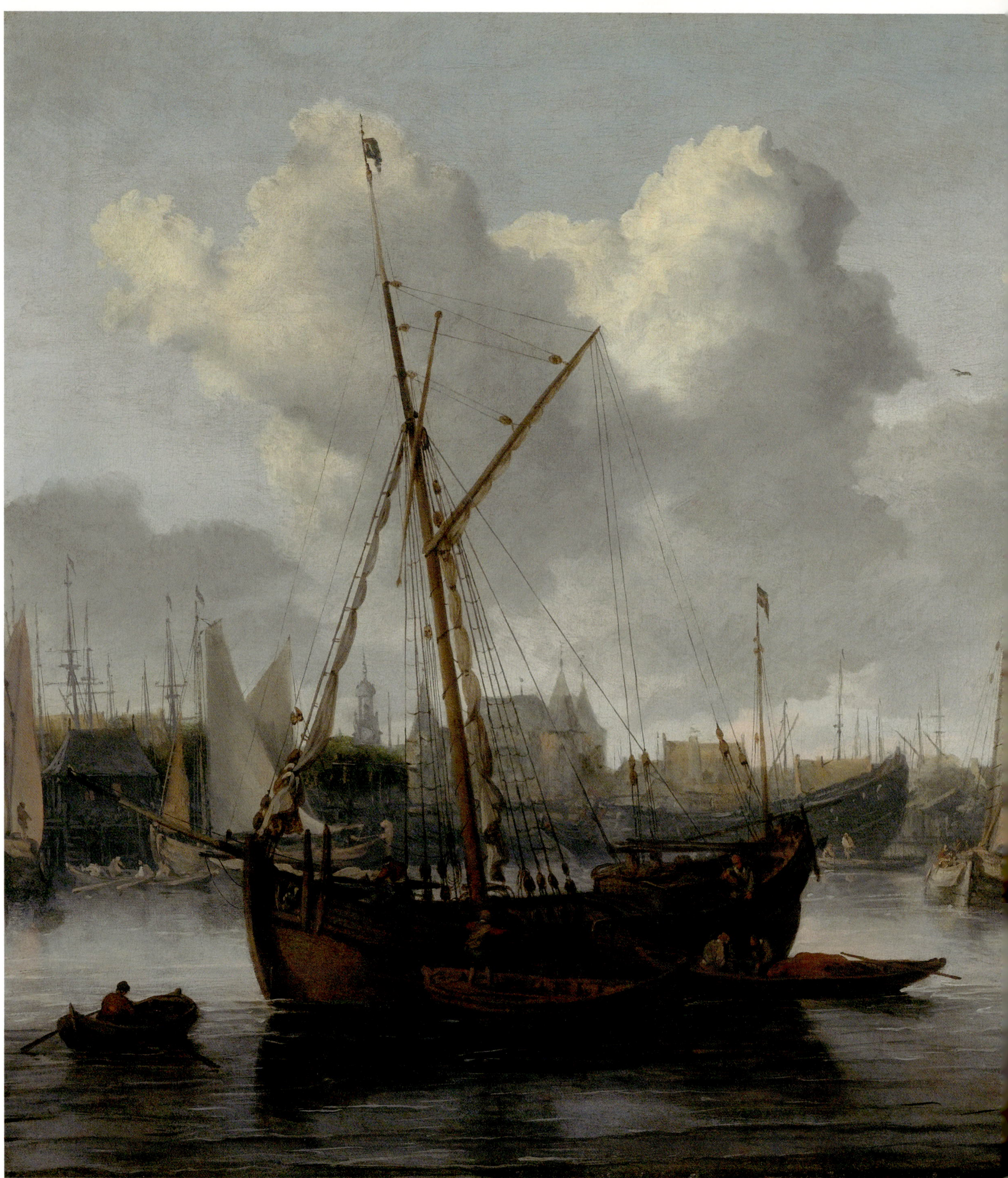

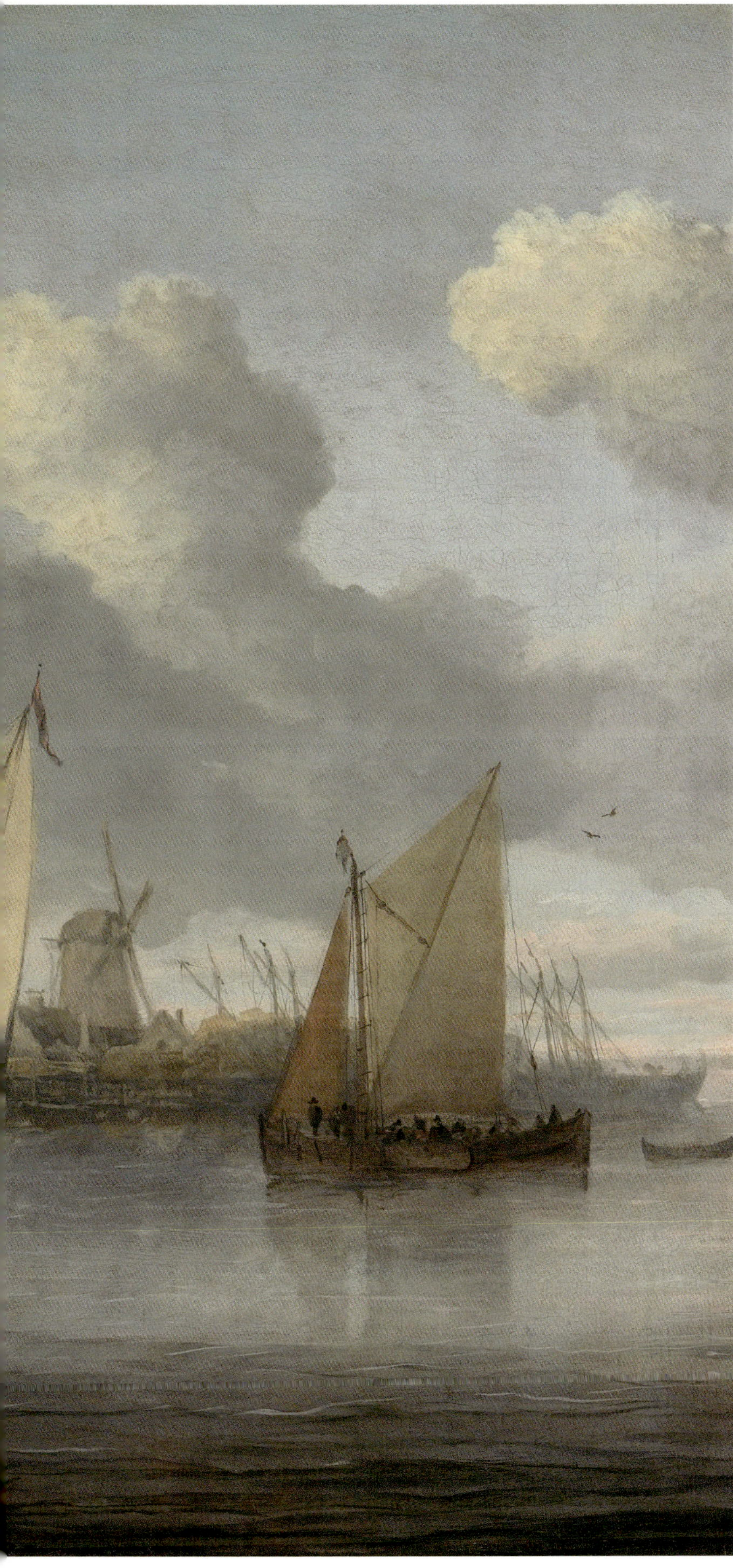

attention to this by leaving the centre of his compositions empty, a new device that Allart adopted. Nevertheless, Mulier I's influence is palpable: the little vessel in the left foreground of Van Everdingen's *Sailing Boats in a Storm* (fig. 63) seems to have been lifted directly from Mulier's *Single-Masters and a Three-Master in a Subsiding Storm* (fig. 66).[26]

Van Everdingen's river views often depict typically Dutch buildings along the banks: windmills, churches and spires. In *Harbour View* (fig. 67), for instance, the Amsterdam Bothuisje (Flounder Shed) is pictured on the extreme left. The gatehouse with round towers at the corners to its right looks something like the Waag (Weigh House) in the same city. Nevertheless, the combination of buildings on the quayside is not a true view of Amsterdam.[27] Sometimes, though, a scene can be identified as an existing place. For instance, Allart pictured his birthplace, Alkmaar (fig. 68), and his home town, Haarlem (fig. 69), from the water below a blanket of grey and white clouds.[28] This type of cityscape —a skyline beneath a high, cloudy sky, with water in the foreground—was developed by the marine specialist Hendrick Vroom in the first decades of the seventeenth century. Van Everdingen must have seen his view of Alkmaar from the Schermeer, which was installed in Alkmaar Town Hall in 1638 (fig. 70).[29]

Allart also made a drawing of Alkmaar (fig. 71) from exactly the same south-eastern quarter, that is from the Zeglis—an important waterway on which many products were carried to the market in Alkmaar.[30] In both compositions the relationship between water, town and sky is roughly equal, but on paper Alkmaar is closer than it is on canvas.

67

Allart van Everdingen, *Harbour View*, oil on canvas, 68.5 x 96.8 cm, New York, Collection of Aliis Inserviendo Consumor Foundation (cat. no. 92)

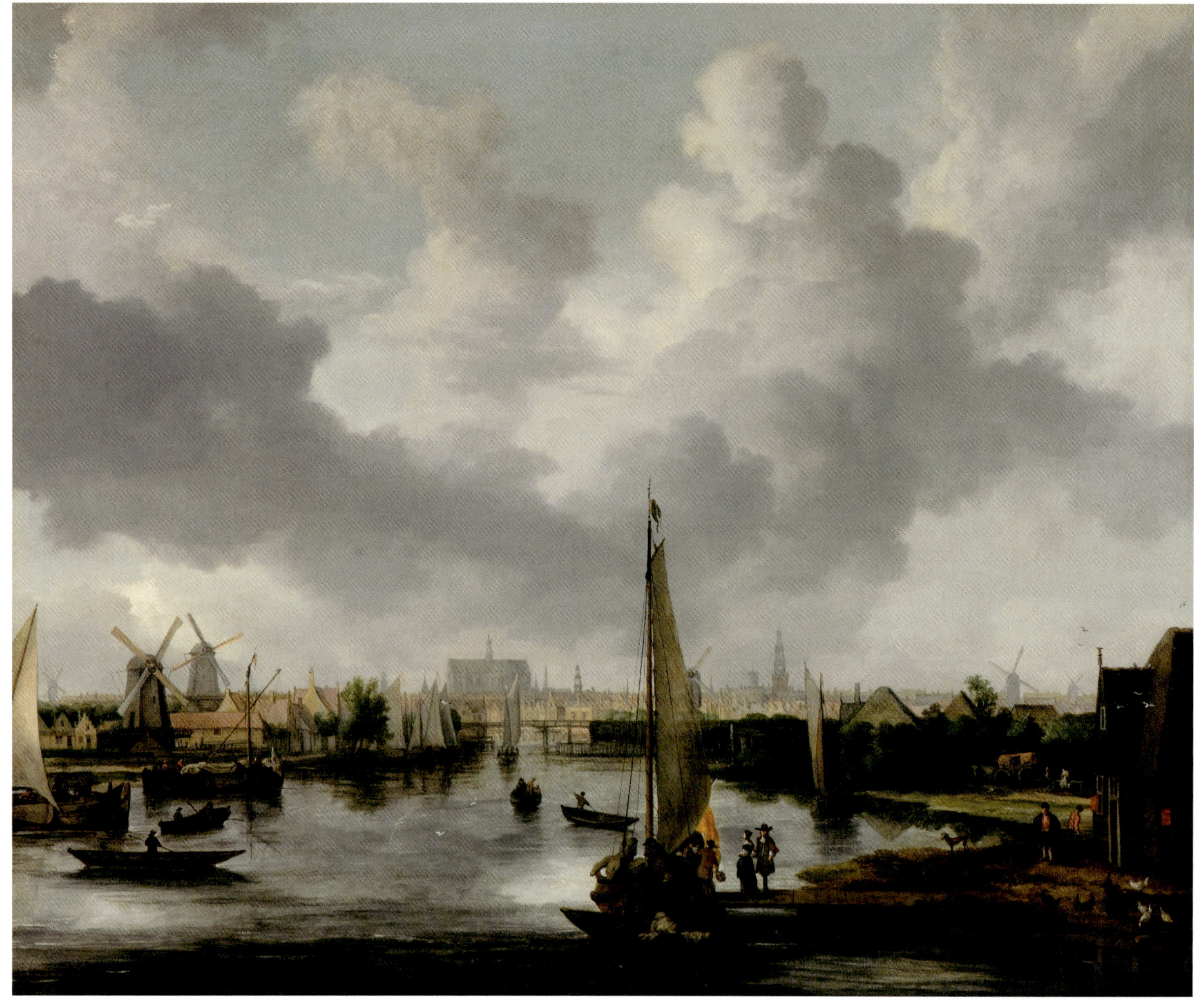

As a result, the tall buildings in the skyline are more prominent, particularly the Grote Sint-Laurenskerk (Great St Lawrence's Church) in the centre, the Waag tower on the right and the windmill between them. The activity on the Zeglis, very evident in the painting, is much less conspicuous in the drawing. Given the absence of dates, it is not possible to establish the exact relationship between the two cityscapes. What we can be sure of, however, is that the carefully finished drawing was made as a work of art in its own right, not as a preliminary study for the painting.[31]

An infrared reflectogram mosaic of the work was made in 2019 to explore the creation of the painted view of Alkmaar (fig. 72).[32] Infrared reflectography (IRR) is an imaging technique using a camera that is sensitive to infrared radiation to 'see through' the paint layers on a canvas or panel. If there is an underdrawing —the artist's initial drawing—it may show up. The IRR montage of Van Everdingen's painting revealed that he had originally planned only low sloops without sails on the water in the centre foreground—a logical structure for a cityscape that he also used for his drawing: the rowing

68

Allart van Everdingen, *View of Alkmaar from the Zeglis*, oil on canvas, 102.5 x 124 cm, Paris, Fondation Custodia, Frits Lugt Collection, inv. no. 6036 (on loan to the Stedelijk Museum Alkmaar) (cat. no. 94)

69
Allart van Everdingen,
*View of Haarlem from the
Noorder Buiten Spaarne*,
oil on canvas on panel,
39 x 65.5 cm, Haarlem,
Frans Hals Museum, inv.
no. OS I-82 (cat. no. 52)

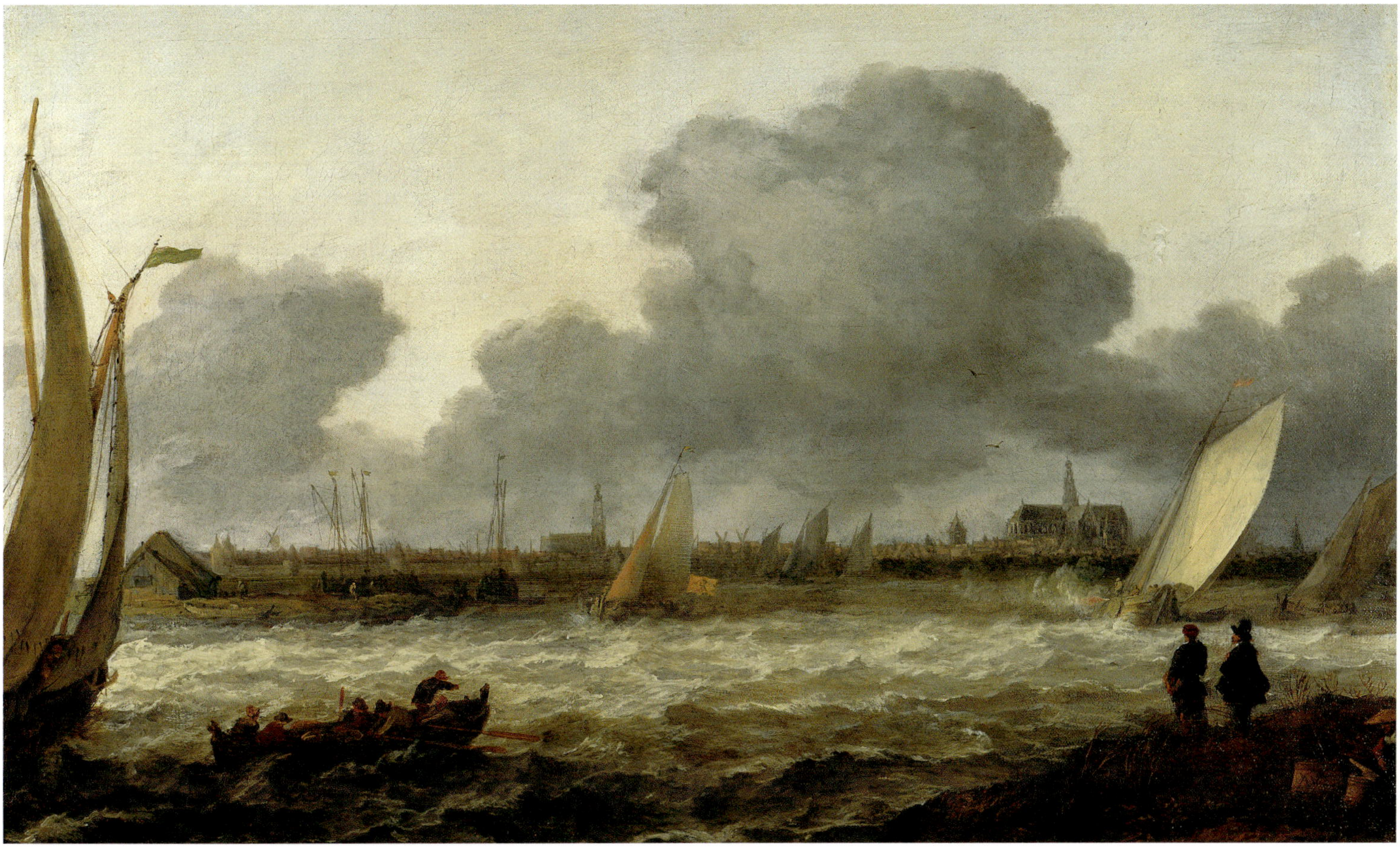

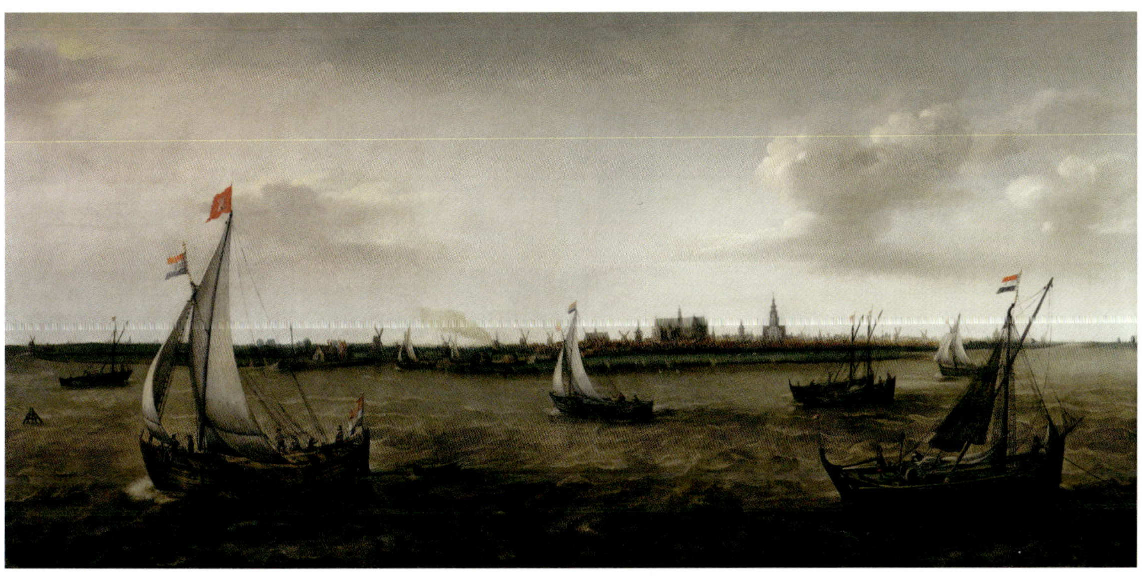

70
Hendrick Cornelisz
Vroom, *View of Alkmaar
from the Schermeer
before Construction of
the Dykes*, 1638, oil on
canvas, 103 x 209.5, cm,
Stedeliik Museum
Alkmaar, inv. no. 21321

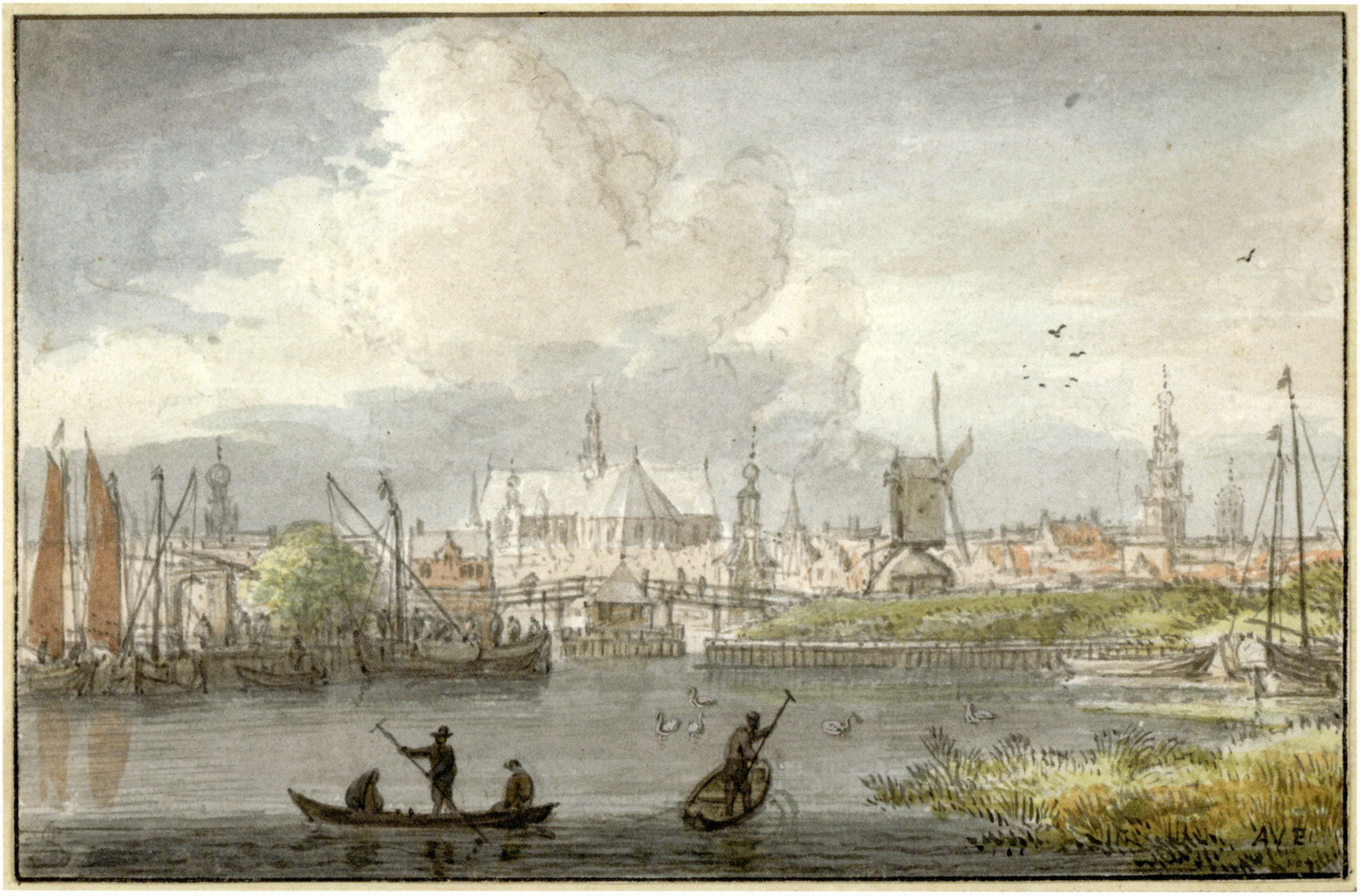

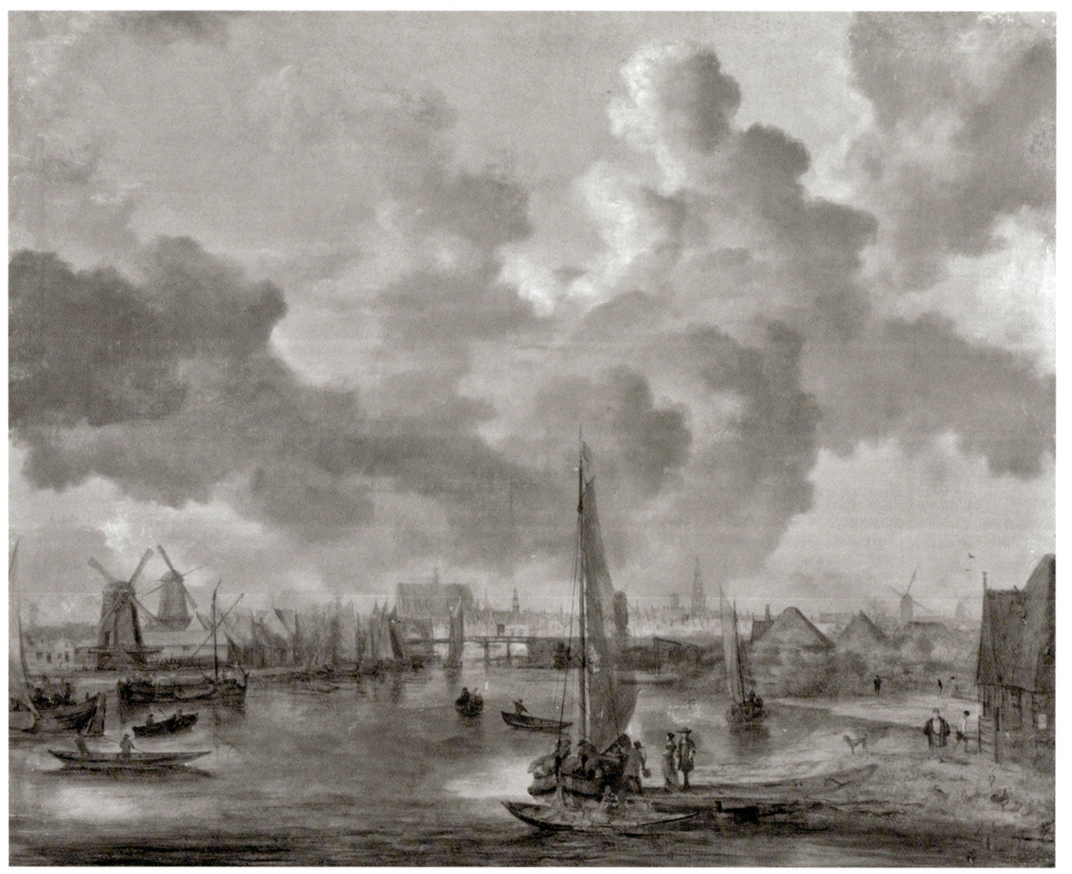

71
Allart van Everdingen, *View of Alkmaar from the Zeglis*, pen and grey ink, watercolour, heightened with white, 112 x 178 mm, Vienna, The Albertina Museum, inv. no. 9582 (cat. no. 102)

< 72
Infrared reflectogram mosaic of Allart van Everdingen, *View of Alkmaar from the Zeglis* (fig. 68, cat. no. 94)

boats in the foreground lead the viewer into the composition without obstructing the view of the town in the background. When the painting was more advanced, however, he decided to introduce a boat with a tall mast in the foreground, slightly to the right of centre; he evidently felt that his composition needed a prominent vertical element. He changed the long, flat barge originally planned for the foreground into a jetty. An elegantly dressed couple walks along it to the sailing boat—which may be a bojort.[33]

Inhabited Forest Landscapes

In 1652, Allart van Everdingen moved to Amsterdam, a vibrant centre of commerce with a much bigger market for his art than Haarlem. There he explored new possibilities within his specialism, the northern landscape. In Haarlem, alongside desolate and rocky vistas, he pictured more hospitable, populated areas, with wooden houses near waterfalls (figs. 56 and 57). In Amsterdam he took it further and gave trees, buildings and human activity a more prominent

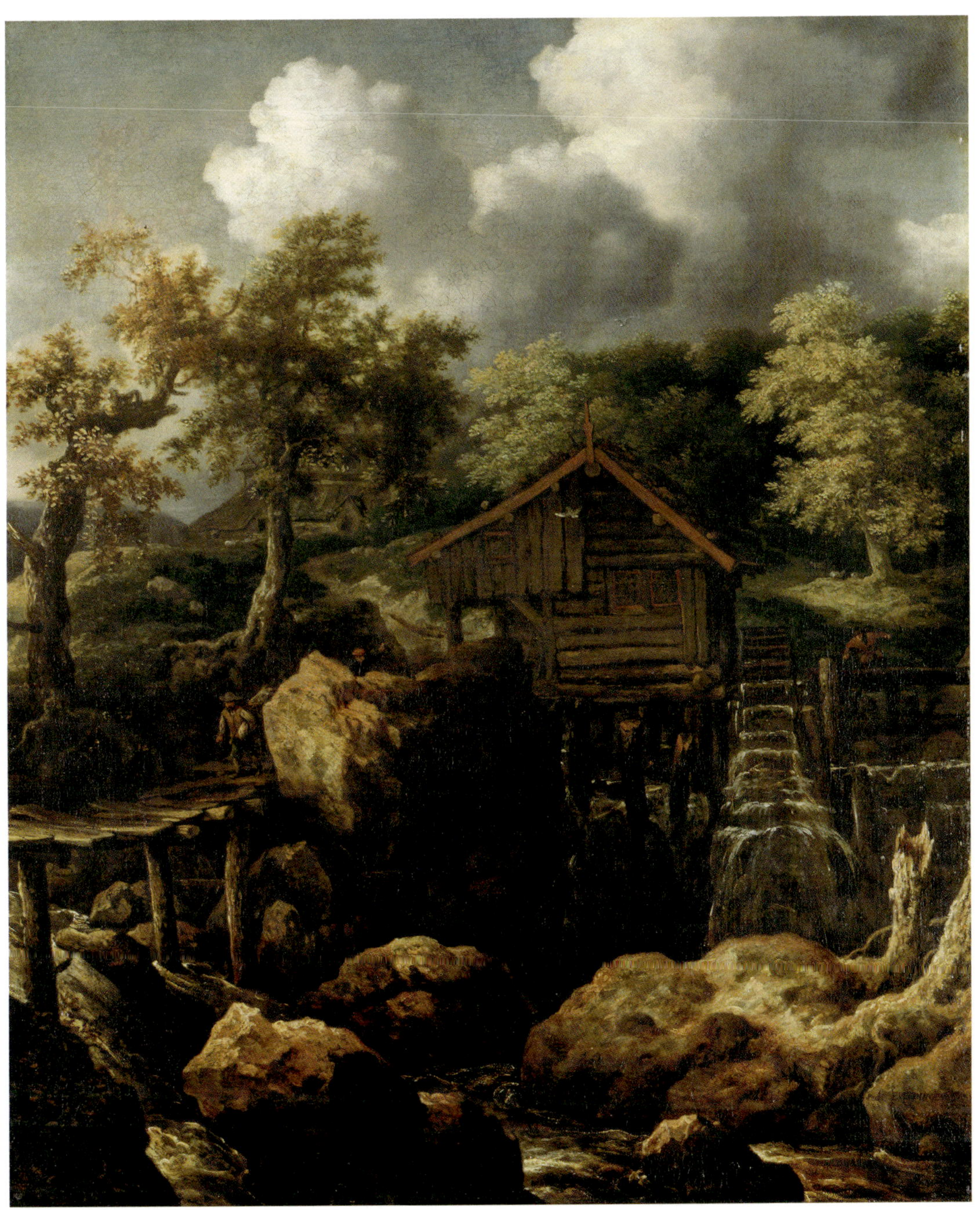

73
Allart van Everdingen,
*Wooded Landscape
with a Watermill*,
oil on canvas, 73 x
61.5 cm, Cologne,
Wallraf-Richartz-
Museum & Fondation
Corboud, inv. no.
WRM 1025 (cat. no. 65)

place in his paintings. In this period he also frequently combined Norwegian motifs with elements that belong in other countries and regions. The result was topographically ambiguous, hybrid landscapes, with a sometimes remarkable sense of tranquillity.[34]

With its log cabin and rocks, the undated *Wooded Landscape with a Watermill* (fig. 73), for instance, is recognizably Norwegian. There is not a pine tree in sight, but the oaks pictured here are likewise native to the south coast of Norway.[35] The brown and olive-green shades in this painting differ from the colours of the earliest dated landscapes and more closely resemble *Trees by the Water* (fig. 62). Both works probably date from the sixteen-fifties.[36] With his idyllic *Landscape with a Watermill* of 1655 (fig. 74) Van Everdingen took a very different path. The large rocks here and there and the mountains in the background appear Scandinavian, but the thatched cottage with the waterwheel in the foreground looks more German than Norwegian.

The horseman's bright red cloak draws the eye to the travellers on the right. The style of these figures differs considerably from the people in, for example, *Wooded Landscape with a Watermill* (fig. 73) or *View of Alkmaar from the Zeglis* (fig. 68): they look more lifelike and are much more detailed. They were, in fact, added to the composition by another artist, probably Nicolaes Berchem (1621/1622-1683), who often populated the work of fellow painters with people and animals.[37]

The infrared reflectogram of this painting (fig. 75) confirms that a second hand worked on it besides Van Everdingen.[38] The design for the painting is clearly visible: an extensive sketch in dark brown brushstrokes. This would have been painted by Allart himself, and he was evidently happy with it as he changed very little of his original composition afterwards. The outline of the tree trunks, the houses, the watermill and the fencing in the underpainting correspond with the position and shape of these components in the finished work. Here and there the underlying sketch has even been allowed to show through, as an area of shadow. The only significant differences are found in the figures on the right, precisely the part of Van Everdingen's composition that was put in by someone else. Allart had indicated a walker beside

the house in the middle ground and a horseman by the fence in the foreground. Berchem was allowed—or took—a good deal of licence in working out these motifs. He painted the rider slightly to the left of the man on the horse in the sketch, gave him a companion on foot and moved the walker further into the background. Around these figures he added a variety of animals—a dog, sheep or goats, cattle—that were not indicated in the underpainting.

In his Amsterdam period Van Everdingen made more of these welcoming landscapes full of rocks and trees, with and without waterfalls (figs. 76 and 77), as it were fusing his new Norwegian landscape type with the existing and valued pictorial tradition of the wooded landscape. One of the leading artists in that genre at the time was Jacob van Ruisdael (1628/1629-1682) (fig. 78).[39] Allart must have been very familiar with his work—the dense foliage and the half-timbered houses in his later landscapes certainly owe a debt to him.

Allart van Everdingen, *Landscape with a Watermill*, 1655, oil on canvas, 66 x 60 cm, Amsterdam, Rijksmuseum, inv. no. SK-A-691 (on loan to the Stedelijk Museum Alkmaar) (cat. no. 3)

Infrared reflectogram of Allart van Everdingen, *Landscape with a Watermill*, 1655 (fig. 74, cat. no. 3)

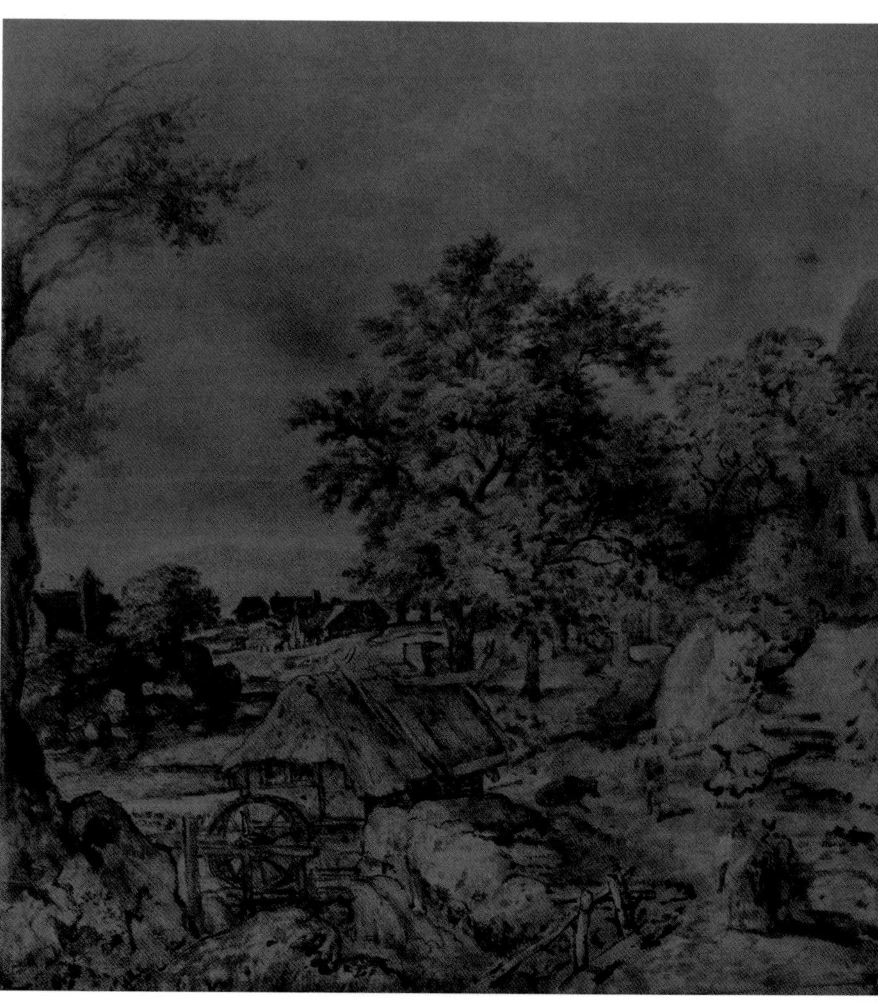

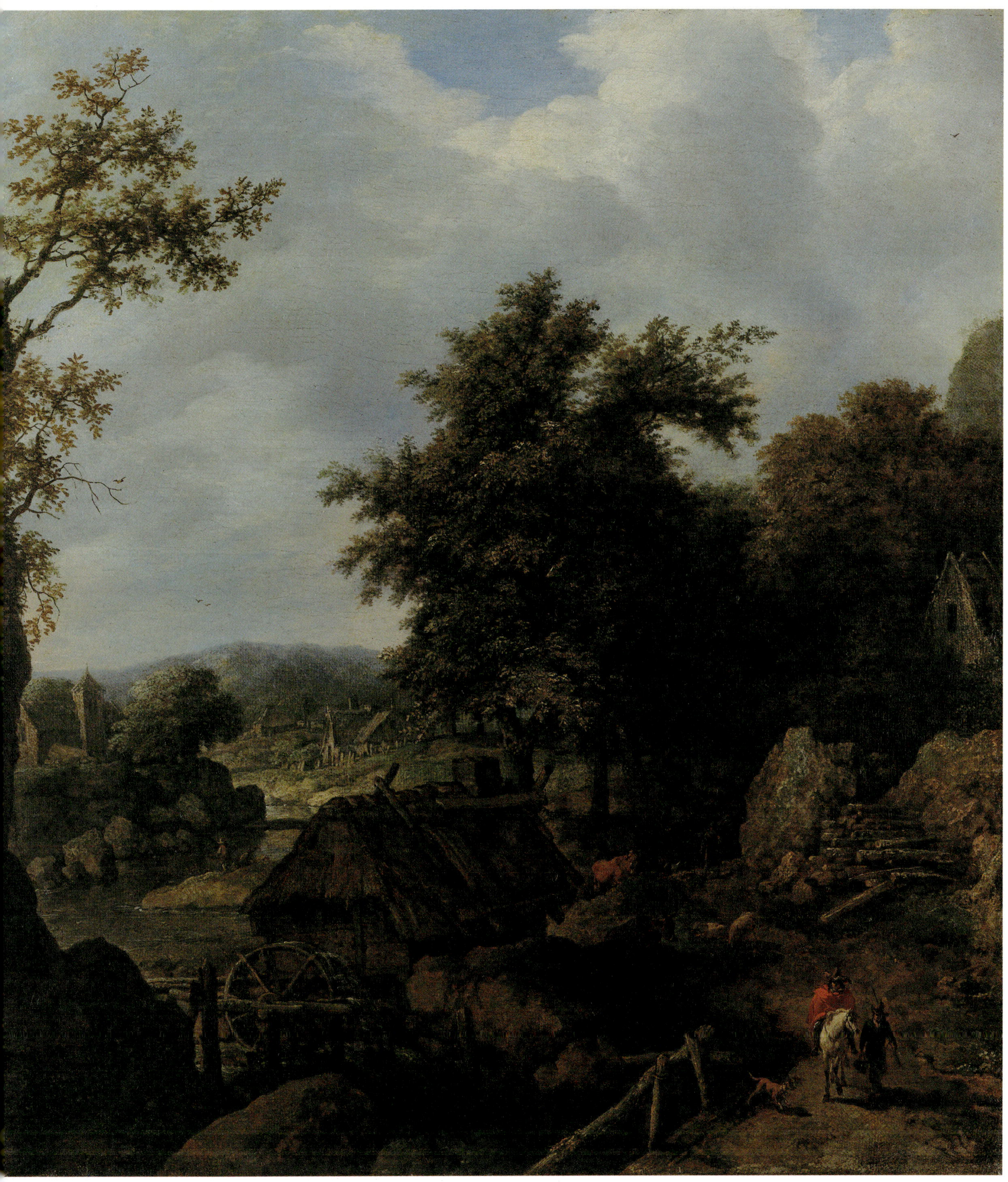

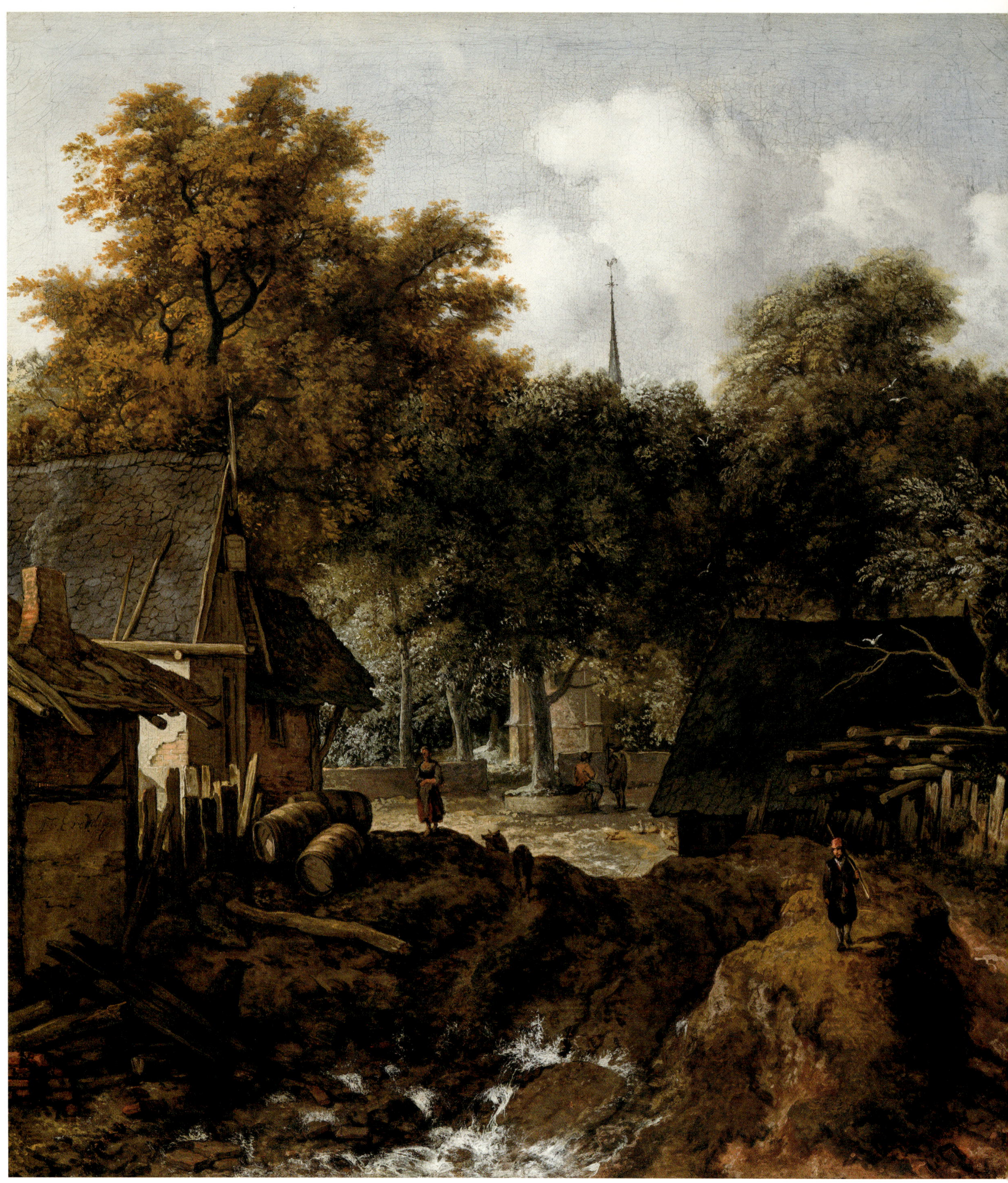

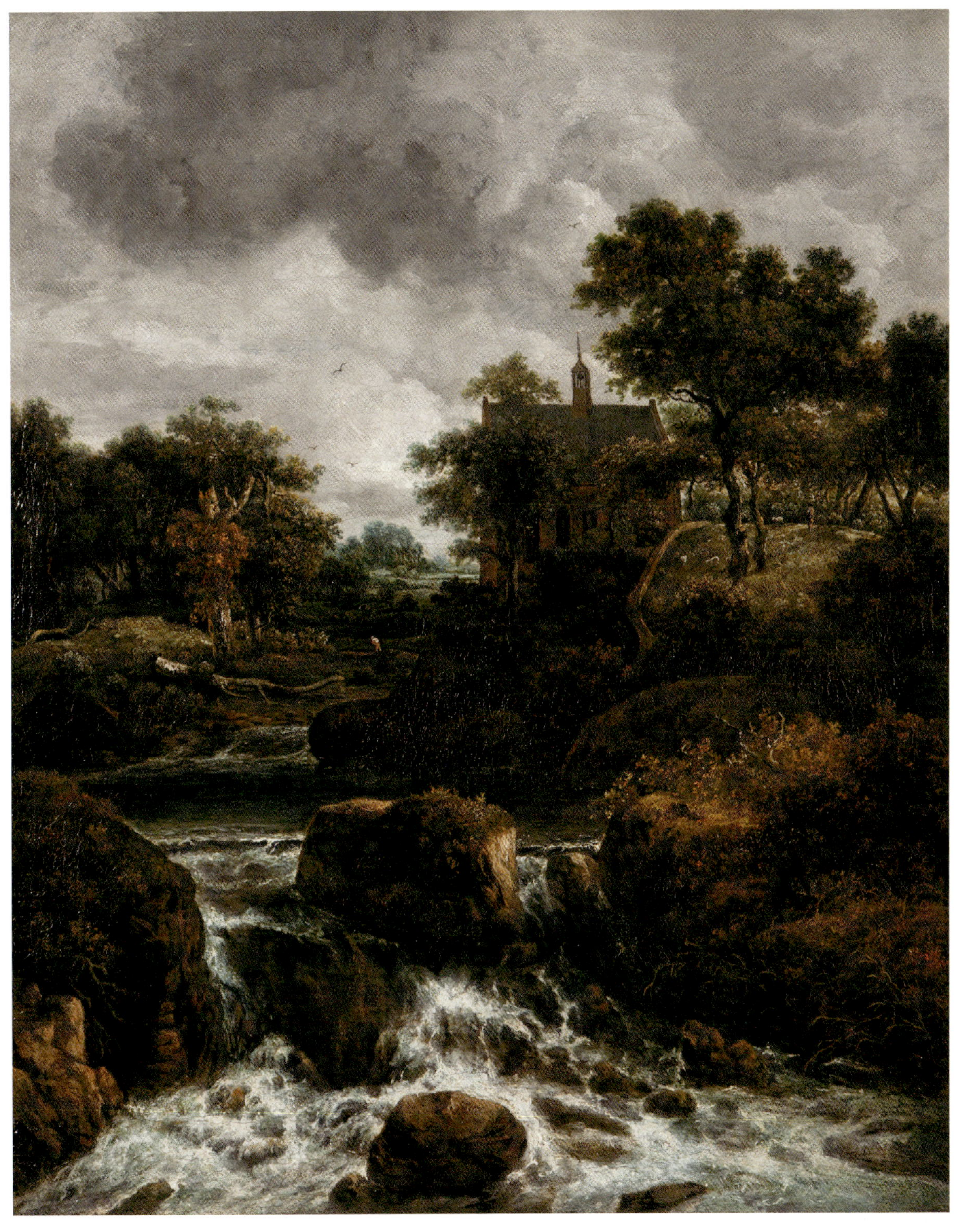

< 76
Allart van Everdingen,
Village View, oil on
canvas, 76 x 66.5 cm,
Budapest, Szépmüvé-
szeti Múzeum, inv. no.
4291 (cat. no. 44)

77
Allart van Everdingen,
*Wooded Landscape with
a Waterfall and a Chapel*,
oil on canvas, 61 x 49.5 cm,
New York, Stein Berre
Collection (cat. no. 93)

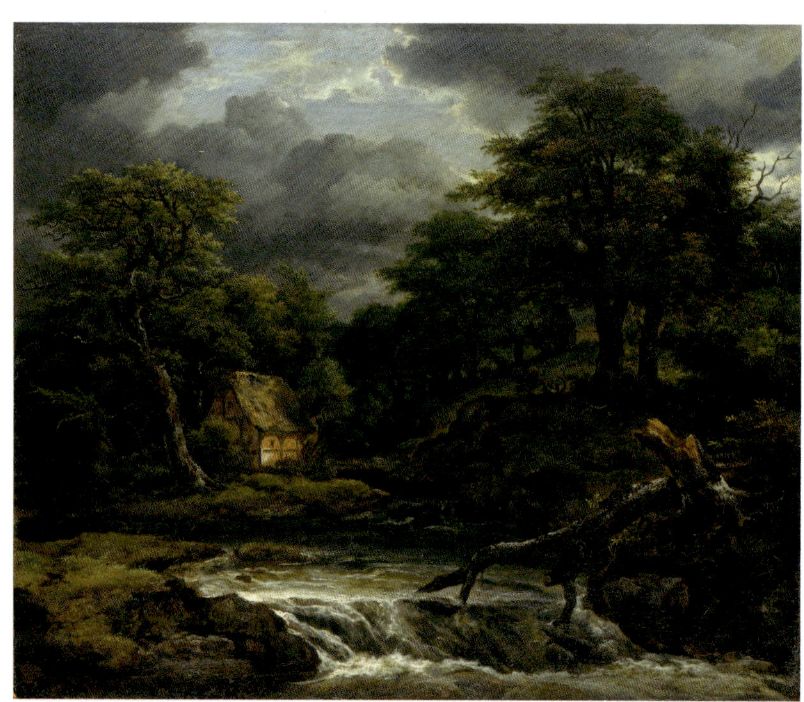

78
Jacob van Ruisdael,
*Wooded Landscape
with a Waterfall and
an Approaching Storm*,
c. 1655, oil on canvas,
56 x 66.8 cm, Frankfurt
am Main, Städel
Museum, inv. no. 754

79
Jacob van Ruisdael,
Chapel by a Waterfall,
c. 1670, oil on canvas,
69 x 53.3 cm, The Hague,
Mauritshuis, inv. no. 153

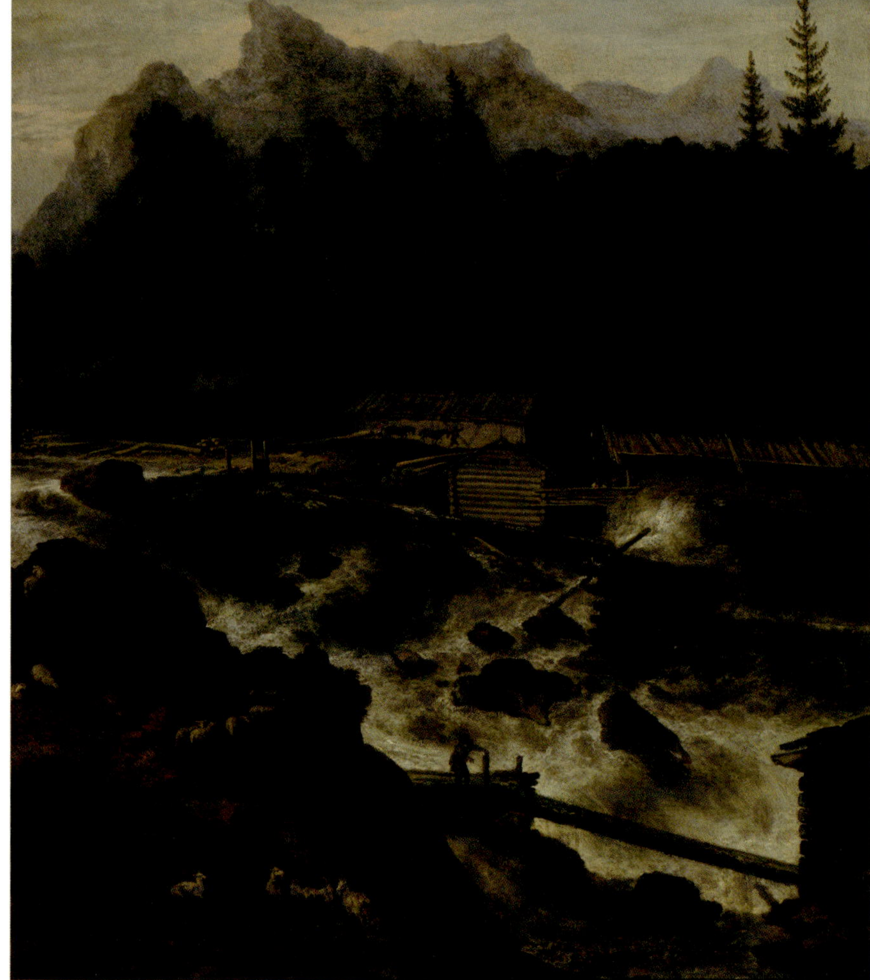

> **80**
Allart van Everdingen,
*Mountain Landscape
with Mölndal Waterfall*,
1670, oil on canvas,
153 x 134 cm, Rouen,
Musée des Beaux-Arts,
inv. no. 850.2

81
Allart van Everdingen,
*Mountain Village on
the Water*, 1664, oil on
panel, 31.8 x 48.1 cm,
The Montreal Museum
of Fine Arts, inv. no.
2013.10 (cat. no. 89)

Conversely, Van Ruisdael drew inspiration from Van Everdingen. He was particularly taken with the waterfall motif and frequently used it in his compositions from the late sixteen-fifties onwards (fig. 33)—never, though, in the typical Norwegian landscapes with log cabins that were Allart's trademark.[40] Remarkably, there is a second version of Van Everdingen's *Wooded Landscape with a Waterfall and a Chapel* (fig. 77) painted by Van Ruisdael (fig. 79). Since both works are undated it is hard to establish precisely how they relate to one another.

Of course, Van Everdingen did not suddenly start producing nothing but topographically indeterminate, charming, inhabited wooded landscapes in Amsterdam. On the contrary, he continued to make the recognizably Scandinavian scenes with which he had made his name in the late sixteen-forties. *Mountain Landscape with Mölndal Waterfall* (fig. 80), for instance, was painted in 1670, on the basis of a drawing the artist had probably sketched on the spot in 1644 (fig. 100).[41] The less obviously Norwegian landscapes are often still quite rocky and rugged. One of the finest examples, which is dated 1664, is in the Montreal Museum of Fine Arts (fig. 81). The paint layers on this panel have become rather transparent over the years, and the artist's underdrawing can be seen with the naked eye. Van Everdingen sketched the

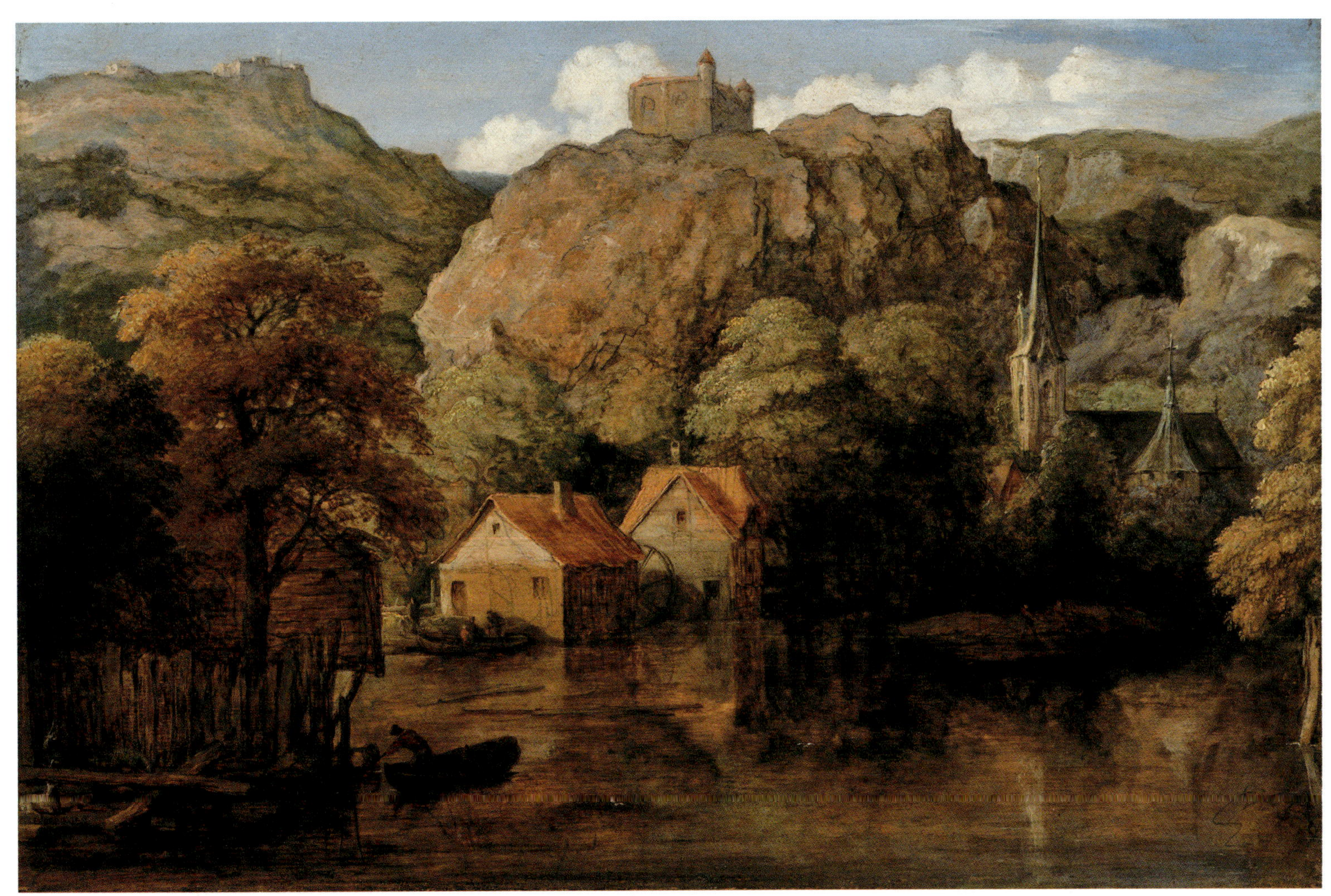

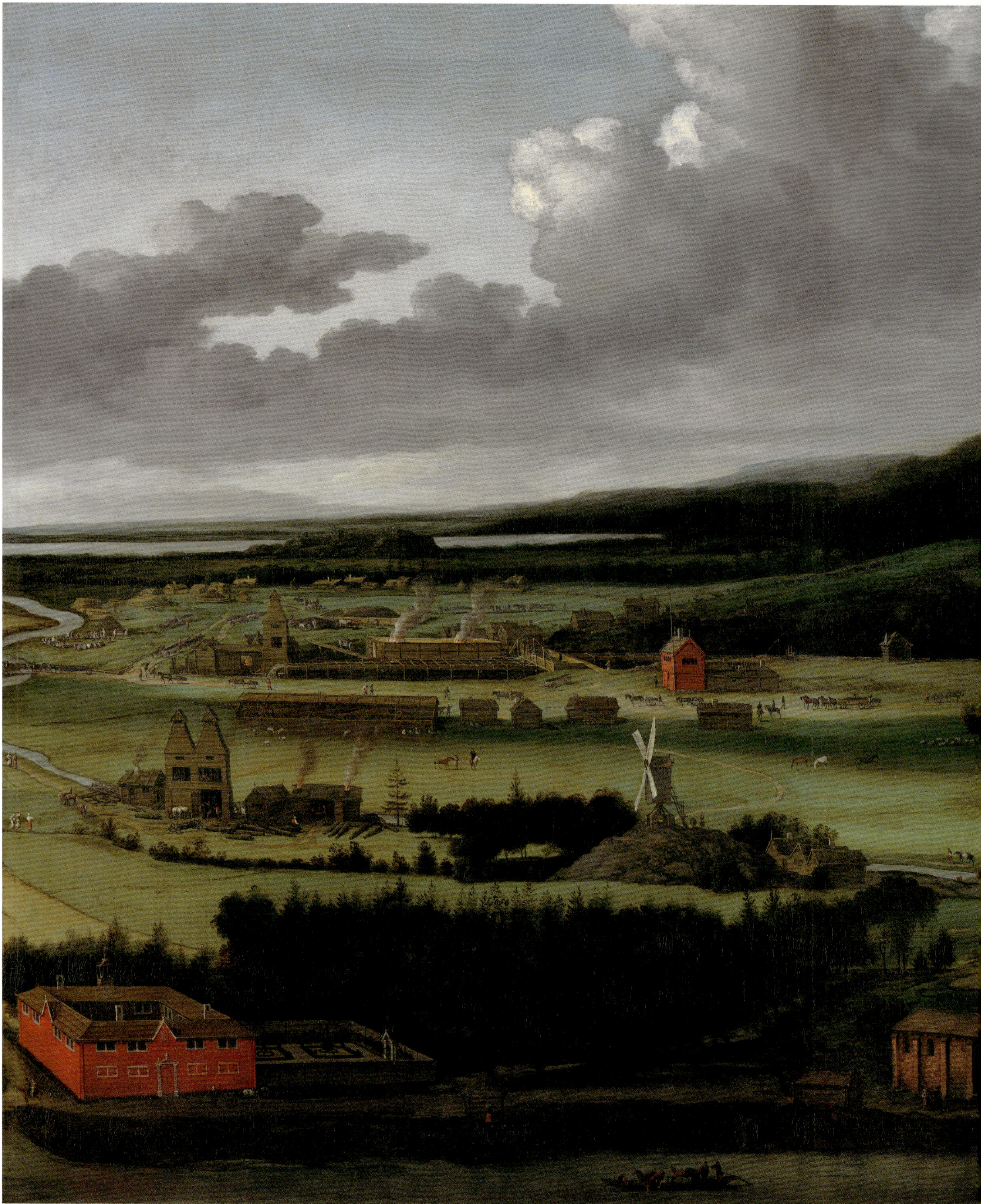

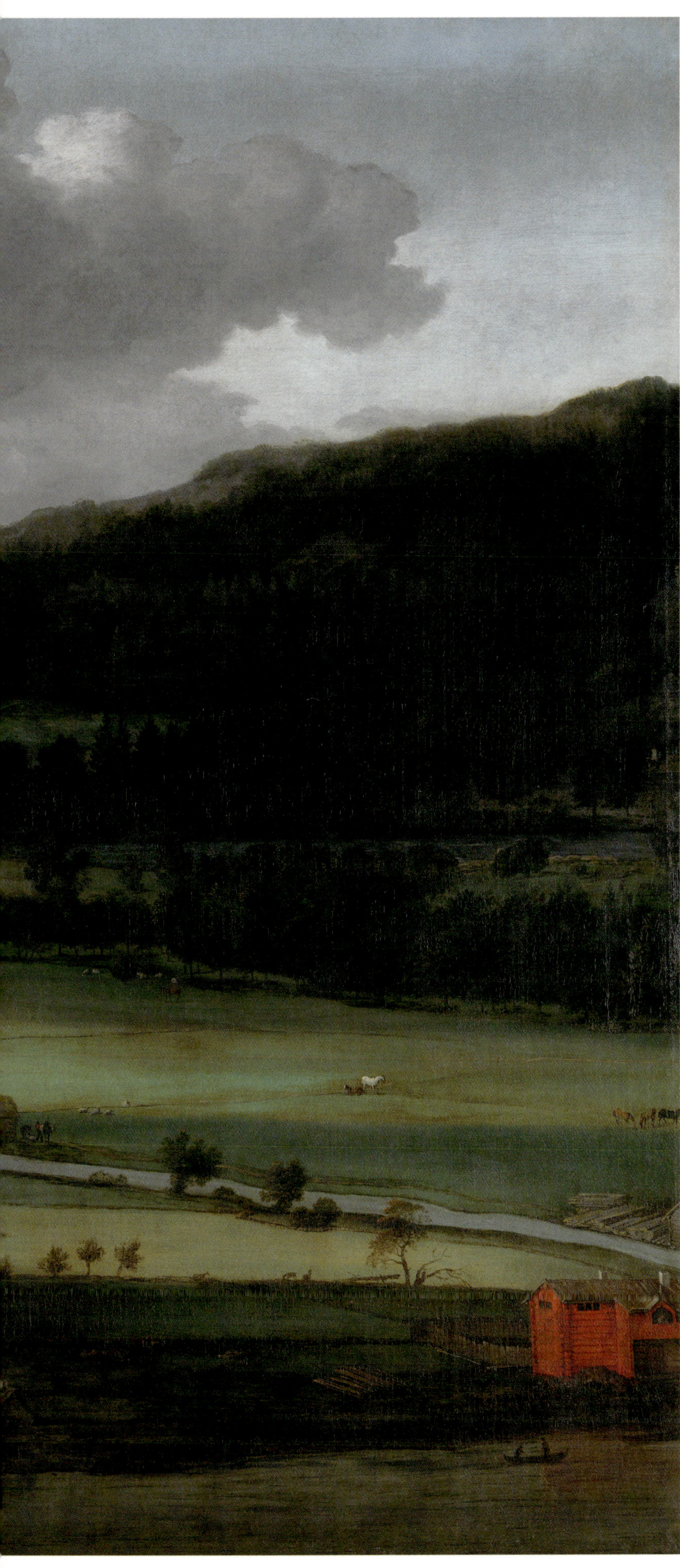

outlines of rocks, houses and trees in flowing lines, and seems to have deviated little from his design when he painted. The only change he made was to move the waterwheel from the nearer to the further of the two houses in the centre.

Companies and Castles

Little is known about the people who bought Van Everdingen's paintings. Most of the works would have been sold on the open market in the art dealership he ran.[42] We know or suspect that a number of works were commissioned. They are generally paintings that prominently feature a company or a castle. The owner of one of these factories or buildings would have ordered such a picture as a status symbol. The most important commission Van Everdingen undertook was the suite of paintings he made for the Trippenhuis—the dual mansion built for the brothers Louys (1605-1684) and Hendrick Trip (1607-1666) on Kloveniersburgwal in Amsterdam between 1660 and 1662.[43]

The Trip family made its fortune trading in iron, copper and armaments from Sweden. When the brothers commissioned artists to make decorations for their new house around 1662, they naturally turned to the master of the Scandinavian landscape for some of the works. Allart made a very large view of the cannon foundry at Julita Bruk that Hendrick Trip leased in the county of Södermanland in Sweden (fig. 82) and four smaller overdoors with waterfalls and cannon foundries (figs. 83-86).[44] The overdoors are still *in situ*. There may well have been a sixth Scandinavian landscape by Van Everdingen hanging in the Trippenhuis (fig. 87).[45] Its palette is quite different, however, and it is believed that it dates from the late sixteen-fifties and was not part of the 1662 commission; it was most likely bought by one of the Trip brothers before that.[46]

82
Allart van Everdingen,
Hendrick Trip's Cannon Foundry at Julita Bruk,
c. 1662, oil on canvas,
192 x 254.5 cm, Amsterdam, Rijksmuseum,
inv. no. SK-A-1510
(cat. no. 4)

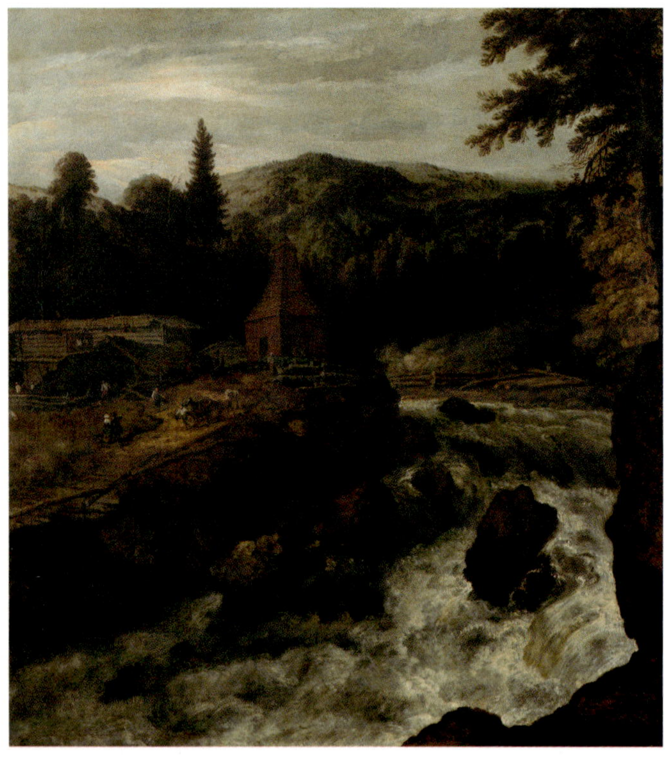

83
Allart van Everdingen, *Cannon Foundry near a Waterfall*,
c. 1662, oil on canvas, 105 x 98.5 cm, Amsterdam,
Trippenhuis (overdoor in the south house)

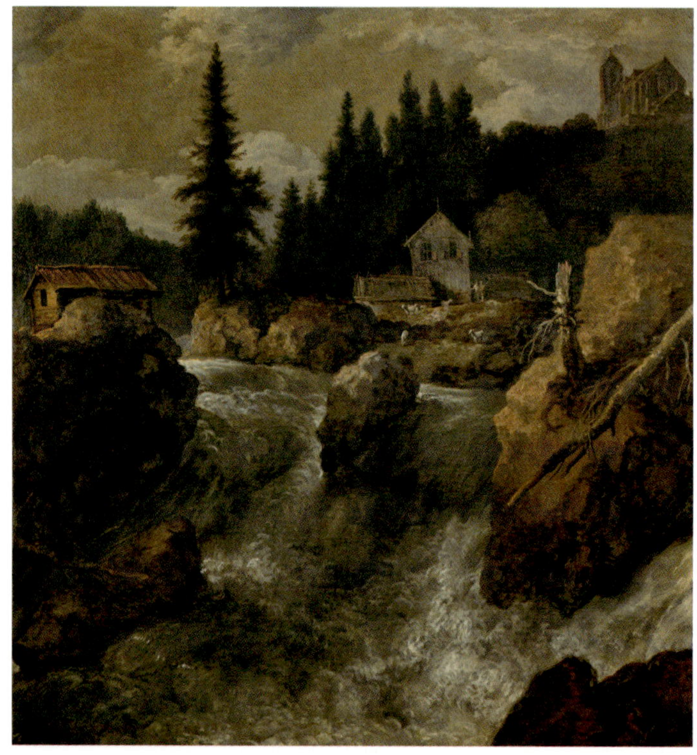

84
Allart van Everdingen, *Waterfall*, c. 1662, oil on canvas,
104.5 x 99 cm, Amsterdam, Trippenhuis (overdoor in
the south house)

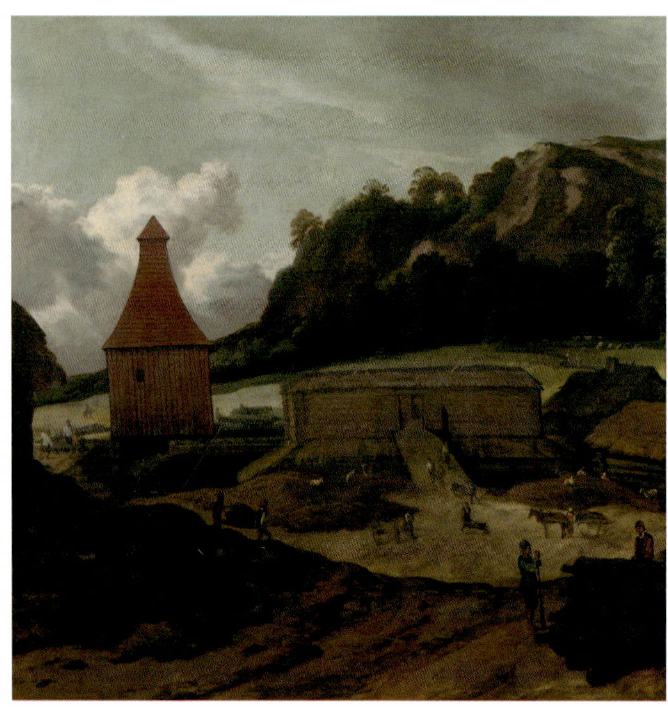

85
Allart van Everdingen, *Cannon Foundry with Ordnance*,
c. 1662, oil on canvas, 101.5 x 101.5 cm, Amsterdam,
Trippenhuis (overdoor in the north house)

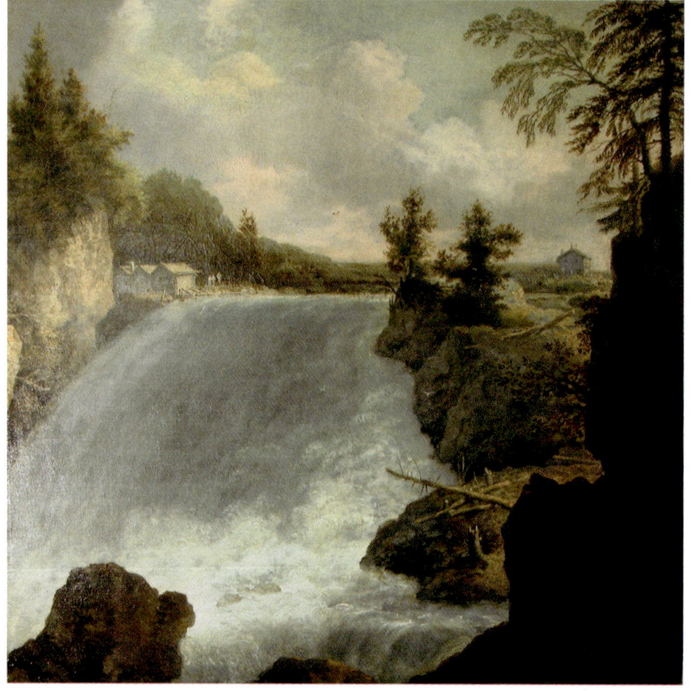

86
Allart van Everdingen, *Waterfall near Trollhättan*,
c. 1662, oil on canvas, 101 x 101.5 cm, Amsterdam,
Trippenhuis (overdoor in the north house)

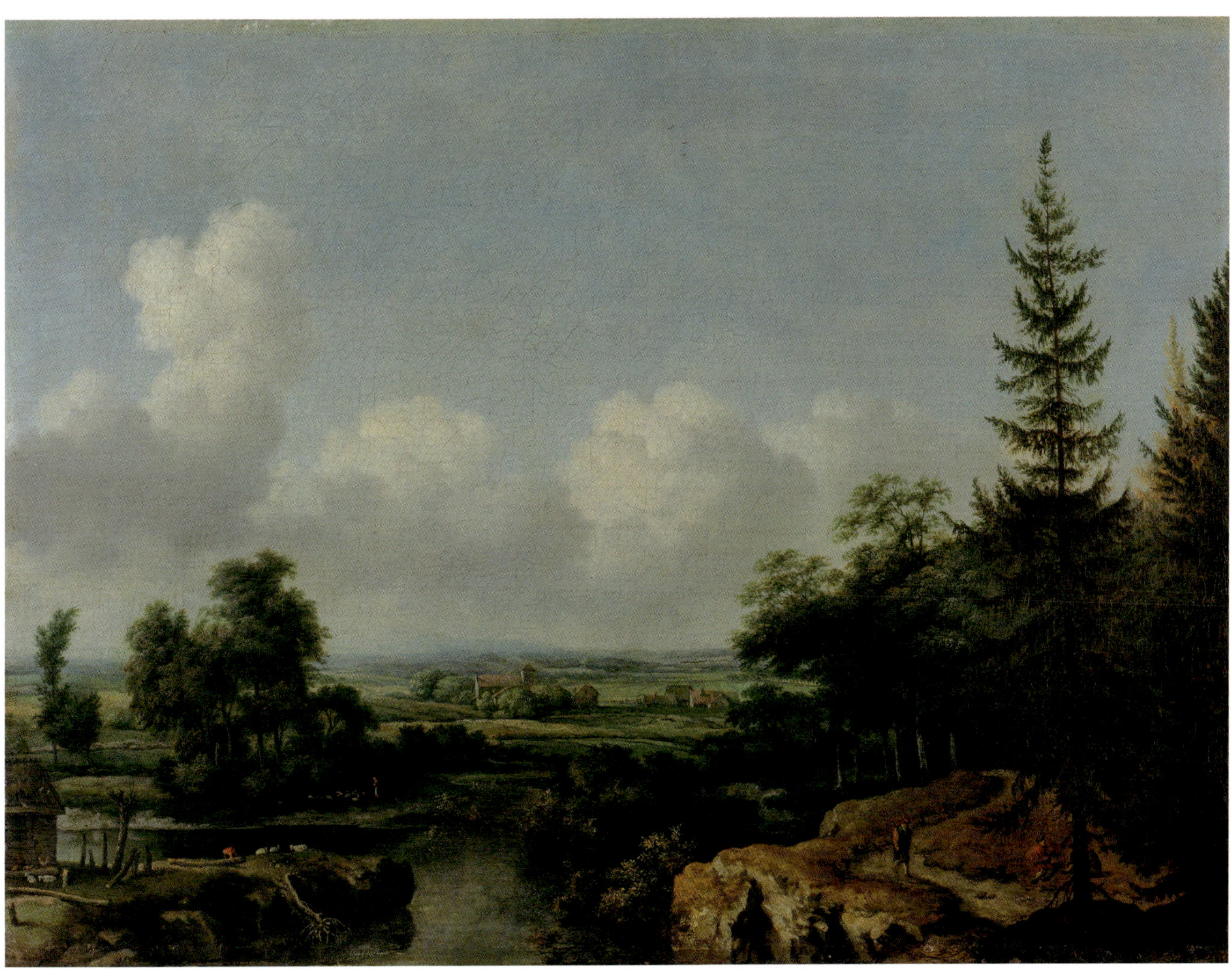

87
Allart van Everdingen,
*Scandinavian Land-
scape*, oil on canvas,
48 x 62.5 cm, Amster-
dam, Rijksmuseum,
inv. no. SK-A-108

The panorama of Hendrick's cannon foundry
(fig. 82) is Van Everdingen's largest known work
and its composition is almost documentary.
It looks like a huge informative map with landmarks and points of interest indicated. It has
sometimes been suggested that Allart visited
Julita Bruk himself to make sketches on the
spot, but there is absolutely no evidence of
a second trip to Scandinavia around 1660.
Besides, Van Everdingen's depiction of the landscape contains topographical errors—the large
lake in the background, for instance, was in
reality much smaller—which makes it unlikely
that he had seen it for himself. He most probably worked from drawn maps of the area,
which may have been provided by the Trip
brothers.[47] They must also have explained

to the painter exactly what happened in their
factory, so that he could imagine it. In the
middle ground of his composition he pictured
labourers using horses and wagons to carry raw
materials like wood and iron ore to the foundry
with its large, smoking furnaces. In front of that,
on the river, are the buildings where the cannon
are cast and bored out—the ordnance stands
in rows by the entrances.

The overdoors are not as cartographic and
cannot be located topographically with any
precision, with one exception: a painting of
a waterfall near Trollhättan (fig. 86) based on
a drawing of that impressive natural phenomenon Van Everdingen had made, possibly on the
spot (fig. 96).[48] Allart's journey through Norway
in 1644 continued to inspire him.

There is also a seventh painting by Van Everdingen that can be associated with the Trip family and probably hung in the Trippenhuis. This extraordinary cityscape (fig. 88) is viewed from behind a balustrade.[49] A curtain above it is looped invitingly to one side; the bright red of the drapery stands out against the clear blue sky and contrasts with the delicate white of the building on the right—the façade of the Trippenhuis. From the balcony we see trees, among them the typical Norway spruces, in a garden below the house and the roofs of Dordrecht in the distance. Van Everdingen painted the walls and roofs of the buildings in the same pastel colours he used in his view of Alkmaar (fig. 68). Dordrecht had a special significance for the Trips: Hendrick and Louys's parents, Jacob Trip (c. 1576-1661) and Margaretha de Geer (1583-1672), were married there, had their children there and were buried there. Jacob and his brother Elias Trip (c. 1570-1636) can be regarded as the founders of the trading house that made

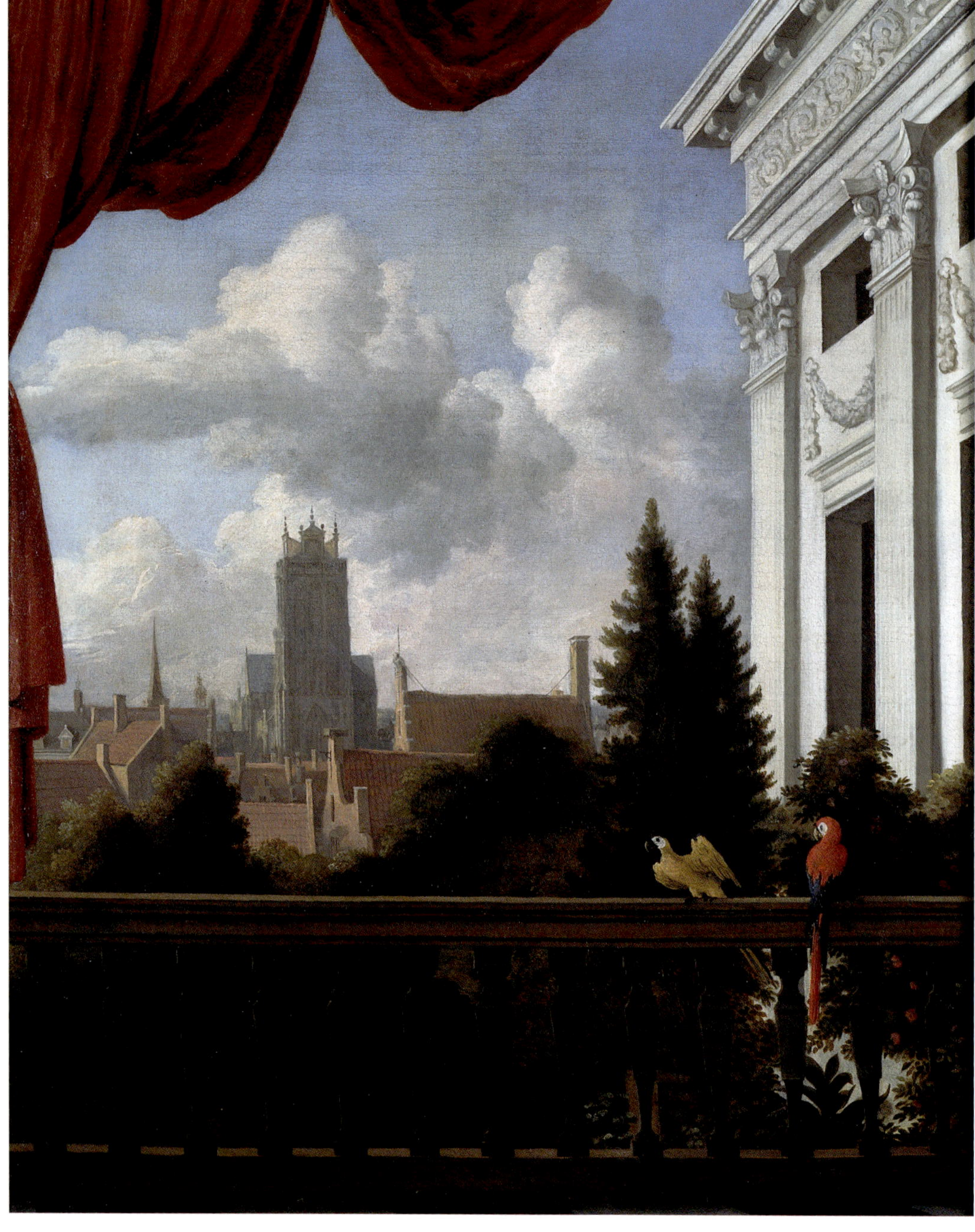

88
Allart van Everdingen, *View of Dordrecht with the Amsterdam Trippenhuis*, oil on canvas, 94 x 76 cm, Academie Minerva Hanzehogeschool Groningen (on loan to the Dordrechts Museum, inv. no. DM/010/953, as a secondary loan from the Groninger Museum, inv. no. 0000.2015) (cat. no. 50)

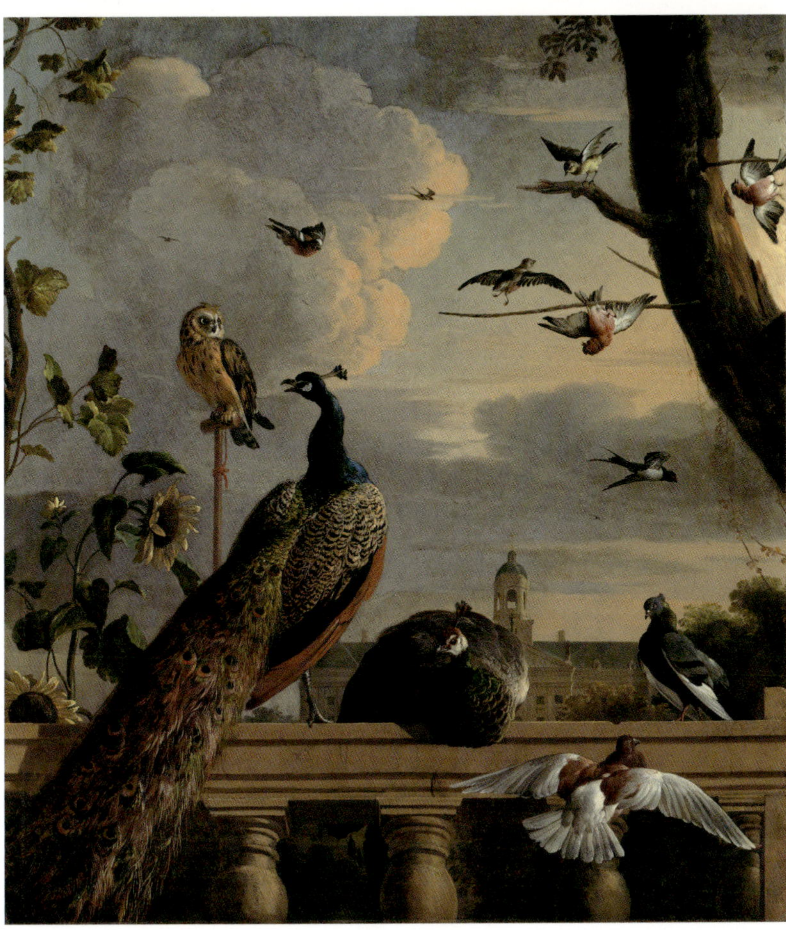

Melchior d'Hondecoeter,
*Birds by a Balustrade
with Amsterdam Town
Hall in the Background*,
1670, oil on canvas,
183.5 x 162 cm,
Amsterdam Museum,
inv. no. SA 35912

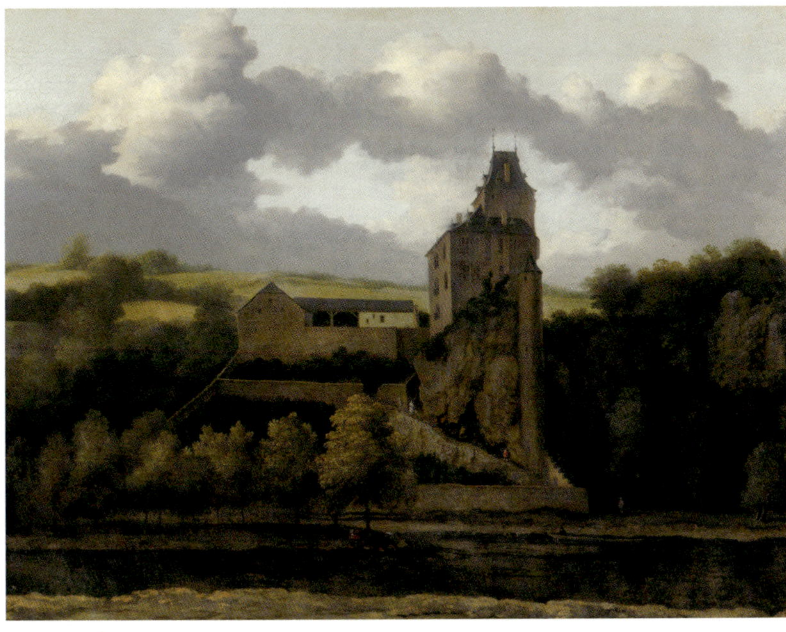

90
Allart van Everdingen,
View of Montjardin Castle,
c. 1655, oil on canvas,
73 x 95.5 cm, The Hague,
Mauritshuis, inv. no. 953
(cat. no. 51)

the family immensely wealthy. Their marriages
to the sisters of the arms magnate Louis de
Geer (1587-1652) certainly helped.

In this townscape, Van Everdingen brought
together three locations—Dordrecht, Amsterdam and Scandinavia—that had meaning for the
Trip family. He also placed two brightly coloured
parrots on the balustrade; birds that were exotic,
exclusive and expensive at that time. In 1670 the
animal specialist Melchior d'Hondecoeter (1636-
1695) made a similar painting of colourful birds
on a balustrade (fig. 89).[50] Amsterdam Town Hall
can be seen in the background. Given the prominent place of the peacocks, symbols of vanity,
and the tethered owl, symbol of wisdom, this
work is often seen as a gibe directed at the
burgomasters of Amsterdam. Their new town
hall, financed with taxpayers' money, testified
to arrogant extravagance rather than wise
government. If the inclusion of the Trippenhuis
in Van Everdingen's painting is considered in
conjunction with D'Hondecoeter's work, the
message could very well be that the Trip family,
thanks to its successful businesses, could afford
to built a magnificent new house with their own
funds, unlike the Amsterdam burgomasters,
who built an impressive town hall with other
people's money.[51]

There is an interesting sidelight on the business contacts between Van Everdingen and the
Trips in the sixteen-sixties; it appears that they
also had a personal relationship. When Allart's
daughter Jacoba was baptized on 18 September
1661, Jacob Trip was one of the witnesses.[52] It
is not clear which Jacob this was: the patriarch
Jacob died in 1661 so it would not have been
him. This leaves two candidates: Hendrick and
Louys's older brother, who would have been
about fifty-seven at the time, and Louys's son,
then twenty-four or twenty-five.

The Mauritshuis in The Hague has a painting
by Van Everdingen that must likewise have been

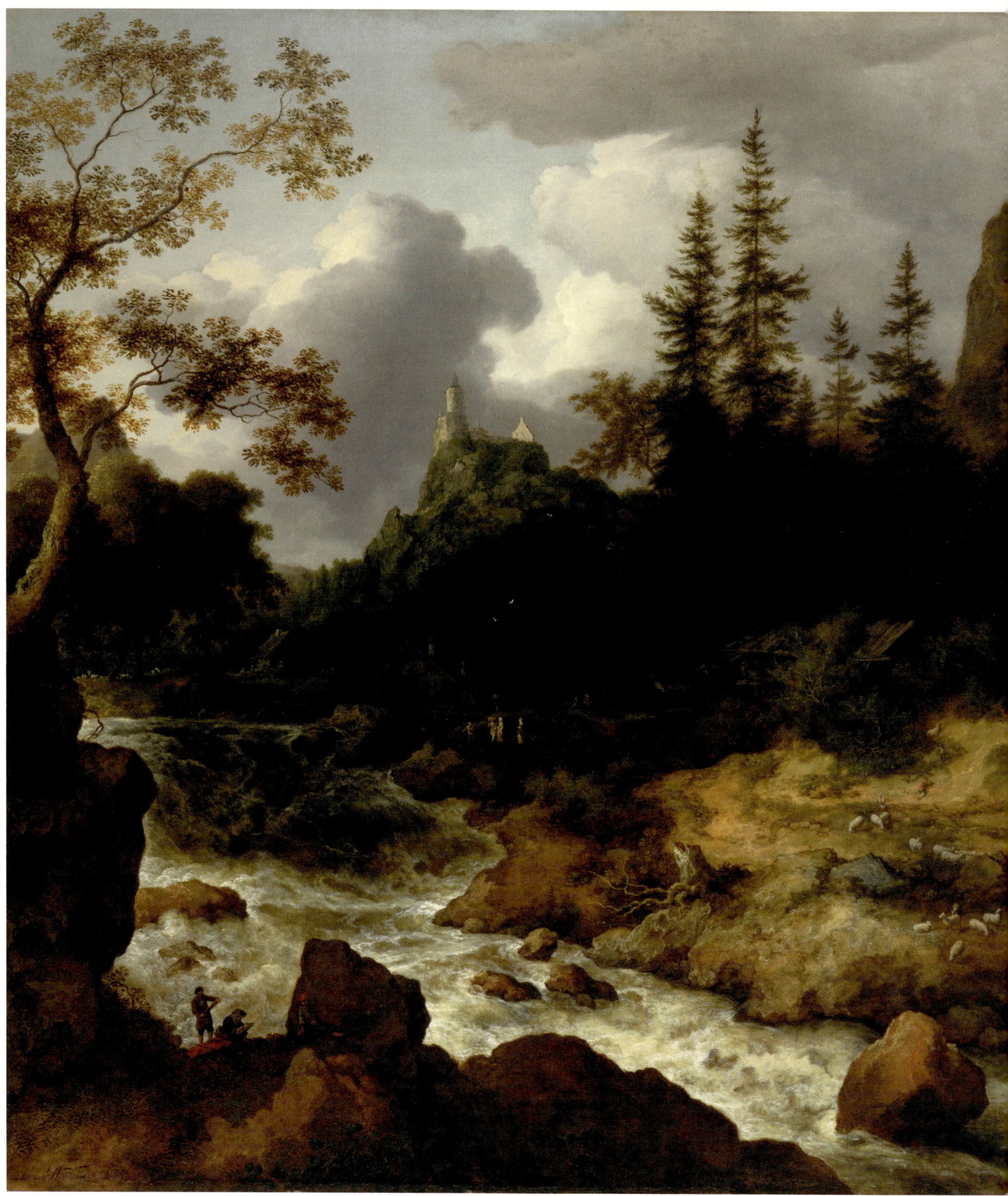

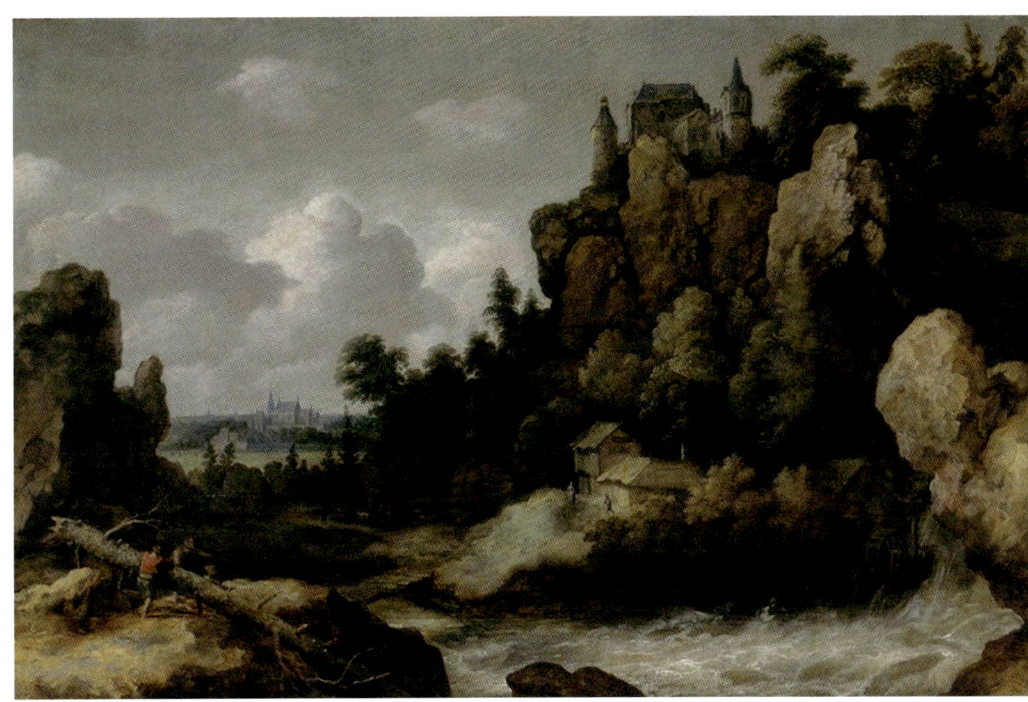

commissioned (fig. 90).[53] It is a view of Mont-jardin Castle, near Sougné-Remouchamps in the Ardennes, beneath a swirling band of cloud. Allart visited the Ardennes in the mid-sixteen-fifties, as some drawings and prints of the springs near Spa attest (figs. 204, 206-208 and 210-213). Louis Gallo da Salamanca came to own the castle in 1654; it may have been he who commissioned Van Everdingen to make the 'portrait' of the castle and prompted his trip to the south.[54]

In the sixteen-sixties, Van Everdingen began including castles in his compositions that cannot be identified as real strongholds (figs. 91-93).[55] With their round towers, light grey walls and slate-grey pitched roofs, they are reminiscent of Bentheim Castle as Jacob van Ruisdael painted it after his visit to the region in 1650 (fig. 94).[56] Allart must have known Van Ruisdael's pictures of the castle and taken inspiration from them. The result was a number of remarkably large paintings, which the artists' biographer Arnold Houbraken certainly had in mind when he wrote disapprovingly at the beginning of the eighteenth century: 'It is to be wished that our Everdingen had not so often worn his paintbrush out on large canvases which frequently get in the way.'[57] And

indeed, these works do not fit well into an ordinary home. In a large space, such as a museum gallery, however, their wall power is unmistakable.

Conclusion

Allart van Everdingen's decision to specialize in the Scandinavian landscape, taken when he was a young artist, was inspired. In the second half of the sixteen-forties, his paintings of rocky areas with waterfalls, pine trees and log cabins were a novelty that helped him establish his name. For many buyers, the attraction of the scenes lay in their foreignness, strangeness and awesomeness. But there must also have been a group of enthusiasts who appreciated these works for their familiarity—Dutchmen who were involved in the trade in timber from Norway, for instance, and the Trip family with their factories and mines in Sweden.

Nevertheless, Van Everdingen's northern mountain landscapes should not be regarded as snapshots *avant la lettre* of the Norwegian coastal region he explored. Even in the earliest, most convincing Scandinavian scenes that Allart painted in Haarlem soon after his return from Norway, he revealed his debt to the pictorial traditions of mountain landscapes that had already developed at the end of the sixteenth century. Van Everdingen's more mature work, created in Amsterdam, is usually less outspokenly Scandinavian. In the sixteen-fifties he began making wooded landscapes in which he combined Norwegian features with, for example, typically German or Dutch elements. He was echoing the work of artists like Jacob van Ruisdael, to share in their success.

What is true of Van Everdingen's many mountain landscapes applies equally to the small group of marines in his painted oeuvre. He began his career with colourful, dramatic scenes of three-masters battling high waves off foreign coasts. Around 1650 he began to concentrate more on Dutch waters with smaller vessels, with the focus on weather, wind and clouds. These works seem to have been painted in the open air, as if Allart simply recorded what he saw around him every day. The breeze filling the sails is almost palpable. Nevertheless, these, too, are artistic constructs, conceived and executed in the workshop.

Van Everdingen selected motifs from Norwegian and Dutch reality that appealed to him and that he had, perhaps, recorded in sketchbooks or on loose sheets of paper. He combined them on his canvases and panels to produce compositions that followed existing, popular pictorial traditions, creating works of art that were sometimes innovative, but never alienating.

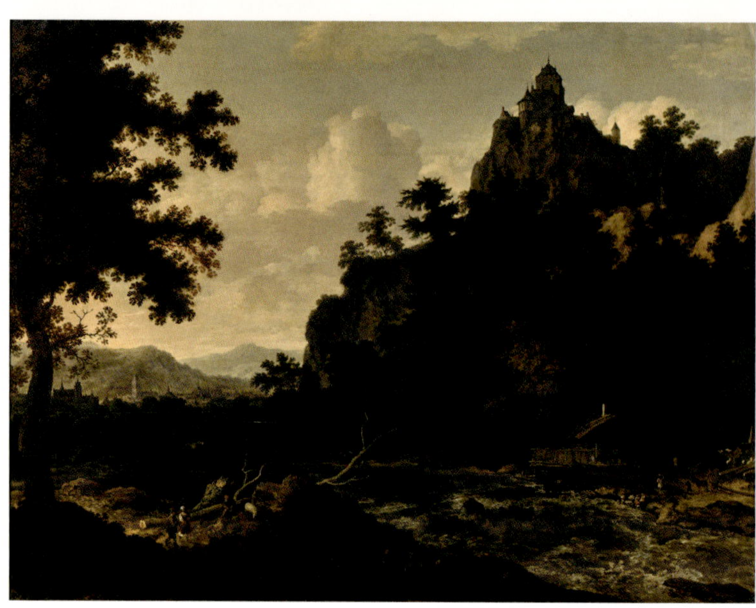

93
Allart van Everdingen, *Mountain Landscape with a River and a Castle*, 1669, oil on canvas, 150 x 200 cm, New York, Collection of Aliis Inserviendo Consumor Foundation

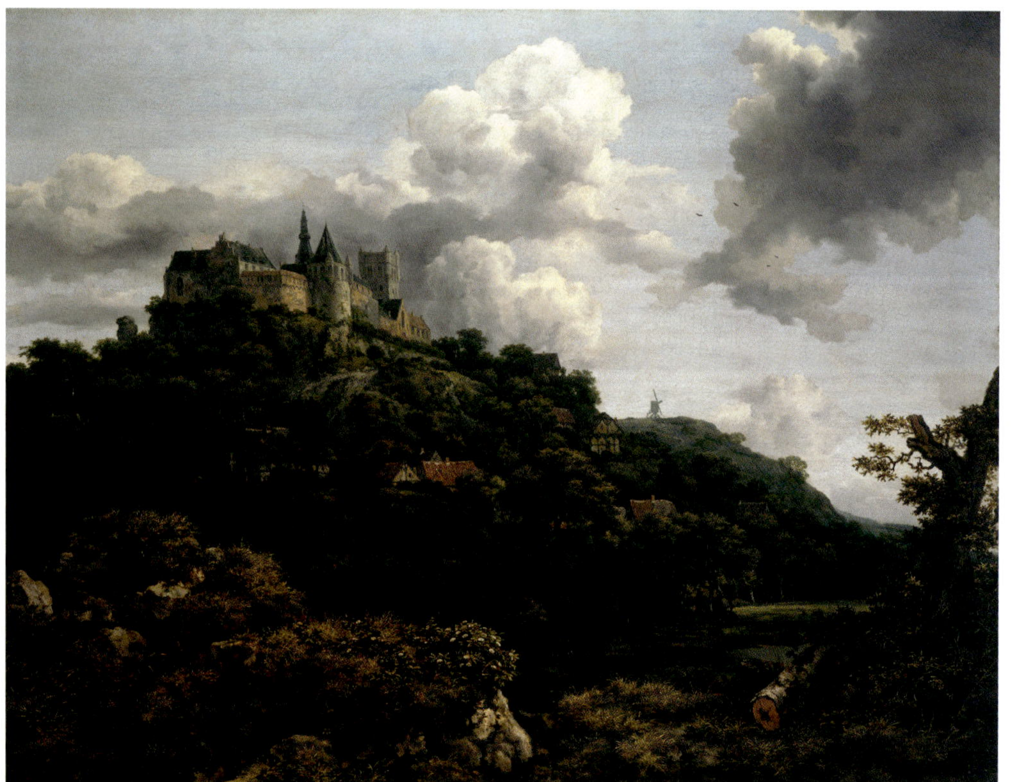

94
Jacob van Ruisdael, *Landscape with Bentheim Castle*, 1653, oil on canvas, 111 x 144 cm, Dublin, National Gallery of Ireland, inv. no. 4531

1 In Davies 2001, 179 paintings are catalogued as 'authentic'. A further twenty-two are attributed to him provisionally; in most cases the present whereabouts of these works are unknown. Davies has consequently not studied them herself and remains non-committal about the attributions. A few more paintings by Van Everdingen surfaced in the trade after 2001; these do not appear in Davies's monograph. Davies published two marines in Davies 2013.

2 For the size and subjects of Van Everdingen's oeuvre see Davies 2001, pp. 13-14.

3 Idem, pp. 41 and 51, and cat. no. 1.

4 For Mulier I see Keyes 1976, Giltaij in Rotterdam/Berlin 1996, pp. 235-237, Van Thiel-Stroman in Köhler et al 2006, pp. 254-255 and Van der Veen in De Beer 2019, vol. 2, pp. 439-443.

5 Cf. Akveld 1996, p. 24.

6 Houbraken 1718-1721, vol. 2, p. 96.

7 On the marine see Rotterdam/Berlin 1996, London 2008 and De Beer 2019; all the information about marine painters in this chapter is taken from these sources unless otherwise stated. On pictures of storms and shipwrecks see also Goedde 1989.

8 Goedde 1989, pp. 84-87 and De Beer 2019a, pp. 27-28.

9 For Roelandt Savery see Prague/Kortrijk 2010.

10 Cf. also Ertz in Essen/Vienna/Antwerp 2003, cat. no. 54 (Joos de Momper II).

11 My thanks to biologist Frans Smeding for his identification of these conifers as Norway spruce (*Picea abies*).

12 My thanks to biologist Frans Smeding for his identification of this tree as the common ash (*Fraxinus excelsior*).

13 Davies 2001, p. 87. For Cornelis Vroom see Van Thiel-Stroman in Köhler et al 2006, pp. 328-332.

14 Davies 2001, cat. no. 40.

15 My thanks to Frans Smeding for his assistance in identifying the species of deer pictured here.

16 Sutton in Amsterdam/Boston/Philadelphia 1987, cat. no. 28 and Chong in idem, cat. no. 68.

17 The 1648 work (fig. 56) is Davies 2001, cat. no. 34; see also Wegener 2000, cat. no. 59.

18 For the wooden architecture in Norway see Holan 1990.

19 Alice Davies calls this motif the 'soaring spruce' (Davies 2001, p. 115).

20 It has been said that this work is of a typically German, Swedish or more generally Scandinavian region (Davies 2001, pp. 144-145). My thanks to Frans Smeding for identifying these trees as larches (*Larix*).

21 Walsh 1991, pp. 100-101. See also Ossing 2019, on clouds in seventeenth-century Dutch painted marines. My thanks to Michiel van Elsas, who helped me understand Van Everdingen's clouds.

22 De Vrij and De Vries wrote in De Vries 1997, cat. no. 20, that this canvas had probably been cut down on all sides; this supposition was repeated in Davies 2001, pp. 62-63. During the recent restoration of the work, however, conservator Jazzy de Groot found remnants of the original tacking edge. In other words, the painting has always been this size. Frans Smeding identified the trees in the painting as elms (*Ulmus*) on the basis of their location by the water, the shape and position of the leaves and the holes made by a woodpecker in the trunk on the left.

23 Sluijter 2013.

24 Davies 2001, pp. 32-33 and 199-202, and Van Thiel-Stroman in Köhler et al 2006, p. 150.

25 Davies dated both the works by Van Everdingen referred to here (Davies 2001, cat. nos. 7 and 9) early, to around 1645 (idem, p. 57). Dendrochronological analysis of the Leipzig panel has revealed that it cannot possibly have been painted before 1655 and probably not until after 1665 (according to Peter Klein in a letter dated 16 June 2011 to Museum der bildenden Künste Leipzig). This information, taken in conjunction with the type of composition, leads me to date this work later. Cf. Nicolaisen 2012, cat. no. 86, in which the date 'um 1643/1644' is retained. I would also place the painting in Frankfurt later than Davies did. For this work see also Krempel 2005, pp. 110-113.

26 De Beer 2019, cat. no. 22.

27 My thanks to Laurens Schoemaker for his analysis of this harbour view.

28 The Haarlem painting is discussed by Biesboer in Köhler et al 2006, cat. no. 136.

29 De Vries 1997, cat. no. 70.

30 Den Bosch/The Hague/Assen 2007, cat. no. 45.

31 Milwaukee 2005, cat. no. 89.

32 The IRR images and the mosaic were made by René Gerritsen on 18 March 2019 with an Osiris camera sensitive to 1700 nm. Lens: Rodenstock, Rodagon IR 150mm f5.6; filter: 1000nm; aperture setting f8; lighting: 2 x 500 watt halogen. The mosaic was composed of four partial images of 16 megapixels each.

33 My thanks to Ron Brand for this suggestion.

34 Davies frequently refers to both changes in Davies 2001, pp. 101-138. See also Stechow 1968, p. 144.

35 Frans Smeding identified the trees in this painting as oaks (the common or sessile oak, *Quercus robur* or *Quercus petraea*) and drew my attention to the fact that in Norway they are confined to the southern coastal strip —the region that Van Everdingen visited.

36 Davies 2001, pp. 62 and 110.

37 Idem, p. 108. For Berchem see Haarlem/Zurich/Schwerin 2006.

38 The IRR image was made by Anna Krekeler on 5 August 2010 with an Osiris camera (Opus Instruments) with an InGaAs detector, sensitive to IR radiation between 900 and 1700 nm. My thanks to Anna for sharing her opinion of the painted design visible on this infrared reflectogram.

39 On Van Ruisdael see Los Angeles/ Philadelphia/London 2005 (with additional literature references) and Van Thiel-Stroman in Köhler et al 2006, pp. 281-286.

40 On the relationship between Van Ruisdael and Van Everdingen see Stechow 1968, pp. 144-145, Davies 2001, pp. 174-179 and Slive 2005, pp. 8-11.

41 The painting is Davies 2001, cat. no. 45.

42 Davies 2001, pp. 35 and 37.

43 For the decorative scheme of the Trippenhuis see Van Run 2019. Specifically on Van Everdingen's paintings for this building: Davies 2001, pp. 125-131. On the Trip family see Klein 1965 and Zandvliet 2006, pp. 21-25 and 69-70 (nos. 7, 8 and 30). All the details about the members of the family and the Trippenhuis in what follows were taken from these publications.

44 The overdoors are Davies 2001, cat. nos. 123-126.

45 Idem, cat. no. 99.

46 Idem, p. 115.

47 This painting and the literature on it are discussed in considerable detail in Davies 2001, pp. 126-127 and 164-167. See also Van der Ham 2005, where it is again concluded that this painting is not a true picture of the situation in all respects.

48 The drawing is Davies 2007, cat. no. 170.

49 Davies 2001, pp. 130-131 and 154-155; Paarlberg in Budapest 2014, cat. no. 27; Van Run 2019, p. 32.

50 For D'Hondecoeter see Rikken 2008; the painting is discussed on pp. 33-36.

51 I base this suggestion on Van Run 2019, pp. 30-32. Van Run not only makes a connection between the cityscapes with balustrades by Van Everdingen and D'Hondecoeter, but also relates them to ceiling paintings including birds in the Trippenhuis. It has recently been discovered that they depict a fable about a raven who flaunts himself in other birds' feathers and is punished for it (idem, pp. 31-32).

52 Van Thiel-Stroman in Köhler et al 2006, p. 151 (note 25).

53 Buvelot 2004, pp. 116-117.

54 Davies 2001, p. 146.

55 The painting dated 1669 is not in Davies 2001.

56 The Hague 2009.

57 Houbraken 1718-1721, vol. 2, p. 96: ''t was te wenschen dat onze Everdingen zyn konstpenceel zoo menigwerf niet had afgesleten op groote doeken welke dikwils in den weg hangen.'

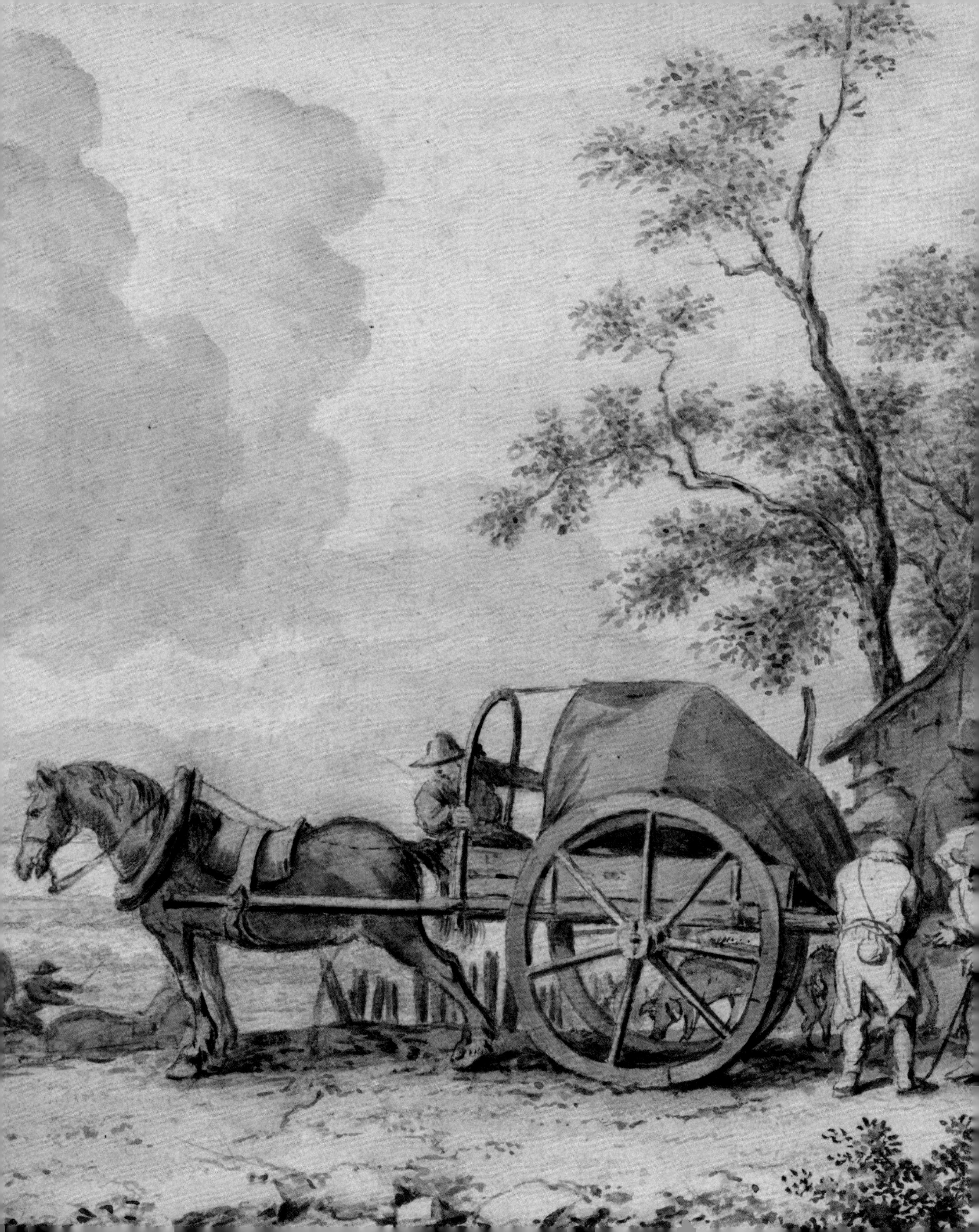

3 METICULOUS AND VERSATILE

Allart van Everdingen the Draughtsman

Yvonne Bleyerveld

< Detail of cat. no. 55

Allart van Everdingen, a very productive painter, was also a prolific draughtsman. We know of more than six hundred and fifty drawings by him, mainly Scandinavian and Dutch landscapes.[1] With this extensive drawn oeuvre, he can hold his own with Dutch landscape painters like Jan van Goyen (1596-1656), Pieter de Molijn (1595-1661) and Nicolaes Berchem (1621/1622-1683), who also all left hundreds of landscape drawings.[2]

Most of Van Everdingen's surviving drawings are works of art in their own right, made for sale, but there are also dozens of drawings associated with his etchings (see the essays by Erik Hinterding and Marjan Pantjes in this catalogue).[3] Allart doubtless also drew preparatory sketches for his paintings and his detailed finished drawings—for sixteenth- and seventeenth-century artists, drawing was the foundation on which their artistic output rested. An important element of their professional training, it was a way of exercising the hand, capturing impressions and collecting motifs. Apart from a set of sketches for a print cycle of Reynard the Fox, however, there are virtually no surviving 'working drawings' by Van Everdingen. They were probably used and reused in the workshop until they were so tattered they had to be thrown away.[4]

As he did in his paintings, Allart van Everdingen pictured rugged Scandinavian landscapes and marines in his drawings, while the Dutch landscape also featured heavily in his drawn oeuvre. The artist drew Dutch river, shore and village views and cityscapes, sometimes with identifiable places in the background, in the tradition of Esaias van de Velde (1587-1630), Jan van Goyen and Pieter de Molijn, who may have been his second teacher. Drawings like these sold well.[5] There is a third group of drawings—hill and mountain landscapes, sometimes with castles or churches—which are difficult to place topographically. In these landscapes, impressions of Scandinavia seem to merge with observations made during a later trip to the Ardennes. Whereas nature predominated in the Scandinavian and 'hybrid' landscapes, the Dutch landscapes and marines are populated by peasants and burghers, fishermen, skaters and bargees. Each group of drawings gives pleasure in its own way.

Most of the hundreds of sheets bear the monogram 'AVE'. Van Everdingen worked in a variety of drawing techniques, although brown ink and a pen or brush were far and away his favourite.[6] It is often possible to see an initial sketch in chalk or graphite under the composition, and the artist used washes in diluted brown or black ink to accentuate darker passages. More than a hundred of his drawings are finished with watercolour, which he applied in transparent or opaque layers.[7] There are two further groups, all scenes in oil paint: a series of brunailles of seascapes and landscapes, and the sketches for the Reynard the Fox print cycle.[8]

Van Everdingen did not date his drawings, which makes it extremely difficult to create some sort of chronology in his large drawn oeuvre. Three drawings attributed to him are dated; they are two works from 1637 and 1639 and a landscape dated 1656. The attributions of these drawings are debatable, however.[9] There is essentially no way of arriving at a chronological order, and the problem is made worse by the fact that there is no obvious stylistic development in the drawn oeuvre. In a few cases, dated paintings connected to a drawing provide points of reference.[10]

This essay aims to shed light on characteristic aspects of Allart van Everdingen's drawn oeuvre and answer the question as to how his work differed from that of other artists. A second question is how his drawings were regarded—in his lifetime and after his death. It goes without saying that any discussion of Van Everdingen's drawn oeuvre must begin with that momentous trip to the north.

Drawings of Scandinavia

While many of his fellow artists went on a study trip to Italy, in his early twenties Allart van Everdingen chose a very different destination. Sailing from a Dutch port in 1644, he boarded a vessel that took him to Norway. When he disembarked there, he doubtless had paper and drawing materials in his luggage to record his impressions during the journey. It is safe to assume that he had drawn in the open air as an apprentice, since this was part of seventeenth-century professional training. Artists in the Republic regularly went outdoors to draw typical Dutch landscapes, villages and towns on the spot, a practice encouraged by seventeenth-century art theoreticians. In his 1604 *Schilder-Boeck*, for instance, Karel van Mander advised young artists to go out and observe natural phenomena and weather conditions, and relax by drawing in nature.[11] The young Allart also had an example to follow—his first teacher Roelandt Savery (1576-1639), who in 1603 had set off with his drawing materials on a ten-year expedition around Prague and the Central European countryside and recorded his impressions.[12] Drawings based on direct observations, in other words 'from life', served as working material in the studio and were used as preparatory studies for a painting, print or finished drawing. Artists who went out and about drew in sketchbooks that were easy to carry or on loose sheets clamped to a drawing board, as we see in a number of Van Everdingen's landscapes (figs. 95, 188 and 197).

It has been suggested that some sixteen drawings of Scandinavian landscapes and motifs by Van Everdingen were made during his trip.[13] They include four sketches done with a brush and grey or black ink, all about the same

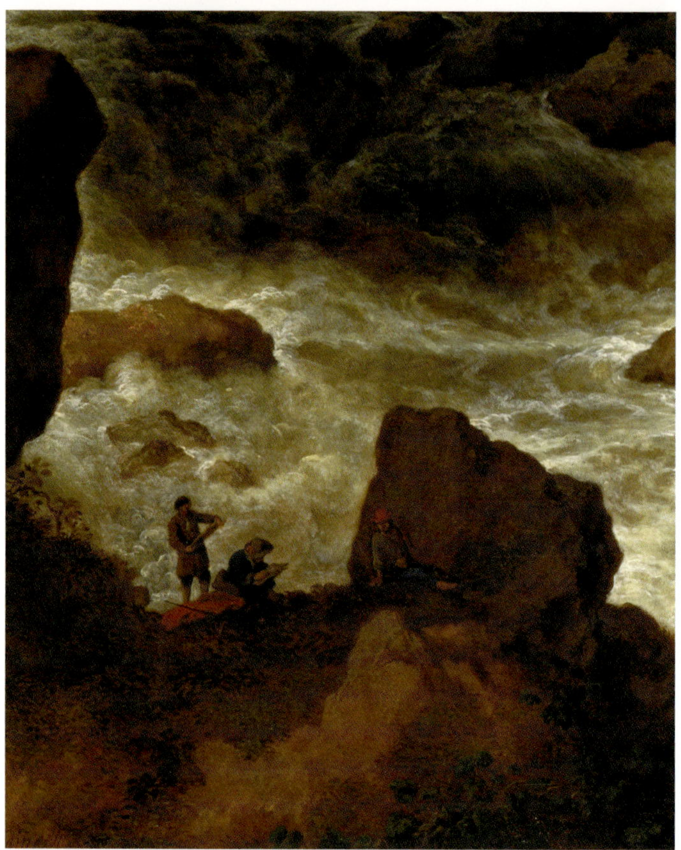

95
Drawing in nature, detail of Allart van Everdingen, *Mountain Landscape with a River and a Castle*, oil on canvas, 219 x 193 cm, Copenhagen, Statens Museum for Kunst, inv. no. MSsp512 (cat. no. 67)

size. Given these similarities, it is generally assumed that they all came from the same sketchbook.[14] Three of them are of identifiable places: a waterfall near Trollhättan (fig. 96) and two views of Risør in Norway (figs. 97 and 98). The fourth is a Norwegian landscape with a log cabin (fig. 99). There is also a larger topographical drawing of a waterfall Mölndal with a system of timber channels used to convey water to watermills (fig. 100). This fine sheet has an inscription on the back in a seventeenth-century hand: 'molendael buÿten gothenburgh na t'leven' ('Mölndal outside Gothenburg from life'). This could have been written by Van Everdingen, but equally well by a later owner of the drawing.

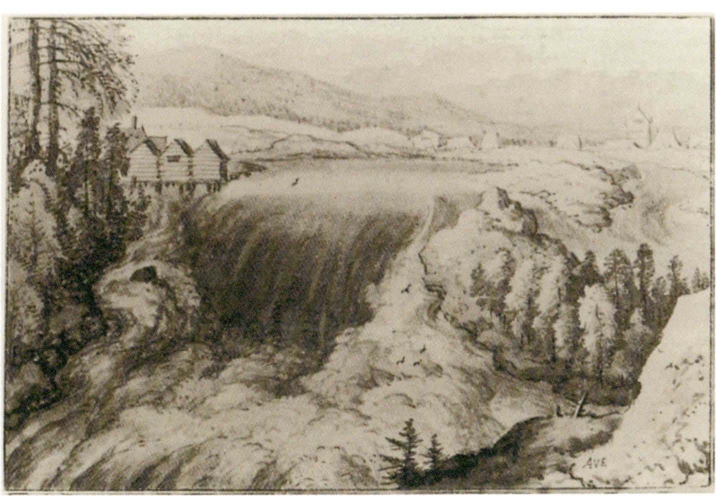

96
Allart van Everdingen, *Waterfall near Trollhättan*, 1644 or shortly thereafter, pen and brush and grey ink, grey wash, 115 x 176 mm, Rotterdam, Museum Boijmans Van Beuningen, inv. no. AvE 4 (PK)

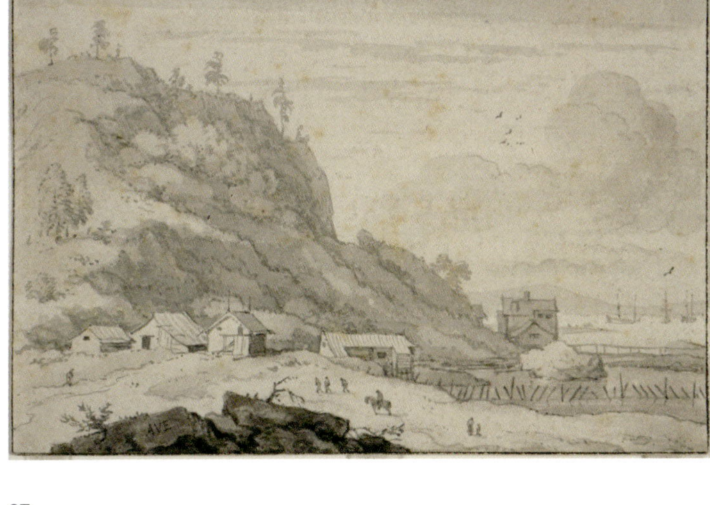

97
Allart van Everdingen, *View of Risør,* 1644 or shortly thereafter, pen and brush and grey ink, grey wash, 115 x 176 mm, Stockholm, Nationalmuseum, inv. no. NMH 851/1938

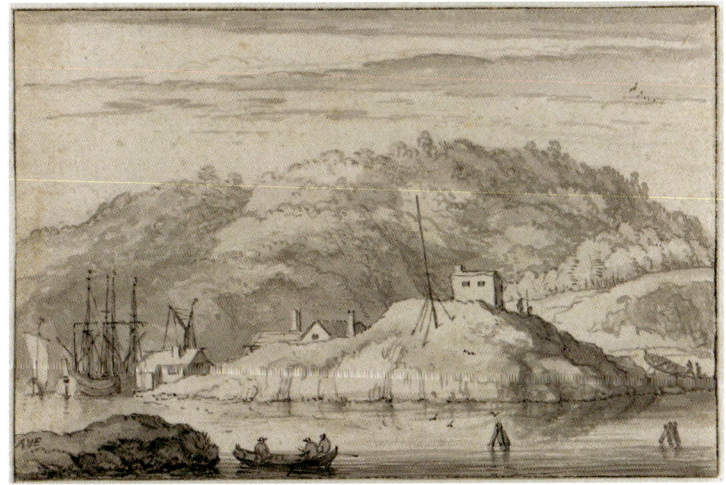

98
Allart van Everdingen, *View of the Harbour at Risør*, 1644 or shortly thereafter, pen and brush and grey ink, grey wash, 115 x 176 mm, Amsterdam, Rijksmuseum, inv. no. RP-T-1957-202 (cat. no. 6)

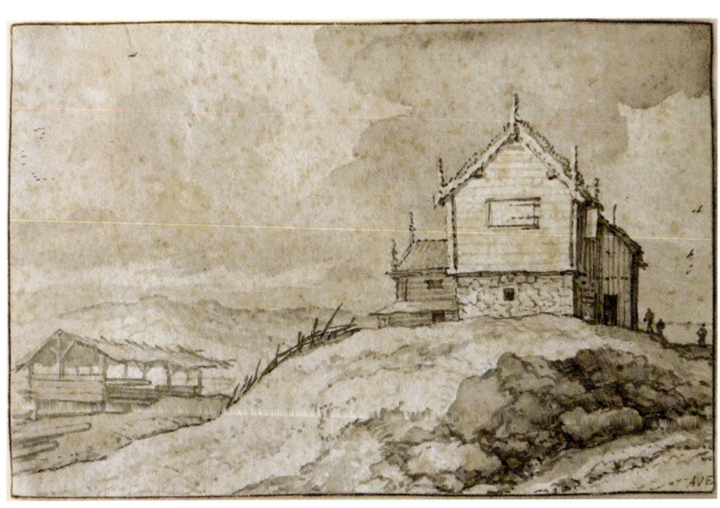

99
Allart van Everdingen, *Norwegian Landscape with a Log Cabin*, 1644 or shortly thereafter, pen and brush and grey ink over traces of black chalk, grey wash, 116 x 176 mm, Boston, Alice I. Davies Collection (cat. no. 45)

It is interesting to note in this context that the Amsterdam artist Jan de Beijer (1703-1780) drew copies of eighteen mountain landscapes and views of water from life by Van Everdingen.[15] It tells us that this group of landscape drawings was still together in the eighteenth century. They were probably sheets related to Allart's trip that came out of a sketchbook. Copies of two drawings of Scandinavian landscapes (figs. 97 and 98) by Jan de Beijer have survived, and one of them carries the inscription 'oostrysen in noorwegen 1644' ('Oostrysen in Norway 1644') (fig. 18, copy after fig. 97).[16]

It is impossible to tell whether the surviving drawings of Scandinavian landscapes were made wholly or in part on the spot. A certain spontaneity in observation and execution has been described as a characteristic of a drawing made from life.[17] However, all the drawings of Scandinavian landscapes by Van Everdingen that we know, including the ones of identifiable locations, are meticulously finished. This suggests that he either drew them outdoors and worked them up with washes afterwards, or they were based on sketches he had done on the spot. If this latter was the case, it could well have happened after he returned to the Republic. A drawing of a waterfall, now in Berlin (fig. 101), appears to be a combination of reality and imagination: the wide river may have been inspired by a waterfall near Trollhättan, but the platform with the two figures on the left was deliberately placed there as a repoussoir to lead the viewer's eye into the scene. Not observed on the spot, in other words, but composed in the workshop.

In any event, the drawn Scandinavian landscapes attest to a journey that made an impression on the artist—the places he visited and the overwhelming nature and typical wooden farmhouses, log cabins, barns and watermills he found in Norway. On his return, Allart van Everdingen must have cherished the drawings of his travels as important reference works when he depicted Scandinavian landscapes and motifs in his paintings, etchings and finished drawings. The wooden house with its stone base in one of the drawings (fig. 99), for instance, appears again in a painting dating from 1648 (fig. 56), made several years after his trip to the north.[18] There are also connections between the drawn *Waterfall near Trollhättan* (fig. 96) and *Waterfall at Mölndal* (fig. 100) on the one hand and painted landscapes with waterfalls dating from around 1662 (fig. 86) and 1670 (fig. 80) on the other.[19] These paintings could have been based directly on the drawings, or both drawings and paintings could have had a common example in the shape of a sketch done on the spot.

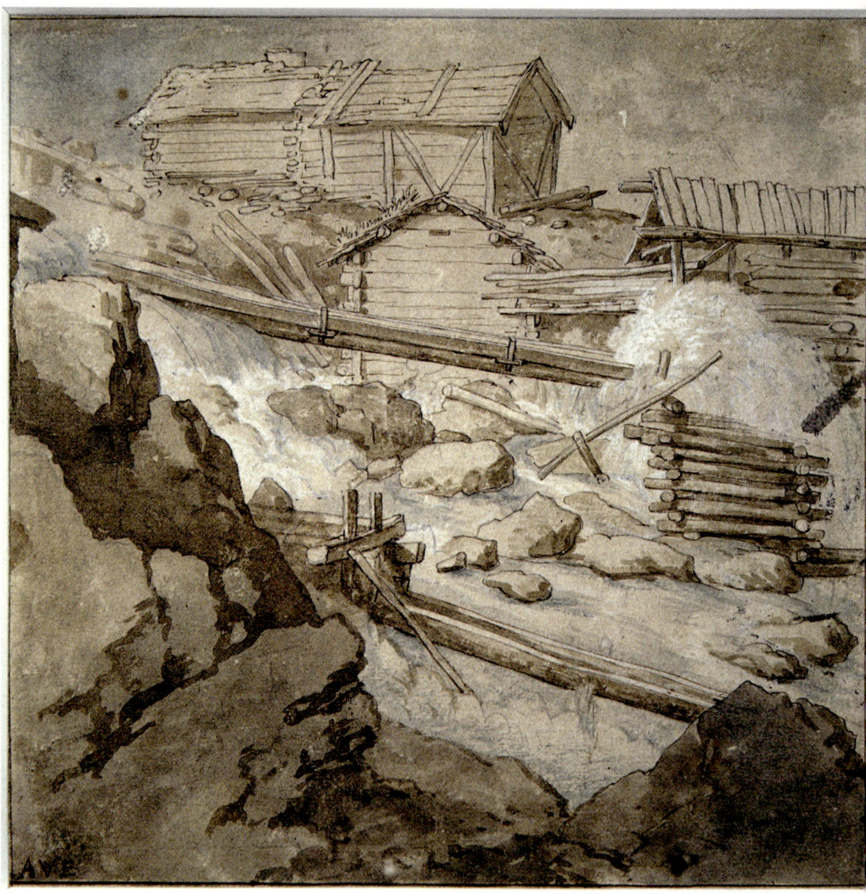

100

Allart van Everdingen, *Waterfall at Mölndal*, 1644 or shortly there-after, pen and brown ink over black chalk, brown and grey wash, blue watercolour, heightened with white, 197 x 194 mm, Mölndal Municipality, inv. no. A-752 (cat. no. 88)

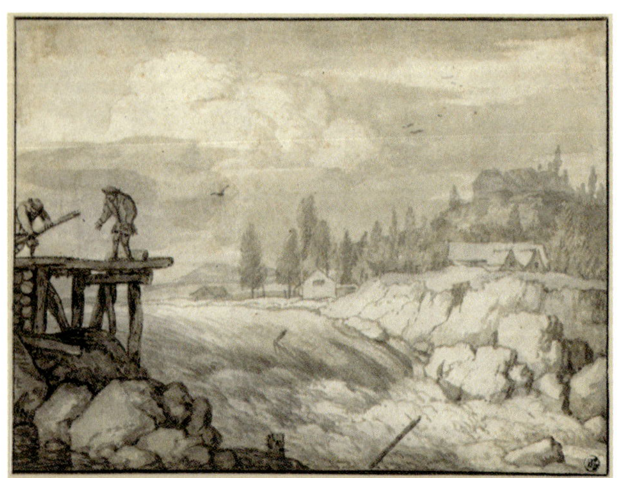

< 101

Allart van Everdingen, *Landscape with a Waterfall, Possibly near Trollhättan*, pen and brush and black and grey-brown ink, grey wash, 121 x 163 mm, Staatliche Museen zu Berlin, Kupferstich-kabinett, inv. no. KdZ 1311 (cat. no. 43)

An Early Drawing?

Although the trip to Norway had an enduring effect on Van Everdingen's artistic output, his drawn oeuvre nevertheless also follows Dutch pictorial traditions. He had been able to study waterfalls and rocks in Roelandt Savery's drawings (figs. 8 and 49). These subjects were already known in the Low Countries through the monumental engravings of penitent saints in the wilderness by Cornelis Cort after Girolamo Muziano dating from 1567 to 1574 (fig. 102).[20] The waterfall at Tivoli near Rome had been a tourist attraction since the sixteenth century and was visited and drawn by artists, including Pieter Bruegel the Elder (1525/1530-1569) and his son Jan Brueghel (1568-1625).[21]

Scandinavian Landscape with an Old Tree Stump (fig. 103) is a work that harks back to an older pictorial tradition. This delicate drawing is almost a portrait of a large old trunk with gnarled roots. The shape of the stump and the

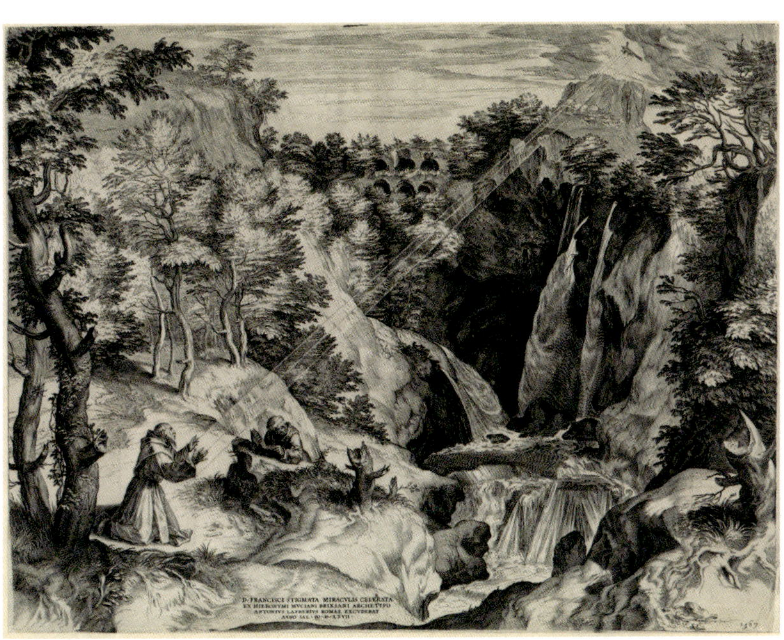

102
Cornelis Cort after Girolamo Muziano, *St Francis Receiving the Stigmata*, 1567, engraving, 411 x 542 mm, Amsterdam, Rijksmuseum, inv. no. RP-P-BI-6528

> 103
Allart van Everdingen, *Scandinavian Landscape with an Old Tree Stump*, brush and grey ink over black chalk, grey wash, 157 x 167 mm, Paris, Fondation Custodia, Frits Lugt Collection, inv. no. 2034 (cat. no. 97)

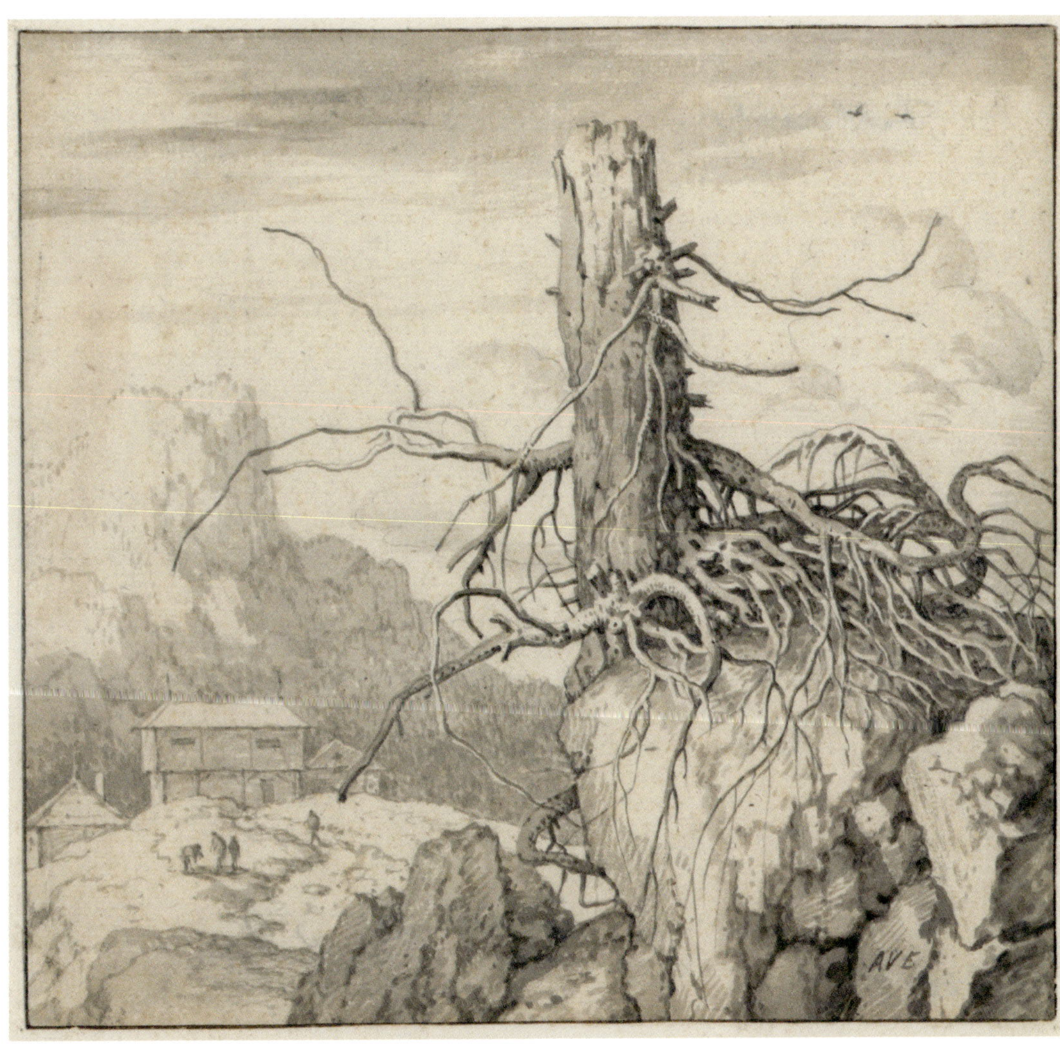

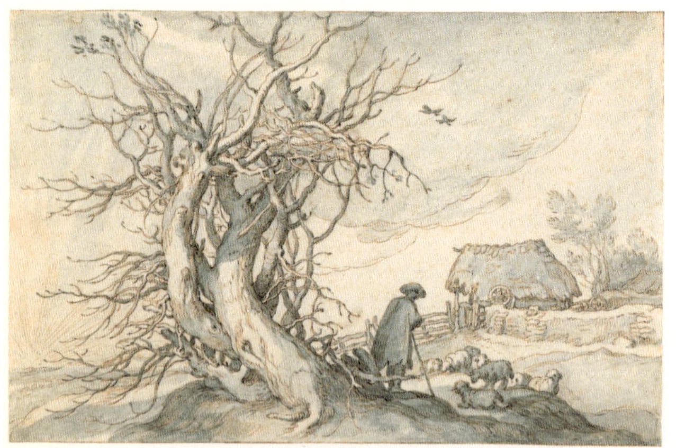

Large Coloured and Monochrome Drawings

It would have been obvious to Allart van Everdingen that he could make money on the open market with his drawings, as he could with his paintings. He had, though, to offer enthusiasts something special, because there must have been huge numbers of drawn landscapes around. Little is known about the seventeenth-century demand for them, although the thousands of surviving landscape drawings from this period suggest that the market must have been lucrative.[25] With his draughtsman's hat on, Van Everdingen had a number of specialisms, and one of these was making drawings on a relatively large scale (roughly 180 x 300 millimetres), which he worked out with great care.[26] He executed these large sheets either in monochrome tints, in other words with a pen and brush and brown or black ink, or in colour —by combining brown or black ink with watercolours in various shades. In both cases he achieved attractive effects that must have pleased art lovers.

In the second half of the seventeenth century, large coloured landscapes were not as familiar as they were to become in the eighteenth.[27] Only a few sixteenth- and seventeenth-century artists had produced coloured landscape drawings, among them Hans Bol

Abraham Bloemaert, *A Shepherd with Sheep near a Dead Tree*, pen and brown ink over a sketch in black chalk, blue wash, 148 x 231 mm, Amsterdam, Rijksmuseum, inv. no. RP-T-1898-A-3740

105
Hendrick Avercamp, *Fishermen by Moonlight*, pen and brown and black ink, watercolour, 144 x 195 mm, Amsterdam, Rijksmuseum, inv. no. RP-T-1948-397

rather curious position of the mature tree, which appears to have grown out of bare rock, tell us that this is an imaginary tree study.[22] Allart had most probably borrowed the motif from drawings by Roelandt Savery and his contemporaries Jacques de Gheyn II (1565-1629), Paulus van Vianen (c. 1570-1613) and Abraham Bloemaert (1566-1651), who also frequently pictured gnarled dead tree trunks and stumps (fig. 104).[23]

This is the only known drawing by Allart to feature a tree trunk so prominently, but the painting *Trees by the Water* (fig. 62) suggests that the subject engaged the artist on more than one occasion.[24] He also frequently included gnarled trees in his etchings (figs. 171, 173 and 174). *Trees by the Water* is regarded as a work dating from the early sixteen-fifties and it is probable that the etchings of gnarled trees were also made during this period. This would suggest that the drawn tree study can likewise be dated quite early.

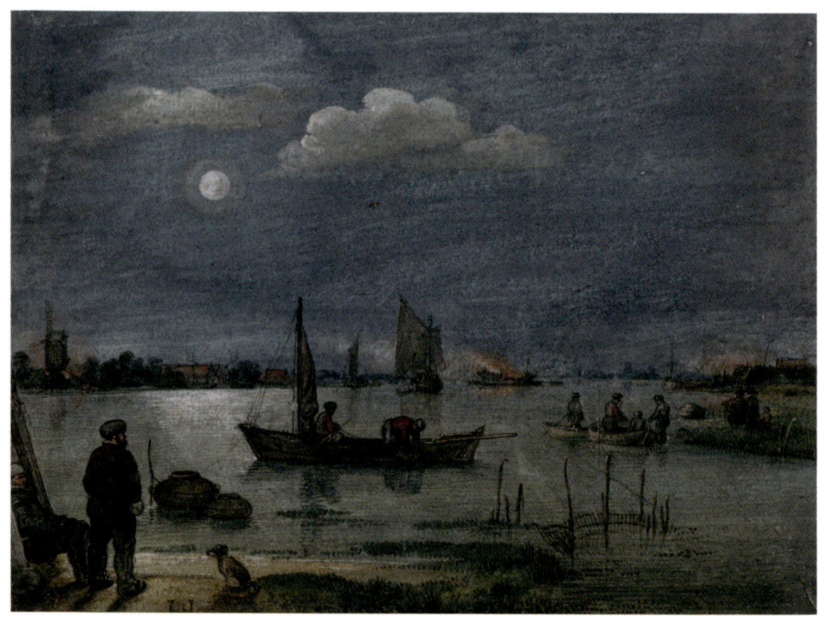

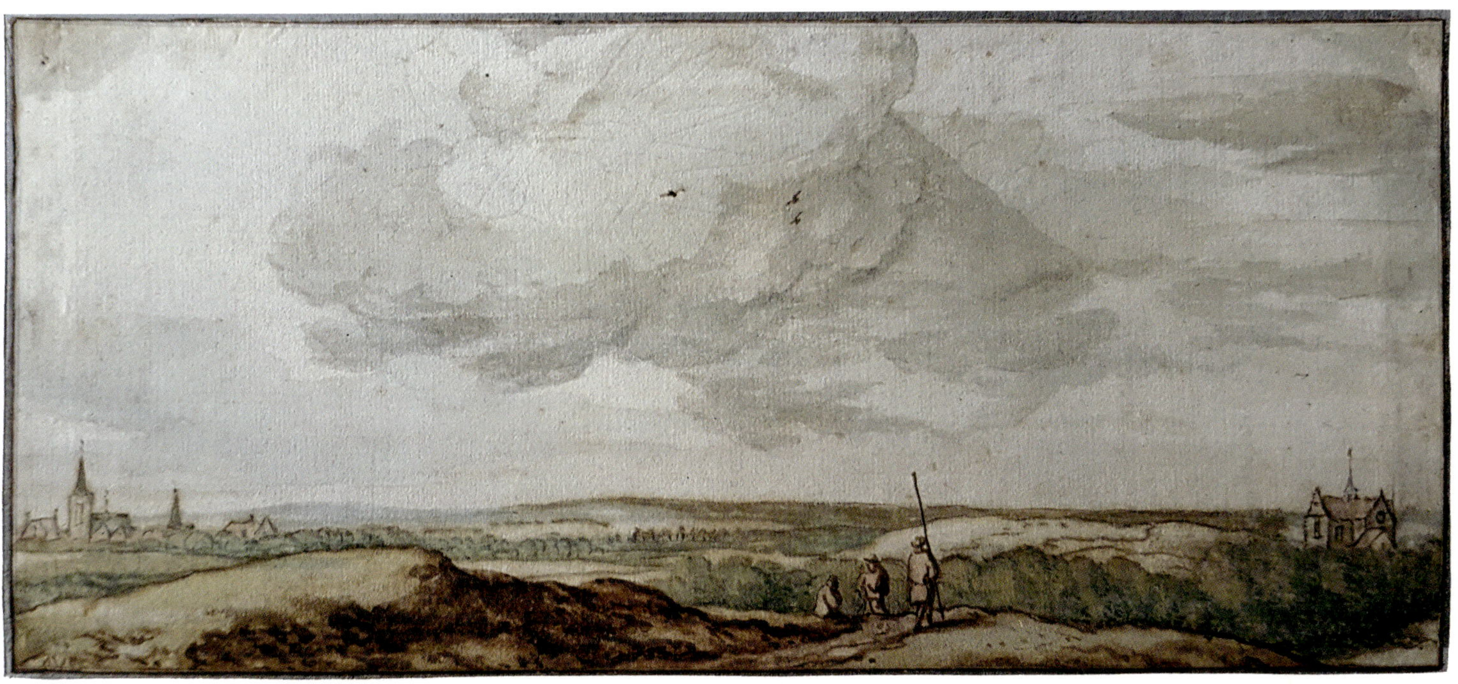

106
Allart van Everdingen,
*Panoramic Landscape
with Three Figures*, pen
and brush and brown
ink, grey wash, water-
colour, 105 x 230 mm,
private collection
(cat. no. 107)

v 107
Pieter de Molijn, *Pano-
ramic Landscape with a
Road beside a Waterway*,
1630, watercolour and
some varnish (egg white?)
over a sketch in black
chalk, 143 x 196 mm,
Amsterdam, Rijksmuseum,
inv. no. RP-T-1948-405

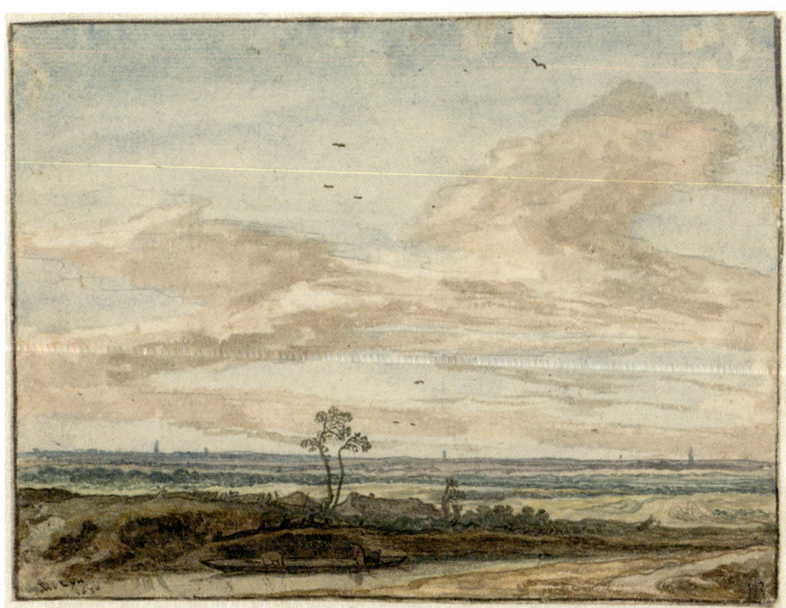

(1534-1593), Abraham Bloemaert (fig. 104), Hendrick Avercamp (1585-1634) (fig. 105) and Anthonie van Borssom (1630-1677).[28] Van Everdingen must have been inspired by Roelandt Savery, who also used colour to enliven his drawn landscapes. He was probably influenced, too, by Pieter de Molijn's coloured drawings. A panoramic landscape by Van Everdingen, in which he used green and blue as well as brown and grey (fig. 106), has much in common with a landscape in light colours by De Molijn (fig. 107). Both drawings have a low horizon, a wide cloudy sky and a palette shading from brown tints in the foreground to bluish grey in the distance. The similarity suggests that Allart's work can be given an early date and that he studied De Molijn's coloured landscapes very closely, either as his pupil or because he had access to them in some other way.

The panoramic landscape shows that Van Everdingen sometimes needed only a few colours. In the *Waterfall at Mölndal* (fig. 100), he confined himself to blue watercolour and accents in white watercolour to convey the sense of fast-flowing water churning through

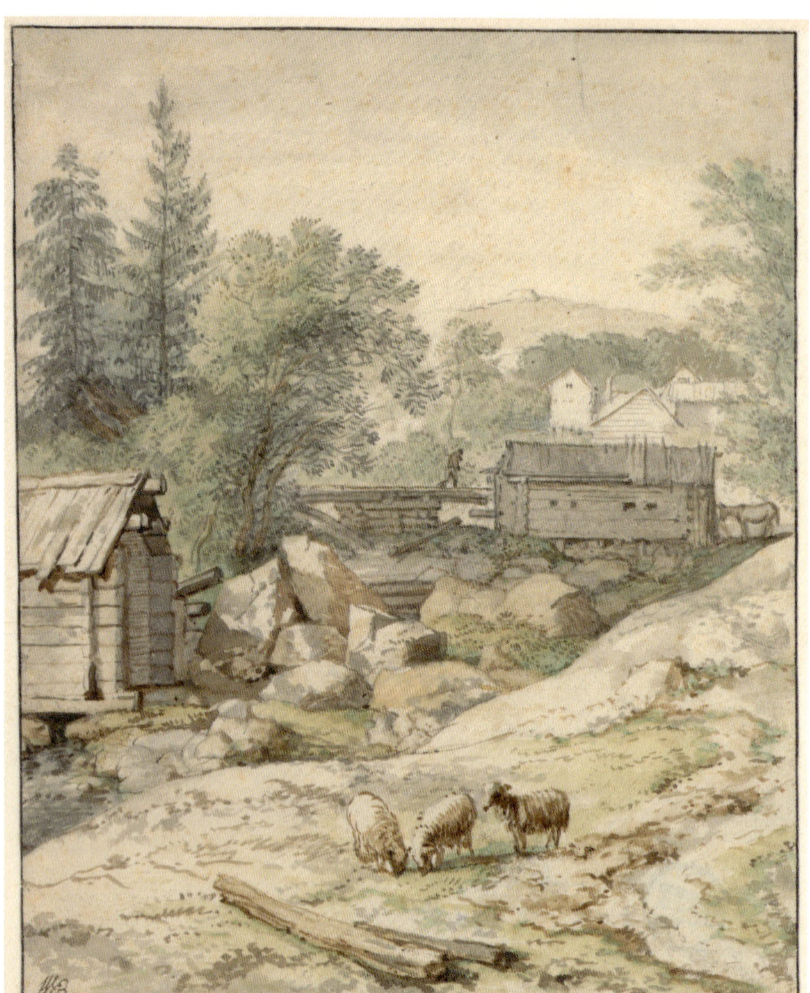

108
Allart van Everdingen, *Scandinavian Landscape with Log Cabins*, pen and brush and brown and grey ink over black chalk, watercolour, 200 x 164 mm, Paris, Fondation Custodia, Frits Lugt Collection, inv. no. 3082 (cat. no. 96)

v 109
Allart van Everdingen, *Scandinavian Landscape with Two Log Cabins by the Water*, brush and brown ink, watercolour, 112 x 168 mm, Haarlem, Teylers Museum, inv. no. Q 030 (cat. no. 54)

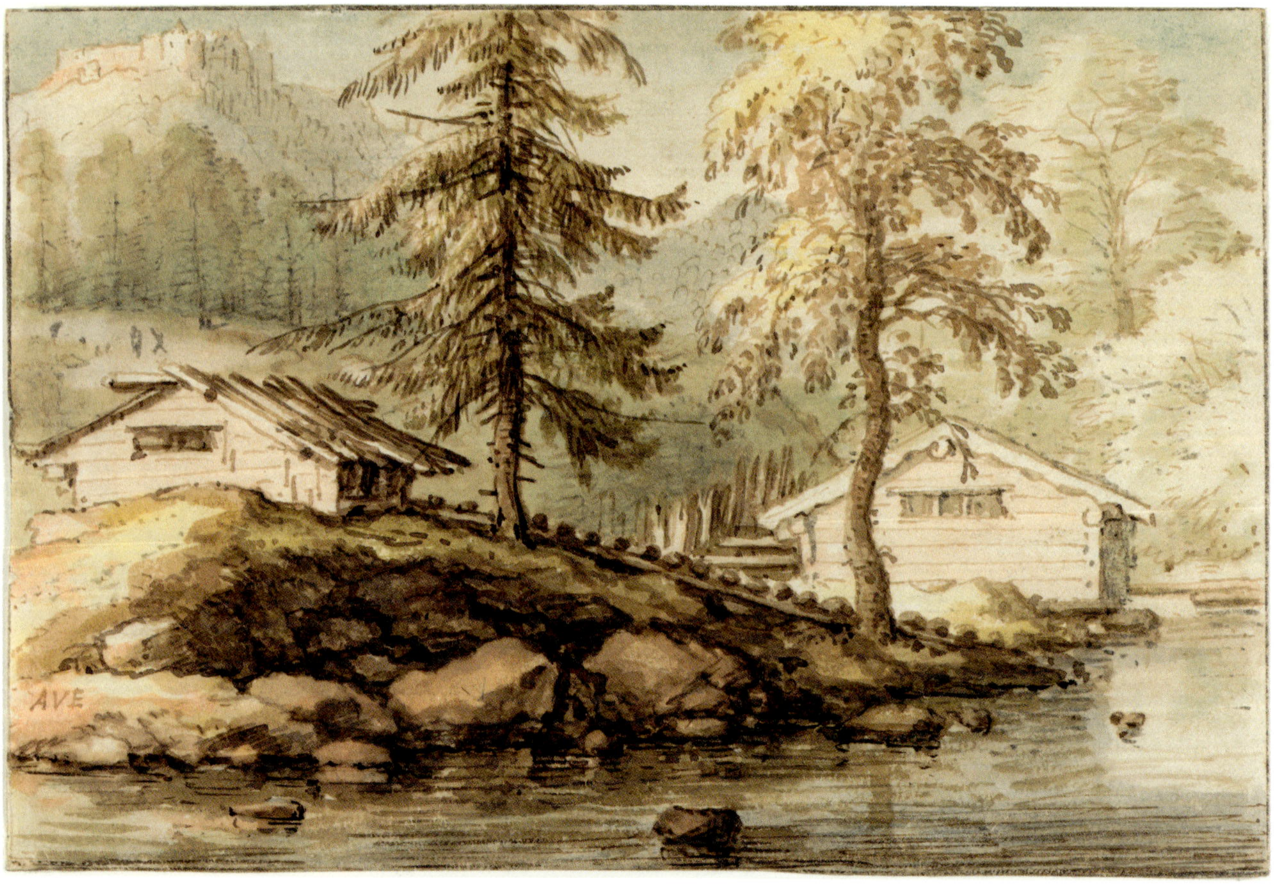

110
Allart van Everdingen, *Figures near a Waterfall in a Mountain Landscape*, pen and brown ink, brown wash, watercolour, heightened with white, 200 x 323 mm, Amsterdam, Stichting Collectie P. & N. de Boer, inv. no. B 477 (cat. no. 40)

the rocks and gushing out of the wooden channel upper right. Van Everdingen built up another Scandinavian landscape with brown ink and black ink diluted to grey, combined with individual touches of watercolour in shades of green and yellow (fig. 108). He used similar colours in a landscape with two log cabins by a river (fig. 109), although there he put more intense layers of colour in the trees and on the river bank in the foreground to suggest depth in the scene.

As well as landscapes in which he used just a few colours, Van Everdingen made drawings he coloured in completely with opaque layers of watercolour. Again, De Molijn could have been his example, for there are two surviving drawings in body colour by him of a similar size

to Van Everdingen's.[29] Allart's use of opaque watercolour produced spectacular results that look like small paintings on paper. One of the highlights in this technique is a landscape with a waterfall flowing between huge rocks (fig. 110). Smoke rises from the chimney of one of the houses on the left; like the foam on the water, it is suggested with white watercolour. The travellers and their donkey on the right convey a sense of the scale of the waterfall and the height of the rocks, and provide colour accents in the predominantly green and brown landscape.

The artist used a similar formula in a marine with a three-master in difficulties in a severe storm (fig. 111). Grey and brown shades predominate, but there are hints of greenish yellow

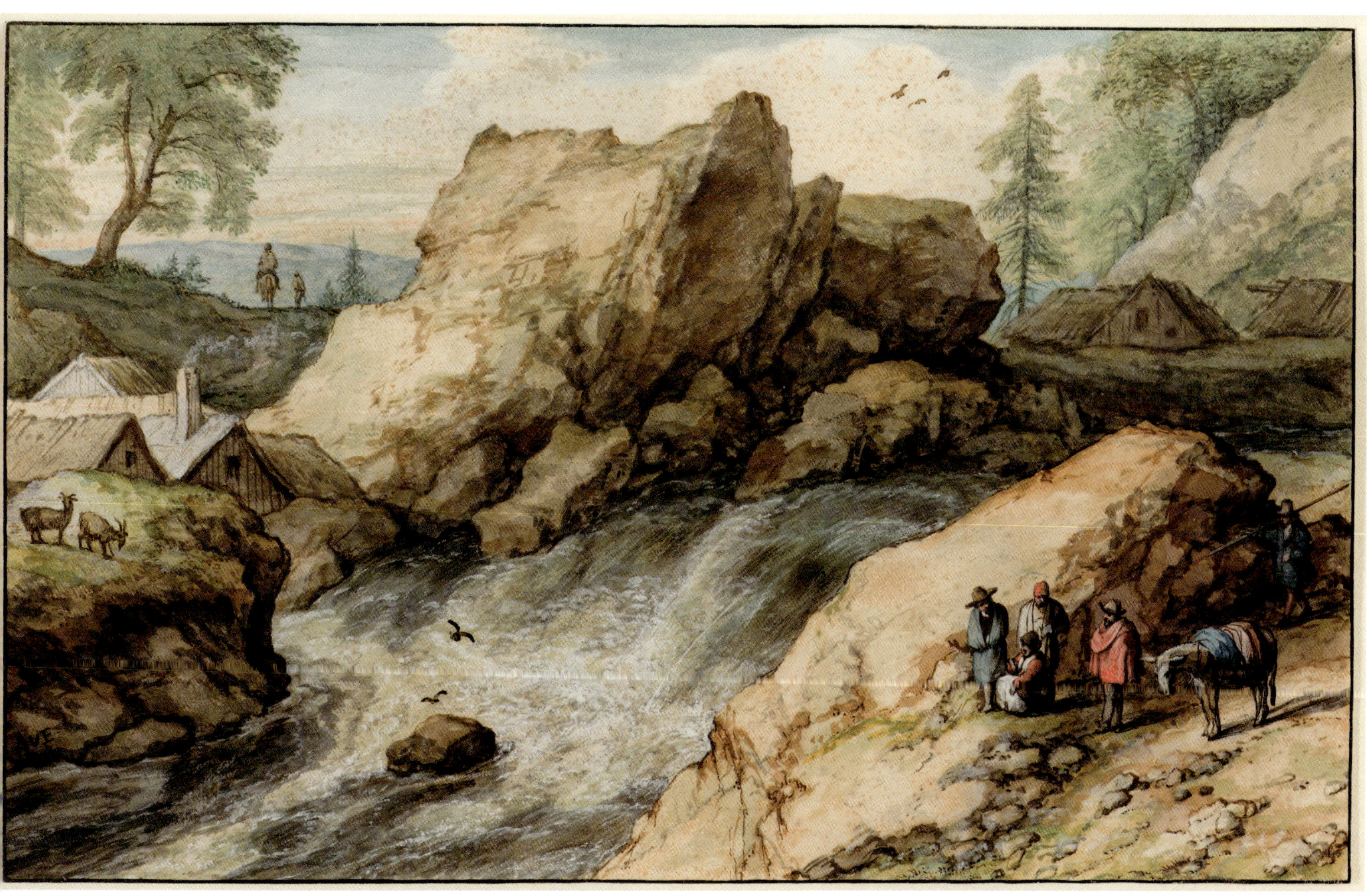

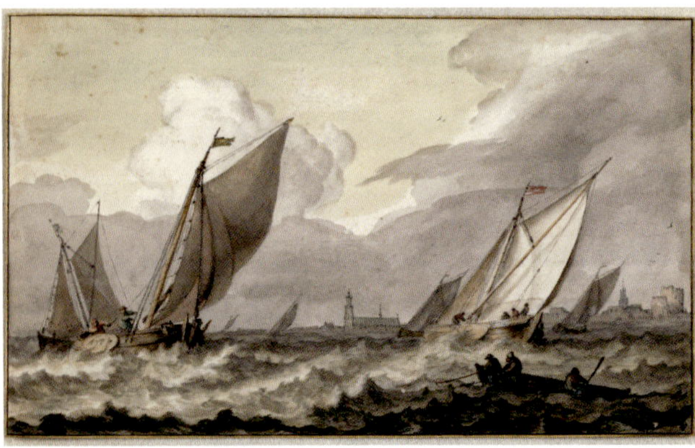

in the waves and in the crevices in the rocks, while the pale coloured clothes of the crew in the lifeboat focus attention on them. There are two more surviving large seascape drawings, with various colours pointing up chiefly grey tones (fig. 112).[30]

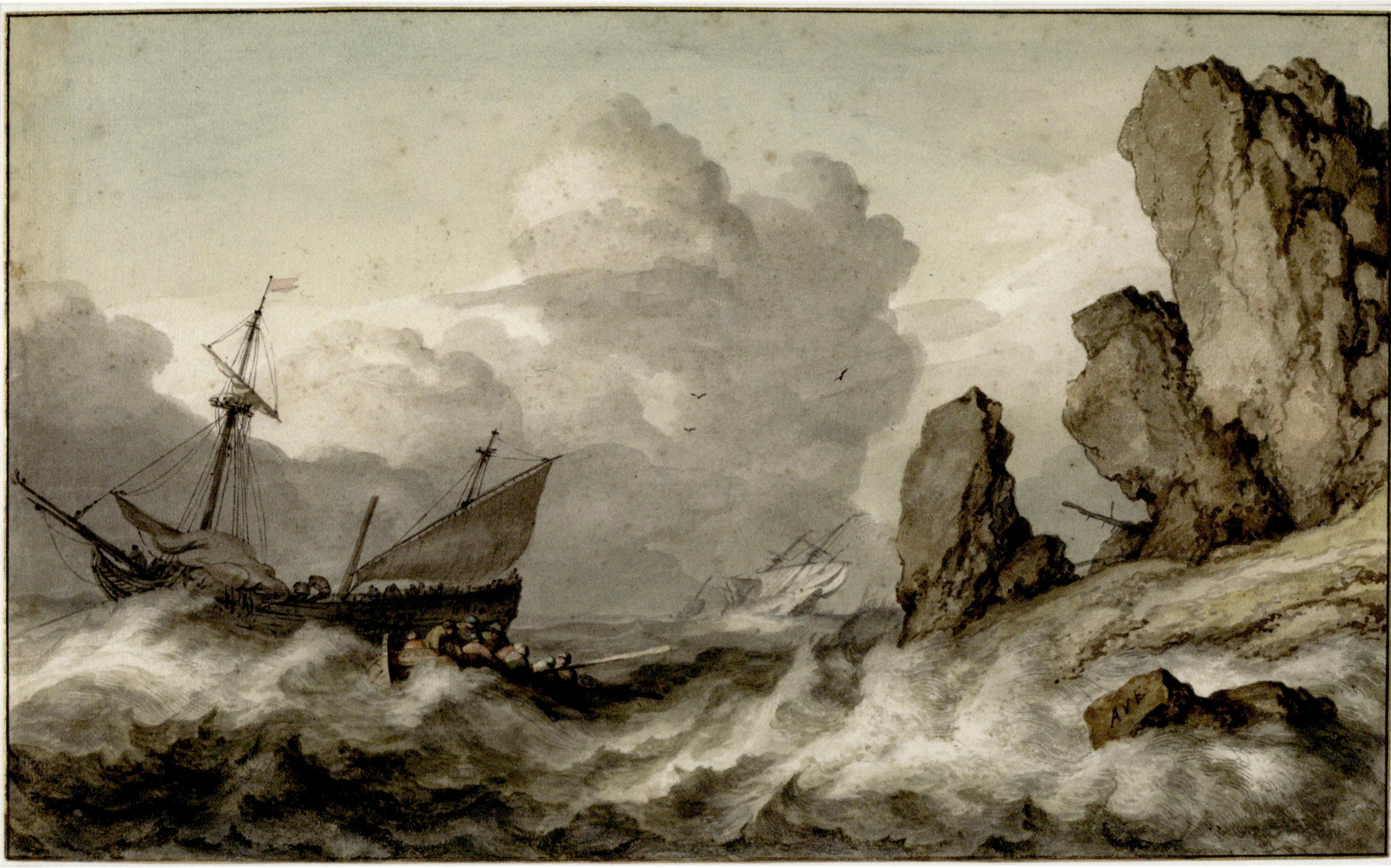

Tower in the Evening (fig. 113) was also done in opaque watercolour. The focus of this drawing is a tower in a town; to the left is a bridge with a shed and to the right a square with trees and buildings. Masts show that this is an inland harbour. The tower cannot be identified, but it is the type that was part of the city walls in Haarlem.[31] Brown and grey shades dominate and suggest that it is evening or late afternoon on a dark winter's day. What brings it to life is the small group of people on the right. The man in the centre holds a lantern that casts a soft light over the bystanders and the porters on either side. The yellowish light and the little mystery of what is happening here add to the atmosphere of the scene.

111
Allart van Everdingen, *Storm at Sea*, brush and grey and brown ink over traces of black chalk, watercolour, 182 x 305 mm, Haarlem, Teylers Museum, inv. no. Q 031 (cat. no. 53)

< 112
Allart van Everdingen, *Sailing Ships on the Coast*, pen and brown ink, brush and grey ink, watercolour, 182 x 306 mm, Chantilly, Musée Condé, inv. no. DE 1073

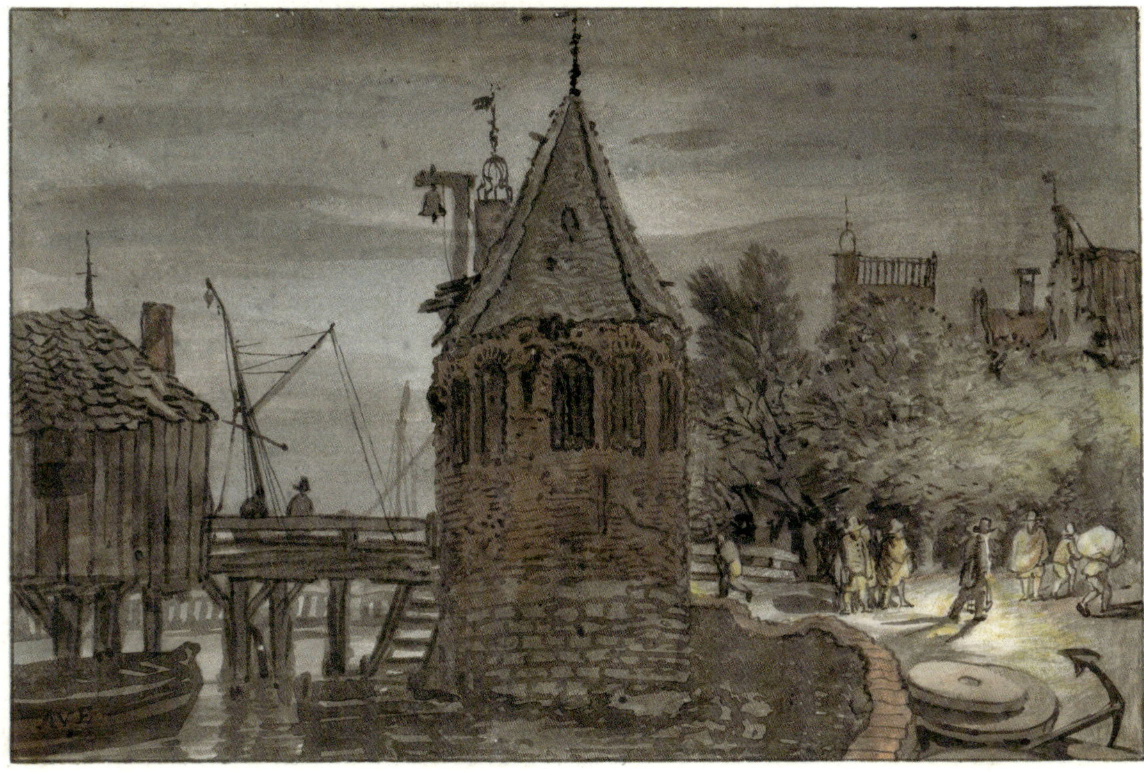

> 113
Allart van Everdingen,
Tower in the Evening,
pen and brush and
black ink, watercolour,
149 x 231 mm, Paris,
Fondation Custodia,
Frits Lugt Collection,
inv. no. 2756 (cat. no. 95)

114
Allart van Everdingen,
Fire in a Town at Night,
pen and brush and
black ink, watercolour,
155 x 232 mm, Staat-
liche Kunstsammlungen
Dresden, Kupferstich-
Kabinett, inv. no. C 1892-8

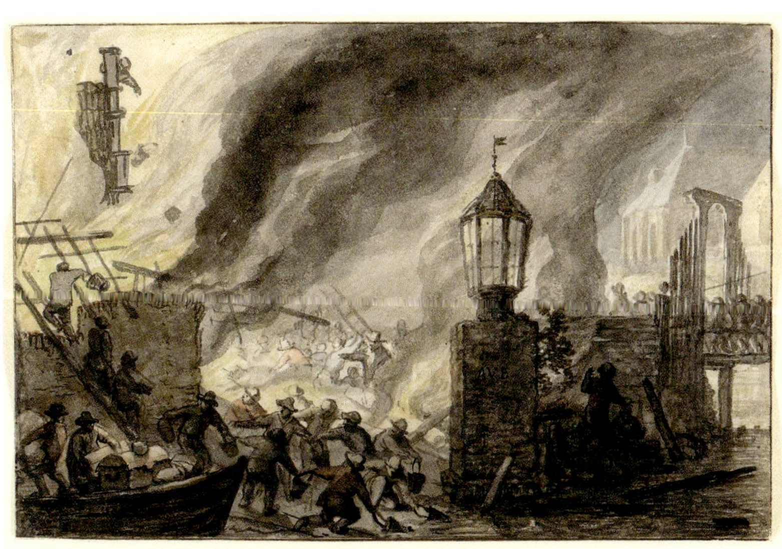

A drawing of a fire in a town (fig. 114) has similar pictorial elements, figures and colours.[32]
A group of men form a human chain in an
attempt to put out a fire with buckets of water,
while valuables are loaded into a boat lower left
and people take to their heels on the right. With
quite loose brushstrokes in black ink and yellow
watercolour, the artist convincingly suggests
flames and smoke, with the wall of a house and
people looming up out of the gloom.

Another large coloured drawing of which
Van Everdingen would have had high hopes
is a winter landscape with sledges and skaters
on a frozen river (fig. 115). The composition is
in the tradition of drawn ice scenes by Hendrick
Avercamp, Jan van Goyen and Pieter de Molijn.
It is full of anecdotal details, such as the man
in the left foreground putting on his skates, the
people chatting by the sledge, the horse eating
out of a nosebag and a group on the right warm-
ing themselves by the tent.

The artist was also able to achieve extraordi-
nary effects simply in shades of brown or grey.
One spectacular example is a seascape in
Vienna (fig. 116), the largest of all the sheets

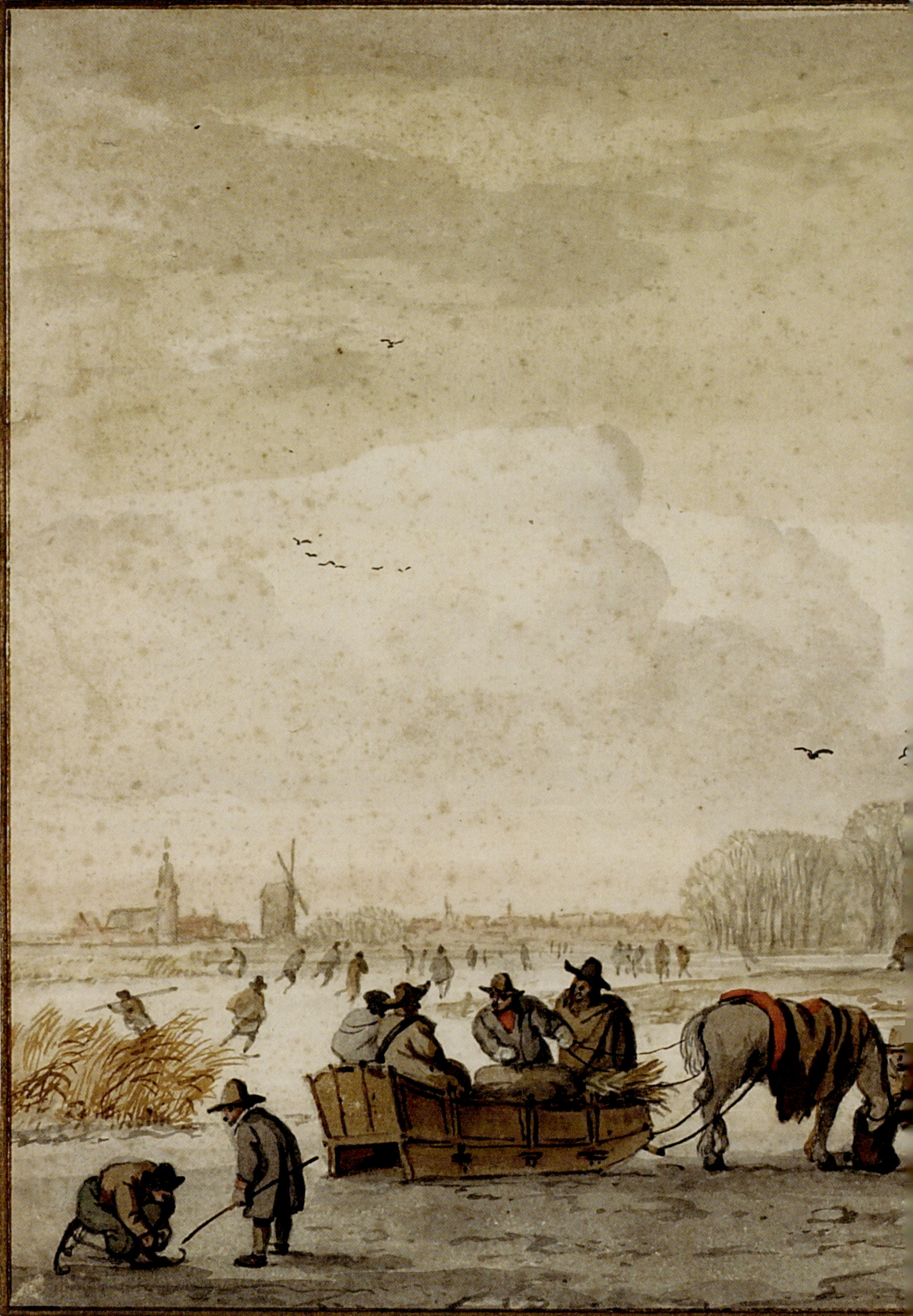

115
Allart van Everdingen,
*Winter Landscape with
Sledges and Skaters*,
brush and grey and
brown ink, watercolour,
180 x 304 mm, Brussels,
Royal Museums of Fine
Arts of Belgium, De Grez
Collection, inv. no.
4060-1282 (cat. no. 47)

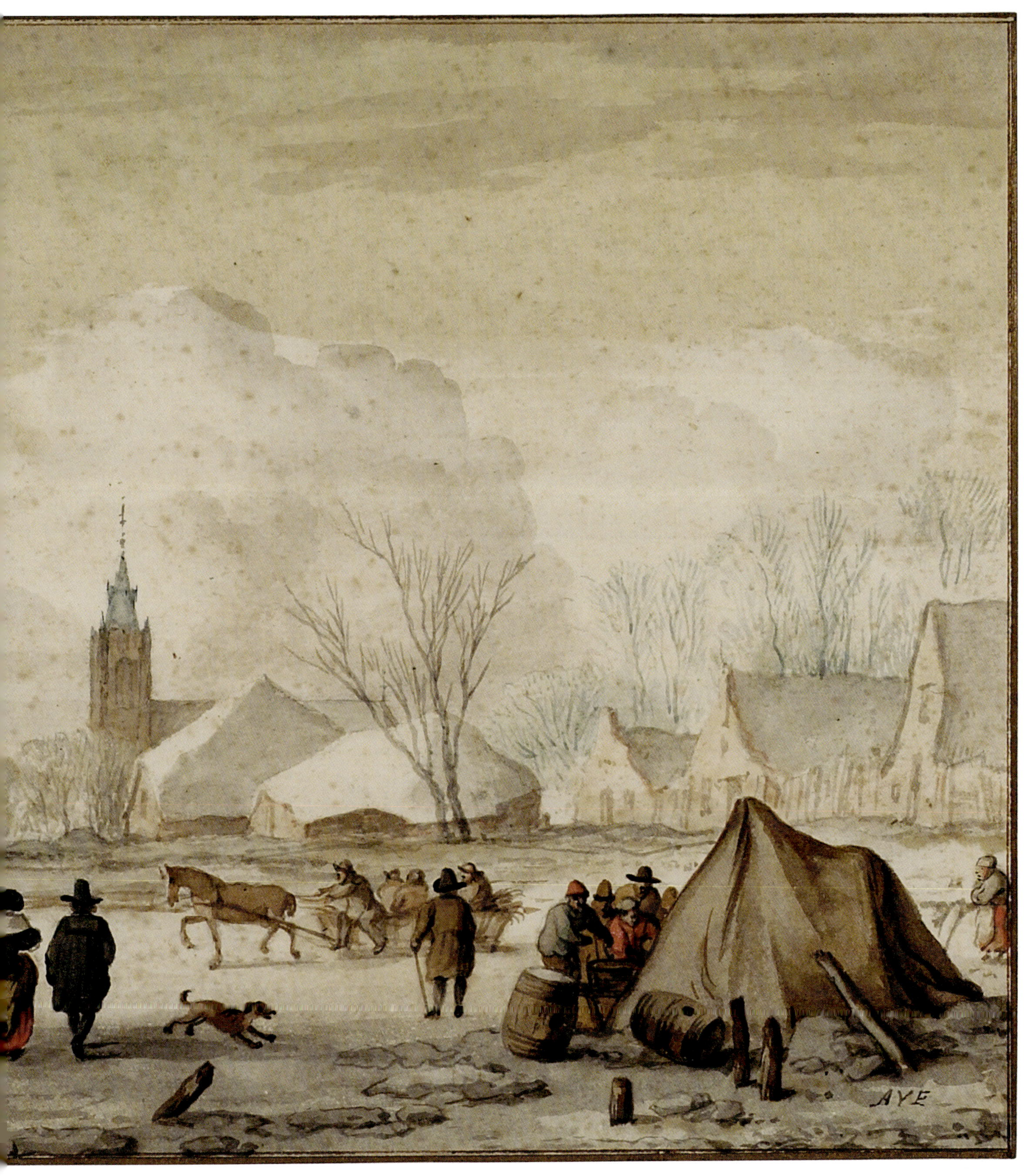

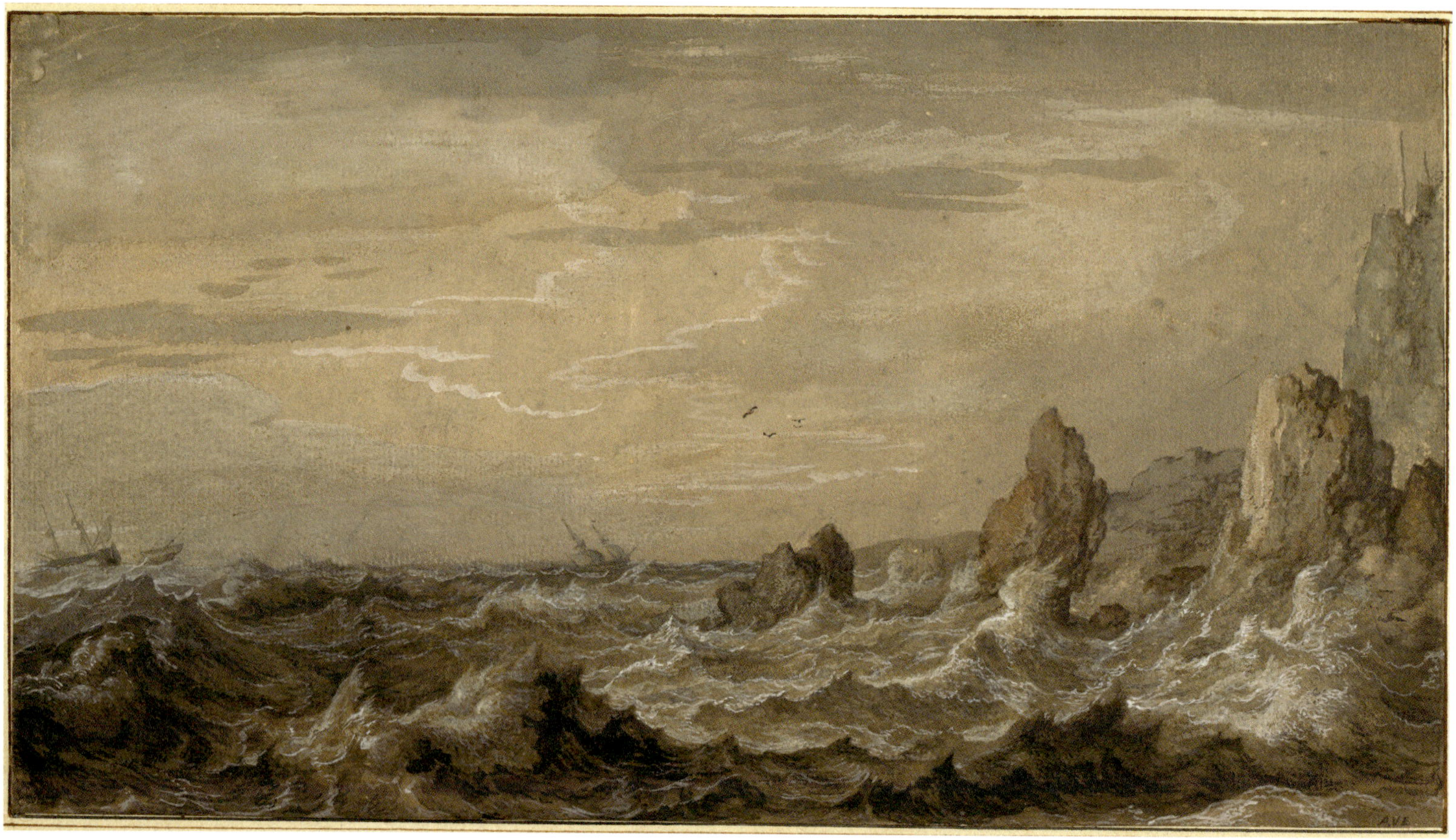

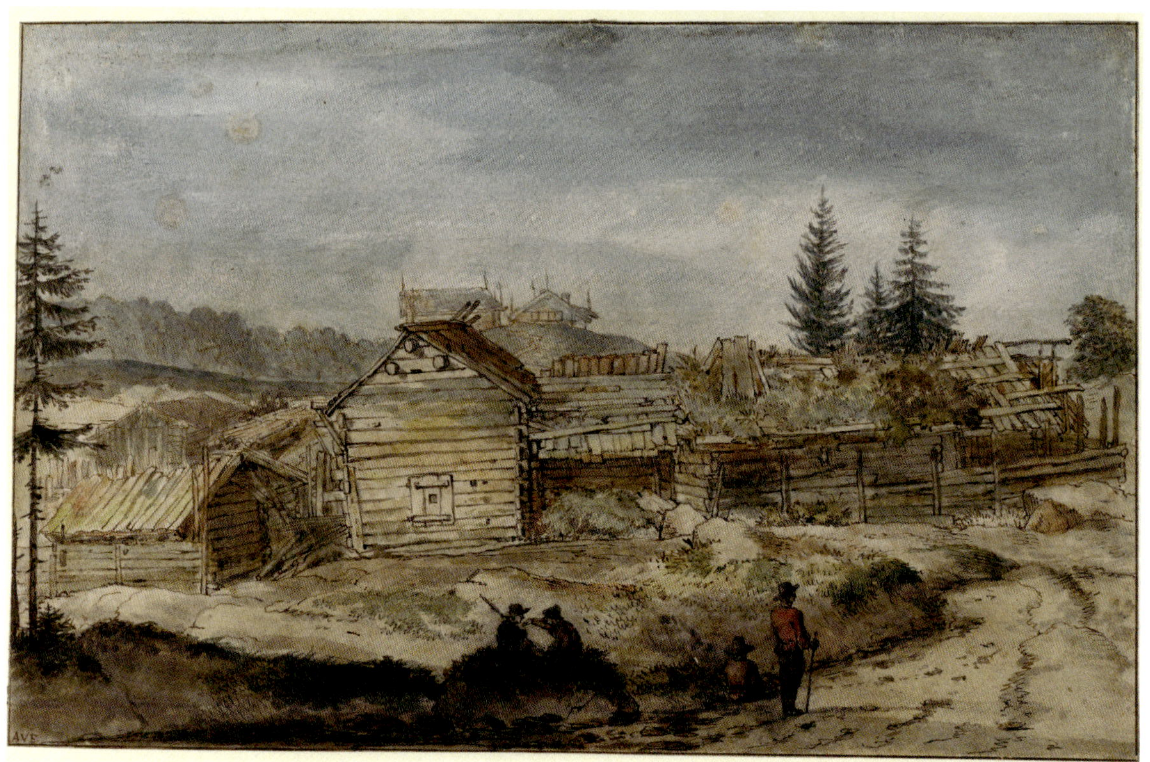

116
Allart van Everdingen,
*Rocky Shore in Stormy
Weather*, brush and
grey and brown ink over
black chalk, grey and
brown wash, heightened
with white, on brown
paper, 225 x 416 mm,
Vienna, The Albertina
Museum, inv. no. 9590
(cat. no. 103)

> 117
Allart van Everdingen,
*Scandinavian Land-
scape with Log Cabins*,
pen and black ink, brush
and grey ink, water-
colour, 193 x 310 mm,
London, The Courtauld
Institute of Art, Witt
Collection, inv. no.
D.1952.RW.2130

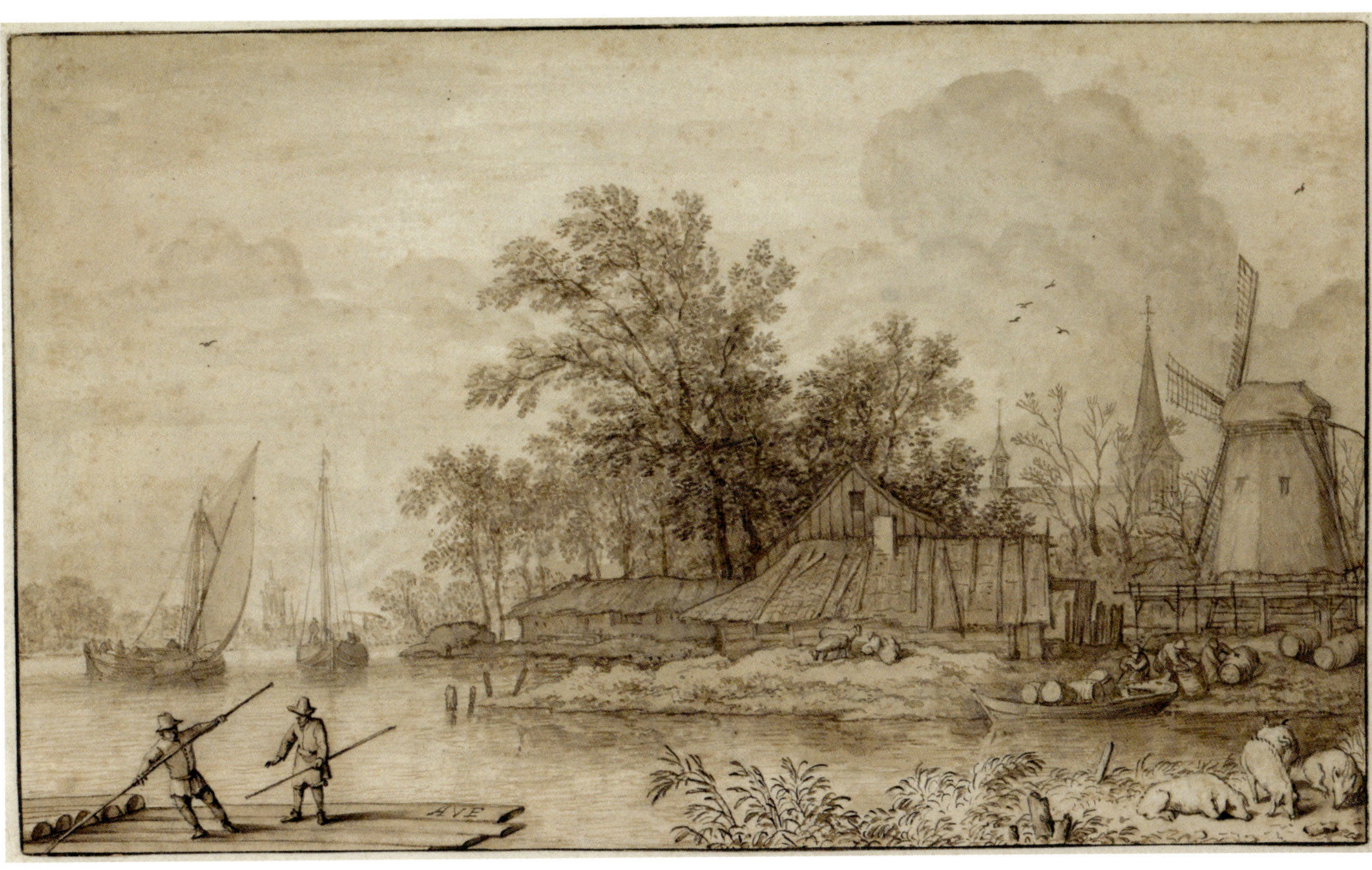

118
Allart van Everdingen, *River View with a Raft and Sailing Barges*, pen and brush and brown ink over black chalk, brown wash, 179 x 302 mm, Paris, Fondation Custodia, Frits Lugt Collection, inv. no. 2648 (cat. no. 98)

in the drawn oeuvre, executed in monochrome hues.[33] In contrast to the marine in Haarlem, (fig. 111), there is virtually no human presence here. In the distance, three ships battle the storm, but the rough seas and the waves crashing on the rocks are the focus. The painterly effect is created by the white body colour applied over the brown and grey to suggest white caps, and the fact that Van Everdingen worked on brown tinted paper, which can be seen in areas of the sky that he left unworked.[34]

In his large coloured and monochrome sheets, Van Everdingen shows himself to be a master draughtsman and master storyteller. They must have been made when the artist's mature style had fully developed—probably after he had settled in Amsterdam in 1652. It was a city where he would have found art lovers who would appreciate these exceptional drawings and where, more to the point, he had a large family to provide for.

People at Work

In his drawings Allart van Everdingen paid a remarkable amount of attention to artisanal and industrial activities and to the places where they happened: small workshops, barns, sheds and wharves.[35] He evidently developed this interest early in his career, for there are a number of drawings of Scandinavian farmhouses, barns and log cabins, surrounded by palings and woodpiles, which show that they captured his imagination even then (fig. 117).[36] His fondness for human industry appears most clearly, however, in his large drawings of Dutch landscapes. In an atmospheric river landscape in pen and brown ink, for example, two men stand on a wooden raft (fig. 118). These raftsmen transport their cargo downstream.[37] In front of the houses and barns beside the windmill, barrels are loaded into a small boat. Two sailing barges move in the background on the left. With the reflections in the water, the composition conveys the feeling of a fine, peaceful day.

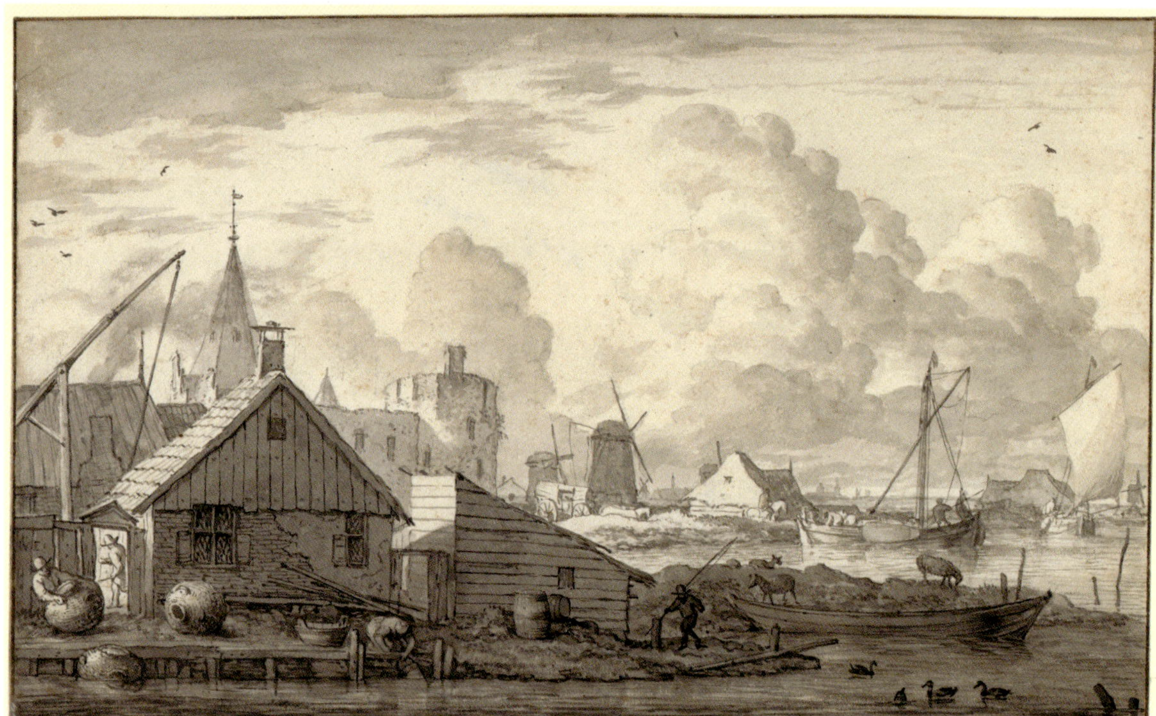

119
Allart van Everdingen, *Activity on the Water*, pen and brush and black ink over black chalk, grey wash, 181 x 300 mm, Staatliche Museen zu Berlin, Kupferstich-kabinett, inv. no. KdZ 12842 (cat. no. 41)

In *Activity on the Water* (fig. 119), we see a few houses and wooden sheds built close to a castle. A man beside a jetty is taking care of *mandbunnen*, large baskets in which fish that have been caught are kept alive (see also fig. 105). A little further along, a woman bends over to fill a bucket with river water. The small build-ing behind them, reached through a gate at the side, may be a smokehouse. Smoking was a popular method of preserving fish, particularly salmon.[38] The tall crane between the buildings was used to load and unload heavy goods. In the background on the right, small cargo vessels ply along the river bank, which is lined with farmhouses and windmills. In short, Van Everdingen has pictured a small seventeenth-century industrial zone in a rural setting, bust-ling with human activity and transport by water.

The large drawing of a group of men caulking a ship in the dark (fig. 120) is intriguing. A rela-tively small inland waterways vessel, coaster or fishing boat has been careened, in other words turned on its side, so the underside of the hull is above water. It was then relatively easy to make it watertight using hemp and tar—oakum— from a floating pontoon. Two men stoke a fire to heat the tar used to pack the joints of the

ship's skin. The sloping bank on the right tells us that the scene is set in a shipyard, vessels were launched or pulled out of the water on a slip like this. The wooden piles to the left of the large three-master provide some shelter so that the shipbuilding and repair work could be done out of the wind. An unusual drawing, this, in the level of detail and the fact that the evening or night scene is lit by the fire under

120
Allart van Everdingen, *Careening a Ship at Night*, pen and brush and black ink over black chalk, grey and brown wash, 181 x 288 mm, Staatliche Museen zu Berlin, Kupferstich-kabinett, inv. no. KdZ 1309 (cat. no. 42)

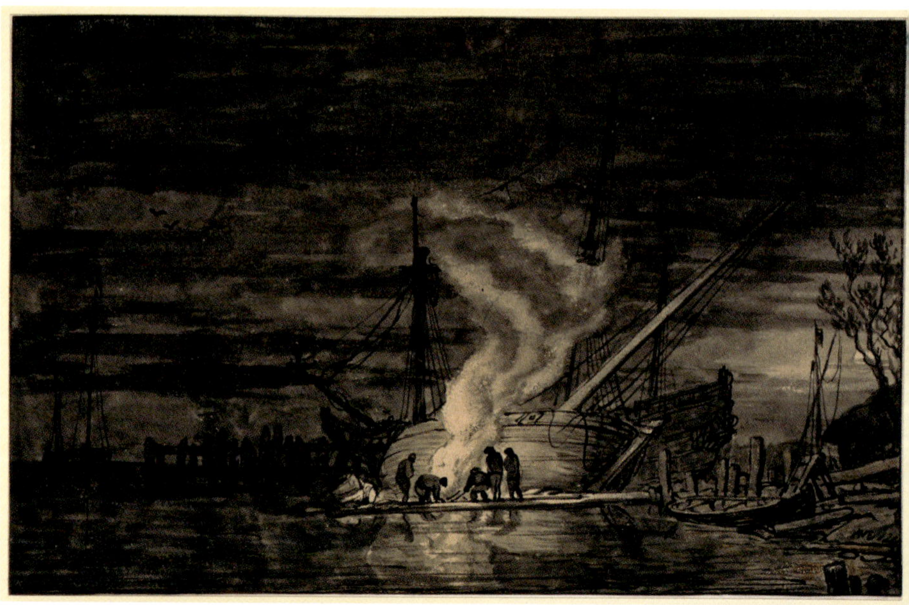

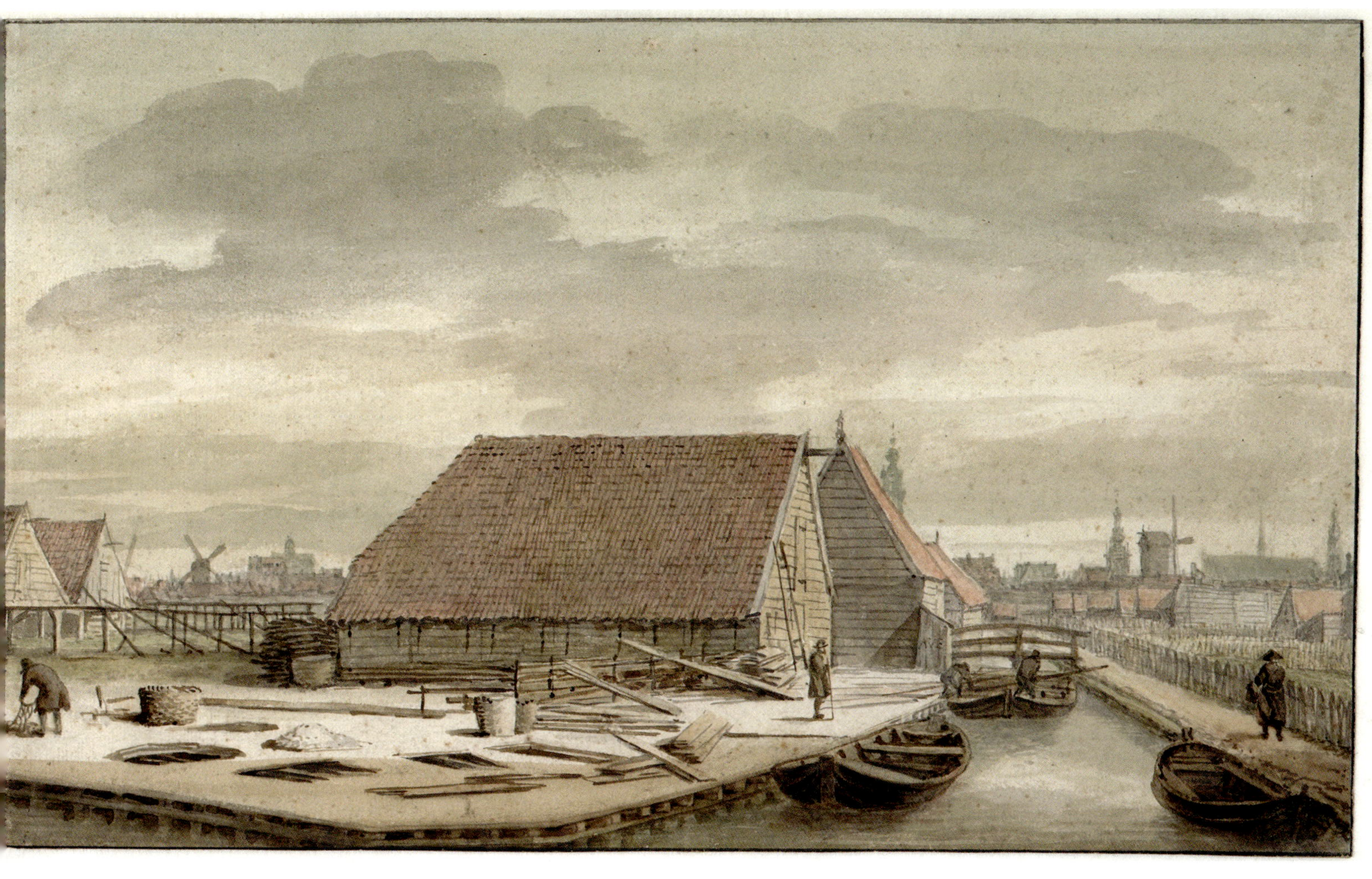

Allart van Everdingen, *Glue Factory on Lange Bleekerspad in Amsterdam*, brush and watercolour over traces of black chalk, 169 x 284 mm, Amsterdam City Archives, accession no. 10055, inv. no. 16 (cat. no. 36)

the tar barrel and the moon behind the tree on the right. The flames create a fine reflection of the men and the hull in the water, set down with swift brushstrokes in diluted ink.[39]

The drawing Van Everdingen made of an Amsterdam glue factory (fig. 121) is exceptional in its subject and detail. It was located on the west side of the city, outside the walls, on Lange Bleekerspad. Small-scale industrial processes that caused appalling smells and water pollution, like glue factories, were located in this rural area.[40] Van Everdingen gave a meticulous picture of the works against the backdrop of the Amsterdam skyline. The Noorderkerk (Northern Church) can be seen on the left, the Westertoren (tower of the Western Church)

appears behind the roof of the shed and on the right—the long, straight outline beside the windmill—the Nieuwe Kerk (New Church) and the Town Hall. The composition was certainly based on observations made on the spot. The sheets of glue were dried in the large shed in the middle and on the racks behind it.[41] In the foreground of the quay are the lime pits used to treat the hides that were one of the raw materials of glue; the ground on the site is white with lime. The planks were used to keep animal waste, another important raw material, under water. It is very likely that this drawing was commissioned by the owner of the glue factory.[42] That was almost certainly Abraham van Beelkamp, who died in 1663, or his widow Elisabeth Croegers, who sold

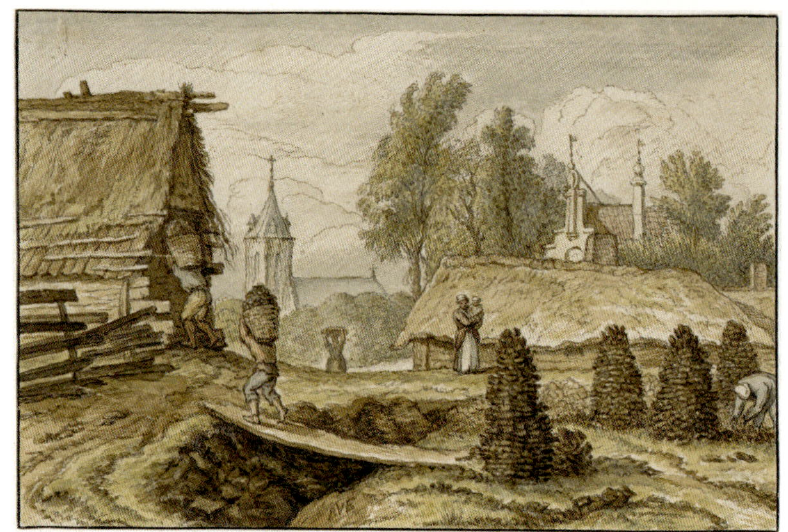

122
Allart van Everdingen,
*Landscape with Peat
Carriers*, pen and
brown ink, brush and
grey ink, watercolour,
155 x 232 mm, London,
The British Museum,
inv. no. 1836.8.11.173

the business in 1669. The drawing must have been made before 1665, since the Amsterdam Town Hall in the background is lacking the great dome that was built between 1662 and 1665.

Van Everdingen was not the only seventeenth-century artist with an eye for early industrial architecture and people at work. Jan van Goyen, for instance, depicted limekilns and breweries in his paintings and drawings.[43] Claes Jansz Visscher (c. 1587-1652) had already pictured peat-cutting around 1608, as had Adriaen van de Venne (1589-1662) in 1626, before Allart did (fig. 122).[44] Caulking a careened ship also appears in drawings and prints by Hendrick Avercamp (in the background of fig. 105), Reinier Zeeman (1623/1624-1664) and Herman Saftleven (c. 1609-1685).[45] Van Everdingen's detailed approach and the

frequency with which he tackled such subjects is unusual, however, and his large drawings of everyday occupations must have been very popular with collectors.

Identifiable Places

Other drawings besides the *Glue Factory* (fig. 121) tell us that Van Everdingen carried around a sketchbook or drawing paper in his own surroundings, as he had in Norway. The *View of Alkmaar from the Zeglis* (fig. 123) proves that he made sketches in the open air just outside his birthplace, Alkmaar. He drew the town from the southeast, with the Grote Sint-Laurenskerk (Great St Lawrence's Church) as the central landmark and the tall tower of the Waag (Weigh House) on the right. The skyline of Allart's later home town, Haarlem, appears in the back-

< 123
Allart van Everdingen,
*View of Alkmaar from
the Zeglis*, pen and
grey ink, watercolour,
heightened with white,
112 x 178 mm, Vienna,
The Albertina Museum,
inv. no. 9582
(cat. no. 102)

124
Allart van Everdingen,
*View of Haarlem from
the North*, pen and
brush and brown and
grey ink over black
chalk, brown and grey
wash, 156 x 271 mm,
Hamburger Kunsthalle,
inv. no. 21908
(cat. no. 57)

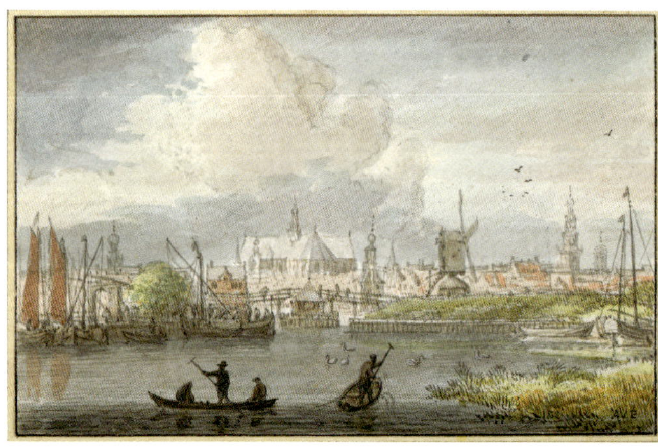

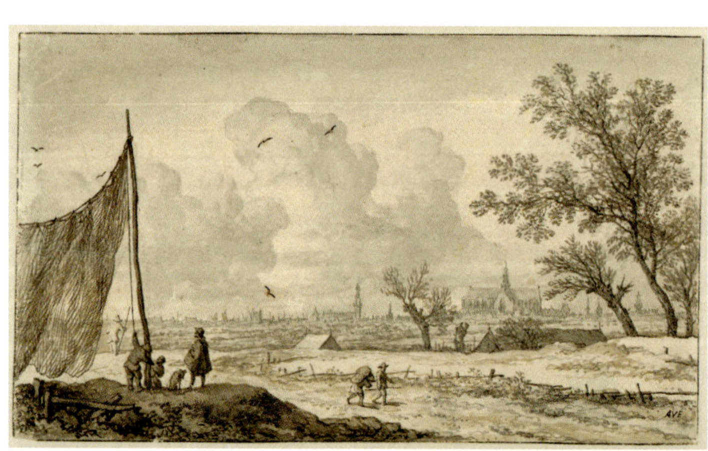

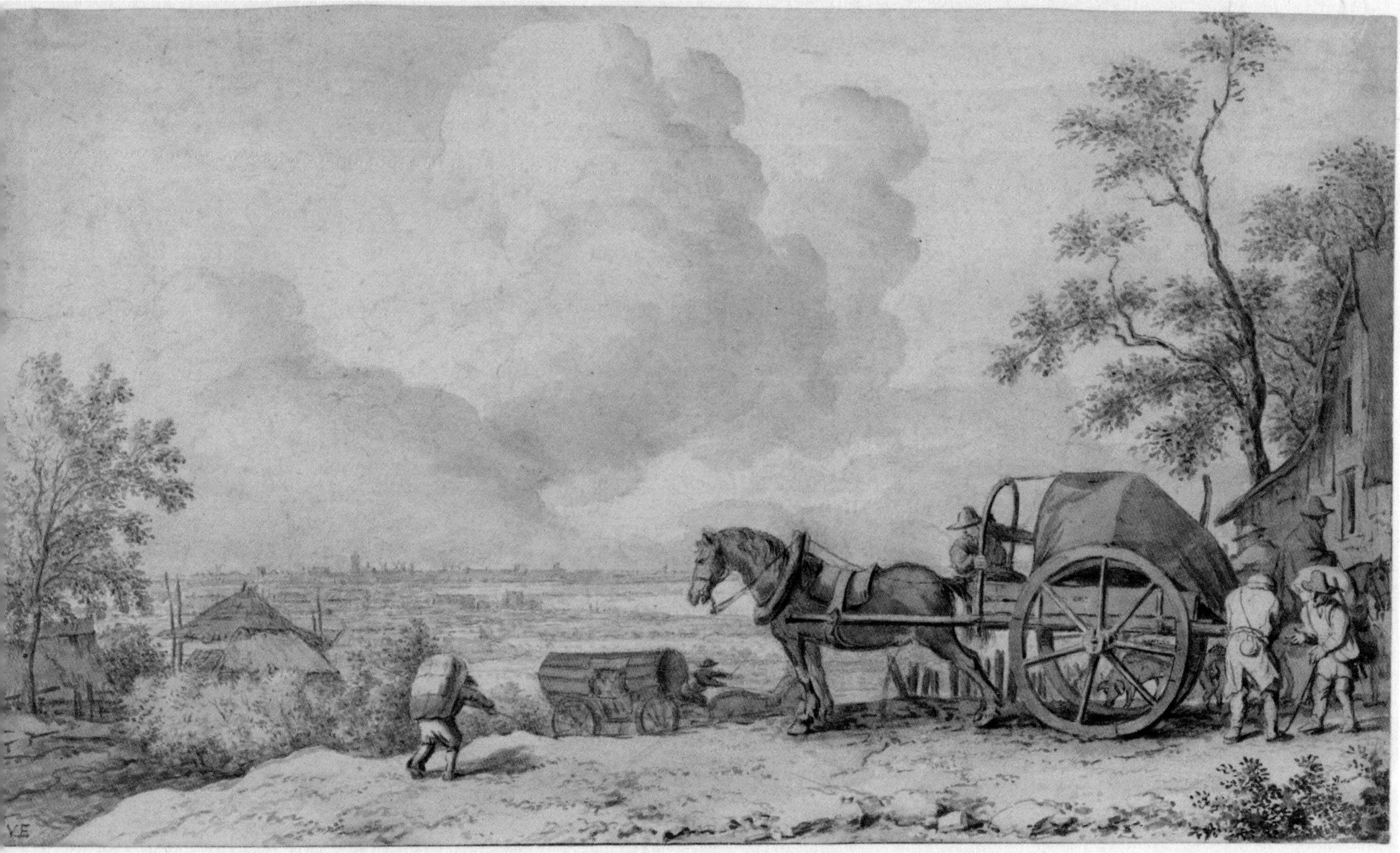

125
Allart van Everdingen,
Landscape with a Cart,
pen and black and grey
ink over black chalk,
grey wash, 175 x 302
mm, Haarlem, Teylers
Museum, inv. no.
KT 2016 031 (cat. no. 55)

v 126
Allart van Everdingen, *Sailing Ship
in a Strong Wind near a Harbour*,
pen and brush and brown ink over
traces of black chalk, brown wash,
125 x 191 mm, Brussels, Royal
Museums of Fine Arts of Belgium,
De Grez Collection, inv. no.
4060-1265 (cat. no. 48)

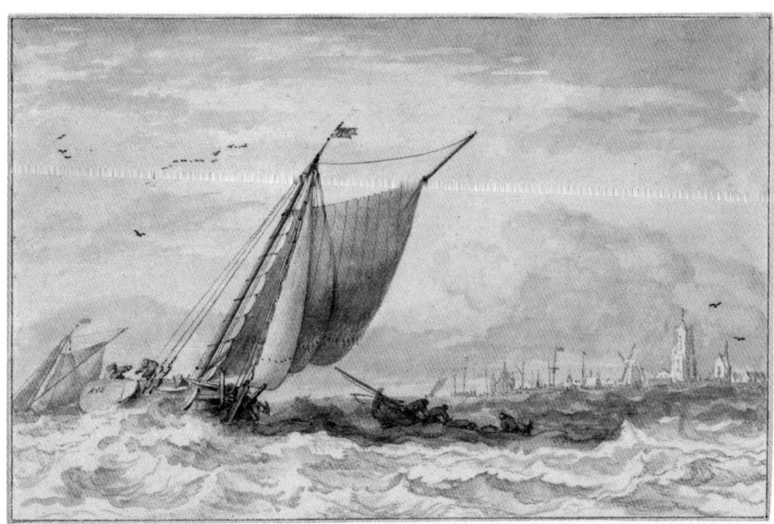

ground of several drawings; one such is a landscape in brown and grey ink with bird-catchers
setting up a net (fig. 124).[46] The town is shown
from the north; the silhouette of the Sint-Bavo-
kerk (St Bavo's Church) is in the centre, with
the spire of the Bakenesserkerk (Bakenesser
Church) to its left. Van Everdingen must have
sat at a slightly elevated vantage point to draw
this view of the town, as the initial composition
for this sheet or as a preparatory sketch for it.

As he did in his paintings, the artist frequently
pictured imaginary towns and villages in his
drawings. The town in the background of a very
delicate scene of a horse and cart has been
erroneously identified as Haarlem (fig. 125),
but this is not the unmistakable skyline with
St Bavo's.[47] It has been cautiously suggested
that a town on the water in a drawing in Brussels
(fig. 126) might be Gorinchem, while an eighteenth-century sale catalogue described it as
a view of the Zuiderzee.[48] Neither suggestion
can be substantiated.

Drawing in the Ardennes

In the mid-sixteen-fifties Allart van Everdingen left the Republic again, this time on a visit to the Ardennes. Although there are no records of this trip in the archives, it can be deduced from some drawings and etchings of Spa and its surroundings and the painting of the nearby Montjardin Castle (fig. 90) that the artist did go to the south. Three preliminary studies for a set of four etchings of springs in and near Spa, which were already famed for their healing effects in the seventeenth century (figs. 204 and 206-208), have survived as oils on paper (figs. 127, 210 and 211).[49] They were most likely based on sketches made on the spot. There is also a second drawing of *The Spring at Sauvenière near Spa* done with a brush and brown ink and water-colour (fig. 212).[50] We should probably regard this as a second preliminary study, although it is also possible that Van Everdingen made this coloured sheet to sell as a work in its own right.

There is no further hard evidence of a trip to the Ardennes. A drawing of Montjardin Castle, which has been regarded as a preliminary study for the painting, was most probably drawn *after* the painted composition and is therefore not a sketch from life.[51] And there is a coloured drawing of a fascinating rock formation (fig. 128), with the inscription 'Capelleken by Beaumont' ('little chapel near Beaumont') on the back in a seventeenth-century hand, but whether this is actually Beaumont is arguable.[52] The building cannot be identified and Beaumont is almost a hundred miles from Spa. Doubts can also be raised about other drawings thought to have been done in the Ardennes or connected with the trip.[53] Yet again, we see how little we know about Van Everdingen's life and the circumstances in which landscapes like these were drawn.

Drawings the Size of a Playing Card

Van Everdingen had another specialism, too; he made small landscape drawings in pen and brown ink that measured around fifty by eighty-five millimetres. More than fifty of these miniature drawings have survived.[54] Six little drawings in Hamburg are typical of this group (figs. 129-134): they are Dutch river and shore views with the usual narrative details, such as peasants on a dyke in a river landscape and fishermen in and on the water. In two seashore views, pinks lie on the beach at ebb tide. In one drawing there is a triangular palisade—a beacon—that served as a navigational aid for shipping.[55] Little drawings like these were sometimes called 'caerteblaetjes' or 'kaarteblaadjes', like Van Everdingen's brunailles of the same size, in other words drawings the size of a playing card.[56]

Seventeenth-century miniature landscape drawings are relatively rare, although small landscape prints were marketed.[57] Van Everdingen may, for instance, have been familiar with the twenty-three etched imaginary landscapes by Herman van Swanevelt (c. 1603-1655), which were sold as a set, with a title page (fig. 165).[58] The small drawn landscapes may also have been sold as sets. The collector

< 127
Allart van Everdingen, *The Spring at Sauvenière near Spa*, c. 1655, pen and brush and brown ink, light and dark grey oil paint, on reddish-brown prepared paper, 128 x 170 mm, Hamburger Kunsthalle, inv. no. 21906 (cat. no. 64)

128
Allart van Everdingen, *Landscape with a Rock (Beaumont?)*, pen and brush in brown ink over traces of black chalk, green and pink water-colour, 95 x 159 mm, Beaux-Arts de Paris, inv. no. Mas. 1635

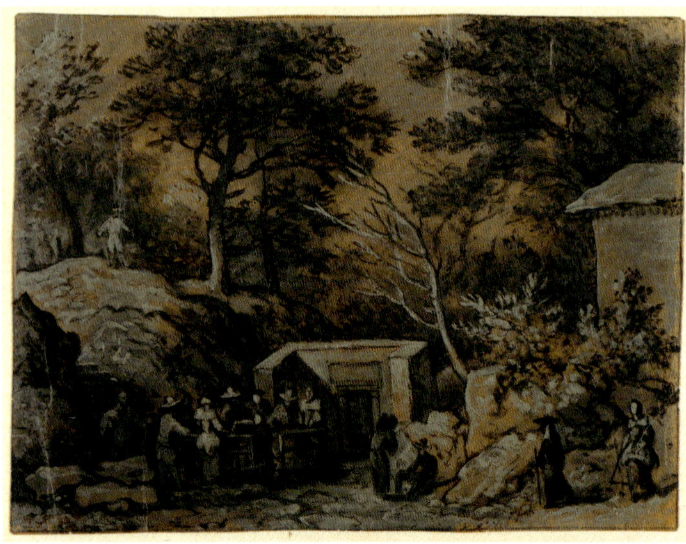

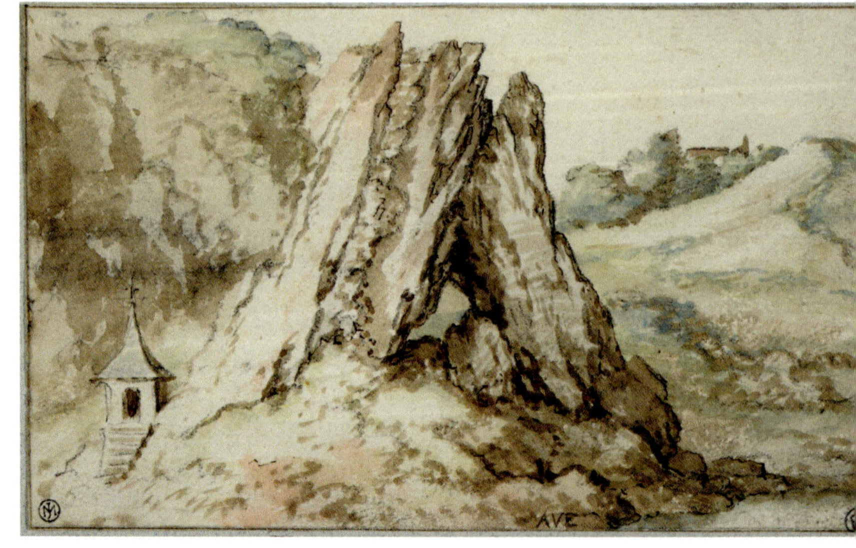

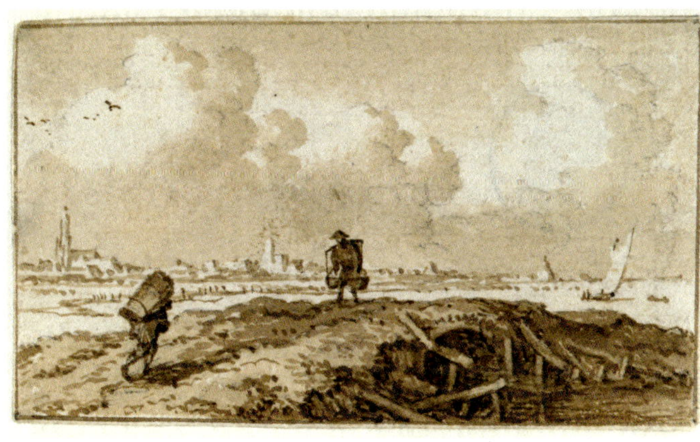

129
Allart van Everdingen, *River Landscape with Two Porters*, pen and brown ink over traces of graphite, brown wash, 48 x 85 mm, Hamburger Kunsthalle, inv. no. 21891 (cat. no. 61)

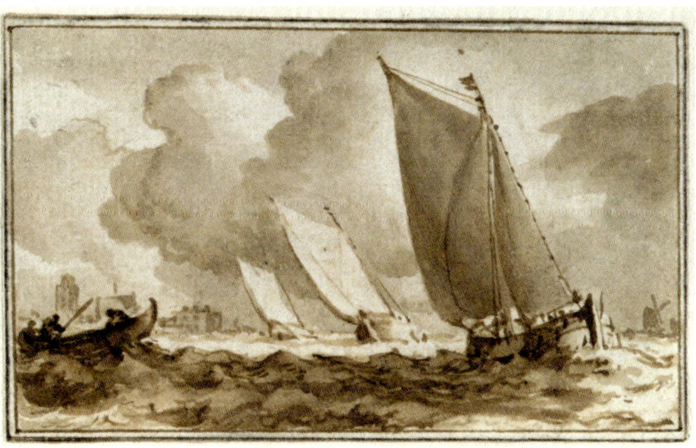

130
Allart van Everdingen, *Three Sailing Ships on Open Water*, pen and brown ink over traces of graphite, brown wash, 51 x 86 mm, Hamburger Kunsthalle, inv. no. 21893 (cat. no. 58)

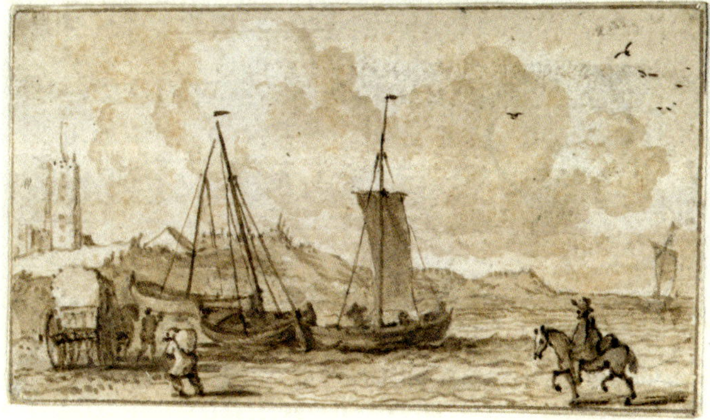

131
Allart van Everdingen, *Shore with Sailing Ships and a Horseman*, pen and brown ink over traces of graphite, brown wash, 48 x 84 mm, Hamburger Kunsthalle, inv. no. 21892 (cat. no. 59)

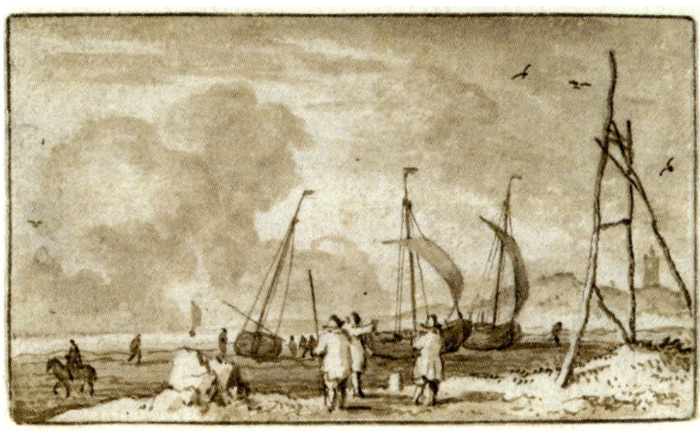

132
Allart van Everdingen, *Shore with a Beacon*, pen and brown ink over traces of graphite, brown wash, 48 x 84 mm, Hamburger Kunsthalle, inv. no. 21896 (cat. no. 60)

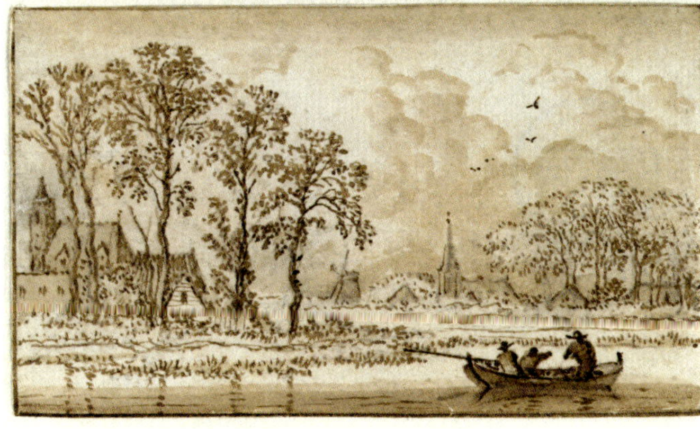

133
Allart van Everdingen, *River Landscape with a Rowing Boat*, pen and brown ink over traces of graphite, brown wash, 48 x 84 mm, Hamburger Kunsthalle, inv. no. 21894 (cat. no. 62)

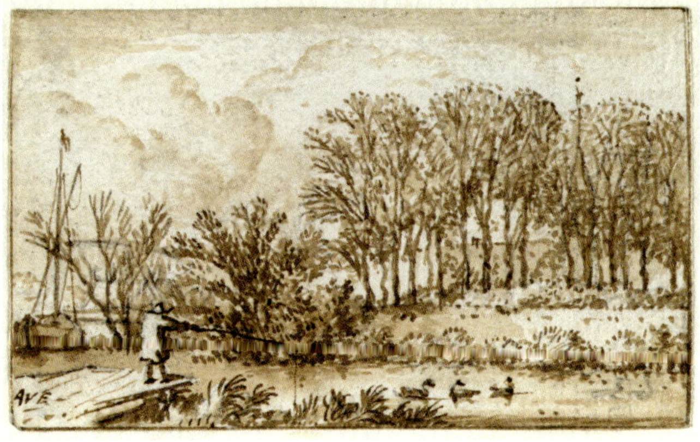

134
Allart van Everdingen, *Landscape with a Fisherman*, pen and brown ink over traces of graphite, brown wash, 49 x 83 mm, Hamburger Kunsthalle, inv. no. 21895 (cat. no. 63)

Sybrand I Feitama (1620-1701) in any event owned twelve 'small landscapes or water views drawn on cards with soot' by Van Everdingen.[59] Descriptions in eighteenth- and nineteenth-century sale catalogues show that these were frequently sold as pairs.[60] The two seashore views in Hamburg (figs. 131 and 132), for example, were listed under the same number at the sale of the collection of the Amsterdam collector Cornelis Ploos van Amstel (1726-1798) in 1800.[61]

The Months of the Year

As well as individual drawings, Van Everdingen made sets of four or twelve sheets of the four elements, the four seasons and the twelve months of the year. This last subject must have sold particularly well, for no fewer than seven complete sets have survived.[62] Van Everdingen may have made sets of the months on commission, for a large set like this was time-consuming and required a considerable outlay on materials.

There is a long tradition of representations of the months of the year going back to medieval cathedral sculptures and late medieval miniatures in books of hours.[63] The subject remained popular in the sixteenth and seventeenth centuries, particularly in printmaking.[64] Sets of drawings were an exclusive alternative to prints. Other artists, such as Esaias van de Velde and Pieter de Molijn, had preceded Van Everdingen with drawn sets.[65] Of the seven surviving complete sets, the drawings in Brussels are the largest (fig. 135). *January* shows men unloading a ship at a town quay and carrying barrels across the ice on a sledge. In *February* a barge ploughs through a frozen river to break the ice, watched by three men and a child on a sled who will soon have to get out of the way. In the sheets for *March* and *April*, Van Everdingen pictured typical spring jobs: pruning trees and moving the livestock. In *May* wealthy people in high spirits go boating, in *June* the farmers shear their sheep and in *July* the hay is brought in.

135

Allart van Everdingen, *The Twelve Months of the Year*, set of twelve drawings, brush and grey ink over graphite, grey wash, each approx. 116 x 180 mm, Brussels, Royal Museums of Fine Arts of Belgium, De Grez Collection, inv. nos. 4060-1270 to 4060-1281 (cat. no. 49)

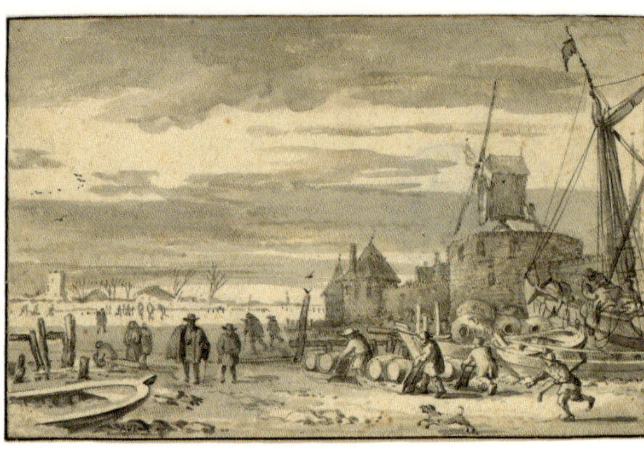

January

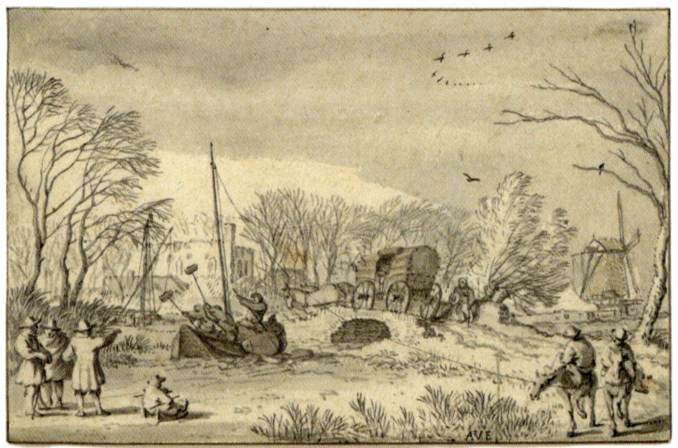

February

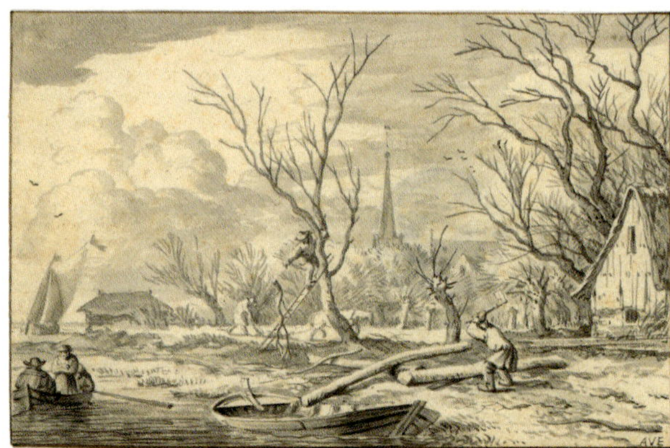

March

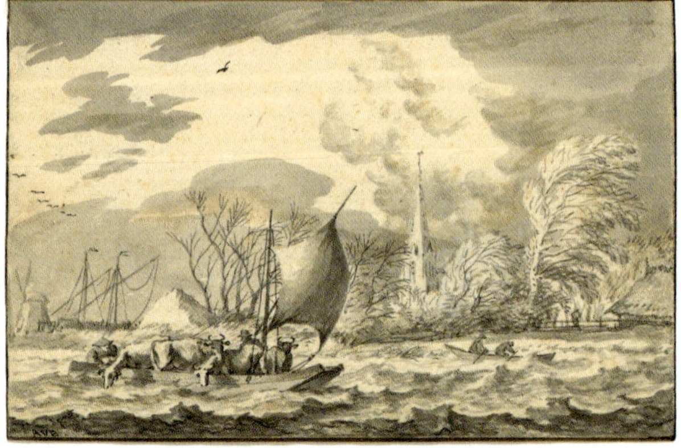

April

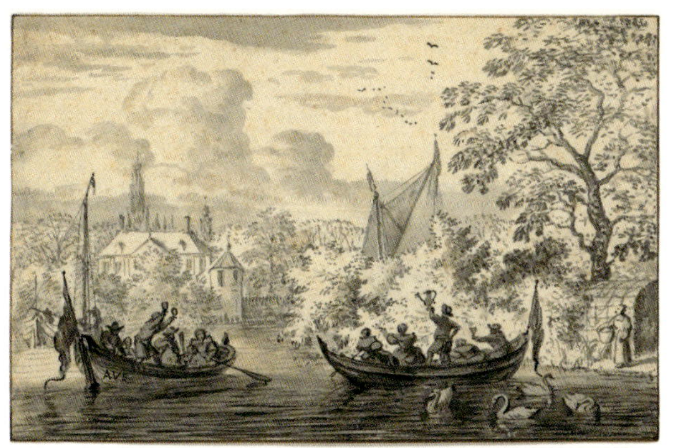

May

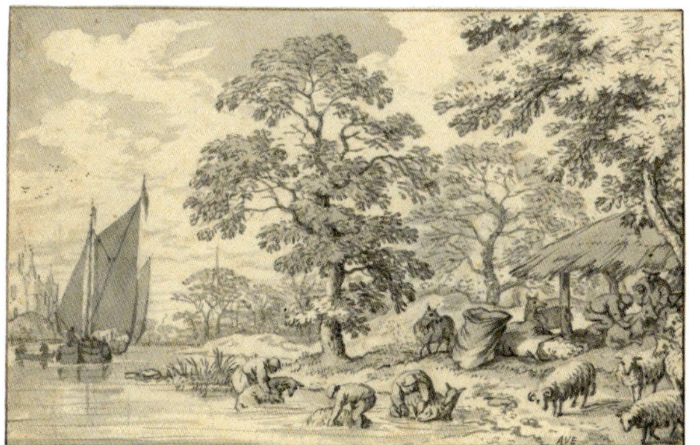

June

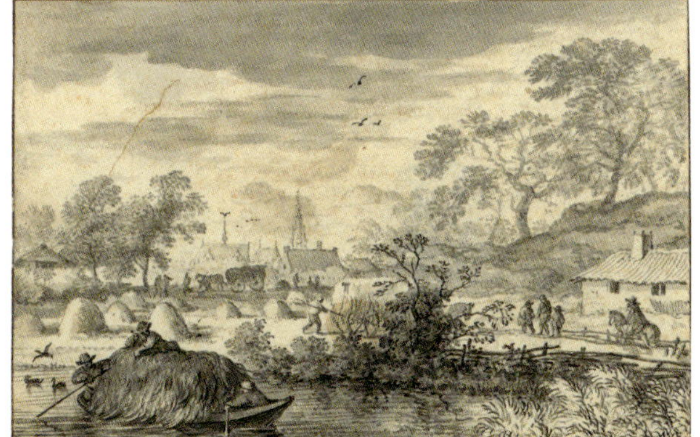

July

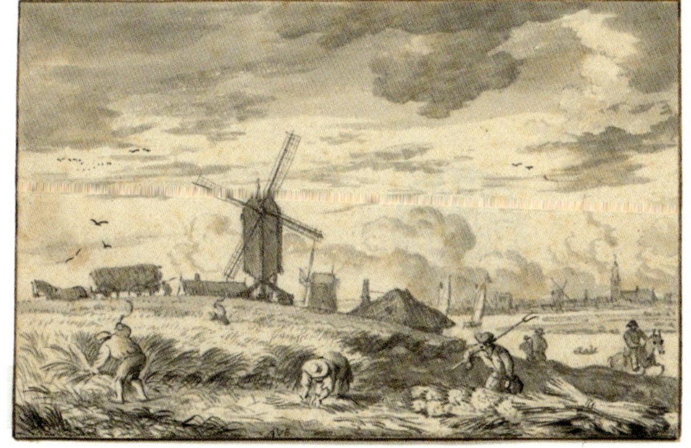

August

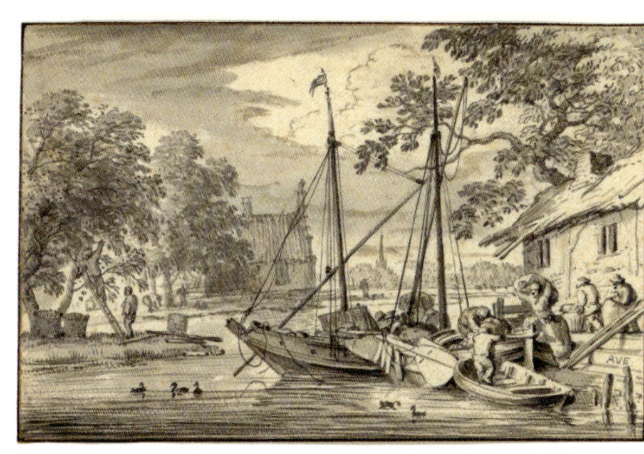

September

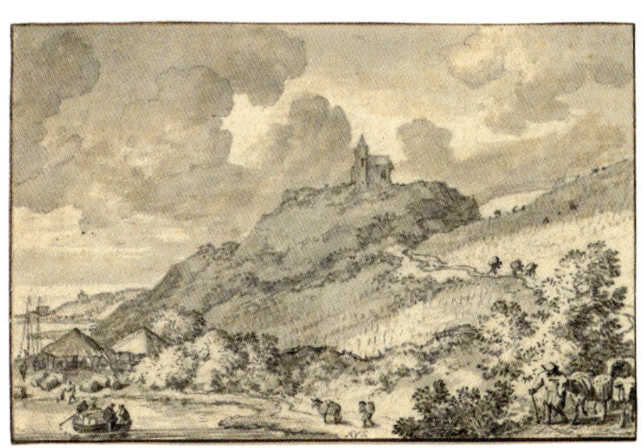

October

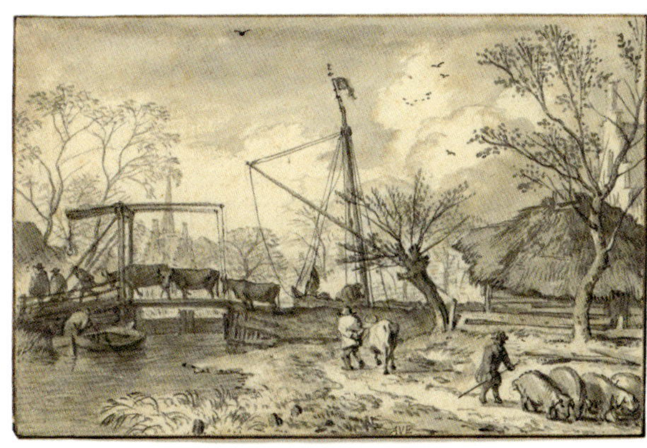

November

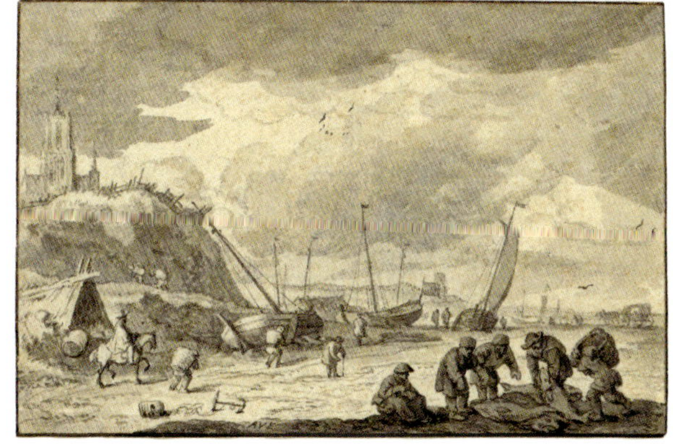

December

In late summer, *August* and *September*, the grain and fruit are harvested. In *October* it is grape-picking time and casks of wine are transported by water in a French or German hilly landscape—there was no grape harvest in the Republic. In *November* the animals are brought back in from the fields, and in *December* fishermen on the beach haul in their catch. These themes, with variations, recur in Allart's sets of the twelve months, and must have given their owners great pleasure with their abundance of pictorial motifs.

The Earliest Collectors and Later Appreciation

Although there is little to go on, it is safe to assume that Allart van Everdingen's drawings were bought by wealthy citizens of Amsterdam and beyond. In the seventeenth-century Republic, they were the leading purchasers of paintings, and the greatest lovers of drawings and prints, which they kept in albums or art books. There are some indications that it was not unusual to buy directly from artists. A drawing by Hendrick Avercamp, for instance, has an inscription to the effect that the owner got it from the artist in 1613 and a sheet attributed to Roelandt Savery has a note saying that it had been purchased in the artist's house in Utrecht in 1641.[66] This route seems all the more likely in Van Everdingen's case because he was an art dealer.[67]

There are a few seventeenth-century collectors whom we know owned drawings by Allart van Everdingen. One is the Amsterdam merchant and marine and landscape painter Jan van de Cappelle (1626-1679), who brought together one of the earliest collections of drawings we know of. He had more than seven thousand sheets, including a portfolio with fifty-two drawings by Allart.[68] Van de Cappelle lived near Van Everdingen, was about the same age and, like him, painted marines; they must certainly have known one another.[69] The Amsterdam silk dyer and collector Constantijn Sennepart (1625-1703) also had drawings by the artist: *Glue Factory* (fig. 121), a coloured village scene with a ruin and a set of the twelve months.[70] Like Van de Cappelle, he was a contemporary of Van Everdingen's and would have bought from him directly, although he probably acquired the *Glue Factory* from a previous owner. The collector Sybrand I Feitama also collected drawings by Van Everdingen, including three complete sets of the twelve months. He bought two of them in 1694 and 1695, in other words long after Allart's death.[71] As far as we know, the collector with the largest number of drawings by Allart van Everdingen was the Amsterdam art dealer Jan Pietersz Zomer (1641-1724). Around 1720, he drew up an inventory of his 'art on paper', but we do not know whether this was his private collection or only his trading stock.[72] Among his seven thousand drawings there were at least a hundred and seventy-five by Van Everdingen.[73] He wrote on the title page that he had amassed his collection over sixty years, which means that he, too, could have bought directly from the artist.

In the eighteenth century, drawings by Allart van Everdingen remained popular with collectors because they satisfied the eighteenth-century taste for finished, preferably coloured drawings.[74] In 1754, for instance, the collector Sybrand II Feitama (1694-1758) had to part with a staggering seven hundred guilders at the Tonneman sale for seven large landscapes by Van Everdingen.[75] In 1744 the French dealer Edmé-François Gersaint (1694-1750) wrote that this Dutch master's drawings were very pleasing and much sought-after and that he was among the artists with the best reputations.[76] Art dealer Christiaan Josi (1768-1828) wrote in 1821 that Allart's drawings (and etchings) were highly regarded and that enthusiasts paid steep prices for them, particularly the large coloured sheets.[77] Some collectors owned large numbers of Allart's drawings. The Hague burgomaster Samuel van Huls (1655-1734), who owned an impressive fifteen thousand drawings, had a hundred and forty-seven sheets by Van Everdingen, while Cornelis Ploos van Amstel had ninety-three of his drawings in his collection.[78]

Van Everdingen's drawings were, moreover, among the sheets by seventeenth-century artists that Ploos van Amstel produced in print, using a special printing technique. Between 1765 and 1787, with the help of assistants, he made forty-six of these 'print drawings', in an edition of three hundred and fifty impressions of each one. Allart van Everdingen is represented in this series by a print drawing after *View of a Village* (fig. 136), a sheet Cornelis Ploos van Amstel owned at the time.[79] It is clear, too, that Allart's work was valued from the many times his drawings and etchings were copied in the eighteenth and nineteenth centuries, for example by Jan de Beijer and by the Hague artist Karel la Fargue (1738-1793).[80] His sets of seasons and months were particular favourites, and the *Glue Factory* (fig. 121) was actually copied twice.[81]

It is clear that Allart van Everdingen, the artist who, according to many an eighteenth- and nineteenth-century sale catalogue could draw so 'finely and pleasingly' and 'skilfully and naturally', continued to be appreciated long after his death.

136
Cornelis Brouwer under the supervision of Cornelis Ploos van Amstel, *View of a Village*, 1782, print drawing, 174 x 277 mm, Amsterdam, Rijksmuseum, inv. no. RP-P-1944-58

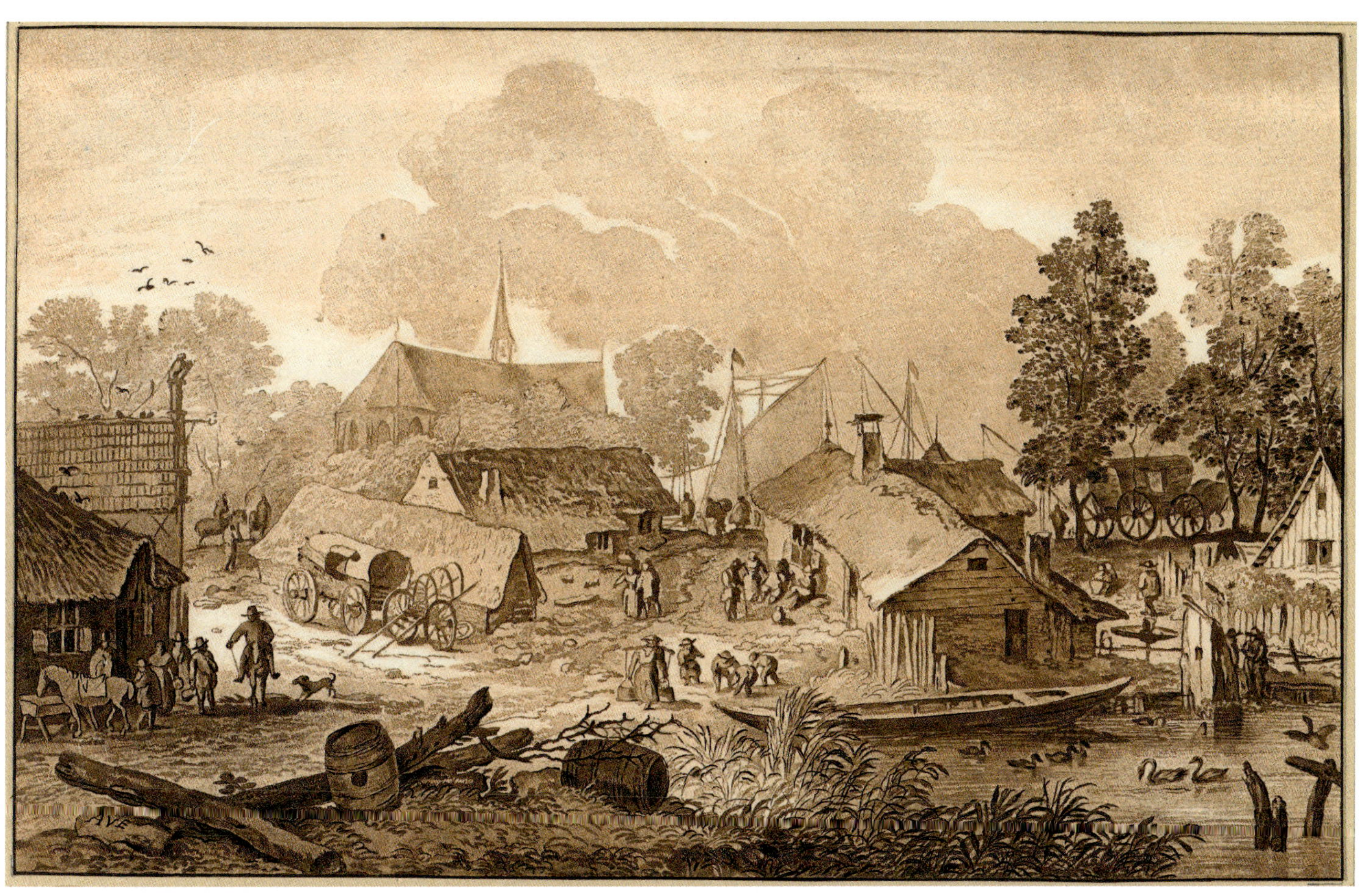

1 Alice Davies catalogued 656 drawings (Davies 2007, p. 10), including the series of small landscapes in oil paint on paper (see Ellis Dullaart's contribution in this book) and the series of sketches for the etchings of Reynard the Fox (the subject of Marjan Pantjes's essay). Some attributions are questionable, however, while several previously unknown drawings by Van Everdingen have surfaced in recent years. The precise number of surviving drawings is consequently difficult to establish.

2 For Van Goyen see Beck 1972-1973 and Beck 1987; for De Molijn see Beck 1998; for Berchem see Stefes 1997.

3 Davies 2007, cat. nos. 575-593.

4 It can be deduced from the inventory of Allart's brother Caesar van Everdingen's estate that he must have made hundreds of preparatory drawings for his paintings—sketches of heads, hands, feet and the like—but they have all been lost (Huys Janssen 2002, pp. 184-187 and Klinkert 2016, p. 13). Hendrick Avercamp may also have had a substantial drawn 'image archive' of figure studies that has vanished (Schapelhouman 2009, pp. 104-107).

5 The same was true of seventeenth-century prints of Dutch landscapes. For the Dutch landscape in seventeenth-century printmaking and painting see Gibson 2000; in sixteenth- and seventeenth-century drawing Bleyerveld 2022; for seventeenth-century topographical prints Amsterdam 1993a.

6 Of the 656 drawings Davies included in her monograph, 369 were executed in this technique (Davies 2007, p. 67).

7 Of the 656 drawings Davies catalogued, 111 are coloured with watercolour (Davies 2007, cat. nos. 1-111). There are no drawings done exclusively in chalk in the oeuvre (idem, p. 130).

8 See the essays by Ellis Dullaart and Marjan Pantjes in this catalogue.

9 Davies 2007, pp. 10-11 and cat. nos. 400, 184 and 73 (respectively). The two early works are not monogrammed and differ stylistically from the rest of the drawn oeuvre. It is moreover difficult to recognize the hand of the later master in drawings supposedly done by a sixteen- or eighteen-year-old artist who was still training. The 1656 drawing (cat. no. 73) was done in a fluid but weak and stylistically anomalous manner. The composition appears to have been worked up later with colours and black ink. It was probably then that the monogram and date were added: the letters in the monogram are more flowing in shape than we are accustomed to seeing in Allart's works. In the light of these arguments, we reject the attribution of these three drawings to Van Everdingen.

10 Watermarks in the paper are likewise of little if any help as far as dating is concerned; see Davies 2007, pp. 36-37 and Erik Hinterding's essay in this catalogue (for watermarks in the paper used for Van Everdingen's etchings).

11 Van Mander 1604, 'Den Grondt der Edel vry Schilder-const', fols. 34r-35r. For this tradition see Buijsen 1992, pp. 46-52 and Bleyerveld 2022.

12 Kotková 2010, pp. 39-40.

13 Davies 2007, p. 15 (summary of the possible trip drawings; NB cat. no. 153 should be 157), see also p. 62. On p. 36 Davies mentions two more possible candidates—cat. nos. 56 and 250.

14 Davies 2007, cat. nos. 169-172.

15 Idem, p. 136, with a reference to sale Metayer Collection, Amsterdam, 16 December 1799, p. 135, album Y.1: 'Agtien stuks fraaije bergachtige Land- and Watergezigten, met verschillende stoffagie; op de schetsen naar 't leven van A. v. Everdingen door J. de Beijer, met sapverven opgeteekend' ('Eighteen fine mountain landscapes and views of water with diverse staffage; copied by J. de Beijer in watercolour from the sketches made from life by A v. Everdingen').

16 For the second copy see Davies 2007, p. 465, fig. 2. We do not know whether these two drawings were originally among the eighteen 'bergachtige Land- and Watergezigten … naar 't leven'.

17 See e.g. Sumowski 1980, p. 370.

18 Davies 2001, p. 46.

19 Idem, pp. 46-47, 170 and cat. nos. 45, 46, 88, 124 and 127.

20 New Hollstein Cornelis Cort 2000, 109; see also nos. 12, 131 (both dated 1573) and 134 (dated 1574).

21 For Pieter Bruegel the Elder see New Hollstein Pieter Bruegel 2006, 49; for Jan Brueghel see Nappi in Brussels/Rome 1995, cat. no. 47.

22 This in contrast to Davies 2001, p. 90, who thinks that the tree stump 'has the freshness of a study executed on the spot'. With thanks to biologist Frans Smeding.

23 Van Hasselt in Brussels/Rotterdam/Paris/ Bern 1968, cat. no. 51. For De Gheyn see most recently Bleyerveld and Veldman 2016, cat. no. 48 (with further literature); for tree studies by Van Vianen and Savery see Schapelhouman and Scholten 2009, pp. 97-102, cat. nos. 6-8 (with further literature); for Bloemaert see Bolten 2007, cat. nos. 1482-1515.

24 Van Everdingen also included an old tree stump on a bare rock in one of the overdoors in the Trippenhuis (fig. 84; Davies 2001, cat. no. 125).

25 Plomp 2001, p. 82.

26 Davies described these drawings as 'masterpiece drawings' (Davies 2007, pp. 36 and 67; see also Bleyerveld 2017, p. 55). Pieter de Molijn was also fond of this format (170/190 x 270/300 mm), alongside a smaller size (140/150 x 185/195 mm), see Robinson in Cambridge 2016, cat. no. 59. Van Everdingen likewise drew a great deal on various different smaller paper sizes.

27 Amsterdam 1993b, p. 156 (under cat. no. 72).

28 For Bol see Hautekeete 2012; for Bloemaert see Bolten 2007; for Avercamp see Schapelhouman 2009; for Van Borssom see Davies 2014.

29 One of them is dated 1629; both measure 202 x 300 mm. See Beck 1998, cat. nos. 15 and 16.

30 One is the drawing in Chantilly pictured here; the other is in Weimar, see Davies 2007, cat. nos. 9 and 10.

31 The tower is reminiscent of the Zanderstoren on the Spaarne in that town; cf. a drawing by Johannes Schouten (dated 1760) in the Noord-Hollands Archief in Haarlem, inv. no. 53-001185 M. With thanks to Laurens Schoemaker.

32 Davies 2007, cat. no. 25.

33 The landscape in opaque watercolour in Frankfurt (Davies 2007, cat. no. 2) is slightly smaller. To my mind, the attribution of a large landscape in Vienna (Davies 2007, cat. no. 1) without a monogram is debatable.

34 Davies considers that the drawing can be regarded as a work of art in its own right, but at the same time as a preliminary study for the painted seascape in Frankfurt (fig. 64) (Davies 2001, pp. 47 and 56). Bisanz-Prakken (in Milwaukee 2005, cat. no. 93) rightly regards the Vienna drawing as a stand-alone work.

35 Van Everdingen's interest in picturing barns, sheds and wharves was previously remarked upon in Bakker, Fleurbaay and Gerlagh 1989, p. 72.

36 Davies 2007, cat. no. 6; see also idem, cat. no. 66 and a drawing sold in London (Sotheby's), 8 July 2009, no. 53 (not in Davies 2007; illustration on the website of the RKD – Netherlands Institute for Art History in The Hague, RKDimages, no. 196503).

37 For this motif see also Davies 2007, cat. nos. 17 and 218 (with rafts in the background).

38 Martens 2004, p. 136.

39 With thanks to Ron Brand. For a similar effect of fire and smoke see Davies 2007, cat. no. 443 and Stefes 2011, cat. no. 313.

40 Frijhoff et al. 2004, p. 96.

41 This fact and all the subsequent information about the drawing were taken from Bakker, Fleurbaay and Gerlagh 1989, cat. no. 16. See also Davies 2007, pp. 50-51.

42 This was suggested by C.P. van Eeghen, see Bakker, Fleurbaay and Gerlagh 1989, cat. no. 16. It would be comparable to Jacob Matham's 1627 pen painting of the Haarlem brewery belonging to Johan Claesz van Loo, which he undoubtedly made as a commission for the brewer. For this work see Torringa in Köhler et al. 2006, cat. no. 303.

43 For limekilns see Beck 1972-1973, vol. 1, cat. nos. 75 and 495; vol. 2, cat. no. 1078; Beck 1987, vol. 3, cat. no. 110a. For a smithy see Beck 1972-1973, vol. 1, cat. nos. 212 and 393b-397.

44 For Allart's drawing see Davies 2007, cat. no. 26; for the print by Claes Jansz Visscher see Hollstein (Claes Jansz Visscher) 123 (in a set of eight prints of Dutch trades, incorporated in the decorative border of a map in 1608); for Van de Venne's drawing see Royalton-Kisch 1988, pp. 254-257.

45 For Zeeman see a drawing (inv. no. RP-T-1889-A-2123), painting (inv. no. SK-A-759)

and etchings (e.g. inv. no. RP-P-1881-A-4737) in the Rijksmuseum; for Saftleven an illustration of a drawing on the website of the RKD – Netherlands Institute for Art History in The Hague, RKDimages, no. 63266 (not in Schulz 1982).

46 Cf. Davies 2007, cat. nos. 121 and 126, where he used a similar composition, with a dark repoussoir in the left or right foreground —in this case fishing nets. Haarlem is also pictured in drawings in Cambridge (Mass.) and Amsterdam (Davies 2007, cat. nos. 125 and 183).

47 As Haarlem in Davies 2007, cat. no. 129.

48 For both see idem, cat. no. 248.

49 Davies 2007, cat. nos. 593, 590 and 591 respectively. See Erik Hinterding's essay in this catalogue.

50 Davies 2007, cat. no. 592 and Sadkov et al. 2010, cat. no. 178—both erroneously as the spring at Watroz.

51 Davies 2001, p. 33; Davies 2007, cat. no. 115. The style of the unsigned drawing (in the Albertina Museum in Vienna) is rather weak.

52 There is a black chalk sketch of a mountain-side on the verso; see Davies 2007, cat. nos. 69 and 69v, and also pp. 10-11 and 113-114, where both scenes are regarded as landscapes in the Ardennes.

53 See Davies 2007, p. 54 and cat. nos. 51 and 111 (two drawings in Rotterdam); p. 66 and cat. no. 203 (drawing in Hamburg, see also Stefes 2011, cat. no. 302); pp. 10, 113-114 and cat. no. 73 (the drawing dated 1656, see the introduction to this essay, including note 9).

54 Davies 2007, cat. nos. 353-399 and cat. nos. 453-456 (set of the four seasons). To these can be added a drawing in a private collection (illustration on the website of the RKD – Netherlands Institute for Art History in The Hague, RKDimages, no. 296851) and a second at the sale of the I.Q. van Regteren Altena Collection, Amsterdam (Christie's), 13 May 2015, no. 240. Neither of them in Davies 2007.

55 There should be a long pole with a basket or buoy at the top of the tripod. For other examples see Davies 2007, cat. nos. 109 and 542; De Beer 2019, cat. nos. 16 and 33.

56 See the annotations in the little book of brunailles (fig. 138). See Broos 1984, p. 26, for an early (c. 1691) use of this term. See also Davies 2007, under cat. nos. 362 and 375. See Schulz 1982, cat. nos. 1315-1327, for a series of figure studies by Herman Saftleven drawn on the back of playing cards measuring about 84 x 53 mm.

57 See e.g. *Four Views Outside Amsterdam* by Claes Jansz Visscher, c. 1610, Hollstein (Claes Jansz Visscher) 140-143; Amsterdam 1993a, cat. no. 9.

58 Hollstein (Herman van Swanevelt) 63-86. According to Steland 2005, p. 57, the sketches for this set can be dated to around 1646.

59 Feitama 1746, p. 15: 'Kleine Land- of Water-gezichjes, op kaarteblaadjes met roet geteekend'. His grandson Sybrand II Feitama (1694-1758) added six little drawings to the set; see idem,

p. 15, and for both collectors Broos 1984 and Broos 1985.

60 See 'Provenance' under Davies 2007, cat. nos. 377, 379, 389, 390, 395 and 397.

61 Sale Cornelis Ploos van Amstel Collection, Amsterdam, 3 March 1800, both under no. GG7. This is confirmed by Christiaan Josi, who wrote that the smallest drawings by the artist were offered as a pair, see Josi 1821, section 'Aldert van Everdingen' (unpaged).

62 One incomplete set of the four elements has survived (Davies 2007, cat. nos. 443-445) and there are one incomplete and two complete sets of the four seasons (Davies 2007, cat. nos. 446-456). The complete sets of the twelve months are in Brussels (fig. 135), Berlin, Rotterdam, Moscow, Amsterdam, Paris and Lawrence (Davies 2007, cat. nos. 457-528 and 555-566). There are also three surviving incomplete sets and a few loose drawings of the months, see Davies 2007, cat. nos. 529-554 and 567-574.

63 See at greatest length 's-Hertogenbosch/ Leuven 2002.

64 For two sets by Hans Bol (c. 1580-1581 and 1585) see e.g. Hautekeete and Van Grieken 2015. For sets by Jan van de Velde (1618) and various engravers after Joachim von Sandrart (1645) see Huys Janssen in 's-Hertogenbosch/ Leuven 2002, cat. nos. 60-71 and 90-93.

65 For Esaias van de Velde see Schapelhouman and Schatborn 1998, cat. nos. 323 and 324; for Pieter de Molijn (two sets dating from 1655 and 1658-1659) see Beck 1998, pp. 23-24 and cat. nos. 84-112.

66 For Avercamp see Plomp 2001, pp. 26-27 and Schapelhouman 2009, pp. 89-90. For Savery see *Dessins anciens* catalogue, Nicolas Schwed Paris, March 2014, no. 8. See also Broos 1984, p. 17, for four drawings that the collector Sybrand I Feitama bought directly from Ludolf Bakhuizen.

67 Davies 2001, pp. 199-201.

68 Bredius 1892, p. 38, cat. no. 18.

69 Davies 2001, p. 37.

70 Davies 2007, cat. nos. 18, 19 and 505-516 respectively. For Sennepart see Broos 1984, pp. 15 and 25-26.

71 Feitama 1746, p. 15, Broos 1984, p. 26 and Broos 1985, p. 118. One of these sets may be the one in Brussels, see Davies 2007, under cat. no. 457.

72 For Zomer see Plomp 1997 and Plomp 2001, pp. 38-39 (with further literature).

73 I am quoting the count in Davies 2007, pp. 19-20 and 461.

74 Plomp 2001, p. 226; Plomp in Haarlem/ Paris 2001, p. 148.

75 Broos 1985, p. 118. Houbraken explicitly mentions coloured drawings by Van Everdingen in the collection of Jeronimus Tonneman (1687-1750), which suggests that he had a special status at that time (Houbraken 1718-1721, vol. 2, p. 96). For Tonneman see Lugt Marques 2863a.

76 Gersaint 1744, p. 22, no. 43: 'Les Desseins de ce Maître Hollandais sont très-agréable, & très recherché par le curieux de la Hollande; c'est un des Maîtres qui y est le plus réputation.' With thanks to Erik Hinterding.

77 Josi 1821, section 'Aldert van Everdingen' (unpaged) and 'Table Alphabetique', p. 7.

78 As appears from the catalogue of Van Huls's sale in 1736, see Davies 2007, p. 20. For Van Huls see Plomp 2001, *passim*. For Ploos van Amstel see Laurentius, Niemeijer and Ploos van Amstel 1980, pp. 345-346.

79 The drawing is in the British Museum in London (Davies 2007, cat. no. 224). For the pen-and-ink drawing see Laurentius, Niemeijer and Ploos van Amstel 1980, p. 271, cat. no. 36.

80 See Davies 2007, pp. 128-144; for La Fargue see also Dumas and Plomp 1998, esp. pp. 37-38.

81 Davies 2007, p. 140. For the copies by Jan Hulswit (1766-1822), who owned *Glue Factory* himself from 1817 onwards, and by Gerrit Lamberts (1776-1850) see idem, p. 136, and Bakker, Fleurbaay and Gerlagh 1989, p. 72 (note 9).

Spotlight 2
A SPECIAL LITTLE BOOK

Ellis Dullaart

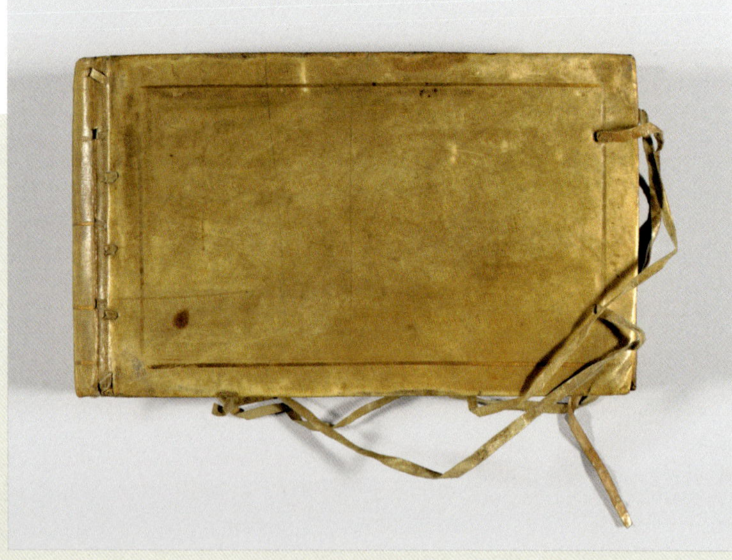

137
Album containing
38 marines, landscapes
and ice scenes by
Allart van Everdingen,
parchment binding,
94 x 160 mm, Amster-
dam, Rijksmuseum,
inv. no. RP-T-1968-99
(cat. no. 5)

The Rijksmuseum in Amsterdam holds an exceptional group of seascapes and landscapes by Allart van Everdingen, painted in oil on paper and bound together in an old parchment binding measuring 94 by 160 millimetres (fig. 137). Each composition measures approximately 47 by 83 millimetres; despite their small size, they are extremely detailed and arresting.[1] Van Everdingen used thin, liquid paint that he applied quickly, often wet in wet. He worked in the brunaille technique—a variant of grisaille—which uses various shades of one principal colour, in this case brown.[2] According to the annotations on the seventh page of the album, mainly written in an eighteenth-century hand, it originally contained forty-seven 'caerte-blaetjes' ('cards') (fig. 138); thirty-eight of them are still together in the Rijksmuseum. The Stichting P. & N. de Boer in Amsterdam has three brunailles in its collection (figs. 139-141), and there is one in a private collection (fig. 142). A fifth loose sheet is known only from photographs (fig. 143).[3] A quick sum tells us that four of the forty-seven brunailles in the original album are missing without trace.

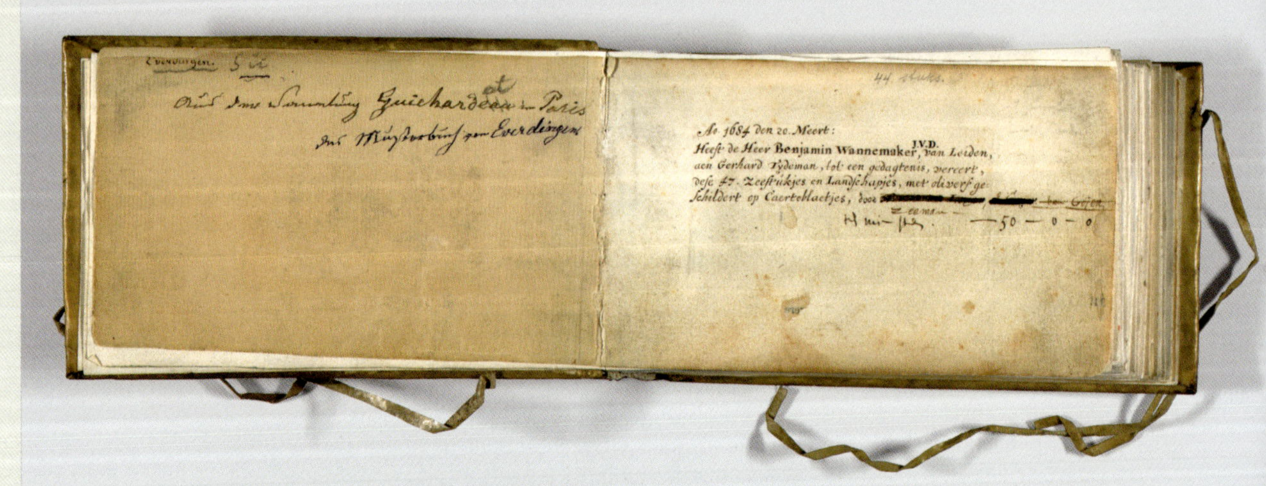

138
Annotations on the
seventh page of the
album (cat. no. 5)

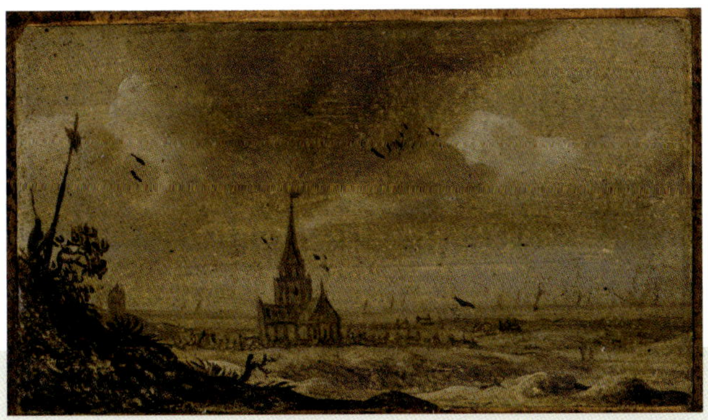

139
Allart van Everdingen, *Church in a Dune Landscape*,
brush and brown and white oil paint on paper, 47 x 83 mm,
Amsterdam, Stichting Collectie P. & N. de Boer, inv. no.
B 650-a (cat. no. 37)

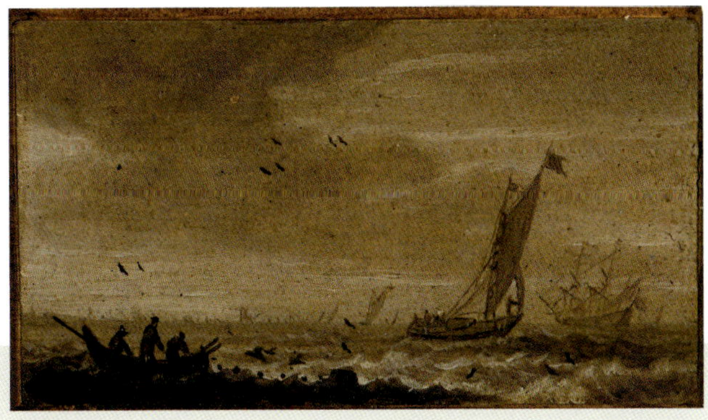

140
Allart van Everdingen, *Seascape with Sailing Boats*,
brush and brown and white oil paint on paper, 47 x 84 mm,
Amsterdam, Stichting Collectie P. & N. de Boer, inv. no.
B 650-b (cat. no. 38)

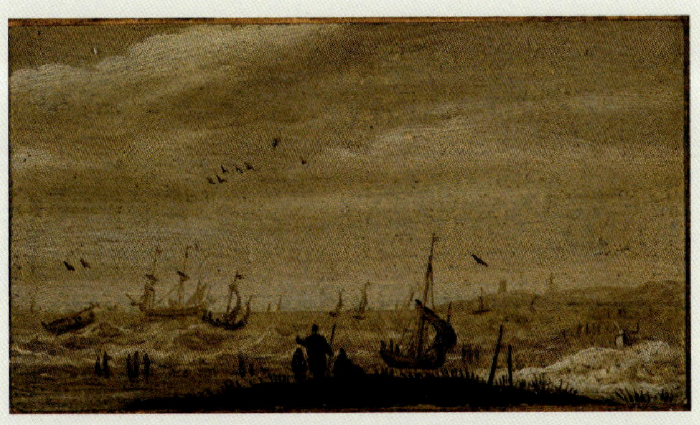

141
Allart van Everdingen, *View of the Beach with Figures
in the Foreground*, brush and brown and white oil paint
on paper, 47 x 84 mm, Amsterdam, Stichting Collectie
P. & N. de Boer, inv. no. B 650-c (cat. no. 39)

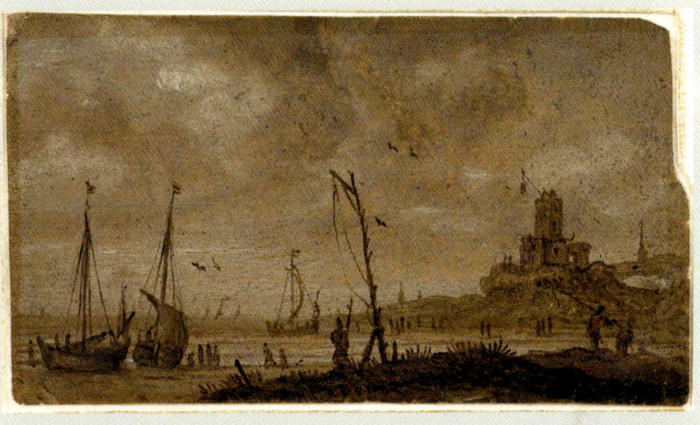

142
Allart van Everdingen, *View of the Beach with a Beacon*,
brush and brown and white oil paint on paper, 46 x 83 mm,
private collection (cat. no. 106)

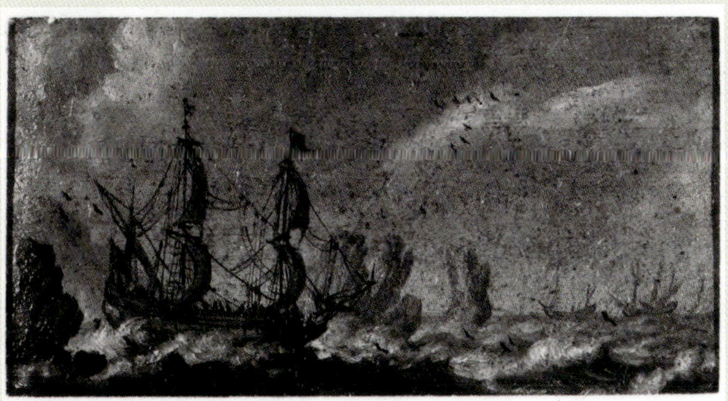

143
Allart van Everdingen, *Seascape with
a Frigate among the Rocks*, brush and
brown and white oil paint on paper,
approx. 47 x 83 mm, whereabouts
unknown

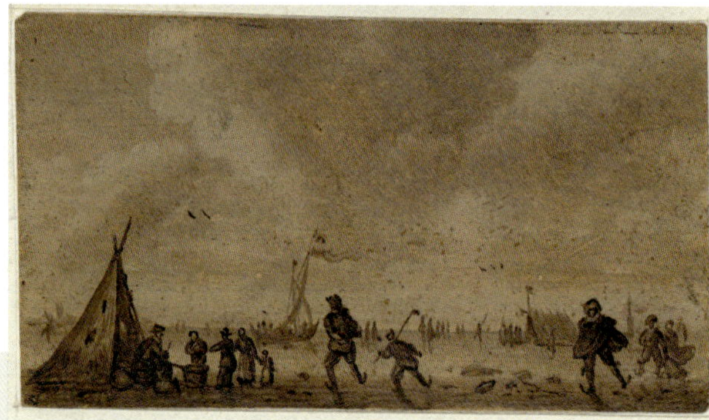

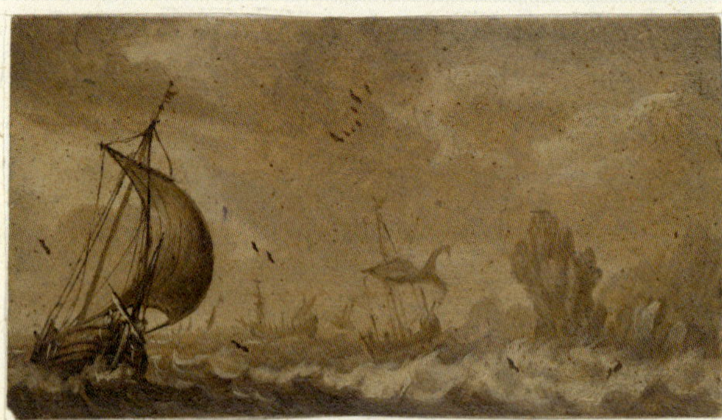

Attribution

The present group of forty-three brunailles consists of seascapes and landscapes, among them several of raging seas with ships near rocky coasts. There are also scenes of vessels on calm water, craggy mountains on the coast, landscapes with farmhouses and country roads, views of the shore and scenes on the ice (fig. 144). Unlike most of Van Everdingen's art-works, the brunailles are not signed. However, comparison with other known work by him confirms that they fit seamlessly in his oeuvre.

The brunailles of seascapes and rocky shorelines (fig. 145), for instance, are akin to a large, finished drawing of the same subject (fig. 111) in terms both of the composition and the way the angry sea is painted. In another drawing, of rocks on the coast and ships in heavy seas in the background (fig. 146), Van Everdingen used a large rock formation in the foreground to create depth in the composition, exactly as he did in the brunailles (fig. 147).[4] The comparison between a drawing in the British Museum (fig. 148) and one specific

144
Allart van Everdingen, *Tent and Skaters on the Ice*, brush and brown and white oil paint on paper, approx. 47 x 83 mm, Amsterdam, Rijksmuseum, inv. no. RP-T-1968-99 (cat. no. 5)

145
Allart van Everdingen, *Ships in a Storm*, brush and brown and white oil paint on paper, approx. 47 x 83 mm, Amsterdam, Rijksmuseum, inv. no. RP-T-1968-99 (cat. no. 5)

> 146
Allart van Everdingen, *Rocky Coast with Ships on a Stormy Sea*, pen and brush and brown ink, brown wash, 115 x 165 mm, The University of North Carolina at Chapel Hill, Ackland Art Museum, The Peck Collection, inv. no. 2017.1.32

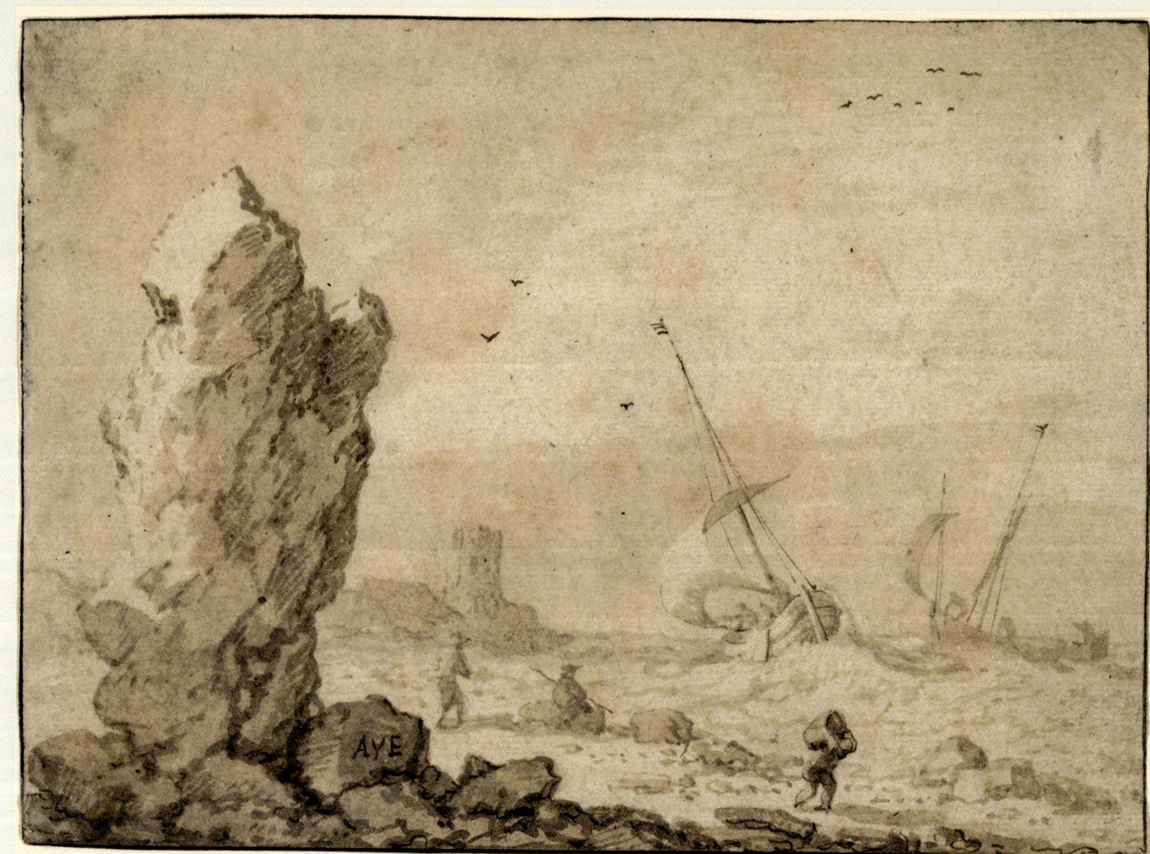

brunaille (fig. 142) reveals interesting compositional similarities.[5] Both sheets feature pinks on the beach and in both cases a dark dune with a beacon in the foreground leads the viewer's eye deeper into the scene, where small figures can be seen on the shore. And Van Everdingen's style is easily recognized in the way he painted the architecture in the brunailles (fig. 149), as a comparison with the buildings in the background of *Panoramic Landscape with Three Figures* (fig. 150) reveals.

Despite the convincing similarities between the brunailles and other, signed work by Van Everdingen, doubts about the attribution of the album have been expressed in the past. There is a name in the eighteenth-century annotations, but it has been crossed out so effectively that it cannot be deciphered. The names of Reinier

147
Allart van Everdingen, *Stormy Sea with a Sinking Ship and a Two-Master among the Rocks*, brush and brown and white oil paint on paper, approx. 47 x 83 mm, Amsterdam, Rijksmuseum, inv. no. RP-T-1968-99 (cat. no. 5)

> 148
Allart van Everdingen, *Coastal View with Sailing Boats on the Beach*, pen and brush and brown ink, brown wash, 104 x 102 mm, London, The British Museum, inv. no. 1836,0811.148

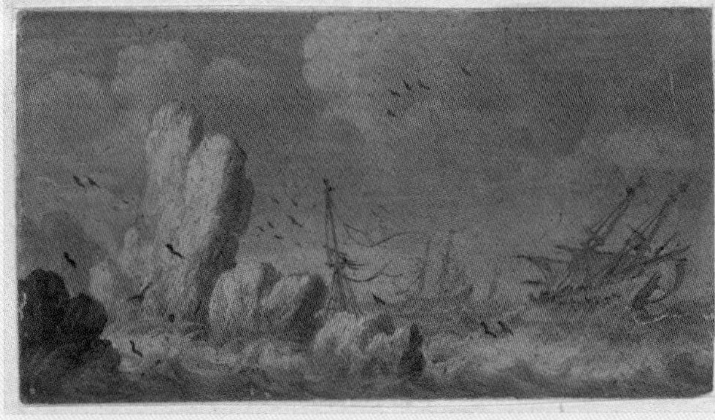

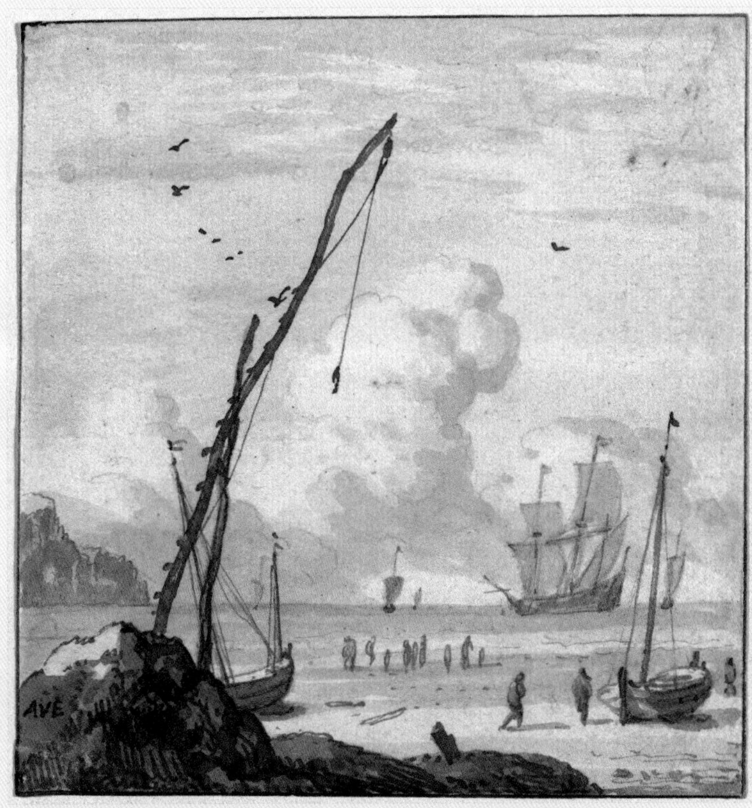

149
Allart van Everdingen, *Ruined Castle on a River*, brush and brown and white oil paint on paper, approx. 47 x 83 mm, Amsterdam, Rijksmuseum, inv. no. RP-T-1968-99 (cat. no. 5)

> 150
Allart van Everdingen, *Panoramic Landscape with Three Figures*, pen and brush and brown ink, grey wash, watercolour, 105 x 230 mm, private collection (cat. no. 107)

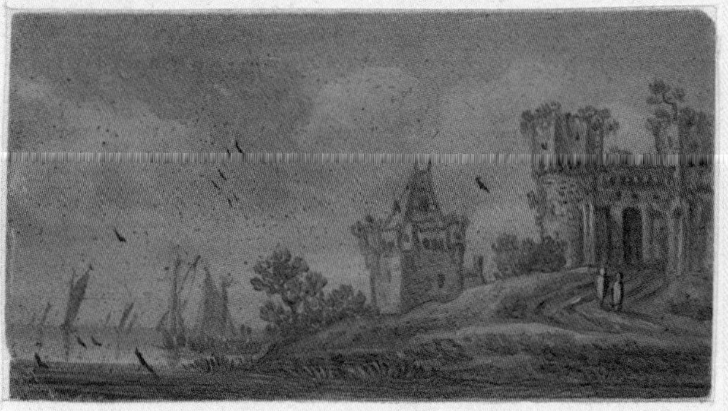

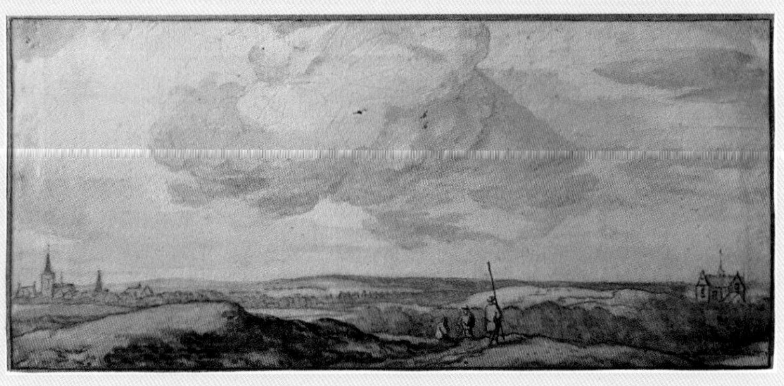

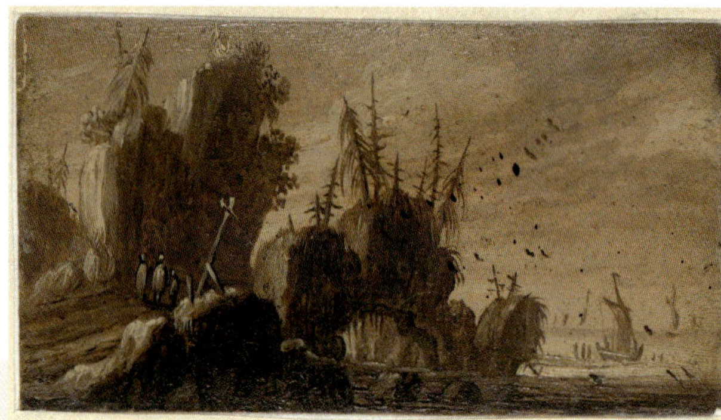

151
Allart van Everdingen, *Rocky Coast with Vegetation and Walkers*, brush and brown and white oil paint on paper, approx. 47 x 83 mm, Amsterdam, Rijksmuseum, inv. no. RP-T-1968-99 (cat. no. 5)

Dating

Van Everdingen dated very few of his works, so it is difficult to establish a chronology in his oeuvre. Nevertheless, on the basis of style and iconography, the brunailles can be dated quite accurately to the 1639-1643 period—immediately after his training ended, but before his trip to Norway.[7]

Many of the scenes show the influence of his teacher, Roelandt Savery (1576-1639). In picturing the craggy rocks with vegetation clinging to them that appear in several brunailles (fig. 151), Savery's work provided enough inspiring examples on which Van Everdingen could base his compositions (fig. 152). The rocky coasts in the work of the Utrecht landscape and marine painter Adam Willaerts (1577-1664) (fig. 46) likewise bear an interesting resemblance to the brunailles. We know that Savery and Willaerts often visited one another's studios.[8] It is safe to assume, therefore, that the young Van Everdingen was familiar with Willaerts's work through Savery.[9] He must also have been inspired by the work of Pieter Mulier I (1595/

Zeeman (1623/1624-1664) and Jan van Goyen (1596-1656) have been added in a different hand, but the latter has also been crossed out. It was not until 1875 that the little book was attributed to Van Everdingen—in the catalogue of the sale of the estate of the dealer in drawings and prints F. Guichardot (died 1875) of Paris.[6] It was probably Guichardot himself who rightly identified Allart's hand in the brunailles.

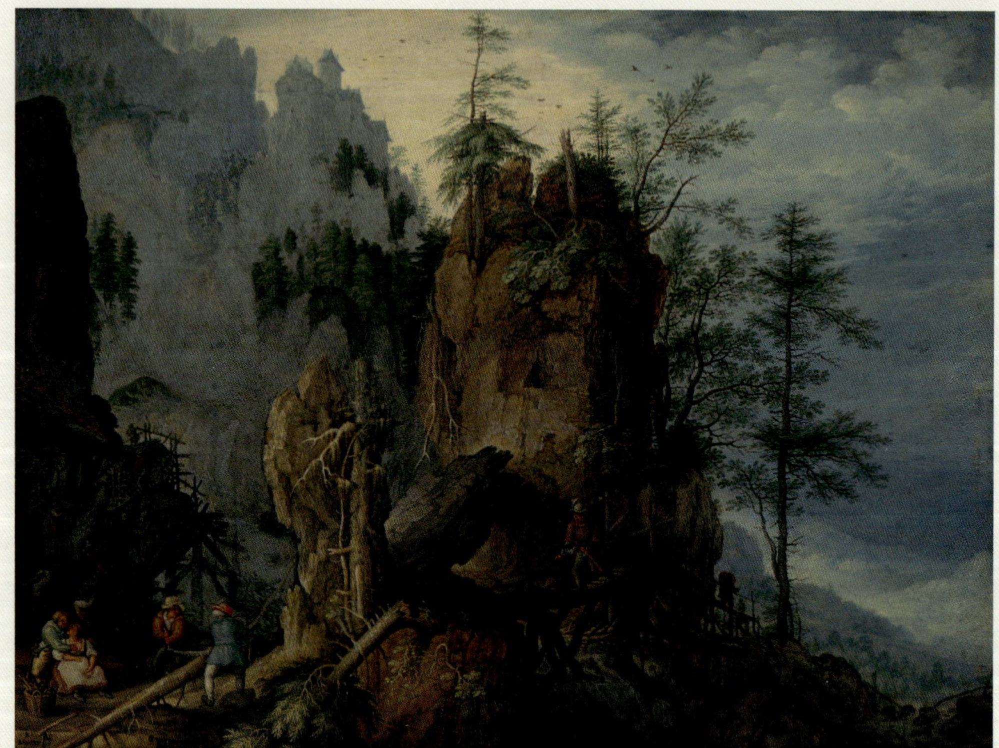

152
Roelandt Savery, *Mountain Landscape with Wood Cutters*, 1610, oil on copper, 26.3 x 35.9 cm, Kunsthistorisches Museum Wien, inv. no. 957

1610-1659/1661) (figs. 12, 43 and 66), who may have been his second teacher. Allart certainly took the subject of wild seas with small ships below a cloudy sky from him, and he also used similar dark foregrounds and strong chiaroscuro in the water in his brunailles (fig. 153).[10] The rock arches that appear in no fewer than thirteen scenes (fig. 154) could probably also trace their origins back to Mulier's oeuvre (fig. 155).[11]

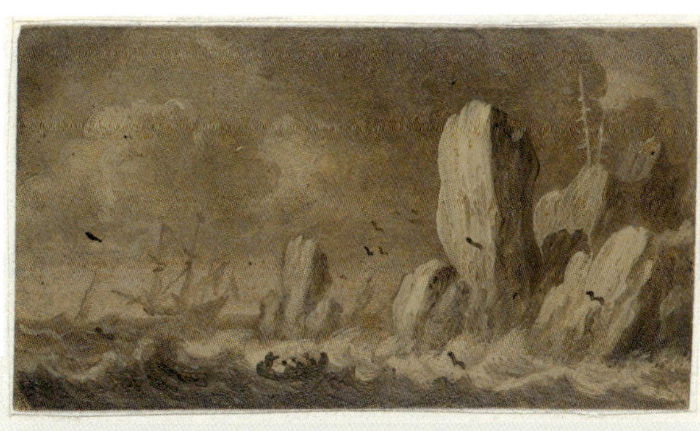

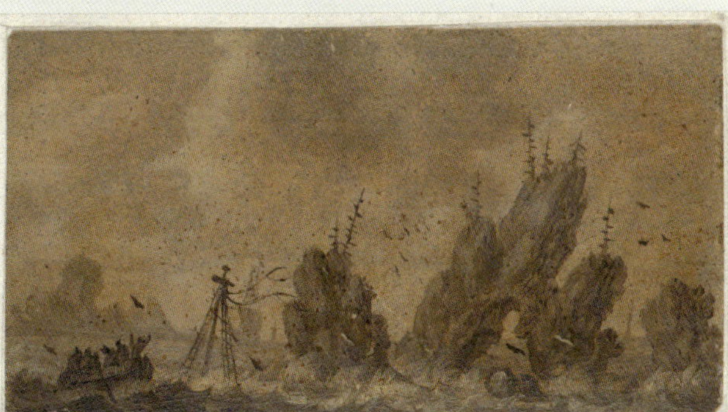

∧ 153
Allart van Everdingen, *Rowing Boat off a Rocky Coast*, brush and brown and white oil paint on paper, approx. 47 x 83 mm, Amsterdam, Rijksmuseum, inv. no. RP-T-1968-99 (cat. no. 5)

< 154
Allart van Everdingen, *Sunken Ship near a Rock Arch, with a Rowing Boat*, brush and brown and white oil paint on paper, approx. 47 x 83 mm, Amsterdam, Rijksmuseum, inv. no. RP-T-1968-99 (cat. no. 5)

∨ 155
Pieter Mulier I, *Ships in a Storm off a Rocky Coast*, oil on panel, 52.5 x 84 cm, whereabouts unknown

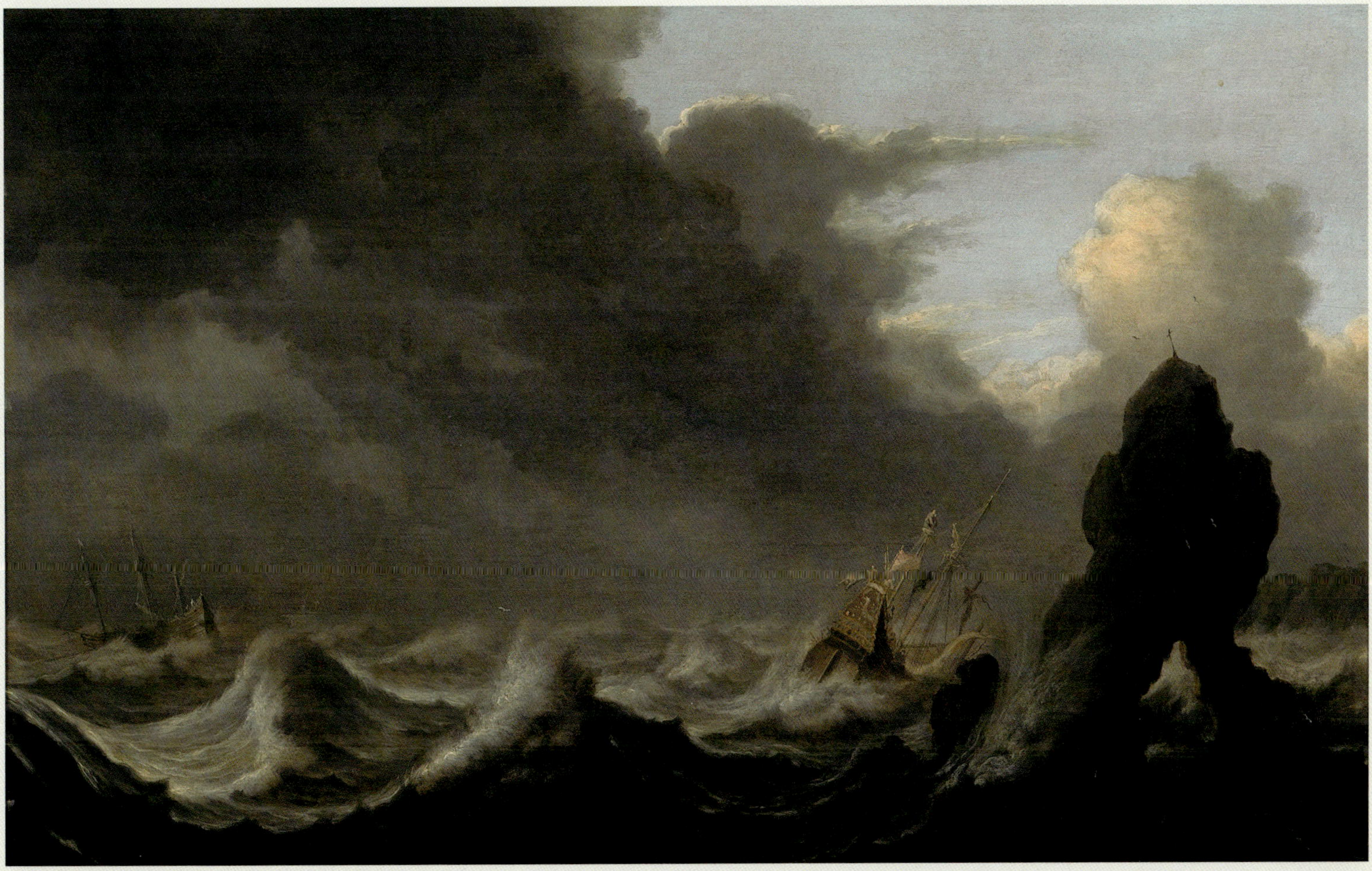

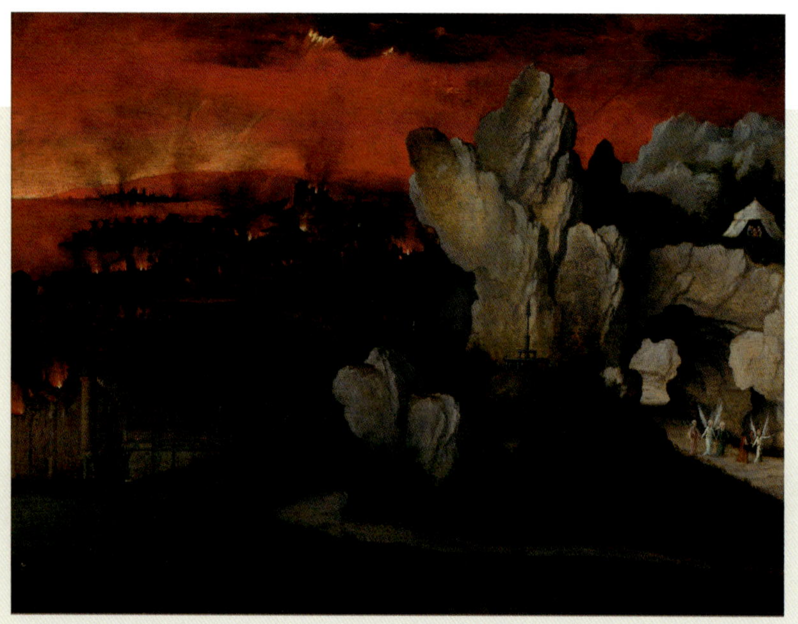

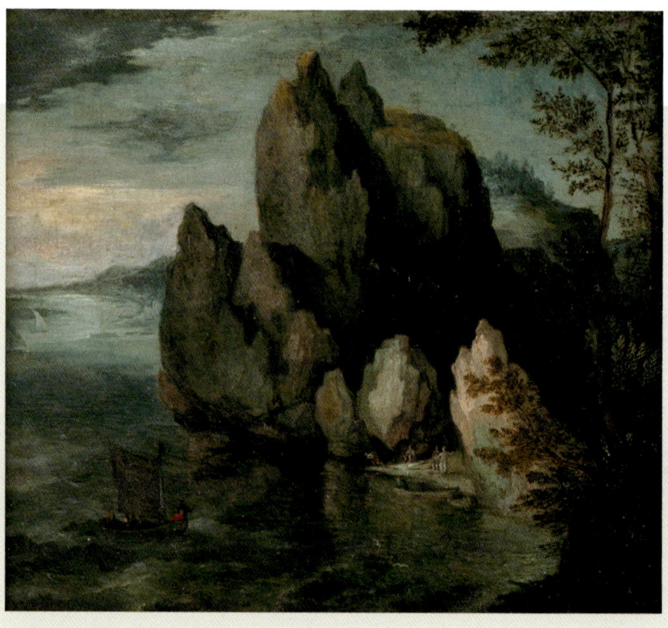

156
Joachim Patinir, *Landscape with Sodom and Gomorrah in Flames,* c. 1520, oil on panel, 22.5 x 30 cm, Amersfoort, Cultural Heritage Agency of the Netherlands, inv. no. NK 2670 (on loan to Museum Boijmans Van Beuningen, Rotterdam)

157
Jan Brueghel, *Seascape with High Rocks,* c. 1592, oil on copper, 10.2 x 11.4 cm, Indianapolis Museum of Art, The Clowes Collection, inv. no. 10014

The shape of most of the rock formations in the brunailles is so unrealistic that it is highly likely they were painted before Van Everdingen's voyage to Scandinavia. They are very reminiscent, for example, of the fantastical rock formations in the work of early Flemish artists like Joachim Patinir (c. 1475/1480-1524) (fig. 156) and Jan Brueghel (1568-1625) (fig. 157). Once Van Everdingen had studied and drawn rocks in Norway, he began to depict them more realistically (fig. 158).[12]

For the landscapes in which water is not a prominent feature, Van Everdingen may have drawn inspiration from the work of Pieter de Molijn (1595-1661) and Jan van Goyen. In technique and composition, Van Everdingen's brunailles of farmhouses and country roads (figs. 159 and 160) echo the drawings and paintings De Molijn made in the sixteen-thirties (fig. 161) and the tonal landscape paintings Van Goyen produced between 1630 and around 1645 (fig. 162).[13]

As well as the parallels with his teachers and contemporaries, there are obvious resemblances between the brunailles and Van Everdingen's own early work (figs. 163 and 164).[14] The similar handling of the choppy sea—short, pointed waves with soft, slightly diffuse whitecaps from which spray seems to blow—is particularly striking in the painted marines of the early sixteen-forties (figs. 42 and 44). The subject of ships in peril off a rocky coast and the compositions with a low horizon and just a few vessels are also comparable.

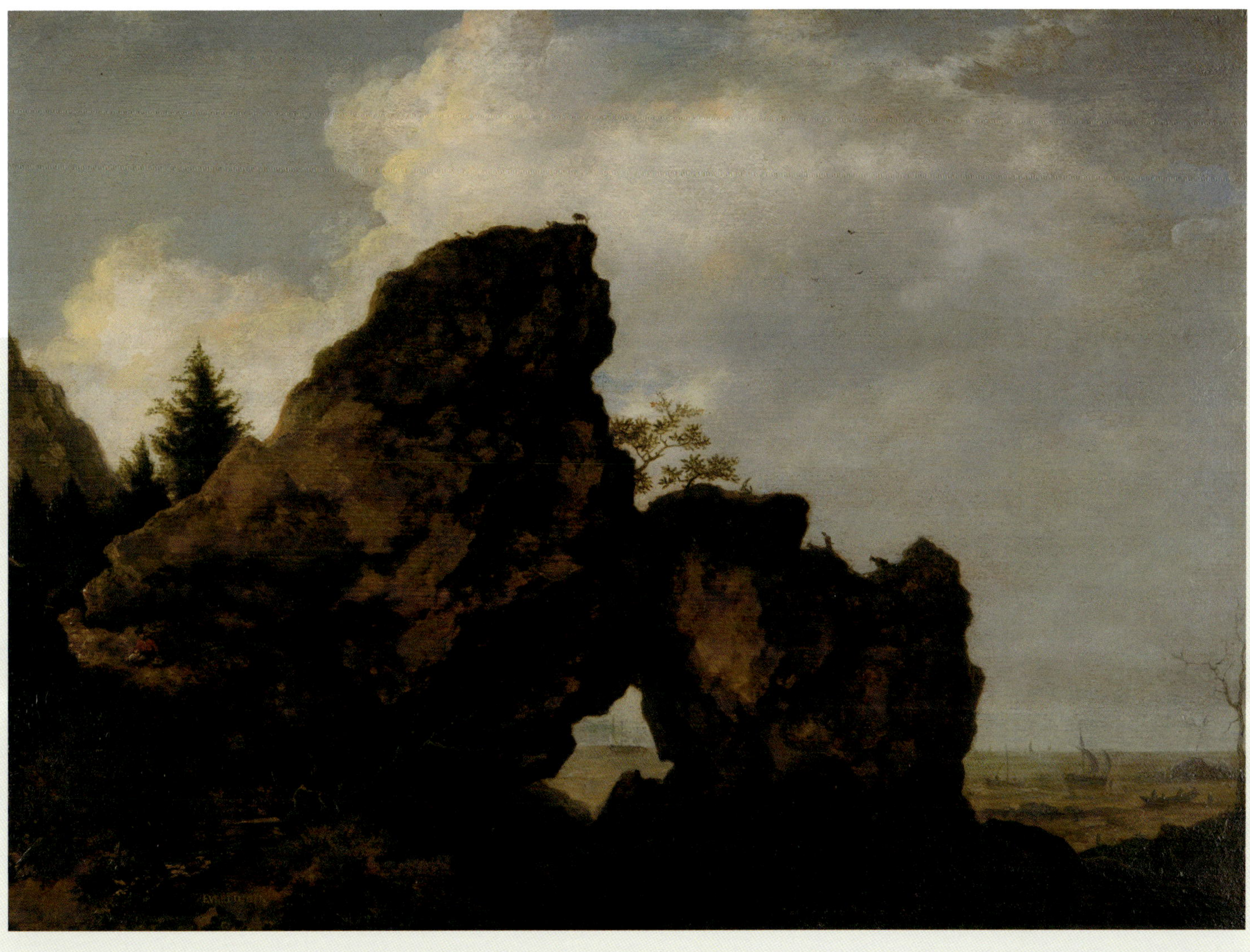

158
Allart van Everdingen,
Rocky Coastal Land-scape, oil on panel,
33 x 45 cm, private
collection (on loan
to the Dordrechts
Museum, inv. no.
DM/017/1279)
(cat. no. 105)

Sketch or End Product?

What was the purpose of Van Everdingen's brunailles? What prompted the artist to make this group of similar scenes? Answers to these questions may be found in the particular technique he used to paint them. Brunaille is a variant of the more usual grisaille technique, in which compositions are painted solely in shades of grey. Artists have painted in grey or brown tones for a variety of reasons since the Middle Ages. In some cases, these pieces were made as works of art in their own right, such as the painted imitation sculptures on the outside of shutters of altarpieces, or they were used as an aid at the design stage in the artistic process. Grisaille and brunaille were an ideal way to set up and try out chiaroscuro effects in a composition, and sixteenth- and seventeenth-

century artists sometimes used them as designs for prints.[15]

It has indeed been suggested that Van Everdingen's brunailles were sketches for prints, similar, for instance, to the twenty-three small imaginary landscapes by Herman van Swanevelt (c. 1603-1655) (fig. 165), or the seventeen beach views and seascapes by Jan Porcellis (c. 1584-1632) (fig. 166).[16] Since, as far as we know, none of the scenes in the brunaille album ever appeared as a print, the suggestion is not very plausible.

An 1898 sale catalogue assumes that the little album of brunailles was made as a pattern book.[17] A pattern book was a collection of examples or models used in artists' workshops as a source of motifs for paintings and highly finished drawings. This hypothesis most probably

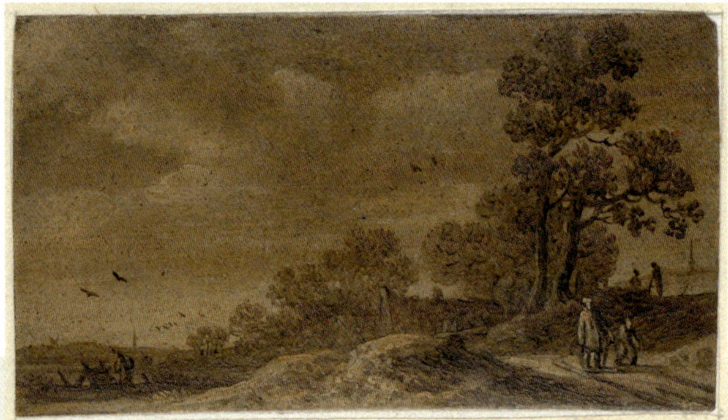

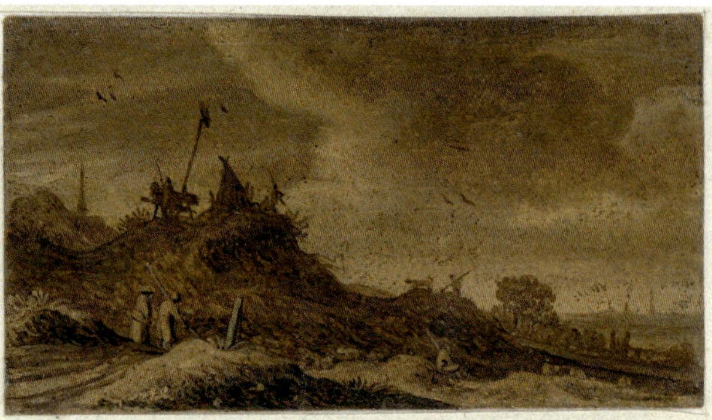

159
Allart van Everdingen, *Figures on a Road in the Dunes*, brush and brown and white oil paint on paper, approx. 47 x 83 mm, Amsterdam, Rijksmuseum, inv. no. RP-T-1968-99 (cat. no. 5)

> 160
Allart van Everdingen, *Dune Landscape*, brush and brown and white oil paint on paper, approx. 47 x 83 mm, Amsterdam, Rijksmuseum, inv. no. RP-T-1968-99 (cat. no. 5)

v 161
Pieter de Molijn, *Dune Landscape with Figures near a Tumbledown Farmhouse*, 1632, black chalk, heightened with white, 192 x 305 mm, Kunstsammlung der Georg-August-Universität Göttingen, inv. no. H 144

does not hold water either, since none of the individual motifs in the brunailles appears in precisely the same way in other works by Van Everdingen.

A third possibility is that Van Everdingen made the brunailles as an exercise, to try out compositions and refine his skills in painting rocks, waves, trees, ships and buildings. The small size and limited palette meant that they did not cost much to make. A final option is that Van Everdingen was commissioned to paint the brunailles or made them as a gift. Might he have created these detailed and meticulously worked out little landscapes and marines as a precious keepsake, perhaps for a friend or acquaintance?

The Adventures of the Album

In any event, the album certainly functioned as a gift in 1684, as the annotations (fig. 138) reveal. They state that the Leiden lawyer Benjamin Wannemaker (born 1647) gave the brunailles to Gerhard (or Gerrit) Tydeman on 20 March 1684:

AD. 1684 the 20th of March:
Mr BENJAMIN WANNEMAKER, [J.V.D.] of Leiden, presents Gerhard Tydeman, as a memento, with these 47 Sea Pieces and Landscapes, painted with oil paint on Cards, by P. [T./A.] v Venner I ...,
.... Van Gojen, Zeeman- at least. – 50 – 0 – 0[18]

Wannemaker's impending move to England on 20 September 1684 may have been what prompted him to present the little book to the publisher and bookseller Gerrit Tydeman (c. 1637-1713) of Zwolle.[19] How they knew one another is not clear, but they may have met through Wannemaker's father, who was also a bookseller. Nor do we have any information as to how and when Wannemaker got hold of the album. Since the brunailles were probably made before he was born in 1647, it seems unlikely he purchased them directly from Van Everdingen, unless they had been hanging around the artist's studio as a youth work for a long time. It is not likely, however, that Wannemaker's father was the first owner and the brunailles were inherited by his son on

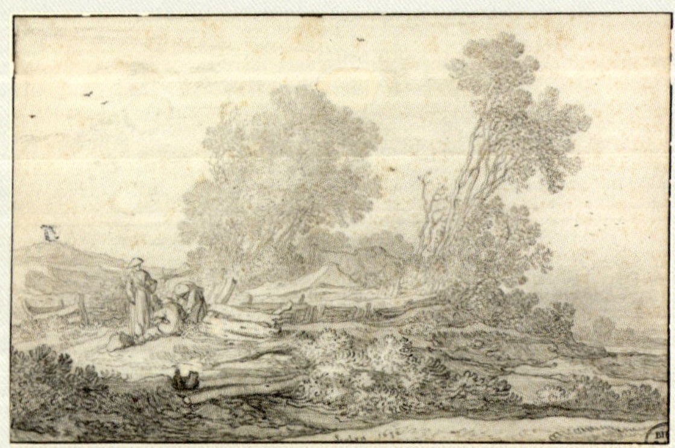

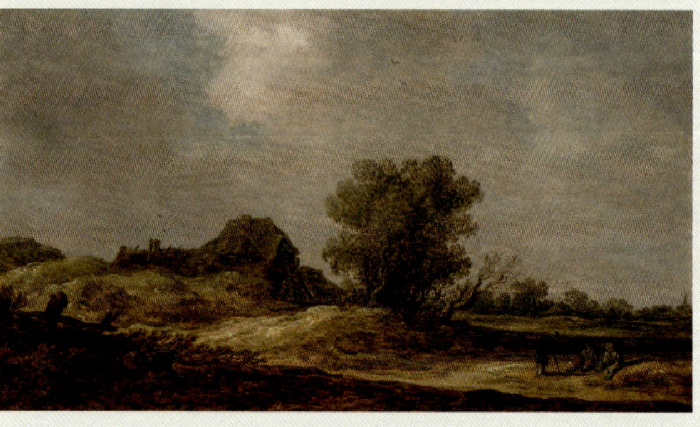

< 162
Jan van Goyen, *Farmhouse in the Dunes*, 1631, oil on panel, 31 x 50 cm, Národní galerie Praha, inv. no. O 2821

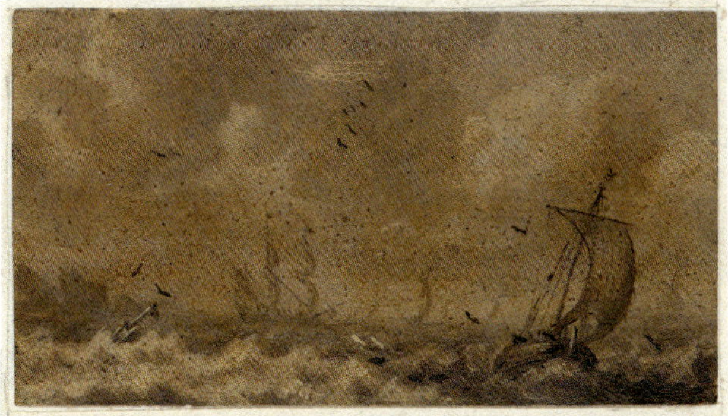

163
Allart van Everdingen,
Sailing Boats on Open Water, brush and brown and white oil paint on paper, approx. 47 x 83 mm, Amsterdam, Rijksmuseum, inv. no. RP-T-1968-99 (cat. no. 5)

v 164
Allart van Everdingen,
Stormy Sea, oil on canvas, 62.9 x 78.6 cm, Philadelphia Museum of Art, John G. Johnson Collection, inv. no. 587

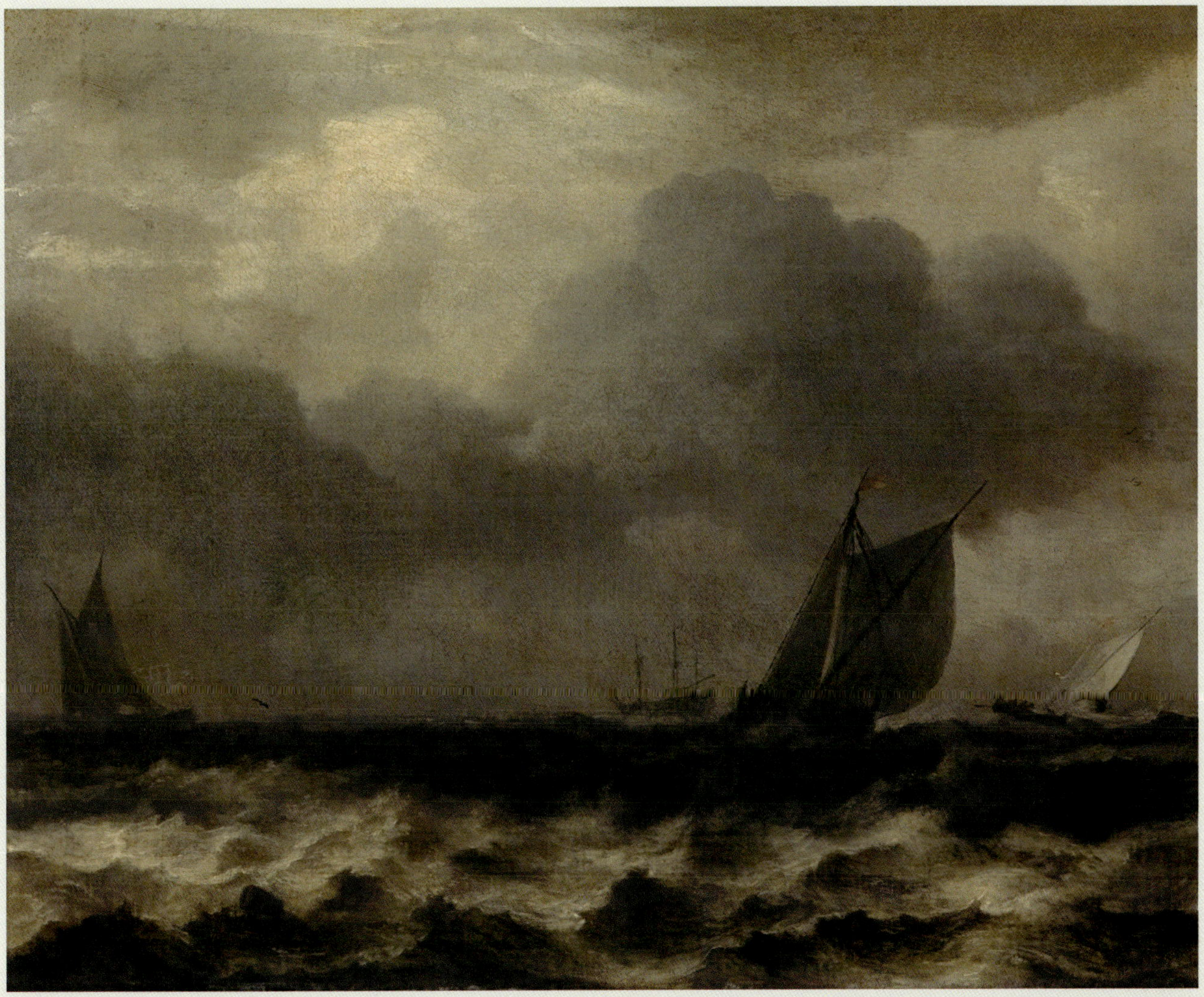

his death in 1662, since they did not appear on the list of goods that were passed down to Wannemaker after his father died.[20]

The fact that the album really was in Tydeman's possession is confirmed by a passage in an eighteenth-century travel journal kept by the German scholar Zacharias Conrad von Uffenbach (1683-1734). During his trip through Lower Saxony, the Northern Netherlands and England, he went to Zwolle in 1710 and visited Tydeman's shop. Von Uffenbach describes at length what was for sale there and also mentions a number of objects that were probably Tydeman's personal property, including 'a small rectangular book, like a family album; with in it some thirty small seascapes painted in oils on cards, mounted on black-painted cardboard and very well made.'[21] This is a pretty accurate description of Van Everdingen's brunaille book, albeit that the black cardboard seems no longer to be present. That was probably lost in the

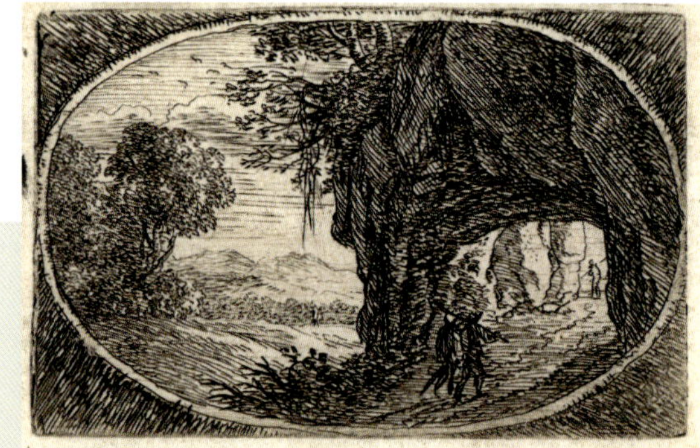

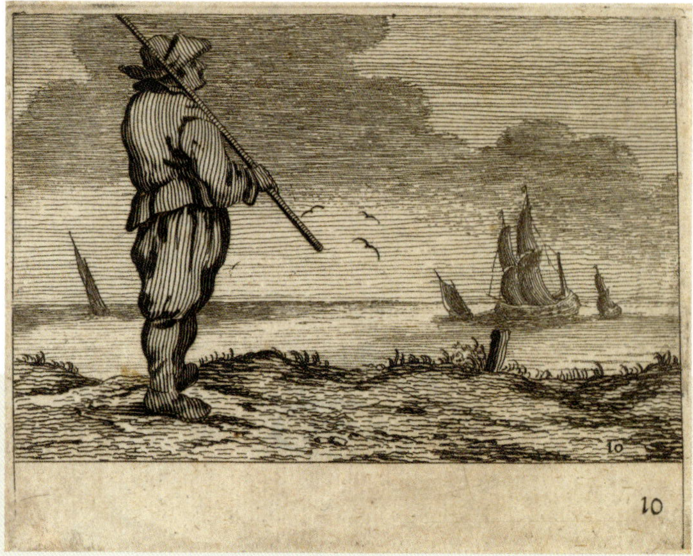

165
Herman van Swanevelt,
*Landscape with a Path
through a Rock*, c. 1646,
etching, 46 x 73 mm,
Amsterdam, Rijks-
museum, inv. no.
RP-P-OB-60.925

> 166
Gillis van Scheyndel I
after Jan Porcellis, *Dune
Landscape with a Man
Watching a Ship,* 1645,
etching, 72 x 93 mm,
Amsterdam, Rijks-
museum, inv. no.
RP-P-1894-A-18329

nineteenth century, when the brunailles were
mounted on new supports.[22] The three sheets in
the Stichting P. & N. de Boer collection do appear
to be mounted on their original supports, which
show traces of dark paint.

There is no information as to who owned
the album in the period from Tydeman's death
in 1713 until the sale of Guichardot's estate in
1875. A few leaves were taken out of the book
in the meantime, for the 1875 sale catalogue
only mentions forty-four.[23] After that, the little
brunaille album changed hands several times
in relatively quick succession before surfacing
again in the Netherlands at the beginning of
the twentieth century.[24] In 1944 it was recorded
as being with the Hague collector Hendrik
Piek (1879-1950). In the summer of 1949,
he removed four brunailles from the album to
loan them to the RKD – Netherlands Institute
for Art History in The Hague for an exhibition.
The fine *Seascape with a Frigate among the
Rocks* (fig. 143) has been missing ever since.[25]
After Piek's death in 1950, the brunaille book
passed to his widow, Wilhelmina Hendrika
Piek-van Ditmar (1881-1968), who in turn left
it to the Dutch State.[26] In 1968 the album was
transferred to the Rijksmuseum, where a year
later the thirty-eight surviving brunailles were
rebound in their parchment binding.[27] It is to
be hoped that the four missing leaves will turn
up one day, so that we have a complete picture
of the original group.

1 Van Everdingen also worked on this very small scale on other occasions; see Yvonne Bleyerveld's essay in this catalogue (figs. 129-134, cat. nos. 58-63).
2 On the technique and history of the grisaille see Buijsen 2018, vol. 1, pp. 128-131 (with further literature).
3 These are two photographs in the image documentation collection at the RKD – Netherlands Institute for Art History in The Hague (BD/RKD/0160 – A. van Everdingen/ folder 5; BD/RKD/0278 – A. van Everdingen/ folder 4). Not in Davies 2007.
4 The drawing: Davies 2007, cat. no. 283; see also Chapel Hill/Ithaca/Worcester 1999, cat. no. 9.
5 The drawing: Davies 2007, cat. no. 325.
6 Guichardot dealt in drawings and prints, and was regularly called in as an expert at sales in the 1844-1868 period. His good reputation as a specialist is evident from a comment in the catalogue compiled for the sale of his estate: 'Les attributions de feu Guichardot, en ce qui concerne les dessins, ont été conservées' ('Where the drawings are concerned, the attributions of the late Guichardot have been retained'). See sale Guichardot Collection, Paris (Delbergue-Cormont), 7-20 July 1875; the brunaille album is listed under no. 130.
7 See also Davies 2007, pp. 87-88.
8 Giltaij in Rotterdam/Berlin 1996, pp. 114 and 116.
9 Davies 2001, pp. 51 and 53.
10 Van Everdingen would probably also have had the seascapes by Jan Porcellis (fig. 65), Simon de Vlieger (c. 1601-1653) and Bonaventura Peeters I (1614-1652) at the back of his mind while painting his brunailles. For examples see De Beer 2019a, pp. 87-99.
11 Van Everdingen also used the rock arch in one of his etchings, see fig. 201 (cat. no. 16). See De Beer 2019a, pp. 97-98, note 301, for a discussion of the pictorial tradition of this motif.

12 See also Davies 2001, p. 55.
13 Tonal or monochrome landscape paintings were swiftly executed with very thin layers of paint in a limited palette of brown, green and grey shades (Beck 1972-1973, vol. 1, pp. 41 and 46-47; Sutton 1987, pp. 35-37; Sluijter 1996, pp. 45-47).
14 The painting: Davies 2001, cat. no. 8.
15 Dirck Barendsz (1534-1592), Anthony van Dyck (1599-1641) and Rembrandt van Rijn (1606-1669) were among the many artists who did this. See also Packer 2017, pp. 137-142; Sliwka 2017, pp. 53-63; Buijsen 2018, vol. 1, p. 127 (with further literature).
16 Van Swanevelt: *Variae Campestru Fantasiae*, c. 1646. See Hollstein (Herman van Swanevelt) 63-86; Steland 2005, p. 57; Wuestman 2007, pp. 66-67. Porcellis: *Verscheyden stranden en water gesichten*, engraved by Gillis van Scheyndel I (c. 1595-before 1660), 1645, see Hollstein (Jan Porcellis) 1-17.
17 Sale Dr August Straeter (1810-1897) Collection, Stuttgart (H.G. Gutekunst), 10-14 May 1898, no. 1117.
18 In the original Dutch:
Ao. 1684 den 20. Meert: / Heeft de Heer Benjamin Wannemaker, J.V.D. van Leiden, / aen Gerhard Tydeman, tot een gedagtenis, vereert, / dese 47. Zeestukjes en Landschapjes, met oliverf ge= / schildert op Caerteblaetjes, door P. [T./A.] v Venner I ..., ... Van Gojen, / Zeeman- / ten minsten. – 50 – 0 – 0
19 Wannemaker was a lawyer at the Court of Holland before he emigrated to England (Erfgoed Leiden en Omstreken, accession no. 0511B: Archief van de Kerkeraad van de Nederlandse Hervormde gemeente te Leiden, inv. no. 361). With thanks to Lisa Lucassen. See also Lunsingh Scheurleer, Fock and Van Dissel 1986-1992, vol. 4b, pp. 520 and 536.
20 Erfgoed Leiden en Omstreken, accession no. 0518: Archief van de Weeskamer te Leiden, inv. no. 19585, Staat van het toebedeelde aan Benjamin Wannemaker.

21 Von Uffenbach 1753-1754, vol. 2, p. 366: 'Unter diesen war ein klein länglicht Büchlein wie ein Stammbuch; in seldigem waren etlich und dreissig auf Charten mit Oelfarbe klein gemalte See-Stückgen, welche auf schwarzgefärbte Pappendeckel geklebet, und sehr wohl gemacht waren.'
22 The paper from which the mounts are made probably dates from the nineteenth century. Most of the endpapers at the front and back of the album are seventeenth century. With thanks to Erik Hinterding.
23 Regrettably we do not know exactly which subjects were depicted on the three leaves that were removed. It is consequently impossible to say whether they were identical to three of the known loose brunailles (figs. 139-142).
24 Sale Dr August Straeter Collection, Stuttgart (H.G. Gutekunst), 10-14 May 1898, no. 1117; purchased for 280 DM by the Prestel gallery, Frankfurt am Main; sale Frankfurt am Main (Prestel), 18-19 November 1921, no. 326.
25 Note in the image documentation of the RKD – Netherlands Institute for Art History in The Hague: '4 stuks uit een plakboek van 47 tekeningen. / door de eigenaar uit elkaar gehaald. / Verz. H. Piek, Den Haag (1944). / Tent. Rijksbureau voor Kunsthistorische Documentatie, 1949' ('4 pieces from an album of 47 drawings, taken apart by the owner. Coll. H. Piek, The Hague (1944). Exh. Rijksbureau voor Kunsthistorische Documentatie, 1949') (BD/RKD/0160 – A. van Everdingen/folder 5). See also the RKD Annual Report for 1949, p. 1.
26 RKD Annual report for 1968, pp. 1-2 (000-000); Cultural Heritage Agency of the Netherlands, Schenkingen en Legaten Archief, W.H. Piek-van Ditmar file.
27 With thanks to Marleen Ram, who checked this for me.

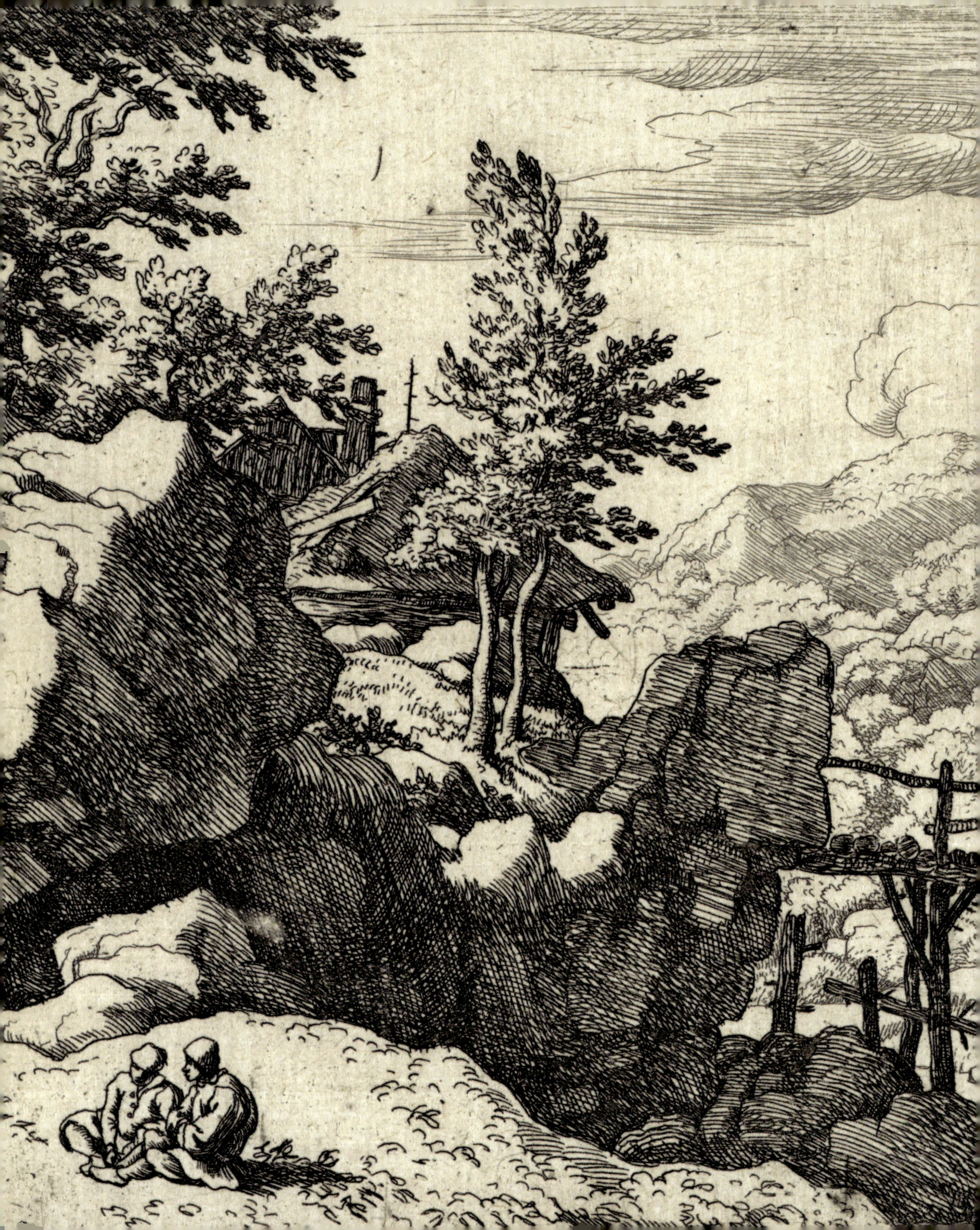

4

'ETCHED IN A MOST LIVELY MANNER'

Allart van Everdingen's Landscape Prints*

Erik Hinterding

< Detail of fig. 176

Allart van Everdingen is known for his paintings and drawings, but he also left a sizable oeuvre of etchings to his own designs. This combination of disciplines was not uncommon in the seventeenth century, for an artist who can draw can also, in theory, etch.[1] Instead of drawing on a sheet of paper, however, he draws on a copper plate. To make an etching, Van Everdingen coated the plate with a mixture of resin and beeswax. So that he could see what he was drawing, he used soot to blacken the surface. Taking an etching needle, he drew in the wax, revealing the bare metal. He bit out these exposed lines in the copper plate in an acid bath and cleaned the remaining ground off the plate. When the plate was inked and pulled through a printing press with a sheet of paper on it, an impression—an etching—appeared on the paper.[2]

In the great majority of the etchings he made, Allart remained true to his specialism; they are landscapes, almost without exception inspired by his trip to Norway in 1644 (fig. 167).[3] He also made a series of prints illustrating the medieval tale of Reynard the Fox. Marjan Pantjes examines that group in the present catalogue; this essay looks in depth at his landscape etchings.

As we shall see, in the eighteenth century the number of landscape prints by Van Everdingen was held at one hundred. Since then a few extremely rare prints have been added to the oeuvre, bringing the total up to a hundred and nine at present.[4] The great majority are signed, usually with his initials 'AVE', and in eleven cases with his full name.[5] This provides a firm anchor for the attribution to the artist. On the other hand, none of the etchings is dated, making it difficult to establish a chronology for the oeuvre. For this reason, the landscapes in the very first oeuvre catalogue, which was compiled by the renowned print connoisseur Adam Bartsch in 1803, were arranged by size, from the smallest to the largest.[6] Bartsch also put prints of virtually the same dimensions together as groups.[7] He arrived at fourteen groups altogether, often of four etchings, but there are also groups of six, eight and even twelve landscapes.[8] He regarded many of the etchings as loose prints.[9] There can be no doubt that Van Everdingen sometimes made his drawings as sets, for example the months of the year.[10] In the case of the four prints of the springs at Spa (figs. 204 and 206-208), putting them together into one group seems convincing

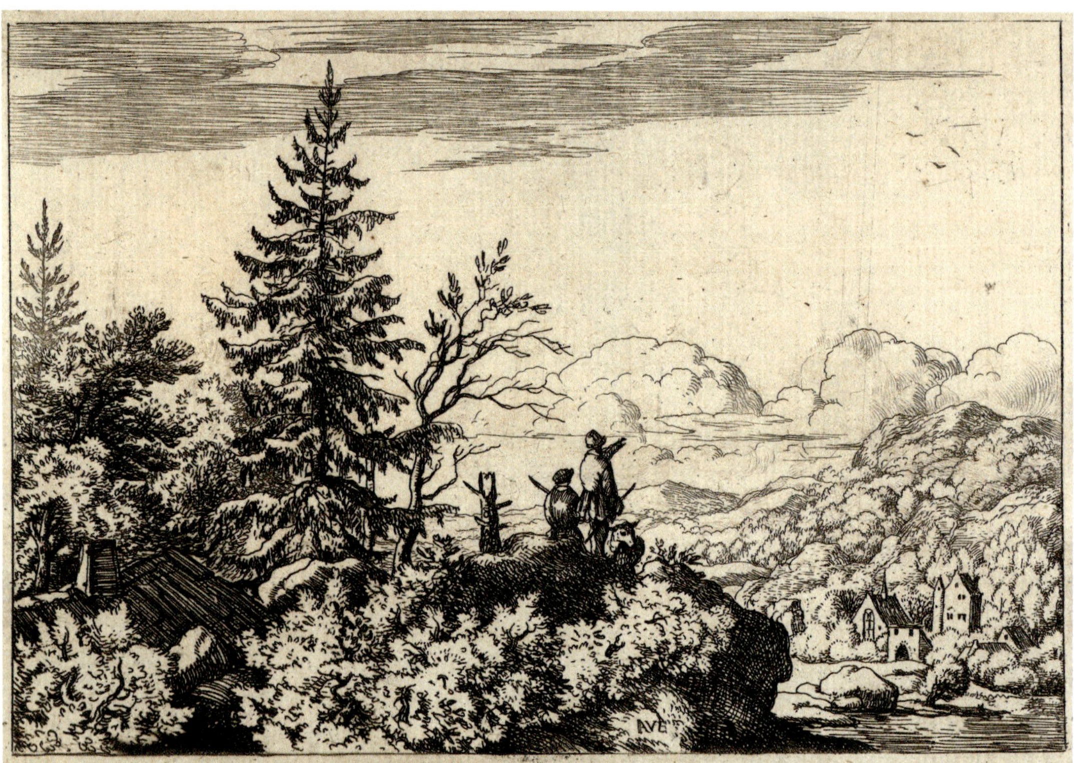

enough, but in other cases it is uncertain whether the precise sequencing does justice to the way the artist originally published them. In the absence of a meaningful alternative, later oeuvre catalogues kept the same order.[11]

In the nineteenth century, people looked to the watermarks in the paper on which the etchings are printed to distinguish early impressions from later ones and at least arrive at a rough dating for the oeuvre. In 1873 the German print dealer Wilhelm Eduard Drugulin noted that the earliest watermarks in Allart van Everdingen's prints were a Paschal Lamb and a small Foolscap with seven slender points to the collar, both of which he dated to around 1645-1650.[12] This almost certainly has to be a little later. The Paschal Lamb that has been found during the present investigation is a proof of *Landscape with a Horseman near a Hamlet* (fig. 168).[13] It is not found in the identical form in the watermark handbooks, but a very similar mark occurs in 1651 or slightly later.[14] The Foolscap with a seven-pointed collar does not appear as a type of watermark before 1650 at all. This variant is

not found until 1651, at first sporadically but increasingly often as the seventeenth century progressed.[15] This suggests that Van Everdingen's earliest etched work has to be dated not to around 1645-1650, but only after 1651. It would therefore seem safe to conclude that Allart began working as a printmaker in Amsterdam, where he lived from 1652 onwards.[16]

Drugulin also mentioned two variants of the Arms of Amsterdam watermark, which he found in impressions of the first state of some eighty landscape etchings and proofs of the Reynard plates.[17] One of these watermarks is an Arms of Amsterdam with the initials 'LA' below it (fig. 169).[18] No identical watermark has been found in the handbooks either, but a very similar mark can be dated to around 1675.[19] That is about he same time as the last mark discussed here: a Foolscap with a seven-pointed collar and a strikingly long middle collar point (fig. 170).[20] Drugulin described the edition with this watermark as 'a general edition of both the landscapes and the finished impressions of Reynard'.[21] This makes it the first full edition

167
Allart van Everdingen, *Two Men on a Hill*, etching, 100 x 146 mm, Amsterdam, Rijksmuseum, inv. no. RP-P-OB-50.343 (Holl. 46 I) (cat. no. 15)

of Allart van Everdingen's etchings, which can be dated to around 1675 or slightly later.[22] Since this was the year the artist died, it must be the first complete edition after his death.

All told, the watermarks are not particularly helpful in determining when Van Everdingen made his etchings. The last Foolscap discussed above does, though, make something else clear. None of the prints on this paper has the strengthened borderlines around the compositions or the shadow passages reinforced with extra lines drawn with a burin, which we shall discuss below. These changes can be securely dated to after 1675 and were therefore not made by Allart van Everdingen or during his lifetime.

Influences

It is possible to identify technical, stylistic and compositional differences that point to a development in the etched work. The obvious first step in finding out which prints belong to the earliest part of the oeuvre is to compare them with the work of the artists from whom Van Everdingen learnt his trade. According to artists' biographer Arnold Houbraken, Roelandt Savery (1576-1639) was his first teacher and Pieter de Molijn (1595-1661) in Haarlem the second.[23] It has not as yet proved possible to find anything in the records to substantiate this assertion, but clear links with the art of both masters can be identified in Van Everdingen's etchings.

Allart's etching *Three Travellers in a Wood* (fig. 171) bears a striking resemblance to Savery's *Gnarled Trees by the Water* (fig. 172).[24]

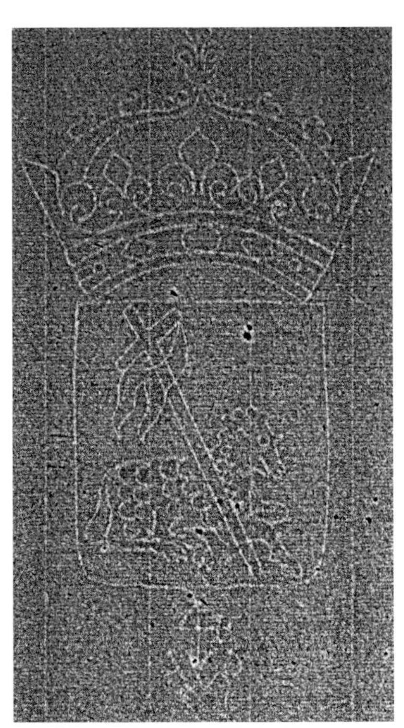

168
Paschal Lamb watermark in Allart van Everdingen, *Landscape with a Horseman near a Hamlet* (fig. 186, cat. no. 7)

169
Arms of Amsterdam watermark in Allart van Everdingen, *Landscape with a Horseman on a Bridge*, Amsterdam, Rijksmuseum, inv. no. RP-P-1879-A-3072 (Holl. 50 I)

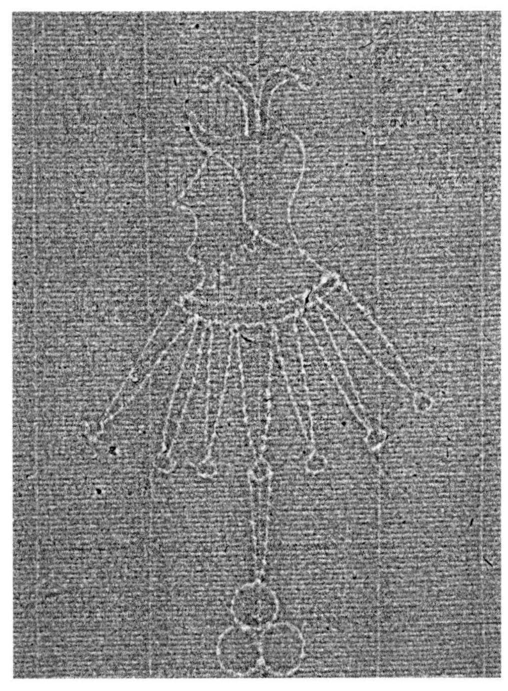

170
Foolscap with seven-pointed collar watermark in Allart van Everdingen, *Landscape with Two Men in the Door of a Log Cabin*, Amsterdam, Rijksmuseum, inv. no. RP-P-OB-50.352 (Holl. 48 II)

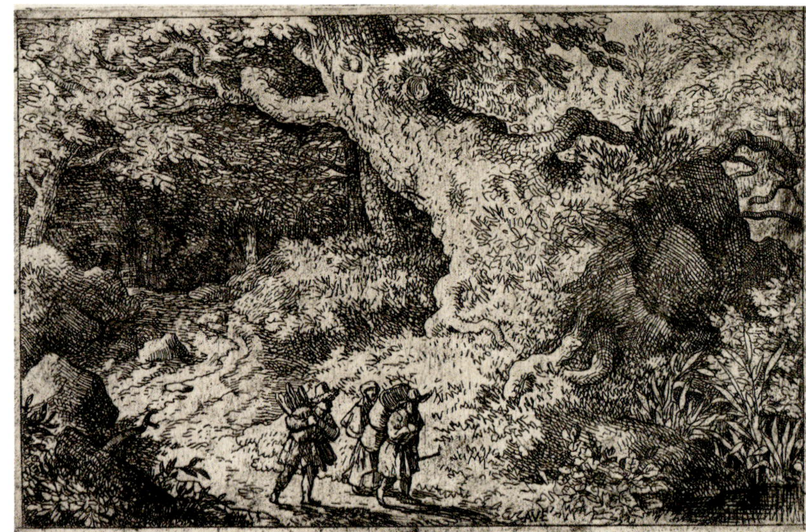

171
Allart van Everdingen,
*Three Travellers in a
Wood*, etching, 105 x
166 mm, Amsterdam
Rijksmuseum, inv. no.
RP-P-OB-50.419
(Holl. 89 II)

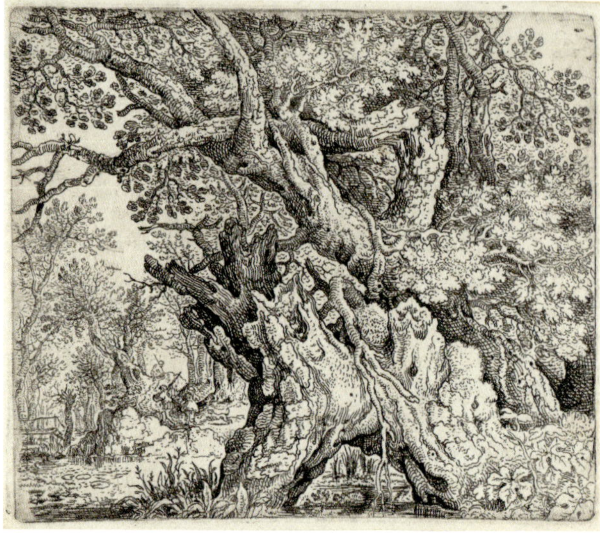

172
Roelandt Savery,
*Gnarled Trees by the
Water*, etching, 124 x
145 mm, Amsterdam,
Rijksmuseum, inv. no.
RP-P-1878-A-1543

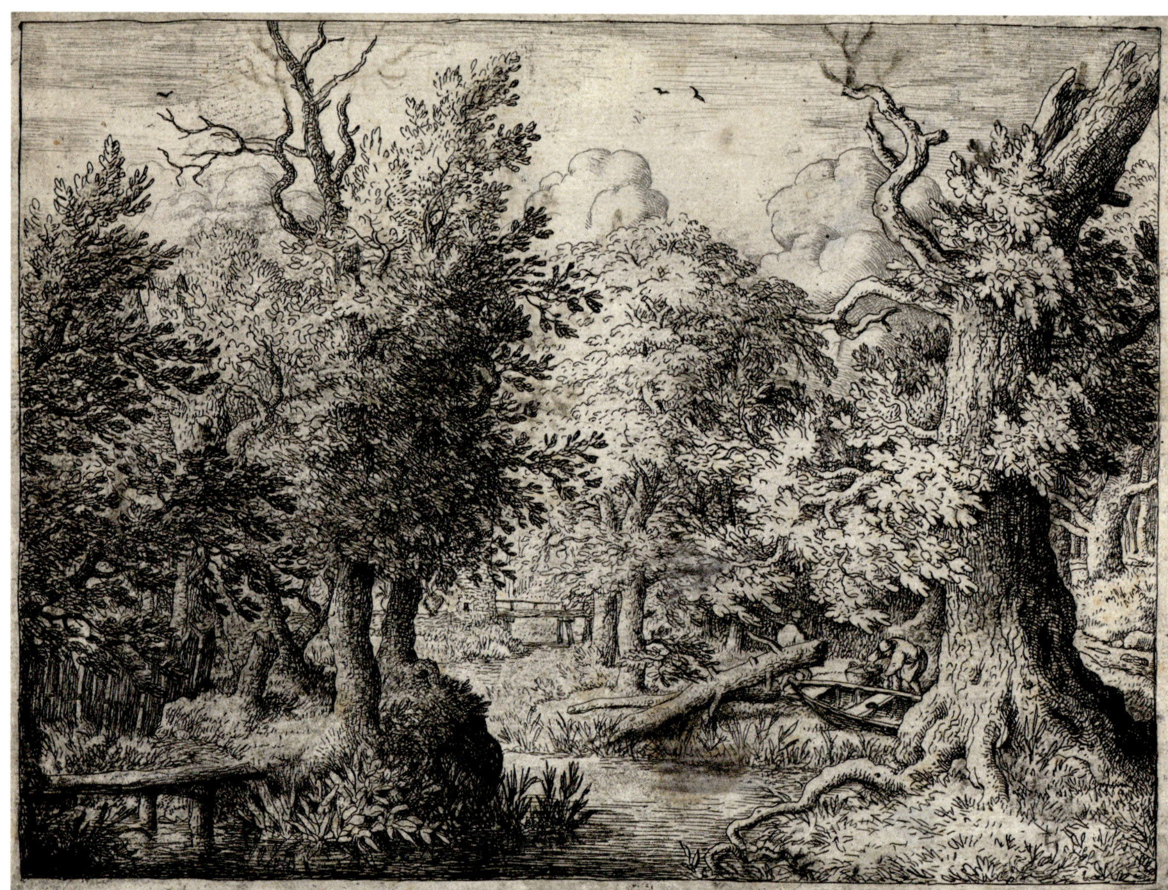

173
Allart van Everdingen,
Stream in the Woods,
etching, retouched
with black chalk, 143 x
194 mm, Amsterdam,
Rijksmuseum, inv. no.
RP-P-OB-50.440
(Holl. 101 I) (cat. no. 25)

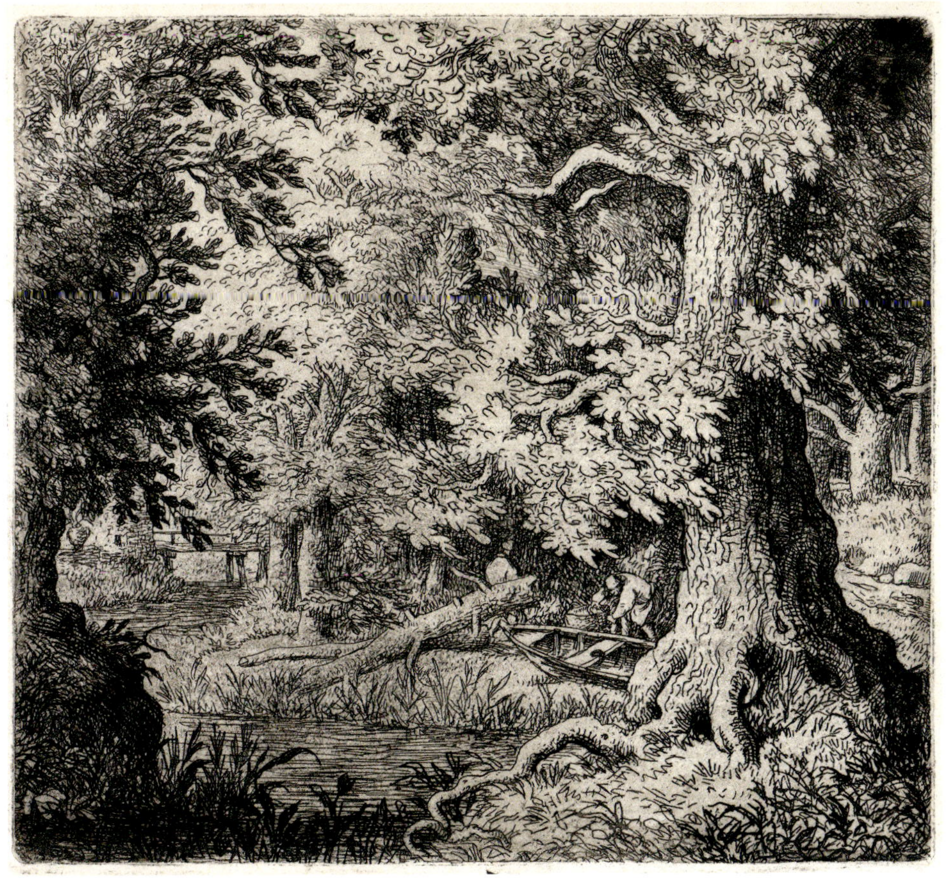

174
Allart van Everdingen, *Stream in the Woods*, etching, 115 x 130 mm, Amsterdam, Rijksmuseum, inv. no. RP-P-OB-50.441 (Holl. 101 VI) (cat. no. 26)

Savery etched the composition to his own design.[25] Both prints feature a giant tree in a wood, with three travellers walking along a path beside it. It is the similarities in style that immediately catch the eye. Like Savery's, Van Everdingen's tree is drawn in a very linear style. Save for a few short dashes, the light passages are left white, while the shadows on the trunk are suggested with regular parallel lines or cross-hatching in an open lozenge pattern, particularly evident on the long roots. Van Everdingen also conveyed the tree canopy—the way the leaves are rendered—in much the same way as Savery. He indicated the foliage in the light with sparse round strokes, that in the shade with small individual groups of leaves on a twig, often three together, which he made darker with a few parallel lines. And, as in Savery's etching, the shadow between the trees and the foliage is reinforced with horizontal lines in a few places.

Roelandt Savery's influence is also unmistakable in *Stream in the Woods* (fig. 173). On the right stands a gnarled tree with exposed roots snaking over the bank. The leaves, both lit and in shadow, are very like those in the previous print (fig. 171). Behind the tree, beside some fallen trunks, two men work near a rowing boat. There is an intriguing building in the centre, possibly a small castle, only a corner of which, connected by a wooden bridge over the water, can be seen through the vegetation. Van Everdingen needed six states (changes to the design on the copper plate) to get the composition right—an exceptionally high number in his etched oeuvre. He evidently struggled before he was happy with the result. In the first state shown here, the composition is essentially complete. The clouds strike a jarring note, etched as they are with a thinner etching needle and in a much more precise style, producing a strange contrast with the more broadly etched wood. Allart must have noticed this at once, for on this impression he used black chalk to sketch in the way he wanted to extend the branches, then pursued the idea in the following states. Step by step he added branches and foliage until the clouds had completely disappeared behind the tree canopy. He also cropped the copper plate on the left and along the top edge, leaving himself with a virtually square image (fig. 174).[26]

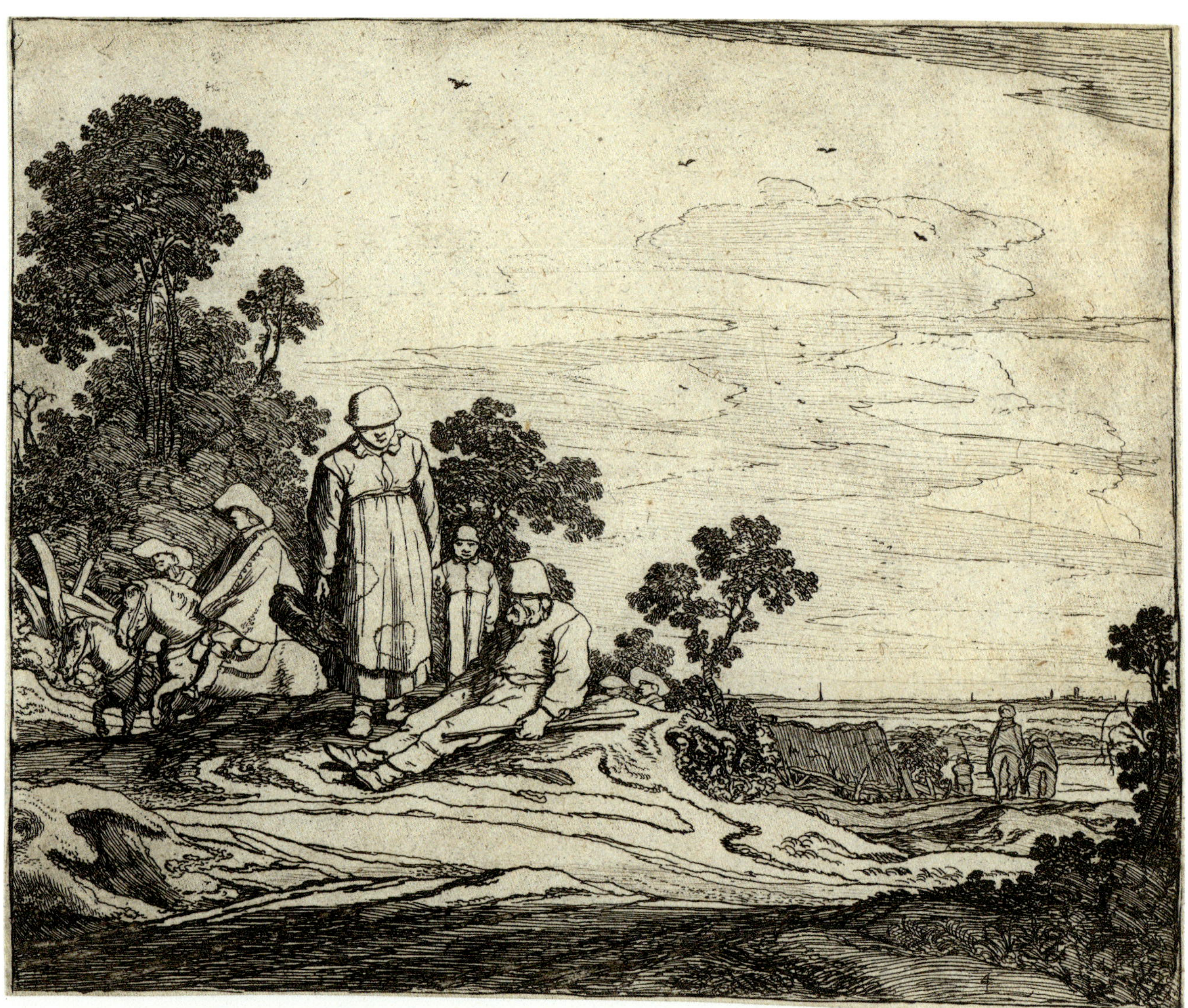

175
Pieter de Molijn, *Land-scape with Horsemen*, 1626, etching, 152 x 187 mm, Amsterdam, Rijksmuseum, inv. no. RP-P-OB-12.613

There are also striking similarities between Van Everdingen's etchings and Pieter de Molijn's etched oeuvre, even though there are no more than four known etchings by De Molijn. *Land-scape with Horsemen* (fig. 175) is typical. Executed like a drawing with a clarity of line, the shadows are usually darkened with parallel lines—sometimes very regularly, as on the roof of the farmhouse on the right, sometimes meandering more calligraphically, as in the foreground.[27] De Molijn indicated light areas with little more than outlines, including the figures, which he shaded only enough to give them the necessary volume. This created harsh contrasts between light and shade. He also divided the composition quite schematically: a dark foreground that acts as a repoussoir, a light middle ground against a backdrop of dark trees and some buildings in the background. He finished by indicating the blue of the sky with a much thinner etching needle than he had used for the landscape. The ramshackle fencing beyond the horsemen on the extreme left is not very prominent in this scene, but it is a conspicuous element in Pieter de Molijn's other etchings.

Like De Molijn's etchings, Allart van Everdingen's *Landscape with a Man on a Bridge* (fig. 176) was drawn with firm, clean lines that describe the composition in rather hard contrasts without intermediate tones. The areas in full light are barely filled, like the little figures in the foreground, which are mostly outlines.

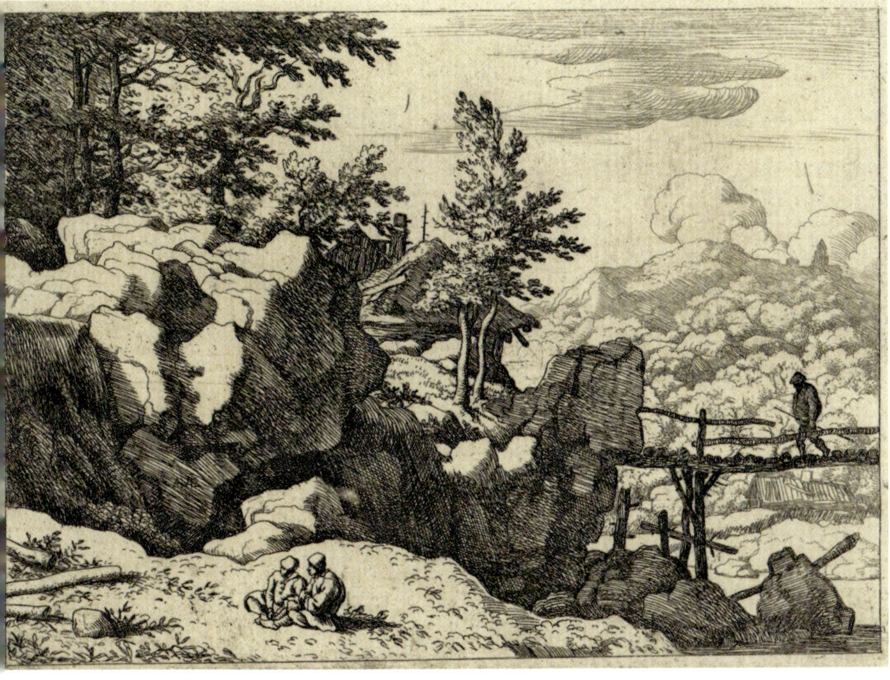

176
Allart van Everdingen, *Landscape with a Man on a Bridge*, etching, 102 x 141 mm, Amsterdam, Rijksmuseum, inv. no. RP-P-OB-50.362 (Holl. 53 I)

The shadows, on the other hand, are often built up from parallel lines, with some open cross-hatching on the rocks to define the deepest areas of shadow there. This passage also acts as a dark middle ground with a light foreground in front of it, while a lighter mountain rises in the distance. As De Molijn did, Van Everdingen indicated the sky with much finer lines than the foreground. The mountain in the background was executed in the same way. There are, though, differences in the foliage. Where Pieter de Molijn represented it like the florets of a cauliflower, which he shaded with regular, gently curved lines, Van Everdingen rendered the leaves more individually, much as Roelandt Savery did.

Many of these characteristics can also be recognized in other etchings by Allart van Everdingen, such as *Landscape with a Log Cabin by a Waterfall* (fig. 177), where the dark areas are created chiefly with parallel lines—going in different directions and sometimes gracefully flowing, but virtually without cross-hatching. Here the strict division of the composition into foreground, middle ground and background has been abandoned. This arrangement is rather more evident in *Landscape with a Sawhorse* (fig. 178), which also has echoes of the fences in Pieter de Molijn's etchings.[28]

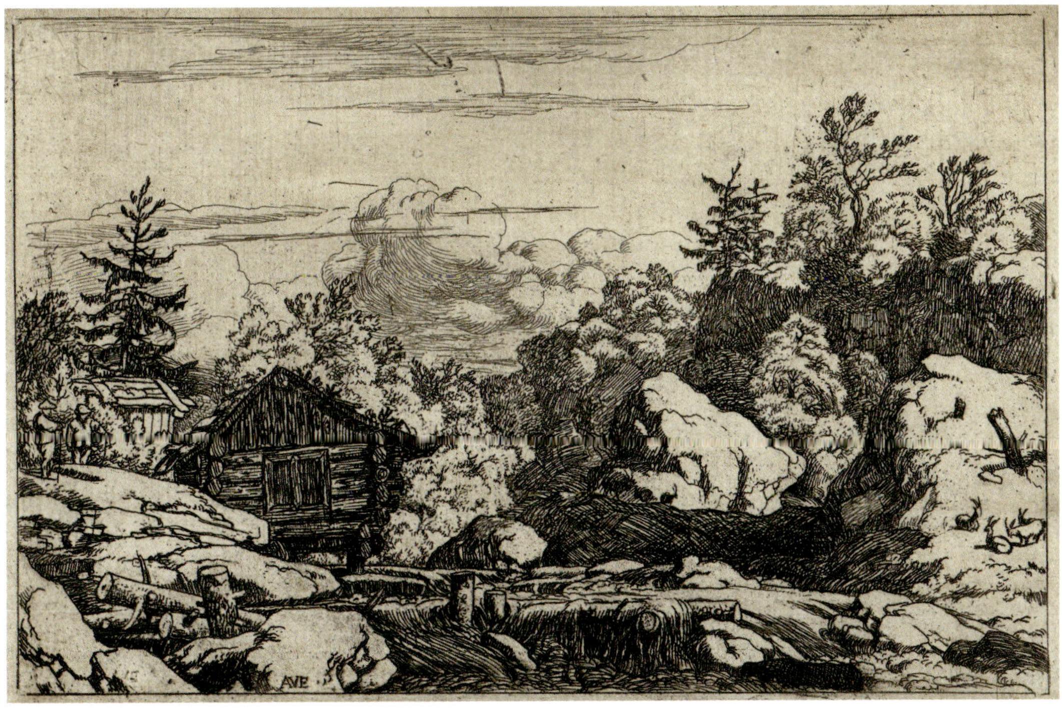

177
Allart van Everdingen, *Landscape with a Log Cabin by a Waterfall*, etching, 92 x 143 mm, Amsterdam, Rijksmuseum, inv. no. RP-P-OB-50.331 (Holl. 36 I)

178
Allart van Everdingen,
*Landscape with a
Sawhorse*, etching,
64 x 113 mm, Amster-
dam, Rijksmuseum,
inv. no. RP-P-OB-50.305
(Holl. 21 I)

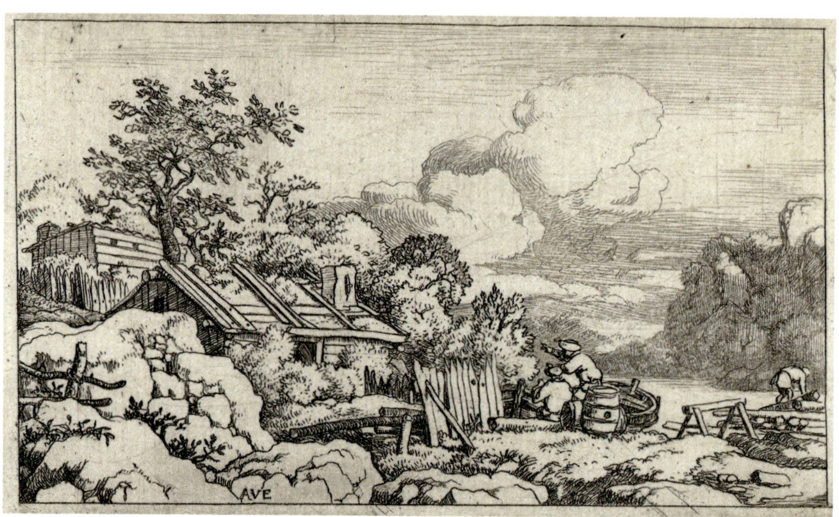

In short, while Allart van Everdingen was clearly influenced by Roelandt Savery in the rendition of trees and leaves in the prints discussed here, he was also indebted to the Haarlem artist Pieter de Molijn for the style, structure and finish of these landscapes. His robust style builds on the stylized landscapes of other Haarlem print-makers like Claes Jansz Visscher (c. 1587-1652), Willem Pietersz Buytenwech (c. 1591-1624) and Esaias van de Velde (1587-1630): clear forms, strong lines, powerful chiaroscuro.[29] The style of Allart van Everdingen's prints that tie in with Pieter de Molijn's can be regarded as an outlier of the vivid etching manner that enjoyed its heyday in the sixteen-twenties and thirties.[30] In that sense, Allart's style is rather old-fashioned, with its roots in Haarlem. It is likely that these prints are also among his early etched works, although this cannot be said with certainty because, at least for the time being, there are no firm anchors.

Thematic Shifts

Whereas Allart van Everdingen never dated his etchings and drawings, he did on occasion put a year on his paintings. Writing in this catalogue, Christi Klinkert took this as the framework for identifying a broad thematic shift in the painted oeuvre. Most of Allart's earliest paintings were seascapes, but in his first landscapes he showed a preference for panoramic vistas, with rough, inhospitable rocks and little sign of human activity (fig. 47). Even before he moved

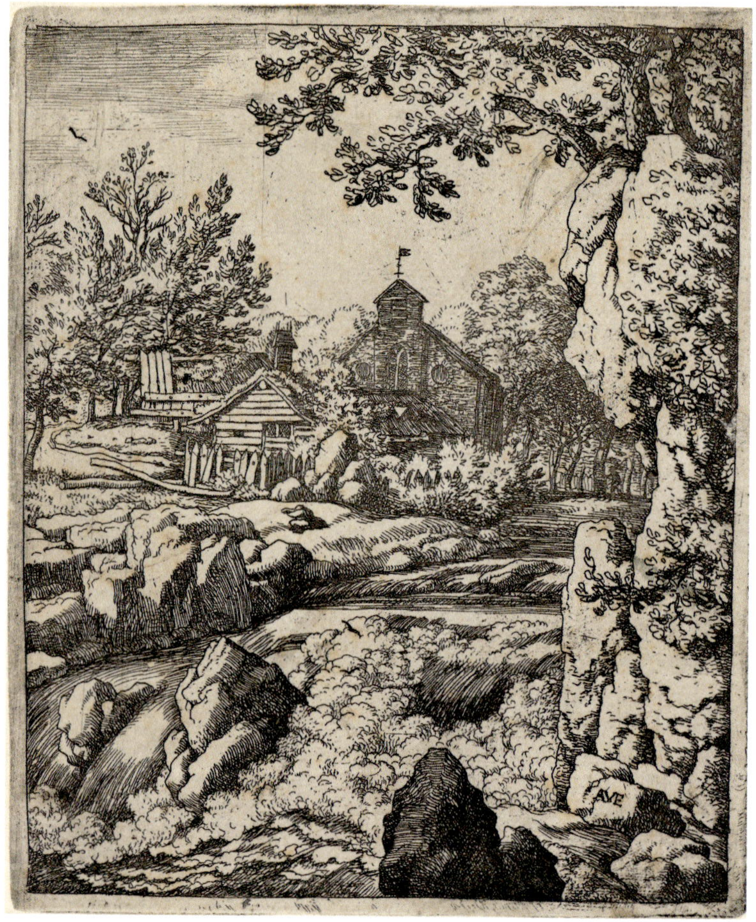

179
Allart van Everdingen,
*Landscape with a
Church and a Water-
fall*, etching, 126 x
106 mm, Amsterdam,
Rijksmuseum, inv. no.
RP-P-OB-50.284
(Holl. 7 Ia) (cat. no. 8)

to Amsterdam, his paintings became more populated and depicted more welcoming Norwegian landscapes, often featuring log cabins with small figures near a waterfall (fig. 57). It may have been soon after he had settled in Amsterdam that he began to combine Norwegian elements with motifs that appear to come from other countries (fig. 74).

Although the etchings are undated, it is possible to detect a similar shift in subject. There are no more seascapes and wild mountain landscapes, but the accessible Norwegian scenes are omnipresent. *Landscape with a Church and a Waterfall* (fig. 179), for instance, features a log cabin with scattered tree trunks beside a stream. As he did in his paintings of waterfalls, Allart van Everdingen opted for a vertical format here. *View of a Village with a Barge* (fig. 180) radiates rural tranquillity, and the artist chose a high, almost square format. Ultimately, though, vertical was not his favourite register for his prints. He usually used a horizontal format, as in his *Landscape with Log Cabins on a Hill* (fig. 181). The buildings are unmistakably Norwegian, with picturesque rickety fences, goats resting in the grass and figures amiably chatting. Since Van Everdingen probably did not start etching until he went

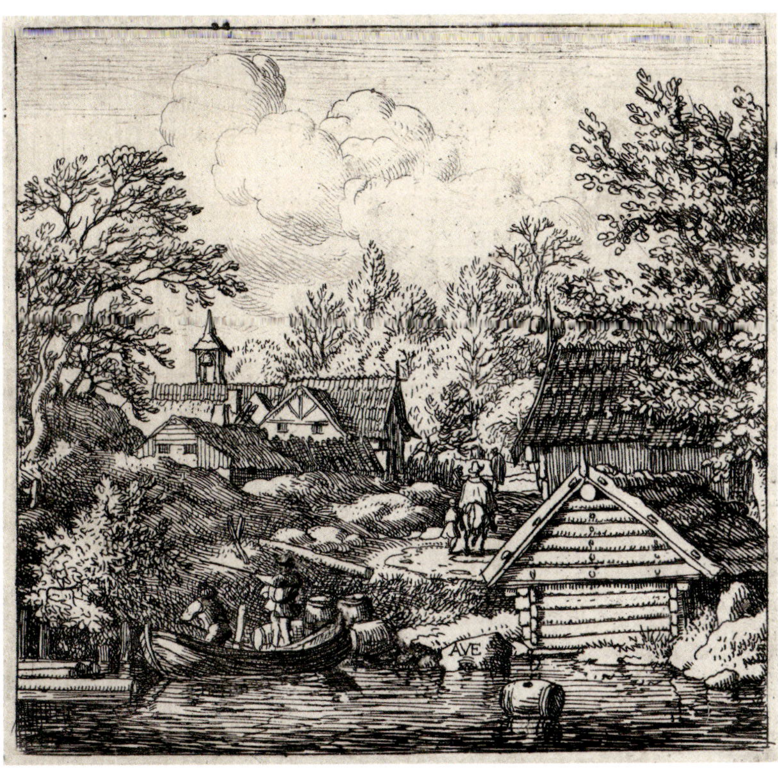

180
Allart van Everdingen,
View of a Village with a Barge, etching, 105 x 111 mm, Amsterdam, Rijksmuseum, inv. no. RP-P-OB-50.303 (Holl. 20 II) (cat. no. 10)

> 181
Allart van Everdingen,
Landscape with Log Cabins on a Hill, etching, 88 x 138 mm, Amsterdam, Rijksmuseum, inv. no. RP-P-OB-50.310 (Holl. 25 I) (cat. no. 11)

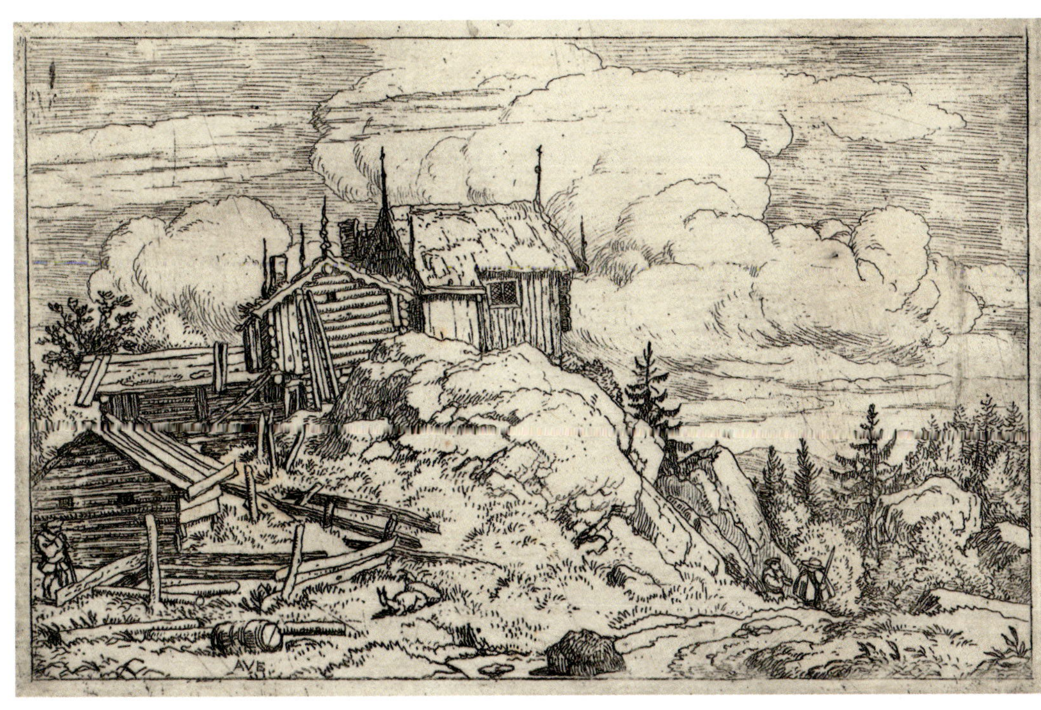

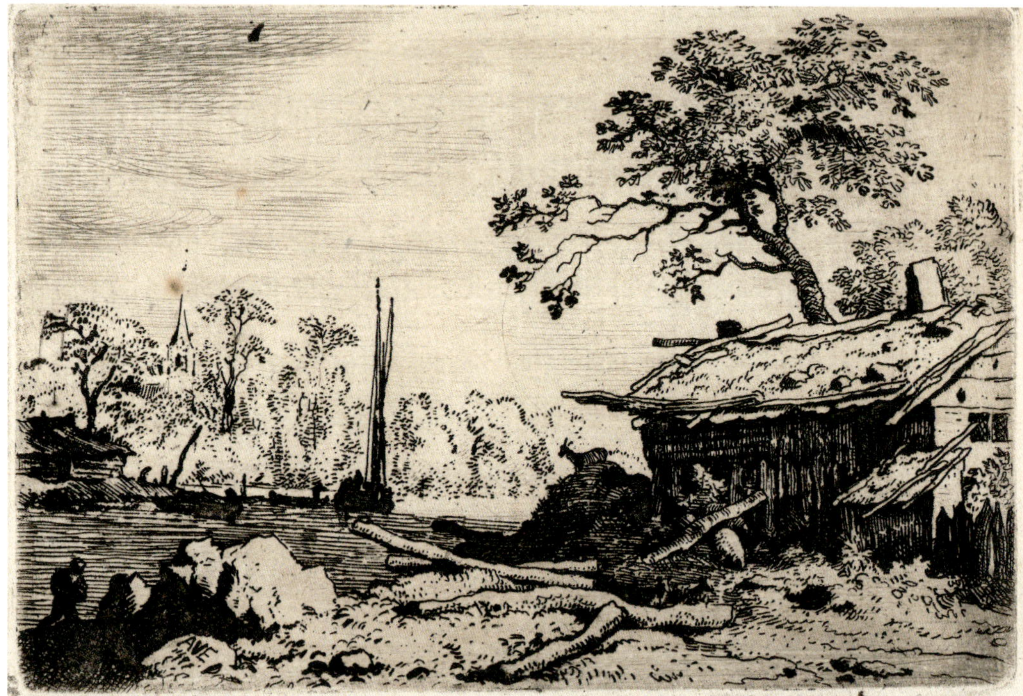

182
Allart van Everdingen, *Tumbledown Hut by the Water*, etching, 91 x 137 mm, Amsterdam, Rijksmuseum, inv. no. RP-P-OB-50.335 (Holl. 38 II)

to Amsterdam, these prints can be counted among the first ones he made there.[31]

As in his paintings, we also find 'hybrid' landscapes in his etchings, where the artist combined motifs from different sources. The mossy roof of the *Tumbledown Hut by the Water* (fig. 182) certainly looks Norwegian, as does the large rock by the water's edge on the left, the scattered tree trunks and the goat on the rock beside the house, but the river with the small boats beyond it and the church spire among the trees could easily be Dutch. A similar sort of lowland prevails in *Landscape with Three Figures Looking at a Rowing Boat*

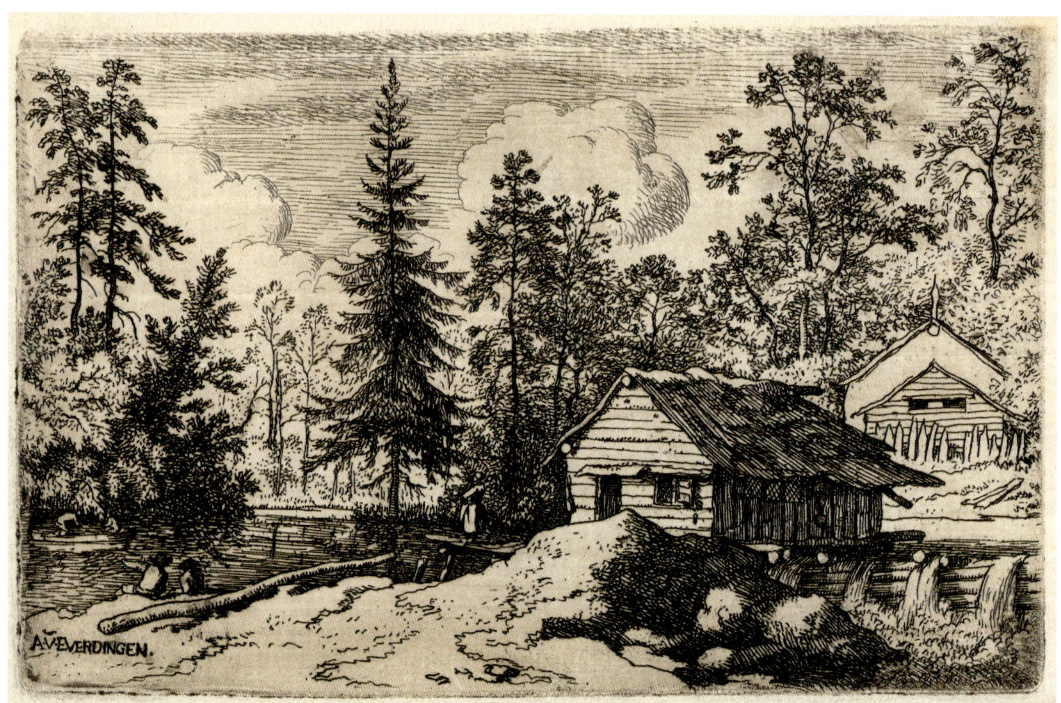

183
Allart van Everdingen, *Landscape with Three Figures Looking at a Rowing Boat*, etching, 92 x 147 mm, Amsterdam, Rijksmuseum, inv. no. RP-P-OB-50.400 (Holl. 75 II)

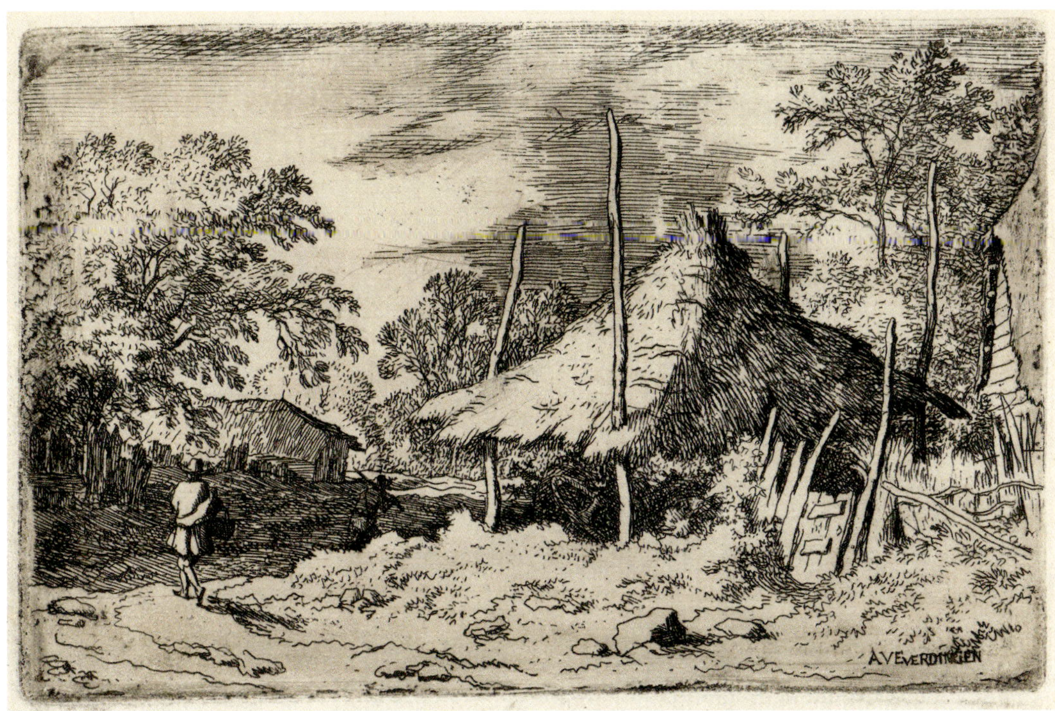

185
Allart van Everdingen,
*Landscape with Two
Houses and a Rowing
Boat*, etching, 75 x
107 mm, Amsterdam,
Rijksmuseum, inv. no.
RP-P-OB-50.291
(Holl. 11 II)

(fig. 183), in which only the weir and the log cabins on the right are reminiscent of Norway. In *Walker near a Haystack* (fig. 184), there are no evidently Norwegian elements at all. As we shall see, there are good reasons for placing the etchings in this group rather later in Allart's Amsterdam period.

Stylistic Changes

As well as these shifts in subject, there are also changes in style in Allart van Everdingen's prints that suggest a development.[32] The vigorous, graphic foliage that calls to mind the work of Allart's teacher Roelandt Savery can be found, for example, in *Landscape with a Church and a Waterfall* (fig. 179) and *View of a Village with a Barge* (fig. 180).[33] These belong in the subject category 'welcoming Norwegian scenes' that can be placed in the first years in Amsterdam, confirming that this is early etched work. After this, the drawing style becomes freer, particularly evident in the way the foliage is done. In *Landscape with Two Houses and a Rowing Boat* (fig. 185), the leaves are no longer round and robustly drawn; now they are indicated with jagged zigzag hatching and short scribbled lines that are reminiscent of the etchings of Jacob van Ruisdael (1628/1629-1682). This etching comes into the category of hybrid landscapes we touched on above. The fact that the etching style is different from that of the pure Norwegian landscapes is evidence that the hybrid landscapes did not appear in Allart's printed work at the same time. They can therefore be placed slightly later in the Amsterdam period.[34] This change in style was not long in coming, it

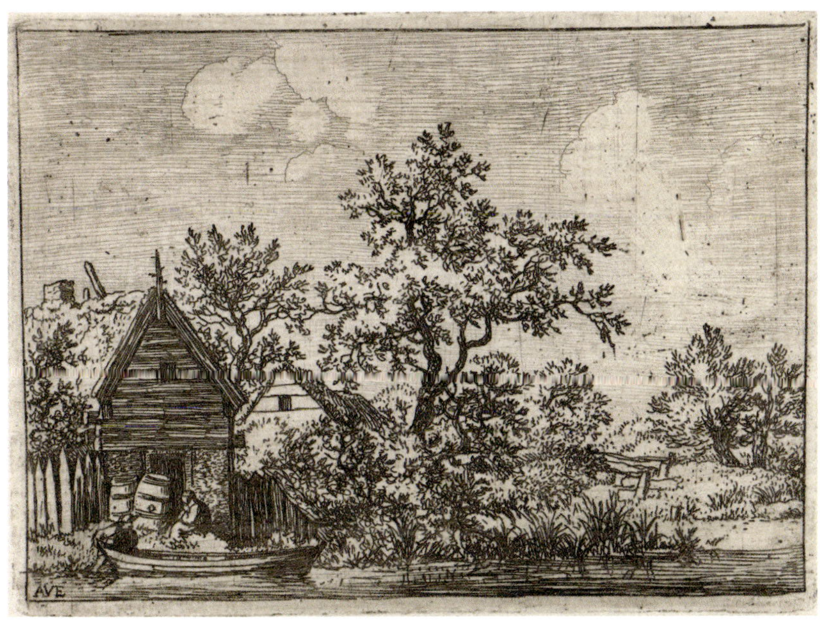

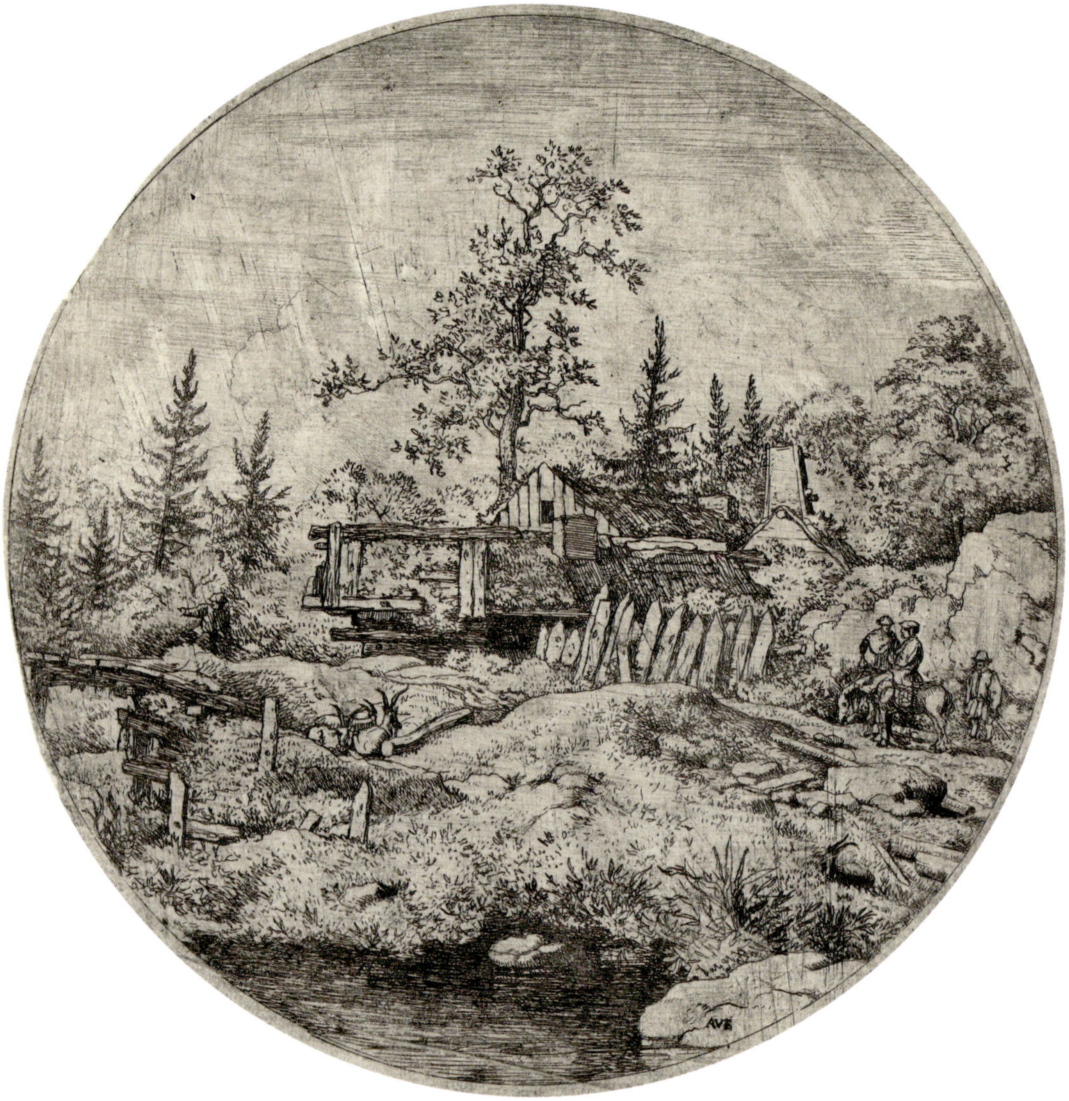

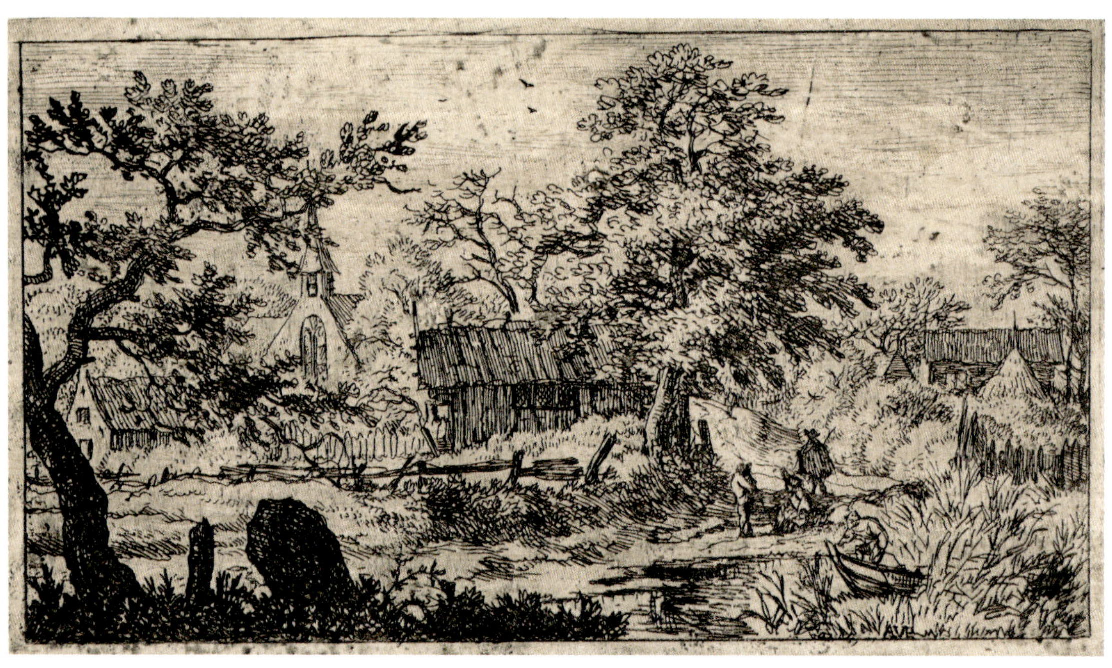

186
Allart van Everdingen,
*Landscape with a Horse-
man near a Hamlet*,
etching, 195 x 193 mm
(sheet, round), Amster-
dam, Rijksmuseum,
inv. no. RP-P-1979-90
(Holl. 4 I) (cat. no. 7)

187
Allart van Everdingen,
*Landscape with a
Rowing Boat in the
Reeds*, etching, 85 x
149 mm, Amsterdam,
Rijksmuseum, inv. no.
RP-P-OB-50.375
(Holl. 61 I)

would seem, witness *Landscape with a Horseman near a Hamlet* (fig. 186), in which (the only one in the oeuvre) the same fanciful foliage can be seen, while the subject is truly Norwegian and not yet hybrid.

There are striking differences to be found even within the group of etchings in this looser style. *Landscape with a Rowing Boat in the Reeds* (fig. 187), for instance, is very freely and sketchily drawn. This raises the question as to whether it should be placed between the Savery-style and the more fiddly prints reminiscent of Van Ruisdael, even if the subject here is undeniably hybrid. The group to which this landscape belongs is also noteworthy because all these prints appear to have been etched on a dirty copper plate, with scratches and irregularities in the surface (fig. 188).[35]

Allart van Everdingen's etching style seems eventually to have emerged as a controlled, efficient manner, which for his drawings Alice Davies described as his 'mature style'.[36] He now described the foliage chiefly with short dashes, and no longer decked out his conifers with loops on the branches, but likewise with short, separate lines. This can be seen in *Walker near a Haystack* (fig. 184) and similarly in *Landscape with Three Figures Looking at a Rowing Boat* (fig. 183).[37] All these etchings belong to the hybrid compositions in his print oeuvre, and

hence later in the Amsterdam period. Precisely when they have to be dated remains uncertain, though. In 1873, Drugulin assumed that Van Everdingen did not make any more prints after 1656.[38] That is unlikely, however, as Marjan Pantjes explains elsewhere in this catalogue, the mezzotints Allart made can be dated to after around 1665.[39] Without hard evidence, it remains impossible to place the artist's prints more accurately and only a rough classification can be made on the basis of stylistic and thematic differences.

Approach

There are remarkably few proof states of Allart van Everdingen's extant etchings. Admittedly, the copper plates were reworked after the artist's death; first of all, the framing lines around the compositions were reinforced, and later the shadows were deepened with new burin lines. It has been assumed that Simon Fokke (1712-1784) was responsible for this, because some new prints by him were added to the Reynard series when it was published by Pieter Schenk II (1693-1775) in 1752.[40] We shall see, though, that there is yet another candidate for working up the plates. True proof states, documenting the earliest stage of the etched design are rare, however. This could indicate that the artist prepared his etchings thoroughly by making drawings.

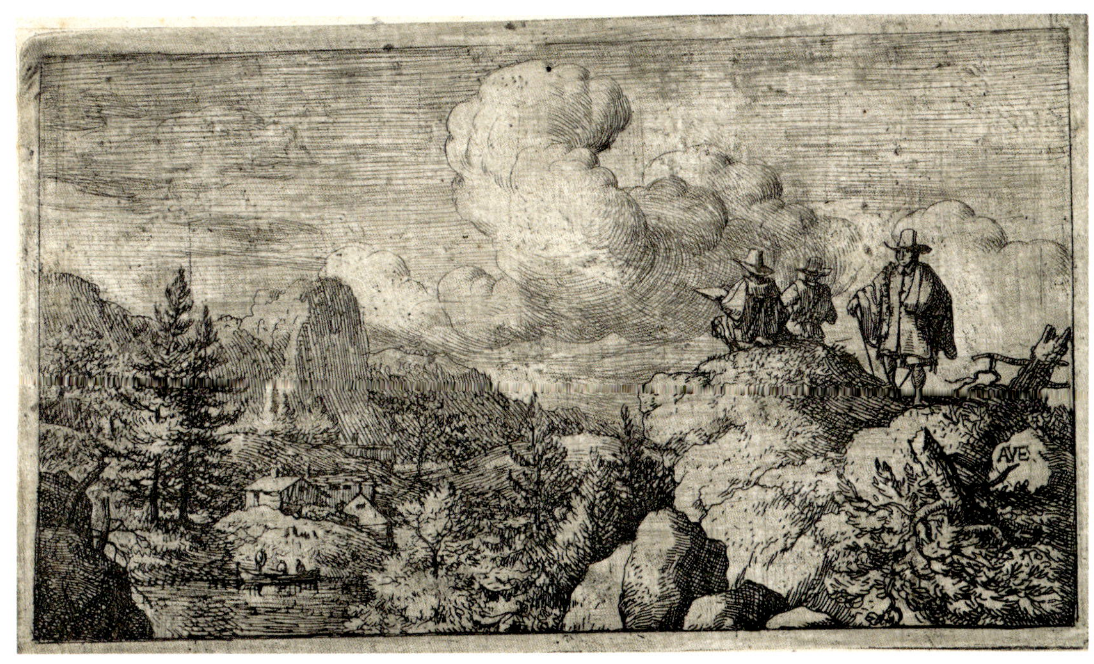

188
Allart van Everdingen, *Landscape with Artists*, etching, 85 x 148 mm, Amsterdam, Rijksmuseum, inv. no. RP-P-OB-50.378 (Holl. 63 III) (cat. no. 19)

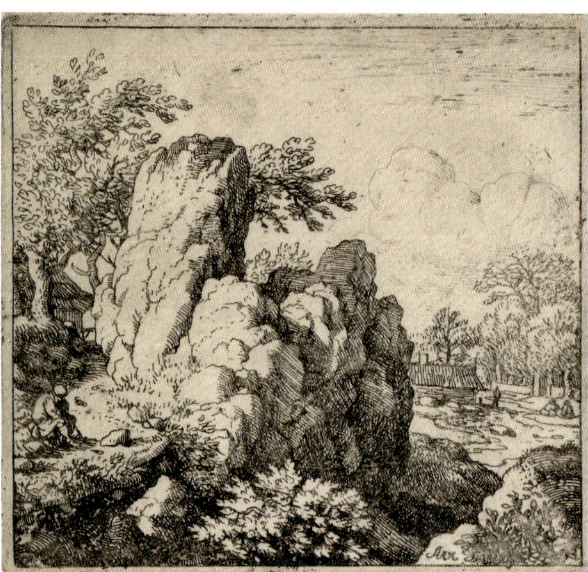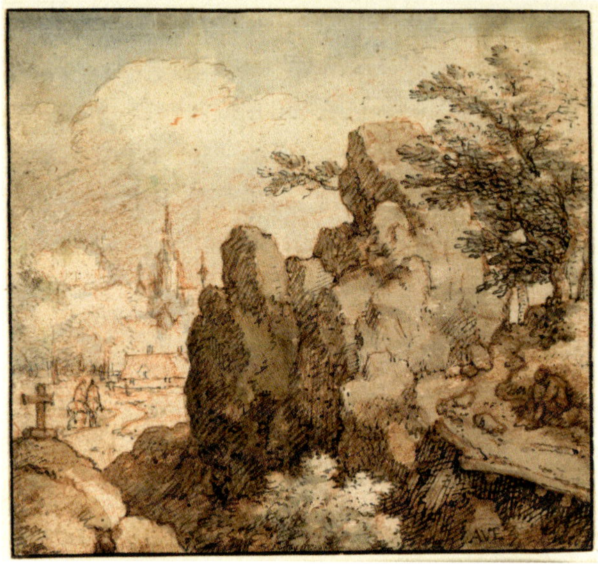

For *Landscape with a Large Rock* (fig. 189), there is indeed a drawn preliminary study, reversed in the etching (fig. 190).[41] The principal lines of the drawing have been indented, an unmistakable sign that the sheet was used to transfer the design on to the copper plate. To that end the back of the paper was coloured all over with red chalk. When the sheet was placed on the copper plate and the outlines were traced over with a hard stylus, red lines were transferred on to the blackened etching ground. These served as a guide for the further working of the etching.

Where there is an indented preliminary study, it is to be expected that the print that results will be very similar to the drawing. In this case, however, there are striking differences which reveal that the artist permitted himself a great deal of licence relative to his original design. The church behind the house in the distance, for instance, did not make it into the etching, any more than the cross on the hill in the corner. The outlines of the rock formation do correspond, but the areas of shadow differ. The top of the rock jutting out on the right is dark, but a patch immediately below it is in full light. it provides a welcome accent in the otherwise shaded rock face. The crown of the tree on the right stretches further over the rock than in the etching, and is also much more heavily shaded. And lastly, the figure below it sits in the shade in the drawing and in the light in the print.

Landscape with Two Carts (fig. 191), for which there is also an indented preliminary study (fig. 192), is very different. The drawing was done with a brush over an underdrawing in graphite and charcoal.[42] The result is extremely tonal —the sky, the mountains in the background and the dark line of trees and buildings on a hill are each indicated in a different shade without any detailing, almost as a silhouette. Only the trees in the foreground are shaded on the left side. This creates unfeasibly hard chiaroscuro; the drawing appears to be chiefly an exercise in dividing light and shade.

The etching is likewise constructed from uniform tonal areas with little detail. The dark line of trees and a church on a hill has been filled with undulating parallel lines in which trees can be made out here and there, without being distinctly separate. Here, too, Van Everdingen allowed himself considerable leeway. The shadows on the trees in the foreground follow the drawing at most approximately, and there are also differences in the distribution of light and dark behind them. Where the sky in Allart van Everdingen's prints is usually indicated with very fine lines, here it is etched with the same thick lines as the landscape below it.

The approach differs so markedly from the drawing and etching discussed above that it would seem unlikely that they were done around the same time. This idea is strengthened by the fact that the back of the drawing was coated with black chalk, not red as in *Landscape with*

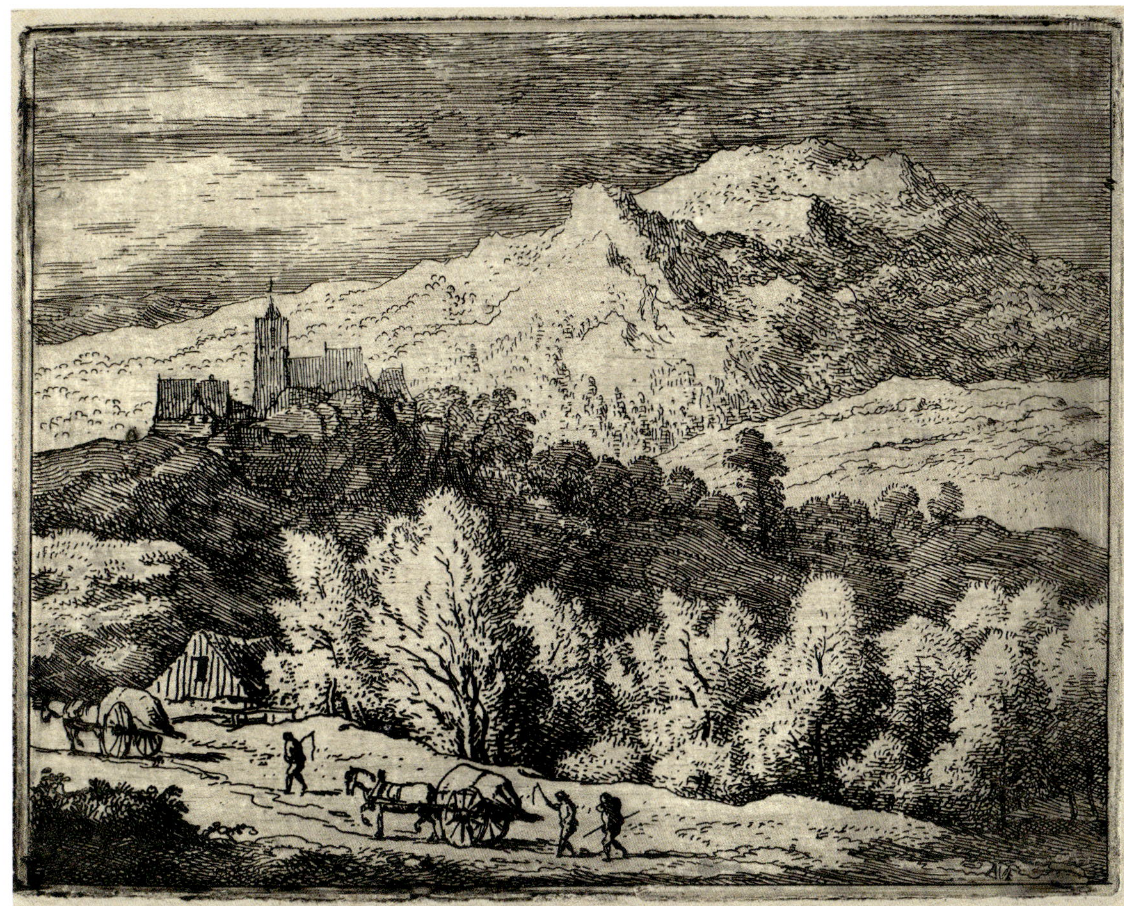

191
Allart van Everdingen, *Landscape with Two Carts*, etching, 122 x 158 mm, Washington, National Gallery of Art, inv. no. 1973.15.147 (Holl. 85 I)

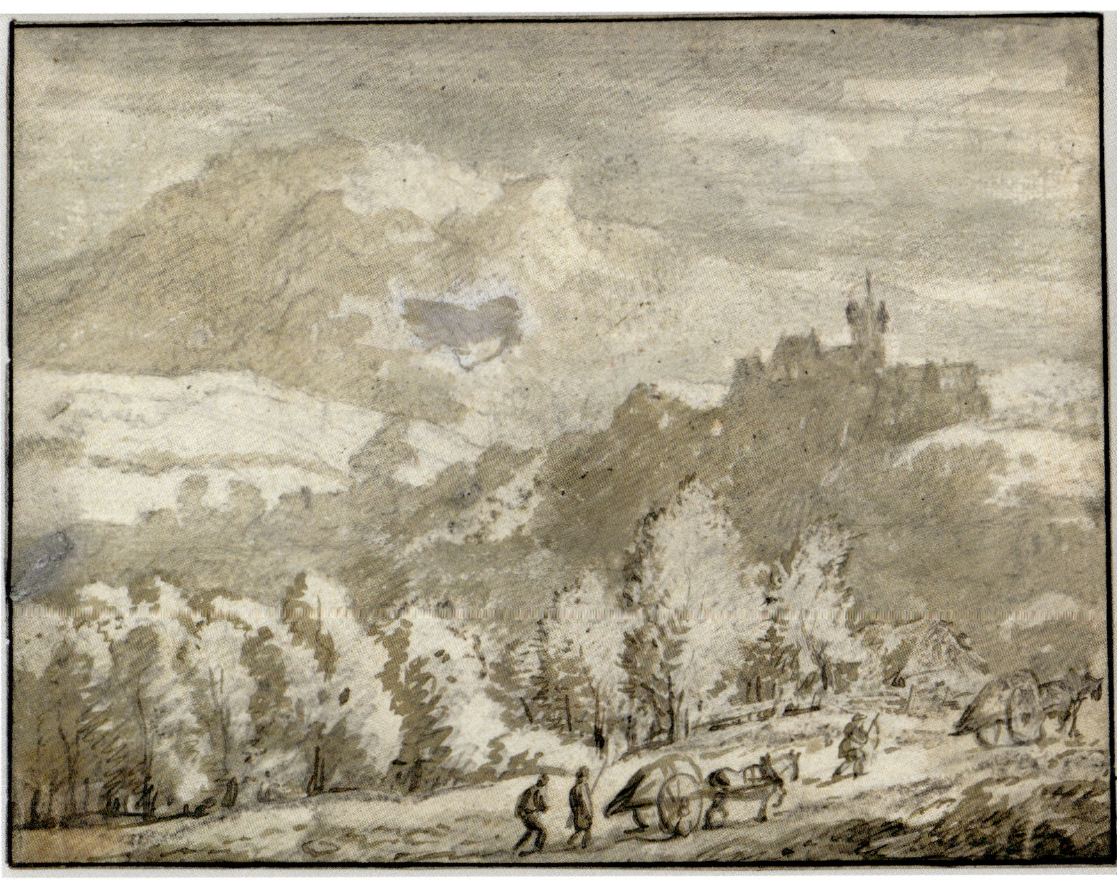

192
Allart van Everdingen, *Landscape with Two Carts*, brush and brown ink, brown and greenish grey wash, heightened with white, over graphite and charcoal, 122 x 165 mm, Klassik Stiftung Weimar, Museen, inv. no. KK 5011

a Large Rock (fig. 190). This tells us that the artist could not have worked with the usual black prepared etching ground, but must have used a white one.[43] This is the only way that the indented black lines would show up on the etching ground.

For the time being it is not possible to attach a date to the etching, but the abstract manner of execution differs from Van Everdingen's other prints, in which he renders trees more as Savery does. The technical control he evidences here is that of an experienced printmaker, suggesting that the etching can be counted among his later work. There are similar characteristics in a number of other etchings, which Bartsch put into the same set as *Landscape with Two Carts* (fig. 191), among them *Landscape with a Church in a Valley* (fig. 193). They would therefore also be later works.[44]

These examples are representative of the total of five surviving indented drawings.[45] There are also non-indented drawings of various etchings that moreover show the scene in the same direction.[46] In these cases, the relationship between drawing and etching is less clear-cut. The buildings in *Three Log Cabins on a Rock* (fig. 194) appear in identical form in a drawing in Berlin (fig. 195).[47] However, the three figures on the right in the drawing do not appear in the etching, while the man and woman on the left by the huts in the etching

are absent from the drawing. The foreground vegetation also differs in the two works. Were the drawing to be a preliminary study for the etching, it is odd that the leaves on the tree on the left are missing in the first state. Van Everdingen drew them in on the print with a brush and grey ink, at the same time indicating with

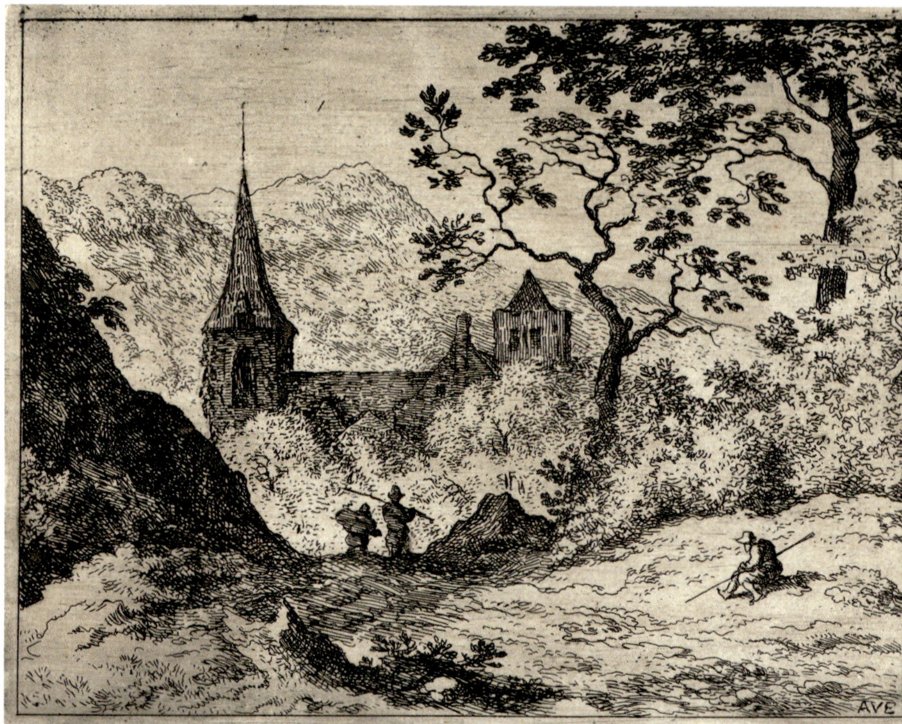

193
Allart van Everdingen, *Landscape with a Church in a Valley*, etching, 126 x 162 mm, Amsterdam, Rijksmuseum, inv. no. RP-P-OB-50.412 (Holl. 84 I)

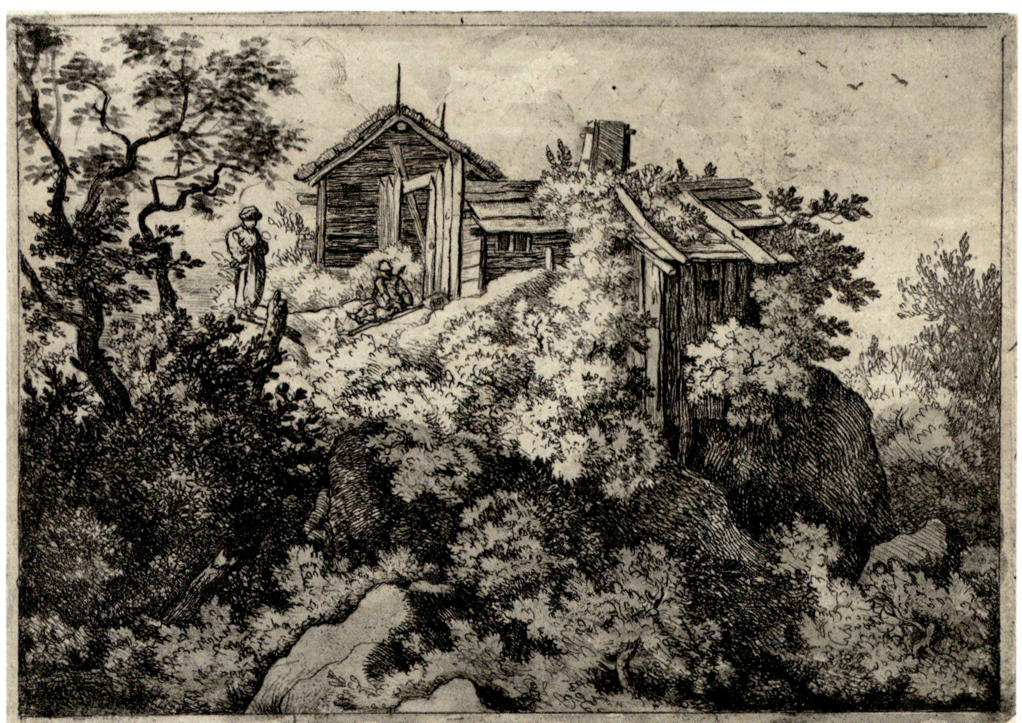

194
Allart van Everdingen, *Three Log Cabins on a Rock*, etching, retouched with brush and grey ink, 98 x 144 mm, Amsterdam, Rijksmuseum, inv. no. RP-P-OB-50.340 (Holl. 41 I) (cat. no. 12)

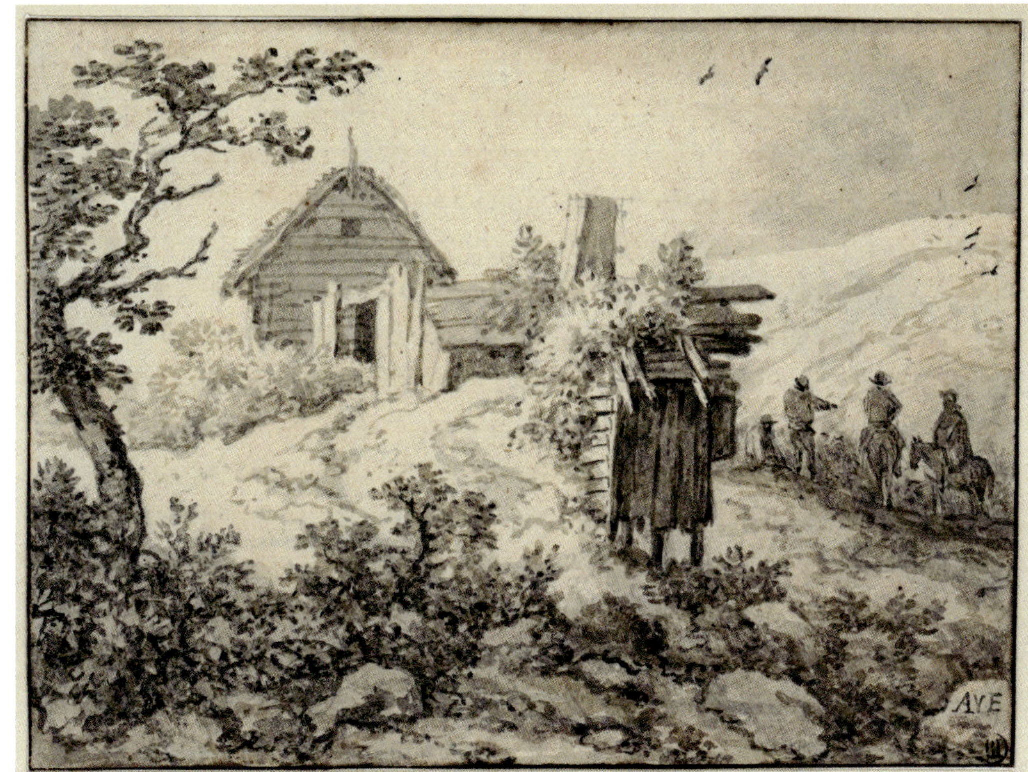

195
Allart van Everdingen, *Three Log Cabins on a Rock*, brush and black and brown ink over black chalk, grey and greyish-brown wash, 107 x 144 mm, Staatliche Museen zu Berlin, Kupferstich-kabinett, inv. no. KdZ 2340

a grey wash that the foreground had to be darker. In the second state, the rocks and bushes were shaded more strongly in that area, while the formerly bare branches on the left now have leaves (fig. 196). It gives us a fascinating insight into the way Van Everdingen worked out his etchings, but it also raises the question as to whether the drawing actually should be regarded as a preliminary study. Of course, it could be an initial idea for an etching, but we know that Allart also made a great many drawings for sale. It is not inconceivable that he sometimes reused an etched composition in a drawing of this kind.

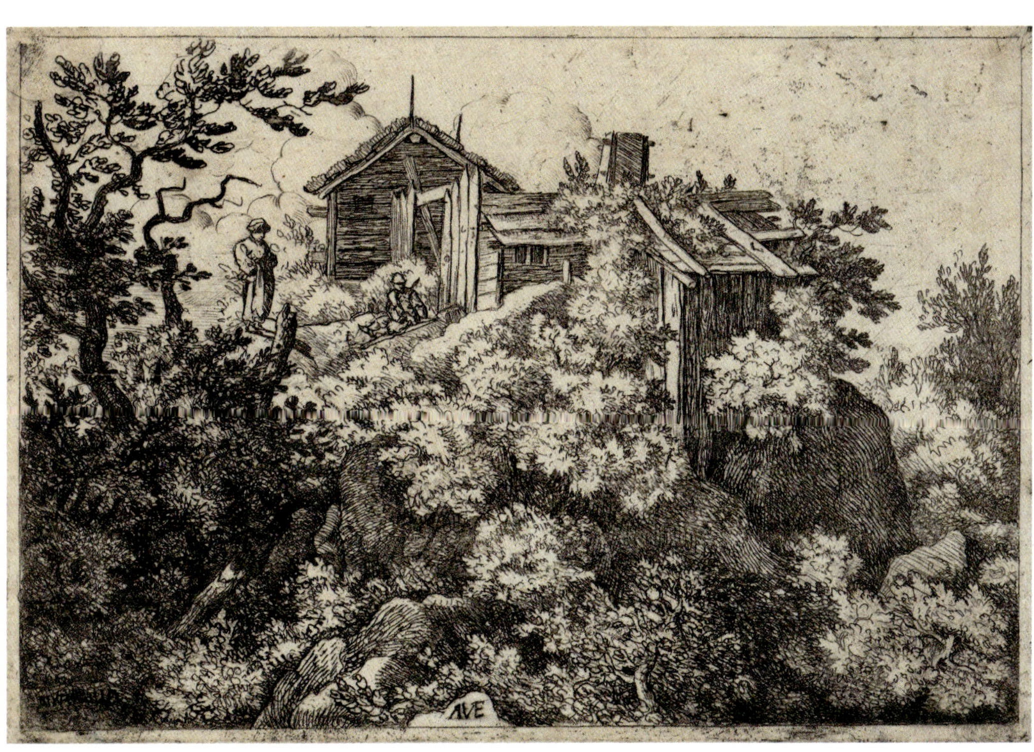

196
Allart van Everdingen, *Three Log Cabins on a Rock*, etching, 99 x 146 mm, Amsterdam, Rijksmuseum, inv. no. RP-P-1879-A-3067 (Holl. 41 II) (cat. no. 13)

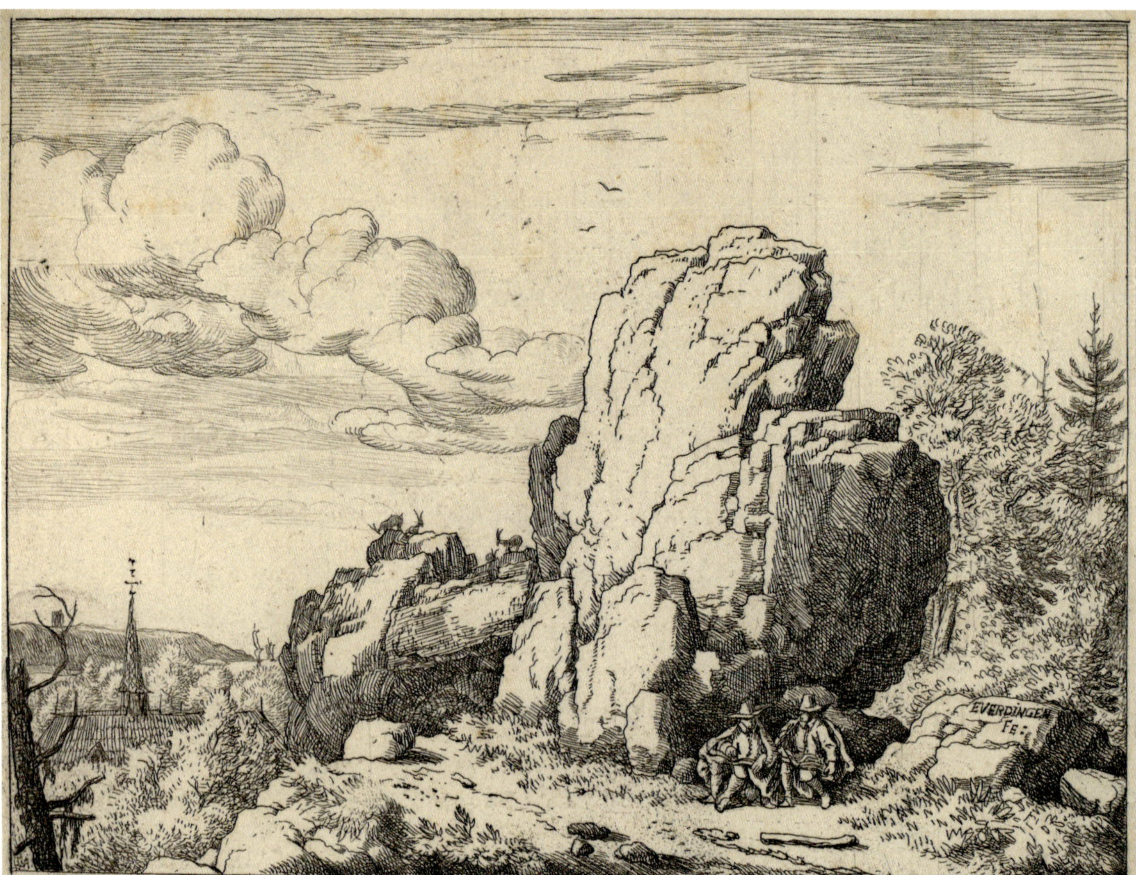

197
Allart van Everdingen,
*Landscape with Two
Artists Sitting at the Base
of a Rock*, etching, 107 x
143 mm, Washington,
National Gallery of Art,
inv. no. 1973.15.103
(Holl. 54 I)

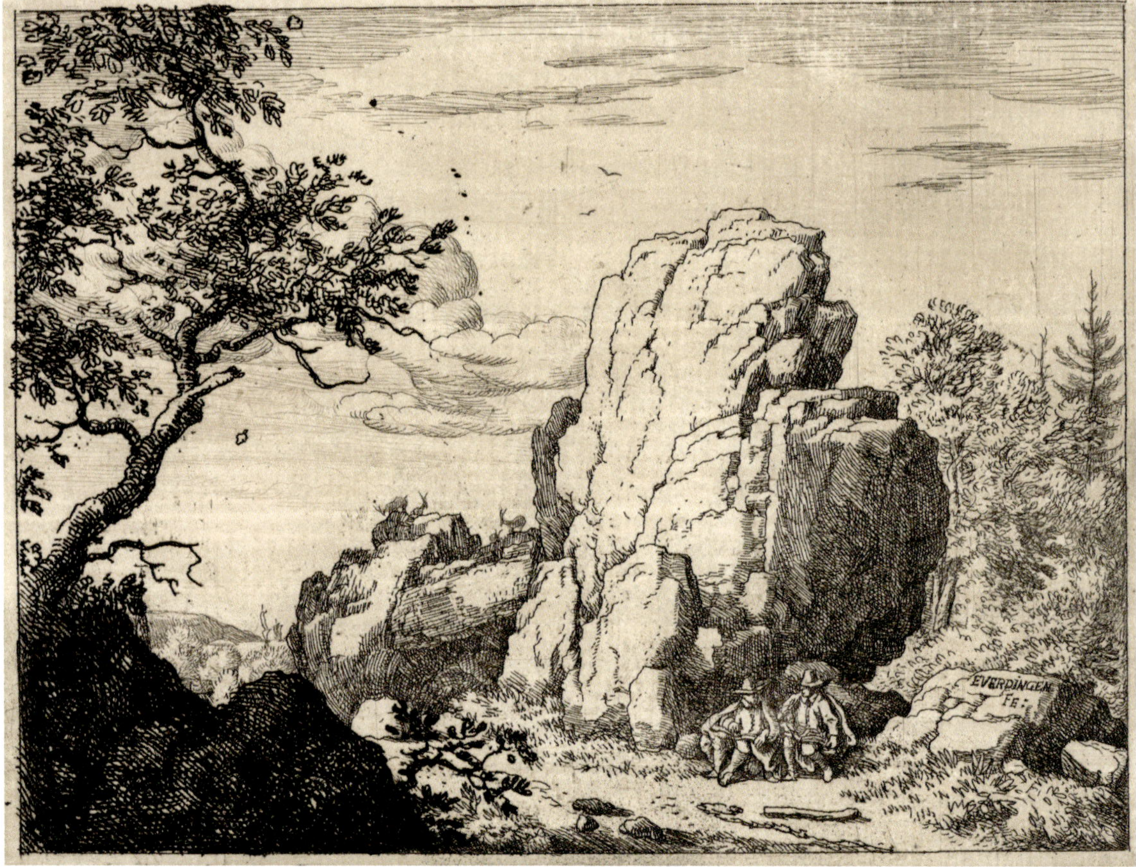

198
Allart van Everdingen,
*Landscape with Two
Artists Sitting at the
Base of a Rock*, etching,
108 x 143 mm, Amster-
dam, Rijksmuseum,
inv. no. RP-P-OB-50.363
(Holl. 54 II) (cat. no. 17)

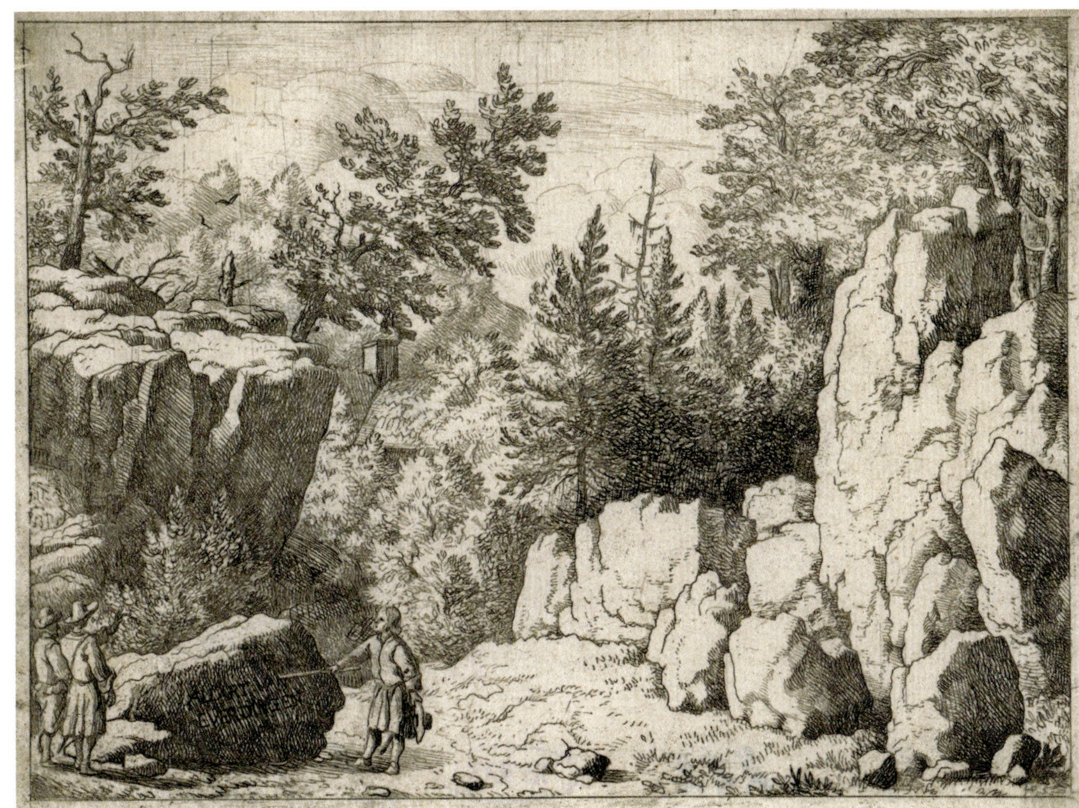

199
Allart van Everdingen, *Landscape with a Man with a Pointer*, etching, 107 x 144 mm, Amsterdam, Rijksmuseum, inv. no. RP-P-1879-A-3074 (Holl. 55 II) (cat. no. 18)

Only nineteen of the huge number of surviving drawings by Allart van Everdingen can be linked to his landscape etchings, and only five of those are indented for transfer.[48] This is in stark contrast to the thirty-five indented preliminary studies for the fifty-seven etchings in the Reynard series.[49] It creates the impression that the artist did not always make preparatory drawings for his landscape prints. The step-by-step manner in which some of them evolved suggests that he often worked directly on the copper plate. The *Stream in the Woods* (figs. 173 and 174) we discussed earlier is a prime example, but there are others. On the left in the first state of *Landscape with Two Artists Sitting at the Base of a Rock* (fig. 197), for instance, there is a vista with a roof and a church spire by a fjord with a sailing boat in the distance. The small figures lead one to wonder whether Van Everdingen pictured himself here, recording the Norwegian landscape in his sketchbook. His name is certainly written in full on the rock beside the men. Seemingly he was not pleased with the open composition, for in the second state the church has largely been concealed

behind a heavily etched tree on a hillock that fills the whole of the left side of the scene (fig. 198). Something similar has happened in *Landscape with a Man with a Pointer* (fig. 199). Here a man, hat respectfully in hand, points out the artist's forename and surname to two other gentlemen. On the tall rock to the left stand two more heavily etched trees and a stump, past which the landscape beyond can be seen. This indicates that they were only added in the second instance. The same is true of the trees on the low rocks to the right of centre. Evidently Allart had not had a strict plan for the execution of this print, but built up the composition as he went along.[50]

Another interesting example is *View of the Sea through an Opening in the Rocks* (fig. 200), which in the first state shows a fortification high on the cliffs in the distance. In the second state the opening in the rocks has been closed slightly with more branches and a considerable mountain has been added behind the distant fort (fig. 201).[51] Topographical accuracy was clearly not Allart van Everdingen's highest priority; his prime concern was a balanced composition.

200
Allart van Everdingen,
*View of the Sea through
an Opening in the Rocks*,
etching, 100 x 148 mm,
Petit Palais, Musée des
Beaux-Arts de la Ville de
Paris, inv. no. GDUT4694
(Holl. 47 I)

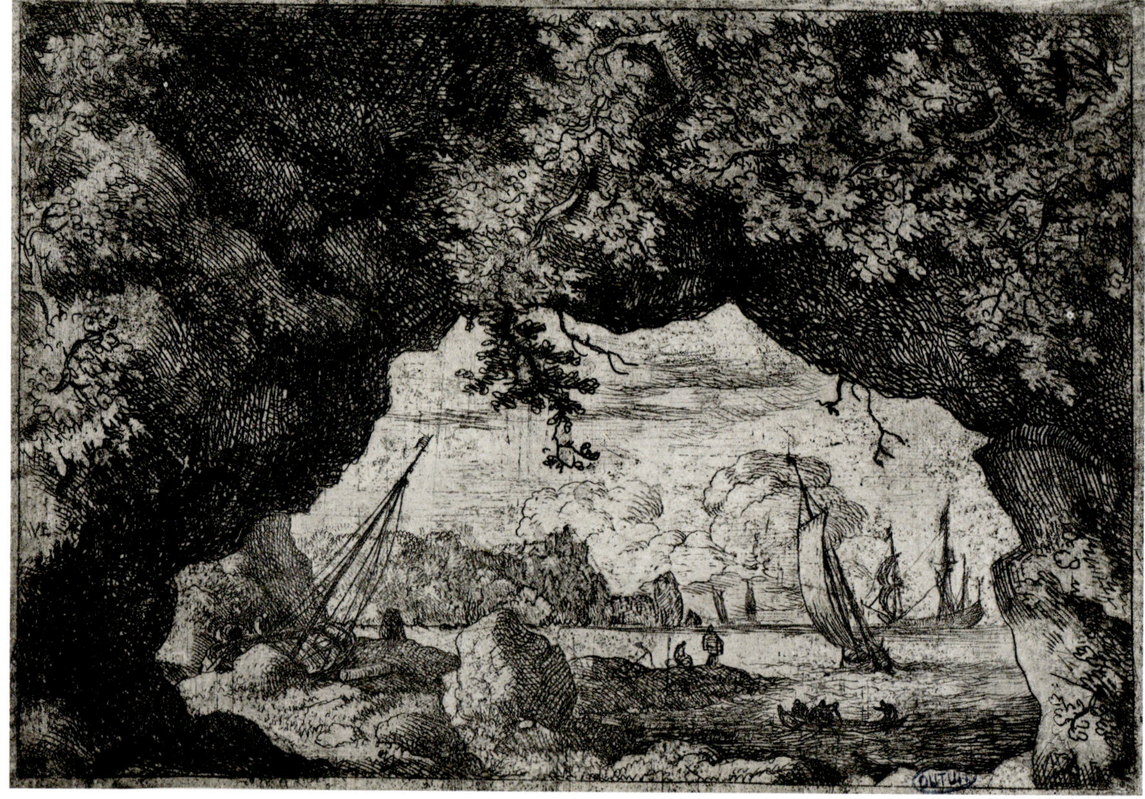

201
Allart van Everdingen,
*View of the Sea through
an Opening in the Rocks*,
etching, 101 x 148 mm,
Amsterdam, Rijksmuseum,
inv. no. RP-P-OB-50.350
(Holl. 47 II) (cat. no. 16)

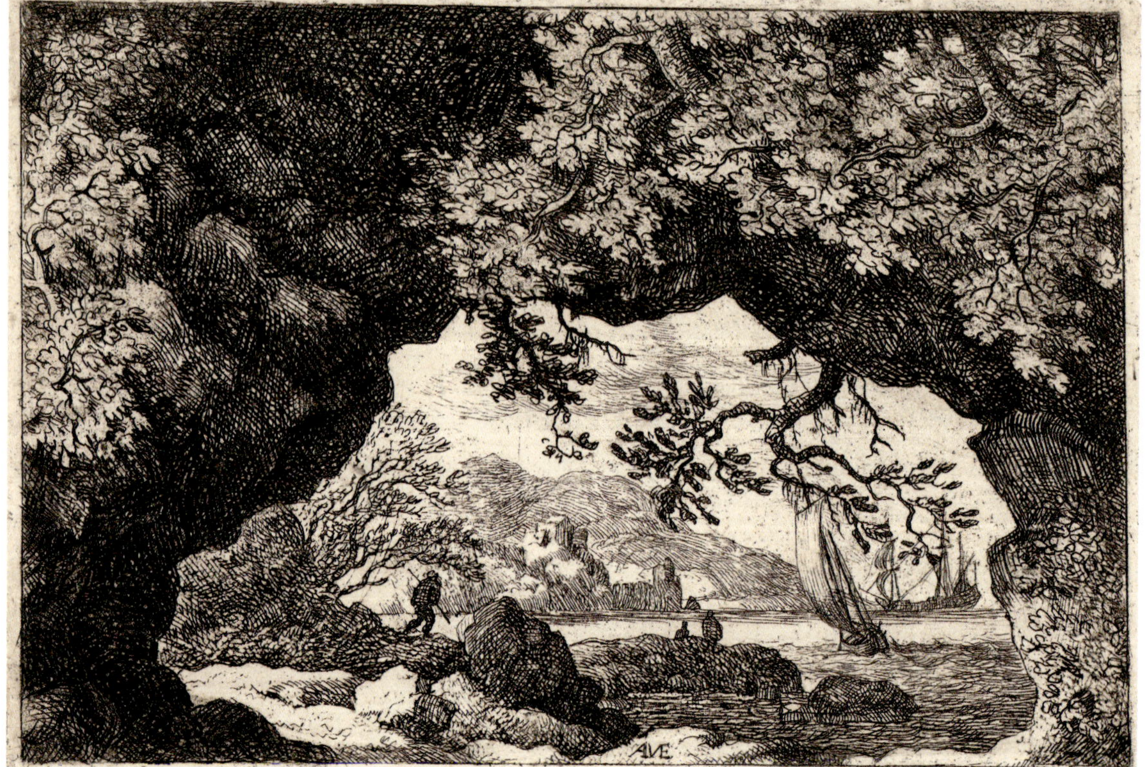

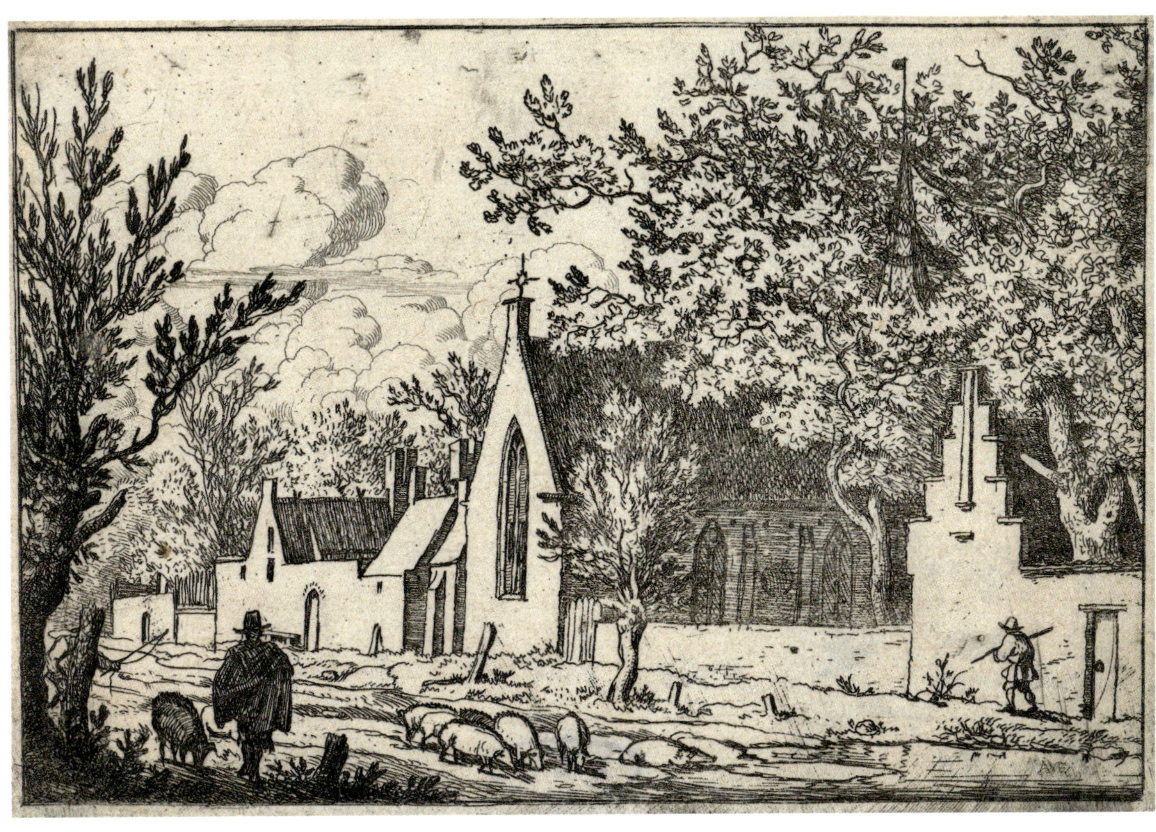

202
Allart van Everdingen, *Swineherd near a Church*, etching, 99 x 145 mm, Amsterdam, Rijksmuseum, inv. no. RP-P-1879-A-3068 (Holl. 43 I) (cat. no. 14)

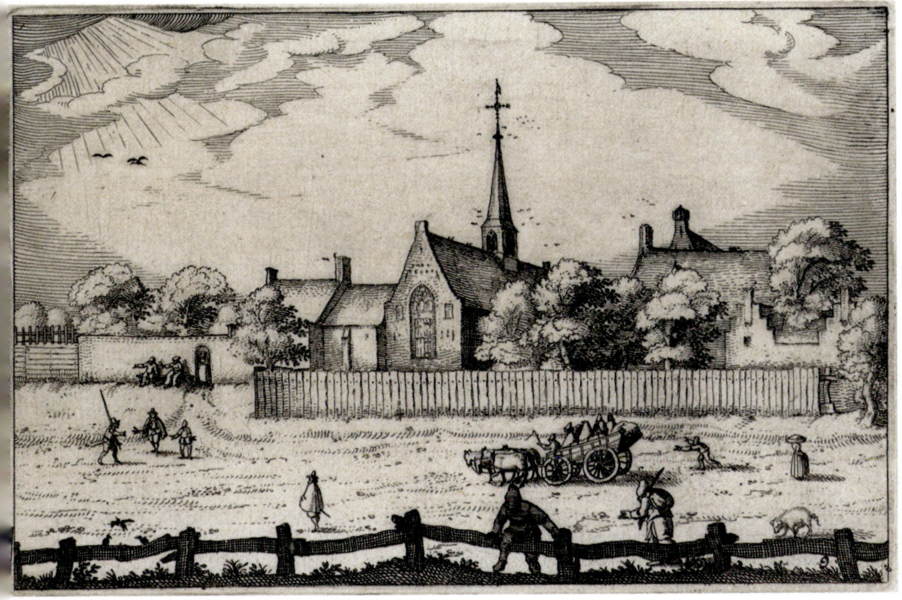

203
Claes Jansz Visscher, *The Leper Hospital in Haarlem*, 1612, etching, 102 x 157 mm, Amsterdam, Rijksmuseum, inv. no. RP-P-1879-A-3470

Identifiable Places

Nevertheless, some of Van Everdingen's etchings do depict existing places. The buildings on the right in *Swineherd near a Church* (fig. 202) bear a striking resemblance to the walls of Haarlem's leper hospital.[52] Comparing Allart's etching with Claes Jansz Visscher's 1612 print of the leper hospital (fig. 203), the stepped gable on the right and the rear wall of the church are easily recognized, as are the staggered walls with a single buttress immediately adjacent to the church.[53] It is also noteworthy that, like Claes Jansz Visscher, Van Everdingen pictured the buildings in the topographically correct orientation. This suggests that he probably worked on the basis of a drawing. The artist lived in Haarlem from 1645 to 1652, so he would certainly have known this spot.[54] The style of the foliage is freer than in Allart's more Saveryesque prints, with swift, sawtooth-like hatching, which means that the etching is almost certainly not an early work.

Four other etchings of identifiable locations show the springs around Spa in the Ardennes. They prove that Allart van Everdingen must have visited the area and this is confirmed by his painting of Montjardin Castle (fig. 90), which is little more than a stone's throw from Spa. The identification of the springs has proven problematic in the past. The one in Spa's main square is the least confusing (fig. 204). The building with the colonnade opposite the cross on the concentric steps can also be seen in the print of Spa that Willem van Nieulandt II (fig. 205) made in 1612.[55] At that time the Sauvenière spring was little more than a hole in the ground surrounded by a wooden fence. In Van Everdingen's print, people have gathered

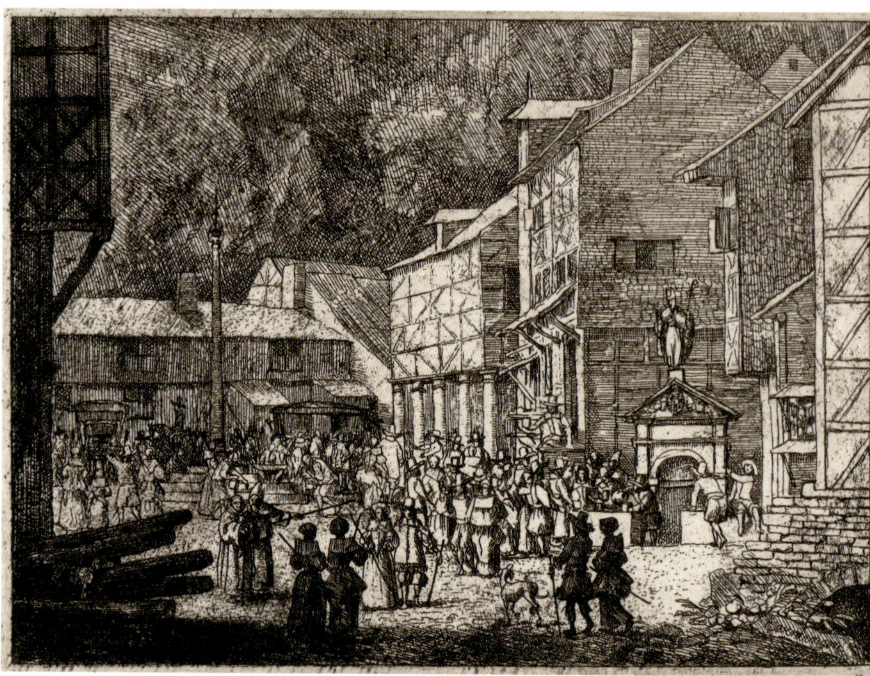

204
Allart van Everdingen, *The Pouhon Spring in the Market Square at Spa*, c. 1655, etching, 131 x 176 mm, Amsterdam, Rijksmuseum, inv. no. RP-P-OB-50.431 (Holl. 96 II) (cat. no. 22)

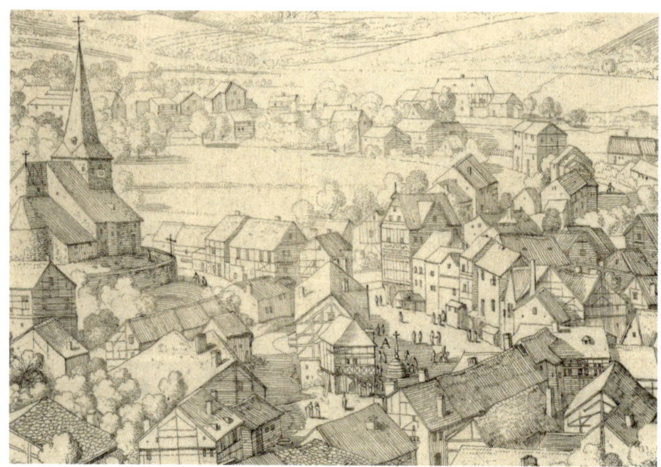

205
Church and market square in Spa, detail of Willem van Nieulandt II after Jan Brueghel, *View of Spa with the Healing Spring*, c. 1612, etching, 452 x 838 mm, Amsterdam, Rijksmuseum, inv. no. RP-P-OB-67.971

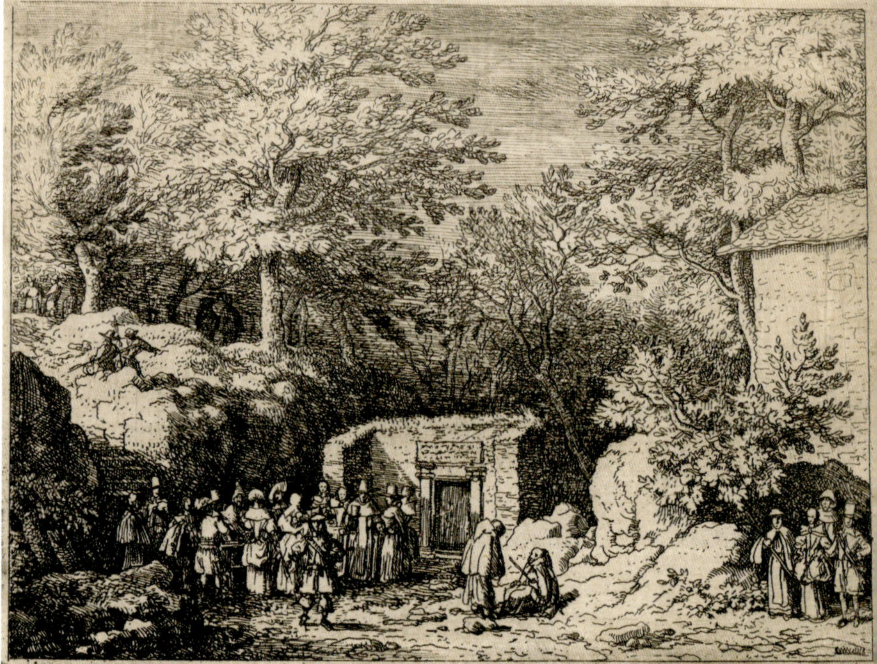

206
Allart van Everdingen, *The Spring at Sauvenière near Spa*, c. 1655, etching, 133 x 175 mm, Amsterdam, Rijksmuseum, inv. no. RP-P-OB-50.434 (Holl. 98 I) (cat. no. 24)

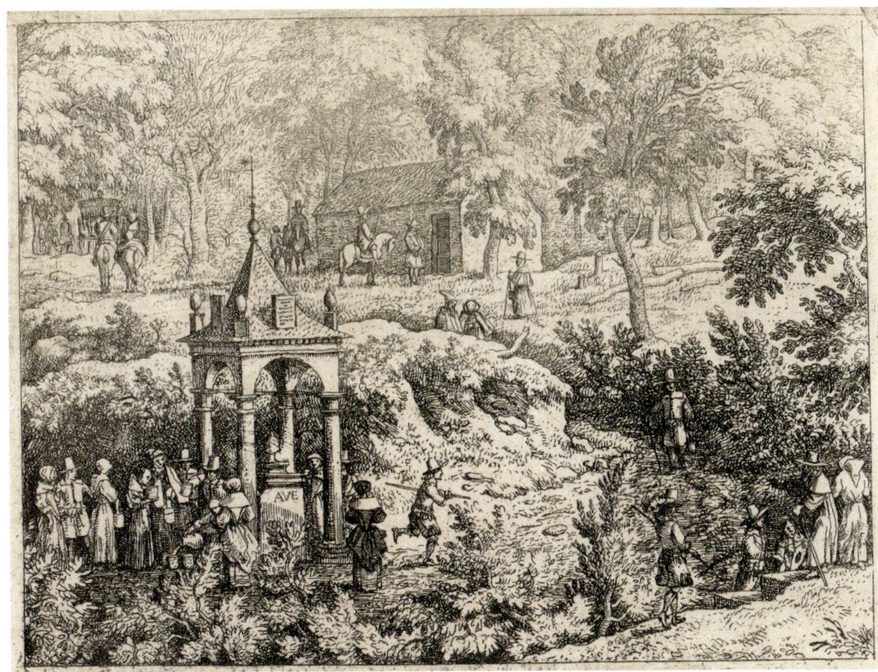

207
Allart van Everdingen,
*The Spring at
Géronstère near Spa*,
c. 1655, etching, 135 x
182 mm, Amsterdam,
Rijksmuseum, inv. no.
RP-P-OB-50.432
(Holl. 97 I) (cat. no. 23)

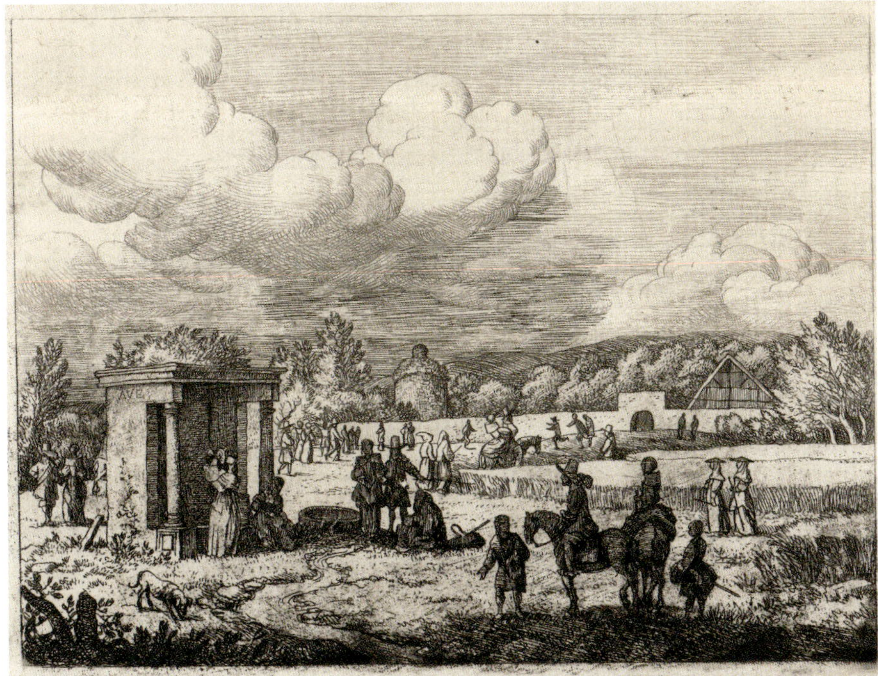

208
Allart van Everdingen,
*The Spring at Tonnelet
near Spa*, c. 1655,
etching, 131 x 177 mm,
Amsterdam, Rijks-
museum, inv. no.
RP-P-OB-50.429
(Holl. 95 II) (cat. no. 21)

there (fig. 206). Immediately behind it lies the
Groesbeeck spring, where a gate was built in
1651.[56] The spring at Géronstère is easily identified by its lowered position and the cupola
that stood over it then (fig. 207). The fourth and
last etching of a spring (fig. 208) has caused
the most confusion: it has been taken to be
the Watroz spring, but is in fact the spring at
Tonnelet.[57] The walled farmstead in the background can also be found in an early eighteenth-
century image of the spring (fig. 209).

The clothes worn by the women in these
etchings enable us to date them—and the trip—
to the mid-sixteen-fifties.[58] This is confirmed
by a detail in the print of the Pouhon spring in
Spa (fig. 204). Atop this spring there is a statue

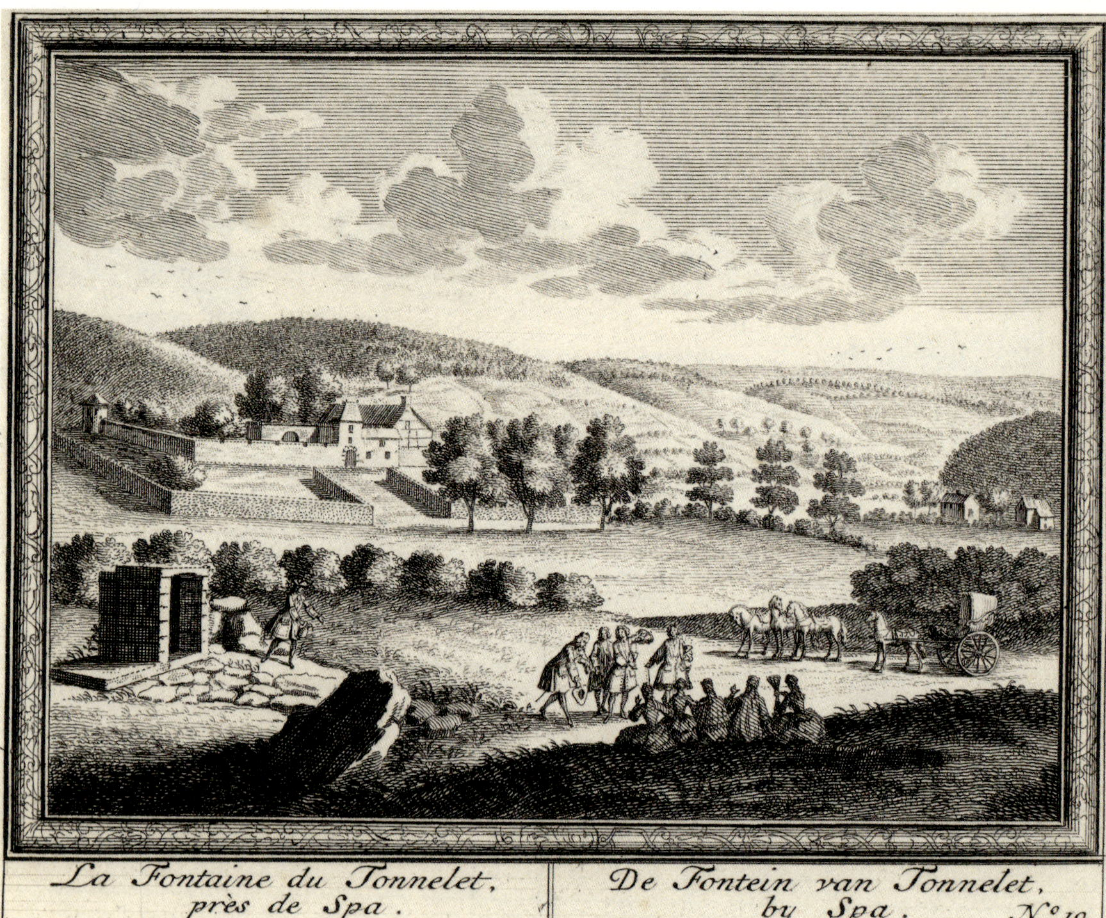

209
Anonymous, *The Spring at Tonnelet near Spa*, 1734, etching, 172 x 198 mm, Amsterdam, Rijksmuseum, inv. no. RP-P-2019-2733-10

210
Allart van Everdingen, *The Pouhon Spring in the Market Square at Spa*, c. 1655, brush and brown and black oil paint, on prepared paper, 122 x 172 mm, London, The British Museum, inv. no. 1836,0811.164

of St Remaclus, the town's patron saint. This statue was removed in 1656, which means that Allart must have visited the region before that.[59]

Van Everdingen must have made the etchings in his Amsterdam workshop on the basis of sketches he had done on the spot. There are surviving drawings for three of the four springs.[60] In the drawing of the spring in the square in Spa (fig. 210), the vantage point is the same as in the etching, but the distribution of the figures and the lighting differ. Where the wall behind the spring on the right of the square is light in the drawing and the spring is not, it is the other way round in the etching. There is a similar reversal on the facade of the building, and the buildings on the other side of the square are light in the drawing and dark in the etching. Since the image in the drawing runs in the same direction as the print, and is moreover quite loosely done, we may wonder whether it actually was the direct example for the print.

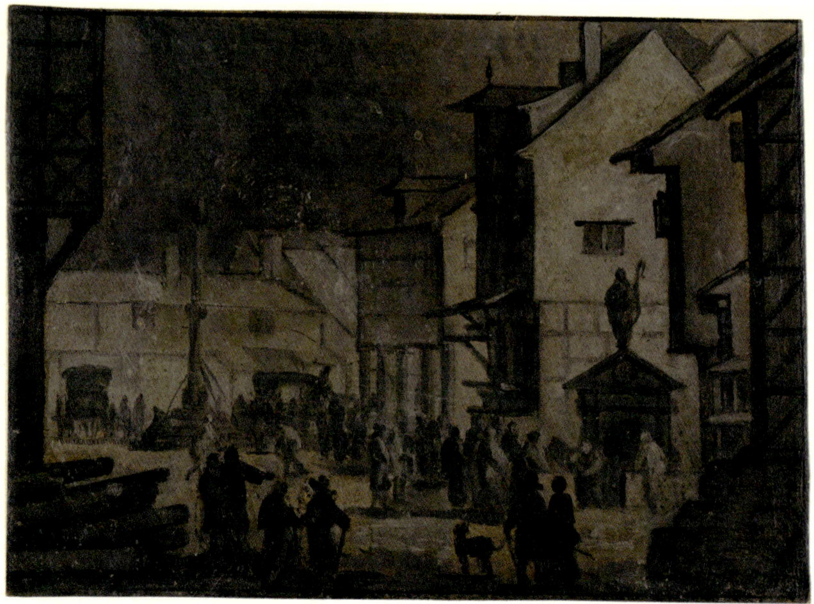

This is definitely not the case with the drawing of the spring at Géronstère (fig. 211), for the place is seen from a different perspective—and at night. It suggests that Van Everdingen made a lot of drawings there and did not use all of them for prints. An interesting aspect of the two drawings of the spring at Sauvenière is that they each show the setting slightly differently. In the drawing in Moscow (fig. 212), the steps seem to come down from slightly further behind the Groesbeeck spring, which reflects the actual situation. In the drawing in Hamburg (fig. 213), the steps come down from the side. It is this drawing that is closest to the etching (even the orientation), and must have been the basis for it—but almost certainly with an indented drawing in mirror image, which has not survived, as an intermediate step.

Reception and Research

A discussion of Allart van Everdingen's etchings would not be complete without looking at the reception of the oeuvre. Remarkably, his prints are totally ignored in the early literature. In 1719, the artists' biographer Arnold Houbraken was the first to discuss the master's life, paintings and drawings, but said not a word about etchings.[61] In the artists' lexicons by Houbraken's successors Jacob Campo Weyerman (1729), Jean-Baptiste Descamps (1754) and Johann

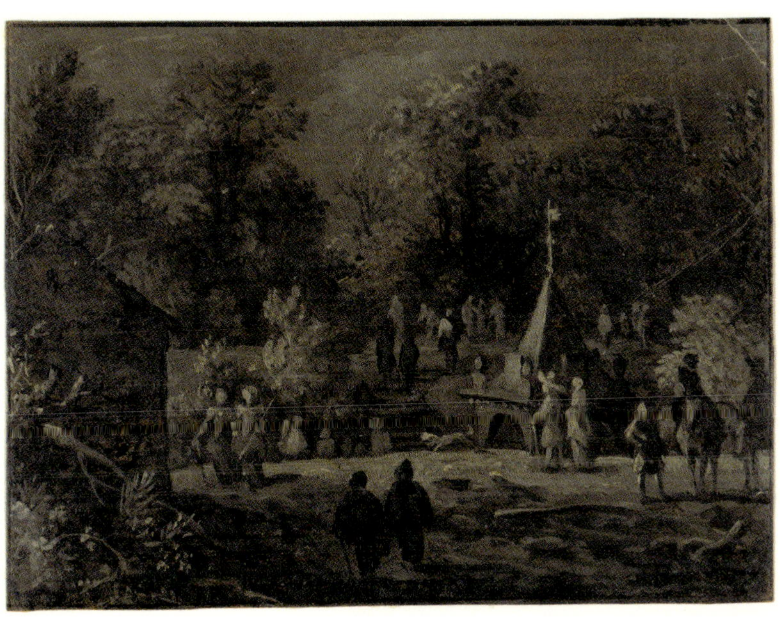

Rudolf Fuessli (1763) there is likewise no mention of Van Everdingen's printmaking in his biography.[62] It was only in 1744 that the French dealer and broker Edmé-François Gersaint wrote of the artist: 'he also executed some of his landscapes as etchings.'[63] And not until 1767 did the French print publisher Pierre-François Basan summarize what he knew about Van Everdingen's etchings at greater length in his *Dictionnaire des Graveurs*: 'He has etched various works to his own designs in a most lively manner, including a set of a hundred small landscapes. And one of fifty-six sheets plus title page whose subjects are derived from a German book titled Reynard's tricks.'[64]

In the period that followed, the number of dictionaries and theoretical treatises for art lovers and collectors rose sharply and Van Everdingen's prints are mentioned more often; Basan's original text is usually easily recognized in them.[65] The observations of the French connoisseur Pierre-Jean Mariette (1694-1775) are particularly interesting, because he also refers to the copper plates: 'It is, so I have been assured, Van Everdingen's heirs who have them, likewise those of the fables, and they hold them, so it is said, very dear.'[66] It is not clear when Mariette wrote this, but it was definitely before 1752, when the publisher Pieter Schenk II in Amsterdam and Leipzig brought out a German translation of this well-known medieval folk tale under the title *Reineke der Fuchs*, illustrated with Van Everdingen's etchings.[67] Schenk owned the Reynard plates at that time.[68]

It seems clear that Schenk did not also own the copper plates of the landscapes, as this group was referred to in 1761 in the estate of the Amsterdam printmaker Pieter Tanjé (1701/1702-1761): 'A Hundred Plates, being the landscapes or the Work of *van Everdingen*'.[69] It would make sense to assume that Tanjé made the most of these plates, although there is no evidence of this in the catalogue of his sale; aside from the copper plates, no impressions of Allart van Everdingen's works are listed. All the same, the fact that Pieter Tanjé—a printmaker—owned these copper plates makes the idea that it was he, not the Simon Fokke referred to above, who was responsible for working up this group a very plausible one.

There is no information about who bought the plates at Pieter Tanjé's sale, but around

1800 they turned up in the possession of Charles Howard Hodges (1764-1837).[70] This painter and printmaker, who worked in the Netherlands, was also an active player in the art trade. On 1 January 1803, with Cornelis Charles Six van Oterleek (1772-1833), he began a 'trade in old and modern prints, copper plates, etc.'[71] He owned, for instance, eighty-eight copper plates by Flemish reproductive engravers such as Lucas Vorsterman, Paulus Pontius and Boëtius à Bolswert, which he printed in 1804 and published under the title *Oeuvres de P.P. Rubens et A. van Dyck ou receuil des principeaux tableaux de ces deux illustres peintres*.[72] He also published the copper plates of Allart van Everdingen's landscape etchings in the form of an album, *Recueil de cent paysages. Inventées, et gravées à l'eau-forte par Aldert van Everdingen*, with a fictitious publisher's address 'Amsterdam par P. van de Boom 1696'.[73] While the copper plates of the Reynard series were reprinted in 1844 and are said to be held in London still, there has been no trace of the landscape plates since Hodges's death.[74]

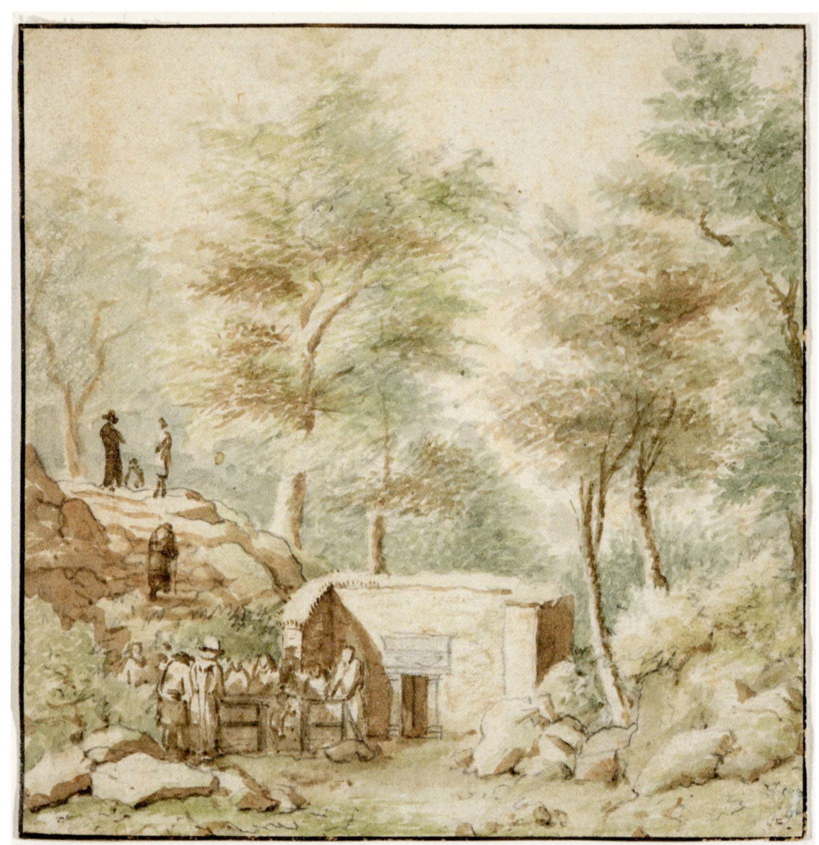

212
Allart van Everdingen, *The Spring at Sauvenière near Spa*, c. 1655, brush and brown ink over traces of black chalk, watercolour, 150 x 148 mm, Moscow, The Pushkin State Museum of Fine Arts, inv. no. 4782

< 213
Allart van Everdingen, *The Spring at Sauvenière near Spa*, c. 1655, pen and brush and brown ink, light and dark grey oil paint, on reddish-brown prepared paper, 128 x 170 mm, Hamburger Kunsthalle, inv. no. 21906 (cat. no. 64)

Nevertheless, it is clear that the copper plates stayed together throughout the eighteenth century, initially as one group with Allart van Everdingen's heirs, later as two separate groups—the landscapes and the Reynard illustrations. This sheds light on the way the artist's prints were collected. Only the seventeenth-century collection history remains shrouded in mist for the time being because virtually no clues have been found for that period. However, it is evident that the landscape etchings were also admired then, for the dilettante Abraham Rutgers (c. 1632-1699) made no fewer than fifty drawings of them.[75] Rutgers used a slightly different paper size for his copies, which meant that he had to make additions of his own at the sides of the scenes to fill the sheets.

An analysis of the mentions in sale catalogues is enlightening for the eighteenth-century collection history. It appears that, particularly in the early years of the century, the oeuvre was sometimes collected without any pretension to completeness. In those cases, the selection of his etchings was kept with the work of such French, Italian and Dutch print artists as Gabriel Perelle, Jacques Callot, Israël Silvestre, Stefano della Bella, Herman van Swanevelt, Nicolaes Berchem and Anthonie Waterloo.[76] Where the Dutch artists were concerned, they were often Italianates who, like Van Everdingen, had concentrated on foreign landscapes.

And yet this selective approach to collecting is not typical. On the contrary, when Van Everdingen's graphic oeuvre appears in sale catalogues, it is usually the complete work—although it is then divided into the landscapes on the one hand and the prints of Reynard the Fox on the other. The earliest mention to have been traced occurs in a 1728 sale catalogue: 'The work of A. van Everdingen, being the Fables of the Animals, and some Landscapes, etched by himself, altogether 81 items, rare'.[77] They also appear in 1754: 'The Meaningful Images of the Animals, besides all the Landscapes, by *A. V. Everdinge*, first Edition, with written Inscriptions'.[78]

Whereas Van Everdingen's etchings appeared at auction only sporadically before 1750, the supply was many times greater between 1750 and 1800.[79] They appear in at least forty-five sales, almost always as a complete set of landscapes and a complete set of Reynard the Fox.[80] Early states were explicitly mentioned for the first time in 1770: 'And another fifteen impressions by this artist, with changes & more, where there is still no sky & which are more or less finished, etc.'[81] After this there are more frequent references to early states, following the same pattern. In each case there are a number of extra impressions alongside a complete set of landscapes or Reynard prints, recommended in such terms as 'very first burr impressions' and 'without skies and less worked'.[82] Strikingly, these are the exceptions. Most of the prints on offer have apparently been worked on and have additions in the sky—in other words they are impressions of the reworked plates. This can only mean that the copper plates were frequently reprinted in the eighteenth century and that it is these impressions that flooded the market in the second half of that century. The fact that the copper plates remained together—albeit in two groups—also explains why impressions of both the landscapes and the Reynard cycle were always offered as complete sets.

With the appearance of the first oeuvre catalogue, compiled by Bartsch in 1803, Allart van Everdingen's landscape prints became an established part of the graphic arts canon. Since then they have been consistently referred to in reviews of his life and work, including publications from the Netherlands.[83] Yet it remains striking that the prints on the market and in print collections are usually in a reworked state. They are, as has become clear, posthumous impressions. This leads us to the remarkable conclusion that Allart van Everdingen himself never made many impressions of his meanwhile very well-known and highly valued etchings.

* The quotation in the title is taken from Basan 1767, p. 189 (see also note 64).

1 A very useful overview of seventeenth-century painters who etched is given in Boston/Saint Louis 1981.

2 For a detailed description of the etching technique see Stijnman 2012, pp. 45-57.

3 For this trip see the essays by Christi Klinkert and Cynthia Osiecki in this catalogue.

4 This count is based on Hollstein (Allart van Everdingen).

5 Prints without a monogram or name: Holl. 1, 31, 32, 64, 86, 87, 88, 91, 93, 94, 108, 110, 111. Prints with the full name: Holl. 37, 51, 52, 54, 55, 67, 75, 77, 81, 96, 103. None of the Reynard prints is signed.

6 Bartsch 1803; illustrations in The Illustrated Bartsch (Allart van Everdingen).

7 E.g. Bartsch 1803, p. 174: '26-29. Suite de quatre estampes', followed by the dimensions of the group. The individual prints are described beneath. See also idem, pp. 243-246, with a 'Table des dimensions des estampes d'Aldert van Everdingen', containing an overview of dimensions, prints and groups.

8 The groups Bartsch identified are B. 7-10 (4), 11-16 (6), 17-20 (4), 21-24 (4), 26-29 (4), 30-33 (4), 34-39 (6), 40-51 (12), 52-55 (4), 57-64 (8), 65-72 (8), 82-87 (6), 90-93 (4), 95-98 (4).

9 The etchings Bartsch described as loose prints are B. 25, 56, 73-81, 88-89, 99-105.

10 Davies 2007, pp. 97-109.

11 See Nagler 1837, pp. 167-171 and Le Blanc 1854, pp. 204-207, who follow Bartsch; Drugulin 1873 made minimal changes to Bartsch's order. Dutuit 1881 did not adopt that, but went back to Bartsch's numbering, because, he said (p. 296), it was better known. Hollstein (Allart van Everdingen) also follows the Bartsch and Dutuit numbering.

12 Drugulin 1873, p. ix.

13 In the present investigation, only the impressions in the Rijksmuseum Print Room have been systematically examined for watermarks. See appendix 'Watermarks in Allart van Everdingen's Etchings'.

14 Hinterding 2006, vol. 2, pp. 165-166 and 394-395.

15 See Voorn 1960, pp. 115-116, who for the first half of the seventeenth century only illustrates foolscaps with five-pointed collars (p. 110), and only foolscaps with seven-pointed collars from the second half of the seventeenth century (p. 143). This latter type only occurs in Rembrandt's prints made after 1650, and is often of French origin (Hinterding 2006, vol. 1, pp. 46-47). The earliest variant with a seven-pointed collar in this oeuvre dates from around 1654 (2), thereafter 1656, 1659 and 1665 (Hinterding 2006, vol. 2, p. 416). Cf. also Laurentius 2007 (seventy-one foolscaps with five-pointed collars and two with a nine-pointed collar from the 1600-1650 period) and Laurentius 2008 (192 foolscaps with seven-pointed collars from the 1650-1700 period).

16 For Allart van Everdingen's residence in Amsterdam from 1652 onwards see Davies 2001, p. 101 and Van Thiel-Stroman in Köhler et al. 2006, p. 149.

17 Drugulin 1873, p. ix.

18 The other variant of the Arms of Amsterdam watermark that Drugulin describes has not been found in the present investigation. The Arms of Amsterdam in general does not appear until 1653 (Voorn 1960, pp. 102 and 130).

19 Laurentius 2008, no. 191.

20 This Foolscap watermark is later than the Arms of Amsterdam. Holl. 18 I has the Arms of Amsterdam, Holl. 18 II this Foolscap.

21 Drugulin 1873, p. x: 'un tirage général, tant des paysages que les épreuves terminées du Reynard'.

22 Drugulin 1873, pp. x-xi, which places the mark around 1675. This agrees with Heawood 1950, nos. 2021 and 2023, Gaudriault 1995, no. 1022. See also Likhachev 1994, nos. 3542-3543.

23 Houbraken 1718-1721, vol. 2, p. 95. For Van Everdingen's teachers see also the first essay in this catalogue.

24 Savery's print: Hollstein (Roelandt Savery) 2.

25 For the preliminary study, which is indented for transfer, see Amsterdam 2000, cat. no. 4 (with further literature).

26 Other prints with echoes of Roelandt Savery are Holl. 81 and 26.

27 Hollstein (Pieter de Molijn) 2.

28 Freedberg 1980, p. 59.

29 Idem, pp. 28-41, Leeflang 1993, pp. 18-19 and Orenstein et al. 1993, pp. 189-195.

30 Hind 1963, p. 190, also places Allart van Everdingen between 'the sterner manner of the Van de Veldes and of Molyn and the errant line of Ruysdael'.

31 See among others Holl. 7-10, 17-20, 21-24, 25, 28, 29. In terms of the chronology within the oeuvre, an order different from Bartsch's sometimes produces equally coherent results, for example (in this order) Holl. 25, 39, 35-37, 34, 36.

32 Drugulin also attempted to classify Allart van Everdingen's etches into stylistic categories (Drugulin 1873, pp. viii-ix). However, his discussion is too cursory and fragmentary to be able to distil a clear pattern from it.

33 Holl. 5, 8-10, 18-20, 26 and 47, for example, also belong in this group.

34 Other examples are Holl. 12-16 and 21-24.

35 The whole series is Holl. 57-64. The series Holl. 65-72 has the same more extreme sketchiness.

36 Cf. Davies 2007, p. 39 and cat. no. 78, indeed drawn in a similar style.

37 Other etchings in this group are Holl. 27-31, 75-78, 85-87 and 93.

38 Drugulin 1873, p. xii. Dutuit rightly questions this (Dutuit 1881, p. 294).

39 Cf. Mansfield 1995, pp. 171-172 who divides the mezzotints into two groups. She dates the first group 'in the late 1650s or early 1660s', and the second 'in the mid- to late 1660s'.

40 Weigel 1843, pp. 80-81.

41 Broos and Schapelhouman 1993, cat. no. 64. The drawings by Allart van Everdingen that are associated with his etchings are discussed in Davies 2007, pp. 110-117, however without any detailed treatment of the prints.

42 Davies 2007, cat. no. 586.

43 For white etching ground see Stijnman 2012, pp. 155-157.

44 There are also indented preliminary studies for two other prints that can be counted among the later work, Davies 2007, cat. nos. 587 (for Holl. 87) and 589 (for Holl. 93bis), which have likewise been coated with black chalk on the back.

45 There is also an indented drawing for Holl. 53 (Davies 2007, cat. no. 583), which is not coloured on the back. Van Everdingen must have used a different method for transferring the design. As well as countless similarities to the drawing, the etching also differs from it in many respects.

46 Davies 2007, cat. nos. 576-582, 584, 585, 588 and 590-593.

47 The drawing: Davies 2007, cat. no. 580.

48 Davies 2007 discusses 656 drawings. For Van Everdingen's drawn oeuvre see Yvonne Bleyerveld's essay in this catalogue.

49 Davies 2007, cat. nos. 599, 601, 603, 604, 611-613, 615, 616, 618-621, 624-626, 628, 629, 632-638, 640-644, 647, 650, 652-654.

50 Another example is Holl. 100, where there is a castle on a hill on the left in the first state that has been concealed behind a pine tree in the foreground in the second. The vista beyond the house on the right has also disappeared in the second state.

51 The reverse also occurred: the castle that can be seen on the high rock in the first state of Landscape with Rocks by the Water (Holl. 62) has vanished in the second.

52 With thanks to Laurens Schoemaker for the identification.

53 Hollstein (Claes Jansz Visscher) 157.

54 Davies 2001, pp. 27-28 and 31; Van Thiel-Stroman in Köhler et al. 2006, p. 149.

55 Hollstein (Willem van Nieulandt II) 114.

56 Dardonville 1830, p. 23

57 Described as Watroz in Hollstein (Allart van Everdingen), for example. Allart's images of the spring at Sauvenière (figs. 212 and 213) have also been taken to be the spring at Watroz (see e.g. Davies 2007, cat. nos. 592 and 593; Sadkov et al. 2010, cat. no. 178; Stefes 2011, cat. no. 304).

58 Derkinderen-Besier 1950, pp. 125 and 149, and fig. 125. With thanks to Sabine Craft-Giepmans.

59 Verreyken 2014, p. 126.

60 Davies 2007, cat. nos. 590-593.

61 Houbraken 1718-1721, vol. 2, pp. 95-96.

62 See Weyerman 1729, vol. 2, pp. 178-179; Descamps 1754, pp. 321-323; Fuessli 1763, p. 174.

63 Gersaint 1744, p. 30: 'il a aussi gravé quelques-uns de ses paysages à l'eau forte.' For Gersaint see Glorieux 2002.

64 Basan 1767, vol. 1, pp. 189-190: 'Il a gravé à l'eau-forte, & d'une maniere très-spirituelle, diverses Pieces de sa composition, entr'autre: Une Suite de 100 petits Paysages. Une autre de 56 p. ps. et t. dont les sujets sont tirés d'un livre allemand, intitulé: les tromperies du Renard.'

65 See e.g. Fuessli 1779, p. 221 and Strutt 1785-1786, vol. 1, p. 280. Von Heinecken 1771, p. 191 mentions Van Everdingen's prints only briefly; Watelet and Levesque 1792, vol. 4, pp. 470-471, do the same.

66 Abecedario 1853-1854, p. 229, 'Ce sont, à ce qu'on m'a assuré, les héritiers d'Everdingen qui les ont, de meme que celles des fables, et ils les tiennent, dit-on, assez chères.'

67 See Marjan Pantjes's essay in this catalogue.

68 Hofmann 1920, p. 188. My thanks to Marjan Pantjes for drawing this article to my attention. In 1798, his son auctioned off copper plates from Schenk's estate, but the sale catalogue has so far not been traced (not mentioned in Lugt) so it is not possible to establish whether Van Everdingen's Reynard plates were among them. See the announcement in the *Oprechte Haerlem-sche Courant* of 23 March 1798: 'Op Donderdag, den 5 April, 1798, zal men te Amsterdam ten Huize van P. SCHENK Pz., in de Kalverstraat, verkoopen: Een aanzienlyke Party KOPERE KONSTPLAATEN, bestaande in *Atlas van Visscher*, in 128 Plaaten, de *Saxische Atlas*, 70 Plaaten, *Bybelgeschiede-nissen*, 46 Plaaten, het Moolen, Sluyzen, Kappen en Trappenboek, met alle Plaaten en beschryving in 't Nederduitsch, Fransch en Hoogduitsch, verscheide Land en anderen Kaarten, Historien, Gezigten, Landschappen, Beelden; alsmede eenige losse en gebonde Boeken, Kaarten, Printen: Nagelaaten door wylen P. SCHENK; de Catalogus is in alle Steden by de voornaamste Boekverkoopers te bekomen, en te Amsterdam by A. Meyer, P. Schenk Pz. en M. Schalekamp.' ('To be sold on Thursday, the 5th April, 1798, in Amsterdam at the House of P. SCHENK Pz., in the Kalverstraat: A considerable consignment of COPPER ENGRAVING PLATES consisting in *Atlas* by *Visscher*, in 128 Plates, the *Saxische Atlas*, 70 Plates, *Biblical Histories*, 46 Plates, The book of Mills, Sluices, Hoods and Staircases, with all the Plates and description in Low German, French and High German, diverse National and other Maps, Histories, Views, Landscapes, Statues; as well as some loose and bound Books, Maps, Prints: Left by the late P. SCHENK; the Catalogue is available from the leading Book-sellers in all Towns, and in Amsterdam from A. Meyer, P. Schenk Pz. and M. Schalekamp.').

69 Sale Pieter Tanjé Collection, 7 December 1761 (Lugt 1183), p. 160, no. 11: 'Hondert Plaaten, zynde de landschapjes of het Werke van *van Everdingen*'.

70 Weigel 1843, p. 80 and sale Charles Howard Hodges Collection, 27 February 1838 (Lugt 14955), p. 76, under 'KOPEREN PLATEN', no. 5: '101 dito [= pieces] dito [= of engravings], van EVERDINGEN'.

71 Van der Feltz 1982, p. 17: 'negotie in oude en moderne printen, koperplaten, enz.'

72 See Muller 1860, pp. 35-36. The album is in the Rijksmuseum library under shelf mark 10 D 4, without a reference to Hodges as the publisher.

73 Rijksmuseum library, shelf mark 301 C 20. Sixteen copies of this album are listed in the catalogue of the sale of Hodges's estate in 1838 (see note 70), p. 72, no. 35.

74 An 1843 edition of the Reynard prints referred to the Englishman Henry Cole as the owner. Hollstein (Allart van Everdingen), p. 203, gives London as the present whereabouts of the Reynard plates. The exact location is unknown.

75 Sale Bubb Kuyper, Haarlem, 28 May-1 June 2018, no. 68/5996. These are drawings after Holl. 4 (2x), 9, 12, 15, 17, 18, 19, 20, 21, 25, 27, 28, 29, 32, 37, 39, 41, 44, 46, 48, 50, 51, 53, 54, 56 (2x), 57 (2x), 61, 62, 64, 65, 66, 68, 70, 72 (2x), 77, 80, 82, 83 (2x), 84, 89, 90, 92, 93 (2x), 99. The only dated drawing is the one of the cat Piet, with the inscription 'Piet slaapt bijt vier op 27 Xbre 85 AR [= 27 oktober 1685 Abraham Rutgers]' ('Piet sleeps by the fire on 27 October 1658 Abraham Rutgers'). The present owner of the drawings is unknown.

76 See e.g. sale Lambert ten Kate Collection, 16 June 1732 (Lugt 416), p. 69, portfolio H; sale Pieter Langendijk Collection, 25 April 1747 (Lugt 663), p. 21, no. 100; sale Jan Wandelaar Collection, 4 September 1759 (Lugt 1059), p. 53, no. 41, and sale (Leendert de?) Neufville Collection, 24 January 1763, p. 217, no. 13, and p. 233.

77 Sale Simon Schijnvoet Collection, 18 February 1728 (Lugt 365), p. 18, no. 81: 'Het werk van A. van Everdingen, zynde de Fabulen der Diere, en eenige Landscapes, door hem zelfs ge-est [*sic*], te samen 81 stuks, raar'. In this case the landscapes do seem to be incomplete. See also the reference to prints by Allart van Everdingen in the handwritten inventory of the art dealer Jan Pietersz Zomer (c. 1720-1724), held in typescript at the RKD – Netherlands Institute for Art History, pp. 84-85: 'Curieuze Gebonden Werken ... S. Het aardige Leven van Reyntje de Vos, van Allard van Everdingen'.

78 Sale Jeronymus Tonneman Collection, 21 October 1754 (Lugt 845), p. 120, no. 25: 'De Zinryke Afbeelding der Dieren, beneffens alle de Landscapes, door A. V. Everdinge, eerste Druk, met geschreeve Schriften'. Also sale Gerrit Schaak Collection, 28 October 1748 (Lugt 689), p. 50, no. 30.

79 Traced mentions in sale catalogues, arranged by year and number in Lugt: 1728 (L. 365), 1732 (L. 416) and 1748 (L. 689).

80 Traced mentions in sale catalogues, arranged by year and number in Lugt: 1752 (L. 799), 1754 (L. 837 and 845), 1755 (L. 869), 1759 (L. 1059), 1760 (L. 1090), 1762 (L. 1219), 1763 (L. 1261 and 1323), 1765 (L. 1438, 1483 and 1486), 1766 (L. 1528 and 1568), 1767 (L. 1594), 1768 (L. 1724), L. 1769 (L. 1778), 1770 (L. 1800 and 1868), 1772 (L. 1984 and 2001), 1773 (L. 2149 and 2206), 1774 (L. 2329), 1775 (L. 2349, 2356, 2446 and 2453), 1777 (L. 2625), 1778 (L. 2899), 1780 (L. 3181 and 3192(2)), 1781 (L. 3280 and 3327), 1782 (L. 3458(2) and 3480), 1784 (L. 3724), 1785 (L. 3860), 1787 (L. 4131(2)), 1789 (L. 4421), 1790 (L. 4620), 1791 (L. 4739), 1793 (L. 5115(2)), 1798 (L. 5718).

81 Sale Nicolaes Marcus Collection, 26 November 1770 (Lugt 1868), p. 458, no. 2260: 'Il y a Quinze Autres Pieces de ce Maître, qui sont avec des Changements & Plusieurs, où il n'y a pas encore de Ciel & qui sont plus ou moins finies, &c.'

82 In the original Dutch: 'allereerste braam-drukken' and 'zonder lugten en minder bewerkt'. Traced catalogues with mentions of early states, arranged by year and number in Lugt: 1770 (L. 1868), 1772 (L. 1984), 1773 (L. 2206), 1774 (L. 2329), 1775 (L. 2349 and 2453), 1793 (L. 5115[2]).

83 Cf. Van Eynden and Van der Willigen 1816-1840, vol. 1, p. 407; Josi 1821, section 'Aldert van Everdingen' (unpaged); Immerzeel 1842-1843, vol. 1, pp. 225-226; Kramm 1858, p. 445.

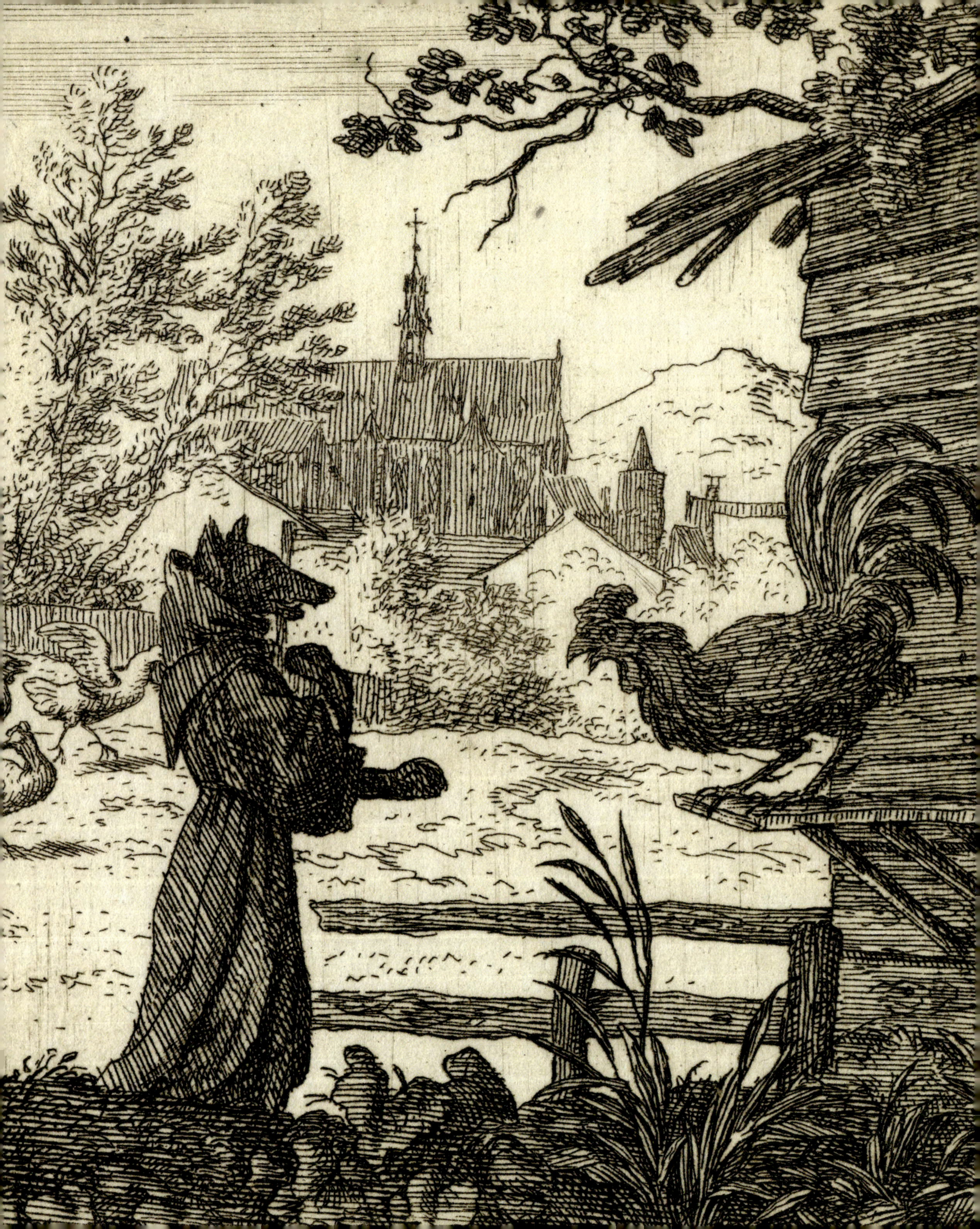

5
REYNARD THE FOX IN PICTURES

Remarkable Drawings and Prints by Allart van Everdingen

Marjan Pantjes

214
Allart van Everdingen, *Design for the title print of Reynard the Fox*, pen and brush and brown ink over traces of black chalk, on brown prepared paper, 147 x 104 mm, London, The British Museum, inv. no. 1836,0811.186 (cat. no. 71)

While Allart van Everdingen was working in Amsterdam, producing paintings, drawings and etchings of landscapes, he also made a series of illustrations for the tale of Reynard the Fox (fig. 214). In these lively animal scenes, probably made between 1665 and 1675, he emerged as an accomplished storyteller.

There are fifty-seven prints in the series, and seventy preparatory drawings for them survive (figs. 215 and 216). This is highly unusual, for in the seventeenth century such sketches were regarded as working material and seldom withstood their treatment in the workshop.[1] Van Everdingen's drawings were made on sixty-one sheets; in nine cases both sides of the paper were used. They are all in the British Museum in London. One drawing—one of the designs for the title print—is signed: the monogram 'AVE' appears in the lower left corner (fig. 217). Impressions of the prints made on the basis of the drawings can be found in several collections.[2]

The tale of Reynard the Fox was conceived as a mirror of human behaviour. It is a collection of stories in which the fox dupes other animals with his sly tricks to get what he wants, usually a good meal for him and his family. The victims

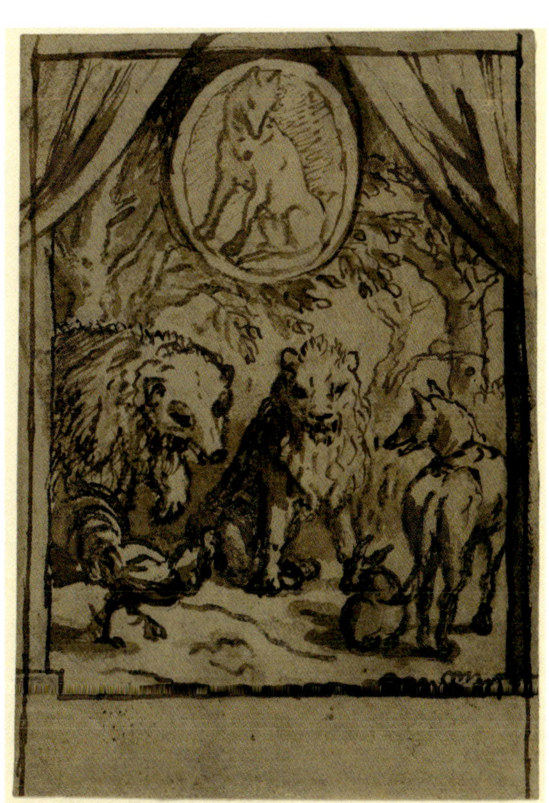

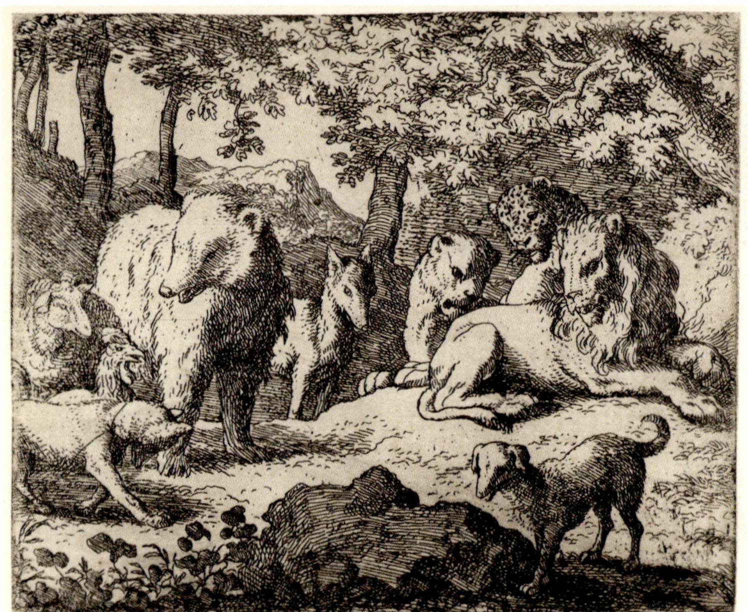

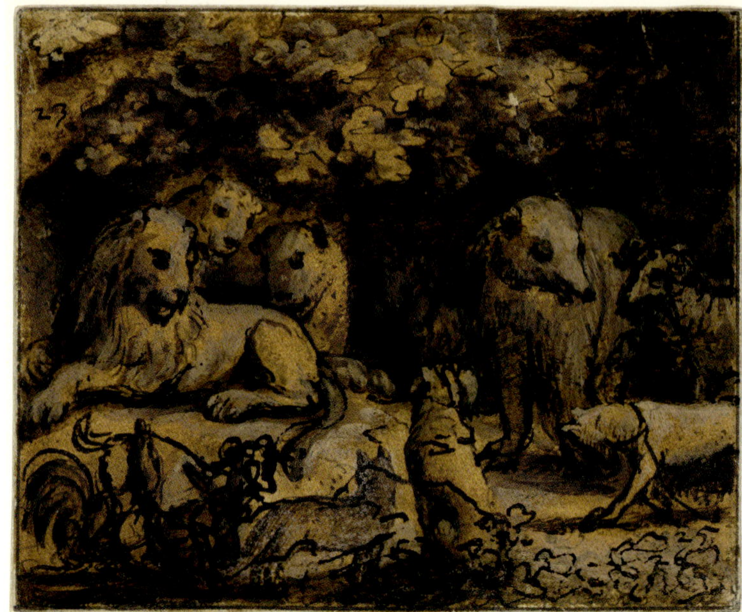

eventually have enough of this and take Reynard to court. However, the cunning fox manages to escape his punishment every time and even gets King Noble the Lion on his side —cleverness overcomes strength!

This essay explores the way Allart van Everdingen set about making his series of prints to illustrate this tale. The drawings and prints are studied side by side for the first time, revealing the choices the artist made in illustrating the cycle in an individual, innovative way.

Reynaerts historie

The literary cycle of Reynard the Fox was already centuries old in Van Everdingen's time. Between around 1170 and 1230 various stories about the animal's cunning tricks appeared in the north of France. This collection of fables is referred to as the *Roman de Renart* and the most popular stories from it formed the basis for the thirteenth-century Middle Dutch poem *Van den vos Reynaerde.* An adaptation of this work called *Reynaerts historie* was published in the late fourteenth century. It was the stand- ard text on Reynard the Fox from the fifteenth century to the end of the nineteenth,[3] and it was on this version of the tale that Allart van Everdingen based his illustrations. In *Bruin the Bear Beaten by Villagers*, for instance, we see people attacking a bear with various implements, including an axe, a spear and a spindle (figs. 236-238). These weapons are

< 215
Allart van Everdingen, *Reynard the Fox's Stay of Execution*, etching, 94 x 116 mm, Amster- dam, Rijksmuseum, inv. no. RP-P-OB-50.474 (Dut. 27 II) (cat. no. 32)

216
Allart van Everdingen, *Reynard the Fox's Stay of Execution*, pen and brush and brown ink over traces of red chalk, brown wash, heightened with light grey, corrections in pen and dark brown ink, on brown prepared paper, 95 x 118 mm, London, The British Museum, inv. no. 1836,0811.208 (cat. no. 80)

v 217
Allart van Everdingen, *Design for the title print of Reynard the Fox*, pen and brush and brown ink, brown wash, heightened with light grey, on brown prepared paper, 94 x 118 mm, London, The British Museum, inv. no. 1836,0811.187 (cat. no. 69)

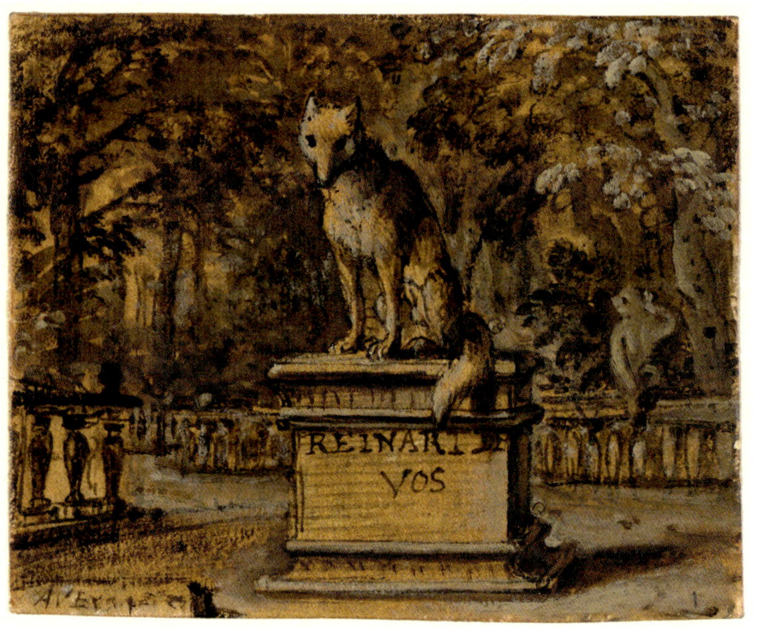

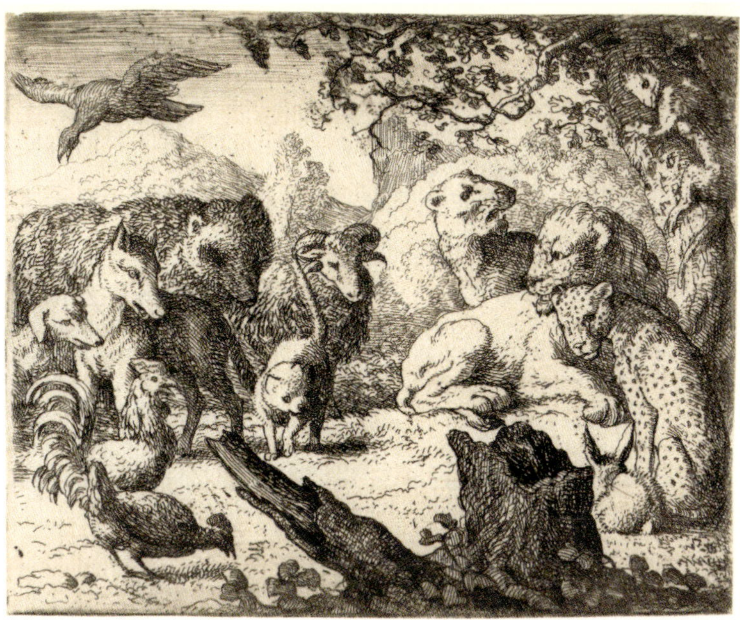

218
Allart van Everdingen,
King Noble the Lion Holds Court, etching,
94 x 117 mm, Amsterdam, Rijksmuseum,
inv. no. RP-P-OB-50.448
(Dut. 2 II) (cat. no. 28)

219
Chanticleer the Cock's Complaint, woodcut
in Heinrich von Alkmar,
Reinke de Vos, Lübeck:
Hans van Ghetelen
1498, fol. 17r, Wolfenbüttel, Herzog August
Bibliothek, sign. A:
32.14 Poet

> 220
Jehan de Gourmont
after Geoffroy Ballain,
The Fight between Reynard the Fox and Isengrim the Wolf,
woodcut in *Reynaert de vos. Een seer ghenouchlicke ende vermakelicke historie: in Franchoyse ende neder Duytsch*, Antwerp:
Christoffel Plantijn
1566, fol. 74v, Munich,
Bayerische Staatsbibliothek, sign. Rar. 714

explicitly mentioned in *Reynaerts historie*, suggesting that Van Everdingen wanted to remain faithful to this telling of the tale.[4]

Reynaerts historie is in two parts. The first part begins on a day when King Noble the Lion is holding court (fig. 218). All the animals appear for this festive occasion—except for Reynard the Fox. The animals seize the opportunity to press charges against the fox for the injuries he has done them, and King Noble decides to put Reynard on trial. The fox manages to manipulate the lion with his lies, is acquitted and returns safe and sound to his den. The second part of the story is broadly a repetition of the first:

the animals accuse Reynard, he is tried again but once more escapes punishment. This time, however, the focus is on the love-hate relationship between Reynard the Fox and Isengrim the Wolf. These animals like to go on the prowl together, but constantly try to trick one another to keep the loot for themselves. This culminates in a decisive fight between Reynard and Isengrim (fig. 244). Against all the odds, the fox wins and is even given a high office at the king's court.[5]

In the late fifteenth century, *Reynaerts historie* began to appear as printed books illustrated with woodcuts.[6] Woodcuts were ideal for use in books: relatively cheap because a great many impressions could be taken from a carved block of wood, they could also be printed on the same press as the text. The earliest known Reynard illustrations, surviving in book fragments dating from between 1487 and 1490, are attributed to the Haarlem Master, an anonymous woodcarver working in Haarlem in the late fifteenth century.[7] His woodcuts were the starting point of a long pictorial tradition (fig. 219). Likewise of influence on later imagery was a series of forty woodcuts made for *Reynaert de vos. Een seer ghenouchlicke ende vermakelicke historie*, an edition published in 1566 by the Antwerp publisher Christoffel Plantijn (c. 1520-1589) (fig. 220).[8] As folk literature, *Reynaerts historie* has retained its appeal down through the centuries.[9] New editions, all illustrated with woodcuts, appeared regularly up to the eighteenth century. In the period from 1603 to 1710, for instance, there are ten known editions from

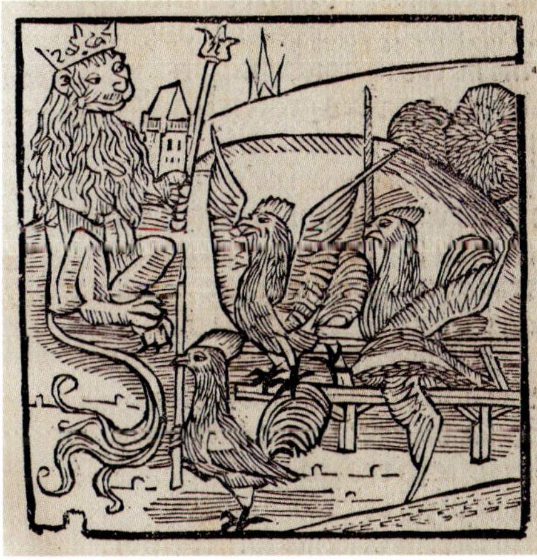

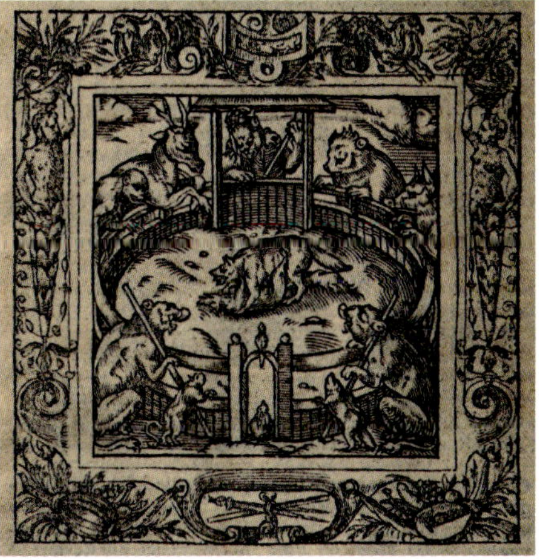

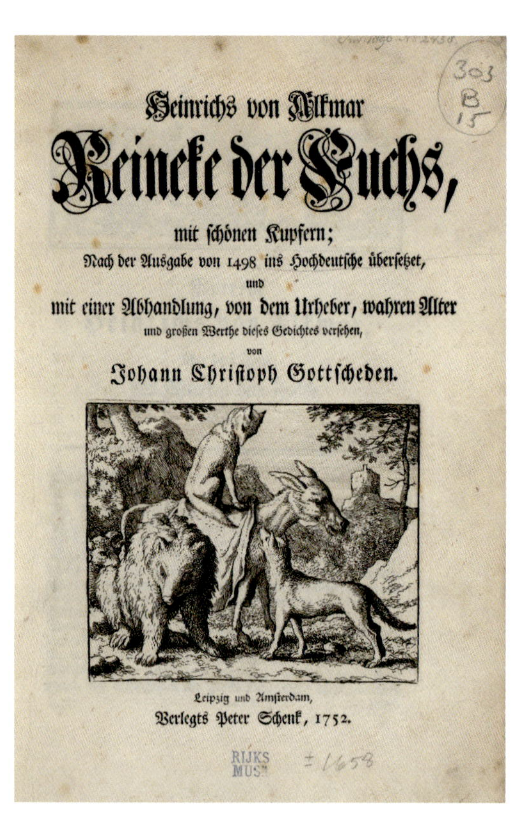

Heinrichs von Alkmar
Reineke der Fuchs,
mit schönen Kupfern;
Nach der Ausgabe von 1498 ins Hochdeutsche übersetzet,
und
mit einer Abhandlung, von dem Urheber, wahren Alter
und großen Werthe dieses Gedichtes versehen,
von
Johann Christoph Gottscheden.

Leipzig und Amsterdam,
Verlegts Peter Schenk, 1752.

the Northern Netherlands, each with some thirty woodcuts, and eight of them were published in Amsterdam, where Allart van Everdingen lived and worked from 1652 onwards.[10] The printing history of *Reynaerts historie* reveals that this version of the Reynard tale in text and images was widespread and well known. Van Everdingen exploited this popularity with his series of prints. Not only did Allart illustrate similar episodes in the story, he also drew on the woodcuts in the printed editions and this is reflected in his sketches and prints.[11]

We do not know why Van Everdingen made his print series of Reynard the Fox—not an obvious subject for an artist who specialized in landscape. It is likely that they were not designed as book illustrations. Etchings are not particularly suited to the purpose and there are no known Dutch editions of the Reynard tale with Allart's prints. The earliest known book in which they appear is the German *Reineke der Fuchs* (fig. 221), published in 1752, long after Van Everdingen's death.[12] The artist most probably made his illustrations to be sold as a set of prints in its own right with a title page with an explanatory text (figs. 214, 217 and 222-224).[13]

In his set of Reynard illustrations, Allart van Everdingen engaged with a tradition of narrative suites of prints, a great many of which were published in the sixteenth and seventeenth centuries. In 1612, for instance, the engraver and publisher Crispijn de Passe I (1564-1637) produced a series titled *Liber Genesis*, a set of sixty engravings including a title print illustrating stories from the Book of Genesis.[14] Before that, in 1602, he brought out a series of no fewer than 134 prints of Ovid's *Metamorphoses*.[15] De Passe was responding to the great popularity of tales from Classical history and mythology at that time.[16] There may also be a connection between Van Everdingen's set of prints and the emergence of books of animal fables, such as the *Vorsteliicke warande der dieren* of 1617. For this edition, Joost van den Vondel (1587-1679) wrote moral verses to accompany more than a hundred prints by Marcus Gheeraerts I (c. 1520-1590/1591).[17]

< 221
Title page of Johann Christoph Gottsched, *Heinrichs von Alkmar Reineke der Fuchs*, Leipzig/Amsterdam: Pieter Schenk 1752, Amsterdam, Rijksmuseum, call number 303 B 15 (cat. no. 27)

222
Allart van Everdingen, *Design for the title print of Reynard the Fox*, pen and brush and brown ink over black chalk, on brown prepared paper, 148 x 104 mm, London, The British Museum, inv. no. 1836,0811.184 (cat. no. 70)

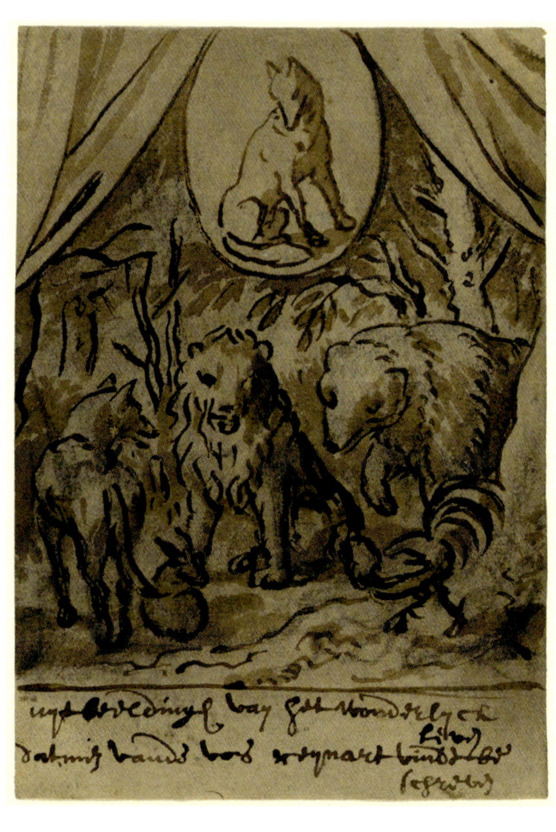

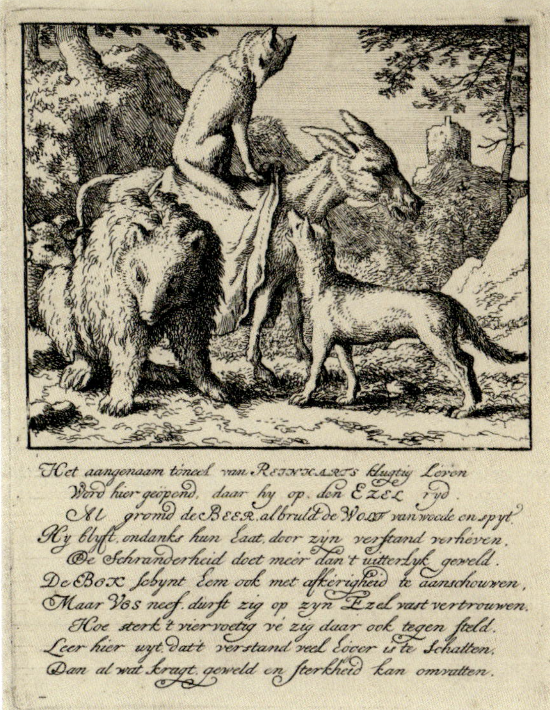

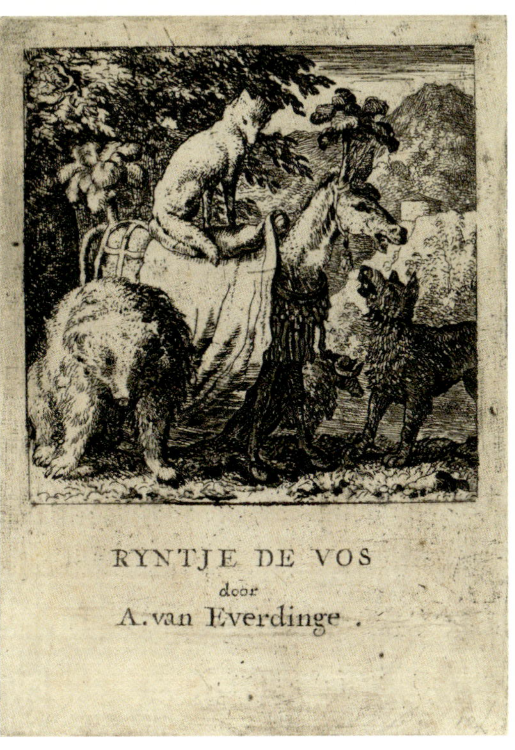

Van Everdingen or an Amsterdam publisher friend may have seen a gap in the market for a series of quality prints of the tale of Reynard the Fox. Regrettably, we do not know exactly what prompted the artist to make these illustrations or who financed the investment in materials and production.

From Drawing to Print

Van Everdingen's designs for the Reynard illustrations divide into two groups: there are sketches in which the artist is working out the right composition and placement of the animals (fig. 225), and more detailed drawings with shadows and highlights (fig. 226). Many of the worked up drawings have a layout in red or black chalk and corrections with a pen and dark brown ink or a brush and light grey oil paint. More than half of the sheets contain signs of indentation for transfer, where the outlines of the drawing were traced so that they could be transferred accurately to the copper plate (fig. 227).[18] The many changes in the drawings show that the artist was looking for the best way of illustrating the story.

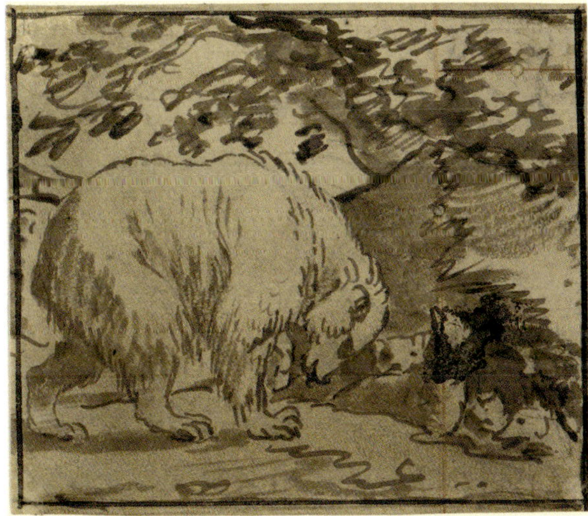

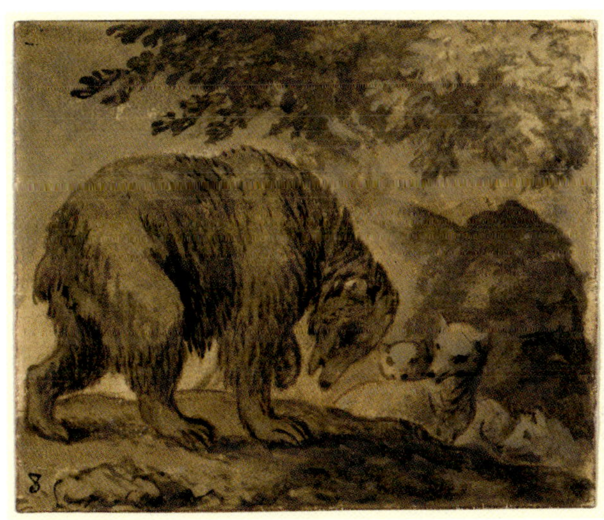

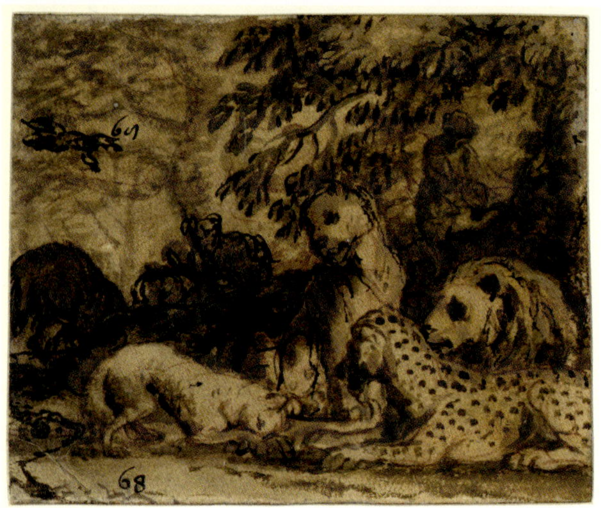

In eight of the fifty-seven prints, Allart van Everdingen used the innovative mezzotint technique, producing the darker impressions with velvety black passages.[20] Mezzotint literally means halftone and is a technique that makes it possible to achieve tonal transitions between light and dark. One of the tools used for this was the roulette: a small metal wheel on a handle with which the printmaker could create patterns of stippling and lines on the copper plate. Van Everdingen's use of the roulette is evident in *Reynard the Fox Tries to Steal a Capon* (fig. 230); a number of diagonal lines built up of short dashes run across Reynard's right rear leg.[21]

It appears that Van Everdingen used several different techniques in the prints with mezzotint, experimenting with tonal effects during the design process.[22] However, it is often difficult to tell which technique he used where and how he achieved certain tonal effects, particularly in the dark areas.

Van Everdingen was most probably one of a group of pioneers in Amsterdam who developed the mezzotint technique, a group that included Wallerant Vaillant (1623-1677) and Abraham Bloteling (1640-1690).[23] Vaillant, a draughtsman, etcher and painter of French descent, brought the technique to Amsterdam around 1665. It is quite possible that Van Everdingen knew him or his work.[24] The use of mezzotint

His search continued as he worked on the copper plates. Sometimes, for instance, he would pull a proof impression on which he added elements to the composition or retouched areas of shadow with a pen, and then etched them into the plate. As far as we know, nine such proofs with corrections survive. In the proof of *Reynard the Fox Accused by the Animals* (fig. 228), for example, we can see that Van Everdingen was trying to find the best placement of the branches and leaves that frame King Noble the Lion and his court. A later state of the print shows the added vegetation, this time etched into the copper plate (fig. 229).[19]

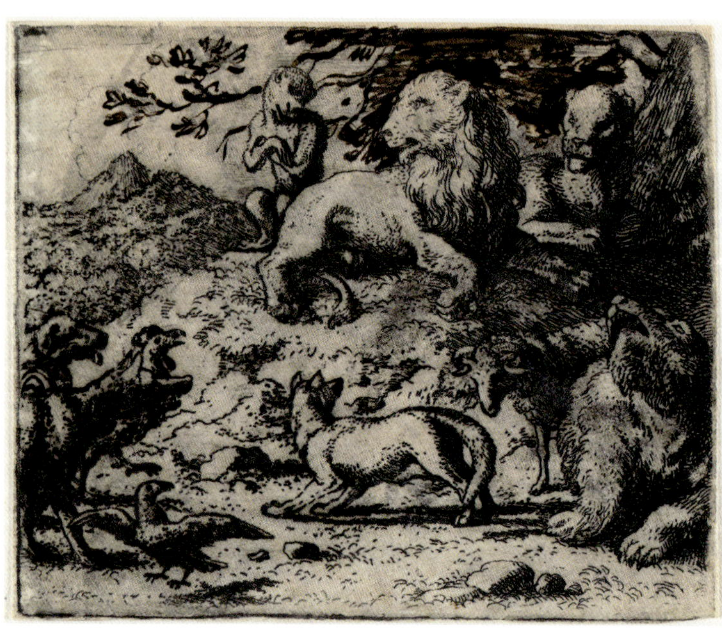

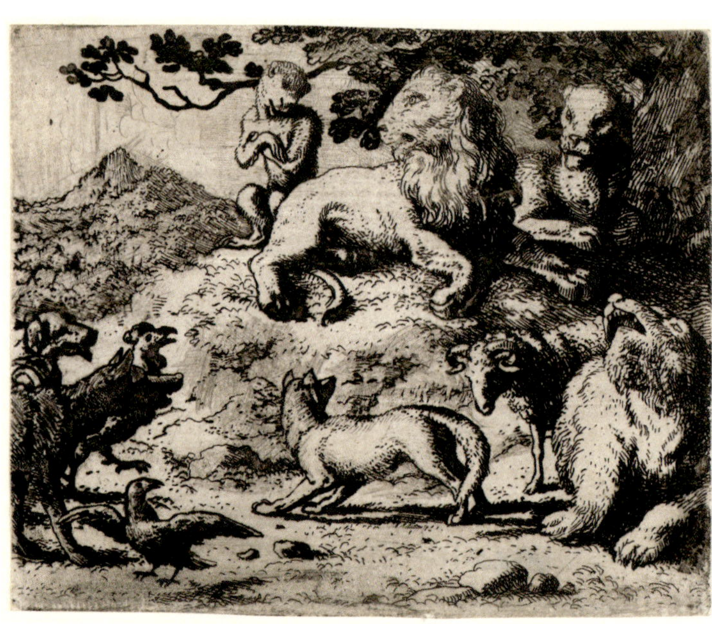

in the Reynard prints dates these illustrations to between around 1665 and Allart's death in 1675.[25]

Focus on Animals and Landscape

As a master of landscape, Van Everdingen stuck to his trade in his Reynard illustrations, devoting considerable attention to the natural surroundings of the animals in the pictures. Many of the designs feature an effective combination of a moment in the story in the foreground and a panoramic view in the background. Allart liked using the repoussoir principle, where a darker foreground 'pushes' a lighter background away—an effective way of creating depth in a scene. We see this in *Bruin the Bear Summonses Reynard the Fox* (fig. 231), where the composition is built up in several layers. Bruin the Bear calls Reynard to come to court. Using a tree stump lower left, Van Everdingen created distance between the viewer and the bear. Bruin himself is in full sunlight, while Reynard skulks in the shadows at the entrance to his den. In the background a mountainous vista unfolds, and the bear is pictured again making his way through the valley as he approaches the fox's den.

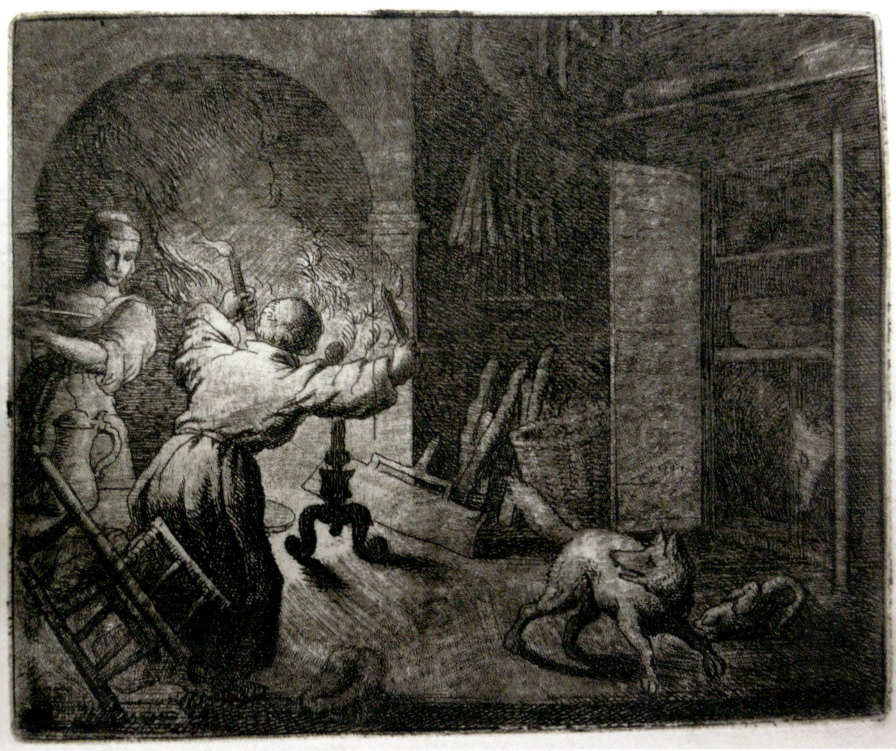

230
Allart van Everdingen,
*Reynard the Fox Tries
to Steal a Capon*,
etching and mezzotint,
95 x 117 mm, Petit
Palais, Musée des
Beaux-Arts de la Ville
de Paris, inv. no.
GDUT10392 (Dut. 20 IV)
(cat. no. 100)

> 231
Allart van Everdingen,
*Bruin the Bear
Summonses Reynard
the Fox*, etching,
96 x 117 mm, Amster-
dam, Rijksmuseum,
inv. no. RP-P-OB-50.454
(Dut. 8 II) (cat. no. 30)

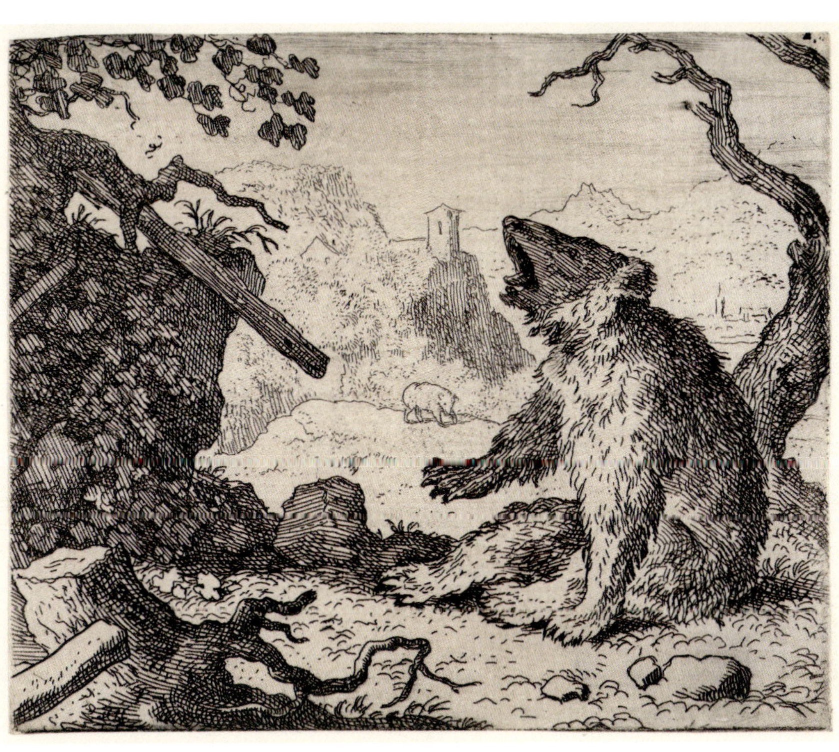

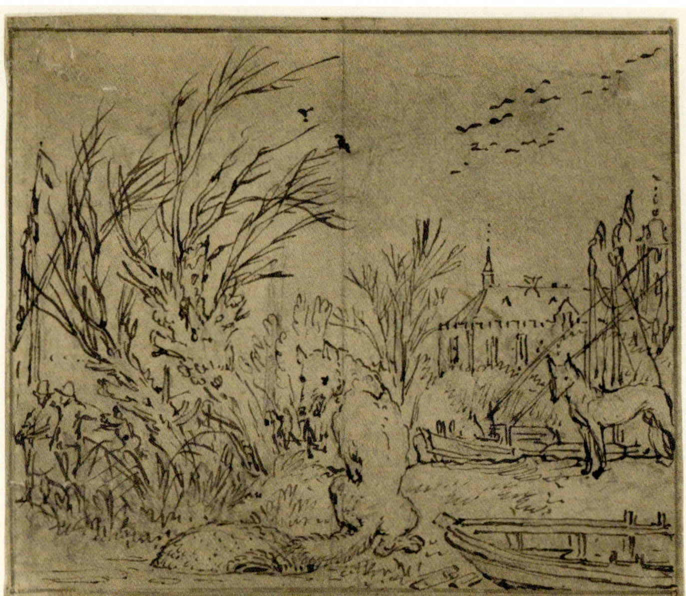

232
Allart van Everdingen,
*Hirsent the She-Wolf
Tricked by Reynard
the Fox*, pen and brown
ink, on brown prepared
paper, 96 x 117 mm,
London, The British
Museum, inv. no.
1836,0811.233
(cat. no. 87)

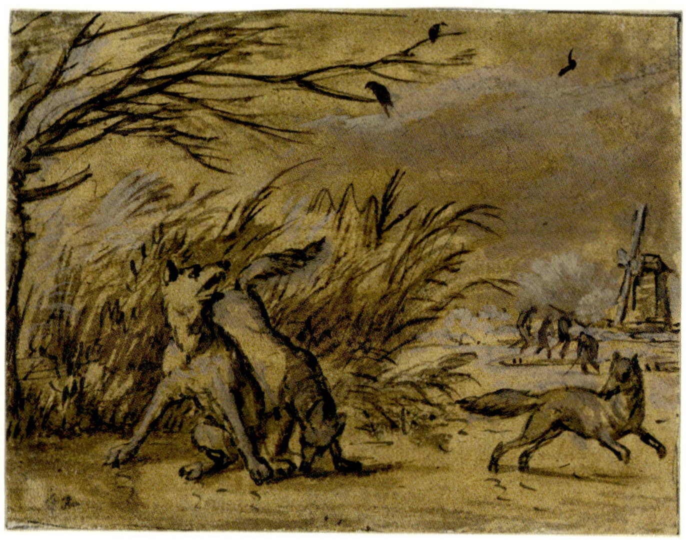

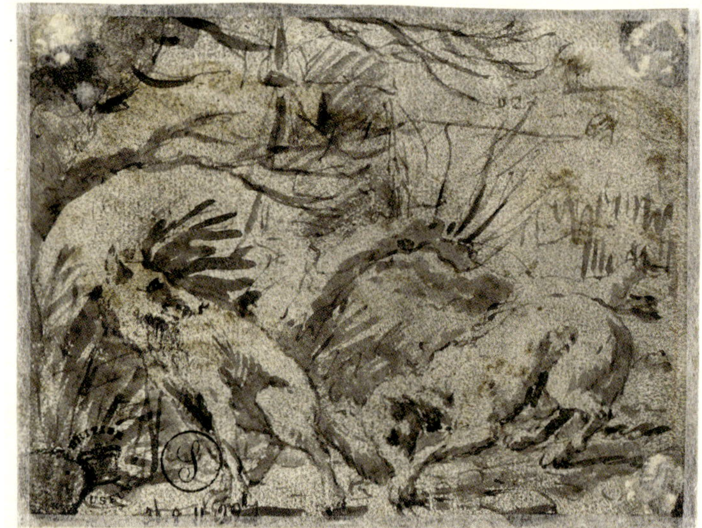

233
Allart van Everdingen,
*Hirsent the She-Wolf
Tricked by Reynard the
Fox*, pen and brush and
brown ink over traces of
red chalk, brown wash,
heightened with light grey,
on brown prepared paper,
90 x 120 mm, London,
The British Museum,
inv. no. 1836,0811.227
(cat. no. 86)

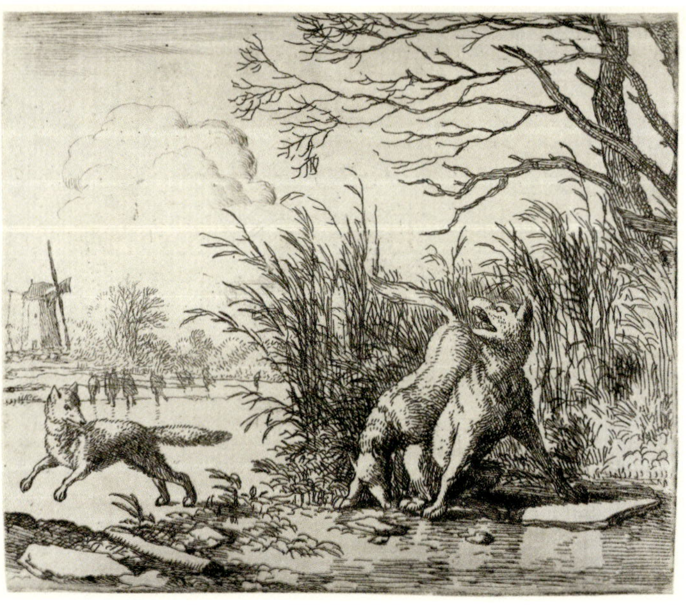

234
Allart van Everdingen,
*Hirsent the She-Wolf
Tricked by Reynard the Fox*,
pen and brush and grey
ink, 90 x 120 mm, London,
The British Museum, inv. no.
1836,0811.227v (cat. no. 86,
verso of fig. 233)

< 235
Allart van Everdingen,
*Hirsent the She-Wolf
Tricked by Reynard
the Fox*, etching, 98 x
118 mm, Amsterdam,
Rijksmuseum, inv. no.
RP-P-OB-50.500
(Dut. 53 II) (cat. no. 35)

Van Everdingen often used a tree trunk as a repoussoir in the foreground of his landscapes (fig. 188). This is just one of the motifs typical of Allart's oeuvre as a whole that are found in the Reynard illustrations—rocks, ships and landmarks like spires, windmills and churches. Some of these appear, for example, in the preparatory drawings and the etching of *Hirsent the She-Wolf Tricked by Reynard the Fox* (figs. 232-235). Reynard had told the wolf that she would catch a lot of fish if she dangled her tail in a hole in the ice to act as a net, but the hole froze over and she was trapped. While Isengrim the Wolf tried in vain to free her, Reynard made good his escape. There are three known designs for this episode, one of which was produced as a print. The first includes motifs like pollard willows, ships' masts, a church and a rowing boat (fig. 232). However, Van Everdingen made a revised design in which the wolves together form a bold triangle in the composition, surrounded by branches and reeds (fig. 233). On the back of this drawing there is a variant of this second design (fig. 234). The boats and quay in the first version have made way for a frozen river in the second (fig. 233); in the background

a small group of skaters near a windmill contextualize the scene. If Reynard was rather passive in the first design, here he is much more dynamic. He seizes the opportunity to escape, slithering across the ice. This was the design that Allart eventually used in the print (fig. 235).

Not all the illustrations feature a distant landscape. In *Bruin the Bear Beaten by Villagers* (fig. 236), Van Everdingen zoomed in close on the drama. Reynard had promised Bruin that he would find a lot of honey in a felled tree trunk on farmer Lamfroit's land, but nothing was further from the truth. Bruin's head and paws became wedged in the hollow trunk, villagers converged on the scene when they heard him bellowing and beat him black and blue. We can see in a highly detailed drawing that Van Everdingen was looking for the best placement of the bear, the tree trunk and the villagers in the composition (fig. 237). Initially he positioned the tree trunk diagonally in the centre of the group of villagers. Then, using dark brown ink, he drew the trunk again in the foreground, where it still formed an obstacle. In the end, Van Everdingen opted for a different arrangement (figs. 236 and 238). The tree trunk was moved to the edge of

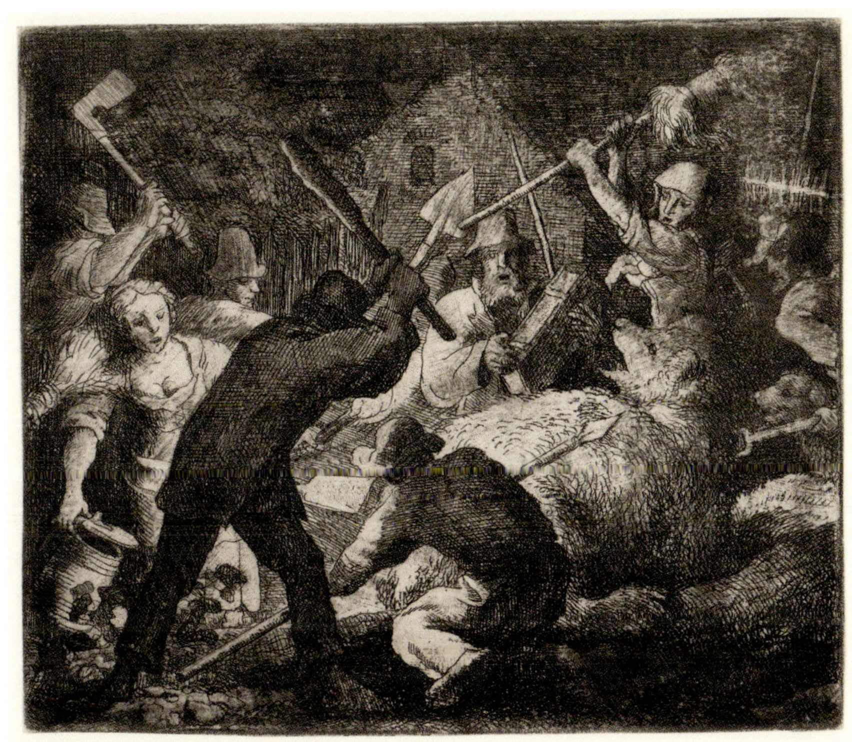

236
Allart van Everdingen, *Bruin the Bear Beaten by Villagers*, etching and mezzotint, 98 x 116 mm, Amsterdam, Rijksmuseum, inv. no. RP-P-OB-50.457 (Dut. 11 III) (cat. no. 31)

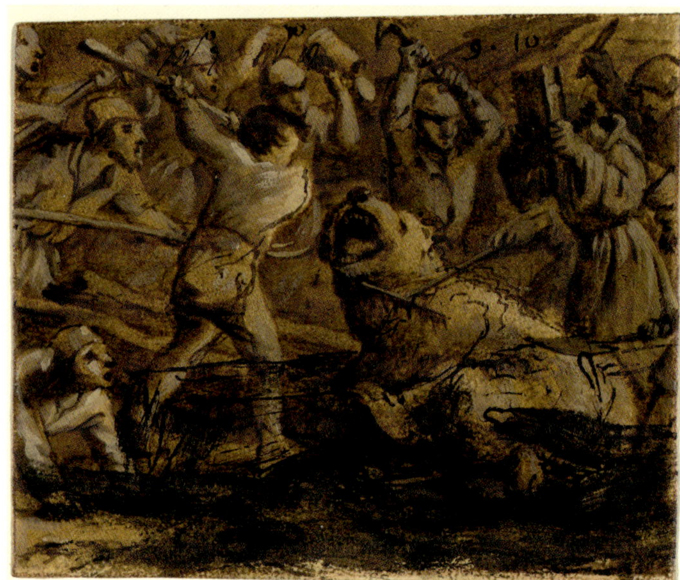

237
Allart van Everdingen, *Bruin the Bear Beaten by Villagers*, pen and brush and brown ink over traces of red chalk, heightened with light grey, brown wash, corrections in pen and dark brown ink, on brown prepared paper, 93 x 114 mm, London, The British Museum, inv. no. 1836,0811.195 (cat. no. 78)

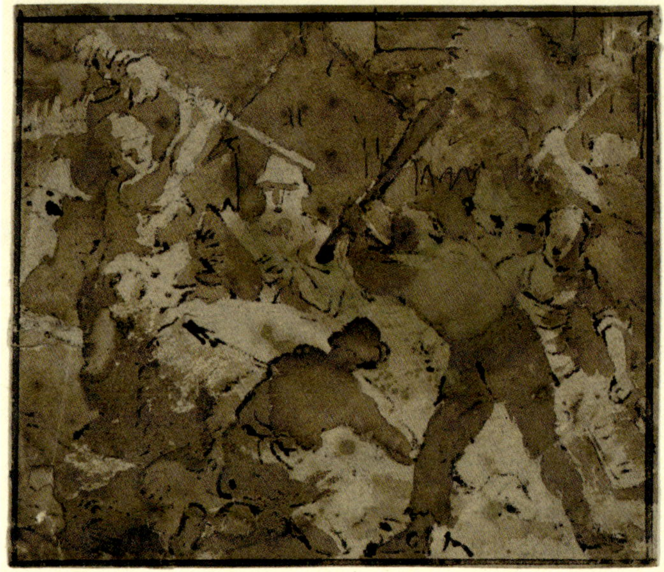

238
Allart van Everdingen, *Bruin the Bear Beaten by Villagers*, pen and brush and brown ink over traces of black chalk, brown wash, on brown prepared paper, 96 x 115 mm, London, The British Museum, inv. no. 1836,0811.194 (cat. no. 77)

the image and the whole focus of the scene shifted to Bruin the Bear, who is lit by the burning torch held by the woman on the left.

Allart van Everdingen rendered the animals in his Reynard pictures very convincingly in lifelike poses (fig. 225) and engaged in natural-looking interactions (fig. 239). We do not know which examples Van Everdingen used for his animals. He probably took inspiration from drawings, prints and paintings by other artists, including work by his teacher Roelandt Savery (1576-1639), and he may have made his own drawings of stuffed and living beasts.[26] Van Everdingen could certainly have seen live wild animals in Amsterdam. Lions, bears, leopards and monkeys were among the exotic creatures that could be seen at markets and fairs, and in menageries.[27]

Van Everdingen let the animals in his illustrations be animals, both in their appearance and in their staging—a departure from the way episodes in the story were depicted in the woodcuts, where the animals were usually given more human features. A good example is the depiction of King Noble the Lion's power and authority. In the pictorial tradition, Noble's royal

status is established by picturing him with a crown and sceptre, much like a heraldic lion (fig. 219). Van Everdingen did not add these attributes, instead portraying the king and his retinue as realistic animals and emphasizing their power by placing them in a stately pose on a higher level than the other animals (fig. 240). This natural 'throne' is usually framed

v 239
Allart van Everdingen, *Reynard the Fox Mocks Bruin the Bear*, pen and brush and brown ink over traces of black chalk, on brown prepared paper, 95 x 117 mm, London, The British Museum, inv. no. 1836,0811.196 (cat. no. 73)

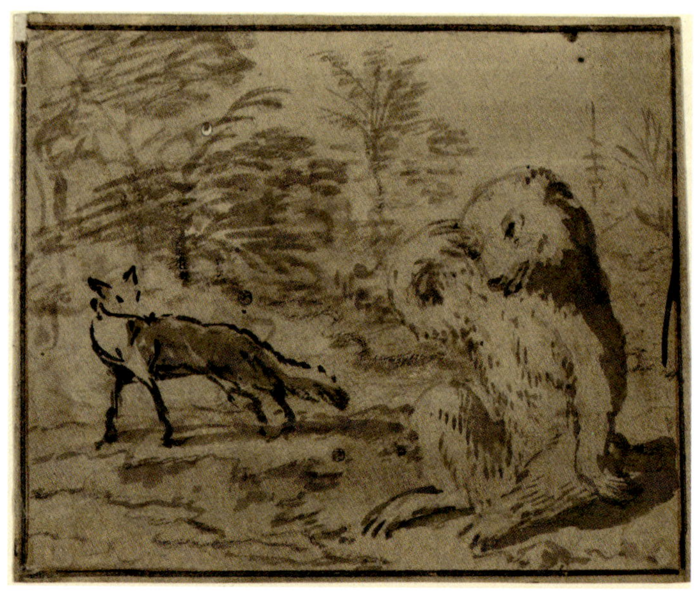

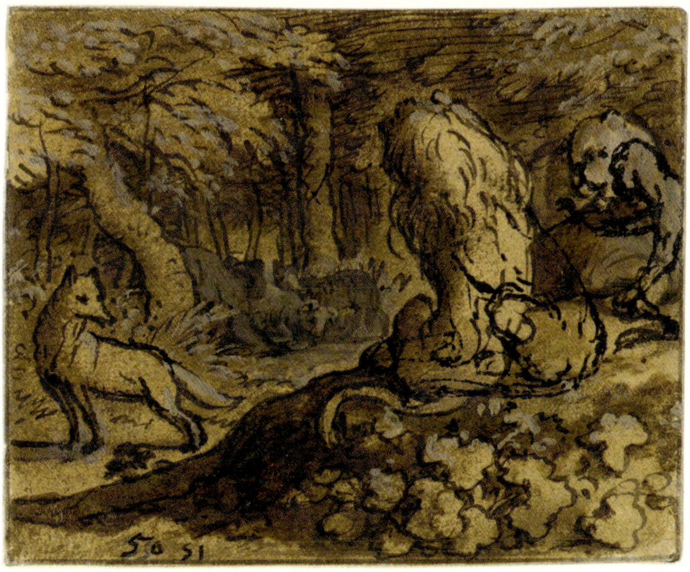

240
Allart van Everdingen, *Reynard the Fox's Defence*, pen and brush and brown ink over traces of red chalk, brown wash, heightened with light grey, corrections in pen and dark brown ink, on brown prepared paper, 94 x 116 mm, London, The British Museum, inv. no. 1836,0811.236 (cat. no. 85)

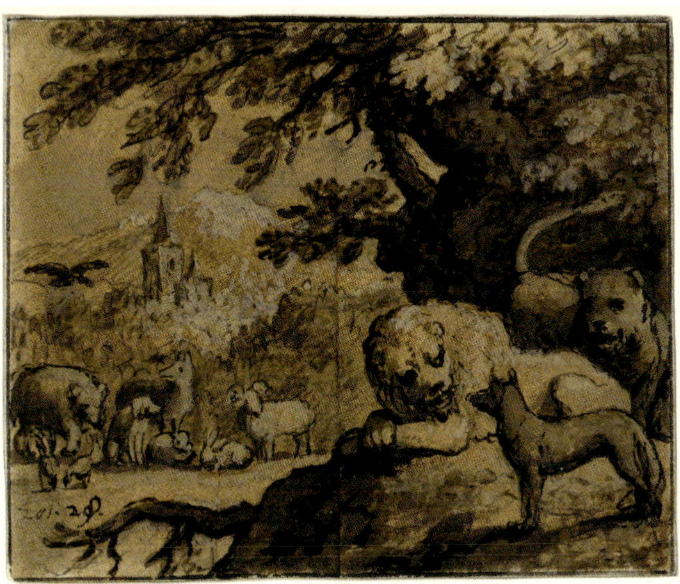

241
Allart van Everdingen, *Reynard the Fox in Conversation with King Noble the Lion*, pen and brush and brown ink, brown wash, heightened with light grey, on brown prepared paper, 95 x 116 mm, London, The British Museum, inv. no. 1852,0519.63 (cat. no. 83)

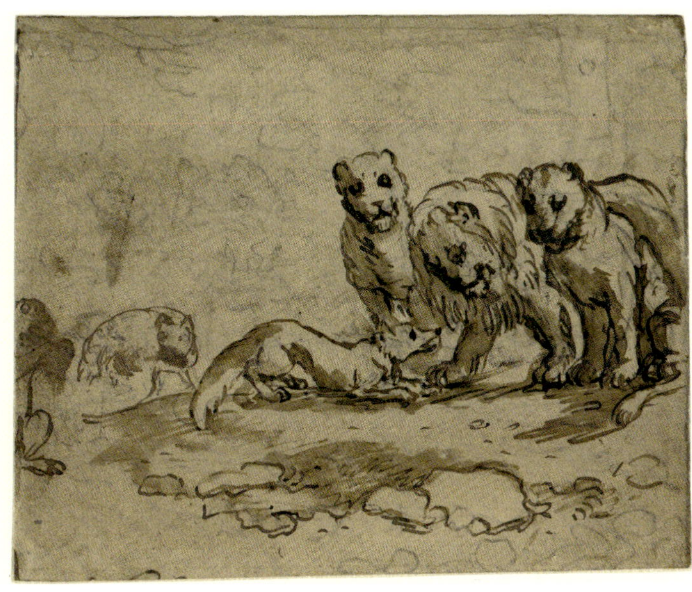

242
Allart van Everdingen, *Reynard the Fox Lies about a Conspiracy against King Noble the Lion*, pen and brush and brown ink over black chalk, on brown prepared paper, 95 x 116 mm, London, The British Museum, inv. no. 1836,0811.235 (cat. no. 82)

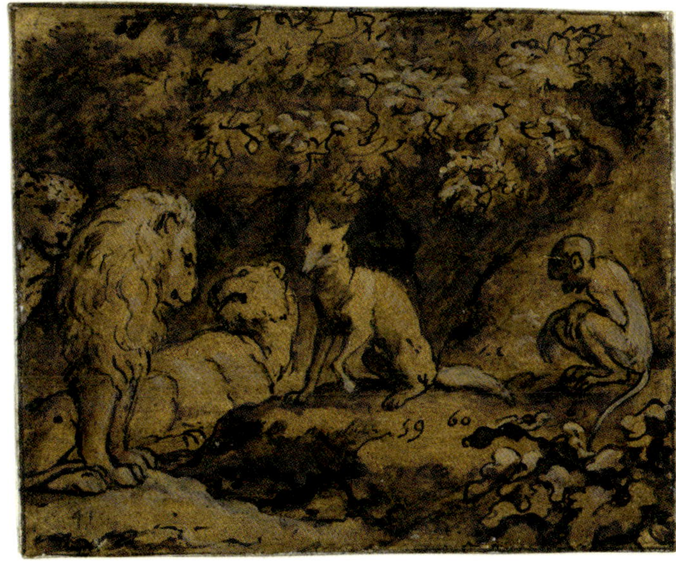

243
Allart van Everdingen, *Reynard the Fox's Defence*, pen and brush and brown ink, brown wash, heightened with light grey, on brown prepared paper, 94 x 116 mm, London, The British Museum, inv. no. 1836,0811.210 (cat. no. 84)

by a strong tree with luxuriant vegetation (fig. 241). In the story, the power seems gradually to shift as the king increasingly believes Reynard's entreaties and lies (fig. 242). The new balance of power is expressed in a number of illustrations, as the fox, not the lion, is placed higher (fig. 243).

The Fight between Reynard the Fox and Isengrim the Wolf (fig. 244) is another example of Allart's realistic depiction of animal interaction. This decisive moment in the tale was often shown as a knightly tournament in a fenced arena (fig. 220). Van Everdingen replaced the arena with a naturally enclosed space—a depression at the bottom of a hill.[28] He shows how Reynard the Fox follows the instructions of the wise she-ape Rukenau to vanquish the strong wolf: Reynard slaps Isengrim's face with his wet tail, then blinds him by kicking sand in his eyes. The tactic enables the fox to win the fight against all the odds.[29]

Van Everdingen's decision to steer clear of human attributes or actions and depict the animals faithfully sometimes makes it difficult to work out which episode in the story he is illustrating. The sketch in which Bruin and Reynard encounter one another on a hill (fig. 245) could equally depict the moment when the bear appears at the fox's den to summons Reynard to attend court and the moment when

Reynard leads Bruin to the farmyard where he says there is honey to be found. The same two scenes could also be pictured in the drawing of Bruin the Bear in sharp profile (fig. 226). It is likewise not always clear which episode is meant in the many illustrations of King Noble the Lion (fig. 241).

Van Everdingen probably realized that his scenes involving animals were sometimes difficult to interpret, for in a few cases he did include human attributes or actions to clarify the situation. In *Reynard the Fox Deceives Chanticleer the Cock* (fig. 246), for example, there was no way he could avoid it.[30] By posing as a pious monk, the fox gains the cock's trust and gets into the monastery garden with hens scratching around. The habit Reynard wears as his disguise is crucial in understanding the illustration. In the first draft of the drawing the fox also held a Bible and a papal brief with a seal. In the correction in dark brown ink, Van Everdingen omitted the attributes and changed the fox's position from full face to profile to show the conversation between him and the cock (fig. 247). In the background Reynard causes mayhem among the hens: we see the result in *Chanticleer the Cock's Complaint* (fig. 248); Coppe the Hen's body is brought to King Noble on a litter.

< 244
Allart van Everdingen,
The Fight between Reynard the Fox and Isengrim the Wolf,
etching, 98 x 116 mm, Petit Palais, Musée des Beaux-Arts de la Ville de Paris, inv. no. GDUT10489 (Dut. 56 III) (cat. no. 101)

245
Allart van Everdingen,
Bruin the Bear Addresses Reynard the Fox, pen and brush and brown ink, brown wash, on brown prepared paper, 95 x 114 mm, London, The British Museum, inv. no. 1836,0811.234 (cat. no. 76)

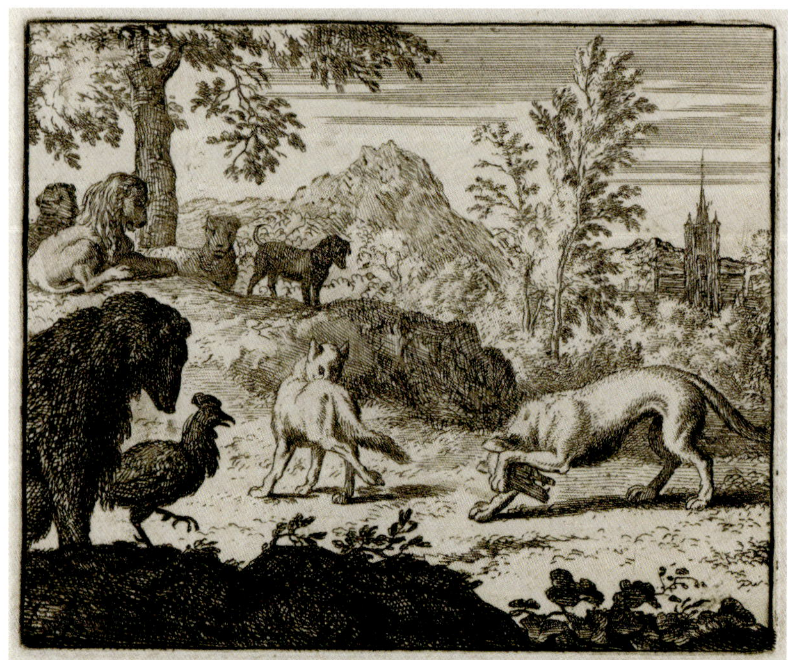

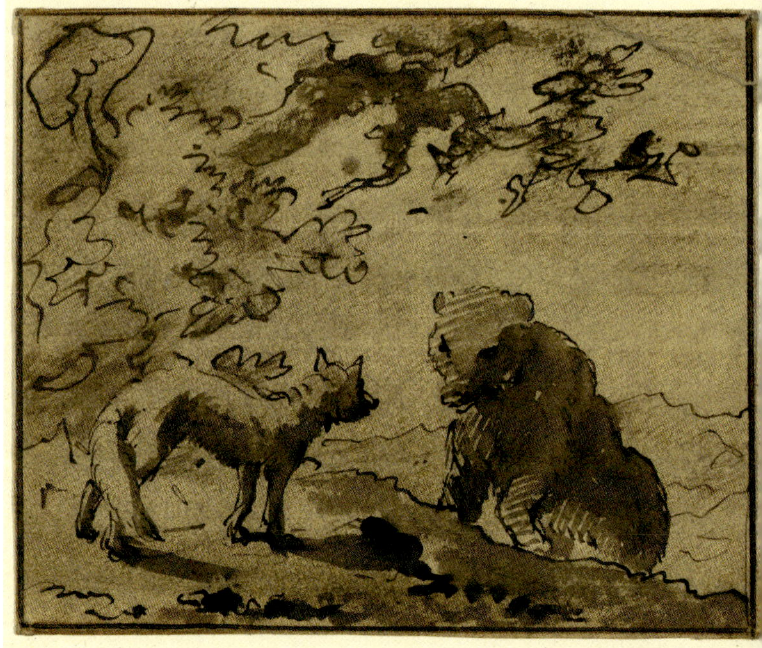

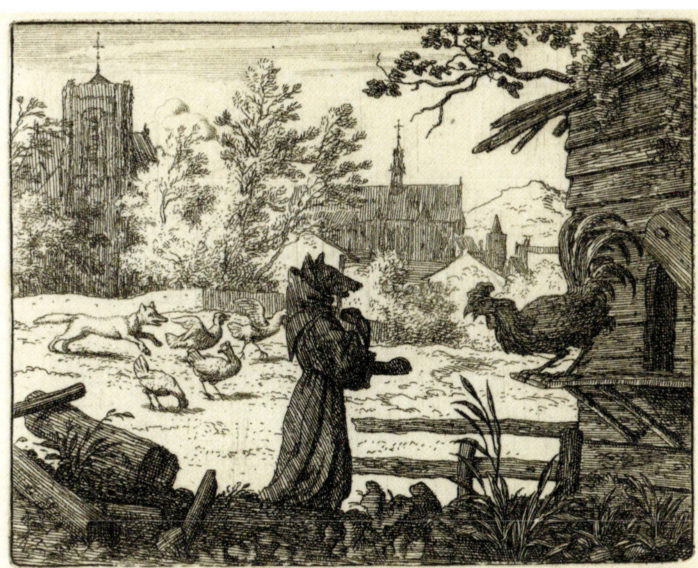

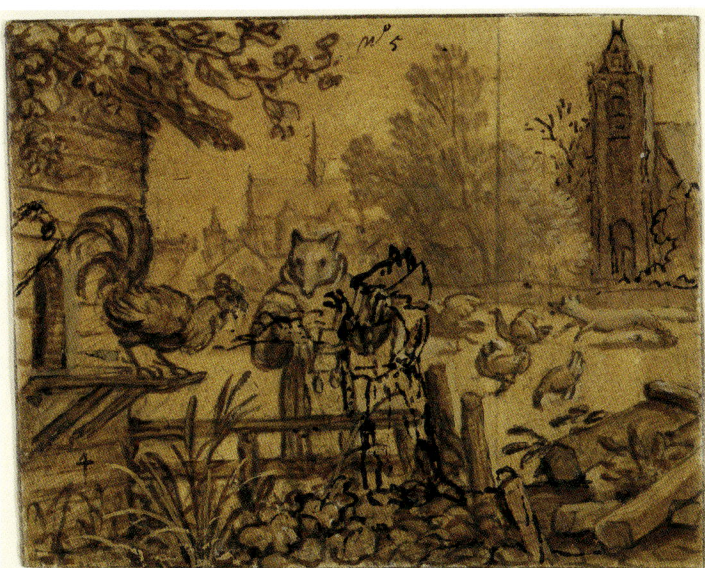

246
Allart van Everdingen,
*Reynard the Fox
Deceives Chanticleer
the Cock*, etching,
95 x 118 mm, Petit
Palais, Musée des
Beaux-Arts de la Ville
de Paris, inv. no.
GDUT10346 (Dut. 6 III)
(cat. no. 99)

247
Allart van Everdingen,
*Reynard the Fox
Deceives Chanticleer
the Cock*, pen and
brush and brown
ink over traces of
red and black chalk,
heightened with light
grey, corrections in pen
and dark brown ink, on
brown prepared paper,
93 x 119 mm, London,
The British Museum,
inv. no. 1836,0811.191
(cat. no. 72)

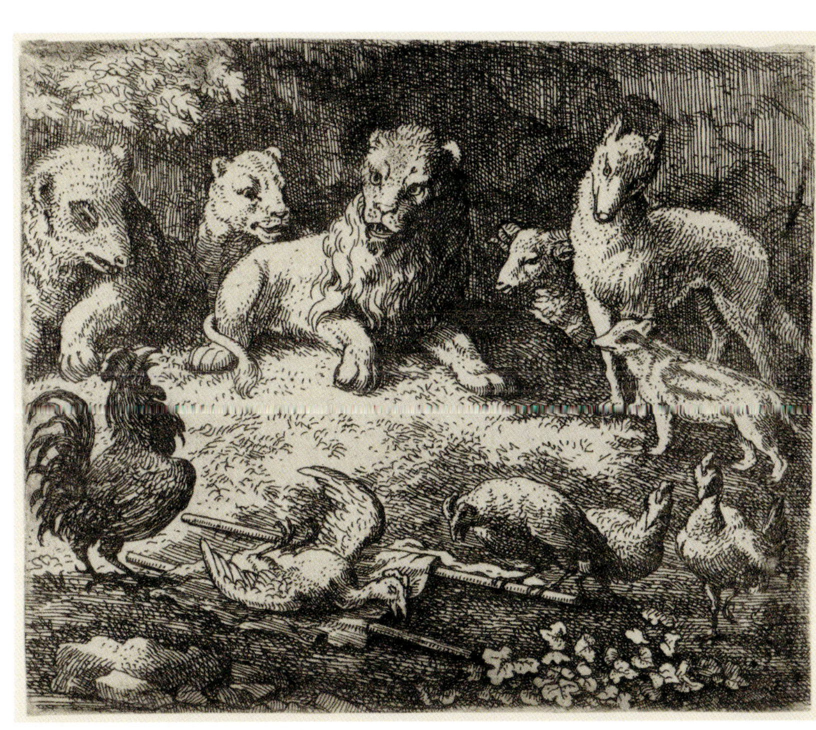

248
Allart van Everdingen,
*Chanticleer the Cock's
Complaint*, etching,
94 x 115 mm, Amster-
dam, Rijksmuseum,
inv. no. RP-P-OB-50.451
(Dut. 5 II) (cat. no. 29)

The Fate of the Copper Plates

The original copper plates of the set of Reynard illustrations probably remained with Van Everdingen's family after his death in 1675.[31] They were bought at auction by the publisher Pieter Schenk II (1693-1775), who used them to illustrate the edition of *Reineke Fuchs* in 1752.[32] His son Pieter Schenk III (1728-1803) may have inherited the plates. In the nineteenth century they turned up in London with the British civil servant and reformer Sir Henry Cole (1808-1882). In 1843 he used them for a children's book titled *The Pleasant History of Reynard the Fox: Told by the Pictures of Aldert van Everdingen*, which he published under the pseudonym Felix Summerly.[33] In the introduction to this book Cole wrote that he had the copper plates.[34] This is confirmed by his diary, in which he recorded the preparations for publication. It is interesting to note that John Linnells, one of the artists with whom he was collaborating, asked more than once if he could have the copper plates.[35] As yet, we do not know whether he actually did get them. Be that as it may, the plates do not now appear to be in Cole's bequest in the Victoria and Albert Museum.[36]

There were a number of reissues of the Reynard tale with Van Everdingen's prints after 1843.[37] In Germany they acquired an influential place in the pictorial tradition of Reynard the Fox, thanks primarily to the imitations by Wilhelm von Kaulbach (1804/1805-1874), who made illustrations after Van Everdingen's examples for the adaptation of the story by the celebrated author Johann Wolfgang Goethe (1749-1832).[38] Goethe was an admirer of Allart van Everdingen's work. After a lengthy search, he was overjoyed to acquire fine impressions of the Reynard series. On 17 April 1783 he wrote to his friend Charlotte von Stein: 'The etchings are there and extraordinarily fine. The Everdingens are first impressions and as if they were made yesterday.'[39]

1 Leeflang 2003, pp. 3 and 17.
2 For the drawings see Hind 1926, cat. nos. 61-121; Davies 2007, pp. 118-127 and cat. nos. 594-665. For the prints see Drugulin 1873, cat. nos. 1-57; Dutuit 1881, cat. nos. 1-57; Hollstein (Allart van Everdingen), p. 203. On the verso of one of the drawings (London, The British Museum, inv. no. 1836,0811.218; Davies 2007, cat. no. 639v) there is a sketch of a landscape. It probably does not belong to the Reynard series and has consequently not been counted for the purposes of this essay. Many of the drawings are numbered in different hands; these numbers may have been added later. There are complete sets of Reynard the Fox prints in the Rijksmuseum in Amsterdam, Museum Boijmans Van Beuningen in Rotterdam, the British Museum in London, the Petit Palais,

Musée des Beaux-Arts de la Ville de Paris in Paris and elsewhere. One moment in the story appears in two different prints (Dut. 51 and 51a). Viewed thus there are fifty-eight prints.
3 Wackers 1993, pp. 269-273. In my research I used the edition Schlusemann and Wackers 2005. In the literature it is usual to refer to *Reynaerts historie* or *Reynaert II*. The editions of this text have appeared under various titles, usually variations of *Reynaerts historie* (Brussels, KBR, sign. Ms. 14601), *Historie van Reynaert die vos* (The Hague, Koninklijke Bibliotheek, sign. I 410) and *Reynaert de vos. Een seer ghenouchlicke ende vermakelicke historie* (Munich, Bayerische Staatsbibliothek, sign. Rar. 714). With thanks to Paul Wackers for his explanation of the literary history of Reynard the Fox.

4 Schlusemann and Wackers 2005, p. 44.
5 Wackers 2002, pp. 331-336.
6 The earliest full text of *Reynaerts historie*, now in the KBR in Brussels (sign. Ms. 14601), was probably printed in Utrecht around 1470. Space for twenty illustrations was reserved in this edition; as far as is known they were never made (Goossens 1983, pp. 6-8).
7 Goossens 1983, p. 9. There are just a few images, which are held in Cambridge University Library (reproduced and discussed in Breul 1927).
8 Verzandvoort 1988-1989.
9 See Cuijpers 2014, esp. the inventories on pp. 20, 35, 44, 55, 91-92, 104 and 114, in which the Reynard story recurs.
10 Menke 1992, pp. 129-137. The same woodcut was often printed several times in the book to illustrate different moments in the story. For

Allart van Everdingen's residence in Amsterdam from 1652 see Davies 2001, p. 101 and Van Thiel-Stroman in Köhler et al. 2006, p. 149.

11 Some of Allart's compositions strongly resemble woodcuts illustrating the same moment in the story, for example *Reynard the Fox and Isengrim the Wolf Steal Fish from a Cart* (Dut. 4). Van Everdingen also usually placed King Noble the Lion by a large tree, the same as in the Plantijn edition. A number of references to the pictorial tradition appear only in a sketch, not in the print based on it. This is the case, for example, in Van Everdingen's illustration *Tibert the Cat Summonses Reynard the Fox* (London, The British Museum, inv. no. 1836,0811.198v; Davies 2007, cat. no. 613v; Dut. 14). The drawing shows the cat with a letter in his mouth, in line with the pictorial tradition; the letter has been left out in the print.

12 See also Verzandvoort 1995.

13 With thanks to Erik Hinterding for this suggestion. The text on a title print in the British Museum in London (inv. no. S.1990, Dut. 1, fig. 223) was engraved in the plate, but not by Van Everdingen. It reads: 'Het aangenaam toneel van REINHARTS klugtig leven / Word hier geöpend, daar hy op den EZEL ryd. / Al gromd de BEER, al bruld de WOLF van woede en spyt, / Hy blyft, ondanks hun haat, door zyn verstand verheven. / De schranderheid doet meer dan 't uitterlyk geweld. / De BOK schynt hem ook met afkerigheid te aanschouwen, / Maar VOS neef, durft zig op zyn Ezel vast vertrouwen, / Hoe sterk 't viervoetig vé zig daar ook tegen steld. / Leer hier wyt, dat 't verstand veel hoger is te schatten, / Dan al wat kragt, geweld en sterkheid kan omvatten.' ('The pleasing drama of REYNARD'S comical life / Is opened here as he rides on the ASS. / Although the BEAR may growl and the WOLF may howl with rage and regret, / His wits make him their superior, despite their hate. / Intelligence does more than outward violence. / The RAM, too, seems to regard him with abhorrence, / But cousin FOX dares to rely upon his Ass, / No matter how hard the four-footed beast resists. / Learn from this that the intellect is valued much more highly / Than anything force, violence and strength can encompass.'). The following text has been added with a pen, possibly in the eighteenth century, on a print in the National Gallery of Art in Washington (inv. no. 1973.15.216, Dut. 1, fig. 224): 'RYNTJE DE VOS / door / A. van Everdinge.' ('REYNARD THE FOX by A. van Everdinge.'). The title prints with under margin were sold as part of the set, see sale Jan Yver Collection, Amsterdam, 30 October 1780 (Lugt 3181), p. 217, no. 1913.

14 Hollstein (Crispijn de Passe) 855. See Veldman 2001, pp. 61-72.

15 Hollstein (Crispijn de Passe) 852. See Veldman 2001, pp. 73-84.

16 For the popularity of series of prints of tales from Ovid's *Metamorphoses* and illustrated editions of Ovid see Sluijter 2000, pp. 23 and 170-181.

17 Gheeraerts's prints were made for the book *De Warachtighe fabulen der dieren* published in Bruges in 1567 (Smith 2018, pp. 4-8). See also Smith 2006 and Feliers 2006, pp. 380-382.

18 Indentation can be seen in thirty-five drawings: Davies 2007, cat. nos. 599, 601, 603, 604, 611-613, 615, 616, 618-621, 624-626, 628, 629, 632-638, 640-644, 647, 650, 652-654. See Erik Hinterding's essay in this catalogue for an explanation of the etching technique and the method of transferring the design.

19 The proofs with corrections are London, The British Museum, inv. nos. 1845,0724.51; 1845,0724.52; 1845,0724.55; 1845,0724.56; 1845,0724.59; 1845,0724.60; S.1993 and S. 1998. With thanks to Olenka Horbatsch and Domenico Pino for their help in analysing the proofs. There is also a proof (without corrections) on the verso of London, The British Museum, inv. no. 1846,0811.222; Davies 2007, cat. no. 645.

20 These are Dut. 10-12, 15, 16, 19, 20 and 54. The quality of the black was dictated primarily by the burrs created when the plate was roughened and the way it was inked (Griffiths 1996, p. 83).

21 A capon is a neutered cockerel.

22 Mansfield 1995, pp. 171-172. During the microscope examination (carried out in the Rijksmuseum's conservation studio on 18 December 2019) no evidence was found of the use of a rocker, a serrated metal tool that is rocked back and forth to roughen the plate.

23 Wuestman 1995, p. 67, Griffiths 1996, p. 85 and Briels 1997, p. 391. Arnold Houbraken described Vaillant as 'een groot yveraar in 't voortzetten en verbeteren van de Schraapkonst, of Swartekonst' ('a great toiler in pursuing and improving the art of scraping, or black art') (Houbraken 1718-1721, vol. 2, p. 103).

24 Wuestman 1995, pp. 66-71.

25 Mansfield 1995, pp. 171-172.

26 On drawings of animals from life see Schatborn 1977. On Savery's pictures of animals see Rikken 2016, esp. pp. 151-173.

27 Winters 2017.

28 The fence in the sketch (London, The British Museum inv. no. 1836,0811.238; Davies 2007, cat. no. 654) that demarcates the scene of the fight was omitted in the print.

29 Schlusemann and Wackers 2005, pp. 366-368 and 384-386.

30 See also the scenes of Reynard the Fox receiving the blessings of Grimbard the Badger and Bellin the Ram (Dut. 18 and 35).

31 This supposition is confirmed in the notes made by the French connoisseur Pierre-Jean Mariette (1694-1775), see Abecedario 1853-1854, p. 229: 'Ce sont, à ce qu'on m'a assuré, les héritiers d'Everdingen qui les ont, de meme que celles des fables, et ils les tiennent, dit-on, assez chères.' ('It is, so I have been assured, Van Everdingen's heirs who have them, likewise those of the fables, and they hold them, so it is said, very dear.').

32 This emerges from a remark by the printer of *Reineke Fuchs*, J.G.I. Breitkopf, in a letter dated 20 February 1782 to Johann Wolfgang Goethe: 'Melde, dass ich die Platten zum Reinicke Fuchs nicht habe, sondern der Kunsthändl[er] Schenk in Amsterdam. Glaube nicht, dass eine andere Edition vorher damit gedruckt worden ist, sondern Schenk hat sie in der Auction erstanden, und angewendet; sie sind vermuthlich vorher vom Künstler genutzt, von Schencken aber nöthig aufgestochen worden, als er sie gedruckt gehabt' ('I can inform you that I don't have the plates for Reinicke Fuchs; the art dealer Schenk in Amsterdam has them. I don't think another edition has been printed with them before, but Schenk bought them at the auction and used them; they were presumably used by the artist before that, but Schenk must have reworked them when he printed them') (Hofmann 1920, p. 188).

33 This was one in a series of children's books with high quality illustrations called 'The Home Treasury' (Summerfield 1980).

34 Summerly 1843, p. 4: 'Everdingen's original copper-plates of REYNARD THE FOX, have recently come into my possession.'

35 The diary is in the National Art Library in London (sign. MSL/1934/4121). The entry for 27 May 1843 reads: 'Called on [Thomas] Webster & gave him Everdingen to show [John] Callcott [Horsley]. [John] Linnells, who renew[e]d his wish to have the Everdingen plates.' On 9 July 1843 he wrote: 'In the Ev[enin]g preparing Everdingens plates for publication.' With thanks to Jonathan Hopson of the Victoria and Albert Museum for his assistance.

36 This was confirmed by Dan Cox and Fahema Begum of the Victoria and Albert Museum. Hollstein (Allart van Everdingen), p. 203, gives London as the location of the plates.

37 Feliers 2006, p. 373.

38 For later iconographic appropriation see Feliers 1994, Verzandvoort 1994a, p. 143, Verzandvoort 1994b and Feliers 2006, pp. 382-385.

39 In the original German: 'Die Küpfer sind da und ausserordentlich schön. Die Eberdingen sind erste Abdrücke und als wie von gestern.' Feliers 2006, p. 371.

Spotlight 3

ALLART VAN EVERDINGEN'S SCANDINAVIAN LANDSCAPES IN ART AND ART THEORY 1700-1850

Paul Knolle

Appreciation of Allart van Everdingen's Scandinavian landscapes can only be described as erratic, and the differences between the developments in the Netherlands and other countries were particularly marked. In his own time, his painted mountain landscapes with waterfalls and pine forests were very popular with Dutch collectors. They were received with such enthusiasm that Jacob van Ruisdael (1628/1629-1682) saw a pecuniary advantage in copying Van Everdingen's choice of subject, even though he had probably never been to Scandinavia.[1] Van Ruisdael was so successful in his endeavour that for long periods in art history Van Everdingen was lost in the long shadow he cast. While Dutch collectors' interest in Van Everdingen's northern paintings swiftly moved on, his drawings and etchings remained popular.[2] In the eighteenth century, outside the Netherlands, particularly in Germany and Norway, the popularity of his 'rugged' landscapes reached heights among artists and collectors that did not diminish until after 1850.[3] Underlying these developments lay all sorts of shifts in opinions about aesthetics and the role of art.

The Netherlands 1700-1850

Despite the diminished enthusiasm on the part of collectors, Dutch artists' biographies dating from the eighteenth and early nineteenth century, without exception, give a positive picture of Allart's Scandinavian paintings.[4] Virtually every author based his account on the brief biography that Arnold Houbraken wrote in 1719 and elaborated on it.[5]

A different sort of writing—the treatise on the national taste of the Dutch School in drawing and painting (1787) by Roeland van Eynden (1747-1819)—is particularly interesting.[6] This artist and author's entry won a competition set by Teylers Tweede Genootschap in Haarlem. The publication appeared at a time when many of his compatriots suggested that art in the Netherlands was in decline. The solution put forward largely entailed encouraging contemporary artists to revive the tradition of seventeenth-century art. If they were to engage with the style and iconography of the earlier age, they would do justice to the nation's taste and improve the quality of art. Collectors rallied around this patriotic reorientation and started buying art by local artists with considerable commitment. With their 'un-Dutch' Scandinavian subjects, Allart van Everdingen's landscapes did not conform to the typical model of the Dutch School and he became as it were a foreigner in his own country.[7] With a view to keeping this unarguably eminent artist on board by a roundabout route, Van Eynden noted that some Dutch painters simply wanted to picture nature 'as it appears in the high Alpine, Swiss or Nordic countries.'[8] Allart van Everdingen 'presents beautiful regions and extensive landscapes of more accuracy and naturalness than Claude Lorrain or Salvator Rosa.'[9] Given his dominant subject matter—mountain landscapes—Van Everdingen did not, admittedly, have a place at the heart of the Dutch School, but his precision and verisimilitude meant that he could be included. At the same time, Van Eynden's comparison of Van Everdingen to Salvator Rosa was in line with international views in those days, as will soon become clear.

At the end of his life, as the co-author of a series of artist's biographies, Van Eynden acknowledged that at least one contemporary Dutch artist, Gerard van Nijmegen (1735-1808), had been inspired by Van Everdingen's Scandi-

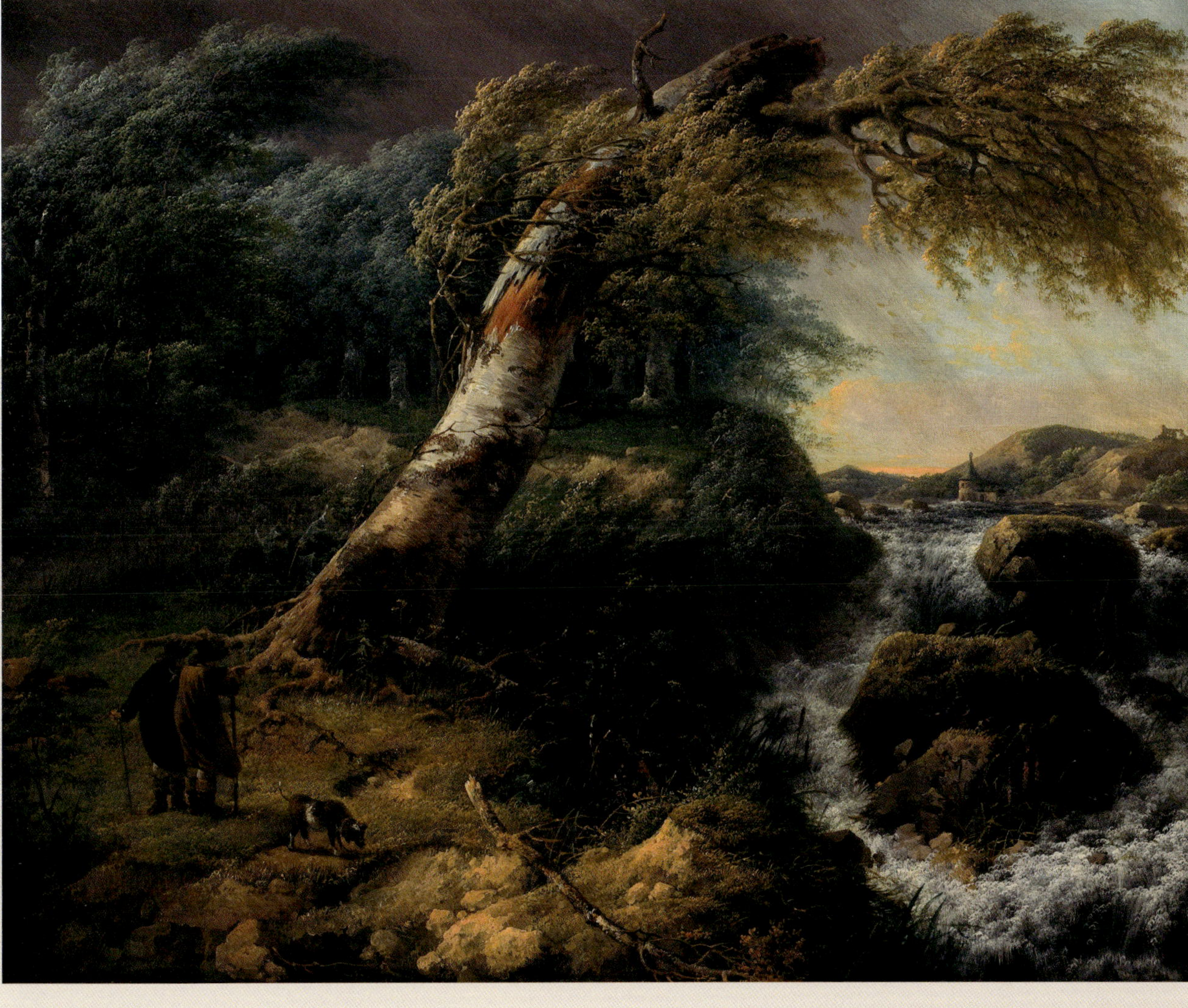

249
Gerard van Nijmegen, *Landscape in a Storm*, 1804, oil on panel, 75 x 92 cm, Enschede, Rijksmuseum Twenthe, inv. no. 4430

navian scenes (fig. 249).[10] Nevertheless the question remains as to whether Dutch painters of wild and grandiose landscapes in the 1780 to 1860 period can really be placed in this Scandinavian, Romantic context. They were actually more inclined to take their inspiration from landscapes along the Rhine and in Italy.[11]

In 1842, when Romantic landscape painting had made an international breakthrough, biographer Johannes Immerzeel praised Van Everdingen, who, he asserted, displayed a rich and poetic imagination in expressing severe storms at sea, waterfalls and thunderstorms.[12] It is striking that Van Everdingen was praised for his poetic imagination in his scenes of untamed nature—this was a quality which, according to foreign critics, most seventeenth-century Dutch artists had lacked.[13]

Van Everdingen and International Romanticism

This poetic imagination fitted well into the contemporary international recognition of Allart's work in Germany, Norway and elsewhere. Since 1760, because of his Scandinavian paintings, Van Everdingen was embraced by foreign artists and art lovers, to whom the sublime—a concept concerned with the aesthetic experience of terrifying situations or locations, such as high mountains—was paramount.[14]

During the second half of the eighteenth century, Van Everdingen and Jacob van Ruisdael took Europe by storm with their 'wild' landscapes. Their paintings and prints were copied and imitated by countless artists. They appeared in important publications on art by eminent authors, who used a vocabulary when describing these works that reflected the emotional attitude to nature at that time. In France, Charles-Jacques-François Lecarpentier (1744-1822), painter and teacher at the École de Dessin et de Peinture in Rouen, praised Allart's work in his *Essai sur le paysage* (1817).[15] In Denmark, at the end of his life, Jens Juel (1745-1802)—who seldom painted inhospitable places—copied a mountain landscape with a river by Allart van Everdingen (fig. 47) that had been acquired for the Royal Gallery in Copenhagen in 1763.[16] In Switzerland, Salomon Gessner (1730-1788) revealed his great admiration for Van Everdingen in his art and in his letter *Brief ueber die Landschaftsmalerei an Herrn Fuesslin* (1772).[17] In his 1775 *Allgemeine Theorie der Schönen Künste*, the Swiss theologian and philosopher Johann Georg Sulzer (1720-1779) mentioned Allart in the same breath as Salvator Rosa, a comparison that would become a cliché: 'There are, as a great connoisseur [Christian Ludwig von Hagedorn (1712-1780), eminent in the German art world] remarked, landscapes by the younger Poussin, by Salvator Rosa, by Van Everdingen, which have something so spectacular about them that they evoke admiration and trepidation that approach the effect of the sublime.'[18] The important Swiss painter of mountain landscapes Alexandre Calame (1810-1864) took inspiration from Van Everdingen and Van Ruisdael and in its turn his work became popular in the Netherlands.[19]

Interestingly, Calame and other painters were also encouraged in a roundabout way by Van Everdingen to paint Alpine landscapes. Inspired by Van Everdingen's and Van Ruisdael's Scandinavian scenes, the Amsterdam painter Jan Hackaert (1628-after 1685) and his friend Conrad Meyer (1618-1689) of Zurich travelled to the canton of Glarus in 1655. With the landscapes inspired by their trip, they set the tone for later painters.[20] Numerous Swiss artists, from Caspar Wolf (1735-1798) to Alexandre Calame, proved receptive to the work of Dutch masters like Hackaert and Van Everdingen.[21]

Germany

Van Everdingen's influence was particularly strong in Germany and Norway. In Germany and Austria, his work was repeatedly copied in the second half of the eighteenth century by printmakers like Johann Georg Wille (1715-1808) and Johann Georg von Dillis (1759-1841), and there are extant painted copies by artists such as Ferdinand Georg Waldmüller (1793-1865) and Andreas Achenbach (1815-1910), who also borrowed motifs from Van Everdingen in their own original work.[22]

He does not, however, appear to have had any profound influence on the figurehead of German Romanticism, Caspar David Friedrich (1774-1840), whose landscapes imbued with religious sentiment are very different from Van Everdingen's more prosaic observations. Some variants of Friedrich's intriguing *Rückenfigur* (fig. 250) are, though, strongly reminiscent of an etching by Allart (fig. 251).[23] Friedrich spent a long time working in Dresden, where an artists' colony grew up. Aside from Friedrich, its members included Johan Christian Dahl (1788-1857) and Carl Gustav Carus (1789-1869), author of *Neun Briefe über Landschaftsmalerei*.[24] Dresden, where several characteristic works by Van Everdingen were to be seen, became the centre of Romantic landscape painting in Germany.[25] Allart van Everdingen's name must often have been mentioned: Friedrich and Dahl lived in the same house for a considerable period and Dahl, inspired by Van Everdingen, became the founder of Norwegian painting.[26]

Allart's northern landscapes were also appreciated by prominent representatives of the German art world. One of the foremost lovers of Allart's work was Johann Wolfgang Goethe (1749-1832). He collected the artist's prints, admired the illustrations of Reynard the Fox and in 1781 copied at least one of Allart's etchings (figs. 252 and 253). Goethe even made a drawing himself that looks very much like a homage to Van Everdingen by way of a monument he designed himself.[27] There is an oft-quoted passage in *Italienische Reise* (*Italian Journey*) in which he describes how, on 11 September 1786, travelling from the Brenner Pass, he saw a landscape that reminded him of Van Everdingen's work.[28] Goethe no doubt communicated his enthusiasm to artists in his circle.

Christian Ludwig von Hagedorn, 'Generaldirektor der Sächsischen Kunstsammlungen und der Kunstakademie' in Dresden from 1764, was another important art expert. Two years earlier he had devoted various passages to Van Everdingen in his *Betrachtungen über die Mahlerey*. Although he was an adherent of Neoclassicism, and thus of the idealized landscape, he wrote that the novelty of depictions of wild, rugged scenery could conjure up emotions and they could contain fine elements that one did not find in more charming surroundings. In this context he mentioned Allart van Everdingen.[29] He directly linked his work to the experience of the sublime, going so far as to write that on these grounds landscape painting should come immediately after history painting in the hierarchy of genres in art.[30] Thus Von Hagedorn, in part because of Van Everdingen's paintings, championed the emancipation of the landscape long before it became generally accepted around 1800.

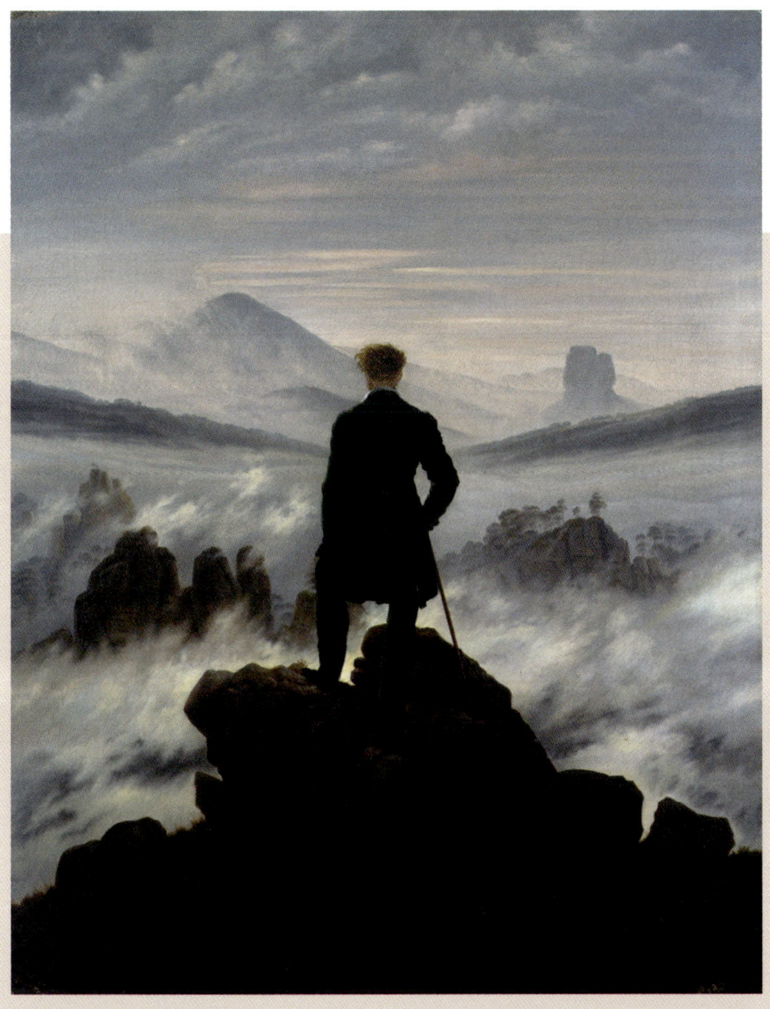

250
Caspar David Friedrich,
*The Wanderer above
the Sea of Fog*, c. 1817,
oil on canvas, 98.4 x
74.8 cm, Hamburger
Kunsthalle, inv. no.
HK-5161

251
Allart van Everdingen,
Landscape with Artists,
etching, 85 x 148 mm,
Amsterdam, Rijksmu-
seum, inv. no.
RP-P-OB-50.378 (Holl.
63 III) (cat. no. 19)

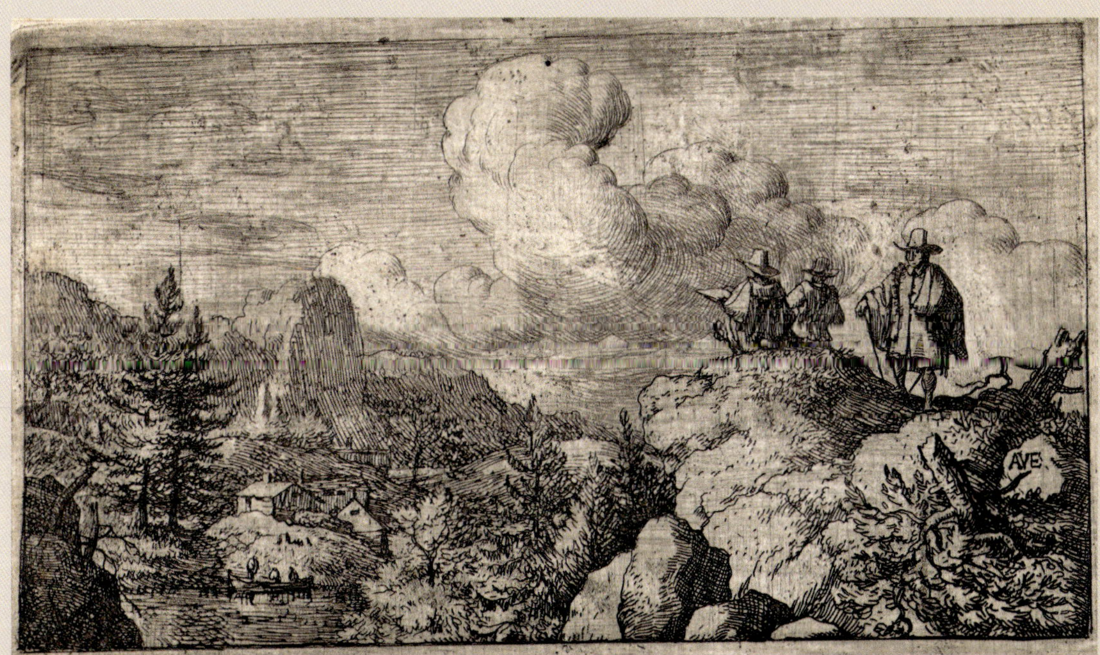

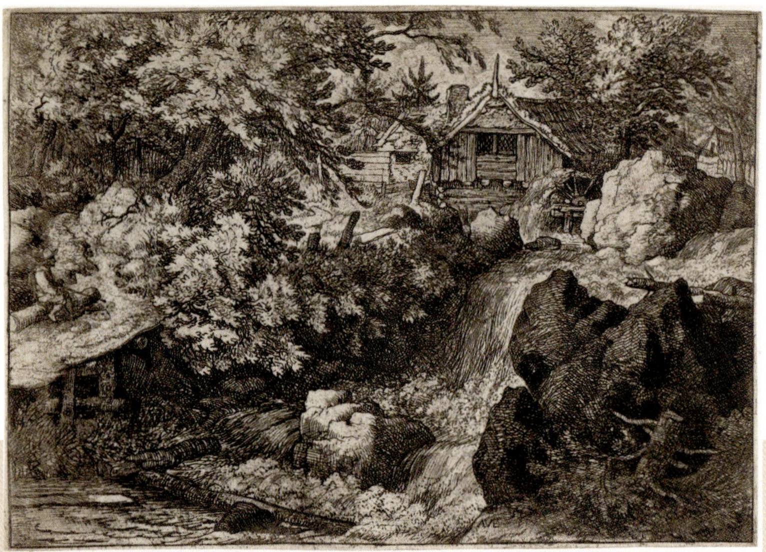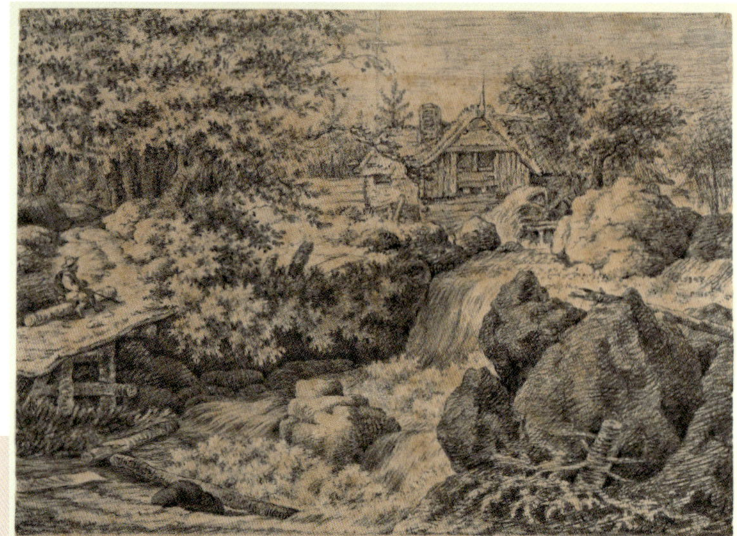

In 1793, the rather conservative lawyer, journalist, diplomat and art critic Friedrich Wilhelm Basilius von Ramdohr (1752 or 1757-1822) placed Van Everdingen in a different category of landscape painters from other Dutchmen, who had concentrated on heavily populated flat landscapes.[31] Von Ramdohr hailed Van Everdingen as the representative of an international genre, not of the Dutch School. He saw him, moreover, possibly echoing Von Hagedorn, as the first artist to make a type of rough northern landscape.

In a letter to Goethe written in December 1805, the German painter Johann Heinrich Menken (1766-1839) even came up with a fashionable comparison to Ossian, the—as it later proved—fictitious author of a Celtic epic. He described Van Ruisdael and Van Everdingen as 'full of the spirit of Ossian'.[32] Ossian's epic poem was associated with wildness, original genius, the sublime.

In short, Van Everdingen's presence in iconic German art criticism from 1760 until well into the nineteenth century is evident.

Norway

At the beginning of the nineteenth century, Norwegian painting acquired an image of its own. More than two centuries after his death, Allart van Everdingen played an important role in this process of emancipation. It was Johan Christian Dahl who, following in Allart's footsteps, began to paint Romantic Norwegian landscapes and was to become one of the greatest European landscape painters of his day. Through him, and pupils like Thomas Fearnley (1802-1842), Norwegian art flourished.[33] As a young landscape painter, Dahl embarked on his training at the Copenhagen art academy in 1811. In this period, he was deeply affected by Van Everdingen's works, some of which could be found in the city in the royal collections and in the collection of Count Adam Gottlob Moltke.[34] According to him, Allart van Everdingen and Jacob van Ruisdael had best expressed the northern sense of nature that he also wanted to convey. Van Everdingen was a particularly attractive example for him because he had studied the Norwegian scenery with a pioneer's eyes as long ago as the seventeenth century. Dahl was to retain his profound respect for these two artists until the end of his life (fig. 254).[35] In 1812 in a letter to one of his patrons in Bergen, Lyder Sagen, he wrote that the landscape painters Van Ruisdael and Van Everdingen were his most important examples, but above all he took pains to study nature.[36] In this he was following, in his turn, the Dutch 'realistic' tradition.[37]

However much Dahl developed his own approach to Norwegian landscapes, his original inspirations, Van Everdingen and Van Ruisdael, remained apparent in his paintings, for instance in the arrangement of rocks and trees (figs. 255 and 256). In 1818, Dahl went to Dresden, where he stayed for two years. There he was influenced by Caspar David Friedrich, although their work

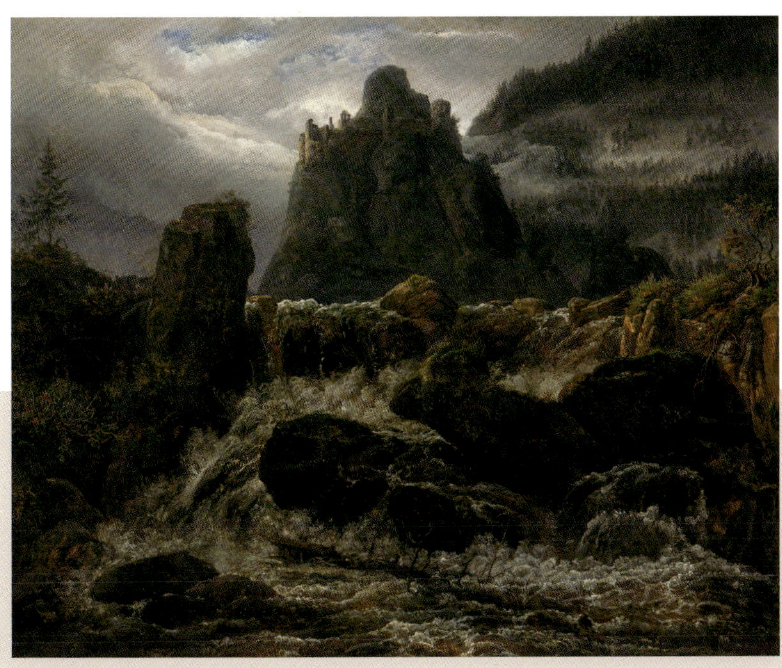

remained very different: like Allart's, Dahl's more or less objective depictions of nature (also called 'Romantic Realism') were quite unlike the often mysterious, moody, subjective landscapes in which Friedrich tried to capture the divine in nature.[38] After a stay in Italy, in 1821 Dahl returned to Dresden, where he was to remain for the rest of his life and, from 1823 onwards, shared a house with Friedrich.[39] Dahl did, though, visit Norway and Denmark regularly and his work was often shown in Copenhagen. In 1824 he became professor of landscape painting at the academy in Dresden. It was there, too, that he met the aforementioned Carl Gustav Carus, physician and painter. With his scenes of bleak, rugged landscape, Dahl tried to say something about the nature and character of Norway, about the life and work of its people and Norway's greatness in the past.

254
Johan Christian Dahl, *Imaginary Land-scape with a Waterfall and a Ruined Castle*, 1819, 53.5 x 65.5 cm, oil on canvas, Bergen, KODE Kunstmuseer og komponisthjem, inv. no. 153

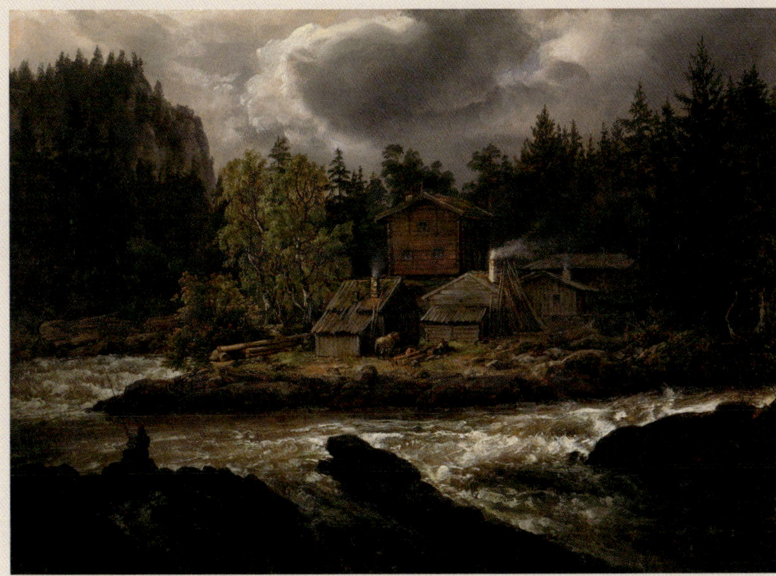

255
Johan Christian Dahl, *View of Hønefossen*, 1847, oil on canvas, 51 x 67.5 cm, Oslo, Nasjonalmuseet, inv. no. NG.M.00980

> 256
Allart van Everdingen, *Norwegian Land-scape with a Waterfall and Watermill*, 1650, oil on canvas, 112.8 x 88.2 cm, Munich, Bayerische Staatsgemälde-sammlungen, Alte Pinakothek, inv. no. 387 (cat. no. 90)

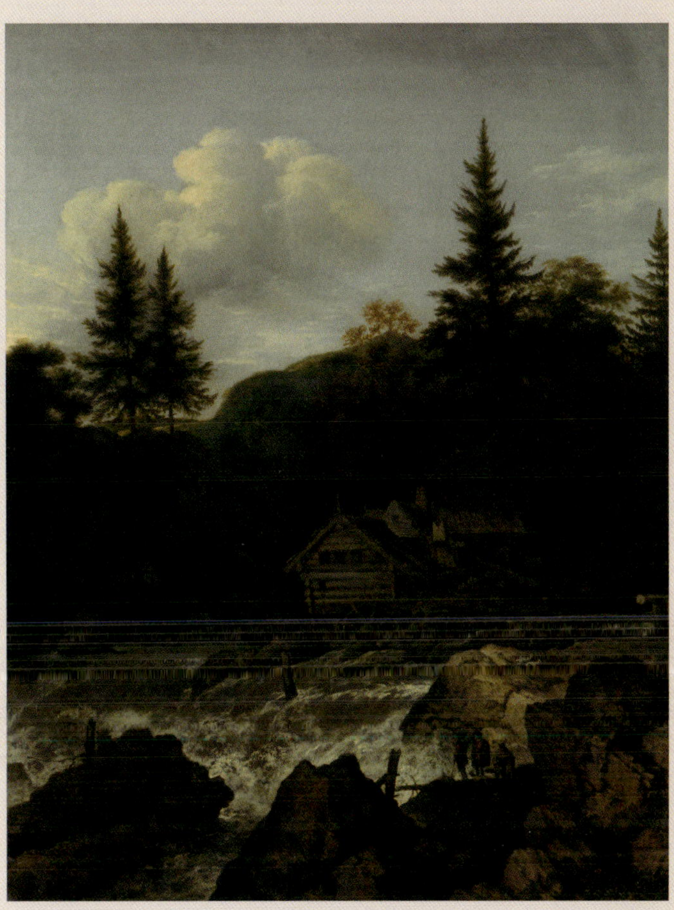

His nationalist sentiments are also evident in his involvement in the preservation of Norwegian monuments and the establishment of a national museum of art.[40]

It is rather ironic that it was a foreign artist like Van Everdingen who helped create Norway's 'national' school of painting. Van Everdingen's role in Norwegian art history was nevertheless acknowledged in Norway in later years. In 1878, for instance, the Norwegian art historian Lorentz Dietrichson described Dahl as 'the innovator of the realistic landscape in the spirit of Van Ruisdael and Van Everdingen'.[41]

In 1894, the eminent Norwegian art historian and critic Andreas Aubert wrote in his book on Dahl and Norwegian painting: 'If we judge the greatness of a landscape painter on the depth of his feeling for nature, of the degree of intimacy with which he lives with nature, Van Everdingen is one of the greatest who have ever lived. In his landscape art and that of Van Ruisdael, the Nordic spirit found its most profound expression very early on. These two landscape painters are more significant in the history of our northern spiritual life than the great Claude Lorrain; they taught us to feel rich in our own Nordic scenery, whereas Claude just fuels a longing for the south.'[42]

Conclusion

By the middle of the nineteenth century, it had become customary to heap Allart van Everdingen with praise for his painted Scandinavian oeuvre at an international level. He had shown himself to be a forerunner of artists who pictured the sublime. He was seen as an example, particularly in Germany and Norway. In Germany, Von Hagedorn praised him as an important player in the struggle for the emancipation of the landscape. In Norway he was even the inspiration for the creation of its national Romantic landscape painting. When artists like Dahl and Fearnley needed a suitable example in their endeavour to achieve an authentic Norwegian art, there was the pioneer Allart van Everdingen, who two centuries before had put Scandinavia on the international map with his outstanding work. And not just that: he was a role model who could in some areas be surpassed; a star who asked for emulation, but whose own work was as solid as a rock.

---

1 Davies 2001, pp. 37-39 and 163-179.
2 For the recognition and collecting of Allart's drawings in the Netherlands see Davies 2007, pp. 19-35, 128-144 and Yvonne Bleyerveld's essay in this catalogue.
3 Davies 2001, p. 197.
4 For Van Everdingen in art literature see Davies 2001, pp. 75-139.
5 Houbraken 1718-1721, vol. 2, pp. 95-96 (discussed at length in the first essay by Christi Klinkert in this catalogue). Jacob Campo Weyerman, for instance, added a lyrical description of his work to the basic information in Houbraken's biography (Weyerman 1729, vol. 2, pp. 178-179).
6 Van Eynden 1787.
7 For these developments see among others Koolhaas-Grosfeld 1982, Knolle 1984a and 1984b, Koolhaas-Grosfeld 1986 and Knolle 1992.
8 Van Eynden 1787, p. 122: 'zo als die zig in de hooge Alpische, Switzersche, of Noordsche landen vertoont.'
9 Idem, p. 124: 'stelt schoone gewesten en uitgestrekte landschappen voor, van meer nauwkeurigheid en natuurlykheid dan Claude Lorrain of Salvator Rosa.'
10 According to Van Eynden and Van der Willigen 1816-1840, vol. 2, p. 248, Gerard van Nijmegen had usually followed the style of Van Ruisdael, Van Everdingen and Pijnacker in his 'Berg- en Boschachtige Landschappen met Watervallen' ('mountainous and wooded landscapes with waterfalls') and was 'gansch niet ongelukkig' ('by no means unfortunate') in so doing. The authors moreover mention several Dutch collections or recent sales of them that included works by Van Everdingen, although the references are not specific enough to establish whether Scandinavian views were among them: Jan van Dijk's drawing collection (sold at auction in 1791), Jan Gildemeester Jansz's collection of drawings sold in 1800 and the collection of the Teylers Genootschap (Van Eynden and Van der Willigen 1816-1840, vol. 3, pp. 409, 431 and 484-485 respectively).
11 See among others Haarlem 2009. As far as Van Everdingen himself is concerned, Blanc 2016 demonstrates that he probably had no access to writings about the sublime, but would have known examples of paintings in which the sublime as an emotion (both terrifying and fascinating at the same time) could be identified. There was no eighteenth- or nineteenth-century Dutch Van Everdingen, as the representative selection of landscape painters in Amsterdam 1997 shows. On Romantic painting in the Netherlands see Groningen 2017 (esp. Reynaerts 2017 in that publication) and the literature referred to in it.
12 Immerzeel 1842-1843, vol. 2, p. 225, where Immerzeel went on to write that nobody had surpassed Van Everdingen 'in het natuurlijk schilderen van zich met de lucht vermengende dampen en rondspattend waterschuim. Zijn geest scheen bij voorkeur zich bezig te houden met het nabootsen der woeste en romantische natuur .... Men noemt hem dan ook om die reden wel eens de Noordsche Salvator Rosa.' ('in the natural painting of mists mingling with the sky and flying spray. His mind seemed to prefer to occupy itself with imitating wild and

romantic nature …. For that reason, people sometimes call him the Nordic Salvator Rosa.').
13 For international views of Dutch art see e.g. Grijzenhout 1992.
14 On the sublime see Denk 2019. Much has been written on mountains as a source of aesthetic pleasure. One of the earliest and best-known publications is Nicolson 1959. See also Herring 2011.
15 According to Lecarpentier, Allart set himself apart from most of his compatriots who practised fine art: 'sa manière, au contraire, est large et forte; il se plaisait à peindre des rochers, des chutes d'eau qui tombent avec un grand fracas et excitent une vapeur humide. Ses sites sont ordinairement sauvages; peu de peintres ont aussi bien rendu les arbres d'hiver qu'*Everdingen*: les sapins, les cyprès produisent un effet on ne peut plus pittoresque dans les tableaux de ce maître, qui sont en général d'un ton doré et transparant; ses eaux sont d'une vérité, d'une fraîcheur qui ne se rencontrent dans les tableaux d'aucun autre peintre de la Hollande.' ('his manner, on the contrary, is broad and strong; he liked to paint rocks, waterfalls that tumble with a great noise and create a damp mist. His settings are usually wild; few painters have rendered winter trees as well as Everdingen: pine trees, cypresses produce an effect that could not be more picturesque than in this artist's pictures, which are generally golden and transparent; his waters are of a truth, of a freshness that is not found in the paintings of any other painter from Holland.' (Lecarpentier 1817, p. 183).
16 Jens Juel's painting is now in private hands, see Poulsen 1991, cat. no. 826. See also Davies 2001, p. 193 and Monrad 2001, pp. 20 and 25.
17 The letter is included in Gessner 1778, pp. 165-194.
18 Sulzer 1775, p. 116: 'Es giebt … Landschaften vom jüngern Poußin, von Salvator Rosa, von Everdingen, die etwas so großes haben, dass sie Bewunderung und einen Schauder erwecken, die der Wirkung des Erhabenen ganz nahe kommen.'
19 Calame's work occurs at the time of the reversal in taste from mountains, from the ugly and terrifying to the source of aesthetic enjoyment that was associated with the appreciation of the sublime. For Calame and his admiration of, in any event, Van Ruisdael see Reynaerts 2017, p. 47; see also Groningen 2017, pp. 78-79.
20 For the connection between Norwegian and Swiss Romantic landscape painting see e.g. London 2011.
21 This was illustrated in the exhibition *Dutch Mountains: From the Dutch Lowlands to the Alps* (Kunstmuseum Winterthur | Reinhart am Stadtgarten 2018-2019).
22 See e.g. Davies 2001, pp. 11-12 and esp. pp. 183-193. For Van Everdingen's role in the genesis of the school of landscape painters in Munich see Heilmann 2013, p. 262.

23 Koerner 2009, pp. 192-197. For figures seen from behind by Friedrich and Dahl see also Birmingham 2006.
24 Carus 1831. See further on this publication Batschman 2002; Deligne 2003 (esp. pp. 176-181 on Van Everdingen); Ševčik 2012. Remarkably, Carus did not include a letter about a waterfall by Van Everdingen until the second edition, published in 1835.
25 In a letter dated 1818, Dahl revealed himself as mildly sceptical about the quality of the works by Van Everdingen that were in Dresden: they were good, but not of the standard of the Van Everdingens in Copenhagen (Bang 1987, vol. 1, p. 237). On Romanticism see Groningen 2017.
26 For the trends in German Romantic landscape painting and the theories about it developed at the time see Bätschmann 2002, pp. 1-73.
27 The current whereabouts of this drawing are unknown. It is reproduced in *De Tweede Ronde* 9 (1988), no. 2, p. 113, which can be accessed at www.dbnl.nl.
28 Goethe 1968, vol. 1, p. 18: 'und so kam ich sehr geschwind, zwischen hohen Felsen, an dem reißenden Eisack herunter. Der Mond ging auf und beleuchtete ungeheuere Gegenstände. Einige Mühlen zwischen uralten Fichten über dem schäumenden Strom waren völlige Everdingen.' ('Very soon we came to the Adige, rushing along between high cliffs. The moon rose and lit up the gigantic masses of the mountains. Some watermills, standing above the foaming river among age-old pines, looked exactly like a painting by Everdingen.'). See also Davies 2001, p. 11 (from where the English translation is taken) and Bonn/Frankfurt/Düsseldorf/Kiel 1986, p. 67. For Goethe and art see Carasso 1992, Frankfurt 1994 (in which among others Maisak 1994, p. 110 on Goethe's copy of Allart's etching), Amsterdam 1999 and Davies 2001, pp. 11-12.
29 Von Hagedorn 1762, vol. 1, pp. 150-151. This passage is also quoted in Honour 1979, albeit in the 1775 French translation. On Van Everdingen see Honour 1979, pp. 59-60 and 332.
30 Von Hagedorn 1762, vol. 1, p. 335.
31 Von Ramdohr 1793, vol. 2, pp. 124-125.
32 Femmel 1980, p. 272, #110: 'Wie gegen Homer Ossian, so verhält sich neben Claude Lorrain – Ruisdael und Everdingen; Claude erreicht den ersteren nicht; Ruisdael und Everdingen sind ossianischen Geistes voll.' ('As Homer is to Ossian, so Ruisdael and Everdingen are to Claude Lorrain; Claude did not equal the first; Ruisdael and Everdingen are full of the spirit of Ossian.').
33 On Dahl and Norwegian landscape painting see among others Bang 1987; Heilmann 1988; Davies 2001, pp. 193-197; Schleswig 2002; Bergen 2018. More specifically on Van Everdingen in Norway: Granberg 1902 and Hauge 1999. On Dahl and Dutch seventeenth-century landscape painters in general see Monrad 2001, pp. 20-35. For Fearnley see Birmingham 2012

and Maastricht/London 2019. Van Everdingen's example is less evident in the work of the third famous nineteenth-century Norwegian landscape painter, Peder Balke (1804-1887), who was also one of Dahl's pupils in Dresden. For Balke see among others Tromsøy/London 2014.
34 For two paintings by Van Everdingen in the royal collection see Lampe 1988, p. 32.
35 Dahl is said to have had two works by Van Everdingen in his studio (Aubert 1947, p. 37). As far as we know, Dahl never copied any of Van Everdingen's works.
36 For the well-known quotation from the letter to Lyder Sagen of 13 June 1812 see Bang 1987, vol. 1, pp. 27 and 232. In a letter he wrote to Georg Kaspar Nagler (1801-1866) in 1835, Dahl returns to his relationship with Van Everdingen's work (Bang 1987, vol. 1, p. 249).
37 In 1812 or 1813 he made copies of two paintings of waterfalls by Van Ruisdael in Count Moltke's collection. Dahl always valued these works highly. They were the most expensive paintings he sold to the Nationalgalerie in 1840. Before he sent them to Oslo, he made copies of them for himself (Aubert 1947, p. 38).
38 For the concept of 'Romantic Realism' see Davies 2001, p. 195.
39 For the personal and artistic relationship between Dahl and Friedrich see Bang 1987, vol. 1, pp. 73-83; Heilmann 1988; Oslo/Dresden 2014.
40 For Dahl's cultural activities aside from painting see Ormhaug 2002. Dahl also studied examples by Van Everdingen when he painted his seascapes (Davies 2001, p. 195).
41 See Aubert 1947, p. 14. This is the German edition of Aubert's book, which was published in Norwegian in 1894.
42 Idem, pp. 36-37: 'Sollen wir die Größe eines Landschaftsmalers nach der Tiefe seines Naturgefühls, nach der Innigkeit seines Zusammenlebens mit der Natur messen, dann gehört Everdingen zu den Größten die gelebt haben. In seiner und in Ruisdaels Landschaftskunst hat der nordische Geist am frühesten seinen tiefsten Ausdruck gefunden. Diese beiden Landschaftsmaler haben eine größere Bedeutung für die Geschichte unseres nordischen Geisteslebens als der große Claude Lorrain; sie haben uns gelehrt, uns reich in unserer eigenen nordischen Natur zu fühlen, während Claude nur die Sehnsucht nach dem Süden nährt.' Aubert made more romanticizing pronouncements about Dahl's work in connection with Van Everdingen's. See e.g. Aubert 1947, p. 125. See also Davies 2001, p. 163. Dahl was often called the northern (or new) Van Everdingen (Aubert 1947, pp. 36-37 and Bang 1987, vol. 1, pp. 44, 263 and 264). Aubert evidently liked to romanticize: he recognized in Van Everdingen and Van Ruisdael Rousseau's and Goethe's sensitivity to nature (Aubert 1947, p. 69).

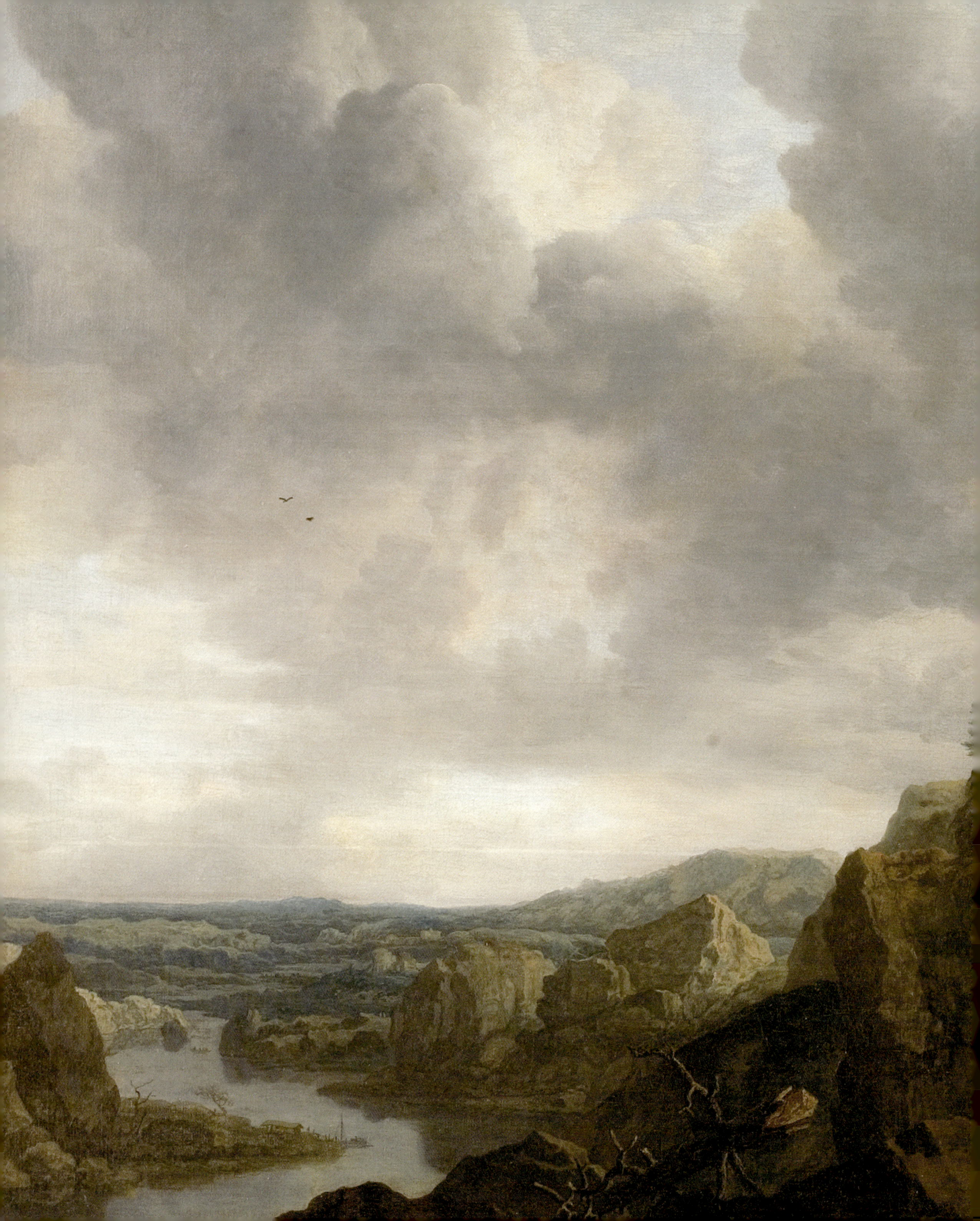

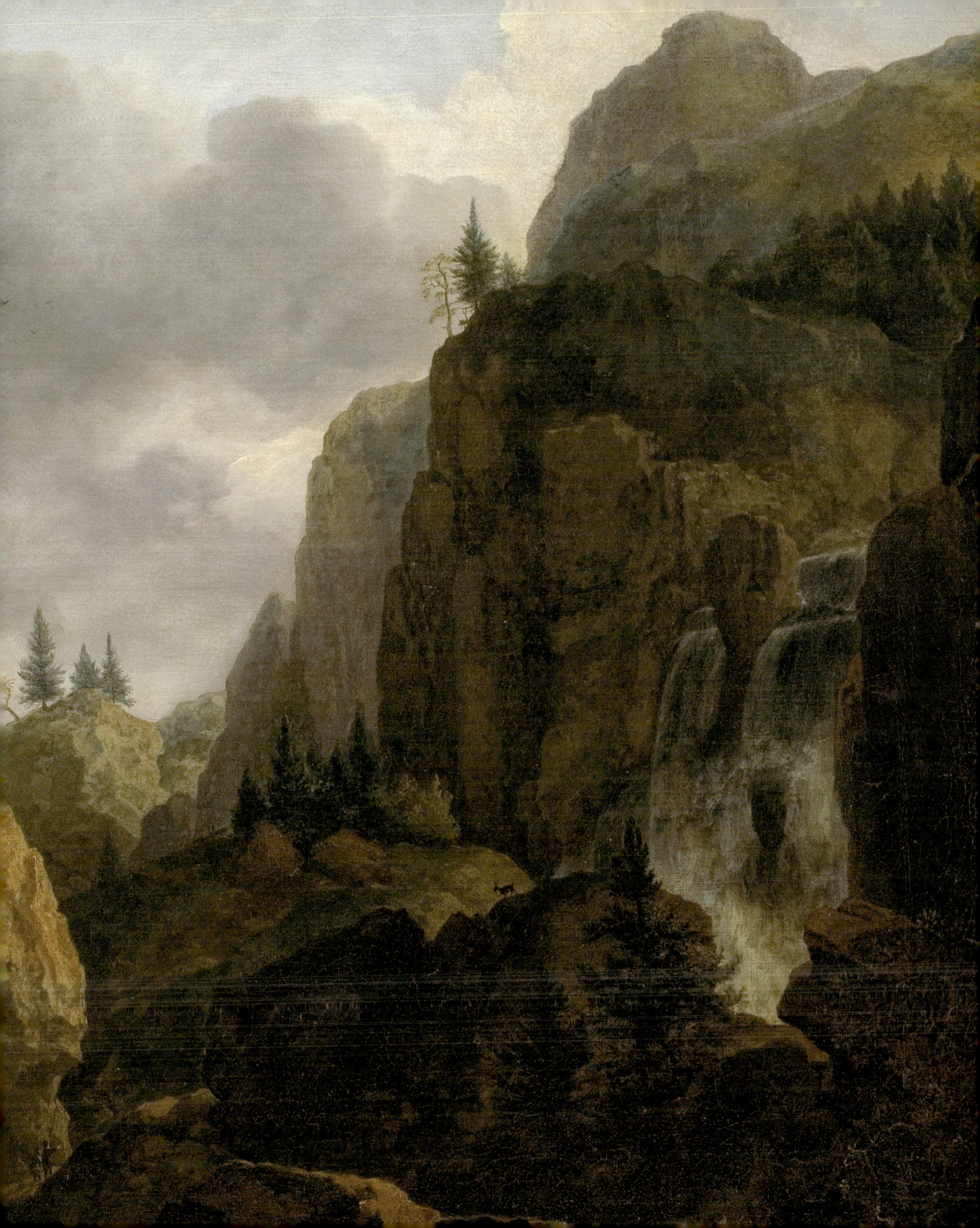

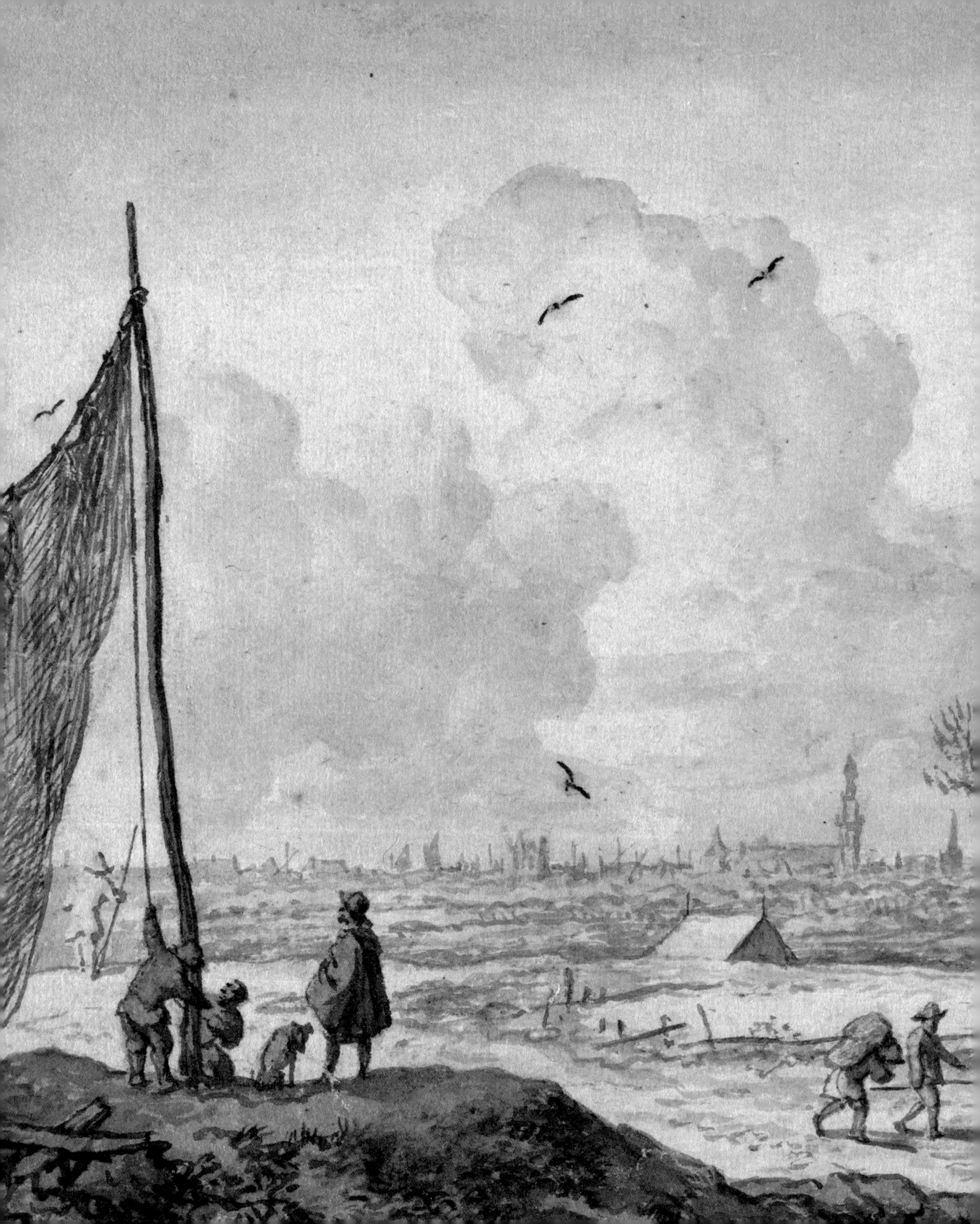

List of Exhibited Works

This is a list of the works of art by Allart van Everdingen that feature in *Allart van Everdingen (1621-1675): The Rugged Landscape / Reynard the Fox*, an exhibition in Stedelijk Museum Alkmaar from 18 September 2021 to 16 January 2022. It presents a cross-section of the whole oeuvre, that is to say paintings and works on paper, Scandinavian and Dutch scenes, landscapes and illustrations of the tale of Reynard the Fox.

The works are arranged by whereabouts and owner. Note: the names of whereabouts and owners follow the alphabetical order of the spelling in the original Dutch catalogue. Please bear this in mind when you look up artworks from Amsterdam City Archives (Stadsarchief Amsterdam), Budapest (Boedapest), Cologne (Keulen), Copenhagen (Kopenhagen) and The Hague (Den Haag). At the time this catalogue was compiled, some paintings were on long-term loans to museums, not with their owners. This is stated in the description of the work in question, after the inventory number.

Where a number of works are listed under a single location, they are arranged by medium (in the order: paintings, brunailles, drawings, prints) and within that by catalogue number. These catalogue numbers are derived from various sources: Davies 2001 for the paintings, Davies 2007 for the brunailles and drawings, Hollstein (Allart van Everdingen) (Holl.) for the landscape prints, Dutuit 1881 (Dut.) for the Reynard the Fox prints. The bibliographic details of these reference works are given in the bibliography at the back of this book.

The entries begin with the following information: title, technique, dimensions, any inscriptions (such as a signature or date), inventory number where available, and credit line, if any. This is followed by a reference to the relevant literature, which begins with the catalogue number in the reference works by Davies, Hollstein or Dutuit referred to above. That is followed by only the most recent relevant literature, because all the earlier works can be found in Davies 2001 and 2007. For the same reason, the provenances of the paintings and drawings are not given here: they are described in detail in Davies 2001 and 2007. Each entry ends with the pages on which the object concerned is discussed or depicted in this book.

Compilers
Yvonne Bleyerveld (drawings)
Ellis Dullaart (brunailles)
Erik Hinterding (prints)
Christi M. Klinkert (paintings)
Marjan Pantjes (drawings and prints of Reynard the Fox)

Alkmaar
Stedelijk Museum Alkmaar

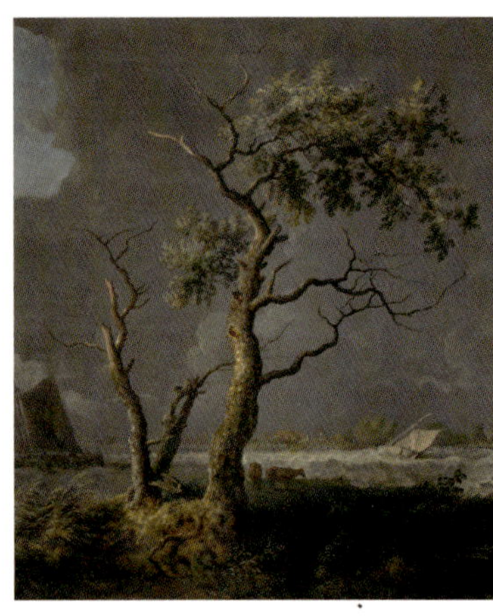

1

Trees by the Water
Oil on canvas; 76.6 x 66.5 cm
Lower left, beside the tree root: A Everdingen
Inv. no. 20918

Davies 2001, cat. no. 17; Giltaij in Tokyo/
Osaka 2018, cat. no. 17

pp. 50-51, 53, 60 and 82

Amsterdam
Amsterdam Museum

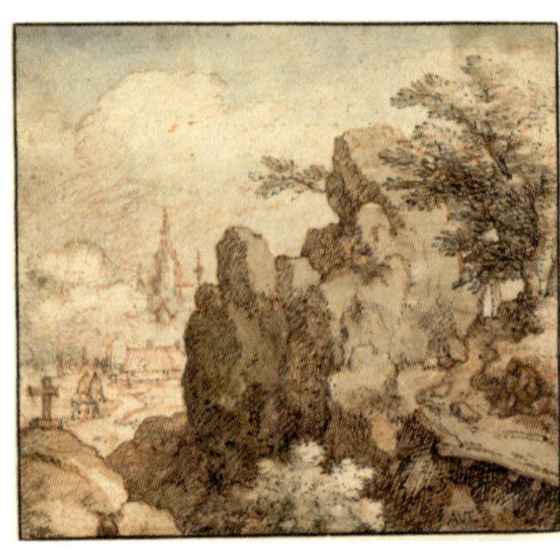

2

Landscape with a Large Rock
Pen and black ink over red chalk, watercolour;
framing lines in pen and black ink; verso
rubbed with red chalk for transfer; outlines
indented for transfer; 100 x 110 mm
Lower right, in pen and black ink: AVE
Inv. no. TA 18001

Davies 2007, cat. no. 575

pp. 130 and 132

Amsterdam
Rijksmuseum

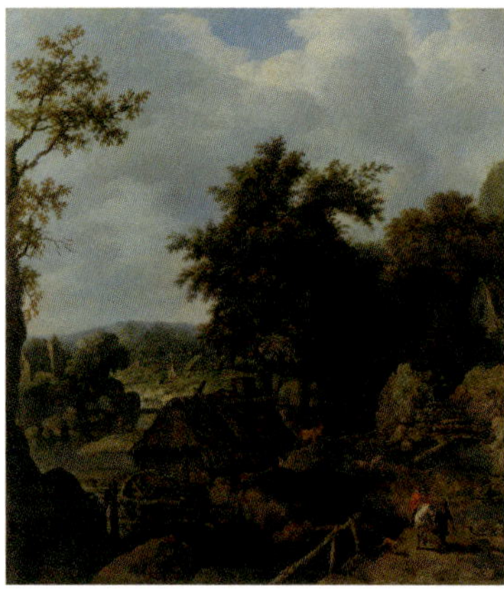

3

Landscape with a Watermill
Oil on canvas; 66 x 60 cm
Lower left: AvEVERDINGEN / 1655
Inv. no. SK-A-691 (Jhr J.S.H. van de Poll
Bequest, Amsterdam), on loan to the
Stedelijk Museum Alkmaar

Davies 2001, cat. no. 42

pp. 60-61 and 125

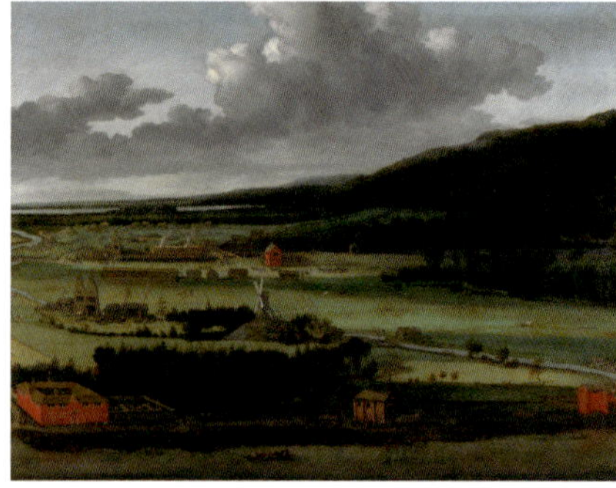

4

*Hendrick Trip's Cannon Foundry
at Julita Bruk*
Oil on canvas; 192 x 254.5 cm
Inv. no. SK-A-1510

Davies 2001, cat. no. 120; Büttner 2004,
pp. 1066-1067; Van der Ham 2005;
Zandvliet 2006, p. 21; Van Run 2019,
p. 16

pp. 27, 29, 66-67 and 69

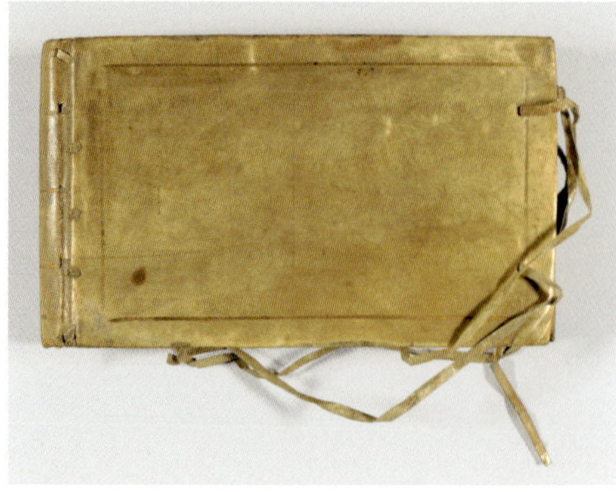

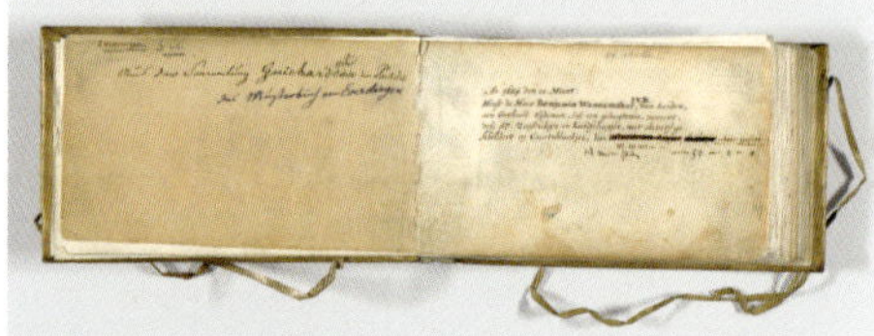

5

Album containing 38 marines, landscapes
and ice scenes
Binding: parchment; 94 x 160 mm
Sheets: brush and brown and white oil paint
on paper; each approx. 46 x 83 mm
Inv. no. RP-T-1968-99

Davies 2007, cat. nos. 402-439

pp. 96, 103 (note 56) and 104-115

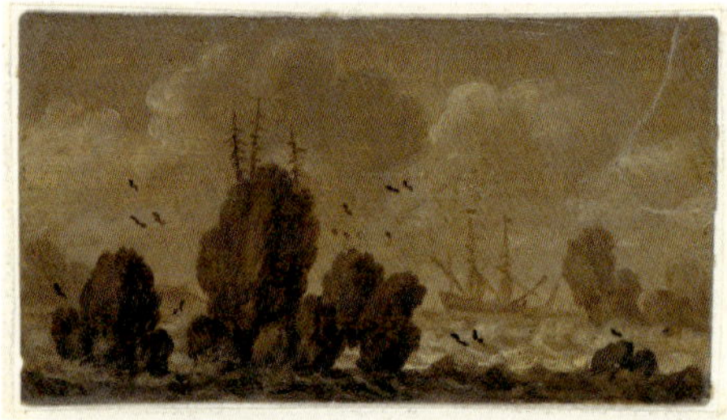

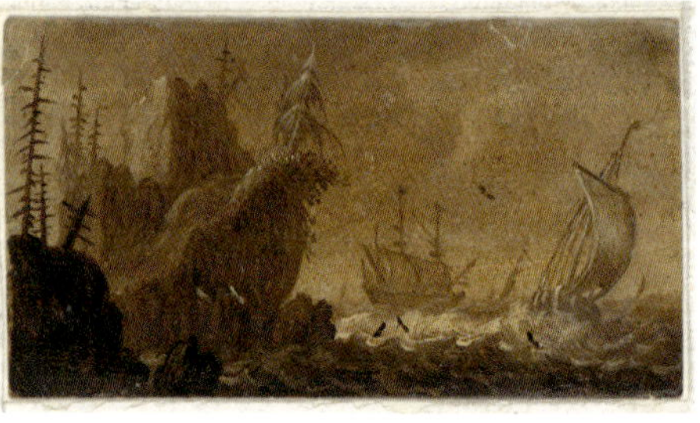

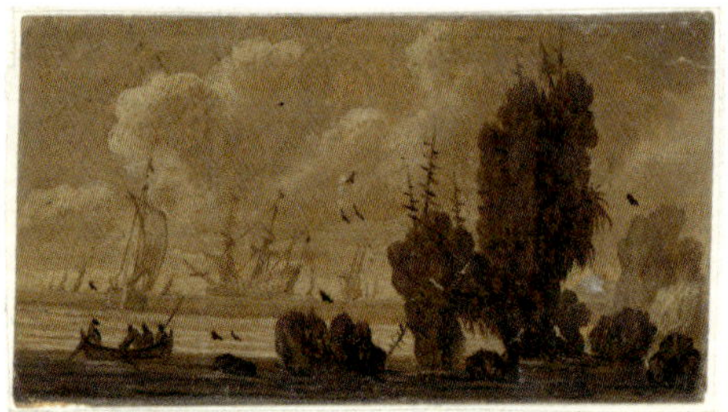

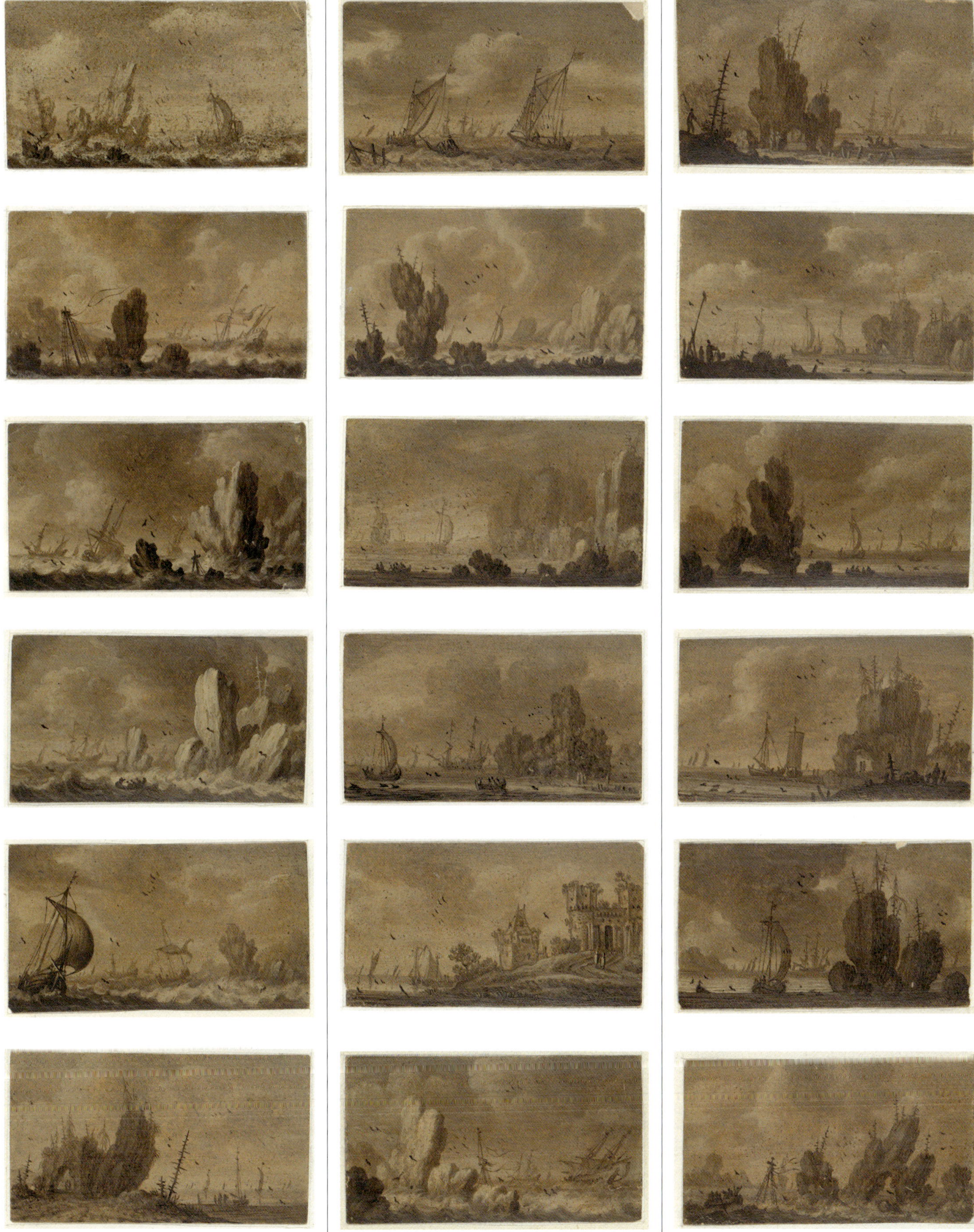

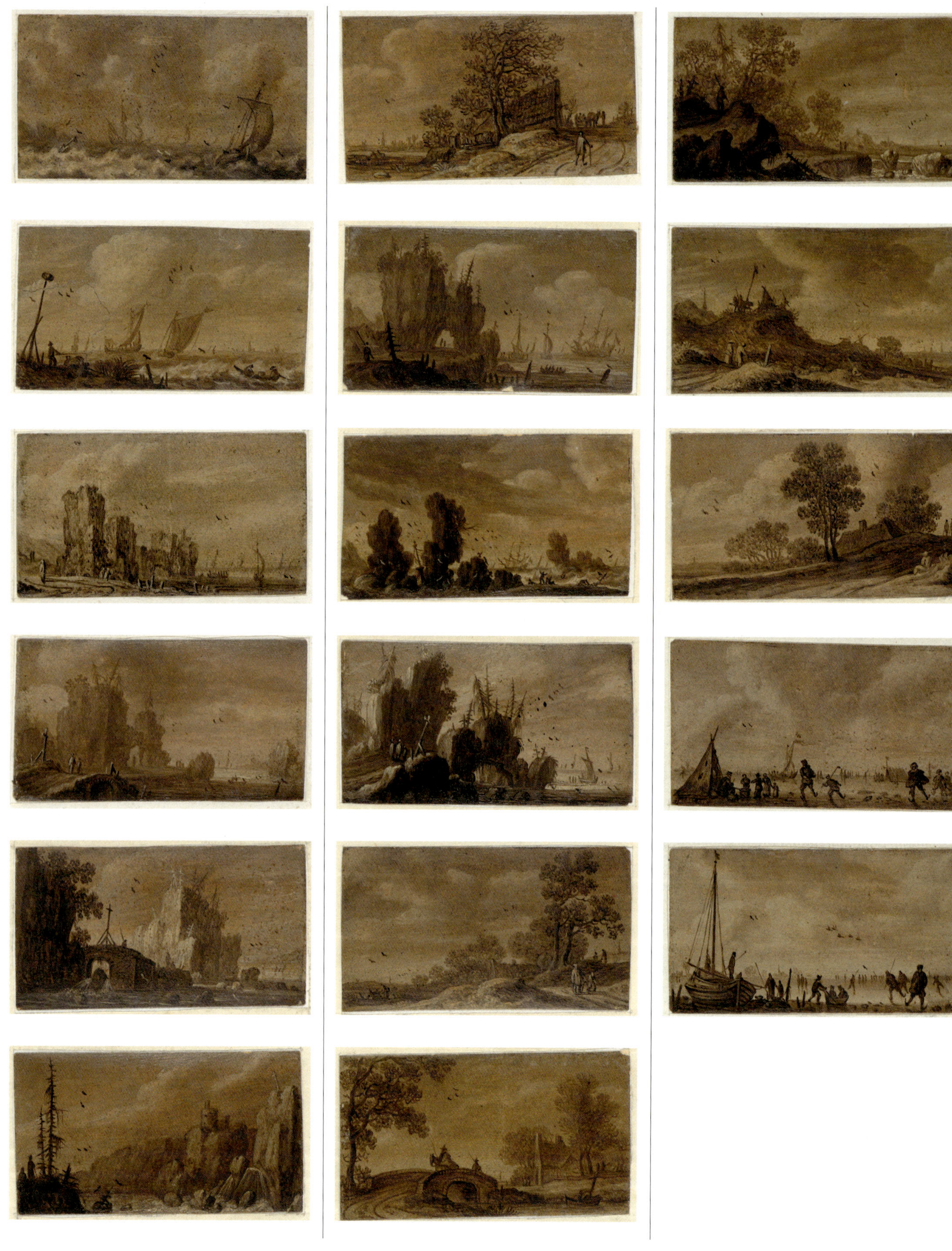

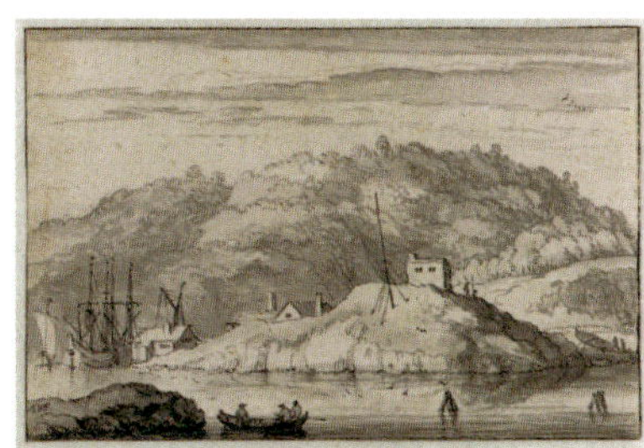

6

View of the Harbour at Risør
Pen and brush and grey ink, grey wash; framing
lines in pen and brown ink; 115 x 176 mm
Lower left, in pen and grey ink: AVE
Inv. no. RP-T-1957-202

Davies 2007, cat. no. 172

pp. 48 and 78-80

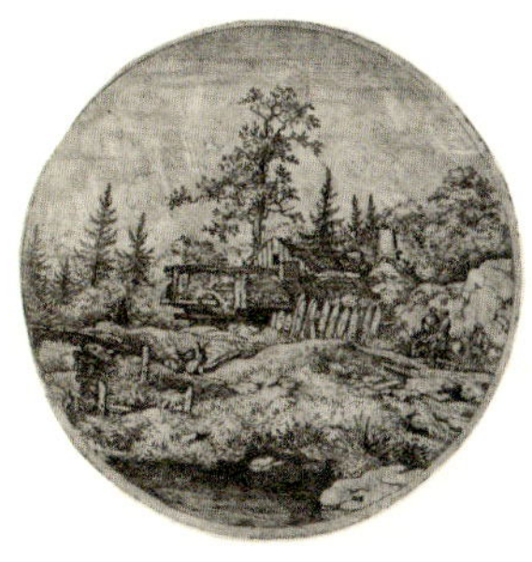

7

Landscape with a Horseman near a Hamlet
Etching; 195 x 193 mm (sheet, round)
Lower right: AVE
Inv. no. RP-P-1979-90

Holl. 4 I; Rosengren 2020, p. 191

pp. 118-119, 128-129 and 192

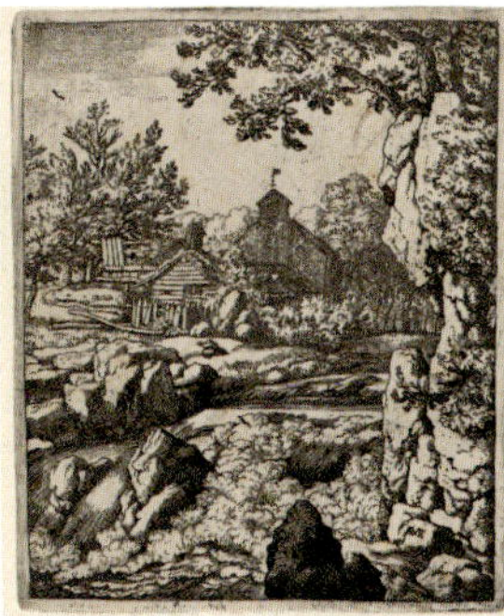

8

Landscape with a Church and a Waterfall
Etching; 126 x 100 mm
Lower right: AVE
Inv. no. RP-P-OB-50.284

Holl. 7 Ia

pp. 124-126

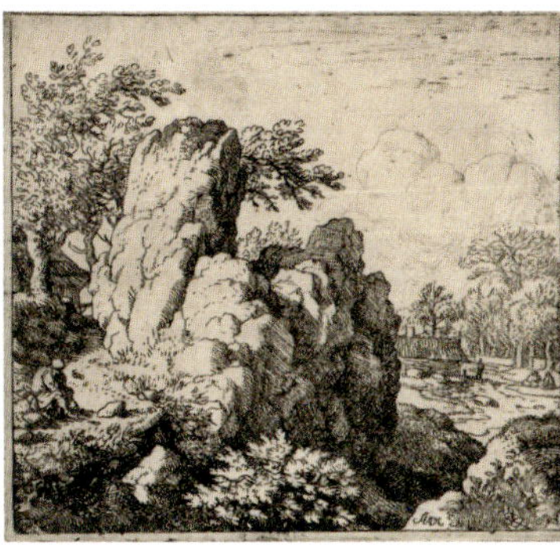

9

Landscape with a Large Rock
Etching; 102 x 111 mm
Lower right: AVE
Inv. no. RP-P-1879-A-3058

Holl. 18 I

pp. 130, 191 and 193

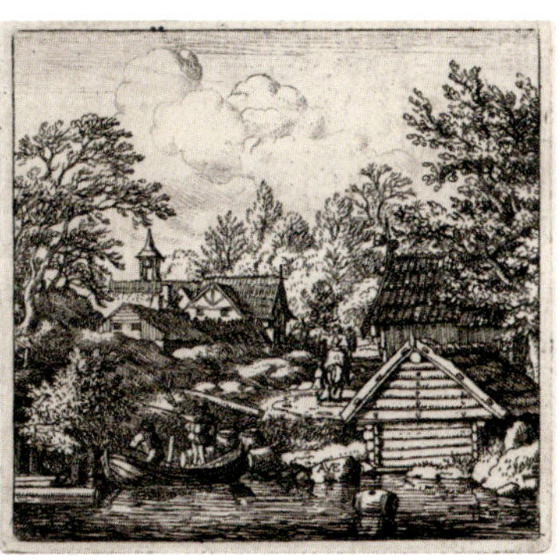

10

View of a Village with a Barge
Etching; 105 x 111 mm
Lower centre on the rock: AVE
Inv. no. RP-P-OB-50.303

Holl. 20 II

pp. 125-126

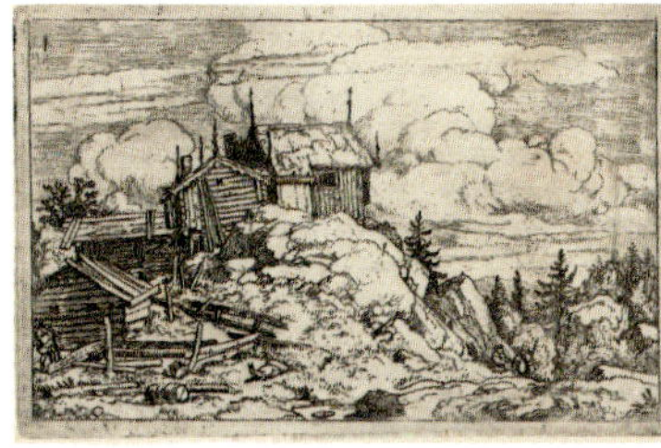

11

Landscape with Log Cabins on a Hill
Etching; 88 x 108 mm
Lower left: AVE
Inv. no. RP-P-OB-50.310

Holl. 25 I

pp. 125-126

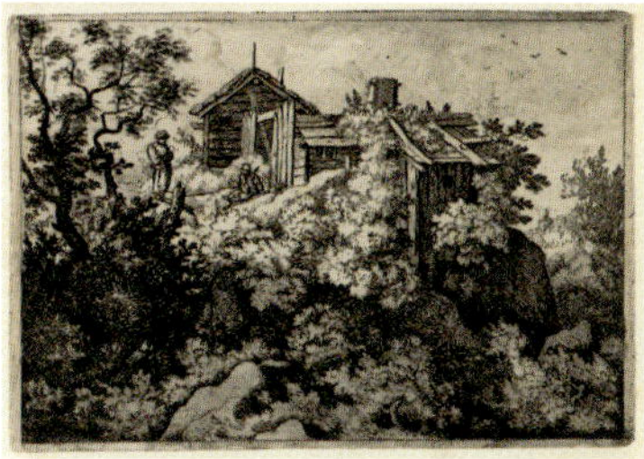

12

Three Log Cabins on a Rock
Etching, retouched with brush and grey ink;
98 x 144 mm
Inv. no. RP-P-OB-50.340

Holl. 41 I

pp. 132-133

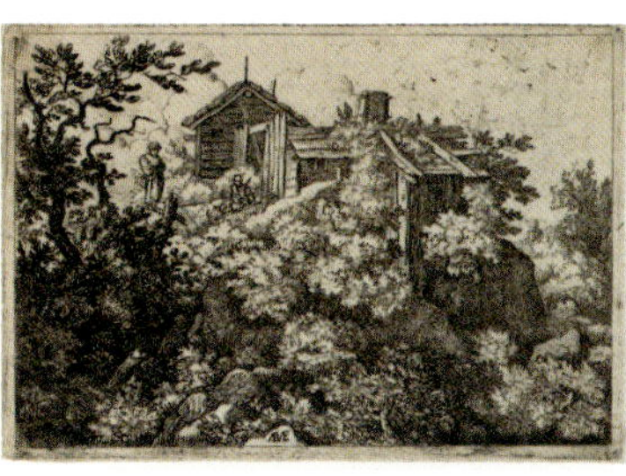

13

Three Log Cabins on a Rock
Etching; 99 x 146 mm
Lower centre: AVE
Inv. no. RP-P-1879-A-3067

Holl. 41 II

pp. 132-133 and 193

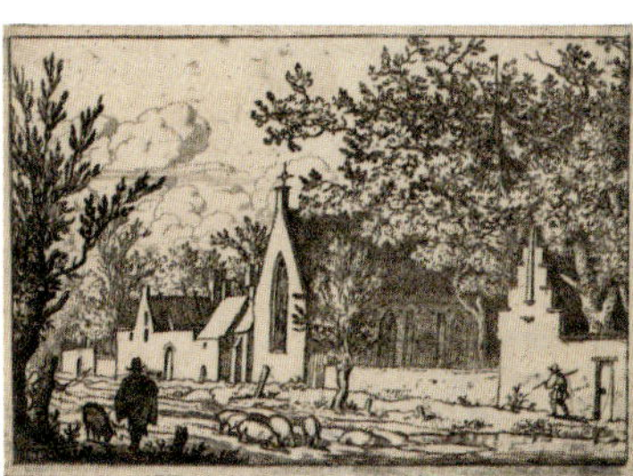

14

Swineherd near a Church
Etching; 99 x 145 mm
Lower right: AVE
Inv. no. RP-P-1879-A-3068

Holl. 43 I

p. 137

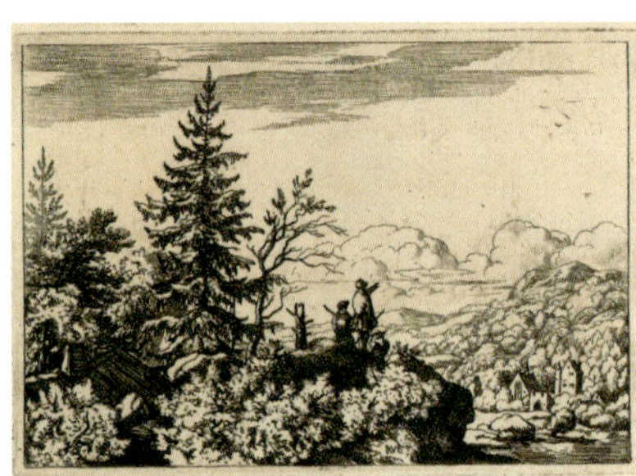

15
Two Men on a Hill
Etching; 100 x 146 mm
Lower centre: AVE
Inv. no. RP-P-OB-50.343

Holl. 46 I

pp. 117-118

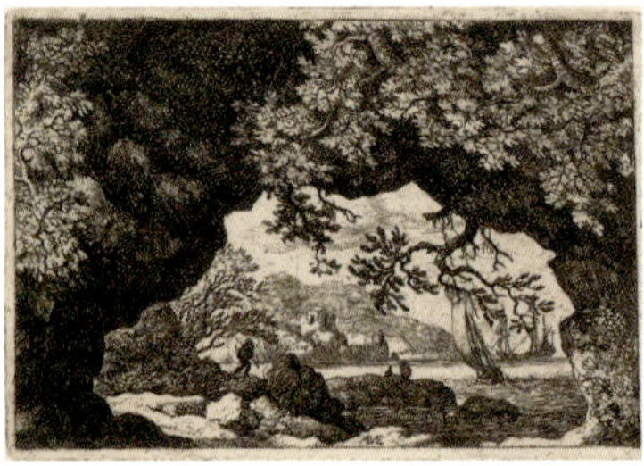

16
*View of the Sea through an Opening
in the Rocks*
Etching; 101 x 148 mm
Lower centre: AVE
Inv. no. RP-P-OB-50.350

Holl. 47 II; Rosengren 2020, pp. 199-200

pp. 115 (note 11) and 135-136

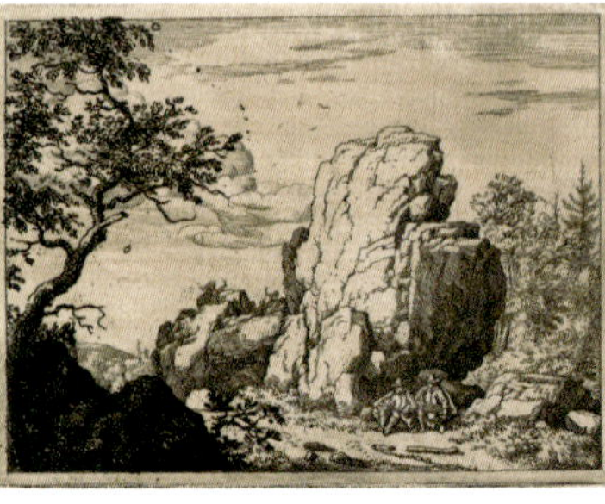

17
*Landscape with Two Artists Sitting
at the Base of a Rock*
Etching; 108 x 143 mm
Lower right, on the rock: EVERDINGEN / FE:
Inv. no. RP-P-OB-50.363

Holl. 54 II

pp. 134-135

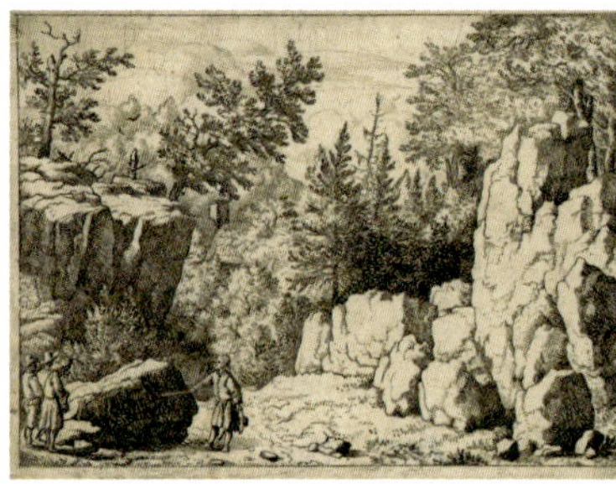

18
Landscape with a Man with a Pointer
Etching; 107 x 144 mm
Lower left, on the rock: ALLART VAN /
EVERDINGEN
Inv. no. RP-P-1879-A-3074

Holl. 55 II; Rosengren 2020, pp. 181-183

pp. 135 and 193

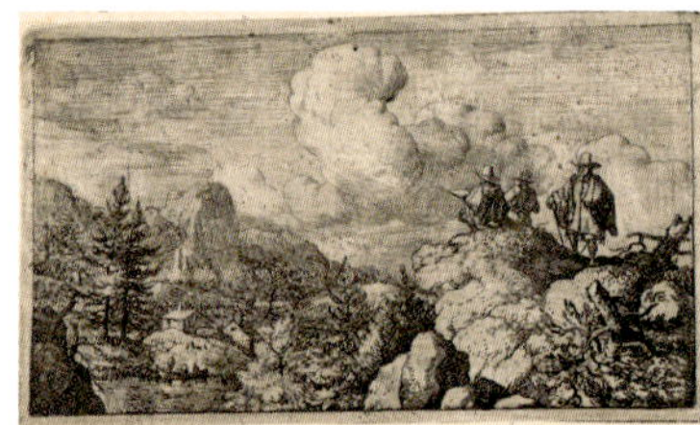

19
Landscape with Artists
Etching; 85 x 148 mm
Centre right: AVE
Inv. no. RP-P-OB-50.378

Holl. 63 III

pp. 78, 129, 155 and 164-165

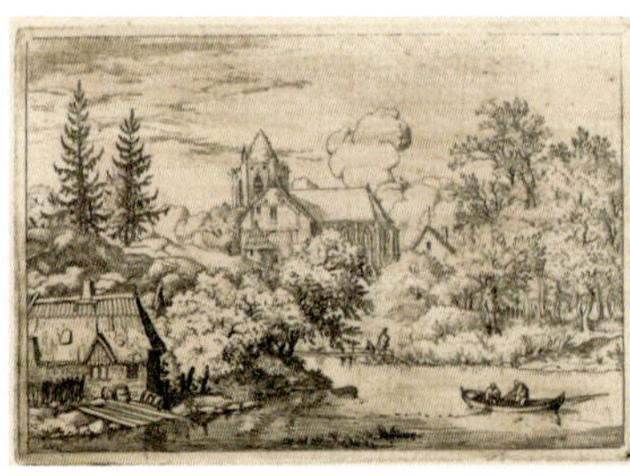

20
River Landscape with a Church
Etching; 100 x 147 mm
Lower left: AVE
Inv. no. RP-P-OB-50.381

Holl. 65 IIa

p. 27

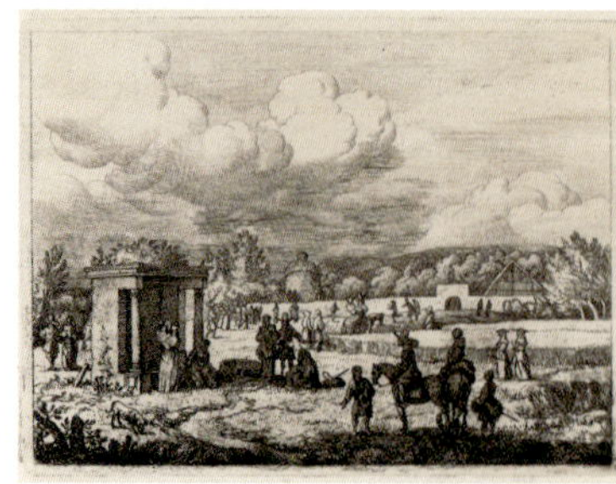

21
The Spring at Tonnelet near Spa
Etching; 131 x 177 mm
Centre left, on the building: AVE
Inv. no. RP-P-OB-50.429

Holl. 95 II

pp. 27, 73, 96, 117 and 137-141

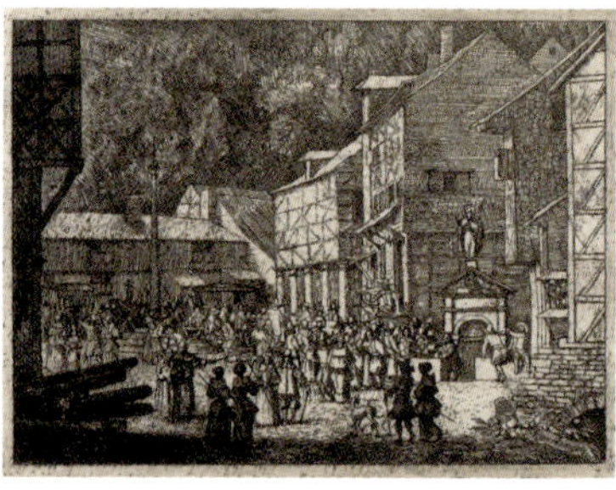

22
The Pouhon Spring in the Market Square at Spa
Etching; 131 x 176 mm
Lower right: Everdingen
Inv. no. RP-P-OB-50.431

Holl. 96 II

pp. 27, 73, 96, 117, 137-141 and 194

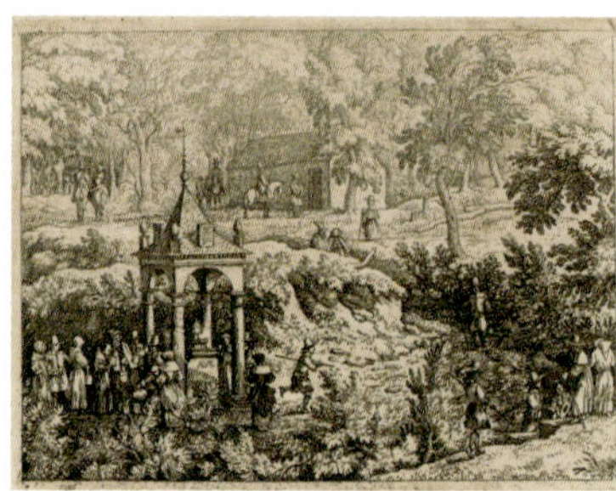

23
The Spring at Géronstère near Spa
Etching; 135 x 182 mm
Left, on the plinth: AVE
Inv. no. RP-P-OB-50.432

Holl. 97 I

pp. 27, 73, 96, 117, 137-141 and 194

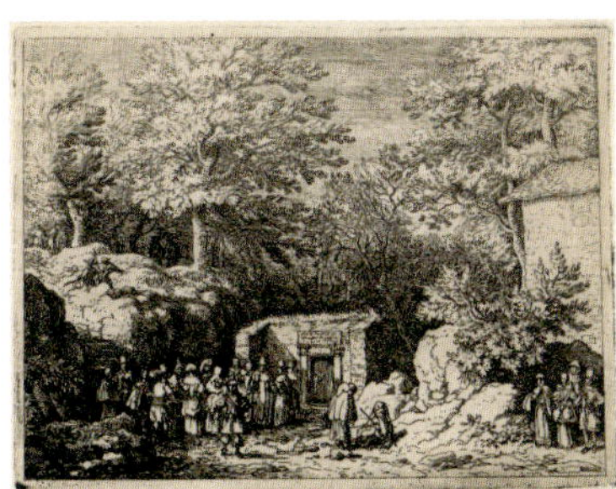

24

The Spring at Sauvenière near Spa
Etching; 133 x 175 mm
Lower left, on the rock: AVE
Inv. no. RP-P-OB-50.434

Holl. 98 I; Boston/Saint Louis 1981, cat. no. 180

pp. 27-28, 73, 96, 117, 137-141 and 194

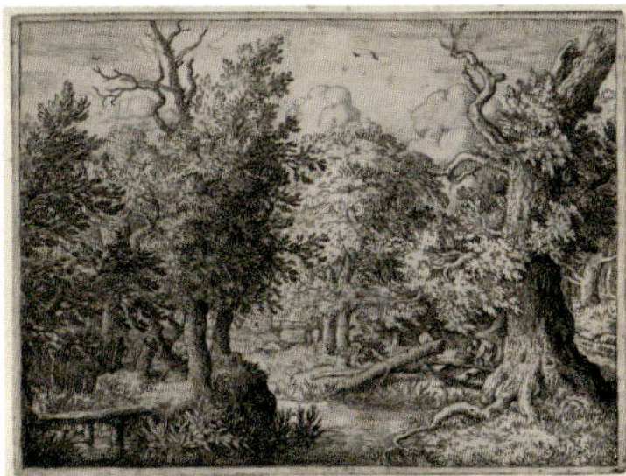

25

Stream in the Woods
Etching, retouched with black chalk;
143 x 194 mm
Lower left, on the bridge: AVE
Inv. no. RP-P-OB-50.440

Holl. 101 I

pp. 82, 120-121 and 135

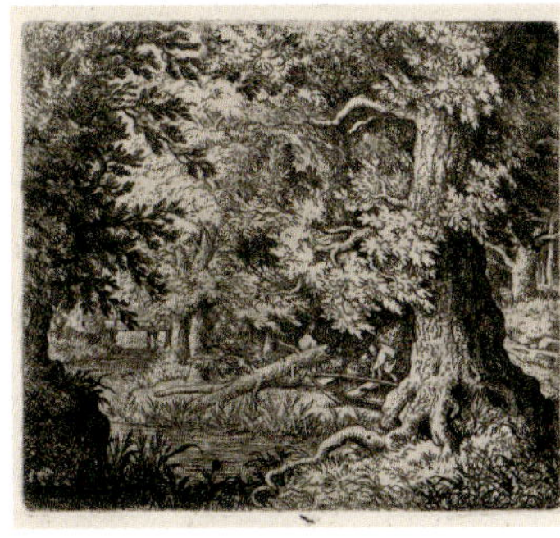

26

Stream in the Woods
Etching; 115 x 130 mm
Inv. no. RP-P-OB-50.441

Holl. 101 VI

pp. 82, 120-121 and 135

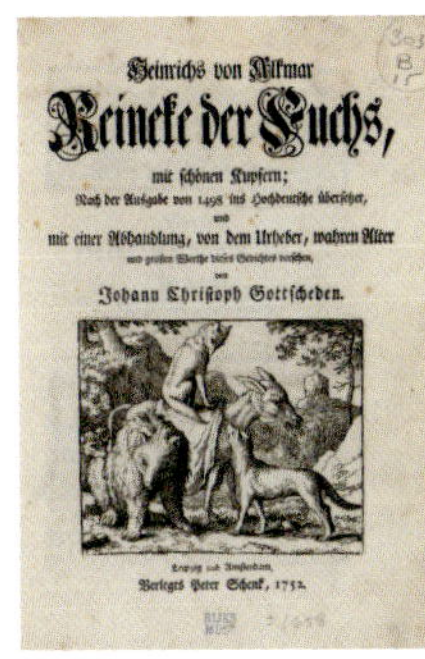

27

Johann Christoph Gottsched, *Heinrichs von Alkmar Reineke der Fuchs*, Leipzig/Amsterdam: Pieter Schenk 1752
Call number 303 B 15

Verzandvoort 1995, pp. 151-155; Feliers 2006, p. 37

pp. 129, 141, 150 and 160

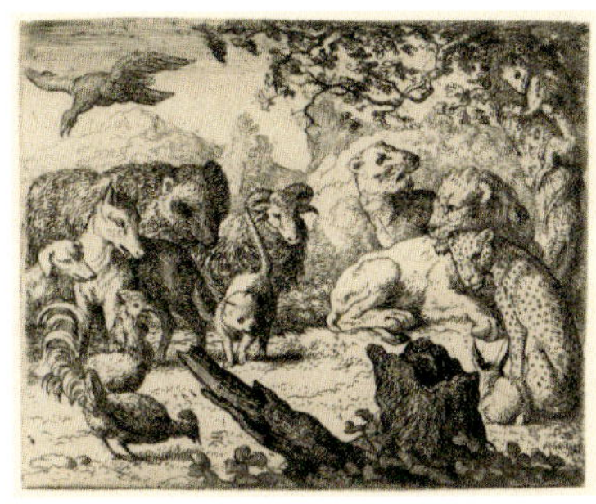

28

King Noble the Lion Holds Court
Etching; 94 x 117 mm
Inv. no. RP-P-OB-50.448

Dut. 2 II; Verzandvoort 1995, p. 159

p. 149

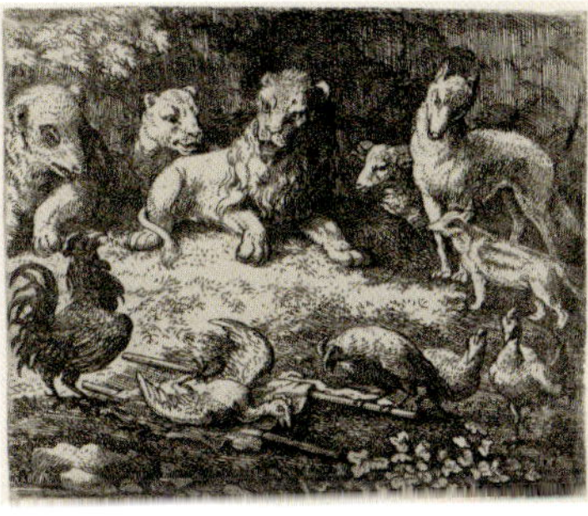

29

Chanticleer the Cock's Complaint
Etching; 94 x 115 mm
Inv. no. RP-P-OB-50.451

Dut. 5 II; Verzandvoort 1995, p. 157

pp. 158-159

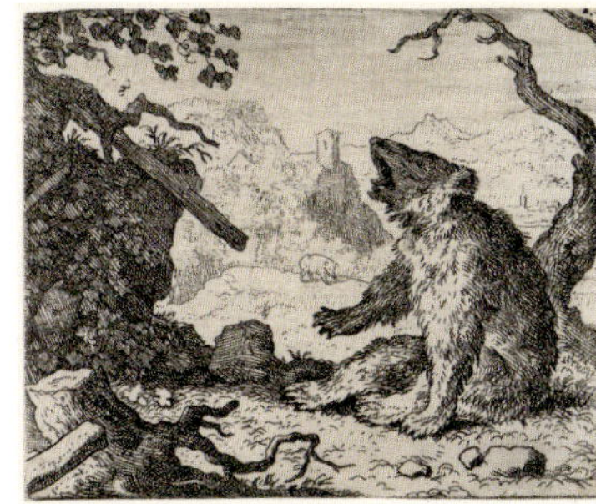

30

Bruin the Bear Summonses Reynard the Fox
Etching; 96 x 117 mm
Inv. no. RP-P-OB-50.454

Dut. 8 II; Verzandvoort 1994a, p. 145; Verzandvoort 1995, p. 161

pp. 153 and 194

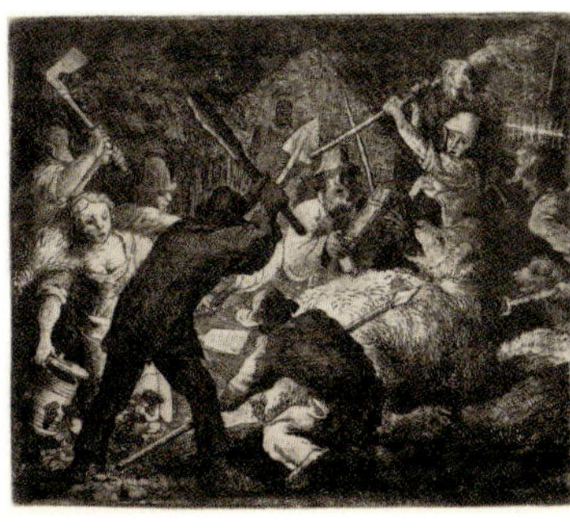

31

Bruin the Bear Beaten by Villagers
Etching and mezzotint; 98 x 116 mm
Inv. no. RP-P-OB-50.457

Dut. 11 III; Verzandvoort 1994a, p. 145; Verzandvoort 1995, p. 161

pp. 148-149 and 155-156

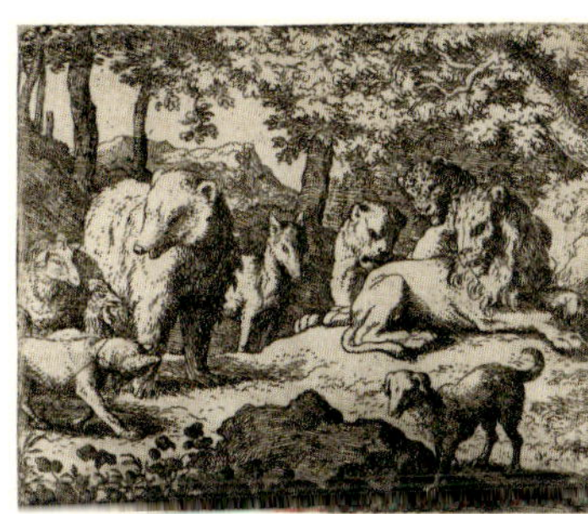

32

Reynard the Fox's Stay of Execution
Etching; 94 x 116 mm
Inv. no. RP-P-OB-50.474

Dut. 27 II; Verzandvoort 1995, p. 158

pp. 147-148 and 194

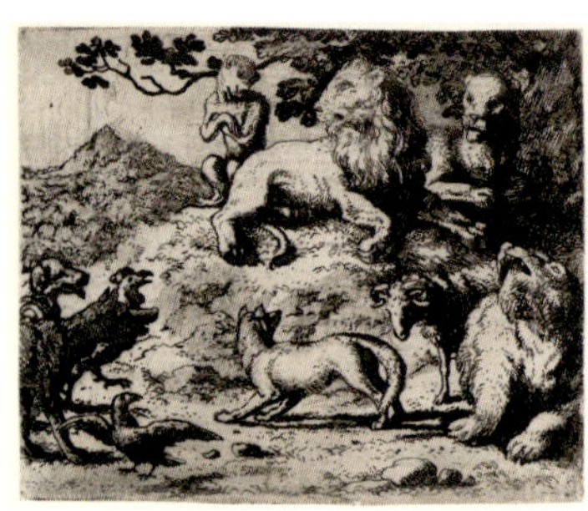

33
Reynard the Fox Accused by the Animals
Etching; 96 x 116 mm
Inv. no. RP-P-OB-50.480

Dut. 33 Ia

pp. 152 and 194

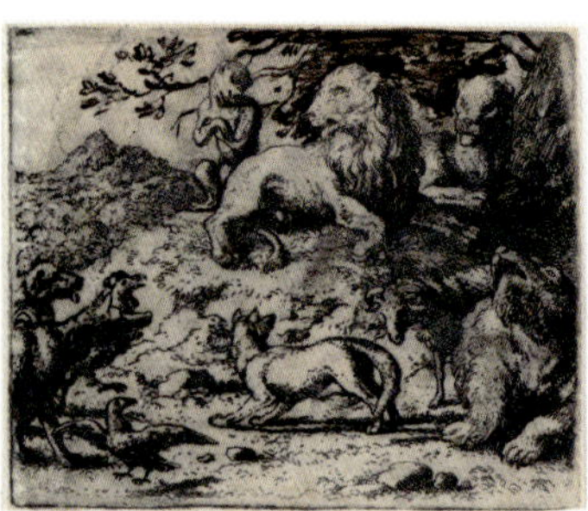

34
Reynard the Fox Accused by the Animals
Etching, retouched with pen and brown ink;
96 x 118 mm
Inv. no. RP-P-2020-11

Dut. 33 (undescribed state before the first)

p. 152

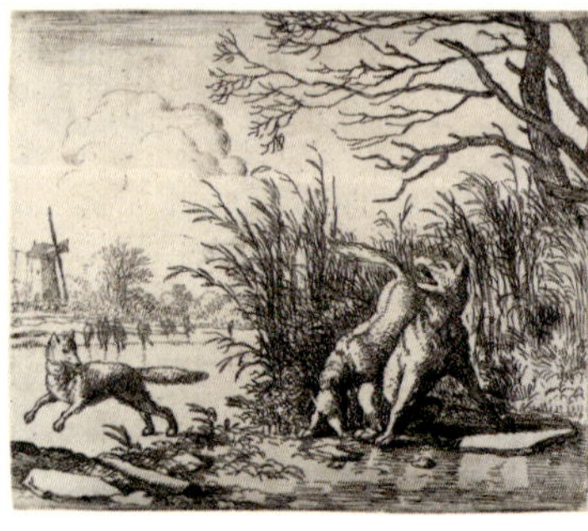

35
*Hirsent the She-Wolf Tricked by Reynard
the Fox*
Etching; 98 x 118 mm
Inv. no. RP-P-OB-50.500

Dut. 53 II

pp. 154-155 and 194

Amsterdam
Amsterdam City Archives

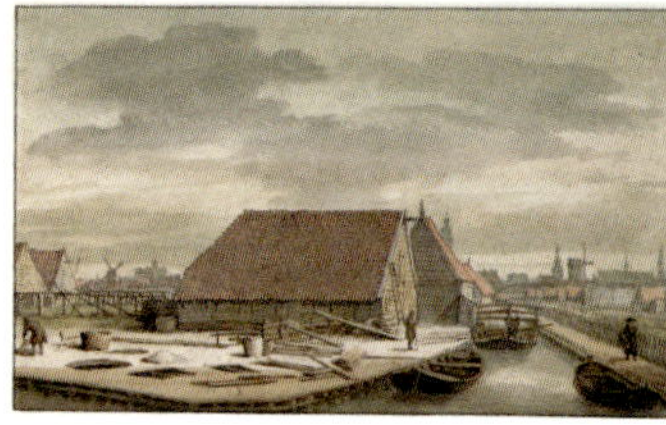

36
*Glue Factory on Lange Bleekerspad
in Amsterdam*
Brush and watercolour over traces of black
chalk; framing lines in pen and grey and
brown ink; 169 x 284 mm
Right, on the hut beside the bridge, in pen
and brown ink: AVE
Accession no. 10055: Van Eeghen Collection,
inv. no. 16

Davies 2007, cat. no. 18

pp. 93-94 and 100-101

Amsterdam
Stichting Collectie
P. & N. de Boer

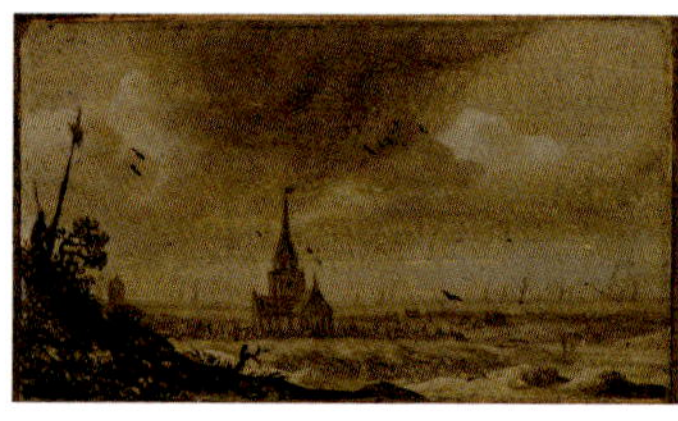

37
Church in a Dune Landscape
Brush and brown and white oil paint on paper;
47 x 83 mm
Inv. no. B 650-a

Davies 2007, cat. no. 440

pp. 104-105 and 115 (note 23)

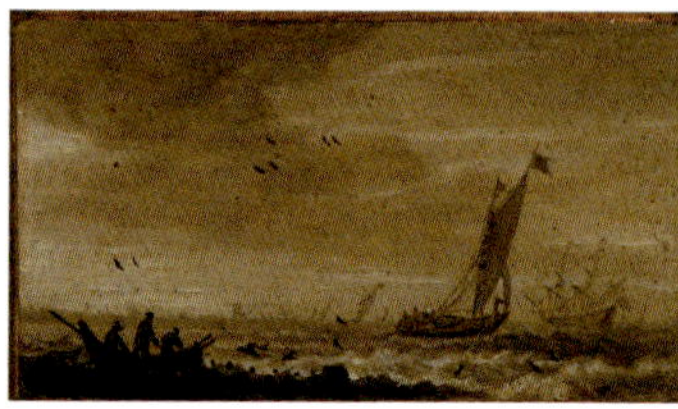

38
Seascape with Sailing Boats
Brush and brown and white oil paint on paper;
47 x 84 mm
Inv. no. B 650-b

Davies 2007, cat. no. 441

pp. 104-105 and 115 (note 23)

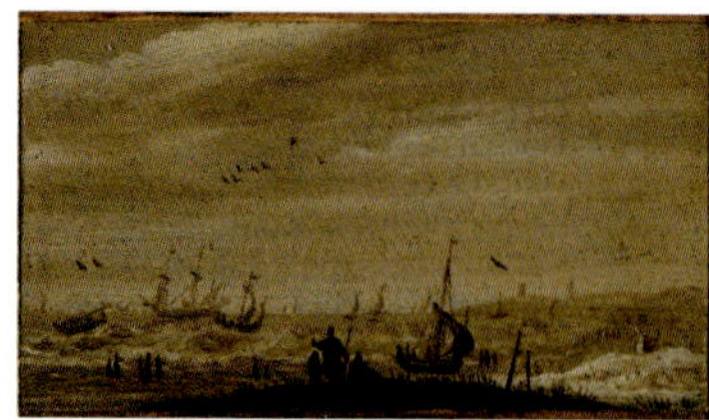

39
View of the Beach with Figures in the Foreground
Brush and brown and white oil paint on paper;
47 x 84 mm
Inv. no. B 650-c

Davies 2007, cat. no. 442

pp. 104-105 and 115 (note 23)

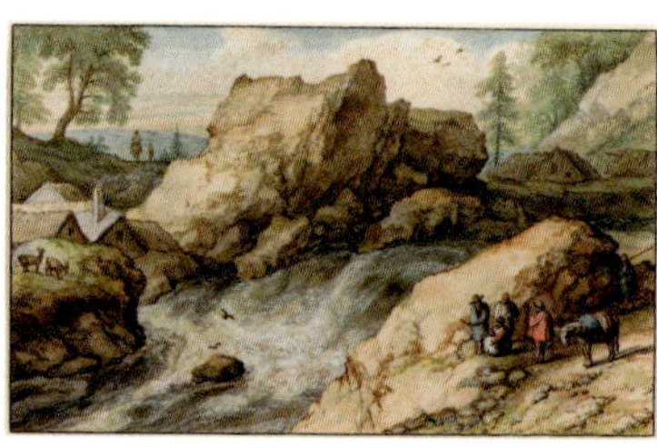

40
*Figures near a Waterfall in a Mountain
Landscape*
Pen and brown ink, brown wash, watercolour,
heightened with white; framing lines in pen
and black ink; 200 x 323 mm
Lower left, in pen and brown ink: AVE
Inv. no. B 477

Davies 2007, cat. no. 3; Blok in Paris 2014,
cat. no. 78; Dumas 2015, p. 218, cat. no. 1

p. 85

Berlin
Staatliche Museen zu Berlin, Kupferstichkabinett

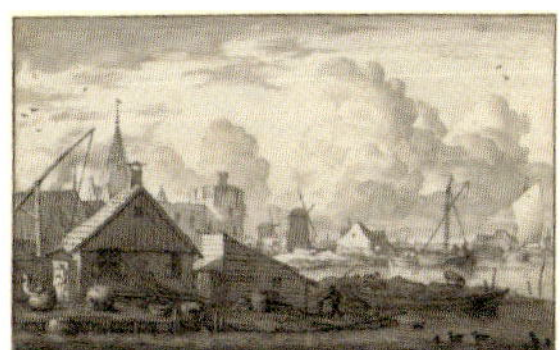

41

Activity on the Water
Pen and brush and black ink over black chalk,
grey wash; framing lines in pen and brown ink;
181 x 300 mm
Left, on the fence, in pen and grey ink: AVE
Inv. no. KdZ 12842

Davies 2007, cat. no. 123

p. 92

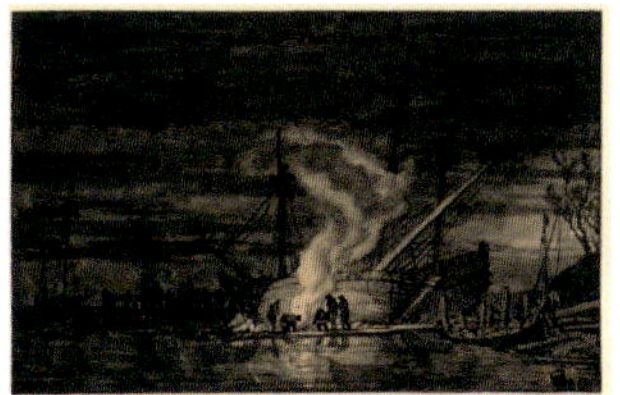

42

Careening a Ship at Night
Pen and brush and black ink over black chalk,
grey and brown wash; framing lines in pen
and black and brown ink; 181 x 288 mm
Lower right, in pen and black ink: AVE
Lower left, in a later hand, in pen and brown ink:
AVE
Inv. no. KdZ 1309

Davies 2007, cat. no. 133

pp. 92-93

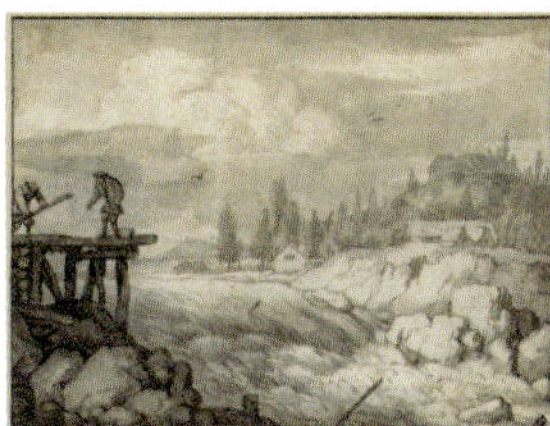

43

*Landscape with a Waterfall, Possibly near
Trollhättan*
Pen and brush and black and grey-brown ink,
grey wash; framing lines in pen and black ink;
121 x 163 mm
Lower left, in pen and grey ink: E
Inv. no. KdZ 1311

Davies 2007, cat. no. 178

p. 80

Budapest
Szépmüvészeti Múzeum

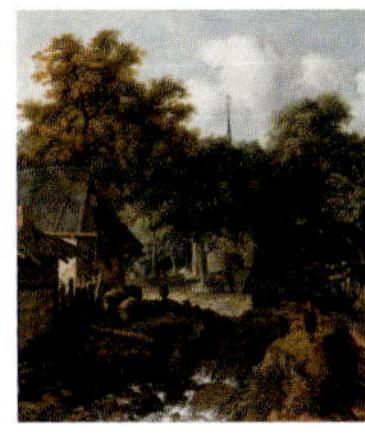

44

Village View
Oil on canvas; 76 x 66.5 cm
Left, on the house: A v.Everdingen
Inv. no. 4291

Davies 2001, cat. no. 128

pp. 60 and 62-63

Boston
Alice I. Davies Collection

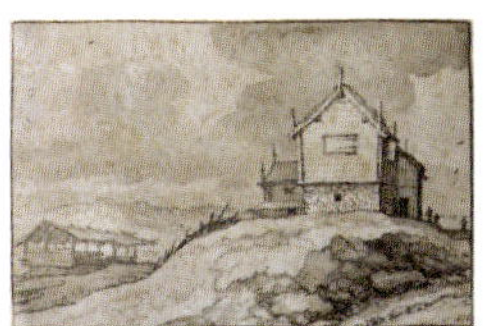

45

Norwegian Landscape with a Log Cabin
Pen and brush and grey ink over traces of
black chalk, grey wash; framing lines in pen
and black ink; 116 x 176 mm
Lower right, in pen and grey ink: AVE

Davies 2007, cat. no. 169

pp. 48-49 and 78-80

Braunschweig
Herzog Anton Ulrich-Museum, Kunstmuseum des Landes Niedersachsen

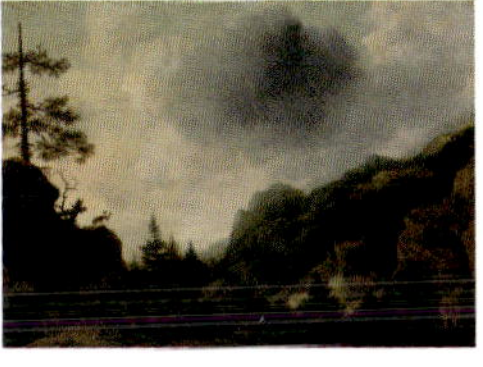

46

Mountain Landscape with a Fallow Deer
Oil on panel; 64.3 x 89 cm
Centre left, on the rock under the bare tree:
A. VAN EVERDINGEN / 1647
Inv. no. GG 364

Davies 2001, cat. no. 28

pp. 2, 32-33 and 44-46

Brussels
Royal Museums of Fine Arts of Belgium

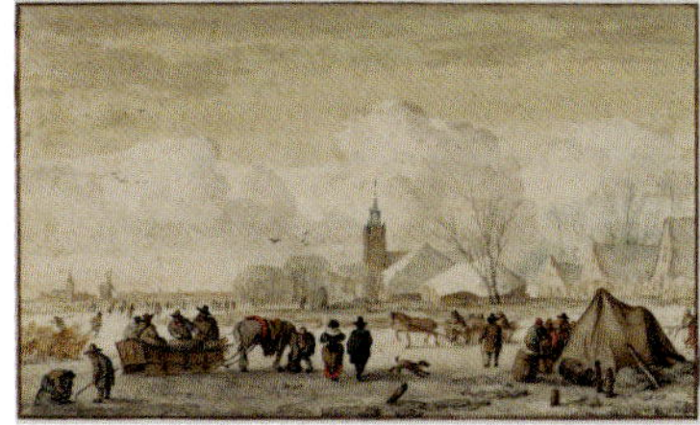

47

Winter Landscape with Sledges and Skaters
Brush and grey and brown ink, watercolour;
framing lines in pen and brown ink and gold;
180 x 304 mm
Lower right, in pen and grey ink: AVE
De Grez Collection, inv. no. 4060-1282

Davies 2007, cat. no. 12

pp. 87-89

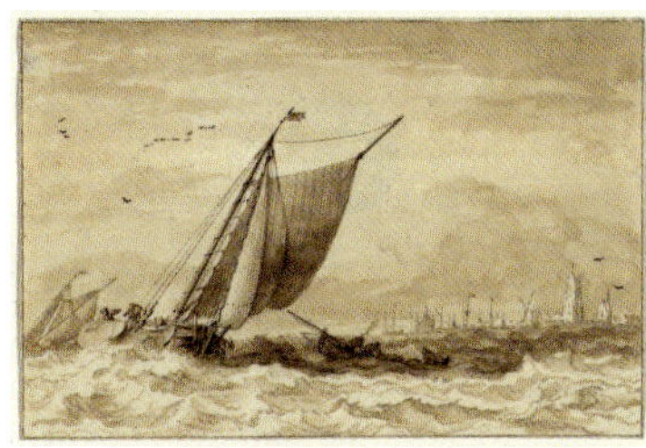

48

Sailing Ship in a Strong Wind near a Harbour
Pen and brush and brown ink over traces of
black chalk, brown wash; framing lines in
pen and brown ink; 125 x 191 mm
Lower left, on the side of the sailing ship,
in pen and brown ink: AVE
De Grez Collection, inv. no. 4060-1265

Davies 2007, cat. no. 248

p. 95

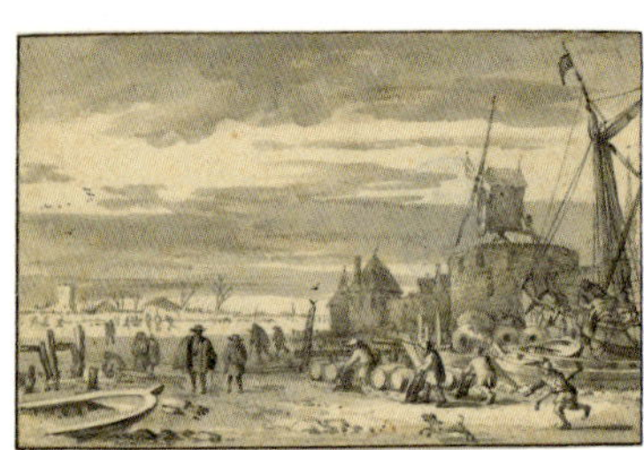

January

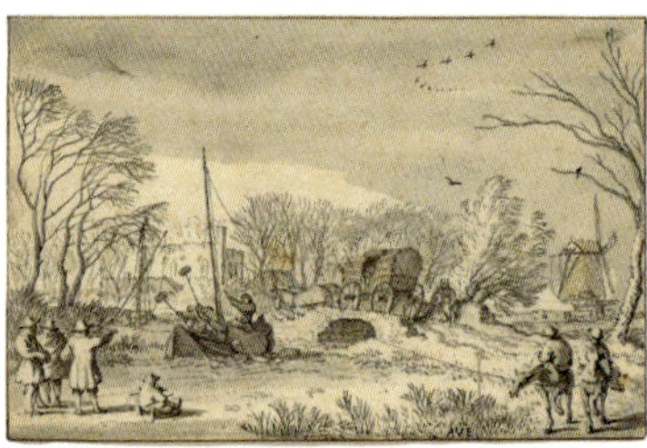

February

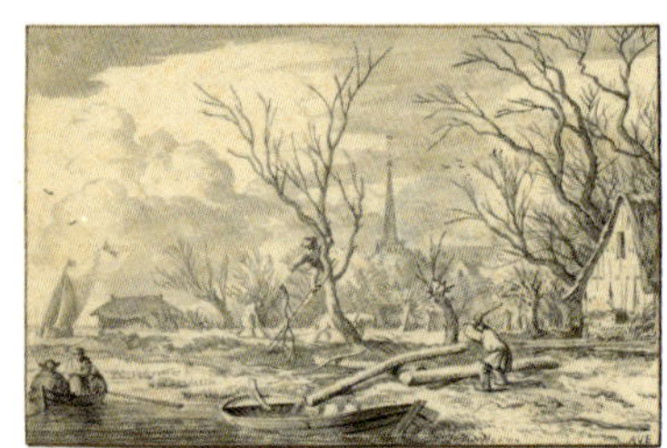

March

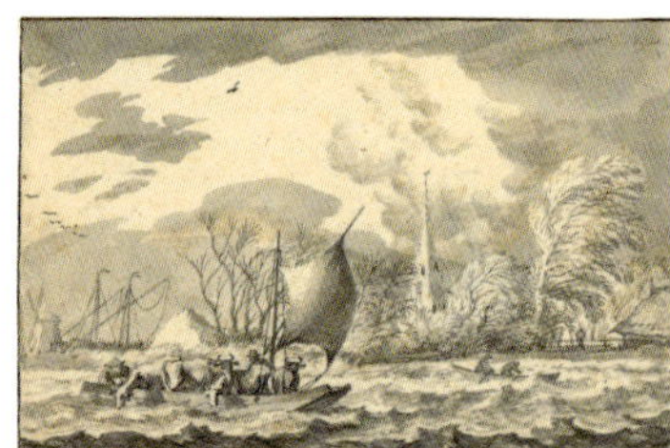

April

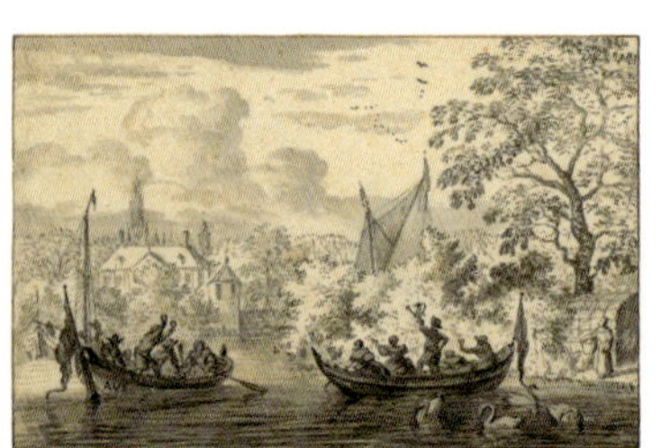

May

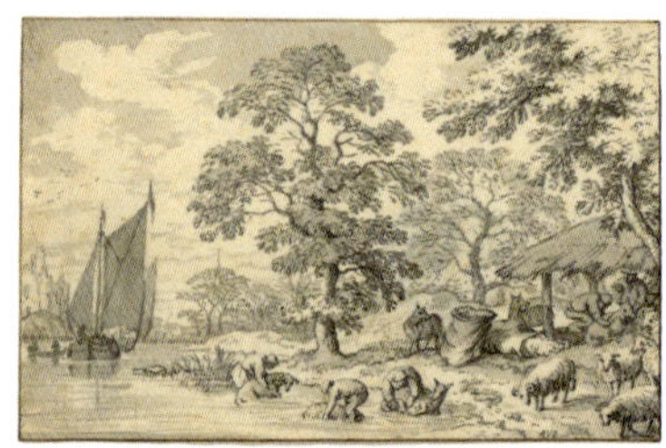

June

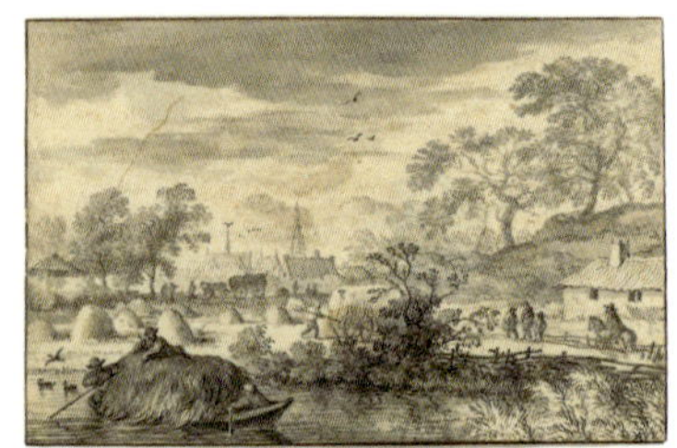

July

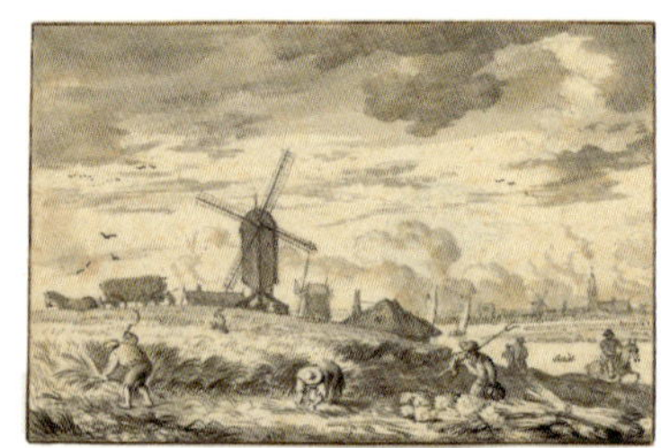

August

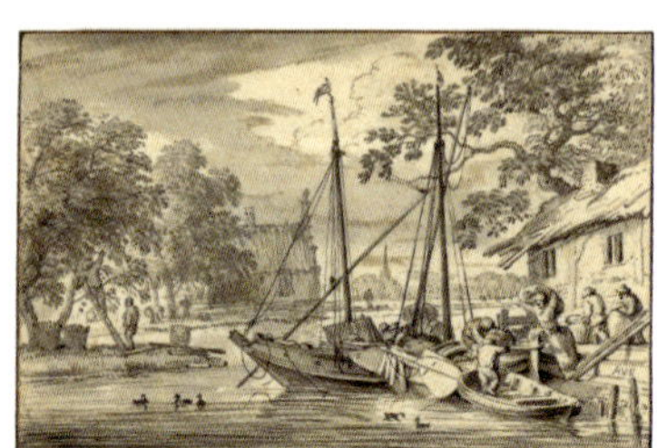

September

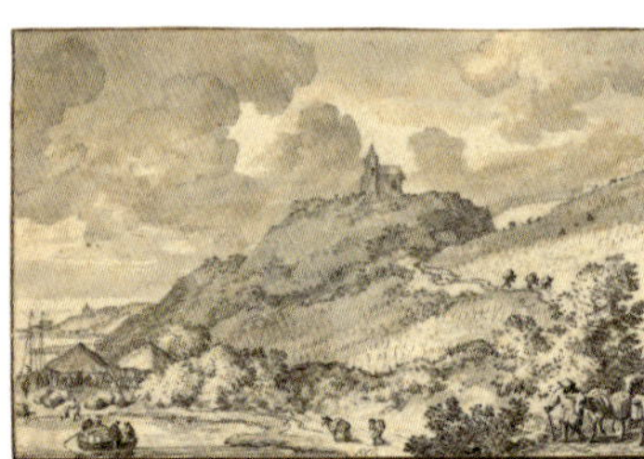

October

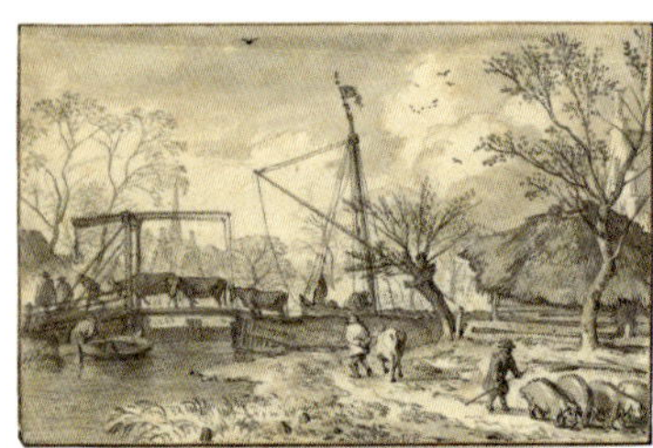

November

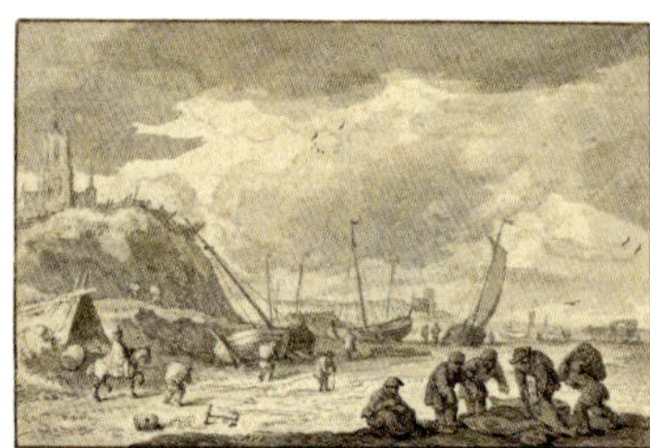

December

49

The Twelve Months of the Year
Brush and grey ink over graphite, grey wash;
framing lines in pen and brown ink; each
approx. 116 x 180 mm
Left, centre or lower right in pen and grey ink:
AVE
De Grez Collection, inv. nos. 4060-1270 to
4060-1281

Davies 2007, cat. nos. 457-468; Vogt in Brussels/
Amsterdam/Aachen 2007, cat. nos. 38 and 39
(*November* and *December*); Bleyerveld 2017,
p. 57 (December)

pp. 98-100

Groningen
Academie Minerva
Hanzehogeschool Groningen

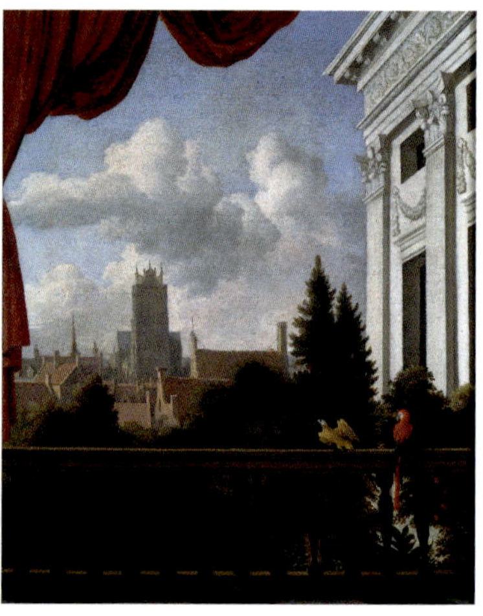

50

*View of Dordrecht with the Amsterdam
Trippenhuis*
Oil on canvas; 94 x 76 cm
Left on the balustrade: A:V:EVERDINGEN.
On loan to the Dordrechts Museum, inv. no.
DM/010/953 (as a secondary loan from the
Groninger Museum, inv. no. 0000.2015)

Davies 2001, cat. no. 178; Paarlberg in Budapest
2014, cat. no. 27; Van Run 2019, pp. 32-33

pp. 70-71

The Hague
Mauritshuis

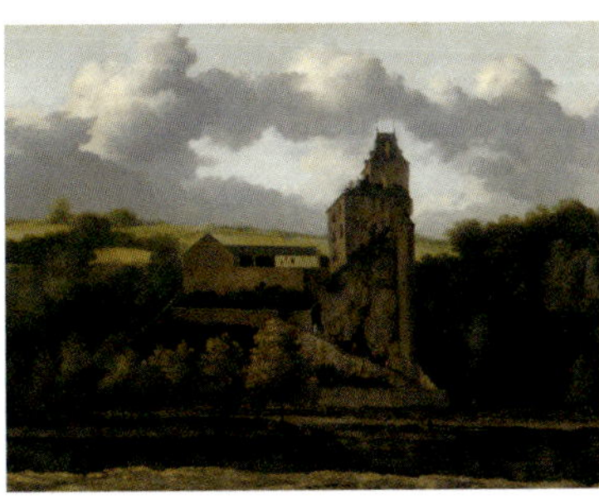

51

View of Montjardin Castle
Oil on canvas; 73 x 95.5 cm
Inv. no. 953

Davies 2001, cat. no. 174; Buvelot 2004,
pp. 116-117

pp. 27, 29, 71, 73, 96 and 138

Haarlem
Frans Hals Museum

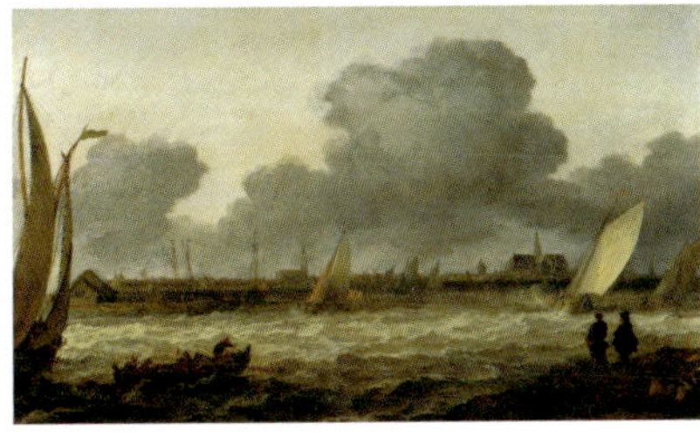

52

*View of Haarlem from the Noorder Buiten
Spaarne*
Oil on canvas on panel; 39 x 65.5 cm
Lower right: AVE
Inv. no. OS I-82 (purchased with the support
of the Vereniging Rembrandt)

Davies 2001, cat. no. 15; Biesboer in Köhler et
al. 2006, cat. no. 136; Haarlem/Munich 2008,
pp. 74-75

pp. 23-24, 55 and 57

Haarlem
Teylers Museum

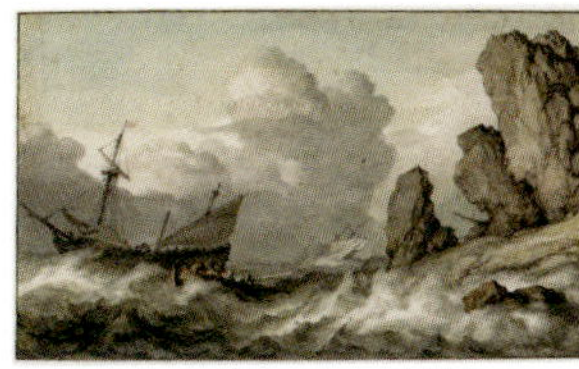

53

Storm at Sea
Brush and grey and brown ink over traces
of black chalk, watercolour; double framing
lines in pen and black ink and brush and gold;
182 x 305 mm
Lower right, on the rock, in pen and grey ink:
AVE
Inv. no. Q 031

Davies 2007, cat. no. 8

Cover and pp. 85-86, 91 and 106

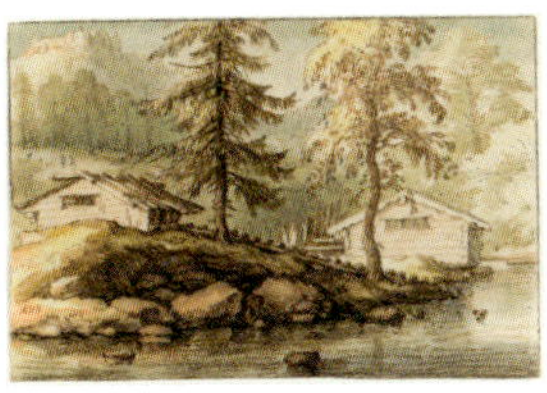

54

*Scandinavian Landscape with Two Log Cabins
by the Water*
Brush and brown ink, watercolour; framing lines
in pen and grey-brown ink; 112 x 168 mm
Lower left, in brush and grey-brown ink: AVE
Inv. no. Q 030

Davies 2007, cat. no. 63

pp. 14 and 84-85

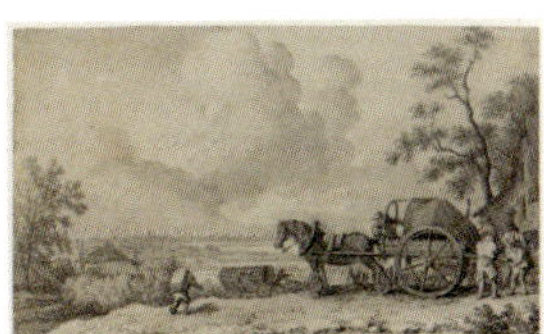

55

Landscape with a Cart
Pen and black and grey ink over black chalk,
grey wash; traces of framing lines in pen and
light brown ink; 175 x 302 mm
Lower left, in pen and black ink: AVE
Inv. no. KT 2016 031 (gift of Matthijs de Clercq)

Davies 2007, cat. no. 129; Plomp in Haarlem
2010, p. 52 and cat. no. 21; Plomp 2015,
pp. 14-15; Dumas 2015, p. 234, no. 94

pp. 76 and 95

Hamburg
Hamburger Kunsthalle

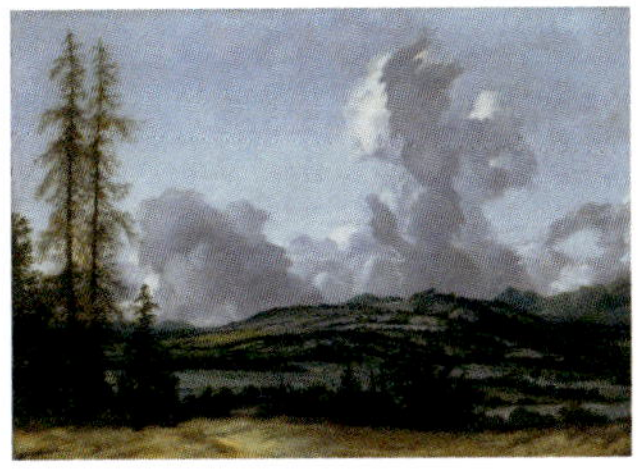

56

Hilly Landscape
Oil on canvas; 72.8 x 102.2 cm
Lower left: A.V.EVERDINGEN
Inv. no. HK-56

Davies 2001, cat. no. 171

p. 50

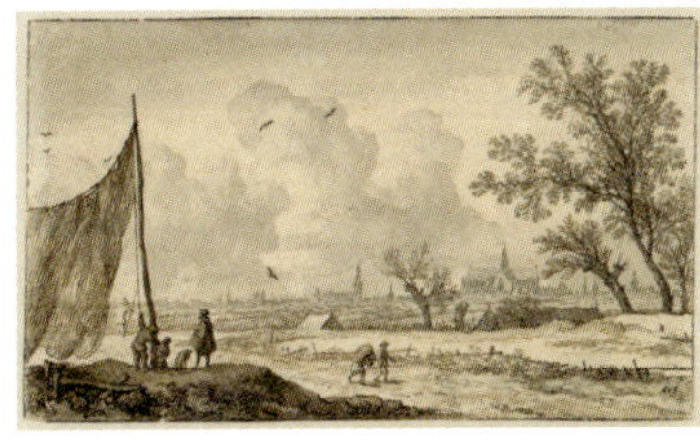

57

View of Haarlem from the North
Pen and brush and brown and grey ink over
black chalk, brown and grey wash; framing lines
in pen and brown ink; 156 x 271 mm
Lower right, in pen and brown ink: AVE
Inv. no. 21908

Davies 2007, cat. no. 140; Stefes 2011,
cat. no. 301

pp. 23-24, 94-95 and 172

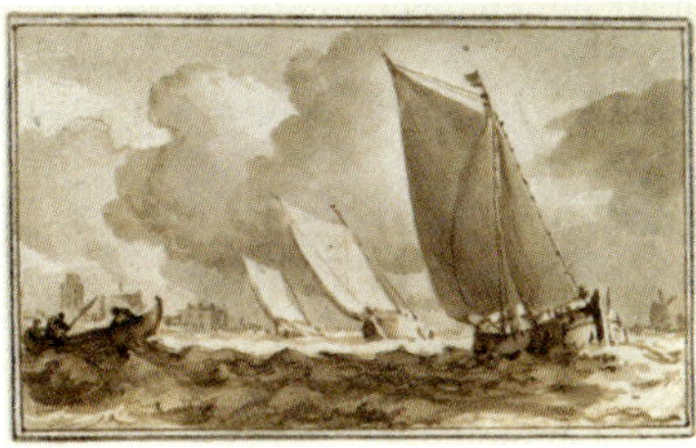

58

Three Sailing Ships on Open Water
Pen and brown ink over traces of graphite,
brown wash; double framing lines in pen
and brown ink and black chalk; 51 x 86 mm
Inv. no. 21893

Davies 2007, cat. no. 366; Stefes 2011,
cat. no. 317

pp. 96-98 and 115 (note 1)

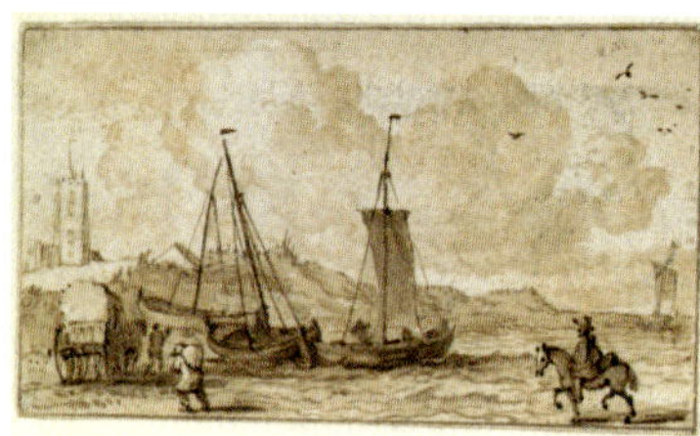

59

Shore with Sailing Ships and a Horseman
Pen and brown ink over traces of graphite,
brown wash; framing lines in pen and brown
ink; 48 x 84 mm
Inv. no. 21892

Davies 2007, cat. no. 367; Stefes 2011,
cat. no. 318

pp. 96-98 and 115 (note 1)

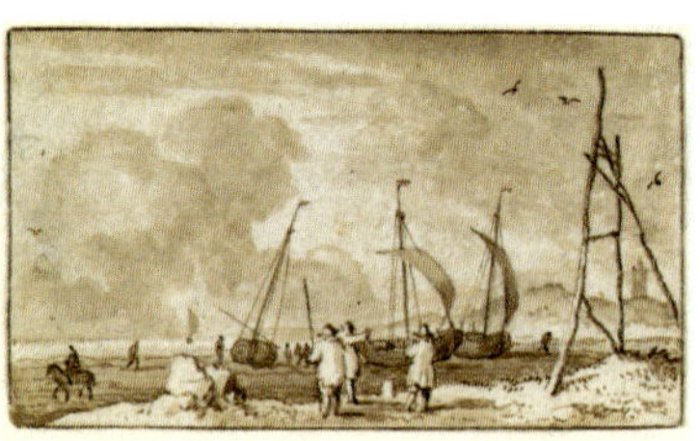

60

Shore with a Beacon
Pen and brown ink over traces of graphite,
brown wash; framing lines in pen and brown
ink; 48 x 84 mm
Inv. no. 21896

Davies 2007, cat. no. 368; Stefes 2011,
cat. no. 319

pp. 96-98 and 115 (note 1)

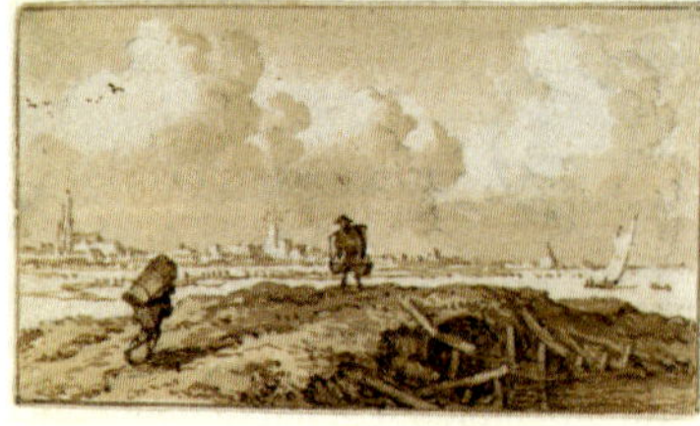

61

River Landscape with Two Porters
Pen and brown ink over traces of graphite,
brown wash; framing lines in pen and brown
ink; 48 x 85 mm
Inv. no. 21891

Davies 2007, cat. no. 369; Stefes 2011,
cat. no. 316

pp. 96-98 and 115 (note 1)

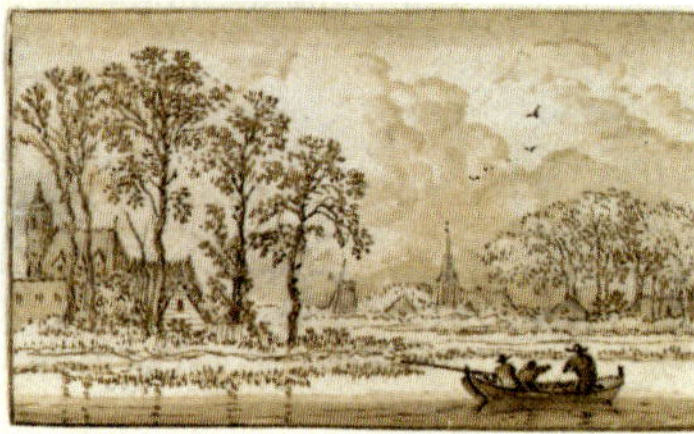

62

River Landscape with a Rowing Boat
Pen and brown ink over traces of graphite,
brown wash; framing lines in pen and brown
ink; 48 x 84 mm
Inv. no. 21894

Davies 2007, cat. no. 382; Stefes 2011,
cat. no. 320

pp. 96-98 and 115 (note 1)

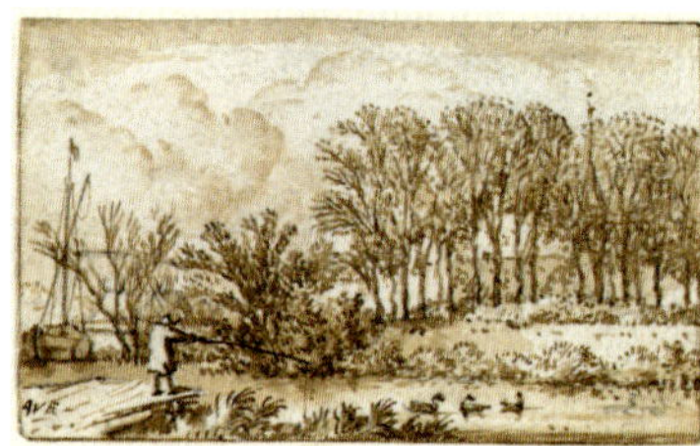

63

Landscape with a Fisherman
Pen and brown ink over traces of graphite,
brown wash; framing lines in pen and brown
ink; 49 x 83 mm
Lower left, in pen and brown ink: AVE
Inv. no. 21895

Davies 2007, cat. no. 383; Stefes 2011,
cat. no. 321

pp. 96-98 and 115 (note 1)

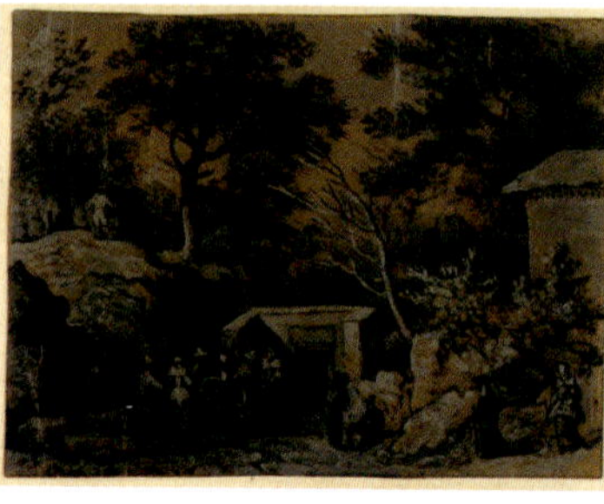

64

The Spring at Sauvenière near Spa
Pen and brush and brown ink, light and dark
grey oil paint, on reddish-brown prepared paper;
remnants of framing lines in pen and brown ink;
128 x 170 mm
Inv. no. 21906

Davies 2007, cat. no. 593; Stefes 2011,
cat. no. 304

pp. 27-28, 73, 96, 140-142 and 144 (note 57)

Cologne
Wallraf-Richartz-Museum
& Fondation Corboud

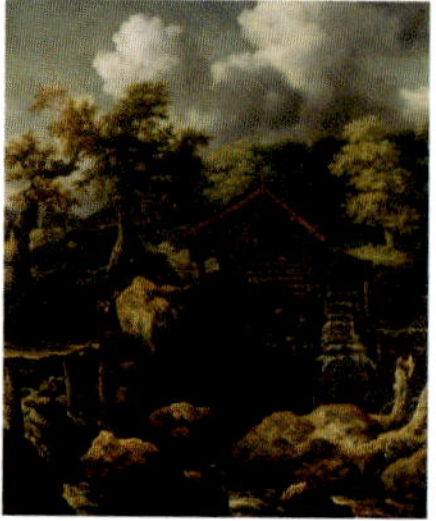

65

Wooded Landscape with a Watermill
Oil on canvas; 73 x 61.5 cm
Lower right: A. EVERDINGEN
Inv. no. WRM 1025

Davies 2001, cat. no. 83

pp. 59-60 and 205

Copenhagen
Statens Museum for Kunst

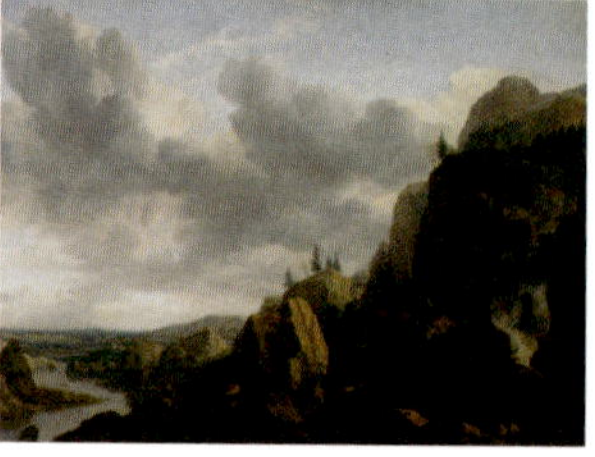

66

Mountain Landscape with a River Valley
Oil on canvas; 82.5 x 111 cm
Lower centre, on the rock under the fallen tree:
A. EVERDINGEN / 1647
Inv. no. KMSsp513

Davies 2001, cat. no. 29; Baarspul in
Copenhagen/Amsterdam 2001, cat. no. 16

pp. 16, 44, 46, 124, 164 and 170-171

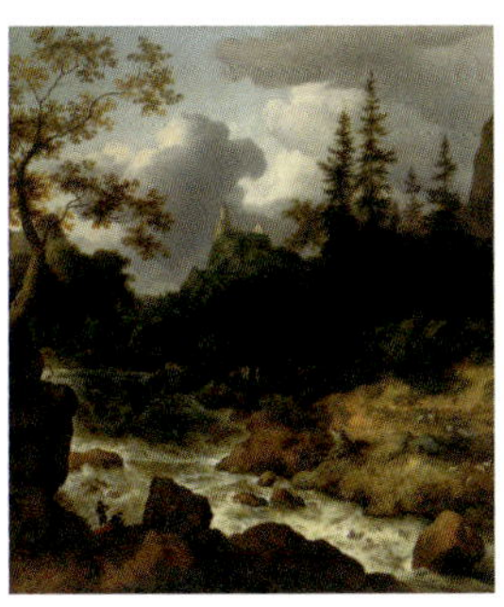

67
Mountain Landscape with a River and a Castle
Oil on canvas; 219 x 193 cm
Lower left: A: v Everdingen
Inv. no. KMSsp512

Davies 2001, cat. no. 107; Monrad in Copen-
hagen/Amsterdam 2001, cat. no. 3; Monrad
2001, pp. 20-22 and 27

Cover and pp. 14, 72-73 and 78

Leipzig
Museum der bildenden Künste
Leipzig

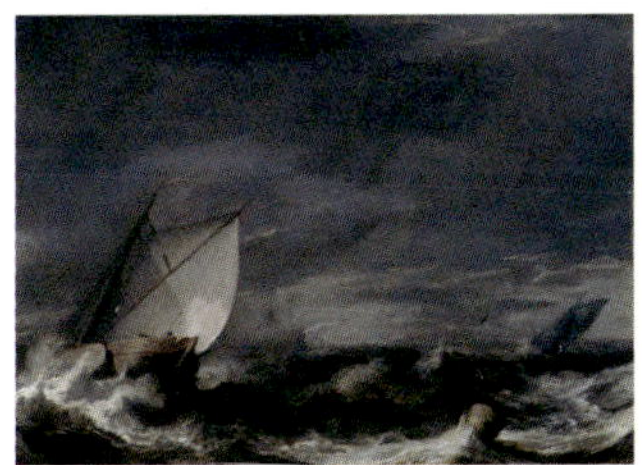

68
Sailing Boats in a Storm
Oil on panel; 26.5 x 37.5 cm
Lower right, on the barrel: AVE
Inv. no. 1007

Davies 2001, cat. no. 7; Nicolaisen 2012,
cat. no. 86; Ossing 2012, fig. 4 (reversed)

pp. 52-53, 55 and 206-207

London
The British Museum

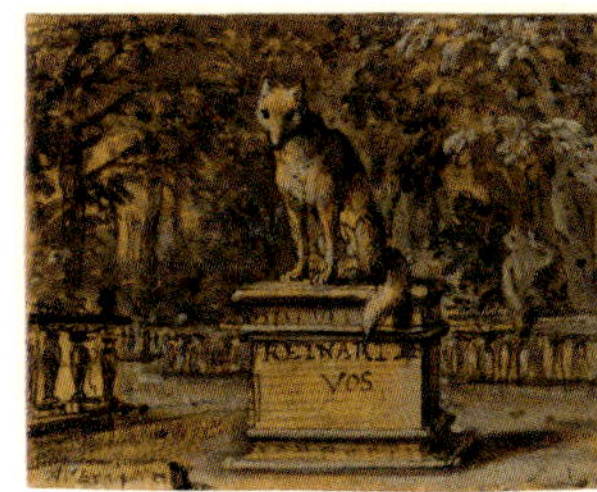

69
Design for the title print of Reynard the Fox
Pen and brush and brown ink, brown wash,
heightened with light grey, on brown prepared
paper; remnants of framing lines in red chalk;
94 x 118 mm
Lower left, in pen and brown ink: AVE
Centre, on the pedestal, in pen and brown ink:
REINART DE / VOS
Inv. no. 1836,0811.187

Davies 2007, cat. no. 594

pp. 147-148 and 150

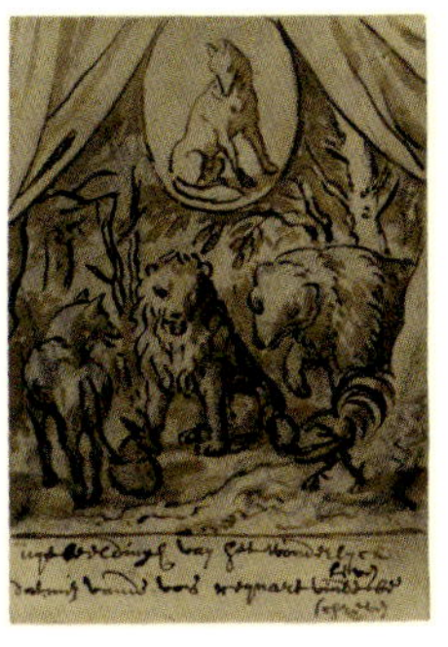

70
Design for the title print of Reynard the Fox
Pen and brush and brown ink over black chalk,
on brown prepared paper; 148 x 104 mm
Below, in pen and brown ink: uytbeeldingh
van het wonderlyck / leven / datmen vande vos
reynart vindt be / schreven
Inv. no. 1836,0811.184

Davies 2007, cat. no. 595

p. 150

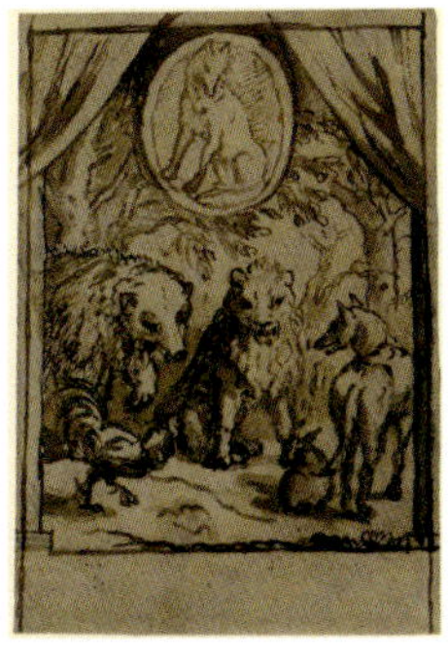

71
Design for the title print of Reynard the Fox
Pen and brush and brown ink over traces of
black chalk, on brown prepared paper; framing
lines in pen and brown ink; 147 x 104 mm
Inv. no. 1836,0811.186

Davies 2007, cat. no. 596

pp. 147 and 150

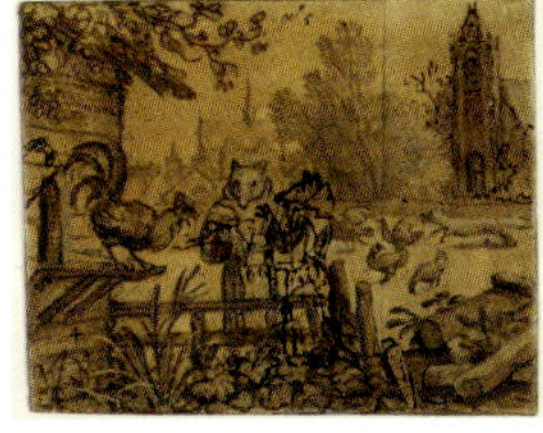

72
Reynard the Fox Deceives Chanticleer the Cock
Pen and brush and brown ink over traces of
red and black chalk, heightened with light grey,
corrections in pen and dark brown ink, on
brown prepared paper; framing lines in pen
and brown ink; outlines indented for transfer;
93 x 119 mm
Inv. no. 1836,0811.191

Davies 2007, cat. no. 603

pp. 158-159

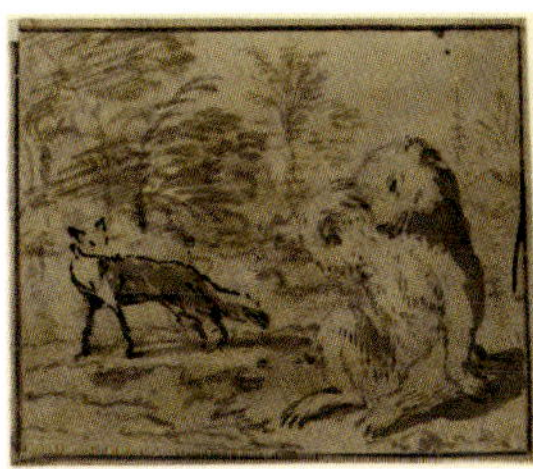

73
Reynard the Fox Mocks Bruin the Bear
Pen and brush and brown ink over traces of
black chalk, on brown prepared paper; framing
lines in pen and brown ink over red chalk;
95 x 117 mm
Inv. no. 1836,0811.196

Davies 2007, cat. no. 605

p. 156

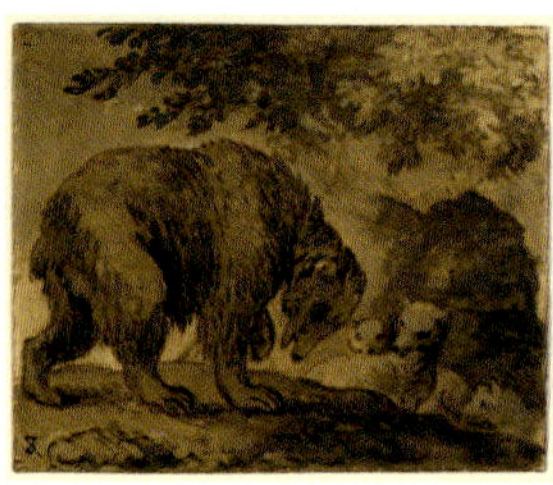

74

Bruin the Bear in Conversation with Reynard the Fox
Pen and brush and brown ink over red chalk, brown wash, heightened with light grey, on brown prepared paper; framing lines in red chalk; 93 x 114 mm
Inv. no. 1852,0519.60

Davies 2007, cat. no. 606

pp. 151 and 158

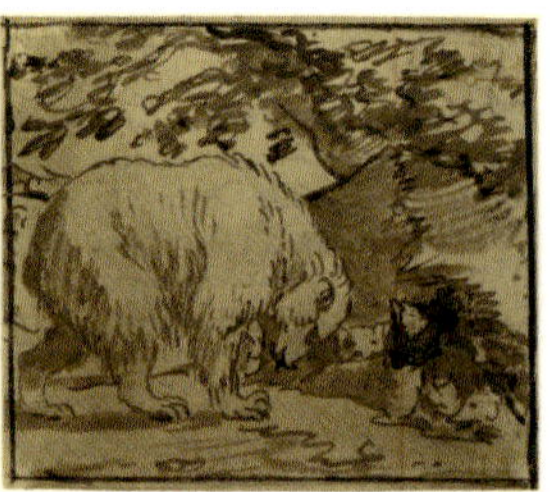

75

Bruin the Bear in Conversation with Reynard the Fox
Pen and brush and brown ink, brown wash, on brown prepared paper; on the right two lines in red chalk; framing lines in pen and brown ink; 97 x 113 mm
Inv. no. 1836,0811.193

Davies 2007, cat. no. 607

pp. 151 and 156

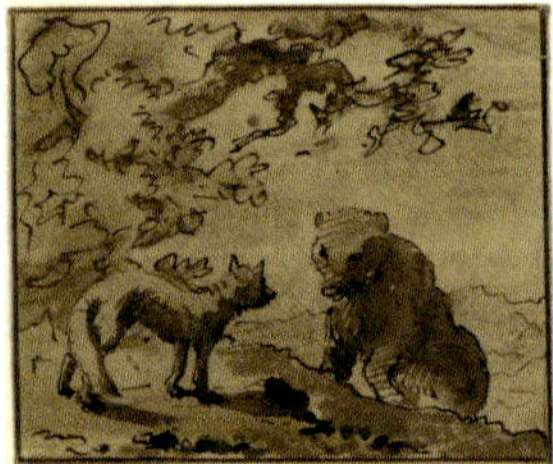

76

Bruin the Bear Addresses Reynard the Fox
Pen and brush and brown ink, brown wash, on brown prepared paper; framing lines in pen and brown ink over red chalk; 95 x 114 mm
Inv. no. 1836,0811.234

Davies 2007, cat. no. 608

p. 158

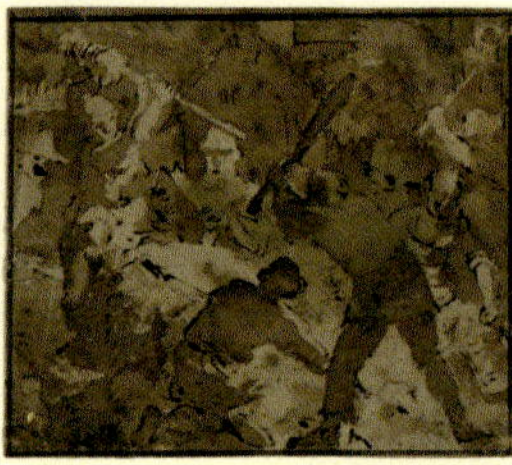

77

Bruin the Bear Beaten by Villagers
Pen and brush and brown ink over traces of black chalk, brown wash, on brown prepared paper; green marks in the middle of the scene; framing lines in pen and brown ink; 96 x 115 mm
Inv. no. 1836,0811.194

Davies 2007, cat. no. 609

pp. 148-149 and 155-156

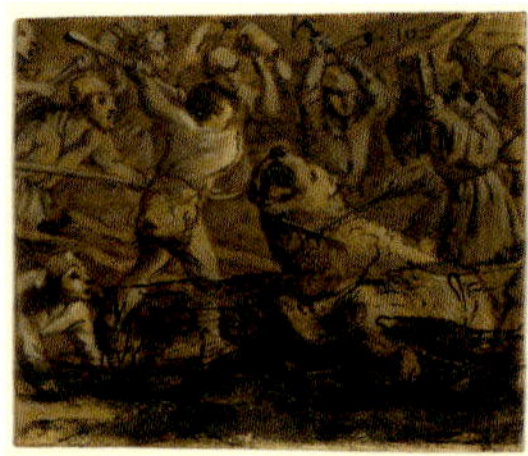

78

Bruin the Bear Beaten by Villagers
Pen and brush and brown ink over traces of red chalk, heightened with light grey, brown wash, corrections in pen and dark brown ink, on brown prepared paper; framing lines in red chalk; 93 x 114 mm
Inv. no. 1836,0811.195

Davies 2007, cat. no. 610

pp. 148-149 and 155-156

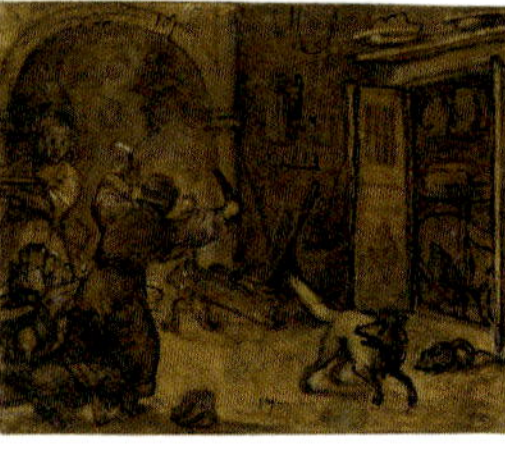

79

Reynard the Fox Tries to Steal a Capon
Pen and brush and brown ink, brown wash, heightened with light grey, corrections in pen and dark brown ink, on brown prepared paper; green marks towards the bottom of the scene; remnants of framing lines in pen and brown ink; 93 x 115 mm
Inv. no. 1836,0811.201

Davies 2007, cat. no. 617

pp. 27-28

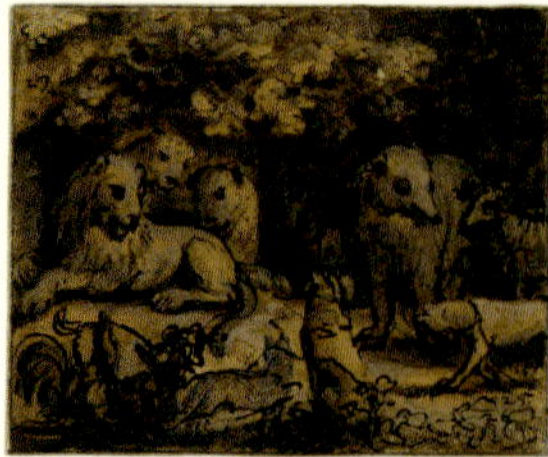

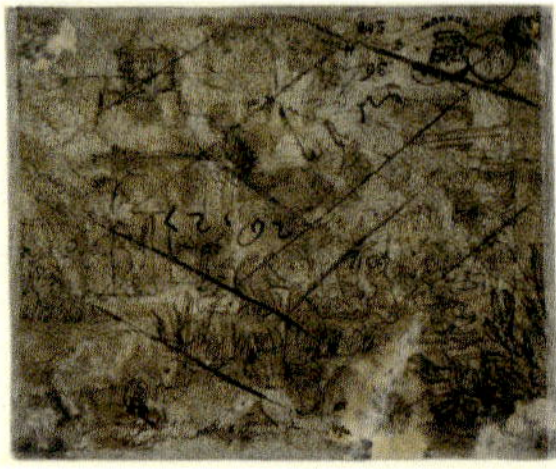

80

Reynard the Fox's Stay of Execution
Pen and brush and brown ink over traces of red chalk, brown wash, heightened with light grey, corrections in pen and dark brown ink, on brown prepared paper; framing lines in pen and brown ink; outlines indented for transfer; 95 x 118 mm
Verso: sketches for *Isengrim the Wolf Rings the Bell*, *Isengrim the Wolf Beaten by Villagers* and *Grimbard the Badger Blesses Reynard the Fox*
Pen and brush and brown ink with conspicuous diagonal lines in pen and brown ink throughout the drawing; rubbed with black chalk for transfer.
Inv. no. 1836,0811.208

Davies 2007, cat. no. 625

pp. 147-148

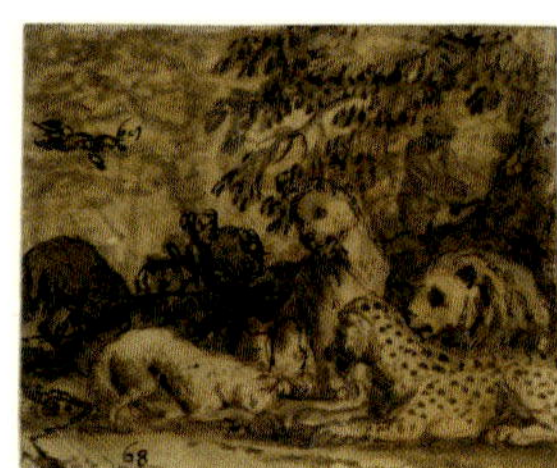

81

Reynard the Fox Lies about a Conspiracy against King Noble the Lion
Pen and brush and brown and grey ink over black and red chalk, brown and grey wash, heightened with light grey, corrections in pen and dark brown ink, on brown prepared paper; remnants of framing lines in red chalk; outlines indented for transfer; 99 x 114 mm
Inv. no. 1836,0811.209

Davies 2007, cat. no. 626

pp. 151-152

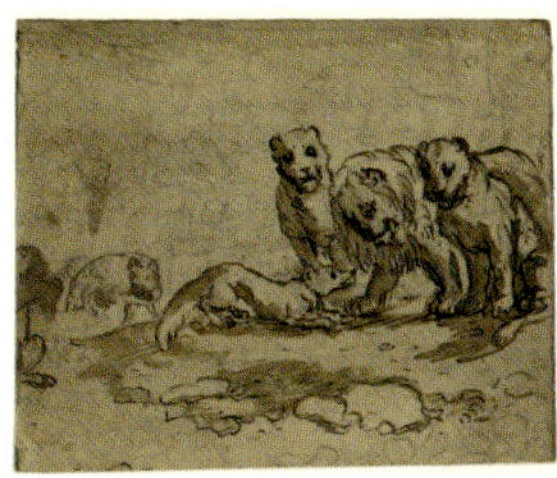

82

Reynard the Fox Lies about a Conspiracy against King Noble the Lion
Pen and brush and brown ink over black chalk, on brown prepared paper; remnants of framing lines in pen and brown ink; 95 x 116 mm
Inv. no. 1836,0811.235

Davies 2007, cat. no. 627

pp. 157-158

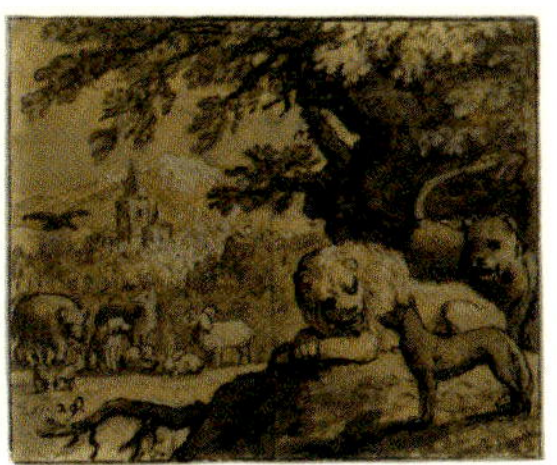

83

Reynard the Fox in Conversation with King Noble the Lion
Pen and brush and brown ink, brown wash, heightened with light grey, on brown prepared paper; framing lines in pen and brown ink; outlines indented for transfer; 95 x 116 mm
Inv. no. 1852,0519.63

Davies 2007, cat. no. 628

pp. 157-158

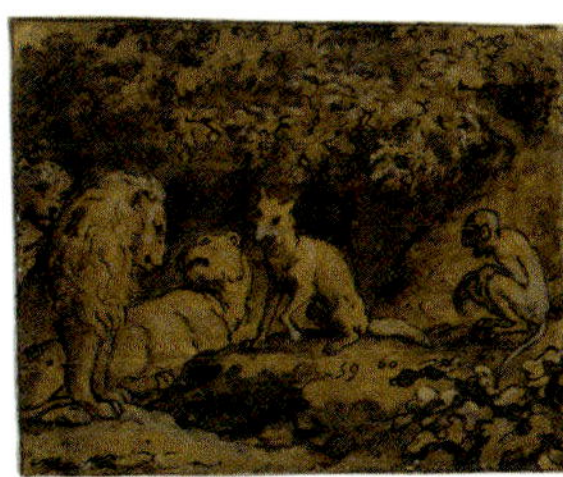

84

Reynard the Fox's Defence
Pen and brush and brown ink, brown wash, heightened with light grey, on brown prepared paper; framing lines in pen and brown ink; outlines indented for transfer; 94 x 116 mm
Inv. no. 1836,0811.210

Davies 2007, cat. no. 629

pp. 157-158

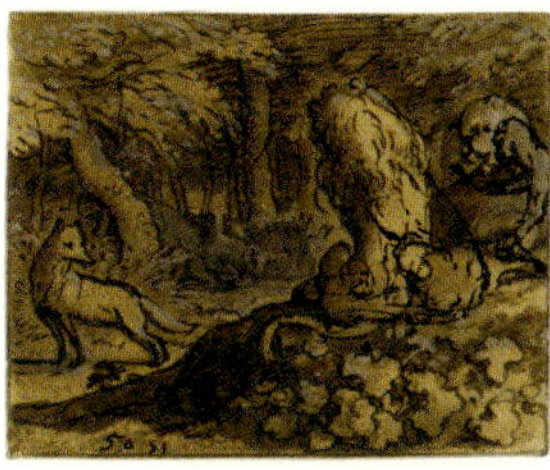

85

Reynard the Fox's Defence
Pen and brush and brown ink over traces of red chalk, brown wash, heightened with light grey, corrections in pen and dark brown ink, on brown prepared paper; framing lines in pen and brown ink; 94 x 116 mm
Inv. no. 1836,0811.236

Davies 2007, cat. no. 630

pp. 156-157

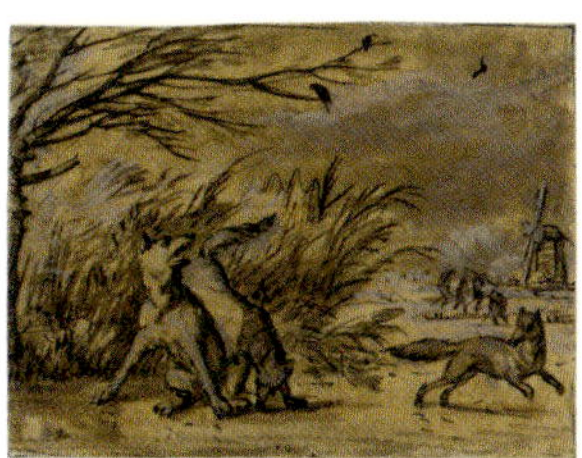

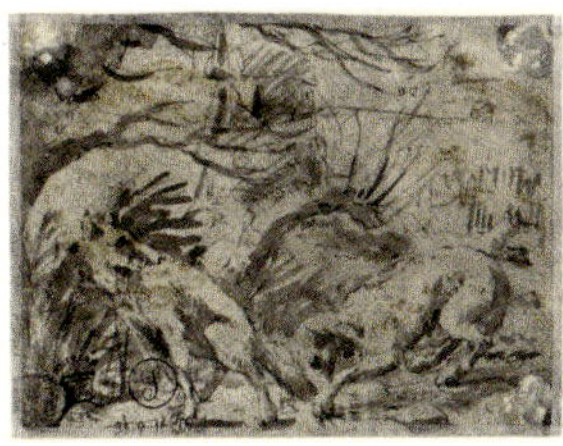

86

Hirsent the She-Wolf Tricked by Reynard the Fox
Pen and brush and brown ink over traces of red chalk, brown wash, heightened with light grey, on brown prepared paper; remnants of framing lines in pen and brown ink; outlines indented for transfer; 90 x 120 mm
Verso: sketch for *Hirsent the She-Wolf Tricked by Reynard the Fox*
Pen and brush and grey ink; rubbed with black chalk for transfer
Inv. no. 1836,0811.227

Davies 2007, cat. no. 650

pp. 154-155

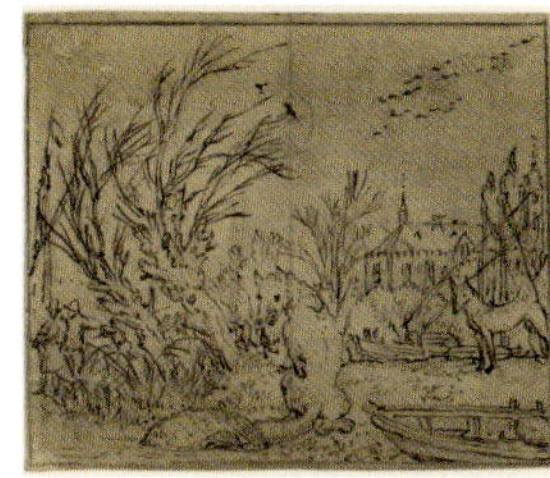

87

Hirsent the She-Wolf Tricked by Reynard the Fox
Pen and brown ink, on brown prepared paper; framing lines in pen and brown ink; 96 x 117 mm
Inv. no. 1836,0811.233

Davies 2007, cat. no. 651

pp. 154-155

Mölndal
Mölndal Municipality

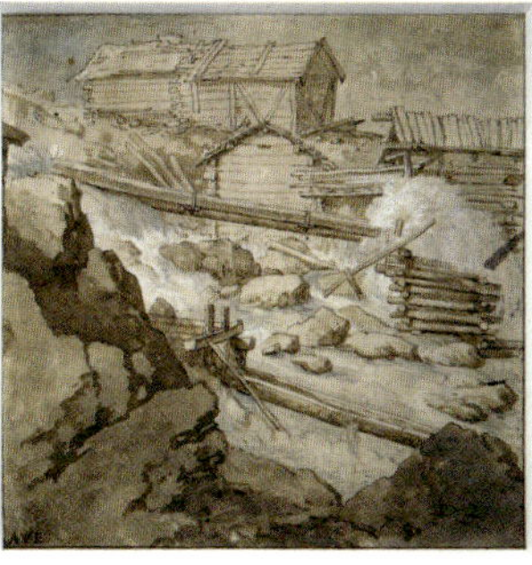

88

Waterfall at Mölndal
Pen and brown ink over black chalk, brown and grey wash, blue watercolour, heightened with white; framing lines in pen and brown ink; 197 x 194 mm
Lower left, in pen and brown ink: AVE
Inv. no. A-752

Davies 2007, cat. no. 21; Magnusson 2018, cat. no.153; Rosengren 2020, pp. 193 and 198

pp. 48, 65, 78-80, 83 and 85

Montreal
The Montreal Museum of Fine Arts

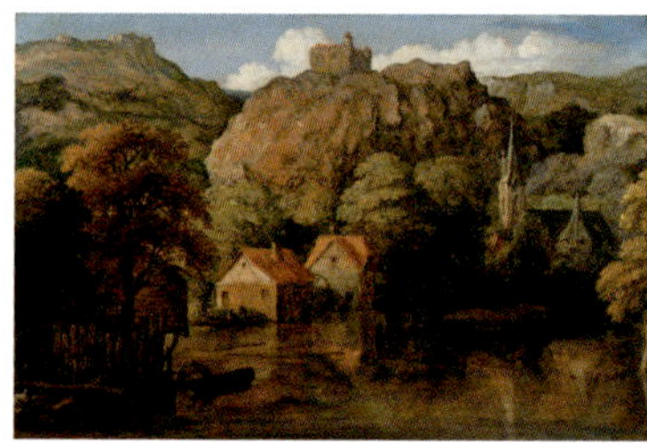

89
Mountain Village on the Water
Oil on panel; 31.8 x 48.1 cm
Lower left, on a tree trunk: […] EVERDINGEN.
1664
Inv. no. 2013.10 (gift of Mr and Mrs
Michal Hornstein)

Davies 2001, cat. no. 44; De Witt 2008,
pp. 128-129 (under cat. no. 74)

pp. 40, 65 and 67

Munich
Bayerische Staatsgemäldesammlungen, Alte Pinakothek

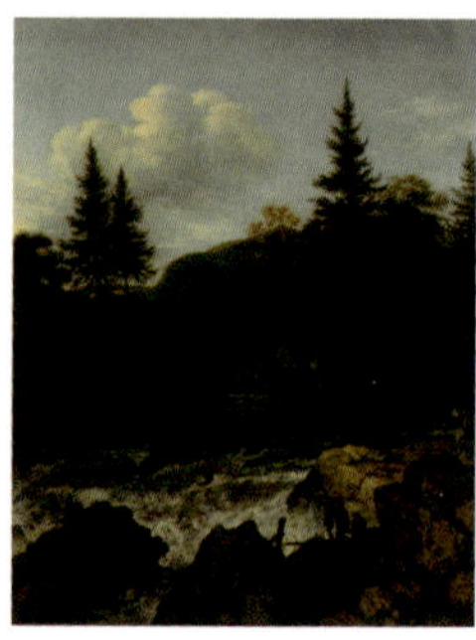

90
*Norwegian Landscape with a Waterfall
and a Watermill*
Oil on canvas; 112.8 x 88.2 cm
Lower right: A v.Everdingen / 1650
Inv. no. 387

Davies 2001, cat. no. 41

pp. 12-13, 48, 59, 125 and 166-167

New York
Collection of Aliis Inserviendo Consumor Foundation

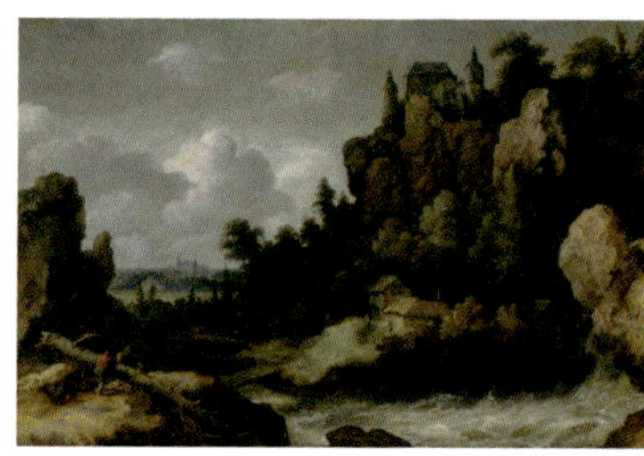

91
Mountain Landscape with a River and a Castle
Oil on canvas; 105.4 x 161.3 cm
Lower centre, on the rock: A v.Everdingen

Davies 2001, cat. no. 133

p. 73

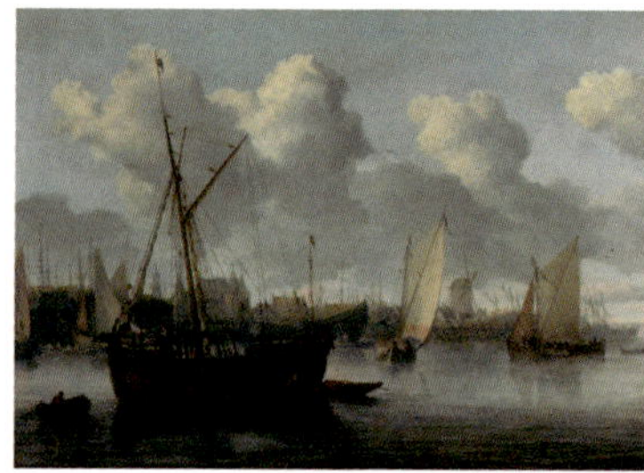

92
Harbour View
Oil on canvas; 68.5 x 96.8 cm
Centre left links, on the leeboard of
the large ship: A.V. EVERDINGEN

Davies 2001, cat. no. 20

pp. 54-55

New York
Stein Berre Collection

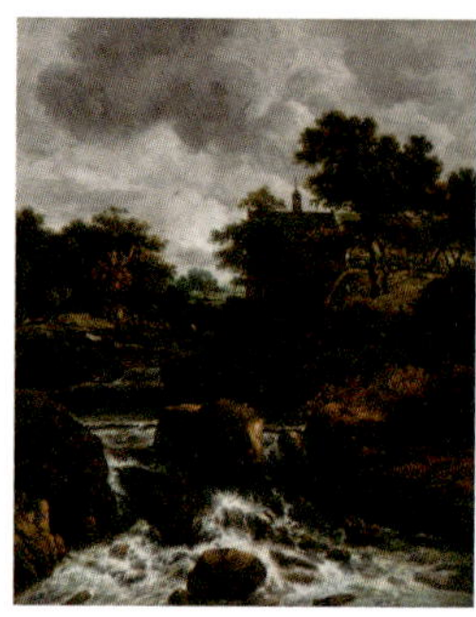

93
Wooded Landscape with a Waterfall and a Chapel
Oil on canvas; 61 x 49.5 cm
Left, on the rock: A.EVERDINGEN

Not in Davies 2001

pp. 60, 63 and 65

Paris
Fondation Custodia

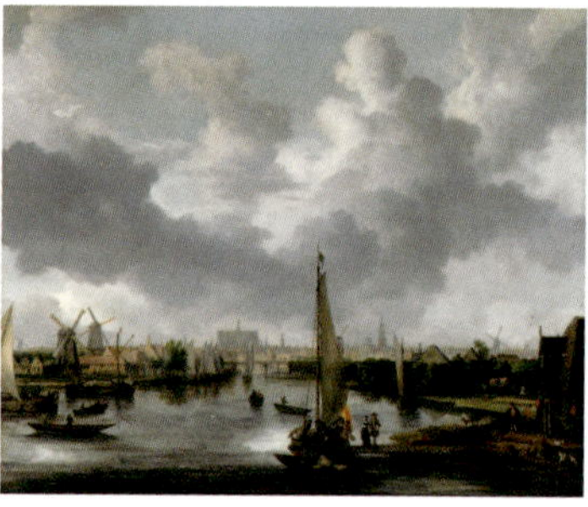

94
View of Alkmaar from the Zeglis
Oil on canvas; 102.5 x 124 cm
Lower right, on the bank under the jetty:
AvEverdingen
Frits Lugt Collection, inv. no. 6036,
on loan to the Stedelijk Museum Alkmaar

Davies 2001, cat. no. 22; Milwaukee 2005,
p. 190 (under cat. no. 89); Den Bosch/
The Hague/Assen 2007, cat. no. 45

pp. 10-11, 55-56, 58-60 and 70

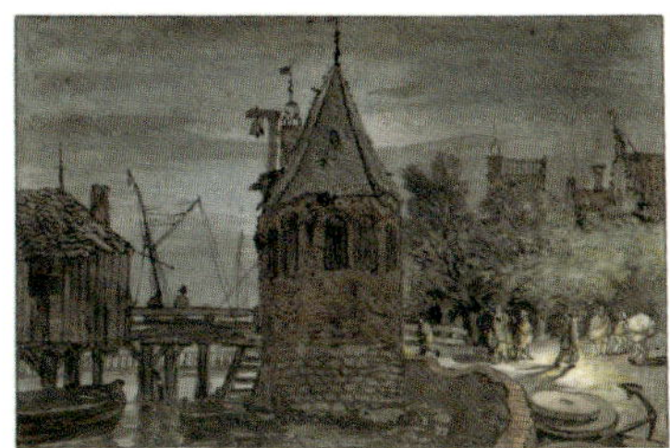

95

Tower in the Evening
Pen and brush and black ink, watercolour;
framing lines in pen and black ink;
149 x 231 mm
Lower left, in pen and black ink: AVE
Frits Lugt Collection, inv. no. 2756

Davies 2007, cat. no. 29

pp. 86 87

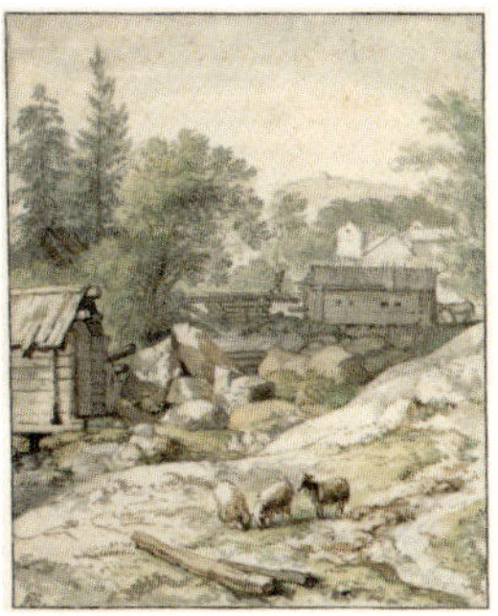

96

Scandinavian Landscape with Log Cabins
Pen and brush and brown and grey ink over
black chalk, watercolour; framing lines in pen
and black ink; 200 x 164 mm
Lower left, in the hand of William Esdaile (Lugt
Marques 2617), in pen and brown ink: WE.
Frits Lugt Collection, inv. no. 3082

Davies 2007, cat. no. 43

pp. 4 and 84-85

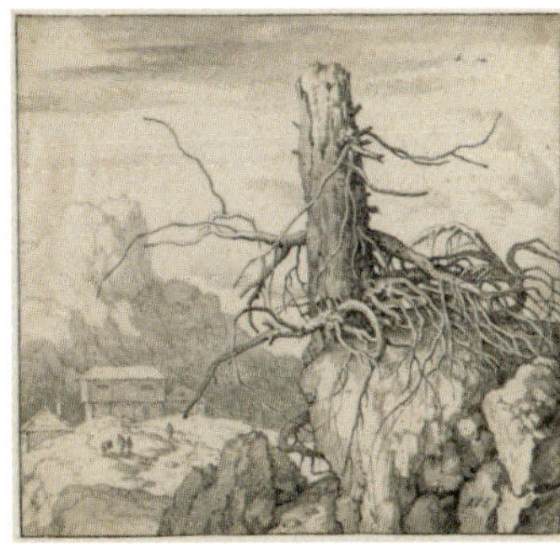

97

*Scandinavian Landscape with an Old Tree
Stump*
Brush and grey ink over black chalk, grey wash;
framing lines in pen and brown and grey ink;
157 x 167 mm
Lower right, in brush and grey ink: AVE
Frits Lugt Collection, inv. no. 2034

Davies 2007, cat. no. 157

pp. 81-82

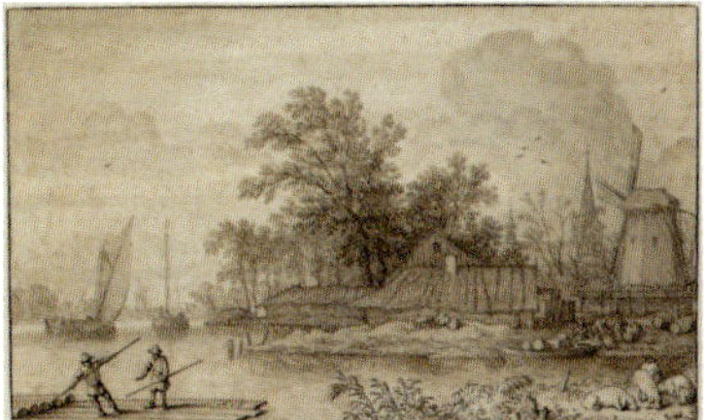

98

River View with a Raft and Sailing Barges
Pen and brush and brown ink over black chalk,
brown wash; framing lines in pen and brown
ink; 179 x 302 mm
Lower left, in pen and brown ink: AVE
Frits Lugt Collection, inv. no. 2648

Davies 2007, cat. no. 217

p. 91

Paris
Petit Palais, Musée des
Beaux-Arts de la Ville de Paris

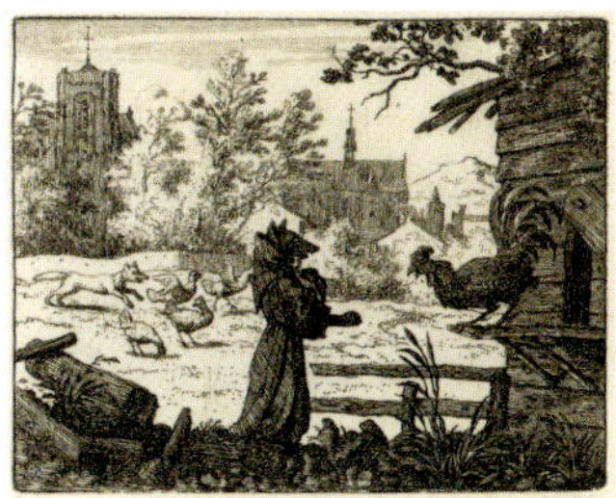

99

Reynard the Fox Deceives Chanticleer the Cock
Etching; 95 x 118 mm
Inv. no. GDUT10346 (Auguste and Eugène
Dutuit Bequest, 1902)

Dut. 6 III; Verzandvoort 1995, pp. 160 and 162;
Feliers 2006, pp. 384-385

pp. 146 and 158-159

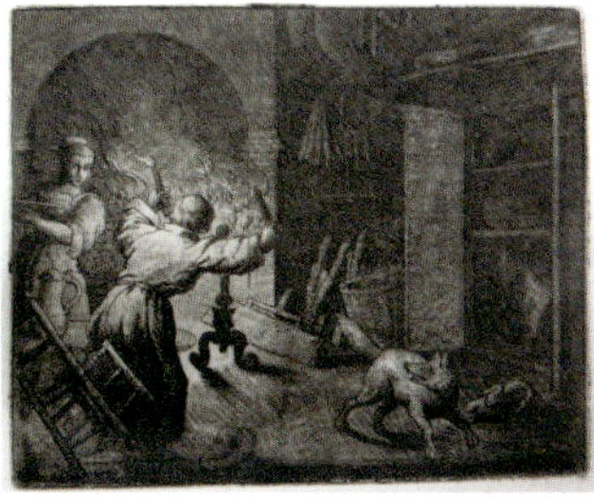

100

Reynard the Fox Tries to Steal a Capon
Etching and mezzotint; 95 x 117 mm
Inv. no. GDUT10392 (Auguste and Eugène
Dutuit Bequest, 1902)

Dut. 20 IV; Verzandvoort 1995, p. 156

pp. 27-28 and 152-153

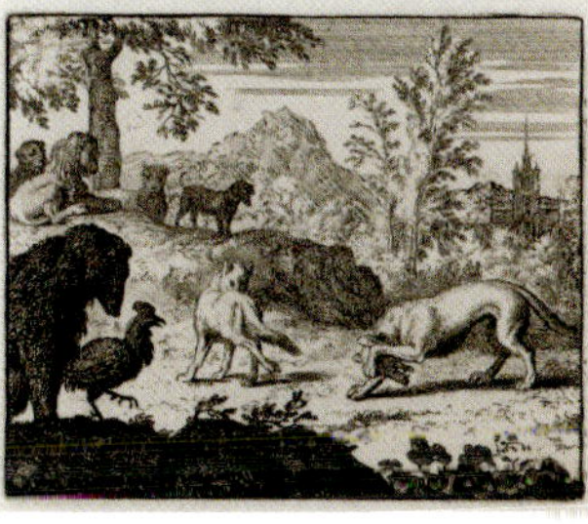

101

*The Fight between Reynard the Fox and
Isengrim the Wolf*
Etching; 98 x 116 mm
Inv. no. GDUT10489 (Auguste and Eugène
Dutuit Bequest, 1902)

Dut. 56 III

pp. 149 and 158

Vienna
The Albertina Museum

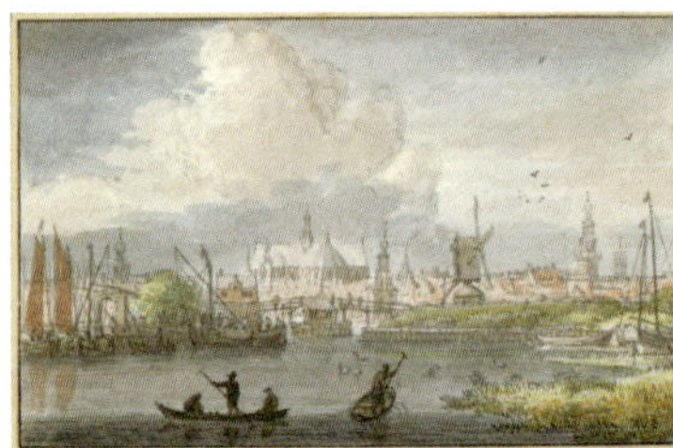

102

View of Alkmaar from the Zeglis
Pen and grey ink, watercolour, heightened
with white; framing lines in pen and black
and brown ink; 112 x 178 mm
Lower right, in brush and black ink: AVE
Inv. no. 9582

Davies 2007, cat. no. 57; Den Bosch/The Hague/
Assen 2007, p. 90 (under cat. no. 45)

pp. 55-56, 58 and 94

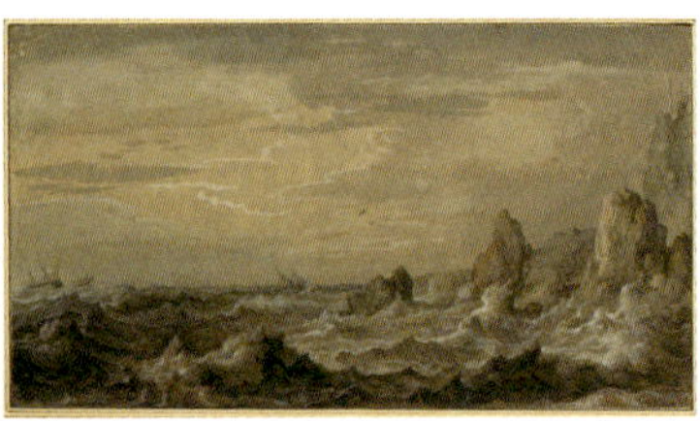

103

Rocky Shore in Stormy Weather
Brush and grey and brown ink over black chalk,
grey and brown wash, heightened with white,
on brown paper; traces of framing lines in pen
and black ink; 225 x 416 mm
Lower right, in brush and brown ink: AVE
Inv. no. 9590

Davies 2007, cat. no. 112

pp. 87 and 90-91

Private Collection

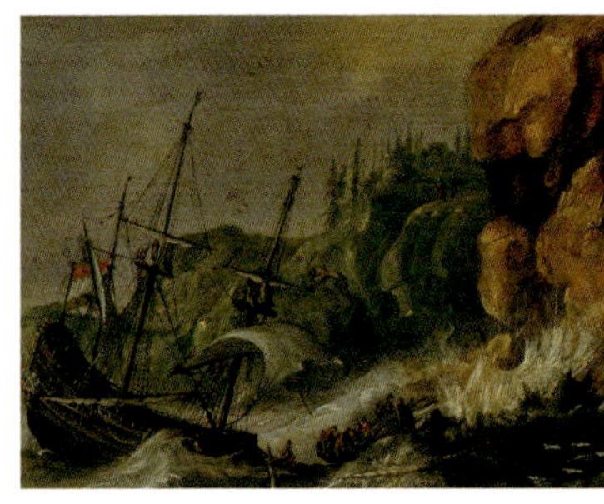

104

Shipwreck off a Rocky Coast
Oil on panel; 34 x 42 cm
Lower right: A.V.Everdingen f

Davies 2001, cat. no. 5

pp. 16, 18, 31, 42-43 and 110

Private Collection

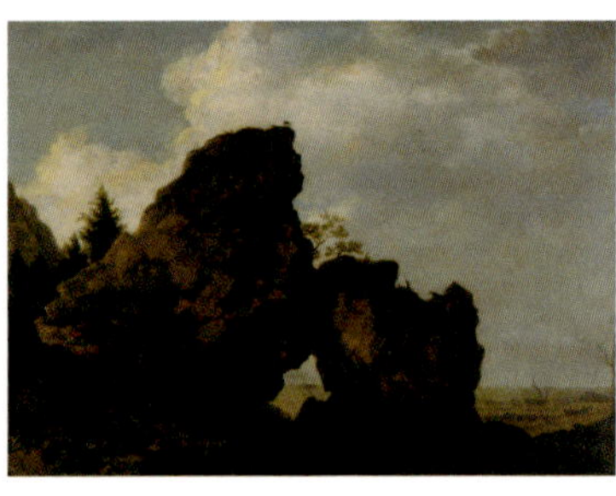

105

Rocky Coastal Landscape
Oil on panel; 33 x 45 cm
Lower left: A.v.EVERDINGEN
On loan to the Dordrechts Museum,
inv. no. DM/017/1279

Davies 2001, cat. no. 115

pp. 46-47 and 110-111

Private Collection

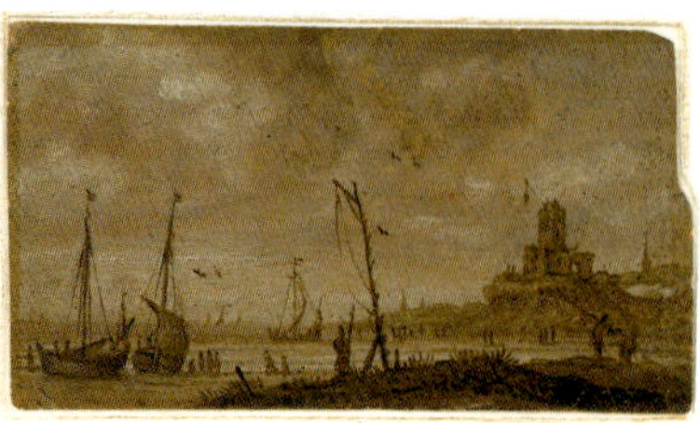

106

View of the Beach with a Beacon
Brush and brown and white oil paint on paper;
46 x 83 mm

Not in Davies 2007

pp. 104-105, 107 and 115 (note 23)

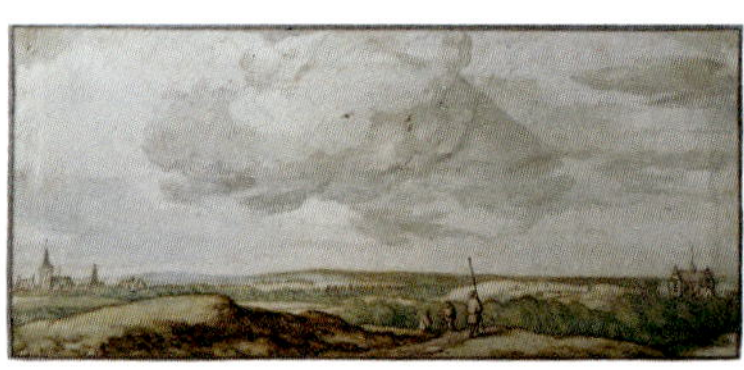

107

Panoramic Landscape with Three Figures
Pen and brush and brown ink, grey wash,
watercolour; framing lines in pen and brown ink;
105 x 230 mm
Lower left, in pen and brown ink: AVE

Davies 2007, cat. no. 65

pp. 83 and 107

Watermarks in Allart van Everdingen's Etchings

This appendix documents the contemporary watermarks in Allart van Everdingen's etchings that are held in the Rijksmuseum Print Room in Amsterdam. Landscape prints are indicated by a number in Hollstein (Allart van Everdingen) (Holl.); prints of Reynard the Fox by a number in Dutuit 1881 (Dut.).

The job of comparing and identifying these watermarks was made considerably easier by the X-rays that Sterre Hoek and Henryk van Hugten took of a large proportion of the marks found. The watermarks are arranged by type (Pascal Lamb, Arms of Amsterdam, Foolscap), then by variant (indicated with a capital letter) and finally by 'twin mark' (indicated with lower-case letters).[1]

In 1951-1952, the book historian Alan Stevenson explained that watermarks are always 'twins'. In the seventeenth century, paper was produced with two moulds—each with the same watermark, but with minute differences—that were used alternately to create a new sheet. A stack of paper therefore always contains two virtually identical watermarks.[2] This is clear to see in the watermarks in Allart van Everdingen's prints. Where more than one watermark of the same type is found, both twin marks have been identified in each case. Without an X-ray it is almost impossible to distinguish the twin marks with certainty. For this reason, the watermarks that were not X-rayed, but could clearly be identified

as a particular type by visual comparison, are listed separately. Each watermark description is accompanied by a reference to very similar marks in watermark manuals. They are intended purely as comparisons; none of these marks is completely identical to those in the paper used for Van Everdingen's etchings.

The watermarks presented here can be only roughly dated. It is, however, clear from a comparison of the prints on the different papers that the Arms of Amsterdam type referred to below must be earlier than the documented Foolscap. The first state of the *Landscape with a Large Rock* (Holl. 18) occurs on paper with the Arms of Amsterdam (cat. no. 9), whereas the second state is found with the Foolscap mark. Finally, it can be inferred from the occurrence of the Foolscap below in two impressions worked up with mezzotint (Holl. 91 and Dut. 54) that this must have been done by Allart van Everdingen himself, not after his death.

Compiler
Erik Hinterding

---

1 The same system was used (and explained) in Hinterding 2006. See vol. 2, pp. 9-11.
2 Stevenson 1951-1952.

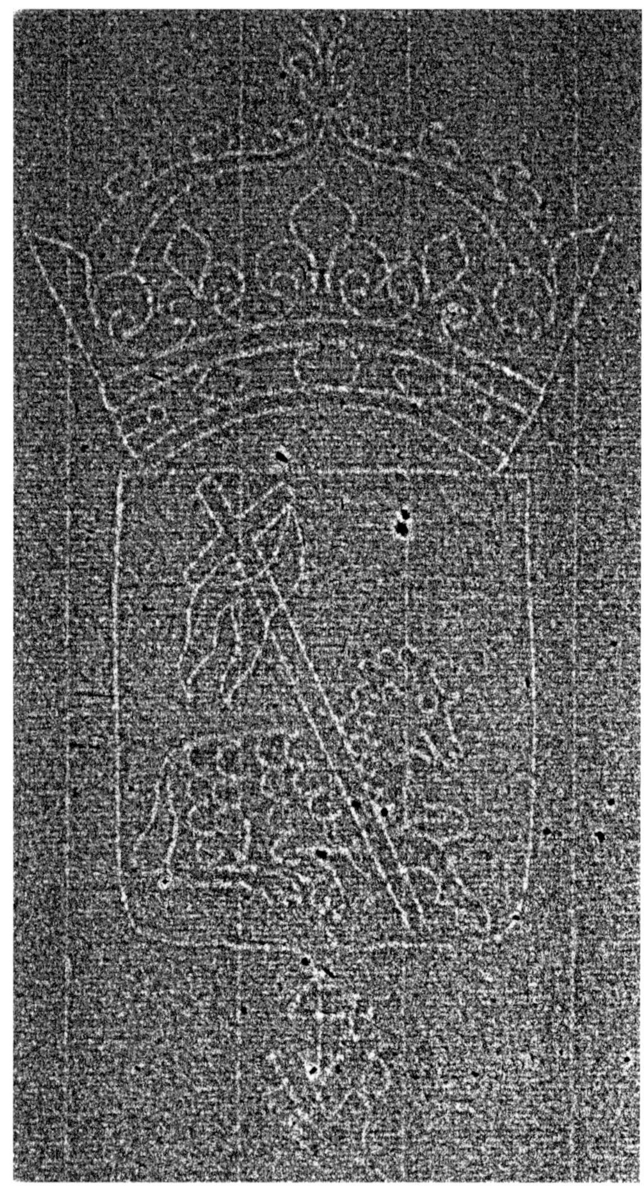

Pascal Lamb, type A.a., inv. no. RP-P-1979-90 (cat. no. 7)

Pascal Lamb

A. The Lamb of God (recumbent lamb with
a flag of the Cross) on a shield. Above the
shield a French crown. Below it '4' and
the initials 'WR'. Probably around 1651.
Cf. Hinterding 2006, vol. 2, pp. 165-166
and 394-395 (c. 1651)

a. Holl. 4 I(5) – inv. no. RP-P-1979-90
(cat. no. 7)

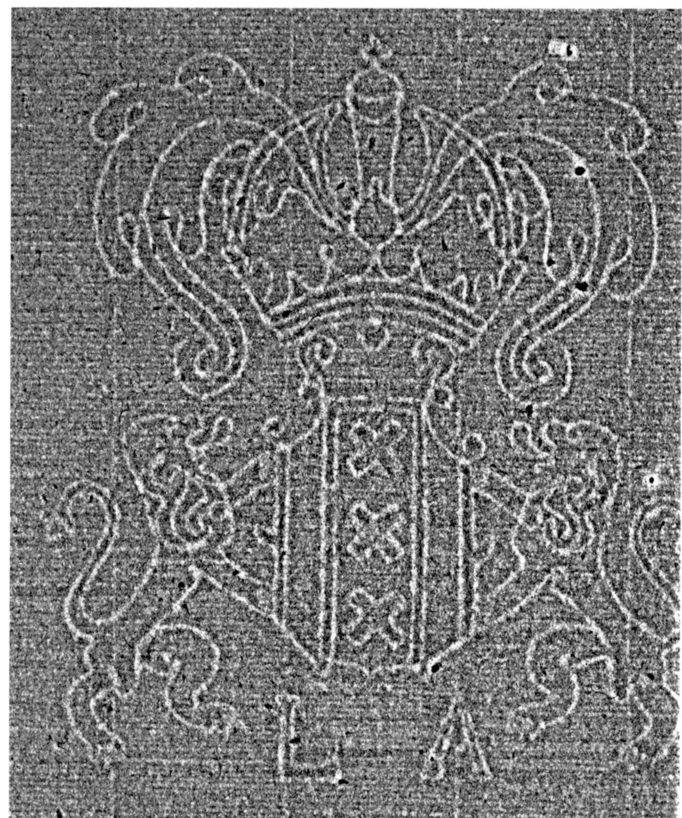

Arms of Amsterdam, type A.a.a., inv. no. RP-P-1879-A-3072

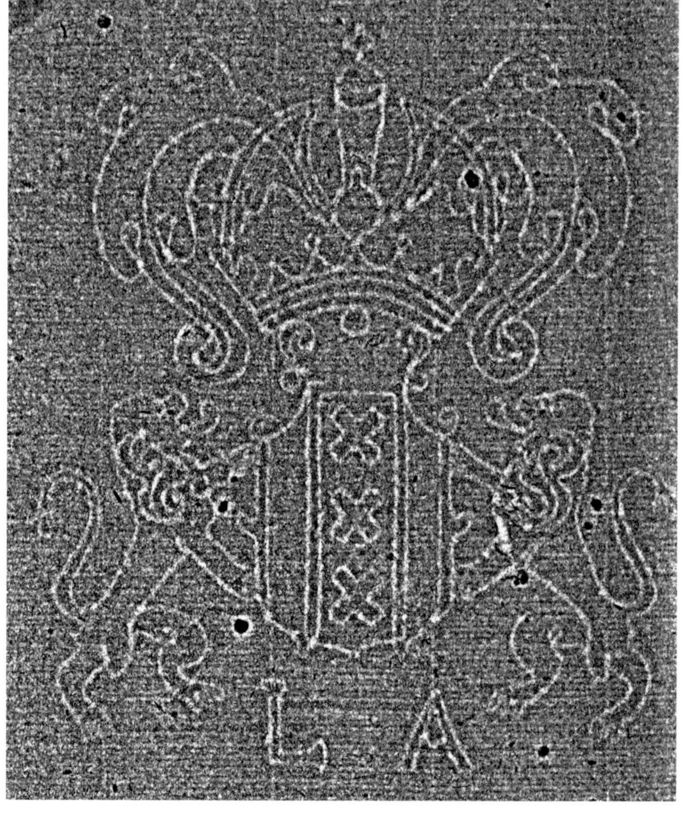

Arms of Amsterdam, type A.a.b., inv. no. RP-P-1879-A-3083

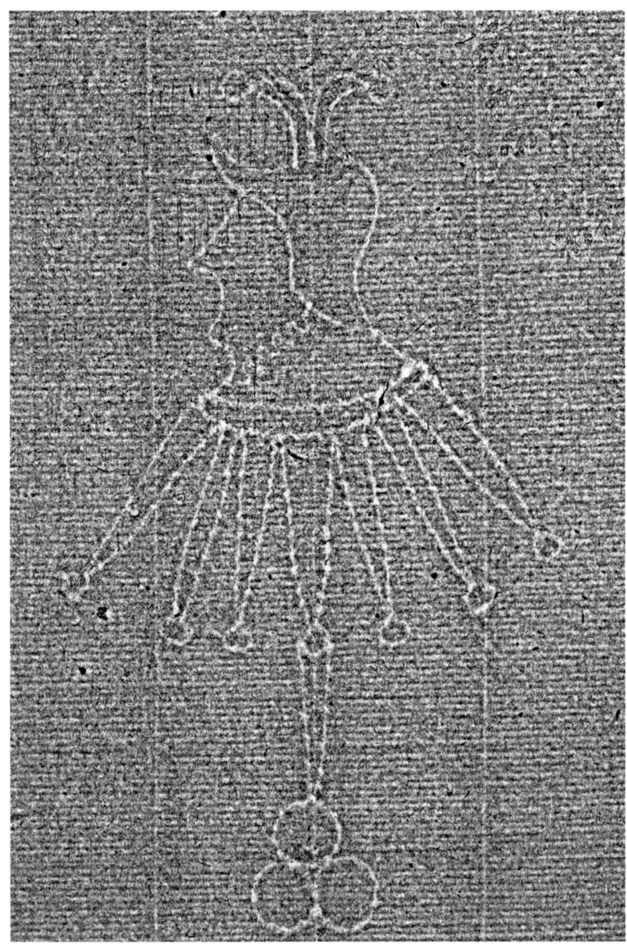

Foolscap, type A'.a.a., inv. no. RP-P-OB-50.352

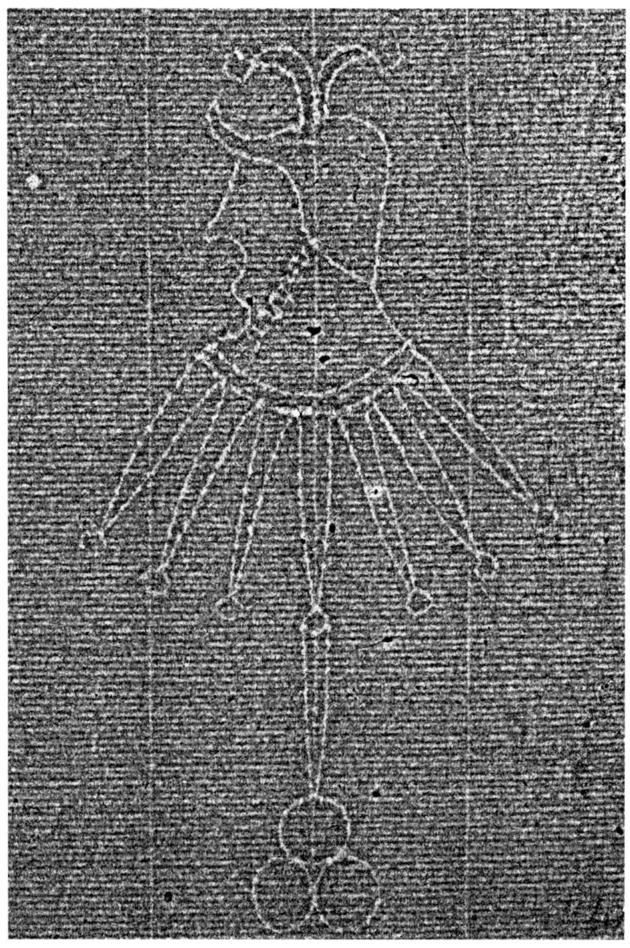

Foolscap, type A'.a.b., inv. no. RP-P-OB-50.423

Arms of Amsterdam

A. Tripartite shield with three St Andrew's crosses below one another in the middle segment. Lions rampant on either side of the shield. Above the shield an imperial crown surrounded with plumes. The initials 'LA' separately below the shield. Probably around 1675.
Cf. Laurentius 2008, nos. 190-191 and 204 (1674-1675), with or without different initials.

Identical watermarks:
a.a. Holl. 18 I(4) – inv. no. RP-P-1879-A 3058
(cat. no. 9)
Holl. 50 I(4) – inv. no. RP-P-1879-A-3072
Holl. 55 II(3) – inv. no. RP-P-1879 A 3074
(cat. no. 18)

Almost identical to the above:
a.b. Holl. 70 II(4) – inv. no. RP-P-1879-A-3083

The same Arms of Amsterdam watermark, but not X-rayed:
Holl. 41 II(5) – inv. no. RP-P-1879-A-3067
(cat. no. 13)

Foolscap with seven-pointed collar

A'. Head of a jester with a seven-pointed collar with bells on the ends of the points. His cap looks like a helmet with two striking small points on top. The middle collar point extends to three rings at the bottom of the watermark. Chain line through the middle of the watermark. Probably around 1675, or slightly later.
Cf. Heawood 1950, nos. 2021 (1674) and 2023 (1676); Likhachev 1994, nos. 3542 and 3543 (1685-1700); Gaudriault 1995, no. 1022 (1675)

Identical watermarks:
a.a. Holl. 2 II(3) – inv. no. RP-P-OB-50.275
Holl. 9 I(3) – inv. no. RP-P-OB-50.288
Holl. 10 II(4) – inv. no. RP-P-OB-50.290
Holl. 13 I(3) – inv. no. RP-P-OB-50.294
Holl. 18 II(4) – inv. no. RP-P-OB-50.301
Holl. 30 II(3) – inv. no. RP-P-OB-50.320
Holl. 31 IV(5) – inv. no. RP-P-OB-50.322
Holl. 36 I(3) – inv. no. RP-P-OB-50.331
Holl. 44 II(3) – inv. no. RP-P-OB-50.345
Holl. 48 II(3) – inv. no. RP-P-OB-50.352
Holl. 52 II(3) – inv. no. RP-P-OB-50.360
Holl. 53 I(2) – inv. no. RP-P-OB-50.362
Dut. 54 III(5) – inv. no. RP-P-OB-50.501
Dut. 57 II(5) – inv. no. RP-P-OB-50.504

Identical watermarks, almost identical to the above:
a.b. Holl. 6 II(3) – inv. no. RP-P-OB-50.282
Holl. 11 II(4) – inv. no. RP-P-OB-50.291
Holl. 81 I(2) – inv. no. RP-P-OB-50.375
Holl. 84 I(2) – inv. no. RP-P-OB-50.412
Holl. 90 I(2) – inv. no. RP-P-OB-50.421
Holl. 91 I(2) – inv. no. RP-P-OB-50.423

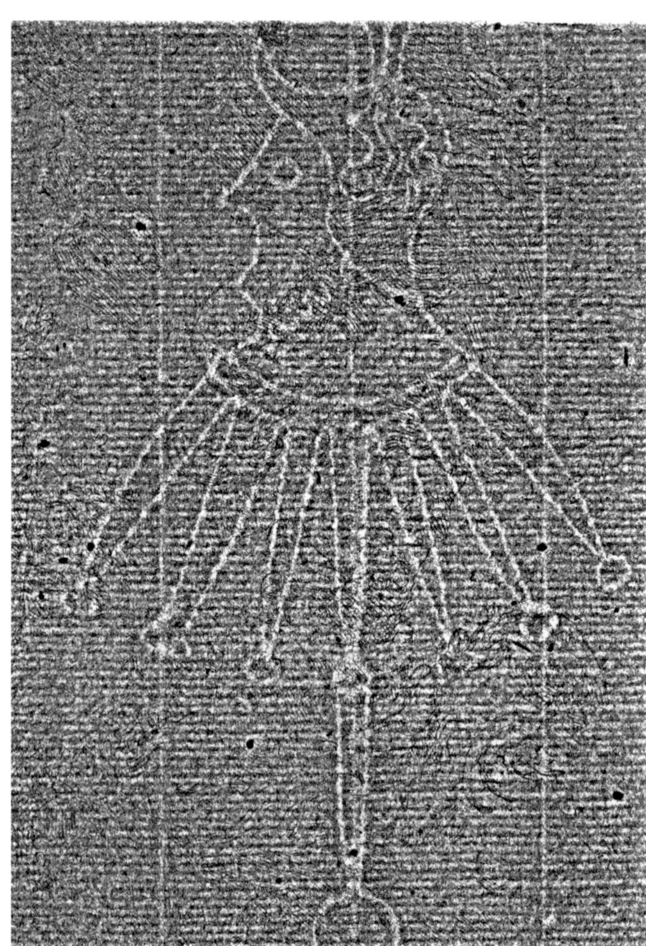

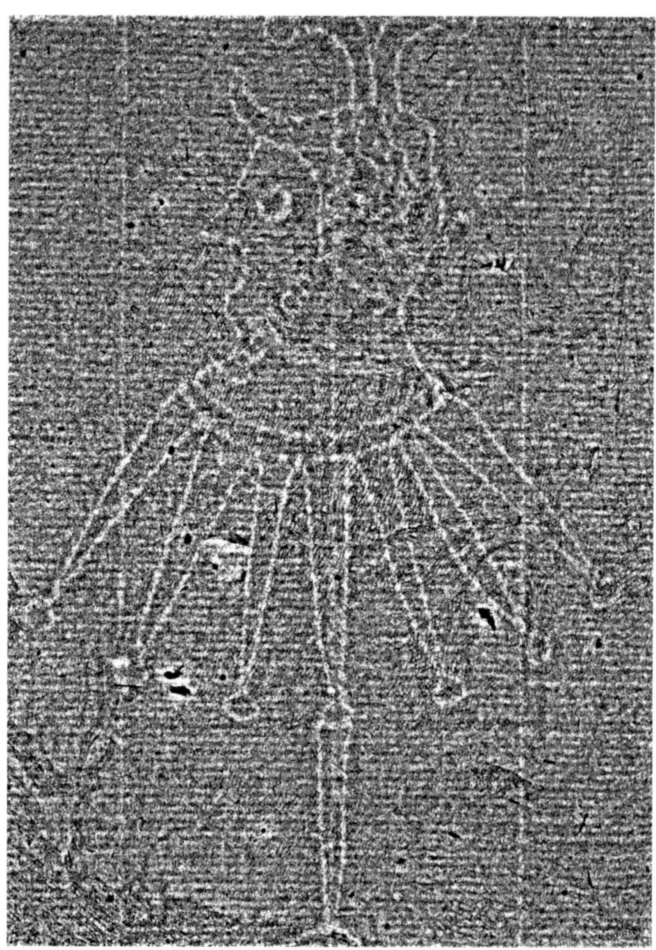

Foolscap, type A'.b.a., inv. no. RP-P-OB-50.459   *Foolscap, type A'.b.b., inv. no. RP-P-OB-50.502*

**Identical watermarks,
closely related to the above:**

b.a. Dut. 13 II(4) – inv. no. RP-P-OB-50.459
Dut. 14 II(4) – inv. no. RP-P-OB-50.460
Dut. 21 II(5) – inv. no. RP-P-OB-50.468
Dut. 53 II(4) – inv. no. RP-P-OB-50.500
(cat. no. 35)
Dut. 56 II(4) – inv. no. RP-P-OB-50.503

Almost identical to the above:

b.b. Dut. 55 II(4) – inv. no. RP-P-OB-50.502

**The same Foolscap watermarks,
but not X-rayed:**

Holl. 15 I(3) – inv. no. RP-P-OB-50.296
Holl. 19 II(4) – inv. no. RP-P-OB-50.304
Holl. 33 I(2) – inv. no. RP-P-OB-50.326
Holl. 38 II(3) – inv. no. RP-P-OB-50.335
Holl. 45 III(5) – inv. no. RP-P-OB-50.347
Holl. 56 III(4) – inv. no. RP-P-OB-50.367
Holl. 57 I(4) – inv. no. RP-P-1879-A-3075
Holl. 58 II(4) – inv. no. RP-P-OB-50.370
Holl. 59 II(3) – inv. no. RP-P-OB-50.372
Holl. 60 II(3) – inv. no. RP-P-OB-50.374
Holl. 66 II(3) – inv. no. RP-P-OB-50.383
Holl. 68 I(2) – inv. no. RP-P-OB-50.387
Holl. 69 III(4) – inv. no. RP-P-OB-50.389
Holl. 72 I(3) – inv. no. RP-P-OB-50.394
Holl. 74 II(3) – inv. no. RP-P-OB-50.398
Holl. 75 II(3) – inv. no. RP-P-OB-50.400
Holl. 79 III(4) – inv. no. RP-P-1882-A-6407
Holl. 80 III(4) – inv. no. RP-P-1882-A-6408
Holl. 89 II(3) – inv. no. RP-P-OB-50.419
Holl. 93 I(2) – inv. no. RP-P-1887-A-12056
Holl. 94 II(4) – inv. no. RP-P-OB-50.427
Holl. 96 II(3) – inv. no. RP-P-OB-50.431 (cat. no. 22)
Holl. 97 I(2) – inv. no. RP-P-OB-50.432 (cat. no. 23)
Holl. 98 I(2) – inv. no. RP-P-OB-50.434 (cat. no. 24)

Holl. 99 III(4) – inv. no. RP-P-OB-50.436
Dut. 4 I(4) – inv. no. RP-P-OB-50.450
Dut. 8 II(4) – inv. no. RP-P-OB-50.454 (cat. no. 30)
Dut. 17 I(4) – inv. no. RP-P-OB-50.463
Dut. 23 II(4) – inv. no. RP-P-OB-50.470
Dut. 25 II(4) – inv. no. RP-P-OB-50.472
Dut. 27 II(4) – inv. no. RP-P-OB-50.474 (cat. no. 32)
Dut. 33 Ia(3) – inv. no. RP-P-OB-50.480 (cat. no. 33)
Dut. 34 III(4) – inv. no. RP-P-OB-50.481
Dut. 35 II(4) – inv. no. RP-P-OB-50.482
Dut. 37 II(4) – inv. no. RP-P-OB-50.484
Dut. 40 I(3) – inv. no. RP-P-OB-50.487
Dut. 41 II(4) – inv. no. RP-P-OB-50.488
Dut. 44 II(4) – inv. no. RP-P-OB-50.491
Dut 45 II(4) – inv. no. RP-P-OB-50.492
Dut. 46 II(4) – inv. no. RP-P-OB-50.493
Dut. 47 II(4) – inv. no. RP-P-OB-50.494
Dut. 49 III(5) – inv. no. RP-P-OB-50.496
Dut. 50 II(4) – inv. no. RP-P-OB-50.497
Dut. 51 I(3) – inv. no. RP-P-OB-50.498

Abecedario 1853-1854
P. de Chennevières and A. de Montaiglon (eds.), *Abecedario de P.J. Mariette et autres notes inédites de cet amateur sur les arts et les artistes*, vol. 2, Paris 1853-1854

Akveld 1996
L.M. Akveld, 'Verklaring van de namen van enige zeventiende-eeuwse Nederlandse scheepstypen, en van sommige van hun constructiedelen', in Rotterdam/Berlin 1996, pp. 21-35

Alkmaar 2015
C.M. Klinkert and A. Taatgen, *Claes Jacobsz van der Heck (ca. 1578-1652). Een Alkmaarse schilder in de Gouden Eeuw*, exh. cat. Alkmaar (Stedelijk Museum Alkmaar) 2015

Alkmaar/Helsinki 2016
C.M. Klinkert and Y. Bleyerveld (eds.), *Caesar van Everdingen (1616/1617-1678). Schilder met een vleiend penseel*, exh. cat. Alkmaar (Stedelijk Museum Alkmaar) / Helsinki (Sinebrychoff Art Museum/Finnish National Gallery) 2016 (English edition: *Caesar van Everdingen (1616/1617-1678): Painting Beauty*)

Allen 1987
E.J. Allen, *The Life and Art of Pieter Molyn*, dissertation University of Maryland 1987

Amburger 1957
E. Amburger, *Die Familie Marselis. Studien zur russischen Wirtschaftsgeschichte*, Giessen 1957

Amsterdam 1993a
B. Bakker and H. Leeflang, *Nederland naar 't leven. Landschapsprenten uit de Gouden Eeuw*, exh. cat. Amsterdam (Museum het Rembrandthuis) 1993

Amsterdam 1993b
M. Schapelhouman and P. Schatborn, *Tekeningen van oude meesters. De verzameling Jacobus A. Klaver*, exh. cat. Amsterdam (Rijksmuseum) 1993

Amsterdam 1997
W. Loos, R.-J. te Rijdt and M. van Heteren, *Langs velden en wegen. De verbeelding van het landschap in de 18de en 19de eeuw*, exh. cat. Amsterdam (Rijksmuseum) 1997

Amsterdam 1999
B. van den Boogert et al., *Goethe & Rembrandt. Tekeningen uit Weimar*, exh. cat. Amsterdam (Museum Het Rembrandthuis) 1999

Amsterdam 2000
E. Runia, *De glorie van de Gouden Eeuw. Nederlandse kunst uit de 17de eeuw. Tekeningen en prenten*, exh. cat. Amsterdam (Rijksmuseum) 2000 (English edition: *The Glory of the Golden Age: Dutch Art in the 17th Century: Drawings and Prints*)

Amsterdam/Boston/Philadelphia 1987
P.C. Sutton, *Masters of 17th-Century Dutch Landscape Painting*, exh. cat. Amsterdam (Rijksmuseum) / Boston (Museum of Fine Arts) / Philadelphia (Philadelphia Museum of Art) 1987

Amsterdam/London 2016
B. Cornelis and M. Schapelhouman, *Adriaen van de Velde: Dutch Master of Landscape*, exh. cat. Amsterdam (Rijksmuseum) / London (Dulwich Picture Gallery) 2016

Aubert 1947
A. Aubert, *Die Nordische Landschaftsmalerei und Johan Christian Dahl*, Berlin 1947

Bakker, Fleurbaay and Gerlagh 1989
B. Bakker, E. Fleurbaay and A.W. Gerlagh, *De verzameling Van Eeghen. Amsterdamse tekeningen 1600-1950*, 2nd revised edition, Amsterdam (Gemeentearchief) / Zwolle 1989

Bang 1987
M.L. Bang, *Johann Christian Dahl 1788-1857: Life and Works*, 3 vols., Oslo 1987

Bartilla 2010
S. Bartilla, '"Wie soudt ghedroomen?" De landschapskunst van Roelandt Savery', in Prague/Kortrijk 2010, pp. 55-75

Bartsch 1803
B.
A. Bartsch, *Le Peintre Graveur*, vol. 2, Vienna 1803, pp. 156-246 (Allart van Everdingen)

Basan 1767
F. Basan, *Dictionnaire des graveurs anciens et modernes depuis l'origine de la gravure; avec une notice des principales estampes qu'ils ont gravées*, 3 vols., Paris 1767

Bätschmann 2002
O. Bätschmann and D. Britt (eds.), *Carl Gustav Carus: Nine Letters on Landscape Painting, Written in the Years 1815-1824; with a Letter from Goethe by Way of Introduction*, Los Angeles 2002

Beck 1972-1973
H.-U. Beck, *Jan van Goyen 1596-1656. Eine Oeuvreverzeichnis in zwei Bänden*, 2 vols., Amsterdam 1972-1973

Beck 1987
H.-U. Beck, *Jan van Goyen 1596-1656. Eine Oeuvreverzeichnis. Ergänzungen zum Katalog der Handzeichnungen und Ergänzungen zum Katalog der Gemälde*, Doornspijk 1987

Beck 1998
H.-U. Beck, *Pieter Molyn 1595-1661. Katalog der Handzeichnungen*, Doornspijk 1998

De Beer 2002
G. de Beer, *Ludolf Backhuysen (1630-1708). Sein Leben und Werk*, Zwolle 2002

De Beer 2019
G. de Beer, *The Golden Age of Dutch Marine Painting: The Inder Rieden Collection*, 4 vols., Leiden 2019

De Beer 2019a
G. de Beer, 'The Inder Rieden Collection and Dutch Marine painting of the Golden Age: The two major tendencies, the innovators, the followers and two influential masters of a related genre', in De Beer 2019, vol. 1, pp. 25-125

Bergen 2018
L. Daatland and T. Myrva (eds.), *J.C. Dahl: The Power of Nature*, exh. cat. Bergen (KODE) 2018

Birmingham 2006
P. Spencer-Longhurst, *Moonrise over Europe: J.C. Dahl and Romantic Landscape*, exh. cat. Birmingham (The Barber Institute of Fine Arts) 2006

Birmingham 2012
A. Sumner and G. Smith (eds.), *In Front of Nature: The European Landscapes of Thomas Fearnley*, exh. cat. Birmingham (The Barber Institute of Fine Arts) 2012

Le Blanc 1854
Le Blanc, *Manuel de l'amateur d'estampes*, vol. 2, Paris 1854

Blanc 2016
J. Blanc, 'The Sensible Natures: Allart Van Everdingen and the Tradition of Sublime Landscape in Seventeenth-Century Dutch Painting', *Journal of Historians of Netherlandish Art* 8 (2016), no. 2, pp. 1-48, accessible online

Bleyerveld 2017
Y. Bleyerveld, 'Een teruggevonden *Strandgezicht met schepen* van Allart van Everdingen in Stedelijk Museum Alkmaar', *Delineavit et Sculpsit* 2017, no. 41, pp. 53-59

Bleyerveld 2022
Y. Bleyerveld, 'On the spot: the appeal of the local', in S. Anderson and J. Seidenstein (eds.), *Crossroads: Drawing the Dutch Landscape*, exh. cat. Cambridge, Massachusetts (Harvard Art Museums) 2022 [forthcoming]

Bleyerveld and Veldman 2016
Y. Bleyerveld and I.M. Veldman, *The Netherlandish Drawings of the 16th Century in Teylers Museum*, Leiden 2016

Boers 2012
M. Boers, *De Noord-Nederlandse kunsthandel in de eerste helft van de zeventiende eeuw*, Hilversum 2012

Bolten 2007
J. Bolten, *Abraham Bloemaert c. 1565-1651: The Drawings*, 2 vols., Leiden 2007

Bonn/Frankfurt/Düsseldorf/Kiel 1986
J. Göres (ed.), *Goethe in Italien*, exh. cat. Bonn (Wissenschaftszentrum) / Frankfurt am Main (Goethehaus) / Düsseldorf (Goethe-Museum Düsseldorf) / Kiel (Landesbibliothek Kiel) 1986

Den Bosch/The Hague/Assen 2007
C. Dumas et al., *Meesters en molens. Van Rembrandt tot Mondriaan*, exh. cat. Den Bosch (Noordbrabants Museum) / The Hague (Museum Bredius) / Assen (Drents Museum) 2007

Boston/Saint Louis 1981
C. Ackley, *Printmaking in the Age of Rembrandt*, exh. cat. Boston (Museum of Fine Arts) / Saint Louis (Saint Louis Art Museum) 1981

Brand and Paul 2020
R. Brand and C. Paul, 'Houthalen met schepen uit de Nederlanden in een Noorse baai', *Scheepshistorie* 2020, no. 28, pp. 26-41

Bredius 1892
A. Bredius, 'De schilder Johannes van de Cappelle', *Oud-Holland* 10 (1892), pp. 26-40

Brenninkmeyer-de Rooij 1984
B. Brenninkmeyer-de Rooij, 'Theorie van de kunst', in Haak 1984, pp. 60-70

Breul 1927
K. Breul (ed.), *The Cambridge Reinaert Fragments (Culemann Fragments)*, Cambridge 1927

Briels 1997
J. Briels, *Vlaamse schilders en de dageraad van Hollands Gouden Eeuw 1585-1630*, Antwerp 1997

Broos 1984
B.P.J. Broos, '"Notitie der Teekeningen van Sybrand Feitama": de boekhouding van drie generaties verzamelaars van oude Nederlandse tekenkunst', *Oud Holland* 98 (1984), pp. 13-39

Broos 1985
B.P.J. Broos, '"Notitie der Teekeningen van Sybrand Feitama", II: "verkocht, verhandeld, veréerd, geruild en overgedaan"', *Oud Holland* 99 (1985), pp. 110-154

Broos and Schapelhouman 1993
B. Broos and M. Schapelhouman, *Oude tekeningen in het bezit van het Amsterdams Historisch Museum, waaronder de collectie Fodor. Nederlandse tekenaars geboren tussen 1600 en 1660*, Amsterdam/Zwolle 1993

Bruijn 1985
J.R. Bruijn, 'The timber trade: the case of Dutch-Norwegian relations in the 17th century', in A. Bang-Andersen, B. Greenhill and E.H. Grude (eds.), *The North Sea: A Highway of Economic and Cultural Exchange: Character—History*, Stavanger/Oslo/Bergen/Tromsø 1985, pp. 123-135

Brussels/Amsterdam/Aachen 2007
S. Hautekeete, *Tekeningen uit de Gouden Eeuw in de verzameling van Jean de Grez*, Brussels (Koninklijke Musea voor Schone Kunsten van België) / Amsterdam (Museum Het Rembrandthuis) / Aachen (Suermondt-Ludwig-Museum) 2007

Brussels/Rome 1995
H. Devisscher et al., *Fiamminghi a Roma 1508-1608. Kunstenaars uit de Nederlanden en het prinsbisdom Luik te Rome tijdens de Renaissance*, exh. cat. Brussels (Paleis voor Schone Kunsten) / Rome (Palazzo delle Esposizione) 1995

Brussels/Rotterdam/Paris/Bern 1968
C. van Hasselt, *Landschaptekeningen van Hollandse meesters uit de XVIIe eeuw uit de particuliere verzameling bewaard in het Institut Néerlandais te Paris*, exh. cat. Brussels (Albert I-Bibliotheek) / Rotterdam (Museum Boymans Van Beuningen) / Paris (Institut Néerlandais) / Bern (Kunstmuseum) 1968

Budapest 2014
I. Ember (ed.), *Rembrandt and the Dutch Golden Age*, exh. cat. Budapest (Szépmüvészeti Múzeum) 2014

Buijsen 1992
E. Buijsen, 'Tussen fantasie en werkelijkheid: 17de eeuwse Hollandse landschapschilderkunst / Between Fantasy and Reality: 17th Century Dutch Landscape Painting', in Tokyo/Kasama/Kumamoto/Leiden 1992, pp. 45-63

Buijsen 2018
E. Buijsen, *De schilderijenproductie van Adriaen Pietersz. van de Venne (1589-1662). Traditie – innovatie – commercie*, 2 vols., dissertation Radboud Universiteit (Nijmegen) 2018

Buijsen et al. 1998
E. Buijsen et al., *Haagse Schilders in de Gouden Eeuw*, The Hague/Zwolle 1998

Bull, Sønstevold and Hammer 1927
E. Bull, V. Sønstevold and S. C. Hammer, *Kristianias historie 1624-1740*, Oslo 1927

Burger-Wegener 1976
C. Burger-Wegener, *Johannes Lingelbach 1622-1674*, unpublished dissertation Freie Universität Berlin 1976

Büttner 2004
N. Büttner, '"Noordsche lantgezigten" – Allaert van Everdingen, Jacob van Ruisdael und die neue Sicht auf die Welt in die Kosmographie', in B. Mahlmann-Bauer (ed.), *Scientiae et artes. Die Vermittlung alten und neuen Wissens in Literatur, Kunst und Musik*, Wiesbaden 2004, vol. 2, pp. 1053-1075, accessible online

Buvelot 2004
Q. Buvelot, *Royal Picture Gallery Mauritshuis: A Summary Catalogue*, The Hague/Zwolle 2004

Bødtker 1938
R. Bødtker, *Norsk fløtnings historie inntil 1860*, Oslo 1938

Bøggild Johannsen 1993
B. Bøggild Johannsen, *Nye Danske kunsthistorie*, vol. 2: *Kongens kunst*, Copenhagen 1993

Cambridge 2016
W. Robinson and S. Anderson, *Drawings from the Age of Bruegel, Rubens, and Rembrandt: Highlights from the Collection of the Harvard Art Museums*, Cambridge, Massachusetts (Harvard Art Museums) 2016

Carasso 1992
D. Carasso, 'Een nieuw beeld. Duitse en Franse denkers over de zeventiende-eeuwse Nederlandse schilderkunst 1775-1860', in Grijzenhout and Van Veen 1992, pp. 161-192

Carus 1831
C.G. Carus, *Neun Briefe über Landschafts-malerei, geschrieben in den Jahren 1815-1824. Zuvor ein Brief von Goethe als Einleitung*, Leipzig 1831

Chapel Hill/Ithaca/Worcester 1999
F.W. Robinson and S. Peck, *Fresh Woods and Pastures New: Seventeenth-Century Dutch Landscape Drawings from the Peck Collection*, exh. cat. Chapel Hill (Ackland Art Museum) / Ithaca, New York (Herbert F. Johnson Museum of Art) / Worcester, Massachusetts (Worcester Art Museum) 1999

Chong 1987
A. Chong, 'The Market for Landscape Painting', in Amsterdam/Boston/Philadelphia 1987, pp. 104-120

Copenhagen/Amsterdam 2001
L.B. Rønberg, K. Monrad and R. Linnet, *Twee Gouden Eeuwen. Schilderkunst uit Nederland en Denemarken*, exh. cat. Copenhagen (Statens Museum for Kunst) / Amsterdam (Rijksmuseum) 2001 (English edition: *Two Golden Ages: Masterpieces of Dutch and Danish Painting*)

Cornelis 1995
B. Cornelis, 'A reassessment of Arnold Houbraken's *Groote Schouburgh*', *Simiolus* 23 (1995), pp. 163-180

Cuijpers 2014
P. Cuijpers, *Van Reynaert de vos tot Tijl Uilenspiegel. Op zoek naar een canon van volksboeken 1600-1900*, Zutphen 2014

Daae 1871
L. Daae, *Det gamle Christiania, 1624-1814*, Christiania [Oslo] 1871

Dardonville 1830
H. Dardonville, *Des eaux minérales de Spa*, Spa/Liège 1830

Davies 1992
A.I. Davies, *Jan van Kessel (1641-1680)*, Doornspijk 1992

Davies 2001
A.I. Davies, *Allart van Everdingen 1621-1675: First Painter of Scandinavian Landscape*, Doornspijk 2001

Davies 2007
A.I. Davies, *The Drawings of Allart van Everdingen: A Complete Catalogue, Including the Studies for Reynard the Fox*, Doornspijk 2007

Davies 2013
A.I. Davies, 'Two Tempests by Allart van Everdingen for Marijke', in Dumas et al. 2013, pp. 93-97

Davies 2014
A.I. Davies, *Anthonie van Borssom (1630-1677): A Catalogue of his Drawings*, Doornspijk 2014

Deligne 2003
A. Deligne, *La terre qui vit. Peinture et savoirs chez Carl Gustav Carus*, Villeneuve-d'Ascq 2003

Denk 2019
C. Denk, 'The Physiognomy of the North—Dahl, Fearnley and Balke', in *Wanderlust: Romantic Landscapes from the Asbjørn Lunde Collection*, exh. cat. Munich (Daxer & Marschall) *s.a.* [2019]

Denmark 1988
S. Heiberg, *Christian IV and Europe: The 19th Art Exhibition of the Council of Europe*, exh. cat. Denmark (exhibition staged over ten Danish institutions, including the Statens Museum for Kunst and Nationalmuseet in Copenhagen) 1988

Derkinderen-Besier 1950
J.H. Derkinderen-Besier, *Spelevaart der mode. De kledij onzer voorouders in de zeventiende eeuw*, Amsterdam 1950

Descamps 1754
J.B. Descamps, *La vie des peintres flamands, allemands et hollandais, avec des portraits gravés and taille-douce*, vol. 2, Paris 1754

Drugulin 1873
W. Drugulin, *Allart van Everdingen. Catalogue raisonné de toutes les estampes qui forment son oeuvre gravé. Supplément au peintre-graveur de Bartsch*, Leipzig 1873

Dumas 2015
C. Dumas, *De Rotterdamse landschapstekenaar Gerard van Rossum (1699-1772) en zijn ver-zameling van voornamelijk zeventiende-eeuwse landschapstekeningen*, The Hague 2015

Dumas and Plomp 1998
C. Dumas and M. Plomp, 'Karel la Fargue (1738-1793) as a forger of seventeenth-century Dutch drawings', *Oud Holland* 112 (1998), pp. 1-76

Dumas et al. 2013
C. Dumas et al. (ed.), *Liber Amicorum Marijke de Kinkelder. Collegiale bijdragen over landschap-pen, marines en architectuur*, The Hague 2013

Dutuit 1881
Dut.
E. Dutuit, *Manuel de l'amateur d'estampes*, vol. 4: *Écoles Flamande et Hollandaise*, Paris 1881, pp. 293-350 (Allart van Everdingen—Landscapes) and pp. 350-380 (Allart van Everdingen—Reynard the Fox)

Erftemeijer 2011
A. Erftemeijer, *De aap van Rembrandt. Kunstenaarsanekdotes van de klassieke oudheid tot heden*, 3rd edition, Haarlem 2011 (originally published 2000)

Essen/Vienna/Antwerp 2003
S. Beele and N. Peeters, *De uitvinding van het landschap. Van Patinir tot Rubens 1520-1650*, exh. cat. Essen (Villa Hügel) / Vienna (Kunst-historisches Museum Wien) / Antwerp (Koninklijk Museum voor Schone Kunsten Antwerpen) 2003

Van Eynden 1787
R. van Eynden, *Antwoord op de vraag van Teylers Tweede Genootschap voor den jaare MDCCLXXXII uitgeschreven over den natio-naalen smaak der Hollandsche school in de teken- en schilderkunst*, Haarlem 1787

Van Eynden and Van der Willigen 1816-1840
R. van Eynden and A. van der Willigen, *Geschiedenis der vaderlandsche schilderkunst, sedert de helft der XVIII eeuw*, 4 vols., Haarlem 1816-1840

Feitama 1746
S. Feitama, *Notitie der Teekeningen, uit de Oudste en latere Aantekeningen, sedert de Jaren 1685 en 1690, somtyds met volle zekerheid, somtyds naar de beste gissinge, of naar myn geheugen, opgemaakt*, handwritten manuscript dated 1746 in RKD – Netherlands Institute for Art History, The Hague

Feliers 1994
W. Feliers, 'Reynaert-ex-libris-kroniek', *Tiecelijn* 7 (1994), pp. 65-67, accessible online at www.dbnl.nl

Feliers 2006
W. Feliers, 'De haas in het Reynaertoeuvre van Allart van Everdingen', *Tiecelijn* 19 (2006), pp. 370-387, accessible online at www.dbnl.nl

Van der Feltz 1982
A.C.A.W. Baron van der Feltz, *Charles Howard Hodges 1764-1837*, Assen 1982

Femmel 1980
G. Femmel, *Goethes Graphiksammlung. Die Franzosen. Katalog und Zeugnisse*, Leipzig 1980

Frankfurt 1994
S. Schulze (ed.), *Goethe und die Kunst*, exh. cat. Frankfurt am Main (Schirn Kunsthalle) 1994

Freedberg 1980
D. Freedberg, *Dutch Landscape Prints*, London 1980

Frijhoff et al. 2004
W. Frijhoff et al., *Geschiedenis van Amsterdam 1578-1650. Centrum van de wereld*, Amsterdam 2004

ALLART VAN EVERDINGEN

Fuessli 1763
J.R. Fuessli, *Allgemeines Künstler-Lexicon, oder: Kurze Nachricht von dem Leben und den Werken der Mahler, [...], etc. etc.*, Zurich 1763

Fuessli 1779
J.R. Fuessli, *Allgemeines Künstlerlexicon, oder: Kurze Nachricht von dem Leben und den Werken der Mahler, [...], etc. etc.*, Zurich 1779

Gaudriault 1995
R. Gaudriault, *Filigranes et autres caractéristiques des papiers fabriqués en France aux XVIIe et XVIIIe siècles*, Paris 1995

Gersaint 1744
E.F. Gersaint, *Catalogue Raisonné des diverses curiosité's du cabinet de feu M. Quentin de Lorangere*, Paris 1744

Gerson 1983
H. Gerson, *Ausbreitung und Nachwirkung der holländischen Malerei des 17. Jahrhunderts*, Amsterdam 1983

Gessner 1778
S. Gessner, 'Brief ueber die Landschaftsmalerey an Herrn Fuesslin', in *Salomon Gessners Schriften*, Zurich 1778, vol. 2, pp. 165-194

Gibson 2000
W. Gibson, *Pleasant Places: The Rustic Landscape from Bruegel to Ruisdael*, Berkeley/ Los Angeles/London 2000

Glorieux 2002
G. Glorieux, *A l'enseigne de Gersaint. Edme-François Gersaint, marchand d'art sur le pont Notre-Dame (1694-1750)*, Seyssel 2002

Goedde 1989
L.O. Goedde, *Tempest and Shipwreck in Dutch and Flemish Art: Convention, Rhetoric, and Interpretation*, University Park, Pennsylvania/ London 1989

Goethe 1968
J.W. Goethe, *Italienische Reise*, 2 vols., Munich 1968 (originally published 1816-1817)

Goossens 1983
J. Goossens, *Die Reynaert-Ikonographie*, Darmstadt 1983

Gottsched 1752
J.C. Gottsched, *Heinrichs von Alkmar Reineke der Fuchs*, Leipzig/Amsterdam 1752

Granberg 1902
O. Granberg, *Allart van Everdingen, och hans "Norska" landskap, det Gamla Julita och Wurmbrandts Kanoner (1902)*, Stockholm 1902

Griffiths 1996
A. Griffiths, *Prints and Printmaking: An Introduction to the History and Techniques*, London 1996

Grijzenhout 1992
F. Grijzenhout, 'Tussen rede en gevoeligheid. De Nederlandse schilderkunst in het oordeel van het buitenland 1660-1800', in Grijzenhout and Van Veen 1992, pp. 27-54

Grijzenhout and Van Veen 1992
F. Grijzenhout and H. van Veen (eds.), *De Gouden Eeuw in perspectief. Het beeld van de Nederlandse zeventiende-eeuwse schilderkunst in later tijd*, Nijmegen/Heerlen 1992

Groningen 2017
D. Jackson, A. Blühm and R. Schenk (eds.), *De Romantiek in het Noorden. Van Friedrich tot Turner*, exh. cat. Groningen (Groninger Museum) 2017

Haak 1984
B. Haak, *Hollandse schilders in de Gouden Eeuw*, Amsterdam 1984

Haarlem 2009
A. Erftemeijer, *Groots en meeslepend. Sublieme landschappen uit de Nederlandse romantiek*, exh. cat. Haarlem (Frans Hals Museum | De Hallen Haarlem) 2009

Haarlem 2010
M. Plomp et al., *From New York With Love: The Drawings Collection of Matthijs de Clercq*, Haarlem (Teylers Museum) 2010

Haarlem/Munich 2008
P. Biesboer, *De Gouden Eeuw begint in Haarlem*, exh. cat. Haarlem (Frans Hals Museum) / Munich (Kunsthalle der Hypo-Kulturstiftung) 2008

Haarlem/Paris 2001
M. van Berge-Gerbaud, M.C. Plomp et al., *Hartstochtelijk verzameld. Beroemde tekeningen in 18de-eeuwse Hollandse collecties*, exh. cat. Haarlem (Teylers Museum) / Paris (Fondation Custodia) 2001

Haarlem/Zurich/Schwerin 2006
P. Biesboer, *Nicolaes Berchem. In het licht van Italië*, exh. cat. Haarlem (Frans Hals Museum) / Zurich (Kunsthaus Zurich) / Schwerin (Staatliches Museum Schwerin) 2006 (English edition: *Nicolaes Berchem: In Light of Italy*)

Von Hagedorn 1762
C.L. von Hagedorn, *Betrachtungen über die Mahlerey*, 2 vols., Leipzig 1762

The Hague 2009
Q. Buvelot, *Jacob van Ruisdael schildert Bentheim*, exh. cat. The Hague (Koninklijk Kabinet van Schilderijen Mauritshuis) 2009

Van der Ham 2005
G. van der Ham, 'Het schilderij en de werkelijkheid', *Bulletin van het Rijksmuseum* 53 (2005), no. 1, pp. 68-73

Hart 1976
S. Hart, *Geschrift en Getal. Een keuze uit de demografisch-, economisch- en sociaal-historische studiën op grond van Amsterdamse en Zaanse archivalia, 1600-1800*, Dordrecht 1976

Hauge 1999
M. Hauge, *En hollender i vår kunsthistorie: Allart van Everdingens grafikk fra Norge*, Oslo 1999

Hautekeete 2012
S. Hautekeete, 'New Insights into the Working Methods of Hans Bol', *Master Drawings* 50 (2012), pp. 329-356

Hautekeete and Van Grieken 2015
S. Hautekeete and J. Van Grieken, *Emblemata Evangelica: Hans Bol*, Brussels 2015

Heawood 1950
E. Heawood, *Watermarks, Mainly of the 17th and 18th Centuries*, Hilversum 1950

Heilmann 1988
C. Heilmann (ed.), *Johan Christian Dahl 1788-1857. Ein Malerfreund Caspar David Friedrichs*, exh. cat. Munich (Neue Pinakothek München) 1988

Heilmann 2013
C. Heilmann, *Natur als Kunst. Frühe Landschaftsmalerei des 19. Jahrhunderts in Deutschland und Frankreich aus der Christoph Heilmann Stiftung im Lenbachhaus München*, Heidelberg 2013

Von Heinecken 1771
K.H. von Heinecken, *Idée générale d'une collection complette d'estampes. Avec une dissertation sur l'origine de la gravure & sur les premiers livres d'images*, Leipzig/ Vienna 1771

Hendriks 1998
M. Hendriks, 'Isaac van Geelkercken', in *Biografisch Woordenboek Gelderland*, vol. 10, Hilversum 1998, pp. 51-54

Herring 2011
S. Herring, 'The Discovery of the Swiss Alps', in London 2011, pp. 53-61

's-Hertogenbosch/Leuven 2002
Y. Bruijnen and P. Huys Janssen (eds.), *De Vier Jaargetijden in de kunst van de Nederlanden 1500-1750*, exh. cat. 's-Hertogenbosch (Noordbrabants Museum) / Leuven (Stedelijk Museum Vander Kelen-Mertens) 2002

Hind 1926
A.M. Hind, *Catalogue of Drawings by Dutch and Flemish Artists Preserved in the Department of Prints and Drawings in the British Museum*, vol. 3, London 1926

Hind 1963
A.M. Hind, *A History of Engraving & Etching from the 15th Century to the Year 1914*, New York 1963

Hinterding 2006
E. Hinterding, *Rembrandt as an Etcher: The Practice of Production and Distribution*, 3 vols., Ouderkerk aan den IJssel 2006

Hofmann 1920
J. Hofmann, 'Allart van Everdingen und Goethes "Reineke Fuchs"', *Zeitschrift für Bücherfreunde* 12 (1920), pp. 188-191

Holan 1990
J. Holan, *Norwegian Wood: A Tradition of Building*, New York 1990

Holden 2012
F. Holden, *Christian IVs by. Livet i Kvadraturen*, Oslo 2012

Hollstein
F.W.H. Hollstein, *Dutch and Flemish Etchings, Engravings and Woodcuts, ca. 1450-1700*, Amsterdam 1949-1987, Roosendaal 1988-1994, Rotterdam 1995-2004 and Ouderkerk aan den IJssel 2006-2010

Hollstein (Allart van Everdingen)
Holl.
F.W.H. Hollstein, *Dutch and Flemish Etchings, Engravings and Woodcuts, ca. 1450-1700*, vol. 6: *Douffet-Floris*, Amsterdam 1952, pp. 154-204

Honour 1979
H. Honour, *Romanticism*, New York/Hagerstown/San Francisco/London 1979

Hos 1961
H.A.J. Hos, 'A. van Everdingen in de Ardennen', *Oud Holland* 76 (1961), pp. 208-220

Houbraken 1718-1721
A. Houbraken, *De groote schouburgh der Nederlantsche konstschilders en schilderessen*, 3 vols., Amsterdam 1718-1721, accessible online at www.dbnl.nl

Huys Janssen 2002
P. Huys Janssen, *Caesar van Everdingen 1616/17-1678*, Doornspijk 2002

The Illustrated Bartsch (Allart van Everdingen)
M.C. Leach and P. Morse, *The Illustrated Bartsch: Netherlandish Artists*, vol. 2, New York 1978, pp. 129-231

Immerzeel 1842-1843
J. Immerzeel Jr., *De levens en werken der Hollandsche en Vlaamsche kunstschilders, beeldhouwers, graveurs en bouwmeesters, van het begin der vijftiende eeuw tot heden*, 3 vols., Amsterdam 1842-1843

De Jager 1990
R. de Jager, 'Meester, leerjongen, leertijd. Een analyse van zeventiende-eeuwse Noord-Nederlandse leerlingcontracten van kunstschilders, goud- en zilversmeden', *Oud Holland* (104) 1990, pp. 69-111

De Jongh 1995
E. de Jongh, *Kwesties van betekenis. Thema en motief in de Nederlandse schilderkunst van de zeventiende eeuw*, Leiden 1995

Josi 1821
C. Josi, *Collection d'imitations de dessins d'après les principaux maîtres hollandais et flamands commencée par C. Ploos van Amstel*, London 1821

Keyes 1976
G.S. Keyes, 'Pieter Mulier the Elder', *Oud Holland* 90 (1976), pp. 230-261

Klein 1965
P.W. Klein, *De Trippen in de 17e eeuw. Een studie over het ondernemersgedrag op de Hollandse stapelmarkt*, Assen 1965

Klinkert 2016
C.M. Klinkert, 'Caesar van Everdingen, de classicist uit Alkmaar', in Alkmaar/Helsinki 2016, pp. 13-33

Knolle 1984a
P. Knolle, 'Cornelis Ploos van Amstel als pleitbezorger van de "Hollandse" iconografie', *Oud Holland* 98 (1984), pp. 43-52

Knolle 1984b
P. Knolle, 'De waardering voor het landschapstuk in de Nederlandse kunsttheorie van de 18de en vroege 19de eeuw', in *Reizen naar Rome. Italië als leerschool voor Nederlandse kunstenaars omstreeks 1800 / Paesaggisti ed altri artisti. Olandesi a Roma intorno al 1800*, exh. cat. Haarlem (Teylers Museum) / Rome (Nederlands Instituut Rome) 1984, pp. 101-123

Knolle 1992
P. Knolle, 'Het kunstkarakter onzer schildernatie. Nationale én internationale oriëntatie bij het stimuleren van de "Hollandse school" 1750-1820', *Documentatieblad Werkgroep achttiende eeuw* 24 (1992), pp. 121-139

Koerner 2009
J.L. Koerner, *Caspar David Friedrich and the Subject of Landscape*, London 2009 (originally published 1990)

Köhler et al. 2006
N. Köhler et al. (eds.), *Painting in Haarlem 1500-1850: The Collection of the Frans Hals Museum*, Ghent 2006

Koolhaas-Grosfeld 1982
E.A. Koolhaas-Grosfeld, 'Nationale versus goede smaak. Bevordering van nationale kunst in Nederland: 1780-1840', *Tijdschrift voor geschiedenis* 95 (1982), pp. 605-636

Koolhaas-Grosfeld 1986
E. Koolhaas-Grosveld, 'Op zoek naar de Gouden Eeuw. De herontdekking van de 17de-eeuwse Hollandse schilderkunst', in L. van Tilborgh and G. Jansen (eds.), *Op zoek naar de Gouden Eeuw. Nederlandse schilderkunst 1800-1850*, exh. cat. Haarlem (Frans Hals Museum) 1986, pp. 29-49

Kotková 2010
O. Kotková, 'Roelandt Savery aan het keizerlijke hof in Praag', in Prague/Kortrijk 2010, pp. 39-53

Kramm 1858
C. Kramm, *De levens en werken der Hollandsche en Vlaamsche kunstschilders, beeldhouwers, graveurs en bouwmeesters, van den vroegsten tot op onzen tijd*, vol. 2, Amsterdam 1858

Krempel 2005
L. Krempel, *Holländische Gemälde im Städel 1550-1800*, vol. 2: *Künstler geboren 1615 bis 1630*, Petersberg/Frankfurt am Main 2005

Lampe 1988
M. Lampe, '1819 – ein kritisches Jahr in Dahls Kunst', in Heilmann 1988, pp. 29-35

Laurentius 2007
T. Laurentius and F. Laurentius, *Watermarks 1600-1650 Found in the Zeeland Archives*, Houten 2007

Laurentius 2008
T. Laurentius and F. Laurentius, *Watermarks 1650-1700 Found in the Zeeland Archives*, Houten 2008

Laurentius, Niemeijer and Ploos van Amstel 1980
T. Laurentius, J.W. Niemeijer and G. Ploos van Amstel, *Cornelis Ploos van Amstel 1726-1797. Kunstverzamelaar en prentenuitgever*, Assen 1980

Lecarpentier 1817
C.-J.-F. Lecarpentier, *Essai sur le paysage, dans lequel on traite des diverses méthodes pour se conduire dans l'étude du paysage, suivi de courtes notices sur les plus habiles peintres and ce genre, ouvrage utile aux amateurs*, Paris 1817

Leeflang 1993
H. Leeflang, 'Het landschap in boek en prent. Perceptie en interpretatie van vroeg zeventiende-eeuwse Nederlandse landschapsprenten', in Amsterdam 1993a, pp. 18-32

Leeflang 2003
H. Leeflang, 'Van ontwerp naar prent. Tekeningen voor prenten van Nederlandse meesters (1550-1700) uit de collectie van het Prentenkabinet van de Universiteit Leiden', *Delineavit et Sculpsit* 27 (2003) (December special edition)

Lesger 1992
C. Lesger, 'Lange-termijn processen en de betekenis van politieke factoren in de Nederlandse houthandel ten tijde van de Republiek', *Economisch- en Sociaal-Historisch Jaarboek* 55 (1992), pp. 105-142

Likhachev 1994
J.S.G. Simmons and B. van Ginneken-van de Kasteele (eds.), *Likhachev's Watermarks: An English-Language Version*, 2 vols., Amsterdam 1994

London 2008
J. Gaschke (ed.), *Turmoil and Tranquillity: The Sea through the Eyes of Dutch and Flemish Masters, 1550-1700*, exh. cat. London (National Maritime Museum, Greenwich) 2008

London 2011
C. Riopelle and S. Herring, *Forests, Rocks, Torrents: Norwegian and Swiss Landscape Paintings from the Lunde Collection*, exh. cat. London (National Gallery) 2011

London 2017
L. Packer and J. Sliwka, *Monochrome: Painting in Black and White*, exh. cat. London (National Gallery) 2017

London/Amsterdam 2006
F. Lammertse and J. van der Veen, *Uylenburgh & zoon. Kunst en commercie van Rembrandt tot De Lairesse 1625-1675*, exh. cat. London (Dulwich Picture Gallery) / Amsterdam (Museum Het Rembrandthuis) 2006 (English edition: *Uylenburgh & Son: Art and Commerce from Rembrandt to De Lairesse 1625-1675*)

Los Angeles/Philadelphia/London 2005
S. Slive, *Jacob van Ruisdael: Master of Landscape*, exh. cat. Los Angeles (Los Angeles County Museum of Art) / Philadelphia (Philadelphia Museum of Art) / London (Royal Academy of Arts) 2005

Lugt
F. Lugt, *Répertoire des catalogues de ventes publiques intéressant l'art ou la curiosité*, 4 vols., The Hague 1938-1987

Lugt Marques
F. Lugt, *Les marques de collections de dessins et d'estampes*, 2 vols., Amsterdam 1921, supplement The Hague 1956, accessible online at http://www.marquesdecollection.fr

Lunsingh Scheurleer, Fock and Van Dissel 1986-1992
T. H. Lunsingh Scheurleer, C. W. Fock and A.J. van Dissel, *Het Rapenburg. Geschiedenis van een Leidse gracht*, 6 vols., Leiden 1986-1992

Maastricht/London 2019
Thomas Fearnley (1802-1842): Oil Sketches from the Collection of Asbjørn Lunde, exh. cat. Maastricht (TEFAF) / London (Masterpiece London) 2019

Magnusson 2018
B. Magnusson, *Dutch Drawings in Swedish Public Collections*, Stuttgart/Stockholm 2018

Maisak 1994
P. Maisak, 'Der Zeichner Goethe oder »Die Practische Liebhaberey in den Künsten«', in Frankfurt 1994, pp. 104-112

Van Mander 1604
K. van Mander, *Het Schilder-Boeck*, Haarlem 1604, accessible online at www.dbnl.nl

Mansfield 1995
E. Mansfield, 'Allart van Everdingen's Mezzotint Incunabula', *Print Quarterly* 12 (1995), pp. 169-179

Martens 2004
P. Martens, 'Visserij en vishandel. De zalm van het Bergse veld', in L.M. Helmus (ed.), *Vis. Stillevens van Hollandse en Vlaamse meesters 1550-1700*, Utrecht (Centraal Museum) / Helsinki (Amos Andersonin Taidemuseo) 2004, pp. 121-138

Menke 1992
H. Menke, *Bibliotheca Reinardiana*, vol. 1: *Die europäischen Reineke-Fuchs-Drucke bis zum Jahre 1800*, Stuttgart 1992

Mey 1878
H.W. Mey, *Wandelingen in Noorwegen. Bijdrage tot de kennis van land en volk*, Haarlem 1878

Mikkelsen 1988
B. Mikkelsen, *Christian IV. En billedbiografi*, Helsingør 1988

Milwaukee 2005
M. Bisanz-Prakken, *Rembrandt and His Time: Masterworks from the Albertina, Vienna*, exh. cat. Milwaukee (Milwaukee Art Museum) 2005

Monrad 2001
K. Monrad, 'De Hollandse dimensie in de landschapschilderkunst van de Deense Gouden Eeuw', in Copenhagen/Amsterdam 2001, pp. 16-71

Muller 1860
F. Muller, *Eenige opmerkingen over de prijzen van boeken en platen op veilingen, naar aanleiding van de verkoopingen der bibliotheken Van Voorst en Van Oosten de Bruyn*, Amsterdam 1860

Munksgaard 1997
J.H. Munksgaard, *Sjøforsvaret av Kristiansand 1550-1940*, Kristiansand 1997

Murdoch 2010
S. Murdoch, *The Terror of the Seas? Scottish Maritime Warfare 1513-1713*, Leiden 2010

Nagler 1837
G.K. Nagler, *Neues Allgemeines Künstler-Lexicon*, vol. 4, Munich 1837

New Hollstein Cornelis Cort 2000
M. Sellink, *The New Hollstein: Dutch and Flemish Etchings, Engravings and Woodcuts 1450-1700: Cornelis Cort*, 3 vols., Rotterdam/Amsterdam 2000

New Hollstein Pieter Bruegel 2006
N.M. Orenstein, *The New Hollstein: Dutch and Flemish Etchings, Engravings and Woodcuts 1450-1700: Pieter Bruegel*, Ouderkerk aan den IJssel/Amsterdam 2006

Nicolaisen 2012
J. Nicolaisen, *Niederländische Malerei 1430-1800. Museum der bildenden Künste Leipzig*, Leipzig 2012

Nicolson 1959
M.H. Nicolson, *Mountain Gloom and Mountain Glory: The Development of the Aesthetics of the Infinite*, Ithaca, New York 1959

Niemeijer 1980
J.W. Niemeijer, 'Artistieke contacten', in Laurentius, Niemeijer and Ploos van Amstel 1980, pp. 168-196

Van Nieuwenhuize 2021
H. van Nieuwenhuize, *Niederländische Seefahrer in schwedischen Diensten. Seeschifffahrt und Technologietransfer im 17. Jahrhundert*, Cologne 2021 [forthcoming]

Orenstein et al. 1993
N. Orenstein et al., 'Print publishers in the
Netherlands 1580-1620', in G. Luijten et al.
(eds.), *Dawn of the Golden Age: Northern
Netherlandish Art 1580-1620*, exh. cat.
Amsterdam (Rijksmuseum) 1993, pp. 167-200

Ormhaug 2002
Knut Ormhaug, 'Johan Christian Dahl und die
Norwegische Kultur. Denkmalpflege – Nationalgalerie – Kunstvereine', in Schleswig 2002,
pp. 137-144

Oslo/Dresden 2014
Dahl und Friedrich. Romantische Landschaften,
exh. cat. Oslo (Nasjonalgalleriet) / Dresden
(Albertinum) 2014

Ossing 2012
F. Ossing, 'Bilder als Klima-Archive?', *System
Erde 2* (2012), no. 1, pp. 90-95, accessible online

Ossing 2019
F. Ossing, 'Between everyday clouds and
embellishments of the sky. Remarks on the
representation of meteorological phenomena
in Dutch marine painting of the seventeenth
century', in De Beer 2019, vol. 1, pp. 127-159

Packer 2017
L. Packer, 'Monochrome painting and printmaking', in London 2017, pp. 137-157

Paris 2014
H. Buijs and G. Luijten (eds.), *Goltzius to
Van Gogh: Drawings and Paintings from
the P. & N. De Boer Foundation*, exh. cat. Paris
(Fondation Custodia) 2014

Plomp 1997
M.C. Plomp, 'Jan Pietersz. Zomer's inscriptions
on drawings', *Delineavit et Sculpsit* 17 (1997),
pp. 13-27

Plomp 2001
M.C. Plomp, *Hartstochtelijk verzameld.
18de-eeuwse Hollandse verzamelaars
van tekeningen en hun collecties*, Paris/
Bussum 2001

Plomp 2015
M.C. Plomp, *The Pleasure of Collecting: On the
Occasion of Matthijs de Clercq's 85 Birthday:
Acquisitions 1997-2015*, Haarlem 2015

Poulsen 1991
E. Poulsen, *Jens Juel*, 2 vols., Copenhagen 1991

Prague/Kortrijk 2010
I. De Jaegere and O. Kotková (eds.), *Roelandt
Savery 1576-1639*, exh. cat. Prague (Národní
Galerie v Praze) / Kortrijk (Broelmuseum) 2010
(English edition: *Roelandt Savery 1576-1639:
A Painter in the Service of Emperor Rudolf II*)

Von Ramdohr 1793
F.W.B. von Ramdohr, *Charis oder Ueber
das Schöne und die Schönheit in den nach-
bildenden Künsten*, 2 vols., Leipzig 1793

Reynaerts 2017
J. Reynaerts, 'Grenzeloos – Nederlandse
romantische landschapsschilderkunst in
Europese context', in Groningen 2017,
pp. 41-55

Rikken 2008
M. Rikken, *Melchior d'Hondecoeter. Vogel-
schilder*, Amsterdam 2008 (English edition:
Melchior d'Hondecoeter: Bird Painter)

Rikken 2016
M.E. Rikken, *Dieren verbeeld. Diervoorstel-
lingen in tekeningen, prenten en schilderijen
door kunstenaars uit de Zuidelijke Nederlanden
tussen 1550 en 1630*, dissertation Leiden
University 2016

Roding 1996
J.G. Roding, 'The North Sea coasts, an architectural unity?', in Roding and Heerma van Voss
1996, pp. 96-106

Roding and Heerma van Voss 1996
J. Roding and L. Heerma van Voss (eds.),
*The North Sea and Culture (1550-1800):
Proceedings of the International Conference
held at Leiden 21-22 April 1995*, Hilversum
1996, pp. 185-198

Rosengren 2020
C. Rosengren, 'The wilderness of Allaert van
Everdingen. Experience and representation of
the north in the age of the baroque', *Lychnos.
Annual of the Swedish History of Science
Society* 2020, pp. 177-205

Rotterdam/Berlin 1996
J. Giltaij and J. Kelch, *Lof der zeevaart.
De Hollandse zeeschilders van de 17e eeuw*,
exh. cat. Rotterdam (Museum Boijmans Van
Beuningen) / Berlin (Staatliche Museen zu
Berlin, Gemäldegalerie im Bodemuseum) 1996
(English edition: *Praise of Ships and the Sea:
The Dutch Marine Painters of the 17th Century*)

Royalton-Kisch 1988
M. Royalton-Kisch, *Adriaen van de Venne's
Album in the Department of Prints and
Drawings in the British Museum*, London 1988

Van Run 2019
T. van Run, 'Nieuw licht op het Trippenhuis:
De verhelderende blik van de dichter-glazen-
maker Salomon Oudart (1633-1699)', *Oud
Holland* 132 (2019), pp. 3-50

Sadkov et al. 2010
V. Sadkov et al., *The Pushkin State Museum
of Fine Arts: Netherlandish, Flemish and
Dutch Drawings of the XVI-XX Centuries*,
Amsterdam 2010

Schapelhouman 1987
M. Schapelhouman, *Nederlandse tekeningen
omstreeks 1600. Catalogus van de Nederlandse
tekeningen in het Rijksprentenkabinet, Rijksmuseum, Amsterdam. Deel III / Netherlandish
Drawings circa 1600: Catalogue of the Dutch
and Flemish Drawings in the Rijksprentenkabinet, Rijksmuseum, Amsterdam. Volume III*,
The Hague 1987

Schapelhouman 2009
M. Schapelhouman, 'De tekeningen. Over-
denkingen bij een oeuvre', in P. Roelofs et al.,
*Hendrick Avercamp. De meester van het
ijsgezicht*, exh. cat. Amsterdam (Rijksmuseum) /
Washington (National Gallery of Art) 2009
(English edition: *Hendrick Avercamp: Master
of the Ice Scene*), pp. 85-117

Schapelhouman and Schatborn 1987
M. Schapelhouman and P. Schatborn, *Land &
water. Hollandse tekeningen uit de 17de eeuw
in het Rijksprentenkabinet / Dutch Drawings
from the 17th Century in the Rijksmuseum Print
Room*, Zwolle 1987

Schapelhouman and Schatborn 1998
M. Schapelhouman and P. Schatborn,
*Dutch Drawings of the Seventeenth Century
in the Rijksmuseum, Amsterdam: Artists born
between 1580 and 1600: Catalogue of the
Dutch and Flemish Drawings in the Rijks-
prentenkabinet, Rijksmuseum, Amsterdam
Volume VI*, 2 vols., Amsterdam/London 1998

Schapelhouman and Scholten 2009
M. Schapelhouman and F. Scholten, 'Eleven
Drawings and a Statue: A Selection from the
Van Regteren Altena Donation', *Bulletin van
het Rijksmuseum* 57 (2009), pp. 89-110

Schatborn 1977
P. Schatborn, 'Beesten nae 't leven',
De kroniek van het Rembrandthuis 29 (1977),
no. 2, pp. 3-31

Schleswig 2002
H. Guratsch (ed.), *Wolken – Wogen – Wehmut.
Johan Christian Dahl 1788-1857. Der Freund
Caspar David Friedrichs*, exh. cat. Schleswig
(Stiftung Schleswig-Holsteinische Landes-
museen Schloß Gottorf) 2002

Schlusemann and Wackers 2005
R. Schlusemann and P. Wackers (eds.),
Reynaerts historie, Münster 2005

Schreiner 1934
J. Schreiner, 'Die Niederländer und die Norwegische Holzausfuhr im 17. Jahrhundert', *Tijdschrift voor Geschiedenis* 49 (1934), pp. 303-328

Schulz 1982
W. Schulz, *Herman Saftleven 1609-1685. Leben und Werke, mit einem kritischen Katalog der Gemälde und Zeichnungen*, Berlin 1982

Ševčik 2012
A.K. Ševčik, *Die Briefe über Landschaftsmalerei von Carl Gustav Carus und ihr wissenschaftlich-ästhetisches Erkenntniskonzept*, dissertation Masaryk University (Brno) 2012, accessible online

Slive 2005
S. Slive, 'Jacob van Ruisdael: Master Land-scapist', in Los Angeles/Philadelphia/London 2005, pp. 1-15

Sliwka 2017
J. Sliwka, 'Studies in light and shadow', in London 2017, pp. 53-73

Sluijter 1996
E.J. Sluijter, 'Jan van Goyen als marktleider, virtuoos en vernieuwer', in C. Vogelaar (ed.), *Jan van Goyen*, exh. cat. Leiden (Stedelijk Museum De Lakenhal) 1996, pp. 38-59

Sluijter 1999
E.J. Sluijter, 'Over Brabantse vodden, econo-mische concurrentie, artistieke wedijver en de groei van de markt voor schilderijen in de eerste helft van de zeventiende eeuw', *Neder-lands Kunsthistorisch Jaarboek* 50 (1999), pp. 112-143

Sluijter 2000
E.J. Sluijter, *De 'heydensche fabulen' in de schilderkunst van de Gouden Eeuw. Schilde-rijen met verhalende onderwerpen uit de klassieke mythologie in de Noordelijke Nederlanden, circa 1590-1670*, Leiden 2000

Sluijter 2013
E.J. Sluijter, '"Dien grooten Raphel in het zeeschilderen!" Over de waardering voor Jan Porcellis' sobere kunst door eigentijdse kenners', in Dumas et al. 2013, pp. 343-358

Smith 2006
P.J. Smith, *Embleemfabels in de Nederlanden (1567-ca. 1670). Het schouwtoneel der dieren*, Hilversum 2006

Smith 2018
P.J. Smith, 'Wandelen in Vondels *Vorsteliicke Warande* (1617)', *Jaarboek van het Genootschap van Bibliofielen* 25 (2018), pp. 35-65

Sogner 1996
S. Sogner, 'Popular contacts between Norway and the Netherlands in the Early Modern Period', in Roding and Heerma van Voss 1996, pp. 185-198

Sogner 2004
S. Sogner, 'Norwegian-Dutch Migrant Relations in the Seventeenth Century', in L. Sicking, H. de Bles and E. des Bouvrie (eds.), *Dutch Light in the "Norwegian Night": Maritime Relations and Migration across the North Sea in Early Modern Times*, Hilversum 2004, pp. 43-56

Spicer 1979
J. Spicer, *The Drawings of Roelandt Savery*, 2 vols., dissertation Yale University (New Haven, Connecticut) 1979

Stechow 1968
W. Stechow, *Dutch Landscape Painting of the Seventeenth Century*, 2nd edition, London 1968

Stefes 1997
A. Stefes, *Nicolaes Pietersz. Berchem (1620-1683). Die Zeichnungen*, s.l. 1997

Stefes 2011
A. Stefes, *Die Sammlungen der Hamburger Kunsthalle Kupferstichkabinett. Band 3. Niederländische Zeichnungen 1450-1850*, 3 vols., Cologne/Weimar/Vienna 2011

Steland 2005
A.C. Steland, 'Herman van Swanevelt als Radierer. Zur Chronologie der Entwürfe und der Drucke', *Oud Holland* 118 (2005), pp. 38-78

Stevenson 1951-1952
A.H. Stevenson, 'Watermarks are twins', *Studies in Bibliography* 4 (1951-1952), pp. 57-91

Stijnman 2012
A. Stijnman, *Engraving and Etching 1400-2000: A History of the Development of Manual Intaglio Printmaking Processes*, London/Houten 2012

Strutt 1785-1786
J. Strutt, *A Biographical Dictionary; Containing an Historical Account of All the Engravers, from the Earliest Period of the Art of Engraving to the Present Time; and a Short List of Their Most Esteemed Works*, 2 vols., London 1785-1786

Stylegar 2016
F.A. Stylegar, *Nieuw Amsterdam. Nordmenn i det hollandske Amerika 1624-1674*, Sandnes 2016

Sulzer 1775
J.G. Sulzer, 'Landschaft. (Zeichnende Künste)', in *Allgemeine Theorie der Schönen Künste*, vol. 2, Leipzig 1775, pp. 114-121

Summerfield 1980
G. Summerfield, 'The making of The Home Treasury', *Children's Literature* 8 (1980), pp. 35-52

Summerly 1843
F. Summerly (ed.), *The Pleasant History of Reynard the Fox: Told by the Pictures of Aldert van Everdingen*, London 1843

Sumowski 1980
W. Sumowski, 'Observations on Jan Lievens' Landscape Drawings', *Master Drawings* 18 (1980), pp. 370-373

Sutton 1987
P.C. Sutton, 'Introduction', in Amsterdam/Boston/Philadelphia 1987, pp. 1-63

Van Thiel 2006
P. van Thiel, 'The Haarlem School', in Köhler et al. 2006, pp. 15-42

Van Tielhof 2002
M. van Tielhof, *The 'Mother of all Trades': The Baltic Grain Trade in Amsterdam from the Late 16th to the Early 19th Century*, Leiden/Boston/Cologne 2002

Tokyo/Kasama/Kumamoto/Leiden 1992
E. Buijsen, *Tussen fantasie en werkelijkheid. 17de Eeuwse Hollandse Landschapschilder-kunst / Between Fantasy and Reality: 17th Century Dutch Landscape Painting*, exh. cat. Tokyo (Tokyo Station Gallery) / Kasama (Kasama Nichido Museum of Art) / Kumamoto (Kumamoto Prefectural Museum of Art) / Leiden (Stedelijk Museum De Lakenhal) 1992

Tokyo/Osaka 2018
A.K. Wheelock, P. Roelofs and G. Wuestman, *Making the Difference: Vermeer and Dutch Art*, exh. cat. Tokyo (The Ueno Royal Museum) / Osaka (Osaka City Museum of Fine Arts) 2018

Tossavainen 1994
J. Tossavainen, *Dutch Forest Products' Trade in the Baltic from the Late Middle Ages to the Peace of Munster in 1648*, unpublished master's thesis University of Jyväskylä 1994

Tromsøy/London 2014
M.I. Lange, K. Ljøgodt and C. Riopelle, *Paintings by Peder Balke*, exh. cat. Tromsøy (Northern Norway Art Museum) / London (National Gallery) 2014

Van Tussenbroek 2012
G. van Tussenbroek, *Historisch hout in Amsterdamse monumenten. Dendrochronologie – houthandel – toepassing*, Publicatiereeks Amsterdamse Monumenten 3, Amsterdam 2012

Tønnessen 1989
Kjeld Tønnessen, *Tollvesenets utvikling på
Agderkysten (fra ca. 1300 til ca. 1930)*,
Kristiansand 1989

Von Uffenbach 1753-1754
Z.C. von Uffenbach, *Merkwürdige Reisen
durch Niedersachsen, Holland und Engelland*,
Frankfurt/Leipzig 1753-1754

Veldman 2001
I.M. Veldman, *Profit and Pleasure: Print Books
by Crispijn de Passe*, Rotterdam 2001

Verreyken 2014
S. Verreyken, 'Tijd om te herbronnen. De impact
van beeldvorming op de stedelijke groei van Spa
in de zeventiende eeuw', *Stadsgeschiedenis* 9
(2014), pp. 113-129

Verzandvoort 1988-1989
E. Verzandvoort, 'Over de door Plantijn gedrukte
uitgaven van *Reynaert de Vos*', *De Gulden
Passer* 66-67 (1988-1989), pp. 237-252,
accessible online at www.dbnl.nl

Verzandvoort 1994a
E. Verzandvoort, 'Bruun de beer op pad. Een
iconografische verkenning', *Tiecelijn* 7 (1994),
pp. 138-155, accessible online at www.dbnl.nl

Verzandvoort 1994b
E. Verzandvoort, 'De vos, Van Everdingen en
Von Kaulbach', in W.N.T.M.B. Gielen, *Johann
Wolfgang von Goethe & Reineke Fuchs*, Hulst
1994, pp. 41-50

Verzandvoort 1995
E. Verzandvoort, 'Allart van Everdingen
(1621-1675) and his illustrations for J.Chr.
Gottsched's *Reineke der Fuchs* (Leipzig, 1752)',
Reinardus 8 (1995), pp. 151-163

Voorn 1960
H. Voorn, *De papiermolens in de provincie
Noord-Holland*, Haarlem 1960

De Vries 1997
S. de Vries (ed.), *De zestiende- en zeventiende-
eeuwse schilderijen van het Stedelijk Museum
Alkmaar. Collectie-catalogus*, Alkmaar/
Zwolle 1997

Wackers 1993
P. Wackers, 'Reynaert de Vos', in W.P. Gerritsen
and A.G. van Melle, *Van Aiol tot de Zwaanridder.
Personages uit de middeleeuwse verhaalkunst
en hun voortleven in literatuur, theater en
beeldende kunst*, Nijmegen 1993, pp. 269-279

Wackers 2002
P. Wackers (ed.), *Reynaert In tweevoud*, vol. 2:
Reynaerts historie, Amsterdam 2002, accessible
online at www.dbnl.nl

Walsh 1991
J. Walsh, 'Skies and Reality in Dutch Land-
scape', in D. Freedberg and J. de Vries (eds.),
*Art in History/History in Art: Studies in
Seventeenth-Century Dutch Culture*,
Santa Monica 1991, pp. 94-117

Watelet and Levesque 1792
C.H. Watelet and P.-C. Levesque, *Dictionnaire
des arts de peinture, sculpture et gravure*,
5 vols., Paris 1792

Wegener 2000
U. Wegener, *Die holländischen und flämischen
Gemälde des 17. Jahrhunderts*, Hannover (Nieder-
sächsisches Landesmuseum Hannover) 2000

Weigel 1843
R. Weigel, *Suppléments au peintre-graveur
de Adam Bartsch*, vol. 1, Leipzig 1843

Weyerman 1729
J.C. Weyerman, *De levens-beschryvingen
der Nederlandsche konst-schilders en konst-
schilderessen, met een uytbreyding over de
schilderkonst der ouden*, 3 vols., The Hague 1729

Widerberg 1924
C.S. Widerberg, *Norges første militæringeniør
Isaac van Geelkerck og hans virke 1644-1656.
Et bidrag til de norske befestningers historie*,
Kristiania [Oslo] 1924

Willemsen 1988
R.T.H. Willemsen, 'Dutch sea trade with Norway
in the seventeenth century', in W.G. Heeres et al.
(eds.), *From Dunkirk to Danzig: Shipping and
Trade in the North Sea and the Baltic, 1350-
1850*, Hilversum 1988, pp. 471-482

Winters 2017
R. Winters, *Exotische dieren in historisch
Amsterdam*, Amsterdam 2017

De Witt 2008
D. de Witt, *The Bader Collection: Dutch and
Flemish Paintings*, Kingston 2008

Wuestman 1995
G. Wuestman, 'The mezzotint in Holland:
"Easily learned, neat and convenient"',
Simiolus 23 (1995), pp. 63-89

Wuestman 2007
G. Wuestman, 'Herman van Swanevelt als
peintre-graveur', in F. de Graaf (ed.), *Het zuiden
tegemoet. De landschappen van Herman van
Swanevelt 1603-1655*, exh. cat. Woerden
(Stadsmuseum Woerden) 2007, pp. 62-71

Zandvliet 2006
K. Zandvliet, *De 250 rijksten van de Gouden
Eeuw. Kapitaal, macht, familie en levensstijl*,
Amsterdam 2006

Photograph Credits

Images of artworks were in principle obtained from the owners of the works. Additional credit lines are given here.

Alkmaar, Stedelijk Museum Alkmaar Figs. 4 and 5: photographs Margareta Svensson; fig. 6: photograph Niels den Haan; fig. 62, cat. no. 1: photograph René Gerritsen

Amersfoort, Cultural Heritage Agency of the Netherlands Fig. 156: former Koenigs Collection, photograph Studio Tromp

Amsterdam, Rijksmuseum Fig. 74, cat. no. 3: Jhr J.S.H. van de Poll Bequest, Amsterdam; fig. 75: infrared reflectogram Anna Krekeler

Amsterdam, Trippenhuis Fig. 32: photograph Roel Backaert; figs. 83-85: photographs Ruth Jongsma and Wim Ruigrok; fig. 86: photograph Ruth Jongsma and Edwin Verweij; all photographs except fig. 32 were commissioned by the Central Government Real Estate Agency; their use courtesy of the Royal Netherlands Academy of Arts and Sciences

Bergen, KODE Art Museums and Composer Homes Fig. 254: photograph Dag Fosse

Berlin, Staatliche Museen zu Berlin, Kupferstichkabinett Figs. 101, 119 and 195, cat. nos. 41 and 43: photographs bpk / Kupferstichkabinett, SMB / Dietmar Katz; fig. 120, cat. no. 42: photograph bpk / Kupferstichkabinett, SMB / Volker-H. Schneider

Braunschweig, Herzog Anton Ulrich-Museum, Kunstmuseum des Landes Niedersachsen Fig. 48, cat. no. 46, illustration on p. 2: photograph B.P. Keiser

Brussels, Royal Museums of Fine Arts of Belgium Figs. 115, 126 and 135, cat. nos. 47-49: photographs Grafisch Buro Lefevre, Heule

Cambridge, Harvard Art Museums/Fogg Museum Fig. 33: gift of Helen Clay Frick, photograph © President and Fellows of Harvard College

Chantilly, Musée Condé Fig. 112: photograph RMN-Grand Palais (domaine de Chantilly) / René-Gabriel Ojéda

Cologne, Wallraf-Richartz-Museum & Fondation Corboud Fig. 73, cat. no. 65, illustration on p. 205: photograph Rheinisches Bildarchiv Köln: rba_c004953

Copenhagen, Statens Museum for Kunst Figs. 2, 38, 47, 91 and 95, cat. nos. 66 and 67, illustrations on pp. 170-171 and on the front cover: photographs SMK Photo / Jakob Skou-Hansen

Dresden, Staatliche Kunstsammlungen Dresden, Kupferstich-Kabinett Fig. 114: photograph bpk / Staatliche Kunstsammlungen Dresden / Andreas Diesend

Dublin, National Gallery of Ireland Fig. 94: gift of Sir Alfred and Lady Clementine Beit, 1987

Enschede, Rijksmuseum Twenthe Figs. 50 and 249: photographs R. Klein Gotink; fig. 249: acquired with the support of the Vereniging Rembrandt

Frankfurt am Main, Städel Museum Fig. 64: photograph bpk / Städel Museum / Ursula Edelmann; fig. 78: photograph bpk / Städel Museum

Göttingen, Kunstsammlung der Georg-August-Universität Göttingen Fig. 161: photograph Katharina Anna Haase

Haarlem, Frans Hals Museum Figs. 21 and 69, cat. no. 52: purchased with the support of the Vereniging Rembrandt, photograph Tom Haartsen

Haarlem, Teylers Museum Fig. 125, cat. no. 55: gift of Matthijs de Clercq, 2016

Hamburg, Hamburger Kunsthalle Figs. 22, 29, 53, 61, 124, 127, 129-134 and 213, cat. nos. 56-64, illustration on p. 172: photographs bpk / Hamburger Kunsthalle / Christoph Irrgang; fig. 250: photograph bpk / Hamburger Kunsthalle / Elke Walford

Hannover, Landesmuseum Hannover Figs. 20 and 56: photographs Landesmuseum Hannover – ARTOTHEK

London, The British Museum Figs. 27, 122, 148, 210, 211, 214, 216, 217, 222, 223, 225-227, 232-234, 237-243, 245 and 247, cat. nos. 69-87: photographs © The Trustees of the British Museum

London, The Courtauld Institute of Art Fig. 117: photograph © The Samuel Courtauld Trust, The Courtauld Gallery, London

London, Greenwich, National Maritime Museum Figs. 12 and 45: acquired with the assistance of H.M. Treasury, the Caird Fund, the Art Fund, the Pilgrim Trust and the Society for Nautical Research Macpherson Fund

Montreal, The Montreal Museum of Fine Arts Fig. 81, cat. no. 89: gift of Mr and Mrs Michal Hornstein

Munich, Bayerische Staatsgemäldesammlungen, Alte Pinakothek Figs. 1, 55, 57 and 256, cat. no. 90: photographs bpk / Bayerische Staatsgemäldesammlungen, Alte Pinakothek

Oslo, Nasjonalmuseet for kunst, arkitektur og design Figs. 24 and 255: photographs Børre Høstland

Paris, Beaux-Arts de Paris Fig. 128: photograph Dist. RMN-Grand Palais / © Beaux-Arts de Paris

Paris, Fondation Custodia Fig. 72: infrared reflectogram mosaic René Gerritsen, made possible in part by Fondation Custodia

Paris, Musée du Louvre Fig. 41: photograph © Réunion des musées nationaux – utilisation soumise à autorisation

Paris, Petit Palais, Musée des Beaux-Arts de la Ville de Paris Figs. 28, 200, 230, 244 and 246, cat. nos. 99-101: Auguste and Eugène Dutuit Bequest, 1902

Private collection Figs. 11 and 44, cat. no. 104: photograph René Gerritsen

Private collection Fig. 23: photograph courtesy of Christie's

Rotterdam, Museum Boijmans Van Beuningen Figs. 14 en 96: photograph Nederlof, taken from Davies 2007 (cat. no. 170)

Rouen, Musée des Beaux-Arts Fig. 80: photograph C. Lancien, C. Loisel / Réunion des Musées Métropolitains Rouen Normandie

Saint-Petersburg, The State Hermitage Museum Fig. 19: photograph Vladimir Terebenin

Stockholm, Nationalmuseum Figs. 13 and 97: photograph Hans Thorwid / Nationalmuseum, Stockholm

Vienna, Kunsthistorisches Museum Wien Fig. 152: photograph KHM-Museumsverband

Washington, National Gallery of Art Fig. 10: Ailsa Mellon Bruce Fund and gift of Arthur K. and Susan H. Wheelock; figs. 36, 197 and 224: Ailsa Mellon Bruce Fund

Whereabouts unknown Fig. 9: photograph Nederlof, taken from Davies 2001 (cat. no. 169); figs. 42, 143 and 155: photographs RKD – Netherlands Institute for Art History

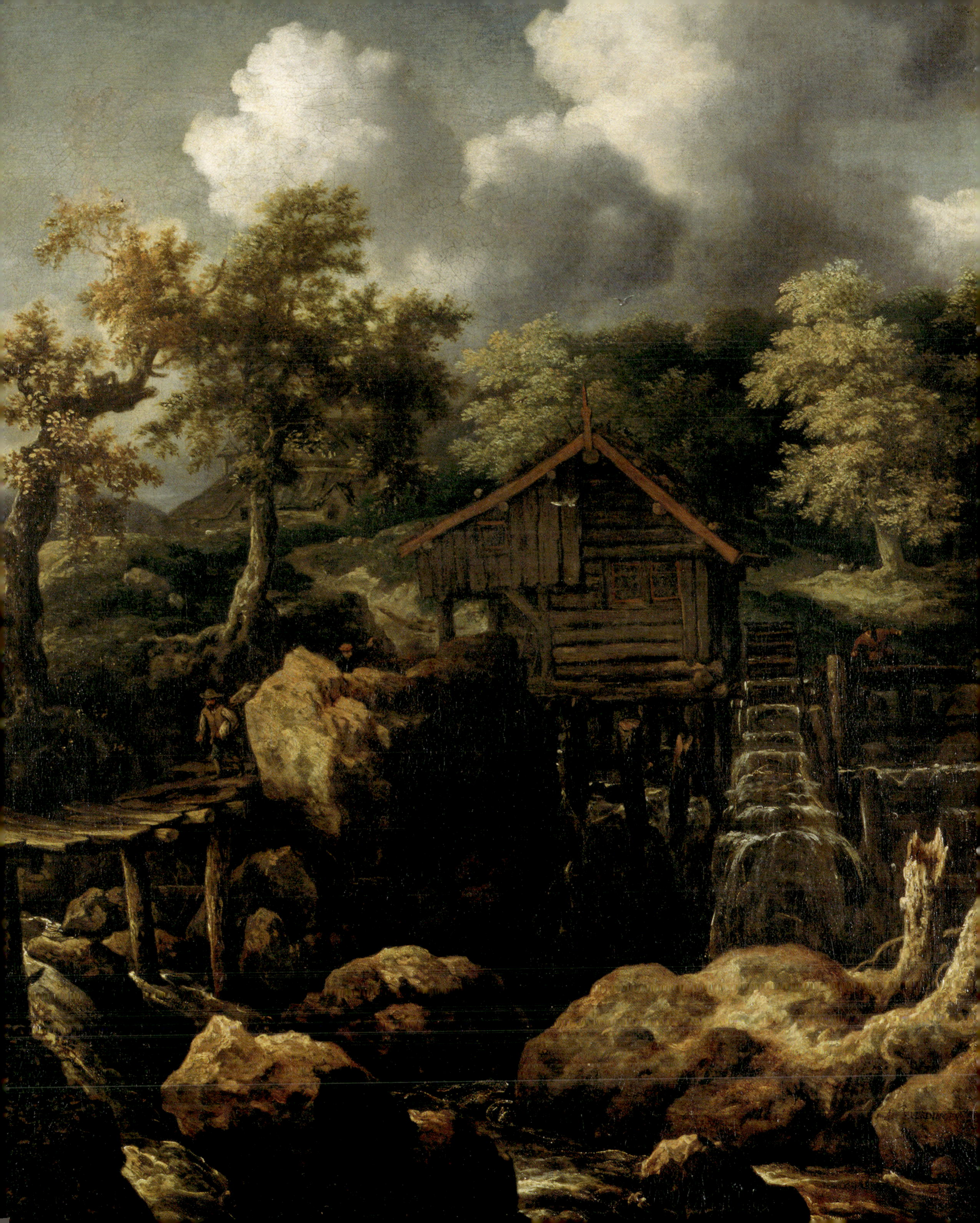

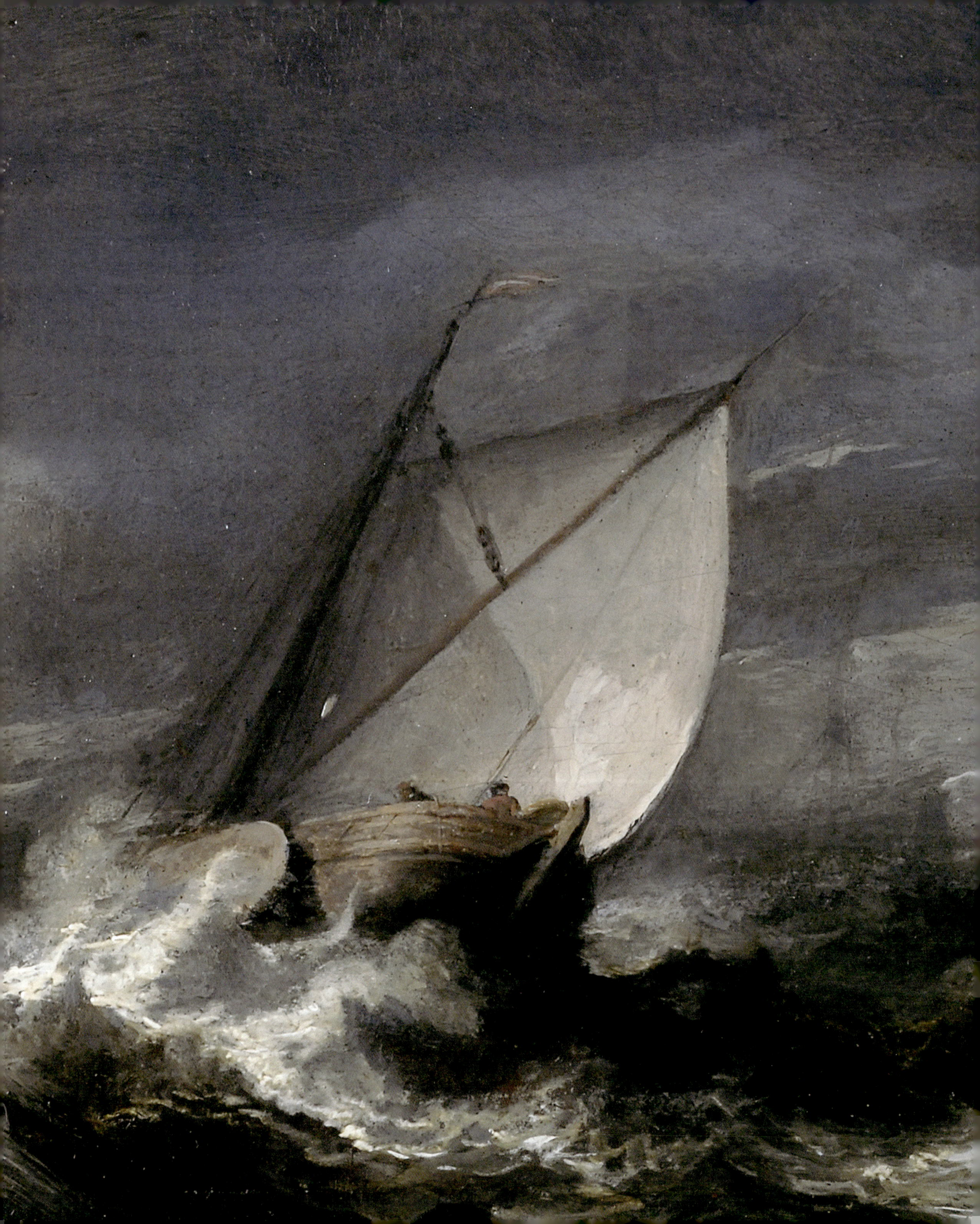

Credits

This book is published to coincide with the exhibition *Allart van Everdingen (1621-1675): The Rugged Landscape / Reynard the Fox (Allart van Everdingen (1621-1675). Het ruige landschap / Reinaert de vos)* in Stedelijk Museum Alkmaar (18 September 2021 – 16 January 2022)

Texts
Christi M. Klinkert, Yvonne Bleyerveld, Ellis Dullaart, Erik Hinterding, Paul Knolle, Cynthia Osiecki, Marjan Pantjes

Copy editing
Christi M. Klinkert and Yvonne Bleyerveld

Picture editing
Olga Kruisbrink

Translation
Lynne Richards

Design
Studio Berry Slok

Lithography (except photographs by Pascal Vossen)
BFC, Bert van der Horst, Amersfoort

Printing
Grafistar

Paper
135 grams Condat Matt Perigord

Publisher
Eelco van Welie, nai010 publishers

Production
Laurence Ostyn, nai010 publishers

Cover illustrations
Front: cat. no. 67 (detail)
Back: cat. no. 53 (detail)

Illustrations
Photographs of landscapes in Sweden and Norway: Pascal Vossen, August-September 2019
Illustrations pp. 2, 4, 10-11, 170-171, 172, 205 and 206-207: (details of) cat. nos. 46, 96, 94, 66, 57, 65 and 68 respectively

nai010 publishers is an internationally orientated publisher specialized in developing, producing and distributing books in the fields of architecture, urbanism, art and design. www.nai010.com

nai010 books are available internationally at selected bookstores and from the following distribution partners:
North, Central and South America – Artbook | D.A.P., New York, USA, dap@dapinc.com
Rest of the world – Idea Books, Amsterdam, the Netherlands, idea@ideabooks.nl

For general questions, please contact nai010 publishers directly at sales@nai010.com or visit our website www.nai010.com for further information.

ISBN 978-94-6208-646-3
NUR 642, 644
BISAC ART015090, ART050020

There is also a Dutch edition of this book, *Allart van Everdingen 1621-1675. Meester van het ruige landschap*
ISBN 978-94-6208-645-6

Allart van Everdingen 1621-1675: Master of the Rugged Landscape is also available as an ebook (PDF)
ISBN 978-94-6208-648-7

Lenders
Amsterdam, Amsterdam City Archives
Amsterdam, Amsterdam Museum
Amsterdam, Rijksmuseum
Amsterdam, Stichting Collectie P. & N. de Boer
Berlin, Staatliche Museen zu Berlin, Kupferstichkabinett
Boston, Alice I. Davies Collection
Braunschweig, Herzog Anton Ulrich-Museum, Kunstmuseum des Landes Niedersachsen
Brussels, Royal Museums of Fine Arts of Belgium
Budapest, Szépművészeti Múzeum
Cologne, Wallraf-Richartz-Museum & Fondation Corboud
Copenhagen, Statens Museum for Kunst
Dordrecht, Dordrechts Museum
Groningen, Academie Minerva Hanzehogeschool Groningen
Groningen, Groninger Museum
Haarlem, Frans Hals Museum
Haarlem, Teylers Museum
The Hague, Mauritshuis
Hamburg, Hamburger Kunsthalle
Leipzig, Museum der bildenden Künste Leipzig
London, The British Museum
Mölndal, Mölndal Municipality
Montreal, The Montreal Museum of Fine Arts
Munich, Bayerische Staatsgemäldesammlungen, Alte Pinakothek
New York, Collection of Aliis Inserviendo Consumor Foundation
New York, Stein Berre Collection
Paris, Fondation Custodia
Paris, Petit Palais, Musée des Beaux-Arts de la Ville de Paris
Vienna, The Albertina Museum
and private lenders